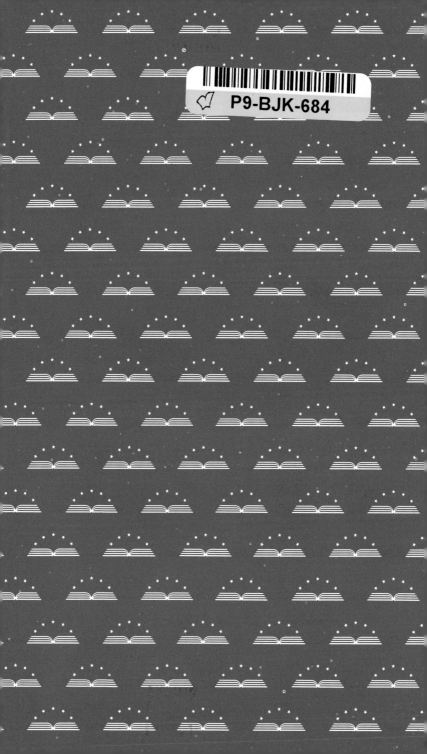

JAMES MADISON

JAMES MADISON

WRITINGS

THE LIBRARY OF AMERICA

The paper used in this publication meets the
minimum requirements of the American National Standard for
Information Sciences—Permanence of Paper for Printed
Library Materials, ANSI Z39.48—1984.

Distributed to the trade in the United States
by Penguin Putnam Inc.
and in Canada by Penguin Books Canada Ltd.

Library of Congress Catalog Number: 98–50372
For cataloging information, see end of Index.
ISBN 1–883011–66–3

First Printing
The Library of America—109

Manufactured in the United States of America

This volume has been published with support from
The John M. Olin Foundation

Contents

THE REVOLUTION
AND THE CONFEDERATION
1772–1787

To William Bradford

My dear Billey,   Orange Virginia Novr. 9th. 1772
   You moralize so prettily that if I were to judge from some
parts of your letter of October 13 I should take you for an old
Philosopher that had experienced the emptiness of Earthly
Happiness. And I am very glad that you have so early seen
through the romantic paintings with which the World is
sometimes set off by the sprightly imaginations of the Ingenious. You have happily supplied by reading and observation the want of experiment and therefore I hope you are
sufficiently guarded against the allurements and vanities that
beset us on our first entrance on the Theatre of Life. Yet however nice and cautious we may be in detecting the follies of
mankind and framing our Oeconomy according to the precepts of Wisdom and Religion I fancy there will commonly
remain with us some latent expectation of obtaining more
than ordinary Happiness and prosperity till we feel the convincing argument of actual disappointment. Tho I will not
determine whether we shall be much the worse for it if we do
not allow it to intercept our views towards a future State, because strong desires and great Hopes instigate us to arduous
enterprizes fortitude and perseverance. Nevertheless a watchful eye must be kept on ourselves lest while we are building
ideal monuments of Renown and Bliss here we neglect to
have our names enrolled in the Annals of Heaven. These
thoughts come into my mind because I am writing to you
and thinking of you. As to myself I am too dull and infirm
now to look out for any extraordinary things in this world for
I think my sensations for many months past have intimated to
me not to expect a long or healthy life, yet it may be better
with me after some time tho I hardly dare expect it and therefore have little spirit and alacrity to set about any thing that is
difficult in acquiring and useless in possessing after one has
exchanged Time for Eternity. But you have Health Youth Fire
and Genius to bear you along through the high tract of public
Life and so may be more interested and delighted in improving on hints that respect the temporal though momentous
concerns of man.

I think you made a judicious choice of History and the Science of Morals for your winter's study. They seem to be of the most universal benefit to men of sense and taste in every post and must certainly be of great use to youth in settling the principles and refining the Judgment as well as in enlarging Knowledge & correcting the imagination. I doubt not but you design to season them with a little divinity now and then, which like the philosopher's stone, in hands of a good man will turn them and every lawful acquirement into the nature of itself, and make them more precious than fine gold. As you seem to require that I should be open and unreserved (which is indeed the only proof of true friendship) I will venture to give you a word of advice though it be more to convince you of my affection for you than from any apprehension of your needing it. Pray do not suffer those impertinent fops that abound in every City to divert you from your business and philosophical amusements. You may please them more by admitting them to the enjoyment of your company but you will make them respect and admire you more by shewing your indignation at their follies and by keeping them at a becoming distance. I am luckily out of the way of such troubles, but I know you are cirrounded with them for they breed in Towns and populous places, as naturally as flies do in the Shambles, because there they get food enough for their Vanity and impertinence.

I have undertaken to instruct my brothers and Sisters in some of the first rudiments of literature, but it does not take up so much of my time but I shall always have leisure to recieve and answer your letters which are very grateful to me I assure you, and for reading any performances you may be kind enough to send me whether of Mr. Freneau or any body else. I think myself happy in your correspondence and desire you will continue to write as often as you can as you see I intend to do by the early and long answer I send you. You are the only valuable friend I have settled in so public a place and must rely on you for an account of all literary transactions in your part of the world.

I am not sorry to hear of Livingston's getting a degree. I heartily wish him well though many would think I had but little reason to do so and if he would be sensible of his opportunities and encouragements I think he might still recover. Lucky and his company after their feeble yet wicked assault upon Mr. Erwin, in my opinion will disgrace the catalogue of names, but they are below contempt and I spend no more words about them.

And now my friend I must take my leave of you, but with such hopes that it will not be long before I receive another epistle from you as make me more cheerfully conclude and Subscribe myself Yr. Sincere and Affecte. friend

Your Direction was right however the addition of Junr. to my name would not be improper.

To William Bradford

My worthy friend,   Jan 24. 1774
    Yours of the 25 of last month came into my hands a few days past. It gave singular pleasure not only because of the kindness expressed in it but because I had reason to apprehend the letter you recd. last from me had miscarried and I should fail in procuring the intelligence I wanted before the Trip I design in the Spring.

I congratulate you on your heroic proceedings in Philada. with regard to the Tea. I wish Boston may conduct matters with as much discretion as they seem to do with boldness: They seem to have great Tryals and difficulties by reason of the obduracy and *ministerialism* of their Governour. However Political Contests are necessary sometimes as well as military to afford excercise and practise and to instruct in the Art of defending Liberty and property. I verily believe the frequent Assaults that have been made on America, Boston especially, will in the end prove of real advantage. If the Church of England had been the established and general Religion in all the Northern Colonies as it has been among us here and uninterrupted tranquility had prevailed throughout the Continent, It is clear to me that slavery and Subjection might and would have been gradually insinuated among us. Union of Religious Sentiments begets a surprizing confidence and Ecclesiastical

Establishments tend to great ignorance and Corruption all of which facilitate the Execution of mischievous Projects. But away with Politicks! Let me address you as a Student and Philosopher & not as a Patriot now. I am pleased that you are going to converse with the Edwards and Henry's & Charles &c&c who have swayed the British Sceptre though I believe you will find some of them dirty and unprofitable Companions unless you will glean Instruction from their follies and fall more in love with Liberty by beholding such detestable pictures of Tyranny and Cruelty. I was afraid you would not easily have loosened your Affections from the Belles Lettres. A Delicate Taste and warm imagination like yours must find it hard to give up such refined & exquisite enjoyments for the coarse and dry study of the Law: It is like leaving a pleasant flourishing field for a barren desert; perhaps I should not say barren either because the Law does bear fruit but it is sour fruit that must be gathered and pressed and distilled before it can bring pleasure or profit. I perceive I have made a very awkward Comparison but I got the thought by the end and had gone too far to quit it before I perceived that it was too much entangled in my brain to run it through. And so you must forgive it. I myself use to have too great a hankering after those amusing Studies. Poetry wit and Criticism Romances Plays &c captivated me much: but I begin to discover that they deserve but a moderate portion of a *mortal's* Time. and that something more substantial more durable more profitable befits a riper Age. It would be exceeding improper for a labouring man to have nothing but flowers in his Garden or to determine to eat nothing but sweet-meats and Confections. Equally absurd would it be for a Scholar and man of Business to make up his whole Library with Books of Fancy and feed his Mind with nothing but such Luscious performances

When you have an Opportunity and write to Mr. Brackinridge pray tell him I often think of him and long to see him and am resolved to do so in the Spring. George Luckey was with me at Christmas and we talked so much about old Affairs & Old Friends that I have a most insatiable desire to see you all. Luckey will accompany me and we are to set off on the 10th. of April if no disaster befalls either of us. I want again to breathe your free Air. I expect it will mend my

Constitution & confirm my principles. I have indeed as good an Atmosphere at home as the Climate will allow: but have nothing to brag of as to the State and Liberty of my Country. Poverty and Luxury prevail among all sorts: Pride ignorance and Knavery among the Priesthood and Vice and Wickedness among the Laity. This is bad enough But It is not the worst I have to tell you. That diabolical Hell conceived principle of persecution rages among some and to their eternal Infamy the Clergy can furnish their Quota of Imps for such business. This vexes me the most of any thing whatever. There are at this in the adjacent County not less than 5 or 6 well meaning men in close Goal for publishing their religious Sentiments which in the main are very orthodox. I have neither patience to hear talk or think of any thing relative to this matter, for I have squabbled and scolded abused and ridiculed so long about it, to so little purpose that I am without common patience. So I leave you to pity me and pray for Liberty of Conscience to revive among us.

I expect to hear from you once more before I see you if time will admit: and want to know when the Synod meets & where: What the Exchange is at and as much about my friends and other Matters as you can and think worth notice. Till I see you Adieu.

NB Our Correspondence is too far advanced to require apologies for bad writing & blots.

January 24. 1774
Your Letter to Mr. Wallace is in my hands and shall be forwarded as soon as possible. I hear nothing from him by Letter or fame.

To William Bradford

My worthy friend   April 1st. 1774. Virginia Orange Cy.
I have another favour to acknowledge in the receipt of your kind Letter of March the 4th. I did not intend to have written again to you before I obtained a nearer communication

with you but you have too much interest in my inclinations ever to be denied a request.

Mr. Brackenridge's illness gives me great uneasiness: I think he would be a loss to *America*: His merit is rated so high by me that I confess if he were gone, I could almost say with the Poet That His Country could furnish such a Pomp for Death no more. But I solace myself from Finley's ludicrous description as you do.

I agree with you that the World needs to be peopled but I should be sorry it should be peopled with bastards as my old friend Dod and —— —— seem to incline. Who could have thought the old monk had been so letcherous. I hope his Religion, like that of some enthusiasts, was not of such a nature as to fan the amorous fire.

Our Assembly is to meet the first of May When It is expected something will be done in behalf of the Dissenters: Petitions I hear are already forming among the Persecuted Baptists and I fancy it is in the thoughts of the Presbyterians also to intercede for greater liberty in matters of Religion. For my part I can not help being very doubtful of their succeeding in the Attempt. The Affair was on the Carpet during the last Session; but such incredible and extravagant stories were told in the House of the monstrous effects of the Enthusiasm prevalent among the Sectaries and so greedily swallowed by their Enemies that I believe they lost footing by it and the bad name they still have with those who pretend too much contempt to examine into their principles and Conduct and are too much devoted to the ecclesiastical establishment to hear of the Toleration of Dissentients, I am apprehensive, will be again made a pretext for rejecting their requests. The Sentiments of our people of Fortune & fashion on this subject are vastly different from what you have been used to. That liberal catholic and equitable way of thinking as to the rights of Conscience, which is one of the Characteristics of a free people and so strongly marks the People of your province is but little known among the Zealous adherents to our Hierarchy. We have it is true some persons in the Legislature of generous Principles both in Religion & Politicks but number not merit you know is necessary to carry points there. Besides, the Clergy are a numerous and powerful body, have great influence at home by reason of their connection with & dependence on the Bishops and Crown and will naturally employ all their art & Interest to depress their rising Adversaries; for such they must consider dissenters who rob them of the good will of the people and may in time endanger their livings & security.

You are happy in dwelling in a Land where those inestimable privileges are fully enjoyed and public has long felt the good effects of their religious as well as Civil Liberty. Foreigners have been encouraged to settle amg. you. Industry and Virtue have been promoted by mutual emulation and mutual Inspection, Commerce and the Arts have flourished and I can not help attributing those continual exertions of Genius which appear among you to the inspiration of Liberty and that love of Fame and Knowledge which always accompany it. Religious bondage shackles and debilitates the mind and unfits it for every noble enterprize every expanded prospect. How far this is the Case with Virginia will more clearly appear when the ensuing Trial is made.

I am making all haste in preparing for my Journey: it appears as if it would be the first of May before I can start which I can the more patiently bear, because I may possibly get Some company by that time and it will answer so exactly with the meeting of the Synod. George Luckey talks of Joining me if I can wait till then. I am resolutely determined to come if it is in my power: If any thing hinders me it will be most likely the indisposition of my Mother who is in a very low state of health and if she should grow worse I am afraid she will be more unwilling to part with my brother as she will be less able to bear a Separation. If it should so unfortunately happen that I should be forced to put off or give out coming, Luckey on his Return to Virginia will bring me whatever publications you think worth sending and among others Calpipnis Letters. But whether I come or not be assured I retain the most ardent affection and esteem for you and the most cordial gratitude for your many generous Kindnesses. It gives me real pleasure when I write to you that I can talk in this Language without the least Affectation and without the suspicion of it, and that if I should omit expressing my love to you your friendship can supply the Omission or if I make use of the

most extravagant expressions of it your Correspondent
Affection can believe them to be sincere. This is a satisfaction
& delight unknown to all who correspond for business or
conveniency; but richly enjoyed by all who make pleasure and
Improvement the business of their Communications.

Farewell

Amendments to the Virginia Declaration of Rights

That Religion or the duty we owe to our Creator, and the
manner of discharging it, being under the direction of reason
and conviction only, not of violence or compulsion, all men
are equally entitled to the full and free exercise of it accordg
to the dictates of Conscience; and therefore that no man or
class of men ought, on account of religion to be invested with
peculiar emoluments or privileges; nor subjected to any penalties or disabilities unless under &c

———

18. That religion, or the duty which we owe to our
CREATOR, and the manner of discharging it, can be directed
only by reason and conviction, not by force or violence; and
therefore, that all men are equally entitled to enjoy the free
exercise of religion, according to the dictates of conscience,
unpunished and unrestrained by the magistrate, Unless the
preservation of equal liberty and the existence of the State are
manifestly endangered; And that it is the mutual duty of all to
practice Christian forbearance, love, and charity towards each
other.

May 29–June 11, 1776

To Thomas Jefferson

Dear Sir   Philadelphia March 27th. 1780

Nothing under the title of news has occurred since I wrote last week by express except that the Enemy on the 1st. of March remained in the neighbourhood of Charlestown in the same posture as when the preceding account came away. From the best intelligence from that quarter there seems to be great encouragement to hope that Clinton's operations will be again frustrated. Our great apprehensions at present flow from a very different quarter. Among the various conjunctures of alarm and distress which have arisen in the course of the revolution, it is with pain I affirm to you Sir, that no one can be singled out more truly critical than the present. Our army threatened with an immediate alternative of disbanding or living on free quarter; the public treasury empty; public credit exhausted, nay the private credit of purchasing Agents employed, I am told, as far as it will bear, Congress complaining of the extortion of the people; the people of the improvidence of Congress, and the army of both; our affairs requiring the most mature & systematic measures, and the urgency of occasions admitting only of temporizing expedients, and those expedients generating new difficulties. Congress from a defect of adequate Statesmen more likely to fall into wrong measures and of less weight to enforce right ones, recommending plans to the several states for execution and the states separately rejudging the expediency of such plans, whereby the same distrust of concurrent exertions that has damped the ardor of patriotic individuals, must produce the same effect among the States themselves. An old system of finance discarded as incompetent to our necessities, an untried & precarious one substituted, and a total stagnation in prospect between the end of the former & the operation of the latter: These are the outlines of the true picture of our public situation. I leave it to your own imagination to fill them up. Believe me Sir as things now stand, if the States do not vigorously proceed in collecting the old money and establishing funds for the credit of the new, that we are undone; and let them be ever so expeditious in doing this, still the

intermediate distress to our army and hindrance to public affairs are a subject of melancholy reflection. Gen Washington
writes that a failure of bread has already commenced in the
army, and that for any thing he sees, it must unavoidably increase. Meat they have only for a short season and as the
whole dependance is on provisions now to be procured, without a shilling for the purpose, and without credit for a
shilling, I look forward with the most pungent apprehensions.
It will be attempted I believe to purchase a few supplies with
loan office Certificates; but whether they will be received is
perhaps far from being certain; and if received will certainly
be a most expensive & ruinous expedient. It is not without
some reluctance I trust this information to a conveyance by
post, but I know of no better at present, and I conceive it to
be absolutely necessary to be known to those who are most
able and zealous to contribute to the public relief.

March 28.
   Authentic information is now recd. that the Enemy in their
passage to Georgia lost all their Horse, the Defiance of 64
guns which foundered at sea, three transports with troops,
although it is pretended these troops and the men of the
Defiance were saved, and 1 transport with Hessians of which
nothing has been heard. By a letter from Mr. Adams dated
Corunna 16 Decr. there seems little probability that Britain is
yet in a humour for peace. The Russian Ambassador at that
Court has been lately changed, and the new one on his way
to London made some stop at Paris whence a rumor has
spread in Europe that Russia was about to employ her mediation for peace. Should there be any reality in it, Mr. Adams
says it is the opinion of the most intelligent persons he had
conversed with that the independance of the United States
would be insisted on as a preliminary: to which G. B. would
accede with much greater repugnance than the cession of
Gibraltar which Spain was determined to make a sine qua
non.
   With respect and regard I am Dr Sir, yrs. sincerely

To Thomas Jefferson

Dear Sir   Philada. April 16th. 1781
    The inclosed paper is a copy of a report from a Committee now lying on the table of Congress for Consideration. The delicacy and importance of the subject makes me wish for your judgment on it before it undergoes the final decision of Congress.

    The necessity of arming Congress with coercive powers arises from the shameful deficiency of some of the States which are most capable of yielding their apportioned supplies, and the military exactions to which others already exhausted by the enemy and our own troops are in consequence exposed. Without such powers too in the general government, the whole confederacy may be insulted and the most salutary measures frustrated by the most inconsiderable State in the Union. At a time when all the other States were submitting to the loss and inconveniency of an embargo on their exports, Delaware absolutely declined coming into the measure, and not only defeated the general object of it, but enriched herself at the expence of those who did their duty.

    The expediency however of making the proposed application to the States will depend on the probability of their complying with it. If they should refuse, Congress will be in a worse situation than at present: for as the confederation now stands, and according to the nature even of alliances much less intimate, there is an implied right of coercion against the delinquent party, and the exercise of it by Congress whenever a palpable necessity occurs will probably be acquiesced in.

    It may be asked perhaps by what means Congress could exercise such a power if the States were to invest them with it? As long as there is a regular army on foot a small detachment from it, acting under Civil authority, would at any time render a voluntary contribution of supplies due from a State, an eligible alternative. But there is a still more easy and efficacious mode. The situation of most of the States is such, that two or three vessels of force employed against their trade will make it their interest to yield prompt obidience to all just requisitions on them. With respect to those States that have little or no foreign trade of their own it is provided that all inland trade with such states as supply them with foreign merchandize may be interdicted and the concurrence of the latter may be enforced in case of refusal by operations on their foreign trade.

There is a collateral reason which interests the States who are feeble in maritime resources, in such a plan. If a naval armament was considered as the proper instrument of general Government, it would be both preserved in a respectable State in time of peace, and it would be an object to mann it with Citizens taken in due proportions from every State. A Navy so formed and under the orders of the general Council of the States, would not only be a guard against aggression & insults from abroad; but without it what is to protect the Southern States for many years to come against the insults & aggressions of their N. Brethren.

I am Dear Sir Yr. sincere friend & obt. servt.

Observations on State Territorial Claims

May 1st. 1782.

The two great objects which predominate in the politics of Congress at this juncture are I. Vermont. II. Western territory.

I The independence of Vermont and its admission into the Confederacy are patronised by the Eastern States (N. Hamshire excepted) 1. from ancient prejudice agst. N York: 2. the interest which Citizens of those States have in lands granted by Vermont. 3. but principally from the accession of weight they will derive from it in Congress. N. Hamshire having gained its main object by the exclusion of its territory East of Connecticut River from the claims of Vermont, is already indifferent to its independence, and will probably soon combine with other Eastern States in its favor.

The same patronage is yielded to the pretensions of Vermont by Pennsylvania & Maryland with the sole view of reinforcing the opposition to claims of Western territory particularly those of Virginia and by N. Jersey & Delaware with the additional view of strengthening the interest of the little States. Both of these considerations operate also on Rhode Island in addition to those above mentioned.

The independence of Vermont and its admission into the Union are opposed by N. York for reasons obvious & well known.

The like opposition is made by Virginia N. Carolina, S. Carolina, and Georgia. The grounds of this opposition are. 1. an habitual jealosy of a predominance of Eastern Interests. 2. the opposition expected from Vermont to Western claims. 3. the inexpediency of admitting so unimportant a State, to an equal vote in deciding on peace & all the other grand interests of the Union now depending. 4. the influence of the example on a premature dismemberment of other States. These considerations influence the four States last mentioned in different degrees. The 2. & 3. to say nothing of the 4. ought to be decisive with Virginia.

II The territorial claims, particularly those of Virginia are opposed by Rhode Island, N. Jersey, Pennsylvania Delaware & Maryland. Rhode Island is influenced in her opposition by 1. a lucrative desire of sharing in the vacant territory as a fund of revenue. 2. by the envy & jealousy naturally excited by superior resources & importance. N. J. Penna: Delaware, Maryland, are influenced partly by the same considerations; but principally by the intrigues of their Citizens who are interested in the claims of land Companies. The decisive influence of this last consideration is manifest from the peculiar, and persivering opposition made agst. Virginia within whose limits those claims lye.

The Western claims, or rather a final settlement of them, are also thwarted by Massachussetts and Connecticut. This object with them is chiefly subservient to that of Vermont, as the latter is with Pennsylvania & Maryland to the former. The general policy and interests of these two States are opposed to the admission of Vermont into the Union, and if the case of the Western territory were once removed, they would instantly divide from the Eastern States in the case of Vermont. Of this Massachussetts & Connecticut are not insensible, and therefore find their advantage in keeping the territorial Controversy pending. Connecticut may likewise conceive some analogy between her claim to the Western Country & that of Virginia, and that the acceptance of the cession of the latter, would influence her sentiments in the controversy between the former & Pennsylvania.

The Western claims are espoused by Virga. N & S. Carolinas, Georgia & N. York, all of these States being interested therein. S. Carolina is the least so. The claim of N. York is very extensive, but her title very flimsy. She urges it more with the hope of obtaining some advantage, or credit, by its cession, than of ever maintaining it. If this Cession should be accepted, and the affair of Vermont terminated, as these are the only ties which unite her with the Southern States, she will immediately connect her policy with that of the Eastern States; as far at least, as the remains of former prejudices will permit.

Memorandum on Conversation Regarding the Continental Army

The evening of this day was spent at Mr. Fitzimmons by Mr. Ghorum, Mr. Hamilton, Mr. Peters, Mr. Carroll & Mr Madison. The conversation turned on the subject of revenue under the consideration of Congress, and on the situation of the army. The conversation on the first subject ended in a general concurrence (Mr. Hamilton excepted) in the impossibility of adding to the impost on trade any taxes that wd. operate equally throughout the States, or be adopted by them. On the second subject Mr. Hamilton & Mr. Peters who had the best knowledge of the temper, transactions & views of the army, informed the company that it was certain that the army had secretly determined not to lay down their arms until due provision & a satisfactory prospect should be afforded on the subject of their pay; that there was reason to expect that a public declaration to this effect would soon be made; that plans had been agitated if not formed for subsisting themselves after such declaration; that as a proof of their earnestness on this subject the Commander was already become extremely unpopular among almost all ranks from his known dislike to every unlawful proceeding, that this unpopularity was daily increasing & industriously promoted by many leading characters; that his choice of unfit & indiscreet persons into his family was the pretext and with some a real motive; but the substantial one a desire to displace him from the respect & confidence of the army in order to substitute Genl.   as the conductor of their efforts to obtain justice. Mr. Hamilton said that he knew Genl. Washington intimately & perfectly, that his extreme reserve, mixed sometimes with a degree of asperity of temper both of which were said to have increased of late, had contributed to the decline of his popularity; but that his virtue his patriotism & his firmness would it might be depended upon never yield to any dishonorable or disloyal plans into which he might be called; that he would sooner suffer himself to be cut into pieces; that he [Mr Hamilton] knowing this to be his true character wished him to be the conductor of the army in their plans for redress, in order that they might be moderated & directed to proper objects, & exclude some other leader who might foment & misguide their councils; that with this view he had taken the liberty to write to the Genl. on this subject and to recommend such a policy to him.

February 20, 1783

Speech in the Continental Congress on Revenue

Mr Madison said that he had observed throughout the proceedings of Congress relative to the establishment of such funds that the power delegated to Congress by the confederation had been very differently construed by different members & that this difference of construction had materially affected their reasonings & opinions on the several propositions which had been made; that in particular it had been represented by sundry members that Congress was merely an Executive body; and therefore that it was inconsistent with the principles of liberty & the spirit of the Constitution, to submit to them a permanent revenue which wd. be placing the purse & the sword in the same hands; that he wished the true doctrine of the confederation to be ascertained as it might perhaps remove some embarrassments; and towards that end would offer his ideas on the subject.

He said that he did not conceive in the first place that the opinion was sound that the power of Congress in cases of revenue was in no respect Legislative, but merely Executive: and in the second place that admitting the power to be Executive a permanent revenue collected & dispensed by them in the discharge of the debts to wch. it sd. be appropriated, would be inconsistent with the nature of an Executive body, or dangerous to the liberties of the republic.

As to the first opinion he observed that by the articles of Confederation Congs. had clearly & expressly the right to fix the quantum of revenue necessary for the public exigences, & to require the same from the States respectively in proportion to the value of their land; that the requisitions thus made were a law to the States, as much as the acts of the latter for complying with them were a law to their individual members: that the fœderal constitution was as sacred & obligatory as the internal constitutions of the several States; and that nothing could justify the States in disobeying acts warranted by it, but some previous abuse or infraction on the part of Congs.; that as a proof that the power of fixing the quantum & making requisitions of money, was considered as a legislative power over the purse, he would appeal to the proposition made by the British Minister of giving this power to the B. Parliamt. & leaving to the American assemblies the privilege of complying in their own modes; & to the reasonings of Congress & the several States on that proposition. He observed further that by the articles of Confederation was delegated to Congs. a right to borrow money indefinitely, and emit bills of Credit which was a species of borrowing, for repayment & redemption of which the faith of the States was pledged & their legislatures constitutionally bound. He asked whether these powers were reconcileable with the idea that Congress was a body merely Executive? He asked what would be thought in G. B. from whose constitution our Political reasonings were so much drawn, of an attempt to prove that a power of making requisitions of money on the Parliament, & of borrowing money for discharge of which the Parlt sd. be bound, might be annexed to the Crown without changing its quality of an Executive branch; and that the leaving to the Parliamt. the mode only of complying with the requisitions of the Crown, would be leaving to it its supreme & exclusive power of Legislation?

As to the second point he referred again to the British Constitution & the mode in which provision was made for the public debts; observing that although the Executive had no authority to contract a debt; yet that when a debt had been authorized or admitted by the parliament a permanent & irrevocable revenue was granted by the Legislature, to be collected & dispensed by the Executive; and that this practice had never been deemed a subversion of the Constitution or a dangerous association of a power over the purse with the power of the Sword.

If these observations were just as he concieved them to be, the establishment of a permanent revenue not by any assumed authority of Congress, but by the authority of the States at the recommendation of Congs: to be collected & applied by the latter to the discharge of the public debts, could not be deemed inconsistent with the spirit of the fœderal constitution, or subversive of the principles of liberty; and that all objections drawn from such a supposition ought to be withdrawn. Whether other objections of sufficient weight might not lie agst. such an establishmt. was another question. For his part altho' for various reasons* he had wished for such a plan as most eligible, he had never been sanguine that it was practicable & the discussions which had taken place had finally satisfied him that it would be necessary to limit the call

---

*Among other reasons privately weighing with him, he had observed that many of the most respectable people of America supposed the preservation of the Confederacy, essential to secure the blessings of the revolution; and permant funds for discharging debts essential to the preservation of Union. A disappointmt to this class wd. certainly abate their ardor & in a critical emergence might incline them to prefer some political connection with G. B. as a necessary cure for our internal instability, again Without permanent & general funds he did not concieve that the danger of convulsions from the army

for a general revenue to duties on commerce & to call for the
deficiency in the most permanent way that could be reconciled with a revenue established within each State separately &
appropriated to the Common Treasury. He said the rule
which he had laid down to himself in this business was to
concur in every arrangemt. that sd. appear necessary for an
honorable & just fulfilment of the public engagements; & in
no measure tending to augment the power of Congress which
sd appear to be unnecessary; and particularly disclaimed the
idea of perpetuating a public debt.

February 21, 1783

To Edmund Randolph

My Dear Sir   Philada. May 1783
   Your favor of the 9th. inst: was duly brought by yesterday's
Mail. My impatience is great to know the reception given to
the propositions of Congress, by the Assembly. I foresaw
some of the topics which are employed against them, & I
dread their effect from the eloquent mouths which will probably enforce them; but I do not despair. Unless those who
oppose the plan, can substitute some other equally consistent
with public justice & honor, and more conformable to the
doctrines of the Confederation, all those who love justice and
aim at the public good will be advocates for the plan. The
greatest danger is to be apprehended from the difficulty of
making the latter class sensible of the impracticability or in-

---

could be effectually obviated, lastly he did not think that any thing wd. be so
likely to prevent disputes among the States with the calamities consequent on
them. The States were jealous of each other, each supposing itself to be on
the whole a creditor to the others: The Eastern States in particular thought
themselves so with regard to the S. States (see Mr. Ghorum in the debates of
this day). If general funds were not introduced it was not likely the balances
wd. be ever be discharged, even if they sd. be liquidated. The consequence
wd. be a rupture of the confederacy. The E. States wd. at sea be powerful &
rapacious, the S. opulent & weak. This wd. be a temptation. the demands on
the S. Sts would be an occasion. Reprisals wd. be instituted. Foreign aid
would be called in by first the weaker, then the stronger side; & finally both
be made subservient to the wars & politics of Europe.

competency of any plan short of the one recommended; the arguments necessary for that purpose being drawn from a general survey of the fœderal system, and not from the interior polity of the States singly.

The letter from the Delegation by the last post to the Govr. apprised the legislature thro' him that negociations for a Treaty of Commerce with G. B. might be expected soon to take place and that if any instructions should be deemed proper no time ought to be lost in giving the subject a legislative discussion. For my own part I wish sincerely that the commercial interests of Virginia were thoroughly investigated & the final sense of the State expressed to its representatives in Congress.

The power of forming Treaties of Commerce with foreign nations is among the most delicate with which Congs. are intrusted, and ought to be exercised with all possible circumspection. Whilst an influence might be expected from them on the event or duration of the war, the public interest required that they should be invited with all the respectable nations of Europe, and that nice calculations of their tendency should be dismissed. The attainment of the object of the war has happily reversed our situation and we ought no longer to enslave ourselves to the policy of the moment. The State of this Country in relation to the Countries of Europe it ought to be observed, will be continually changing, and regulations adapted to its commercial & general interests at present, may hereafter be directly opposed to them. The general policy of America is at present pointed at the encouragement of Agriculture, and the importation of the objects of consumption. The wider therefore our ports be opened and the more extensive the privileges of all competitors in our Commerce, the more likely we shall be to buy at cheap & sell at profitable rates. But in proportion as our lands become settled, and spare hands for manufactures & navigation multiply, it *may* become our policy to favor those objects by peculiar privileges, bestowed on our own Citizens; or at least to introduce regulations inconsistent with foreign engagements suited to the present state of things.

The relative situation of the different States in this respect is another motive to circumspection. The variance of their policy & interests in the article of commerce strikes the first view, and it may with great truth be noted that as far as any concessions may be stipulated in favor of foreign nations they will cheifly be at the expence of those States which will share least in the compensations obtained for them. If for example, restrictions be laid on the Legislative rights of the States to prohibit, to regulate or to tax as they please their imports & exports, & to give such preferences as they please to the persons or vessels employed in them, it is evident that such restrictions will be most felt by those States which have the greatest interest in exports & imports. If on the other side the Citizens of the U.S. should in return for such a stipulation be obliged to navigate & carry, in forbidden channels, is it not equally evident that the benefit must fall to the share of those States which export & consume least, and abound most in resources of ships & seamen.

Nor should it be overlooked that as uniform regulations of the Commerce of the different States, will so differently affect their different interests, such regulations must be a strong temptation to measures in the aggrieved States which may first involve the whole confederacy in controversies with foreign nations, and then in contests with one another. I may safely suggest also to your ear, that a variety of circumstances make it proper to recollect that permanent engagements entered into by the Confederacy with foreign powers, may survive the Confederacy itself; that a question must then arise how far such engagements formed by the States in their fœderal character are binding on each of them separately, and that they may become pretexts for quarrels with particular States, very inconvenient for the latter, or for a general intrusion into American disputes. On the other hand candor suggests that foreign connections, if founded on principles equally corresponding with the policy & interests of the several States might be a new bond to the fœderal compact.

Upon these considerations I think it would be advisable to form all our commercial Treaties in future with great deliberation, to limit their duration to moderate periods, & to restrain our Ministers from acceding finally to them till they shall have previously transmitted them in the terms adjusted, for the revision & express sanction of Congress. In a Treaty of Commerce with G. B. it may be the policy of Virga. in particular to reserve her right as unfettered as possible over her own commerce. The monopoly which formerly tyrannized over it, has left wounds which are not yet healed, & the numerous debts due from the people, & which by the provisional articles they are immediately liable for, may possibly be made instruments for reestablishing their dependence. It cannot therefore be for the interest of the State to preclude it from any regulations which experience may recommend for its thorough emancipation. It is possible that experience may never recommend an exercise of this right, nor do my own sentiments favor in general, any restrictions or preferences in matters of commerce, but those who succeed us will have an equal claim to judge for themselves and will have further lights to direct their judgments. Nor ought the example of old & intelligent nations to be too far or too hastily condemned by an infant & inexperienced one. That of G. B. is in the science of commerce particularly worthy of our attention: And did she not originally redeem the management of her Commerce from the monopoly of the Hanse towns by peculiar exemptions to her own subjects? did she not dispossess the Dutch by a like policy? and does she not still make a preference of her own Vessels & her own mariners the basis of her maritime power? If Holland has followed a different system the reason is plain. Her object is not to exclude rivals from her own navigation but to insinuate herself into that of other nations.

The leading objects in the proposed Treaty with G. B. are 1. a direct commerce with the W. Indies. 2. the carrying trade between the different parts of her dominions. 3. a like trade between these & other parts of the world. In return for these objects we have nothing to offer of which we could well deprive her, but to secure to her subjects an entire equality of privileges with our own Citizens. With regard to the 1. object it may be observed, that both the temper & the interest of the nation leave us little ground to apprehend an exclusion from it. The French have so much the advantage of them from the facility of raising food as well as the other produce of their Islands, that the English will be under the necessity of admitting supplies from the U.S. into their Islands, and they surely will prefer paying for them in commodities to paying for them in cash. With regard to the 2 & 3 objects it may be observed that altho' they present great advantages, they present them only to those States which abound in maritime resources. Lastly with regard to the concession to be made on the part of the U.S. it may be observed that it will affect cheifly, if not solely, those States which will share least in the advantages purchased by it. So striking indeed does this contrast appear that it may with certainty be inferred that If G. B. were negociating a Treaty with the former States only, she would reject a mutual communication of the privileges of natives, nor is it clear that her apprehensions on this side, will not yet lead her to reject such a stipulation with the whole.

If this subject should be taken up by the Legislature, I hope that altho' not a member, your attention & aid will be given to it. If it sh. not be taken up publickly, I wish for your own private sentiments & those of the most intelligent members which you may be able to collect.

We have no European intelligence. Sr. G. Carlton in a letter to Gel. W. avows the same sentiments as were expressed in the conference relative to the negroes, but repeats his caution agst. their being understood as the national construction of the Treaty.

I send you herewith three more copies of the pamphlet of Congress which I have procured since my last. If Majr. Moore & Mr. F. Strother sd. be in the Assembly, I beg the favor of you to present one with my compliments to each of them. The third you will dispose of as you may think best.

In reviewing the freedom of some of the remarks which I have hazarded above, I am almost induced to recall them till I can cover them with cypher. As there is little danger attending the mail at present, and your own [   ] will take care of such as may be improper to be reverberated to this place, I shall upon the whole let them stand.

To Lafayette

My Dear Sir   Orange March 20th. 1785.
Your favour of the 15th. continued on the 17th of December came very slowly but finally safe to hand. The warm expressions of regard which it contains are extremely flattering

to me, and the more so as they so entirely correspond with my own wishes for every thing which may enter into your happiness.

You have not erred in supposing me out of the number of those who have relaxed their anxiety concerning the navigation of the Mississippi. If there be any who really look on the use of that river, as an object not to be sought or desired by the United States I can not but think they frame their policies on both very narrow and very delusive foundations. It is true, if the States which are to be established on the waters of the Mississippi were to be viewed in the same relation to the Atlantic States as exists between the heterogeneous and hostile Societies of Europe, it might not appear strange that a distinction or even an opposition of interests should be set up. But is it true that they can be viewed in such a relation? Will the settlements which are beginning to take place on the branches of the Mississippi, be so many distinct Societies, or only an expansion of the same Society? So many new bodies or merely the growth of the old one? Will they consist of a hostile or a foreign people, or will they not be a bone of our bones, and flesh of our flesh? Besides the confederal band, within which they will be comprehended, how much will the connection be strengthened by the ties of friendship, of marriage and consanguinity? ties which it may be remarked, will be even more numerous, between the ultramontane and the Atlantic States than between any two of the latter. But viewing this subject through the medium least favorable to my ideas, it still presents to the U. States sufficient inducements to insist on the navigation of the Mississippi. Upon this navigation depends essentially the value of that vast field of territory which is to be sold for the benefit of the common Treasury: and upon the value of this territory when settled will depend the portion of the public burdens of which the old States will be relieved by the new. Add to this the stake which a considerable proportion of those who remain in the old states will acquire in the new by adventures in land either on their own immediate account or that of their descendents.

Nature has given the use of the Mississippi to those who may settle on its waters, as she gave to the United States their independence. The impolicy of Spain may retard the former

as that of G. Britain did the latter. But as G. B. could not defeat the latter, neither will Spain the former. Nature seems on
all sides to be reasserting those rights which have so long
been trampled on by tyranny & bigotry. Philosophy & Commerce are the auxiliaries to whom she is indebted for her triumphs. Will it be presumptuous to say that those nations will
shew most wisdom as well as acquire most glory, who, instead
of forcing her current into artificial channels, endeavour to ascertain its tendency & to anticipate its effects. If the United
States were to become parties to the occlusion of the Mississippi they would be guilty of treason against the very laws
under which they obtained & hold their national existence.

The repugnance of Spain to an amicable regulation of the
use of the Mississippi, is the national offspring of a system,
which every body but herself has long seen to be as destructive to her interest, as it is dishonorable to her character. An
extensive desart seems to have greater charms in her eye, than
a flourishing but limited empire, nay than an extensive flourishing empire. Humanity cannot suppress the wish that some
of those gifts which she abuses were placed by just means, in
hands that would turn them to a wiser account. What is metamorphosis wd. the liberal policy of France work in a little time
on the Island of N. Orleans? It would to her be a fund of as
much real wealth, as Potosi has been of imaginary wealth to
Spain. It would become the Grand Cairo of the New World.

The folly of Spain is not less displayed in the means she em-
ploys than in the ends she prefers. She is afraid of the growth
and neighbourhood of the U. States because it may endanger
the tranquility of her American possessions: and to obviate
this danger she proposes to shut up the Mississippi. If her
prudence bore any proportion to her jealousy she would see,
that if the experiment were to succeed, it would double the
power of the U. States to disturb her, at the same time that it
provoked a disposition to exert it; she would see that the only
offensive weapon which can render the U. States truly formidable to her, is a navy, and that if she could keep their inhabitants from crossing the Appalachian, she would only drive to
the sea most of those swarms which would otherwise direct
their course to the Western wilderness. She would reflect too
that as it is impossible for her to destroy the power which she

dreads, she ought only to consult the means of preventing a future exertion of it. What are those means? Two & two only. The first is a speedy concurrence in such a treaty with the U. S. as will produce a harmony, & remove all pretexts for interrupting it. The second, which would in fact result from the first, consists in favouring the extension of their settlements. As these become extended the members of the Confederacy must be multiplied, and along with them the Wills which are to direct the machine. And as the wills multiply, so will the chances against a dangerous union of them. We experience every day the difficulty of drawing thirteen States into the same plans. Let the number be doubled & so will the difficulty. In the multitude of our Counsellors, Spain may be told, lies her safety.

If the temper of Spain be unfriendly to the views of the U. States, they may certainly calculate on the favorable sentiments of the other powers of Europe at least of all such of them as favored our Independence. The chief advantages expected in Europe from that event center in the revolution it was to produce in the commerce between the new & old world. The commerce of the U. S. is advantageous to Europe in two respects, first by the unmanufactured produce which they export; secondly by the manufactured imports which they consume. Shut up the Mississippi and discourage the settlements on its waters and what will be the consequence? First, a greater quantity of subsistance must be raised within the antient settlemts., the culture of tobacco indigo & other articles for exportation be proportionably diminished, and their price proportionably raised on the European consumer. Secondly the hands without land at home being discouraged from seeking it where alone it could be found, must be turned in a great degree to manufacturing, our imports proportionably diminished, and a proportional loss fall on the European manufacturer. Establish the freedom of the Mississippi, and let our emigrations have free course, and how favorably for Europe will the consequence be reversed. First the culture of every article for exportation will be extended, and the price reduced in favour of her Consumers. Secondly, our people will increase without an increase of our Manufacturers, and in the same proportion will be increased the employment & profit of hers.

These consequences would affect France in common with the other commercial nations of Europe: but there are additional motives which promise the U. States her friendly wishes and offices. Not to dwell on the philanthropy which reigns in the heart of her Monarch and which has already adorned his head with a crown of laurels. He cannot be inattentive to the situation into which a controversy between his antient and new allies would throw him, nor to the use which would be made of it by his watchful adversary. Will not all his Councils then be employed to prevent this controversy? Will it not be seen that as the pretensions of the parties directly interfere, it can be prevented only by dissuasive interposition on one side or the other, that on the side of the U. S. such an interposition must from the nature of things be unavailing, or if their pretensions cd. for a moment be lulled they wd. but awake with fresh energy, and consequently that the mediating influence of France ought to be turned wholly on the side of Spain. The influence of the French Court over that of Spain is known to be great & America it is supposed to be greater than perhaps it really is. The same may be said of the intimacy of the Union between the two nations. If this influence should not be exerted, this intimacy may appear to be the cause. The United States consider Spain as the only favorite of their ally of whom they have found to be jealous, and whilst France holds the first place in their affections they must at least be mortified at any appearance that the predilection may not be reciprocal.

The Mississippi has drawn me into such length that I fear you will have little patience left for any thing else. I will spare it as much as possible. I hear nothing from Congress except that Mr. Jay has accepted his appt. and that no successor has yet been chosen to Dr. Franklyn. Our Legislature made a decent provision for the remittances due for 1785 from Va. to the Treasy. of the U. S. and very extensive provision for opening our inland navigation: they have passed an Act vesting in Genl. Washington a considerable interest in each of the works on Js. River & Potowmac but with an honorary rather than lucrative aspect. Whether he will accept it or not I cannot say. I meant to have sent you a copy of the Act, but have been disappointed in getting one from Richmd. They also passed an act for reforming our juridical system which promises Salutary effects, and did not pass the Act for the corrupting Religious system. Whether they passed an act for paying British debts or not they do not know themselves. Before the bill for that purpose had got through the last usual forms, the want of members broke up the House. It remains therefore in a situation which has no precedent, & without a precedent lawyers & legislators are as much at a loss, as a mariner without his compass. The subjects in which you interested yourself were all referred to the Executive with power to do what I hope they will do better than the Assembly. I understood before I left Richmd. that you wd. receive officially from the Govr. a copy of the Resolutions which I sent you. I recd. a letter a few days ago from Mr. Mercer written in the bosom of wedlock at Mr. Spriggs; another at the same time from Monroe, who was well at New York. I have nothing to say of myself but that I have exchanged Richmond for Orange as you will have seen by the above date; that I enjoy a satisfactory share of health; that I spend the chief of my time in reading, & the chief of my reading on Law; that I shall hear with the greatest pleasure of your being far better employed, & that I am with most affect. esteem Yr. Obedt [   ] & Sert.

Memorial and Remonstrance Against Religious Assessments

To the Honorable the General Assembly of the
Commonwealth of Virginia
A Memorial and Remonstrance

We the subscribers, citizens of the said Commonwealth, having taken into serious consideration, a Bill printed by order of the last Session of General Assembly, entitled "A Bill establishing a provision for Teachers of the Christian Religion," and conceiving that the same if finally armed with the sanctions of a law, will be a dangerous abuse of power, are bound as faithful members of a free State to remonstrate against it, and to declare the reasons by which we are determined. We remonstrate against the said Bill,

1. Because we hold it for a fundamental and undeniable truth, "that Religion or the duty which we owe to our Creator and the manner of discharging it, can be directed only by reason and conviction, not by force or violence." The Religion then of every man must be left to the conviction and conscience of every man; and it is the right of every man to exercise it as these may dictate. This right is in its nature an unalienable right. It is unalienable, because the opinions of men, depending only on the evidence contemplated by their own minds cannot follow the dictates of other men: It is un-alienable also, because what is here a right towards men, is a duty towards the Creator. It is the duty of every man to ren-der to the Creator such homage and such only as he believes to be acceptable to him. This duty is precedent, both in order of time and in degree of obligation, to the claims of Civil Society. Before any man can be considered as a member of Civil Society, he must be considered as a subject of the Gov-ernour of the Universe: And if a member of Civil Society, who enters into any subordinate Association, must always do it with a reservation of his duty to the General Authority; much more must every man who becomes a member of any partic-ular Civil Society, do it with a saving of his allegiance to the Universal Sovereign. We maintain therefore that in matters of Religion, no mans right is abridged by the institution of Civil Society and that Religion is wholly exempt from its cog-nizance. True it is, that no other rule exists, by which any question which may divide a Society, can be ultimately deter-mined, but the will of the majority; but it is also true that the majority may trespass on the rights of the minority.

2. Because if Religion be exempt from the authority of the Society at large, still less can it be subject to that of the Legis-lative Body. The latter are but the creatures and vicegerents of the former. Their jurisdiction is both derivative and limited: it is limited with regard to the co-ordinate departments, more necessarily is it limited with regard to the constituents. The preservation of a free Government requires not merely, that the metes and bounds which separate each department of power be invariably maintained; but more especially that nei-ther of them be suffered to overleap the great Barrier which defends the rights of the people. The Rulers who are guilty of

such an encroachment, exceed the commission from which they derive their authority, and are Tyrants. The People who submit to it are governed by laws made neither by themselves nor by an authority derived from them, and are slaves.

3. Because it is proper to take alarm at the first experiment on our liberties. We hold this prudent jealousy to be the first duty of Citizens, and one of the noblest characteristics of the late Revolution. The free men of America did not wait till usurped power had strengthened itself by exercise, and entangled the question in precedents. They saw all the consequences in the principle, and they avoided the consequences by denying the principle. We revere this lesson too much soon to forget it. Who does not see that the same authority which can establish Christianity, in exclusion of all other Religions, may establish with the same ease any particular sect of Christians, in exclusion of all other Sects? that the same authority which can force a citizen to contribute three pence only of his property for the support of any one establishment, may force him to conform to any other establishment in all cases whatsoever?

4. Because the Bill violates that equality which ought to be the basis of every law, and which is more indispensible, in proportion as the validity or expediency of any law is more liable to be impeached. If "all men are by nature equally free and independent," all men are to be considered as entering into Society on equal conditions; as relinquishing no more, and therefore retaining no less, one than another, of their natural rights. Above all are they to be considered as retaining an "*equal* title to the free exercise of Religion according to the dictates of Conscience." Whilst we assert for ourselves a freedom to embrace, to profess and to observe the Religion which we believe to be of divine origin, we cannot deny an equal freedom to those whose minds have not yet yielded to the evidence which has convinced us. If this freedom be abused, it is an offence against God, not against man: To God, therefore, not to man, must an account of it be rendered. As the Bill violates equality by subjecting some to peculiar burdens, so it violates the same principle, by granting to others peculiar exemptions. Are the Quakers and Menonists the only sects who think a compulsive support of their

Religions unnecessary and unwarrantable? Can their piety alone be entrusted with the care of public worship? Ought their Religions to be endowed above all others with extraordinary privileges by which proselytes may be enticed from all others? We think too favorably of the justice and good sense of these denominations to believe that they either covet pre-eminences over their fellow citizens or that they will be seduced by them from the common opposition to the measure.

5. Because the Bill implies either that the Civil Magistrate is a competent Judge of Religious Truth; or that he may employ Religion as an engine of Civil policy. The first is an arrogant pretension falsified by the contradictory opinions of Rulers in all ages, and throughout the world: the second an unhallowed perversion of the means of salvation.

6. Because the establishment proposed by the Bill is not requisite for the support of the Christian Religion. To say that it is, is a contradiction to the Christian Religion itself, for every page of it disavows a dependence on the powers of this world: it is a contradiction to fact; for it is known that this Religion both existed and flourished, not only without the support of human laws, but in spite of every opposition from them, and not only during the period of miraculous aid, but long after it had been left to its own evidence and the ordinary care of Providence. Nay, it is a contradiction in terms; for a Religion not invented by human policy, must have pre-existed and been supported, before it was established by human policy. It is moreover to weaken in those who profess this Religion a pious confidence in its innate excellence and the patronage of its Author; and to foster in those who still reject it, a suspicion that its friends are too conscious of its fallacies to trust it to its own merits.

7. Because experience witnesseth that ecclesiastical establishments, instead of maintaining the purity and efficacy of Religion, have had a contrary operation. During almost fifteen centuries has the legal establishment of Christianity been on trial. What have been its fruits? More or less in all places, pride and indolence in the Clergy, ignorance and servility in the laity, in both, superstition, bigotry and persecution. Enquire of the Teachers of Christianity for the ages in which it appeared in its greatest lustre; those of every sect, point to the

ages prior to its incorporation with Civil policy. Propose a restoration of this primitive State in which its Teachers depended on the voluntary rewards of their flocks, many of them predict its downfall. On which Side ought their testimony to have greatest weight, when for or when against their interest?

8. Because the establishment in question is not necessary for the support of Civil Government. If it be urged as necessary for the support of Civil Government only as it is a means of supporting Religion, and it be not necessary for the latter purpose, it cannot be necessary for the former. If Religion be not within the cognizance of Civil Government how can its legal establishment be necessary to Civil Government? What influence in fact have ecclesiastical establishments had on Civil Society? In some instances they have been seen to erect a spiritual tyranny on the ruins of the Civil authority; in many instances they have been seen upholding the thrones of political tyranny: in no instance have they been seen the guardians of the liberties of the people. Rulers who wished to subvert the public liberty, may have found an established Clergy convenient auxiliaries. A just Government instituted to secure & perpetuate it needs them not. Such a Government will be best supported by protecting every Citizen in the enjoyment of his Religion with the same equal hand which protects his person and his property; by neither invading the equal rights of any Sect, nor suffering any Sect to invade those of another.

9. Because the proposed establishment is a departure from that generous policy, which, offering an Asylum to the persecuted and oppressed of every Nation and Religion, promised a lustre to our country, and an accession to the number of its citizens. What a melancholy mark is the Bill of sudden degeneracy? Instead of holding forth an Asylum to the persecuted, it is itself a signal of persecution. It degrades from the equal rank of Citizens all those whose opinions in Religion do not bend to those of the Legislative authority. Distant as it may be in its present form from the Inquisition, it differs from it only in degree. The one is the first step, the other the last in the career of intolerance. The magnanimous sufferer under this cruel scourge in foreign Regions, must view the Bill as a Beacon on our Coast, warning him to seek some

other haven, where liberty and philanthrophy in their due extent, may offer a more certain repose from his Troubles.

10. Because it will have a like tendency to banish our Citizens. The allurements presented by other situations are every day thinning their number. To superadd a fresh motive to emigration by revoking the liberty which they now enjoy, would be the same species of folly which has dishonoured and depopulated flourishing kingdoms.

11. Because it will destroy that moderation and harmony which the forbearance of our laws to intermeddle with Religion has produced among its several sects. Torrents of blood have been spilt in the old world, by vain attempts of the secular arm, to extinguish Religious discord, by proscribing all difference in Religious opinion. Time has at length revealed the true remedy. Every relaxation of narrow and rigorous policy, wherever it has been tried, has been found to assuage the disease. The American Theatre has exhibited proofs that equal and compleat liberty, if it does not wholly eradicate it, sufficiently destroys its malignant influence on the health and prosperity of the State. If with the salutary effects of this system under our own eyes, we begin to contract the bounds of Religious freedom, we know no name that will too severely reproach our folly. At least let warning be taken at the first fruits of the threatened innovation. The very appearance of the Bill has transformed "that Christian forbearance, love and charity," which of late mutually prevailed, into animosities and jealousies, which may not soon be appeased. What mischiefs may not be dreaded, should this enemy to the public quiet be armed with the force of a law?

12. Because the policy of the Bill is adverse to the diffusion of the light of Christianity. The first wish of those who enjoy this precious gift ought to be that it may be imparted to the whole race of mankind. Compare the number of those who have as yet received it with the number still remaining under the dominion of false Religions; and how small is the former! Does the policy of the Bill tend to lessen the disproportion? No; it at once discourages those who are strangers to the light of revelation from coming into the Region of it; and countenances by example the nations who continue in darkness, in shutting out those who might convey it to them. Instead of

Levelling as far as possible, every obstacle to the victorious progress of Truth, the Bill with an ignoble and unchristian timidity would circumscribe it with a wall of defence against the encroachments of error.

13. Because attempts to enforce by legal sanctions, acts obnoxious to so great a proportion of Citizens, tend to enervate the laws in general, and to slacken the bands of Society. If it be difficult to execute any law which is not generally deemed necessary or salutary, what must be the case, where it is deemed invalid and dangerous? And what may be the effect of so striking an example of impotency in the Government, on its general authority?

14. Because a measure of such singular magnitude and delicacy ought not to be imposed, without the clearest evidence that it is called for by a majority of citizens, and no satisfactory method is yet proposed by which the voice of the majority in this case may be determined, or its influence secured. "The people of the respective counties are indeed requested to signify their opinion respecting the adoption of the Bill to the next Session of Assembly." But the representation must be made equal, before the voice either of the Representatives or of the Counties will be that of the people. Our hope is that neither of the former will, after due consideration, espouse the dangerous principle of the Bill. Should the event disappoint us, it will still leave us in full confidence, that a fair appeal to the latter will reverse the sentence against our liberties.

15. Because finally, "the equal right of every citizen to the free exercise of his Religion according to the dictates of conscience" is held by the same tenure with all our other rights. If we recur to its origin, it is equally the gift of nature; if we weigh its importance, it cannot be less dear to us; if we consult the "Declaration of those rights which pertain to the good people of Virginia, as the basis and foundation of Government," it is enumerated with equal solemnity, or rather studied emphasis. Either then, we must say, that the Will of the Legislature is the only measure of their authority; and that in the plenitude of this authority, they may sweep away all our fundamental rights; or, that they are bound to leave this particular right untouched and sacred: Either we must say, that they may controul the freedom of the press, may abolish the

Trial by Jury, may swallow up the Executive and Judiciary Powers of the State; nay that they may despoil us of our very right of suffrage, and erect themselves into an independent and hereditary Assembly or, we must say, that they have no authority to enact into law the Bill under consideration. We the Subscribers say, that the General Assembly of this Commonwealth have no such authority: And that no effort may be omitted on our part against so dangerous an usurpation, we oppose to it, this remonstrance; earnestly praying, as we are in duty bound, that the Supreme Lawgiver of the Universe, by illuminating those to whom it is addressed, may on the one hand, turn their Councils from every act which would affront his holy prerogative, or violate the trust committed to them: and on the other, guide them into every measure which may be worthy of his blessing, may redound to their own praise, and may establish more firmly the liberties, the prosperity and the happiness of the Commonwealth.

c. June 20, 1785

To James Monroe

Dear Sir   Orange Aug: 7th. 1785
   I received the day before yesterday your favour of the 26th July. I had previously recd. the Report on the proposed change of the 9th. art: of the Confederation, transmitted by Col: Grayson, and in my answer to him offered such ideas on the subject as then occurred. I still think the probability of success or failure ought to weigh much with Congress in every recommendation to the States; of which probability Congress, in whom information from every State centers, can alone properly judge. Viewing in the abstract the question whether the power of regulating trade, to a certain degree at least, ought to be vested in Congress, it appears to me not to admit of a doubt, but that it should be decided in the affirmative. If it be necessary to regulate trade at all, it surely is necessary to lodge the power, where trade can be regulated with effect, and experience has confirmed what reason foresaw, that it can never be so regulated by the States acting in their separate ca-

pacities. They can no more exercise this power separately, than they could separately carry on war, or separately form treaties of alliance or Commerce. The nature of the thing therefore proves the former power, no less than the latter, to be within the reason of the fœderal Constitution. Much indeed is it to be wished, as I conceive, that no regulations of trade, that is to say, no restrictions or imposts whatever, were necessary. A perfect freedom is the System which would be my choice. But before such a system will be eligible perhaps for the U. S. they must be out of debt; before it will be attainable, all other nations must concur in it. Whilst any one of these imposes on our Vessels seamen &c in their ports, clogs from which they exempt their own, we must either retort the distinction, or renounce not merely a just profit, but our only defence against the danger which may most easily beset us. Are we not at this moment under this very alternative? The policy of G. B. (to say nothing of other nations) has shut against us the channels without which our trade with her must be a losing one; and she has consequently the triumph, as we have the chagrin, of seeing accomplished her prophetic threats, that our independence, should forfeit commercial advantages for which it would not recompence us with any new channels of trade. What is to be done? Must we remain passive victims to foreign politics; or shall we exert the lawful means which our independence has put into our hands, of extorting redress? The very question would be an affront to every Citizen who loves his Country. What then are those means? Retaliating regulations of trade only. How are these to be effectuated? only by harmony in the measures of the States. How is this harmony to be obtained? only by an acquiescence of all the States in the opinion of a reasonable majority. If Congress as they are now constituted, can not be trusted with the power of digesting and enforcing this opinion, let them be otherwise constituted: let their numbers be encreased, let them be chosen oftener, and let their period of service be shortened; or if any better medium than Congress can be proposed, by which the wills of the States may be concentered, let it be substituted; or lastly let no regulation of trade adopted by Congress be in force untill it shall have been ratified by a certain proportion of the States. But let us not sacrifice the end to the means: let us not rush on certain ruin in order to avoid a possible danger. I conceive it to be of great importance that the defects of the fœderal system should be amended, not only because such amendments will make it better answer the purpose for which it was instituted, but because I apprehend danger to its very existence from a continuance of defects which expose a part if not the whole of the empire to severe distress. The suffering part, even when the minor part, can not long respect a Government which is too feeble to protect their interest; But when the suffering part come to be the major part, and they despair of seeing a protecting energy given to the General Government, from what motives is their allegiance to be any longer expected. Should G. B. persist in the machinations which distress us; and seven or eight of the States be hindered by the others from obtaining relief by fœderal means, I own, I tremble at the anti-fœderal expedients into which the former may be tempted. As to the objection against intrusting Congress with a power over trade, drawn from the diversity of interests in the States, it may be answered. 1. that if this objection had been listened to, no confederation could have ever taken place among the States, 2. that if it ought now to be listened to, the power held by Congress of forming Commercial treaties by which 9 States may indirectly dispose of the Commerce of the residue, ought to be immediately revoked. 3 that the fact is that a case can scarcely be imagined in which it would be the interest of any 2/3ds of the States to oppress the remaining 1/3d. 4. that the true question is whether the commercial interests of the States do not meet in more points than they differ. To me it is clear that they do: and if they do there are so many more reasons for, than against, submitting the commercial interest of each State to the direction and care of the Majority. Put the West India trade alone, in which the interest of every State is involved, into the scale against all the inequalities which may result from any probable regulation by nine States, and who will say that the latter ought to preponderate? I have heard the different interest which the Eastern States have as Carriers pointed out as a ground of caution to the Southern States who have no bottoms of their own agst their concurring hastily in retaliations on G. B. But will the present system of G. B. ever give the Southern States bottoms:

and if they are not their own Carriers I shod. suppose it no mark either of folly or incivility to give our custom to our brethren rather than to those who have not yet entitled themselves to the name of friends.

In detailing these sentiments I have nothing more in view than to prove the readiness with which I obey your requests. As far as they are just they must have been often suggested in the discussions of Congress on the subject. I can not even give them weight by saying that I have reason to believe they would be relished in the public Councils of this State. From the trials of which I have been a witness I augur that great difficulties will be encountered in every attempt to prevail on the Legislature to part with power. The thing itself is not only unpalatable, but the arguments which plead for it have not their full force on minds unaccustomed to consider the interests of the State as they are interwoven with those of the Confederacy much less as they may be affected by foreign politics whilst those wch. plead agst. it, are not only specious, but in their nature popular: and for that reason, sure of finding patrons. Add to all this that the mercantile interest which has taken the lead in rousing the public attention of other States, is in this so exclusively occupied in British Commerce that what little weight they have will be most likely to fall into the opposite scale. The only circumstance which promises a favorable hearing to the meditated proposition of Congs. is that the power which it asks is to be exerted agst. G. B, and the proposition will consequently be seconded by the animosities which still prevail in a strong degree agst. her. I am My dear Sir very sincerely Yr friend & servt.

To Caleb Wallace

Dr. Sir   Orange Augt. 23d. 1785

Your favour of the 12th. of July was safely deliverd to me by Mr. Craig. I accept with pleasure your propos'd exchange of Western for Eastern intelligence and though I am a stranger to parental ties can sufficiently concieve the happiness of which they are a source to congratulate you on Your possession of two fine sons & a Daughter. I do not smile at the Idea of transplanting myself into your wilderness. Such a change of my abode is not indeed probable. Yet I have no local partialities which can keep me from any place which promises the greatest real advantages but If such a removal was not even possible I should nevertheless be ready to communicate, as you desire my Ideas towards a constitution of Government for the State in embryo. I pass over the general policy of the measure which calls for such a provision. It has been unanimously embraced by those who being most interested in it must have but consider'd it, & will I dare say be with equal unanimity acceded to by the other party which is to be consulted. I will first offer some general remarks on the Subject, & then answer your several queries.

1. *The Legislative department* ought by all means, as I think to include a Senate constituted on such principles as will give *wisdom* and steadiness to legislation. The want of these qualities is the grievance complained of in all our republics. The want of *fidelity* in the administration of power having been the grievance felt under most Governments, and by the American States themselves under the British Government. It was natural for them to give too exclusive an attention to this primary attribute. The Senate of Maryland with a few amendments is a good model. Trial has I am told verified the expectations from it. A Similar one made a part of our constitution as it was originally proposed but the inexperience & jealousy of our then Councils, rejected it in favour of our present Senate a worse could hardly have been substituted & yet bad as it is, it is often a useful bitt in the mouth of the house of Delegates. Not a single Session passes without instances of sudden resolutions by the latter of which they repent in time to intercede privately with the Senate for their Negative. For the other branch models enough may be found. Care ought however to be taken against its becoming to numerous, by fixing the number which it is never to exceed. The quorum, wages, and privileges of both branches ought also to be fixed. A majority seems to be the natural quorum. The wages of the members may be made payable for   years to come in the medium value of wheat, for   years preceeding as the same shall from period to period be rated by a respectable Jury

appointed for that purpose by the Supreme Court. The privileges of the members ought not in my opinion to extend beyond an exemption of their persons and equipage from arrests during the time of their actual Service. If it were possible it would be well to define the extent of the Legislative power but the nature of it seems in many respects to be indefinite. It is very practicable however to enumerate the essential exceptions. The Constitution may expresly restrain them from medling with religion—from abolishing Juries from taking away the Habeus corpus—from forcing a citizen to give evidence against himself, from controuling the press, from enacting retrospective laws at least in criminal cases, from abridging the right of suffrage, from seizing private property for public use without paying its full Value from licensing the importation of Slaves, from infringing the Confederation &c &c.

As a further security against fluctuating & indegested laws the Constitution of New York has provided a Council of Revision. I approve much of such an institution & believe it is considered by the most intelligent citizens of that state as a valuable safeguard both to public interests & to private rights. Another provision has been suggested for preserving System in Legislative proceedings which to some may appear still better. It is that a standing commtee composed of a few select & skilful individuals should be appointed to prepare bills on all subjects which they may judge proper to be submitted to the Legislature at their meetings & to draw bills for them during their Sessions. As an antidote both to the jealousy & danger of their acquiring an improper influence they might be made incapable of holding any other Office Legislative, Executive, or Judiciary. I like this Suggestion so much, that I have had thoughts of proposing it to our Assembly, who give almost as many proofs as they pass laws of their need of some such Assistance.

2 *The Executive Department* Though it claims the 2d place is not in my estimation entitled to it by its importance all the great powers which are properly executive being transferd to the Fœderal Government. I have made up no final opinion whether the first Magistrate should be chosen by the Legislature or the people at large or whether the power should be vested in one man assisted by a council or in a council of which the President shall be only primus inter pares. There

are examples of each in the U. States and probably advantages & disadvantages attending each. It is material I think that the number of members should be small & that their Salaries should be either unalterable by the Legislature or alterable only in such manner as will not affect any individual in place. Our Executive is the worst part of a bad Constitution. The Members of it are dependant on the Legislature not only for their wages but for their reputation and therefore are not likely to withstand usurpations of that branch; they are besides too numerous and expensive, their organization vaugue & perplexed & to crown the absurdity some of the members may without any new appointment continue in Office for life contrary to one of Articles of the Declaration of Rights.

3d *The Judiciary Department* merits every care. Its efficacy is Demonstrated in G. Brittain where it maintains private Right against all the corruptions of the two other departments & gives a reputation to the whole Government which it is not in itself entitled to. The main points to be attended to are 1. that the Judges should hold their places during good behavior. 2. that their Salaries should be either fixed like the wages of the Representatives or not be alterable so as to affect the Individuals in Office. 3 that their Salaries be liberal. The first point is obvious: without the second the independance aimed at by the first will be Ideal only: without the 3d. the bar will be superior to the bench which destroys all security for a Systematick administration of Justice. After securing these essential points I should think it unadvisable to descend so far into detail as to bar any future Modification of this department which experience may recommend. An enumeration of the principal courts with power to the Legislature to Institute inferior Courts may suffice. The Admiralty business can never be extensive in your situation and may be refer'd to one of the other Courts. With regard to a Court of Chancery as distinct from a Court of Law, the reasons of Lord Bacon on the affirmative side outweigh in my Judgment those of Lord Kaims on the other side. Yet I should think it best to leave this important question to be decided by future lights without tying the hands of the Legislature one way or the other. I consider our county courts as on a bad footing and would never myself consent to copy them into another constitution.

All the States seem to have seen the necessity of providing for Impeachments but none of them to have hit on an unexceptionable Tribunal. In some the trial is referd to the Senate in others to the Executive, in others to the Judiciary department. It has been suggested that a tribunal composed of members from each Department would be better than either and I entirely concur in their opinion. I proceed next to your queries.

1 "Whether is a representation according to number, or property, or in a joint proportion to both the most Safe? or is a representation by counties preferable to a more equitable mode that will be difficult to adjust?" Under this question may be consider'd 1. the right of Suffrage. 2 the mode of suffrage. 3 the plan of representation. As to the 1. I think the extent which ought to be given to this right a matter of great delicacy and of critical Importance. To restrain it to the landholders will in time exclude too great a proportion of citizens; to extend it to all citizens without regard to property, or even to all who possess a pittance may throw too much power into hands which will either abuse it themselves or sell it to the rich who will abuse it. I have thought it might be a good middle course to narrow this right in the choice of the least popular, & to enlarge it in that of the more popular branch of the Legislature. There is an example of this Distinction in N. Carolina if in none of the States. How it operates or is relished by the people I cannot say. It would not be surprising if in the outset at least it should offend the sense of equallity which reigns in a free Country. In a general vein I see no reason why the rights of property which chiefly bears the burden of Government & is so much an object of Legislation should not be respected as well as personal rights in the choice of Rulers. It must be owned indeed that property will give influence to the holder though it should give him no legal priviledges and will in generall be safe on that as well as other Accounts, expecially if the business of Legislation be guarded with the provisions hinted at. 2 as to the mode of suffrage I lean strongly to that of the ballot, notwithstanding the objections which be against it. It appears to me to be the only radical cure for those arts of Electioneering which poison the very fountain of Liberty. The States in which the Ballot has been the Standing mode are the only instances in which elections are tolerably

chaste and those arts in disgrace. If it should be thought improper to fix this mode by the constitution I should think it at least necessary to avoid any constitutional bar to a future adoption of it.* 3 By the plan of representation I mean 1. the classing of the Electors 2 the proportioning of the representatives to each class. The first cannot be otherwise done than by geographical description as by Counties. The second may esily be done in the first instance either by comprizing within each county an equal number of electors; or by proportioning the number of representatives of each county to its number of electors. The dificulty arises from the disproportionate increase of electors in different Counties. There seem to be two methods only by which the representation can be equalized from time to time. The 1 is to change the bounds of the counties. The 2d to change the number of representatives allotted to them respectavely, as the former would not only be most troublesome & expensive, but would involve a variety of other adjustments. The latter method is evidently the best. Examples of a Constitutional provision for it exists in several of the States. In some it is to be executed periodically in others pro re nata. The latter seems most accurate and very practicable. I have already intimated the propriety of fixing the number of representatives which ought never to be exceeded. I should suppose 150 or even 100 might safely be made the ne plus ultra for Kentuckey.

  2 "Which is to be preferd an Anual, Trienniel, or Septennial Succession to Offices or frequent elections without limitations in choice or that the Officers when chosen should continue quamdiu se bene gesserint?" The rule ought no doubt to be different in the different Departments of power. For one part of the Legislature Annual Elections will I suppose be held indispensably though some of the ablest Statemen & soundest Republicans in the U States are in favour of triennial. The great danger in departing from Annual elextions in this case lies in the want of some other natural term to limit the departure. For the other branch 4 or 5 Years may be the period. For neither branch does it seem necessary or proper to prohibit an indefinite reeligibility. With regard to the Executive if the elec-

*The Constitutn of N York directs an experiment on this Subject.

tions be frequent & particularly, if made as to any member of
it by the people at large a reeligibility cannot I think be objected to. If they be unfrequent, a temporary or perpetual incapacitation according to the degree of unfrequency at least in
the case of the first Magistrate may not be amiss. As to the
Judiciary department enough has been said & as to the
Subordinate officers civil & Military, nothing need be said
more than that a regulation of their appointments may under
a few restrictions be safely trusted to the Legislature.

3. "How far may the same person with propriety be employed in the different departments of Government in an infant Country where the counsel of every individual may be
needed?" Temporary deviations from fundamental principles
are always more or less dangerous. When the first pretext fails,
those who become interested in prolonging the evil will rarely
be at a loss for other pretexts. The first precedent too familiar-
izes the people to the irregularity, lessens their veneration for
those fundamental principles, & makes them a more easy prey
to Ambition & self Interest. Hence it is that abuses of every
kind when once established have been so often found to perpetuate themselves. In this caution I refer cheifly to an improper
mixture of the three great departments within the State. A
Delegation to Congress is I conceive compatible with either.

4 "Should there be a periodical review of the Constitution?" Nothing appears more eligible in theory nor has sufficient trial perhaps been yet made to condemn it in practise.
Pensylvania has alone adopted the expedient. Her citizens are
much divided on the subject of their constitution in general
& probably on this part of it in particular I am inclind to
think though am far from being certain, that it is not a
favourite part even with those who are fondest of their
Constitution. Another plan has been thought of which might
perhaps Succeed better and would at the same time be a
safeguard to the equilibrium of the constituent Departments
of Government. This is that a Majority of any two of the
three departments should have authority to call a plenipotentiary convention whenever they may think their constitutional
powers have been Violated by the other Department or that
any material part of the Constitution needs amendment. In
your situation I should think it both imprudent & indecent

not to leave a door open for at least one revision of your first Establishment; imprudent because you have neither the same resources for supporting nor the same lights for framing a good establishment now as you will have 15 or 20 Years hence; indecent because an handfull of early settlers ought not to preclude a populous Country from a choice of the Government under which they & their Posterity are to live. Should your first Constitution be made thus temporary the objections against an intermediate union of officers will be proportionably lessen'd. Should a revision of it not be made thus necessary & certain there will be little probability of its being ever revised. Faulty as our Constitution is as well with regard to the Authority which formed it as the manner in which it is formed the Issue of an experiment has taught us the difficulty of amending it; & Although the issue might have proceeded from the unseasonableness of the time yet it may be questioned whether at any future time the greater depth to which it will have stricken its roots will not counterballance any more auspicious circumstances for overturning it.

5 & 6 "Or will it be better unalterably to fix some leading Principles in Government and make it consistant for the Legislature to introduce such changes in lessor matters as may become expedient? can censors be provided that will impartially point out differences in the Constitutions & the Violations that may happen." Answers on these points may be gatherd from what has been already said.

I have been led to offer my sentiments in this loose forms rather than to attempt a delineation of such a plan of Government as would please myself not only by my Ignorance of many local circumstances & opinions which must be consulted in such a work but also by the want of sufficient time for it. At the receipt of your letter I had other employment and what I now write is in the midst of preparations for a Journey of business which will carry me as far as Philadelphia at least & on which I shall set out in a day or two.

I am sorry that it is not in my power to give you some satisfactory information concerning the Mississippi. A Minister from Spain has been with Congress for some time & is authorised as I understand to treat on what ever subjects may concern the two nations. If any explanations or propositions have passed between him & the Minister of Congress, they are as yet on the list of Cabinett Secrets. As soon as any such shall be made public & come to my knowledge I shall take the first opportunity of transmitting them. Wishing you & your family all happiness I am Dr Sir Yours friend & Servant

The Constitutions of the several States were printed in a small Volume a year or two ago by order of Congs. A perusal of them need not be recommended to you. Having but a single copy I cannot supply you. It is not improbable that you may be already possessed of one. The Revisall of our laws by Jefferson, Withe & Pendleton beside their Value in improving the legal code may suggest some things worthy of being attended to in framing a Constitution.

To George Washington

Dear Sir   Richmond Decr. 9. 1785
   Your favour of the 30. Novr. was received a few days ago. This would have followed much earlier the one which yours acknowledges had I not wished it to contain some final information relative to the commercial propositions. The discussion of them has consumed much time, and though the absolute necessity of some such general system prevailed over all the efforts of its adversaries in the first instance, the stratagem of limiting its duration to a short term has ultimately disappointed our hopes. I think it better to trust to further experience and even distress, for an adequate remedy, than to try a temporary measure which may stand in the way of a permanent one, and must confirm that transatlantic policy which is founded on our supposed distrust of Congress and of one another. Those whose opposition in this case did not spring from illiberal animosities towards the Northern States, seem to have been frightened on one side at the idea of a perpetual & irrevocable grant of power, and on the other flattered with a hope, that a temporary grant might be renewed from time to time, if its utility should be confirmed by the experiment. But we have already granted perpetual & irrevocable powers of a much more extensive nature than those now proposed

and for reasons not stronger than the reasons which urge the latter. And as to the hope of renewal, it is the most visionary one that perhaps ever deluded men of sense. Nothing but the peculiarity of our circumstances could ever have produced those sacrifices of sovereignty on which the fœderal Government now rests. If they had been temporary, and the expiration of the term required a renewal at this crisis, pressing as the crisis is, and recent as is our experience of the value of the confederacy, sure I am that it would be impossible to revive it. What room have we then to hope that the expiration of temporary grants of commercial powers would always find a unanimous disposition in the States, to follow their own example. It ought to be remembered too that besides the caprice, jealousy, and diversity of opinions, which will be certain obstacles in our way, the policy of foreign nations may hereafter imitate that of the Macedonian Prince who effected his purposes against the Grecian confederacy by gaining over a few of the leading men in the smaller members of it. Add to the whole, that the difficulty now found in obtaining a unanimous concurrence of the States in any measure whatever, must continually increase with every increase of their number and perhaps in a greater ratio, as the Ultramontane States may either have or suppose they have a less similitude of interests to the Atlantic States than these have to one another. The propositions however have not yet received the final vote of the House, having lain on the table for sometime as a report from the Commee. of the whole. The question was suspended in order to consider a proposition which had for its object a Meeting of Politico-Commercial Commissrs from all the States for the purpose of digesting and reporting the requisite augmentation of the power of Congress over trade. What the event will be cannot be foreseen. The friends to the original propositions are I am told rather increasing, but I despair of a majority in any event for a longer term than 25 years for their duration. The other scheme will have fewer enemies and may perhaps be carried. It seems naturally to grow out of the proposed appointment of Commssrs for Virga. & Maryd, concerted at Mount Vernon for keeping up harmony in the commercial regulations of the two States. Maryd has ratified the Report, but has invited into the plan Delaware and Penna.

who will naturally pay the same compliment to their neighbours &c. &c. Besides these general propositions on the subject of trade, it has been proposed that some intermediate measures should be taken by ourselves, and a sort of navigation act will I am apprehensive be attempted. It is backed by the mercantile interest of most of our towns except Alexandria which alone seems to have liberality or light on the subject. It was refused even to suspend the measure on the concurrence of Maryland or N. Carolina. This folly however can not one would think, brave the ruin which it threatens to our Merchts. as well as people at large, when a final vote comes to be given.

We have got thro' a great part of the Revisal, and might by this time have been at the end of it had the time wasted in disputing whether it could be finished at this Session been spent in forwarding the work. As it is, we must content ourselves with passing a few more of the important bills, leaving the residue for our successors of the next year. As none of the bills passed are to be in force till Jan. 1787, and the residue unpassed will probably be least disputable in their nature, this expedient tho' little eligible, is not inadmissible. Our public credit has had a severe attack and a narrow escape. As a compromise it has been necessary to set forward the half tax till March, and the whole tax of Sepr. next till Novr. ensuing. The latter postponement was meant to give the planters more time to deal with the Merchts in the sale of their Tobo., and is made a permanent regulation. The Assize bill is now depending. It has many enemies and its fate is precarious. My hopes however prevail over my apprehensions. The fate of the Port bill is more precarious. The failure of an interview between our Commssrs and Commssrs on the part of N. Carolina has embarrassed the projected Canal between the Waters of the two States. If N. C. were entirely well disposed the passing an Act suspended on & referred to her legislature would be sufficient, and this course must, I suppose be tried, tho' previous negociation would have promised more certain success. Kentucky has made a formal application for independence. Her memorial has been considered, and the terms of separation fixed by a Come. of the whole. The substance of them is that all *private* rights & interests derived from the laws of Virginia shall be secured that the unlocated lands shall be applied to the objects to which the laws of Va. have appropriated them—that nonresidents shall be subjected to no higher taxes than residents—that the Ohio shall be a common high way for Citizens of the U. S. and the jurisdiction of Kentucky & Virga. as far as the remaing. territory of the latter will lie thereon, be concurrent only with the new States on the opposite Shore—that the proposed State shall take its due share of our State debts—and that the separation shall not take place unless these terms shall be approved by a Convention to be held to decide the question, nor untill Congs. shall assent thereto, and fix the terms of their admission into the Union. The limits of the proposed State are to be the same with the present limits of the district. The apparent coolness of the Representatives of Kentucky as to a separation since these terms have been defined indicates that they had some views which will not be favored by them. They disliked much to be hung up on the will of Congs. I am Dr. Sir with highest esteem and unfeigned regard. Yr. obedt. & hble Servt.

To James Monroe

Dear Sir   Orange 19th. March 1786
    I am just favored with yours of the 11 & 16. of Feby. A newspaper since the date of the latter has verified to me your inauguration into the mysteries of Wedlock, of which you dropped a previous hint in the former. You will accept my sincerest congratulations on this event, with every wish for the happiness it promises. I join you cheerfully in the purchase from Taylor, as preferable to taking it wholly to myself. The only circumstance I regret is that the first payment will rest with you alone if the conveyance should be accelerated. A few months will elapse inevitably before I shall be able to place on the spot my half of the sum, but the day shall be shortened as much as possible. I accede also fully to your idea of extending the purchase in that quarter. Perhaps we may be able to go beyond the thousand acres you have taken into view. But ought we not to explore the ground before we venture too far? Proximity of situation is but presumptive evidence of the quality of soil. The value of land depends on a variety of little circumstances which can only be judged of from inspection,

and a knowledge of which gives a seller an undue advantage over an uninformed buyer. Can we not about the last of May or June take a turn into that district. I am in a manner determined on it myself. It will separate you but for a moment from New York, and may give us lights of great consequence. I have a project in my head, which if it hits your idea and can be effectuated may render such an excursion of decisive value to us. I reserve it for oral communication.

"The Question of policy" you say "is whether it will be better to correct the vices of the Confederation, by recommendation gradually as it moves along, or by a Convention. If the latter should be determined on, the powers of the Virga. Commssrs are inadequate." If all on whom the correction of these vices depends were well informed and well disposed, the mode would be of little moment. But as we have both ignorance and iniquity to control, we must defeat the designs of the latter by humouring the prejudices of the former. The efforts for bringing about a correction thro' the medium of Congress have miscarried. Let a Convention then be tried. If it succeeds in the first instance, it can be repeated as other defects force themselves on the public attention, and as the public mind becomes prepared for further remedies. The Assembly here would refer nothing to Congress. They would have revolted equally against a plenipotentiary commission to their deputies for the Convention. The option therefore lay between doing what was done and doing nothing. Whether a right choice was made time only can prove. I am not in general an advocate for temporizing or partial remedies. But a rigor in this respect, if pushed too far may hazard every thing. If the present paroxism of our affairs be totally neglected our case may become desperate. If any thing comes of the Convention it will probably be of a permanent not a temporary nature, which I think will be a great point. The mind feels a peculiar complacency, in seeing a good thing done when it is not subject to the trouble & uncertainty of doing it over again. The Commission is to be sure not filled to every man's mind. The History of it may be a subject for some future tête atête. You will be kind enough to forward the letter for Mr. Jefferson and to be assured that I am with the sincerest affection Yr friend & Servt.

To Thomas Jefferson

Dear Sir   Philada. Aug: 12th. 1786

My last of the 19th. of June intimated that my next would be from N. York or this place. I expected it would rather have been from the former which I left a few days ago, but my time was so taken up there with my friends and some business that I thought it best to postpone it till my return here. My ride through Virga. Maryd. & Pena. was in the midst of harvest. I found the crops of wheat in the upper parts of the two former considerably injured by the wet weather which my last described as so destructive in the lower parts of those States. The computed loss where I passed was about one third. The loss in the Rye was much greater: It was admitted however that the crops of both would have been unusually large but for this casualty. Throughout Pena. the wheat was unhurt, and the Rye very little affected. As I came by the way of Winchester & crossed the Potowmac at Harpers Ferry I had an opportunity of viewing the magnificent scene which nature here presents. I viewed it however under great disadvantages. The air was so thick that distant objects were not visible at all, and near ones not distinctly so. We ascended the mountain also at a wrong place, fatigued ourselves much in traversing it before we gained the right position, were threatened during the whole time with a thunder storm, and finally overtaken by it. Had the weather been favorable the prospect would have appeared to peculiar advantage, being enriched with the harvest in its full maturity, which filled every vale as far as the eye could reach. I had the additional pleasure here of seeing the progress of the works on the Potowmac. About 50 hands were employed at these falls or rather rapids, who seemed to have overcome the greatest difficulties. Their plan is to slope the fall by opening the bed of the river, in such a manner as to render a lock unnecessary, and by means of ropes fastened to the rocks, to pull up & ease down the boats where the current is most rapid. At the principal falls 150 hands I was told were at work, and that the length of the canal will be reduced to less than a mile, and carried through a vale which does not require it to be deep. Locks will here be unavoidable. The Undertakers are very sanguine. Some of

them who are most so talk of having the entire work finished
in three years. I can give no particular account of the progress
on James River, but am told it is very flattering. I am still less
informed of what is doing with North Carolina towards a
Canal between her & our waters. The undertaking on the
Susquehannah is said to be in such forwardness as to leave no
doubt of its success. A negociation is set on foot between
Pena. Maryd. & Delaware for a canal from the head of
Chesapeak to the Delaware. Maryd. as I understand heretofore opposed the undertaking, and Pena. means now to make
her consent to it a condition on which the opening of the
Susquehannah within the limits of Pena. will depend. Unless
this is permitted the opening undertaken within the limits of
Maryland will be of little account. It is lucky that both parties
are so dependent on each other as to be thus mutually forced
into measures of general Utility. I am told that Pena. has
complied with the joint request of Virga. and Maryland for a
Road between the head of Potowmac and the waters of the
Ohio and the secure & free use of the latter through her jurisdiction. These fruits of the Revolution do great honour to
it. I wish all our proceedings merited the same character.
Unhappily there are but too many belonging to the opposite
side of the acct. At the head of these is to be put the general
rage for paper money. Pena. & N. Carolina took the lead in
this folly. In the former the sum emitted was not considerable, the funds for sinking it were good, and it was not made
a legal tender. It issued into circulation partly by way of loan
to individuals on landed security, partly by way of payment to
the public Creditors. Its present depreciation is about 10 or 12
Per Ct. In N. Carolina the sums issued at different times has
been of greater amount, and it has constantly been a tender.
It issued partly in payments to military creditors, and latterly
in purchases of Tobo. on public account. The Agent I am informed was authorized to give nearly the double of the current price, and as the paper was a tender, debtors ran to him
with their Tobo. and the Creditors paid the expence of the
farce. The depreciation is said to be 25 or 30 Per Ct. in that
State. S. Carolina was the next in order. Her emission was in
the way of loans to individuals, and is not a legal tender. But
land is there made a tender in case of suits, which shuts the

Courts of Justice, and is perhaps as great an evil. The friends of the emission say that it has not yet depreciated, but they admit that the price of commodities has risen, which is evidently the form in which depreciation will first shew itself. New Jersey has just issued £30,000 (dollar at 7/6), in loans to her Citizens. It is a legal tender. An addition of £100,000 is shortly to follow on the same principles. The terror of popular associations stifles as yet an overt discrimination between it & specie; but as this does not operate in Philada. & N. York where all the trade of N. J. is carried on, its depreciation has already commenced in those places & must soon communicate itself to N. J. New York is striking £200,000 (dollr. at 8/-) on the plan of loans to her Citizens. It is made a legal tender in case of suits only. As it is but just issuing from the press, its depreciation exists only in the foresight of those who reason without prejudice on the subject. In Rhode Island £100,000 (dolr. at 6/.) has lately been issued in loans to individuals. It is not only made a tender, but severe penalties annexed to the least attempt direct or indirect to give a preference to specie. Precautions dictated by distrust in the rulers, soon produced it in the people. Supplies were witheld from the Market, the Shops were shut, popular meetings ensued, and the State remains in a sort of Convulsion. The Legislature of Massts. at their last Session rejected a paper emission by a large majority. Connecticut & N. Hampshire also have as yet foreborne, but symptoms of the danger it is said begin to appear in the latter. The Senate of Maryd. has hitherto been a bar to paper in that State. The clamor for it is now universal, and as the periodical election of the Senate happens at this crisis, and the whole body is unluckily by their constitution to be chosen at once, it is probable that a paper emission will be the result. If in spite of the zeal exerted agst. the old Senate a majority of them should be reelected, it will require all their firmness to withstand the popular torrent. Of the affairs of Georga. I know as little as of those of Kamskatska. Whether Virga. is to remain exempt from the epidemic malady will depend on the ensuing Assembly. My hopes rest chiefly on the exertions of Col. Mason and the failure of the experiments elsewhere. That these must fail is morally certain; for besides the proofs of it already visible in some States, and the intrinsic defect of the paper in all, this fictitious money will rather feed than cure the spirit of extravagance which sends away the coin to pay the unfavorable balance, and will therefore soon be carried to market to buy up coin for that purpose. From that moment depreciation is inevitable. The value of money consists in the uses it will serve. Specie will serve all the uses of paper. Paper will not serve one of the essential uses of specie. The paper therefore will be less valuable than specie. Among the numerous ills with which this practice is pregnant, one I find is that it is producing the same warfare & retaliation among the States as were produced by the State regulations of commerce. Massts. & Connecticut have passed laws enabling their Citizens who are debtors to Citizens of States having paper money, to pay their debts in the same manner as their Citizens who are Creditors to Citizens of the latter States are liable to be paid their debts.

The States which have appointed deputies to Annapolis are N. Hampshire, Massts. R. Island, N. Y. N. J. Pena. Delaware & Virga. Connecticut declined not from a dislike to the object, but to the idea of a Convention, which it seems has been rendered obnoxious by some internal Conventions which embarrassed the Legislative Authority. Maryd. or rather her Senate negatived an appointment because they supposed the measure might interfere with the plans or prerogatives of Congs. N. Carolina has had no Legislative meeting since the proposition was communicated. S. Carolina supposed she had sufficiently signified her concurrence in a general regulation of trade by vesting the power in Congs. for 15 years. Georgia— Many Gentlemen both within & without Congs. wish to make this Meeting subservient to a Plenipotentiary Convention for amending the Confederation. Tho' my wishes are in favor of such an event, yet I despair so much of its accomplishment at the present crisis that I do not extend my views beyond a Commercial Reform. To speak the truth *I almost despair even of this*. You will find the *cause in a measure* now before *Congress of which you will receive* the *details* from *Colo. Monroe*. I content myself with *hinting* that it is a *proposed treaty with Spain* one *article of* which *shuts the Mississipi for twenty five or thirty years*. Passing by the other *southern states figure* to yourself the *effect of such a stipulation* on the *assembly of Virginia* already *jealous* of *northern policy* and which will be composed of about *thirty members from* the *western waters;* of a majority of others attached to the *western country from interests* of their *own, of their friends or their constituents* and of many others who though indifferent to the *Missisipi will zealously* play off the *disgust of* its *friends against federal measures.* Figure to yourself its effect on the *people at large* on the *western waters* who are impatiently waiting for a *favorable result* to the *negociation with Guardoqui:* & who will consider themselves as *sold by* their *Atlantic brethren.* Will it be an unnatural consequence if they consider *themselves as absolved* from every *federal tie* and *court some protection* for their *betrayed rights?* This *protection* will appear more attainable from the *maritime power* of *Britain* than from *any other quarter* and *Britain* will be *more ready than any other nation* to *seize an opportunity of embroiling our affairs.* What may be the motive *with Spain to satisfy herself* with a *temporary occlusion* of the *Missisipi* at the same time that *she holds forth* our *claim to it as absolutely inadmissible is matter* of *conjecture only.* The *patrons* of the *measure in Congress* contend that the *minister* who at present *governs the Spanish councils* means only to *disembarass himself at the expence* of *his successors.* I should rather suppose *he means to work a total* separation of *interest and affection between* the *western and eastern settlements* and to *foment* the jealousy *between the eastern* & *southern States.* By the former the *population of* the *western country* it may be expected, will be *checked* and the *Missisipi so far secured* and by both the general *security of Spanish America* be promoted. As far as I can learn the *assent of nine states* in *Congress* will not at this time be *got to the proposed treaty* but an *unsuccessful attempt* by *six or seven* will *favor the views of Spain* and be *fatal I fear* to an *augmentation of* the *federal authority,* if not to the *little now existing.* My personal situation is rendered by this business particularly *mortifying.* Ever since I have been *out of Congress I have been inculcating* on our *assembly a confidence* in the *equal attention of Congress* to the *rights and* interests of *every part of the republic* and on the *western members* in particular, the necessity of making the Union *respectable by new powers* to *Congress* if they wished *Congress to negociate with effect for the Missisipi.* I leave to Col. Monroe the giving you a particular account of the Impost. The Acts of Penna. Delaware & N. York must be revised & amended in material points before it can be put in force, and even then the fetters put on the collection by some other States will make it a very awkward business. Your favor of 25th. of April from London found me here. My letter from Richmd. at the close of the Assembly will have informed you of the situation in which British debts stand in Virga. Unless Congs. say something on the subject I do not think any thing will be done by the next Session. The expectations of the British Merchants coincide with the information I had recd.; as your opinion of the steps proper to be taken by the Assembly, do with those for which I have ineffectually contended. The merits of Mr. P. will ensure every attention from me to his claim as far as general principles will admit. I am afraid that these will insuperably bar his wishes. The Catalogues sent by Mr. Skipwith I do not expect to receive till I get back to Virga. If you meet with "Graecorum Respublicae ab Ubbone Emmio descriptae," Lugd. Batavorum, 1632, pray get it for me.

My trip to N. Y. was occasioned chiefly by a plan concerted between Col. Monroe & myself for a purchase of land on the Mohawk. Both of us have visited that district, and were equally charmed with it. The soil is perhaps scarcely inferior to that of Kentucky, it lies within the body of the Atlantic States, & at a safe distance from every frontier. It is contiguous to a branch of Hudson's River which is navigable with trifling portages which will be temporary, to tide-water, and is not more than ten, 15 or 20 miles from populous settlements where land sells at £8 & £10 per Acre. In talking of this Country sometime ago with *General Washington* he considered it in the same light with Monroe and myself, intimating that if he had money to spare and was disposed to deal in land, this is the very spot which his fancy had selected out of all the U. S. We have made a small purchase, and nothing *but the difficulty of raising a* sufficient *sum restrained us* from *making a large one.* In searching for the *means of overcoming this difficulty,* one has occurred which we have agreed that *I should mention to you* and which if *you should think as we do* is *recomended* by the prospect of *advantage to your self as well as to us.* We mention it *freely because we trust* that *if it does* not *meet your sanction you will as freely tell us so.* It is that the *aid of your credit* in *your private capacity* be *used for borrowing* say, *four or five thousand louis* more or less, on the *obligation of Monro* and myself, with *your suretyship* to be laid out by *Monro and myself* for *our triple emolument*: an *interest* not *exceeding six per cent* to be *paid annually* and the *principal within a term* not less than *eight or ten years*. To guard agst. accidents a private *instrument* might be *executed among ourselves specifying* all necessary *covenants*. We have not taken the resolution of *submitting this plan without well examining* the expediency of *your becoming a party to it* as well as the *prospect of its succeeding*. There can certainly be *no impropriety in your* taking *just means of bettering your fortune* nor can *we discover any in your doing this on* the *Mohawk* more than *on James River*. For the prospect of *gain by* the *rise of* the *land beyond* the *interest of the money we calculate* on the present *difference of price* between the *settled and vacant land* far beyond any *possible* difference in the *real value*. The former as has been noted *sells for eight or ten pounds per acre*. The latter distinguished only by its being a little *higher up* the *river* & its being *uninhabited* was *bought by us for* one *dollar and a half* and there is little doubt that *by taking a larger* quantity, still *better bargains may be got*. This comparative *cheapness* proceeds from causes which are accidental & temporary. The *lands in question* are chiefly in the *hands of men who hold large quantities*, and who are either *in debt* or *live in* the *city at an expence* for which *they have no other resource* or are *engaged in transactions* that *require money*. The scarcity of *specie which* enters *much into the cheapness* is probably but temporary also. As it is the *child of extravagance* it will become the *parent of economy* which will regain us our due share of the *universal medium*. The same vicicitude which can only be retarded by our *short lived substitutes of paper* will be attended also by such a *fall in the rate of exchange* that *money drawn by bills* from *Europe now* and *repaid a few years hence* will probably *save one years interest at least* & I will only add that scarce an instance has happened in which *purchases of new lands of good quality* and *in good situations* have not *well rewarded the adventurers*. With these remarks which determine *our judgments we submit to your better one* the *project to which they relate*. Wishing you every possible happiness I remain Dr Sir your affectionate friend & Servt.

Mrs. House & Mrs. Trist desire to be particularly remembered to yourself & Miss Patsy. I left with Col. Monroe letters for you both from Mrs. T. which will probably go by the same packet with this.

To James Monroe

Dear Sir   Annapolis Sepr. 11. 1786

I have two letters from you not yet acknowledged, one of the 1st the other of the 3d. inst. Nothing could be more distressing than the issue of the business stated in the latter. If the affirmative vote of 7 States sd. be pursued it will add the insult of Trick to the injury of the thing itself. Our prospect here makes no amends for what is done with you. Delaware N. J. & Va. alone are on the ground. Two Commissrs. attend from N. Y. & one from Pa. Unless the sudden attendance of a much more respectable number takes place it is proposed to break up the Meeting with a recommendation of another time & place, & an *intimation* of the expediency of extending the plan to other defects of the Confederation. In case of a speedy dispersion I shall find it requisite to ride back as far as Philada. before I proceed to Virga. from which place, if not from this, I will let you know the Upshot here. I have heard that Col. Grayson was stopped at Trenton by indisposition on his way to the Assembly of Pena. I hope he is well again, and wd. write to him but know not whither to address a letter to him. Adieu Yr. Affy.

To George Washington

Dear Sir   Richmond Decr. 7th. 1786

Notwithstanding the communications in your favor of the 18th. Ult: which has remained till now to be acknowledged, it was the opinion of every judicious friend whom I consulted that your name could not be spared from the Deputation to the Meeting in May in Philada. It was supposed that in the first place, the peculiarity of the mission and its acknowledged pre-eminence over every other public object, may possibly reconcile your undertaking it, with the respect which is justly due & which you wish to pay to the late officers of the army; and in the second place that although you should find that or any other consideration an obstacle to your attendance on the service, the advantage of having your name in the front of the appointment as a mark of the earnestness of Virginia, and an invitation to the most select characters from every part of the Confederacy, ought at all events to be made use of. In these sentiments I own I fully concurred, and flatter myself that they will at least apologize for my departure from those held out in your letter. I even flatter myself that they will merit a serious consideration with yourself, whether the difficulties which you enumerate ought not to give way to them.

The affair of the Mississippi which was brought before the Assembly in a long Memorial from the Western Members & some of the Officers, has undergone a full consideration of both houses. The Resolutions printed in the papers, were agreed to unanimously in the H. of Delegates. In the Senate I am told the language was objected to by some members as too pointed. They certainly express in substance the decided sense of this Country at this time on the subject, and were offered in the place of some which went much farther and which were in other respects exceptionable. I am entirely convinced from what I observe here, that unless the project of Congs. can be reversed, the hopes of carrying this State into a proper federal System will be demolished. Many of our most federal leading men are extremely soured with what has already passed. Mr. Henry, who has been hitherto the Champion of the federal cause, has become a cold advocate, and in the event of an actual sacrifice of the Misspi. by Congress, will unquestionably go over to the opposite side. I have a letter from Col. Grayson of late date which tells me that nothing further has been done in Congs. and one from Mr. Clarke of N. Jersey, which informs me that he expected every hour, instructions from his Legislature for reversing the vote given by the Delegates of that State in favor of the Project.

The temper of the Assembly at the beginning of the Session augured an escape of every measure this year, not consonant to the proper principles of Legislation. I fear now that the conclusion will contradict the promising outset. In admitting Tobo. for a commutable, we perhaps swerved a little from the line in which we set out. I acquiesced in the measure myself, as a prudential compliance with the clamours within doors & without, and as a probable means of obviating more hurtful experiments. I find however now that it either had no such tendency, or that schemes were in embrio which I was not aware of. A bill for establishing district Courts has been clogged with a plan for installing all debts now due, so as to make them payable in three annual portions. What the fate of the experiment will be I know not. It seems pretty certain that if it fails the bill will fail with it. It is urged in support of this measure that it will be favorable to debtors & creditors both, and that without it, the bill for accelerating Justice would ruin the former, and endanger the public repose. The objections are so numerous and of such a nature, that I shall myself give up the bill rather than pay such a price for it. With unfeigned affection & the higst. respt. I am Dr. Sir Yr. Obedt. & hble servt.

To Edmund Pendleton

Dear Sir   New York Feby. 24. 1787.

If the contents of the Newspapers of this place find their way into the gazettes of Richmond you will have learnt that the expedition of Genl: Lincoln against the insurgents has effectually dispersed the main body of them. It appears however that there are still some detachments which remain to be subdued, & that the Government of Massts. consider very strong precautions as necessary agst. further eruptions. The principal incendiaries have unluckily made off. By some it is said they are gone to Canada; by others that they have taken shelter in Vermont, and by some that they are opening a communication with the upper parts of this State. The latter suggestion has probably some color, as the Governor here has thought proper to offer rewards for them after the example of Govr. Bowdoin. We have no interesting information from Europe.

The only step of moment taken by Congs. since my arrival has been a recommendation of the proposed meeting in May

for revising the federal articles. Some of the States, considering this measure as an extraconstitutional one, had scruples
agst. concurring in it without some regular sanction. By
others it was thought best that Congs. should remain neutral
in the business, as the best antidote for the jealousy of an
ambitious desire in them to get more powers into their hands.
This suspence was at length removed by an instruction from
this State to its delegates to urge a Recommendatory Resolution in Congress which accordingly passed a few days ago.
Notwithstanding this instruction from N. York, there is room
to suspect her disposition not to be very federal, a large majority of her House of delegates having very lately entered
into a definitive refusal of the impost, and the instruction itself having passed in the Senate by a casting vote only. In consequence of the sanction given by congs. Massts. it is said will
send deputies to the Convention, and her example will have
great weight with the other N. England States. The States
from N. Ca. to N. Jersey inclusive have made their appointments, except Maryd. who has as yet only determined that she
will make them. The Gentlemen here from S. Ca. & Georgia,
expect that those States will follow the general example. Upon
the whole therefore it seems probable that a meeting will take
place, and that it will be a pretty full one. What the issue of it
will be is among the other arcana of futurity and nearly as in-
scrutable as any of them. In general I find men of reflection
much less sanguine as to a new than despondent as to the
present System. Indeed the present System neither has nor deserves advocates; and if some very strong props are not applied will quickly tumble to the ground. No money is paid
into the public Treasury; no respect is paid to the federal authority. Not a single State complies with the requisitions, several pass them over in silence, and some positively reject them.
The payments ever since the peace have been decreasing, and
of late fall short even of the pittance necessary for the Civil list
of the Confederacy. It is not possible that a Government can
last long under these circumstances. If the approaching Convention should not agree on some remedy, I am persuaded
that some very different arrangement will ensue. The late turbulent scenes in Massts. & infamous ones in Rhode Island,
have done inexpressible injury to the republican character in

that part of the U. States; and a propensity towards Monarchy is said to have been produced by it in some leading minds. The bulk of the people will probably prefer the lesser evil of a partition of the Union into three more practicable and energetic Governments. The latter idea I find after long confinement to individual speculations & private circles, is beginning to shew itself in the Newspapers. But tho' it is a lesser evil, it is so great a one that I hope the danger of it will rouse all the real friends to the Revolution to exert themselves in favor of such an organization of the Confederacy, as will perpetuate the Union, and redeem the honor of the Republican name.

I shall follow this introductory letter with a few lines from time to time as a proper subject for them occurs. The only stipulation I exact on your part is that you will not consider them as claiming either answers or acknowledgments; and that you will believe me to be with sincerest wishes for your health and every other happiness Yr. Affecte. friend & servt.

To Thomas Jefferson

Dear Sir   N. York. March 19th. 1787
My last was of the 15th. of Feby. and went by the Packet. This will go to England in the care of a French gentleman who will consign it to the care of Mr. Adams.

The appointments for the Convention go on auspiciously. Since my last Georgia, S. Carolina, N. York, Massts. and N. Hampshire have come into the measure. The first and last of these States have commissioned their delegates to Congress, as their representatives in Convention. The deputation of Massts. consists of Messrs. Ghoram, Dana, King, Gerry, and Strong. That of N. York, Messrs. Hamilton Yates & Lansing. That of S. Carolina, Messrs. J. Rutledge, Laurens, Pinkney (General) Butler, and Chas. Pinkney lately member of Congress. The States which have not yet appointed are R. Island, Connecticut, and Maryland. The last has taken measures which prove her intention to appoint, and the two former it is not doubted will follow the example of their neighbours. I just learn from the Governor of Virginia that Mr. Henry has resigned his place in the deputation from that State, and that Genl. Nelson is put into it by the Executive who were authorized to fill vacancies. The Governor, Mr. Wythe & Mr. Blair will attend, and some hopes are entertained of Col. Mason's attendance. Genl. Washington has prudently authorized no expectations of his attendance, but has not either precluded himself absolutely from stepping into that field if the crisis should demand it. What may be the result of this political experiment cannot be foreseen. The difficulties which present themselves are on one side almost sufficient to dismay the most sanguine, whilst on the other side the most timid are compelled to encounter them by the mortal diseases of the existing constitution. These diseases need not be pointed out to you who so well understand them. Suffice it to say that they are at present marked by symptoms which are truly alarming, which have tainted the faith of the most orthodox republicans, and which challenge from the votaries of liberty every concession in favor of stable Government not infringing fundamental principles, as the only security against an opposite extreme of our present situation. I think myself that it will be expedient in the first place to lay the foundation of the new system in such a ratification by the people themselves of the several States as will render it clearly paramount to their Legislative authorities. 2dly. Over & above the positive power of regulating trade and sundry other matters in which uniformity is proper, to arm the federal head with a negative *in all cases whatsoever* on the local Legislatures. Without this defensive power experience and reflection have satisfied me that however ample the federal powers may be made, or however Clearly their boundaries may be delineated, on paper, they will be easily and continually baffled by the Legislative sovereignties of the States. The effects of this provision would be not only to guard the national rights and interests against invasion, but also to restrain the States from thwarting and molesting each other, and even from oppressing the minority within themselves by paper money and other unrighteous measures which favor the interest of the majority. In order to render the exercise of such a negative prerogative convenient, an emanation of it must be vested in some set of men within the several States so far as to enable them to give a temporary sanction to laws of immediate necessity. 3dly. to change the principle of Representation in the federal system. Whilst the execution of the Acts of Congs. depends on the several legislatures, the equality of votes does not destroy the inequality of importance and influence in the States. But in case of such an augmentation of the federal power as will render it efficient without the intervention of the Legislatures, a vote in the general Councils from Delaware would be of equal value with one from Massts. or Virginia. This change therefore is just. I think also it will be practicable. A majority of the States conceive that they will be gainers by it. It is recommended to the Eastern States by the actual superiority of their populousness, and to the Southern by their expected superiority. And if a majority of the larger States concur, the fewer and smaller States must finally bend to them. This point being gained, many of the objections now urged in the leading States agst. renunciations of power will vanish. 4thly. to organise the federal powers in such a manner as not to blend together those which ought to be exercised by separate departments. The limited powers now vested in Congs. are frequently mismanaged from the want of such a distribution of them: What would be the case, under an enlargement not only of the powers, but the number, of the federal Representatives? These are some of the leading ideas which have occurred to me, but which may appear to others as improper, as they appear to me necessary.

Congress have continued so thin as to be incompetent to the despatch of the more important business before them. We have at present nine States and it is not improbable that something may now be done. The report of Mr. Jay on the mutual violations of the Treaty of peace will be among the first subjects of deliberation. He *favors the British claim of interest* but *refers* the *question to the court*. The amount of the *report which is an able one* is that the *treaty should* be *put in force* as a *law and the exposition of it* left like that *of other laws to the ordinary tribunals.*

The *Spanish project sleeps. A* perusal of the *attempt of seven states* to make a *new treaty by repealing* an *essential condition of the old* satisfied me that Mr. *Jay's caution* would *revolt at so irregular a sanction.* A late accidental conversation with *Guardoqui proved to me* that the *negociation is arrested.* It may appear strange that a member of *Congress should be indebted to a foreign minister* for *such information yet such* is the *footing on which the intemperance* of *party has put the matter* that it rests wholly with *Mr. Jay how far he* will *communicate with Congress* as well as *how far he will negociate with Guardoqui.* But although it appears that the intended *sacrifice of* the *Missisipi will not be made,* the *consequences of the intention* and the *attempt are likely to be very serious.* I have already made known to you the light in which the subject was *taken up by Virginia.* Mr. *Henry's disgust exceeded all measure* and I am not singular in ascribing his refusal to *attend the Convention* to the *policy of keeping himself free* to *combat or espouse the result of it according* to the result *of the Missisipi business. Among other circumstances North Carolina also* has given *pointed instructions* to *her delegates, so has New Jersey. A proposition* for the *like purpose* was a *few days ago made in the legislature of Pensylvania* but went off without a *decision on its merits. Her delegates in Congress are equally divided* on the subject. The tendency of this *project* to *foment distrusts among the Atlantic states* at a *crisis when harmony* and *confidence ought to have been* studiously *cherished* has not been more *verified than its predicted effect* on the *ultramontane settlements.* I have credible information that the people *living on the western waters are already in great agitation and are* taking *measures for uniting their consultations.* The *ambition* of *individuals* will *quickly mix itself* with the *original motives of resentment and interest. A communication will gradually* take place *with their British neighbors.* They will be *led to set up for themselves* to *seise on the vacant lands to entice* emigrants *by bounties* and an *exemption from federal burdens* and in all respects to *play the part of Vermont on a larger theatre.* It is *hinted to me* that *British partisans* are already *feeling the pulse* of some of the *West settlements.* Should these *apprehensions not be imaginary Spain may have equal reason* with the *United States to rue the unnatural attempt to shut the Missisipi. Guardoqui has been admonished* of *the danger* and I believe *is not insensible to it tho'* he *affects to be otherwise* and *talks* as if the dependence of *Britain on the commercial favors of his court* would *induce her to play into the hands of Spain.* The eye of *France also can not fail to watch over the western prospects.* I learn from those who *confer here with Otto and de la forest* that they *favor the open-*

ing of the Missisipi disclaiming *at the same time any authority to* speak the *sentiments of their court*. I find that the *Virginia delegates during the Missisipi discussions* last *fall entered into very confidential interviews with these gentlemen*. In one of them the *idea was communicated to Otto* of *opening the Missisipi for exports* but *not for imports* and *of giving to France and Spain* some *exclusive privileges in the trade*. He *promised* to transmit it to *Vergennes to obtain his sentiments* on the *whole matter* and *to communicate them to the delegates*. Not long *since Grayson called on him* and *revived the subject*. He as*sured* G—that *he had received no answer* from *France* and signified his *wish that you might pump the Count de Vergennes observing that he would deny to you his having received any information from America*. I *discover thro* several *channels that it would be* very *grateful to the French politicians here to see our negociations with Spain shifted into your hands* and *carried on under the mediating auspices of their court*.

Van Berkel has remonstrated against the late *acts of Virginia giving privileges to French wines* and *brandies in French bottoms contending* that the *Dutch are entitled* by *their treaty to equal exemptions* with the *most favored nation without being subject to a compensation for them*. Mr. *Jay has reported against this construction* but considers the *act of Virginia as violating the treaty* first *because it appears to be gratuitous* not *compensatory on the face of it*. Secondly *because the states have no right to form tacit compacts* with *foreign nations*. No decision of Congress has yet taken place on the subject.

The expedition under General Lincoln agst. the insurgents has effectually succeeded in dispersing them. Whether the calm which he has restored will be durable or not is uncertain. From the precautions taking by the Govt. of Massts. it would seem as if their apprehensions were not extinguished. Besides disarming and disfranchising for a limited time those who have been in arms, as a condition of their pardon, a military corps is to be raised to the amount of 1000, or 1500 men, and to be stationed in the most suspected districts. It is said that notwithstanding these specimens of the temper of the Government, a great proportion of the offenders chuse rather to risk the consequences of their treason, than submit to the conditions annexed to the amnesty, that they not only appear openly on public occasions but distinguish themselves by badges of their character, and that this insolence is in many instances countenanced by no less decisive marks of popular favor than elections to local offices of trust & authority.

A proposition is before the Legislature of this State now sitting for renouncing its pretensions to Vermont, and urging the admission of it into the confederacy. The different parties are not agreed as to the form in which the renunciation should be made, but are likely to agree as to the substance. Should the offer be made, and Vermont should not reject it altogether I think they will insist on two stipulations at least, 1st. that their becoming parties to the Confederation shall not subject their boundaries, or the rights of their citizens to be questioned under the 9th. art: 2dly. that they shall not be subject to any part of the public debts already contracted.

The Geographer and his assistants have returned surveys on the federal lands to the amount of about 800,000 Acres which it is supposed would sell pretty readily for public securities, and some of it lying on the Ohio even for specie. It will be difficult however to *get the proper steps taken by Congress so many of the states having* now *lands of their own at market.* It is supposed that this consideration had *some share in the zeal for shutting the Missisipi. New Jersey* and some others *having no western lands* which *favored this measure* begin now to *penetrate the secret.*

A letter from the Govr. of Virga. informs me that the project of paper money is beginning to recover from the blow given it at the last Session of the Legislature. *If Mr. H. espouses it of which* there is *little doubt I think an emission will take place.* The Governor mentions the death of Col A. Cary speaker of the Senate.

This letter will be accompanied by another inclosing a few Peccan Nuts. When I sent the latter to the Gentleman who is charged with it, I doubted whether I should be able to finish this in time, and I only succeed by having written to the last moment. Adeiu. Yrs. Afey.

Vices of the Political System of the United States

April. 1787

Vices of the
Political system
of the U. States

Observations by J. M. (a copy taken by
permission by Danl. Carroll & sent to
Chs Carroll of Carrollton)

1. Failure of the
States to comply
with the
Constitutional
requisitions.

1. This evil has been so fully experienced
both during the war and since the peace,
results so naturally from the number and
independent authority of the States and
has been so uniformly examplified in
every similar Confederacy, that it may be
considered as not less radically and permanently inherent in, than it is fatal to the
object of, the present System.

2. Encroach-
ments by the
States on
the federal
authority.

2. Examples of this are numerous and
repetitions may be foreseen in almost
every case where any favorite object of a
State shall present a temptation. Among
these examples are the wars and Treaties
of Georgia with the Indians—The un-
licensed compacts between Virginia and
Maryland, and between Pena. & N.
Jersey—the troops raised and to be kept
up by Massts.

3. Violations of
the law of na-
tions and of
treaties.

3. From the number of Legislatures, the
sphere of life from which most of their
members are taken, and the circumstances
under which their legislative business is
carried on, irregularities of this kind must
frequently happen. Accordingly not a year
has passed without instances of them in
some one or other of the States. The
Treaty of peace—the treaty with France—
the treaty with Holland have each been
violated. [See the complaints to Congress
on these subjects]. The causes of these ir-

regularities must necessarily produce frequent violations of the law of nations in other respects.

As yet foreign powers have not been rigorous in animadverting on us. This moderation however cannot be mistaken for a permanent partiality to our faults, or a permanent security agst. those disputes with other nations, which being among the greatest of public calamities, it ought to be least in the power of any part of the Community to bring on the whole.

4. Trespasses of the States on the rights of each other.

4. These are alarming symptoms, and may be daily apprehended as we are admonished by daily experience. See the law of Virginia restricting foreign vessels to certain ports—of Maryland in favor of vessels belonging to her own citizens—of N. York in favor of the same.

Paper money, instalments of debts, occlusion of Courts, making property a legal tender, may likewise be deemed aggressions on the rights of other States. As the Citizens of every State aggregately taken stand more or less in the relation of Creditors or debtors, to the Citizens of every other States, Acts of the debtor State in favor of debtors, affect the Creditor State, in the same manner, as they do its own citizens who are relatively creditors towards other citizens. This remark may be extended to foreign nations. If the exclusive regulation of the value and alloy of coin was properly delegated to the federal authority, the policy of it equally requires a controul on the States in the cases above mentioned. It must have been meant 1. to preserve uniformity in the circulating medium throughout the nation. 2. to prevent those frauds on the citizens of other States, and the subjects of foreign powers, which might disturb the tranquility at home, or involve the Union in foreign contests.

The practice of many States in restricting the commercial intercourse with other States, and putting their productions and manufactures on the same footing with those of foreign nations, though not contrary to the federal articles, is certainly adverse to the spirit of the Union, and tends to beget retaliating regulations, not less expensive & vexatious in themselves, than they are destructive of the general harmony.

5. want of concert in matters where common interest requires it.

5. This defect is strongly illustrated in the state of our commercial affairs. How much has the national dignity, interest, and revenue suffered from this cause? Instances of inferior moment are the want of uniformity in the laws concerning naturalization & literary property; of provision for national seminaries, for grants of incorporation for national purposes, for canals and other works of general utility, wch. may at present be defeated by the perverseness of particular States whose concurrence is necessary.

6. want of Guaranty to the States of their Constitutions & laws against internal violence.

6. The confederation is silent on this point and therefore by the second article the hands of the federal authority are tied. According to Republican Theory, Right and power being both vested in the majority, are held to be synonimous. According to fact and experience a minority may in an appeal to force, be an overmatch for the majority. 1. If the minority happen to include all such as possess the skill and habits of military life, & such as possess the great pecuniary resources, one

third only may conquer the remaining two thirds. 2. One third of those who participate in the choice of the rulers, may be rendered a majority by the accession of those whose poverty excludes them from a right of suffrage, and who for obvious reasons will be more likely to join the standard of sedition than that of the established Government. 3. Where slavery exists the republican Theory becomes still more fallacious.

7. want of sanction to the laws, and of coercion in the Government of the Confederacy.

7. A sanction is essential to the idea of law, as coercion is to that of Government. The federal system being destitute of both, wants the great vital principles of a Political Constitution. Under the form of such a Constitution, it is in fact nothing more than a treaty of amity of commerce and of alliance, between so many independent and Sovereign States. From what cause could so fatal an omission have happened in the articles of Confederation? from a mistaken confidence that the justice, the good faith, the honor, the sound policy, of the several legislative assemblies would render superfluous any appeal to the ordinary motives by which the laws secure the obedience of individuals: a confidence which does honor to the enthusiastic virtue of the compilers, as much as the inexperience of the crisis apologizes for their errors. The time which has since elapsed has had the double effect, of increasing the light and tempering the warmth, with which the arduous work may be revised. It is no longer doubted that a unanimous and punctual obedience of 13 independent bodies, to the acts of the federal Government, ought not be calculated on. Even during the war, when

external danger supplied in some degree the defect of legal & coercive sanctions, how imperfectly did the States fulfil their obligations to the Union? In time of peace, we see already what is to be expected. How indeed could it be otherwise? In the first place, Every general act of the Union must necessarily bear unequally hard on some particular member or members of it. Secondly the partiality of the members to their own interests and rights, a partiality which will be fostered by the Courtiers of popularity, will naturally exaggerate the inequality where it exists, and even suspect it where it has no existence. Thirdly a distrust of the voluntary compliance of each other may prevent the compliance of any, although it should be the latent disposition of all. Here are causes & pretexts which will never fail to render federal measures abortive. If the laws of the States, were merely recommendatory to their citizens, or if they were to be rejudged by County authorities, what security, what probability would exist, that they would be carried into execution? Is the security or probability greater in favor of the acts of Congs. which depending for their execution on the will of the state legislatures, wch. are tho' nominally authoritative, in fact recommendatory only.

8. Want of ratification by the people of the articles of Confederation.

8. In some of the States the Confederation is recognized by, and forms a part of the constitution. In others however it has received no other sanction than that of the Legislative authority. From this defect two evils result: 1. Whenever a law of a State happens to be repugnant to an act of Congress, particularly when the

latter is of posterior date to the former, it will be at least questionable whether the latter must not prevail; and as the question must be decided by the Tribunals of the State, they will be most likely to lean on the side of the State.

2. As far as the Union of the States is to be regarded as a league of sovereign powers, and not as a political Constitution by virtue of which they are become one sovereign power, so far it seems to follow from the doctrine of compacts, that a breach of any of the articles of the confederation by any of the parties to it, absolves the other parties from their respective obligations, and gives them a right if they chuse to exert it, of dissolving the Union altogether.

9. Multiplicity of laws in the several States.

9. In developing the evils which viciate the political system of the U. S. it is proper to include those which are found within the States individually, as well as those which directly affect the States collectively, since the former class have an indirect influence on the general malady and must not be overlooked in forming a compleat remedy. Among the evils then of our situation may well be ranked the multiplicity of laws from which no State is exempt. As far as laws are necessary, to mark with precision the duties of those who are to obey them, and to take from those who are to administer them a discretion, which might be abused, their number is the price of liberty. As far as the laws exceed this limit, they are a nuisance: a nuisance of the most pestilent kind. Try the Codes of the several States by this test, and what a luxuriancy of legislation do they present. The short period of independency has

filled as many pages as the century which
preceded it. Every year, almost every session, adds a new volume. This may be the
effect in part, but it can only be in part, of
the situation in which the revolution has
placed us. A review of the several codes
will shew that every necessary and useful
part of the least voluminous of them
might be compressed into one tenth of
the compass, and at the same time be rendered tenfold as perspicuous.

10. mutability of the laws of the States.

10. This evil is intimately connected with
the former yet deserves a distinct notice as
it emphatically denotes a vicious legislation. We daily see laws repealed or superseded, before any trial can have been
made of their merits; and even before a
knowledge of them can have reached the
remoter districts within which they were
to operate. In the regulations of trade this
instability becomes a snare not only to
our citizens but to foreigners also.

11. Injustice of the laws of States.

11. If the multiplicity and mutability of
laws prove a want of wisdom, their injustice betrays a defect still more alarming:
more alarming not merely because it is a
greater evil in itself, but because it brings
more into question the fundamental principle of republican Government, that the
majority who rule in such Governments,
are the safest Guardians both of public
Good and of private rights. To what
causes is this evil to be ascribed?

These causes lie 1. in the Representative bodies.
2. in the people them-
selves.

1. Representative appointments are sought
from 3 motives. 1. ambition 2. personal interest. 3. public good. Unhappily the two

first are proved by experience to be most prevalent. Hence the candidates who feel them, particularly, the second, are most industrious, and most successful in pursuing their object: and forming often a majority in the legislative Councils, with interested views, contrary to the interest, and views, of their Constituents, join in a perfidious sacrifice of the latter to the former. A succeeding election it might be supposed, would displace the offenders, and repair the mischief. But how easily are base and selfish measures, masked by pretexts of public good and apparent expediency? How frequently will a repetition of the same arts and industry which succeeded in the first instance, again prevail on the unwary to misplace their confidence?

How frequently too will the honest but unenlightened representative be the dupe of a favorite leader, veiling his selfish views under the professions of public good, and varnishing his sophistical arguments with the glowing colours of popular eloquence?

2. A still more fatal if not more frequent cause lies among the people themselves. All civilized societies are divided into different interests and factions, as they happen to be creditors or debtors— Rich or poor—husbandmen, merchants or manufacturers—members of different religious sects—followers of different political leaders—inhabitants of different districts—owners of different kinds of property &c &c. In republican Government the majority however composed, ultimately give the law. Whenever therefore an apparent interest or common passion

unites a majority what is to restrain them
from unjust violations of the rights and interests of the minority, or of individuals?
Three motives only 1. a prudent regard to
their own good as involved in the general
and permanent good of the Community.
This consideration although of decisive
weight in itself, is found by experience to
be too often unheeded. It is too often forgotten, by nations as well as by individuals
that honesty is the best policy. 2dly. respect for character. However strong this
motive may be in individuals, it is considered as very insufficient to restrain them
from injustice. In a multitude its efficacy is
diminished in proportion to the number
which is to share the praise or the blame.
Besides, as it has reference to public opinion, which within a particular Society, is
the opinion of the majority, the standard
is fixed by those whose conduct is to be
measured by it. The public opinion without the Society, will be little respected by
the people at large of any Country. Individuals of extended views, and of national
pride, may bring the public proceedings
to this standard, but the example will
never be followed by the multitude. Is it
to be imagined that an ordinary citizen or
even an assembly-man of R. Island in estimating the policy of paper money, ever
considered or cared in what light the measure would be viewed in France or Holland; or even in Massts or Connect.? It
was a sufficient temptation to both that it
was for their interest: it was a sufficient
sanction to the latter that it was popular in
the State; to the former that it was so
in the neighbourhood. 3dly. will Religion
the only remaining motive be a sufficient

restraint? It is not pretended to be such on men individually considered. Will its effect be greater on them considered in an aggregate view? quite the reverse. The conduct of every popular assembly acting on oath, the strongest of religious Ties, proves that individuals join without remorse in acts, against which their consciences would revolt if proposed to them under the like sanction, separately in their closets. When indeed Religion is kindled into enthusiasm, its force like that of other passions, is increased by the sympathy of a multitude. But enthusiasm is only a temporary state of religion, and while it lasts will hardly be seen with pleasure at the helm of Government. Besides as religion in its coolest state, is not infallible, it may become a motive to oppression as well as a restraint from injustice. Place three individuals in a situation wherein the interest of each depends on the voice of the others, and give to two of them an interest opposed to the rights of the third? Will the latter be secure? The prudence of every man would shun the danger. The rules & forms of justice suppose & guard against it. Will two thousand in a like situation be less likely to encroach on the rights of one thousand? The contrary is witnessed by the notorious factions & oppressions which take place in corporate towns limited as the opportunities are, and in little republics when uncontrouled by apprehensions of external danger. If an enlargement of the sphere is found to lessen the insecurity of private rights, it is not because the impulse of a common interest or passion is less predominant in this case with the majority; but because a common interest or passion is less apt to be felt and the requisite combinations less easy to be formed by a great than by a small number. The Society becomes broken into a greater variety of interests, of pursuits, of passions, which check each other, whilst those who may feel a common sentiment have less opportunity of communication and concert. It may be inferred that the inconveniences of popular States contrary to the prevailing Theory, are in proportion not to the extent, but to the narrowness of their limits.

The great desideratum in Government is such a modification of the Sovereignty as will render it sufficiently neutral between the different interests and factions, to controul one part of the Society from invading the rights of another, and at the same time sufficiently controuled itself, from setting up an interest adverse to that of the whole Society. In absolute Monarchies, the prince is sufficiently, neutral towards his subjects, but frequently sacrifices their happiness to his ambition or his avarice. In small Republics, the sovereign will is sufficiently controuled from such a Sacrifice of the entire Society, but is not sufficiently neutral towards the parts composing it. As a limited Monarchy tempers the evils of an absolute one; so an extensive Republic meliorates the administration of a small Republic.

An auxiliary desideratum for the melioration of the Republican form is such a process of elections as will most certainly extract from the mass of the Society the purest and noblest characters which it contains; such as will at once feel most strongly the proper motives to pursue the end of their appointment, and be most capable to devise the proper means of attaining it.

12. Impotence
of the laws of
the States

To George Washington

Dear Sir   New York April 16 1787

I have been honoured with your letter of the 31 of March, and find with much pleasure that your views of the reform which ought to be pursued by the Convention, give a sanction to those which I have entertained. Temporising applications will dishonor the Councils which propose them, and may foment the internal malignity of the disease, at the same time that they produce an ostensible palliation of it. Radical attempts, although unsuccessful, will at least justify the authors of them.

Having been lately led to revolve the subject which is to undergo the discussion of the Convention, and formed in my mind *some* outlines of a new system, I take the liberty of submitting them without apology, to your eye.

Conceiving that an individual independence of the States is utterly irreconcileable with their aggregate sovereignty; and that a consolidation of the whole into one simple republic would be as inexpedient as it is unattainable, I have sought for some middle ground, which may at once support a due supremacy of the national authority, and not exclude the local authorities wherever they can be subordinately useful.

I would propose as the ground-work that a change be made in the principle of representation. According to the present form of the Union in which the intervention of the States is in all great cases necessary to effectuate the measures of Congress, an equality of suffrage, does not destroy the inequality of importance, in the several members. No one will deny that Virginia and Massts. have more weight and influence both within & without Congress than Delaware or Rho. Island. Under a system which would operate in many essential points without the intervention of the State legislatures, the case would be materially altered. A vote in the national Councils from Delaware, would then have the same effect and value as one from the largest State in the Union. I am ready to believe that such a change would not be attended with much difficulty. A majority of the States, and those of greatest influence, will regard it as favorable to them. To the Northern States it will be recommended by their present populousness; to the Southern by their expected advantage in this respect. The lesser States must in every event yield to the predominant will. But the consideration which particularly urges a change in the representation is that it will obviate the principal objections of the larger States to the necessary concessions of power.

I would propose next that in addition to the present federal powers, the national Government should be armed with positive and compleat authority in all cases which require uniformity; such as the regulation of trade, including the right of taxing both exports & imports, the fixing the terms and forms of naturalization, &c &c.

Over and above this positive power, a negative *in all cases whatsoever* on the legislative acts of the States, as heretofore exercised by the Kingly prerogative, appears to me to be absolutely necessary, and to be the least possible encroachment on the State jurisdictions. Without this defensive power, every positive power that can be given on paper will be evaded & defeated. The States will continue to invade the national jurisdiction, to violate treaties and the law of nations & to harrass each other with rival and spiteful measures dictated by mistaken views of interest. Another happy effect of this prerogative would be its controul on the internal vicisitudes of State policy; and the aggressions of interested majorities on the rights of minorities and of individuals. The great desideratum which has not yet been found for Republican Governments, seems to be some disinterested & dispassionate umpire in disputes between different passions & interests in the State. The majority who alone have the right of decision, have frequently an interest real or supposed in abusing it. In

Monarchies the sovereign is more neutral to the interests and views of different parties; but unfortunately he too often forms interests of his own repugnant to those of the whole. Might not the national prerogative here suggested be found sufficiently disinterested for the decision of local questions of policy, whilst it would itself be sufficiently restrained from the pursuit of interests adverse to those of the whole Society? There has not been any moment since the peace at which the representatives of the union would have given an assent to paper money or any other measure of a kindred nature.

The national supremacy ought also to be extended as I conceive to the Judiciary departments. If those who are to expound & apply the laws, are connected by their interests & their oaths with the particular States wholly, and not with the Union, the participation of the Union in the making of the laws may be possibly rendered unavailing. It seems at least necessary that the oaths of the Judges should include a fidelity to the general as well as local constitution, and that an appeal should lie to some national tribunals in all cases to which foreigners or inhabitants of other States may be parties. The admiralty jurisdiction seems to fall entirely within the purview of the national Government.

The national supremacy in the Executive departments is liable to some difficulty, unless the officers administering them could be made appointable by the supreme Government. The Militia ought certainly to be placed in some form or other under the authority which is entrusted with the general protection and defence.

A Government composed of such extensive powers should be well organized and balanced. The Legislative department might be divided into two branches; one of them chosen every   years by the people at large, or by the legislatures; the other to consist of fewer members, to hold their places for a longer term, and to go out in such a rotation as always to leave in office a large majority of old members. Perhaps the negative on the laws might be most conveniently exercised by this branch. As a further check, a council of revision including the great ministerial officers might be superadded.

A national Executive must also be provided. I have scarcely

ventured as yet to form my own opinion either of the manner in which it ought to be constituted or of the authorities with which it ought to be cloathed.

An article should be inserted expressly guarantying the tranquillity of the States against internal as well as external dangers.

In like manner the right of coercion should be expressly declared. With the resources of Commerce in hand, the national administration might always find means of exerting it either by sea or land; But the difficulty & awkwardness of operating by force on the collective will of a State, render it particularly desirable that the necessity of it might be precluded. Perhaps the negative on the laws might create such a mutuality of dependence between the General and particular authorities, as to answer this purpose. Or perhaps some defined objects of taxation might be submitted along with commerce, to the general authority.

To give a new System its proper validity and energy, a ratification must be obtained from the people, and not merely from the ordinary authority of the Legislatures. This will be the more essential as inroads on the *existing Constitutions* of the States will be unavoidable.

The inclosed address to the States on the subject of the Treaty of peace has been agreed to by Congress, & forwarded to the several Executives. We foresee the irritation which it will excite in many of our Countrymen; but could not withold our approbation of the measure. Both, the resolutions and the address, passed without a dissenting voice.

Congress continue to be thin, and of course do little business of importance. The settlement of the public accounts, the disposition of the public lands, and arrangements with Spain, are subjects which claim their particular attention. As a step towards the first, the treasury board are charged with the task of reporting a plan by which the final decision on the claims of the States will be handed over from Congress to a select set of men bound by the oaths, and cloathed with the powers, of Chancellors. As to the Second article, Congress have it themselves under consideration. Between 6 & 700 thousand acres have been surveyed and are ready for sale. The mode of sale however will probably be a source of different opinions; as will the mode of disposing of the unsurveyed residue. The Eastern gentlemen remain attached to the scheme of townships. Many others are equally strenuous for indiscriminate locations. The States which have lands of their own for sale, are *suspected* of not being hearty in bringing the federal lands to market. The business with Spain is becoming extremely delicate, and the information from the Western settlements truly alarming.

A motion was made some days ago for an adjournment of Congress for a short period, and an appointment of Philada. for their reassembling. The excentricity of this place as well with regard to E. and West as to N. & South has I find been for a considerable time a thorn in the minds of many of the Southern members. Suspicion too has charged some important votes on the weight thrown by the present position of Congress into the Eastern Scale, and predicts that the Eastern members will never concur in any substantial provision or movement for a proper permanent seat for the national Government whilst they remain so much gratified in its temporary residence. These seem to have been the operative motives with those on one side who were not locally interested in the removal. On the other side the motives are obvious. Those of real weight were drawn from the apparent caprice with which Congress might be reproached, and particularly from the peculiarity of the existing moment. I own that I think so much regard due to these considerations, that notwithstanding the powerful ones on the other side, I should have assented with great repugnance to the motion, and would even have voted against it if any probability had existed that by waiting for a proper time, a proper measure might not be lost for a very long time. The plan which I shd. have judged most eligible would have been to fix on the removal whenever a vote could be obtained but so as that it should not take effect until the commencement of the ensuing federal year. And if an immediate removal had been resolved on, I had intended to propose such a change in the plan. No final question was taken in the case. Some preliminary questions shewed that six States were in favor of the motion. Rho. Island the 7th. was at first on the same side, and Mr. Varnum one of her delegates continues so. His colleague was overcome by the solicitations of his Eastern breathren. As neither Maryland nor South Carolina were on the floor, it seems pretty evident that N. York has a very precarious tenure of the advantages derived from the abode of Congress.

We understand that the discontents in Massts which lately produced an appeal to the sword, are now producing a trial of strength in the field of electioneering. The Governor will be displaced. The Senate is said to be already of a popular complexion, and it is expected the other branch will be still more so. Paper money it is surmised will be the engine to be played off agst. creditors both public and private. As the event of the Elections however is not yet decided, this information must be too much blended with conjecture to be regarded as matter of certainty.

I do not learn that the proposed act relating to Vermont has yet gone through all the stages of legislation here; nor can I say whether it will finally pass or not. In truth, it having not been a subject of conversation for some time, I am unable to say what has been done or is likely to be done with it. With the sincerest affection & the highest esteem I have the honor to be Dear Sir Your devoted Servt.

FRAMING AND RATIFYING
THE CONSTITUTION
1787–1789

The Virginia Plan

Resolutions proposed by Mr. Randolph in Convention
May 29, 1787

1. Resolved that the Articles of Confederation ought to be so corrected & enlarged as to accomplish the objects proposed by their institution; namely, "common defence, security of liberty and general welfare."

2. Resd. therefore that the rights of suffrage in the National Legislature ought to be proportioned to the Quotas of contribution, or to the number of free inhabitants, as the one or the other rule may seem best in different cases.

3. Resd. that the National Legislature ought to consist of two branches.

4. Resd. that the members of the first branch of the national Legislature ought to be elected by the people of the several States every   for the term of   ; to be of the age of   years at least, to receive liberal stipends by which they may be compensated for the devotion of their time to public service; to be ineligible to any office established by a particular State, or under the authority of the United States, except those peculiarly belonging to the functions of the first branch, during the term of service, and for the space of   after its expiration; to be incapable of re-election for the space of   after the expiration of their term of service, and to be subject to recall.

5. Resold. that the members of the second branch of the National Legislature ought to be elected by those of the first, out of a proper number of persons nominated by the individual Legislatures, to be of the age of   years at least; to hold their offices for a term sufficient to ensure their independency; to receive liberal stipends, by which they may be compensated for the devotion of their time to public service; and to be ineligible to any office established by a particular State, or under the authority of the United States, except those peculiarly belonging to the functions of the second branch, during the term of service, and for the space of   after the expiration thereof.

6. Resolved that each branch ought to possess the right of

originating Acts; that the national Legislature ought to be impowered to enjoy the Legislative Rights vested in Congress by the Confederation & moreover to legislate in all cases to which the separate States are incompetent, or in which the harmony of the United States may be interrupted by the exercise of individual Legislation; to negative all laws passed by the several States, contravening in the opinion of the National Legislature the articles of Union, and to call forth the force of the Union agst. any member of the Union failing to fulfill its duty under the articles thereof.

7. Resd. that a National Executive be instituted; to be chosen by the National Legislature for the term of   years, to receive punctually at stated times a fixed compensation for the services rendered, in which no increase or diminution shall be made so as to affect the Magistracy, existing at the time of increase or diminution, and to be ineligible a second time; and that besides a general authority to execute the National laws, it ought to enjoy the Executive rights vested in Congress by the Confederation.

8. Resd. that the Executive and a Convenient number of the National Judiciary, ought to compose a Council of revision with authority to examine every act of the National Legislature before it shall operate, & every act of a particular Legislature before a Negative thereon shall be final; and that the dissent of the said Council shall amount to a rejection, unless the Act of the National Legislature be again passed, or that of a particular Legislature be again negatived by   of the members of each branch.

9. Resd. that a National Judiciary be established to consist of one or more supreme tribunals, and of inferior tribunals to be chosen by the National Legislature, to hold their offices during good behaviour; and to receive punctually at stated times fixed compensation for their services, in which no increase or diminution shall be made so as to affect the persons actually in office at the time of such increase or diminution. That the jurisdiction of the inferior tribunals shall be to hear & determine in the first instance, and of the supreme tribunal to hear and determine in the dernier resort, all Piracies & felonies on the high seas, captures from an enemy; cases in which foreigners or citizens of other States applying to such

jurisdictions may be interested, or which respect the collection of the National revenue; impeachments of any national officers, and questions which may involve the national peace and harmony.

10. Resolvd. that provision ought to be made for the admission of States lawfully arising within the limits of the United States, whether from a voluntary junction of Government & Territory or otherwise, with the consent of a number of voices in the National legislature less than the whole.

11. Resd. that a Republican Government & the territory of each State, except in the instance of a voluntary junction of Government & territory, ought to be guaranteed by the United States to each State.

12. Resd. that provision ought to be made for the continuance of Congress and their authorities and privileges, until a given day after the reform of the articles of Union shall be adopted, and for the completion of all their engagements.

13. Resd. that provision ought to be made for the amendment of the Articles of Union whensoever it shall seem necessary, and that the assent of the National Legislature ought not to be required thereto.

14. Resd. that the Legislative Executive & Judiciary powers within the several States ought to be bound by oath to support the articles of Union.

15. Resd. that the amendments which shall be offered to the Confederation, by the Convention ought at a proper time, or times, after the approbation of Congress to be submitted to an assembly or assemblies of Representatives, recommended by the several Legislatures to be expressly chosen by the people to consider & decide thereon.

Speech in the Federal Convention on Factions

Mr. Madison considered an election of one branch at least of the Legislature by the people immediately, as a clear principle of free Govt. and that this mode under proper regulations had the additional advantage of securing better representatives, as well as of avoiding too great an agency of the State Governments in the General one. He differed from the member from Connecticut (Mr. Sharman) in thinking the objects mentioned to be all the principal ones that required a National Govt. Those were certainly important and necessary objects; but he combined with them the necessity, of providing more effectually for the security of private rights, and the steady dispensation of Justice. Interferences with these were evils which had more perhaps than any thing else produced this convention. Was it to be supposed that republican liberty could long exist under the abuses of it practiced in some of the States. The gentleman (Mr. Sharman) had admitted that in a very small State, faction & oppression wd. prevail. It was to be inferred then that wherever these prevailed the State was too small. Had they not prevailed in the largest as well as the smallest tho' less than in the smallest; and were we not thence admonished to enlarge the sphere as far as the nature of the Govt. would admit. This was the only defence agst. the inconveniencies of democracy consistent with the democratic form of Govt. All civilized Societies would be divided into different Sects, Factions, & interests, as they happened to consist of rich & poor, debtors & creditors, the landed the manufacturing the commercial interests, the inhabitants of this district or that district, the followers of this political leader or that political leader, the disciples of this religious Sect or that religious Sect. In all cases where a majority are united by a common interest or passion, the rights of the minority are in danger. What motives are to restrain them? A prudent regard to the maxim that honesty is the best policy is found by experience to be as little regarded by bodies of men as by individuals. Respect for character is always diminished in proportion to the number among whom the blame or praise is to be divided. Conscience, the only remaining tie, is known to be inadequate in individuals: In large numbers little is to be expected from it. Besides, Religion itself may become a motive to persecution & oppression. These observations are verified by the Histories of every Country antient & modern. In Greece & Rome the rich & poor, the creditors & debtors, as well as the patricians & plebians alternately oppressed each other with equal unmercifulness. What a source of oppression was the relation between the parent Cities of Rome, Athens & Carthage, & their respective provinces: the former possessing the power, & the latter being sufficiently distinguished to be separate objects of it? Why was America so justly apprehensive of Parliamentary injustice? Because G. Britain had a separate interest real or supposed, & if her authority had been admitted, could have pursued that interest at our expence. We have seen the mere distinction of colour made in the most enlightened period of time, a ground of the most oppressive dominion ever exercised by man over man. What has been the source of those unjust laws complained of among ourselves? Has it not been the real or supposed interest of the major number? Debtors have defrauded their creditors. The landed interest has borne hard on the mercantile interest. The Holders of one species of property have thrown a disproportion of taxes on the holders of another species. The lesson we are to draw from the whole is that where a majority are united by a common sentiment and have an opportunity, the rights of the minor party become insecure. In a Republican Govt. the Majority if united have always an opportunity. The only remedy is to enlarge the sphere, & thereby divide the community into so great a number of interests & parties, that in the 1st. place a majority will not be likely at the same moment to have a common interest separate from that of the whole or of the minority; and in the 2d place, that in case they shd have such an interest, they may not be apt to unite in the pursuit of it. It was incumbent on us then to try this remedy, and with that view to frame a republican system on such a scale & in such a form as will controul all the evils wch. have been experienced.

June 6, 1787

Speech in the Federal Convention on the Revisionary Power

Mr. Madison 2ded. the motion. He observed that the great difficulty in rendering the Executive competent to its own defence arose from the nature of Republican Govt. which could not give to an individual citizen that settled pre-eminence in the eyes of the rest, that weight of property, that personal interest agst. betraying the national interest, which appertain to an hereditary magistrate. In a Republic personal merit alone could be the ground of political exaltation, but it would rarely happen that this merit would be so pre-eminent as to produce universal acquiescence. The Executive Magistrate would be envied & assailed by disappointed competitors: His firmness therefore wd. need support. He would not possess those great emoluments from his station, nor that permanent stake in the public interest which wd. place him out of the reach of foreign corruption: He would stand in need therefore of being controuled as well as supported. An association of the Judges in his revisionary function wd both double the advantage and diminish the danger. It wd. also enable the Judiciary Department the better to defend itself agst. Legislative encroachments. Two objections had been made 1st. that the Judges ought not to be subject to the bias which a participation in the making of laws might give in the exposition of them. 2dly. that the Judiciary Departmt. ought to be separate & distinct from the other great Departments. The 1st. objection had some weight; but it was much diminished by reflecting that a small proportion of the laws coming in question before a Judge wd. be such wherein he had been consulted; that a small part of this proportion wd. be so ambiguous as to leave room for his prepossessions; and that but a few cases wd. probably arise in the life of a Judge under such ambiguous passages. How much good on the other hand wd. proceed from the perspicuity, the conciseness, and the systematic character wch. the Code of laws wd. receive from the Judiciary talents. As to the 2d. objection, it either had no weight, or it applied with equal weight to the Executive & to the Judiciary revision of the laws. The maxim on which the objection was founded required a separation of the Executive as well as of the Judiciary from the Legislature & from each other. There wd. in truth however be no improper mixture of these distinct powers in the present case. In England, whence the maxim itself had been drawn, the Executive had an absolute negative on the laws; and the supreme tribunal of Justice (the House of Lords) formed one of the other branches of the Legislature. In short, whether the object of the revisionary power was to restrain the Legislature from encroaching on the other co-ordinate Departments, or on the rights of the people at large; or from passing laws unwise in their principle, or incorrect in their form, the utility of annexing the wisdom and weight of the Judiciary to the Executive seemed incontestable.

June 6, 1787

To Thomas Jefferson

Dear Sir   Philada. June 6th. 1787.
   The day fixed for the meeting of the Convention was the 14th. ult. On the 25th. and not before seven States were assembled. General Washington was placed unâ voce in the chair. The Secretaryship was given to Major Jackson. The members present are from Massachussetts Mr. Gherry, Mr. Ghorum, Mr. King, Mr. Strong. From Connecticut Mr. Sherman Docr. S. Johnson, Mr. Elseworth. From N. York Judge Yates, Mr. Lansing, Col. Hamilton. N. Jersey, Governour Livingston, Judge Brearly, Mr. Patterson, Attorney Genl. [Mr. Houston & Mr. Clarke are absent members.] From Pennsylvania Doctr. Franklyn, Mr. Morris, Mr. Wilson, Mr. Fitzimmons, Mr. G. Clymer, Genl. Mifflin, Mr. Governeur Morris, Mr. Ingersoll. From Delaware Mr. Jno. Dickenson, Mr. Reed, Mr. Bedford, Mr. Broom, Mr. Bassett. From Maryland Majr. Jenifer only. Mr. McHenry, Mr. Danl. Carrol, Mr. Jno. Mercer, Mr. Luther Martin are absent members. The three last have supplied the resignations of Mr. Stone, Mr. Carrol of Carolton, and Mr. T. Johnson as I have understood the case. From Virginia Genl. Washington,

Governor Randolph, Mr. Blair, Col. Mason, Docr. McClurg, J Madison. Mr. Wythe left us yesterday, being called home by the serious declension of his lady's health. From N. Carolina, Col. Martin late Governor, Docr. Williamson, Mr. Spaight, Col. Davy. Col. Blount is another member but is detained by indisposition at N. York. From S. Carolina Mr. John Rutlidge, General Pinkney, Mr. Charles Pinkney, Majr. Pierce Butler, Mr. Laurens is in the Commission from that State, but will be kept away by the want of health. From Georgia Col. Few, Majr. Pierce, formerly of Williamsbg. & aid to Genl. Greene, Mr. Houston. Mr. Baldwin will be added to them in a few days. Walton and Pendleton are also in the deputation. N. Hamshire has appointed Deputies but they are not expected; the State treasury being empty it is said, and a substitution of private resources being inconvenient or impracticable. I mention this circumstance to take off the appearance of backwardness, which that State is not in the least chargeable with, if we are rightly informed of her disposition. Rhode Island has not yet acceded to the measure. As their Legislature meet very frequently, and can at any time be got together in a week, it is possible that caprice if no other motive may yet produce a unanimity of the States in this experiment.

In furnishing you with this list of names, I have exhausted all the means which I can make use of for gratifying your curiosity. It was thought expedient in order to secure unbiassed discussion within doors, and to prevent misconceptions & misconstructions without, to establish some rules of caution which will for no short time restrain even a confidential communication of our proceedings. The names of the members will satisfy you that the States have been serious in this business. The attendance of Genl. Washington is a proof of the light in which he regards it. The whole Community is big with expectation. And there can be no doubt but that the result will in some way or other have a powerful effect on our destiny.

Mr. Adams' Book which has been in your hands of course, has excited a good deal of attention. An edition has come out here and another is in the press at N. York. It will probably be much read, particularly in the Eastern States, and contribute with other circumstances to revive the predilections of this Country for the British Constitution. Men of learning find nothing new in it. Men of taste many things to criticize. And men without either not a few things, which they will not understand. It will nevertheless be read, and praised, and become a powerful engine in forming the public opinion. The name & character of the Author, with the critical situation of our affairs, naturally account for such an effect. The book also has merit, and I wish many of the remarks in it, which are unfriendly to republicanism, may not receive fresh weight from the operations of our Governments.

I learn from Virga. that the appetite for paper money grows stronger every day. Mr. H—n—y is an avowed patron of the scheme, and will not fail I think to carry it through unless the County [Prince Edward] which he is to represent shall bind him hand and foot by instructions. I am told that this is in contemplation. He is also said to be unfriendly to an acceleration of Justice. There is good reason to beleive *too that hostile* to *the object of the convention* and that *he wishes either a partition or total dissolution of the confederacy.*

I sent you a few days ago by a Vessel going to France a box with peccan Nuts planted in it. Mr Jno. Vaughn was so good as to make the arrangements with the Capt: both for their preservation during the voyage & the conveyance of them afterwards. I had before sent you via Eangland a few nuts sealed up in a letter.

Mr. Wythe gave me favorable accounts of your Nephew in Williamsburg. And from the Presidt. of Hampden Sidney who was here a few days ago I recd. information equally pleasing as to the genius, progress, and character of your younger Nephew.

I must beg you to communicate my affecte. respects to our friend Mazzei, and to let him know that I have taken every step for securing his claim on Dorhman, which I judged most likely to succeed. There is little doubt that Congress will allow him more, than he owes Mr. Mazzei, and I have got from him such a draught on the Treasury board as I think will ensure him the chance of that fund. Dorman is at present in Virga. where he has also some claims & expectations, but they are not in a transferrable situation. I intended to have written to Mazzei and must beg his pardon for not doing it. It is really out of my power at this time. Adieu Yrs Affy

Remarks in the Federal Convention on the Senate

MR. MADISON.   If the motion (of Mr. Dickenson) should be agreed to, we must either depart from the doctrine of proportional representation; or admit into the Senate a very large number of members. The first is inadmissible, being evidently unjust. The second is inexpedient. The use of the Senate is to consist in its proceeding with more coolness, with more system, & with more wisdom, than the popular branch. Enlarge their number and you communicate to them the vices which they are meant to correct. He differed from Mr. D. who thought that the additional number would give additional weight to the body. On the contrary it appeared to him that their weight would be in an inverse ratio to their number. The example of the Roman Tribunes was applicable. They lost their influence and power, in proportion as their number was augmented. The reason seemed to be obvious: They were appointed to take care of the popular interests & pretensions at Rome, because the people by reason of their numbers could not act in concert; were liable to fall into factions among themselves, and to become a prey to their aristocratic adversaries. The more the representatives of the people therefore were multiplied, the more they partook of the infirmities of their constituents, the more liable they became to be divided among themselves either from their own indiscretions or the artifices of the opposite factions, and of course the less capable of fulfilling their trust. When the weight of a set of men depends merely on their personal characters; the greater the number the greater the weight. When it depends on the degree of political authority lodged in them the smaller the number the greater the weight. These considerations might perhaps be combined in the intended Senate; but the latter was the material one.

———

Mr. Madison could as little comprehend in what manner family weight, as desired by Mr. D. would be more certainly conveyed into the Senate through elections by the State

Legislatures, than in some other modes. The true question was in what mode the best choice wd. be made? If an election by the people, or thro' any other channel than the State Legislatures promised as uncorrupt & impartial a preference of merit, there could surely be no necessity for an appointment by those Legislatures. Nor was it apparent that a more useful check would be derived thro' that channel than from the people thro' some other. The great evils complained of were that the State Legislatures run into schemes of paper money &c. whenever solicited by the people, & sometimes without even the sanction of the people. Their influence then, instead of checking a like propensity in the National Legislature, may be expected to promote it. Nothing can be more contradictory than to say that the Natl. Legislature witht. a proper check, will follow the example of the State Legislatures, & in the same breath, that the State Legislatures are the only proper check.

June 7, 1787

Remarks in the Federal Convention on the Power to Negative State Laws

Mr. Madison seconded the motion. He could not but regard an indefinite power to negative legislative acts of the States as absolutely necessary to a perfect system. Experience had evinced a constant tendency in the States to encroach on the federal authority; to violate national Treaties; to infringe the rights & interests of each other; to oppress the weaker party within their respective jurisdictions. A negative was the mildest expedient that could be devised for preventing these mischeifs. The existence of such a check would prevent attempts to commit them. Should no such precaution be engrafted, the only remedy wd. lie in an appeal to coercion. Was such a remedy eligible? Was it practicable? Could the national resources, if exerted to the utmost enforce a national decree agst. Massts. abetted perhaps by several of her neighbours? It wd. not be possible. A small proportion of the Community, in a compact situation, acting on the defensive, and at one of its

extremities might at any time bid defiance to the National authority. Any Govt. for the U. States formed on the supposed
practicability of using force agst. the unconstitutional proceedings of the States, wd. prove as visionary & fallacious as
the Govt. of Congs. The negative wd. render the use of force
unnecessary. The States cd. of themselves then pass no operative act, any more than one branch of a Legislature where
there are two branches, can proceed without the other. But in
order to give the negative this efficacy, it must extend to all
cases. A discrimination wd. only be a fresh source of contention between the two authorities. In a word, to recur to
the illustrations borrowed from the planetary system, This
prerogative of the General Govt. is the great pervading principle that must controul the centrifugal tendency of the States;
which without it, will continually fly out of their proper orbits
and destroy the order & harmony of the political System.

————

Mr. Madison observed that the difficulties which had been
started were worthy of attention and ought to be answered
before the question was put. The case of laws of urgent necessity must be provided for by some emanation of the power
from the Natl. Govt. into each State so far as to give a temporary assent at least. This was the practice in Royal Colonies
before the Revolution and would not have been inconvenient;
if the supreme power of negativing had been faithful to the
American interest, and had possessed the necessary information. He supposed that the negative might be very properly
lodged in the senate alone, and that the more numerous &
expensive branch therefore might not be obliged to sit constantly. He asked Mr. B. what would be the consequence to
the small States of a dissolution of the Union wch. seemed
likely to happen if no effectual substitute was made for the
defective System existing, and he did not conceive any effectual system could be substituted on any other basis than that
of a proportional suffrage? If the large States possessed the
Avarice & ambition with which they were charged, would the
small ones in their neighbourhood, be more secure when all
controul of a Genl. Govt was withdrawn.

June 8, 1787

Speech in the Federal Convention on the New Jersey Plan

Mr. Madison.   Much stress had been laid by some gentlemen on the want of power in the Convention to propose any other than a *federal* plan. To what had been answered by others, he would only add, that neither of the characteristics attached to a *federal* plan would support this objection. One characteristic was that in a *federal* Government, the power was exercised not on the people individually; but on the people *collectively*, on the *States*. Yet in some instances as in piracies, captures &c. the existing Confederacy, and in many instances, the amendments to it proposed by Mr. Patterson, must operate immediately on individuals. The other characteristic was that a *federal* Govt. derived its appointments not immediately from the people, but from the States which they respectively composed. Here too were facts on the other side. In two of the States, Connect. and Rh. Island, the delegates to Congs. were chosen, not by the Legislatures, but by the people at large; and the plan of Mr. P. intended no change in this particular.

It had been alledged (by Mr. Patterson), that the Confederation having been formed by unanimous consent, could be dissolved by unanimous Consent only. Does this doctrine result from the nature of compacts? Does it arise from any particular stipulation in the articles of Confederation? If we consider the federal union as analogous to the fundamental compact by which individuals compose one Society, and which must in its theoretic origin at least, have been the unanimous act of the component members, it cannot be said that no dissolution of the compact can be effected without unanimous consent. A breach of the fundamental principles of the compact by a part of the Society would certainly absolve the other part from their obligations to it. If the breach of *any* article by *any* of the parties, does not set the others at liberty, it is because, the contrary is *implied* in the compact itself, and particularly by that law of it, which gives an indefinite authority to the majority to bind the whole in all cases. This latter circumstance shews that we are not to consider the federal

Union as analogous to the social compact of individuals: for if it were so, a Majority would have a right to bind the rest, and even to form a new Constitution for the whole, which the Gentn: from N. Jersey would be among the last to admit. If we consider the federal Union as analogous not to the social compacts among individual men: but to the conventions among individual States, What is the doctrine resulting from these conventions? Clearly, according to the Expositors of the law of Nations, that a breach of any one article, by any one party, leaves all the other parties at liberty, to consider the whole convention as dissolved, unless they choose rather to compel the delinquent party to repair the breach. In some treaties indeed it is expressly stipulated that a violation of particular articles shall not have this consequence, and even that particular articles shall remain in force during war, which in general is understood to dissolve all subsisting Treaties. But are there any exceptions of this sort to the Articles of confederation? So far from it that there is not even an express stipulation that force shall be used to compell an offending member of the Union to discharge its duty. He observed that the violations of the federal articles had been numerous & notorious. Among the most notorious was an act of N. Jersey herself; by which she *expressly refused* to comply with a constitutional requisition of Congs.—and yielded no farther to the expostulations of their deputies, than barely to rescind her vote of refusal without passing any positive act of compliance. He did not wish to draw any rigid inferences from these observations. He thought it proper however that the true nature of the existing confederacy should be investigated, and he was not anxious to strengthen the foundations on which it now stands.

Proceeding to the consideration of Mr. Patterson's plan, he stated the object of a proper plan to be twofold. 1. to preserve the Union. 2. to provide a Governmt. that will remedy the evils felt by the States both in their united and individual capacities. Examine Mr. P.s plan, & say whether it promises satisfaction in these respects.

1. Will it prevent those violations of the law of nations & of Treaties which if not prevented must involve us in the calamities of foreign wars? The tendency of the States to these vio-

lations has been manifested in sundry instances. The files of Congs. contain complaints already, from almost every nation with which treaties have been formed. Hitherto indulgence has been shewn to us. This cannot be the permanent disposition of foreign nations. A rupture with other powers is among the greatest of national calamities. It ought therefore to be effectually provided that no part of a nation shall have it in its power to bring them on the whole. The existing Confederacy does not sufficiently provide against this evil. The proposed amendment to it does not supply the omission. It leaves the will of the States as uncontrouled as ever.

2. Will it prevent encroachments on the federal authority? A tendency to such encroachments has been sufficiently exemplified among ourselves, as well in every other confederated republic antient and Modern. By the federal articles, transactions with the Indians appertain to Congs. Yet in several instances, the States have entered into treaties & wars with them. In like manner no two or more States can form among themselves any treaties &c. without the consent of Congs. Yet Virga. & Maryd. in one instance—Pena. & N. Jersey in another, have entered into compacts, without previous application or subsequent apology. No State again can of right raise troops in time of peace without the like consent. Of all cases of the league, this seems to require the most scrupulous observance. Has not Massts, notwithstanding, the most powerful member of the Union, already raised a body of troops? Is she not now augmenting them, without having even deigned to apprize Congs. of Her intention? In fine have we not seen the public land dealt out to Cont. to bribe her acquiescence in the decree constitutionally awarded agst. her claim on the territory of Pena.? For no other possible motive can account for the policy of Congs. in that measure? If we recur to the examples of other confederacies, we shall find in all of them the same tendency of the parts to encroach on the authority of the whole. He then reviewed the Amphyctionic & Achæan confederacies among the antients; and the Helvetic, Germanic & Belgic among the moderns, tracing their analogy to the U. States—in the constitution and intent of their federal authorities—in the tendency of the particular members to usurp on these authorities; and to bring confusion & ruin on the whole.

He observed that the plan of Mr. Pat—son besides omitting a controul over the States as a general defence of the federal prerogatives was particularly defective in two of its provisions. 1. Its ratification was not to be by the people at large, but by the *legislatures*. It could not therefore render the Acts of Congs. in pursuance of their powers, even legally *paramount* to the Acts of the States. 2. It gave to the federal Tribunal an appellate jurisdiction only—even in the criminal cases enumerated. The necessity of any such provision supposed a danger of undue acquittals in the State tribunals. Of what avail cd. an appellate tribunal be, after an acquittal? Besides in most if not all of the States, the Executives have by their respective *Constitutions* the right of pardg. How could this be taken from them by a *legislative* ratification only?

3. Will it prevent trespasses of the States on each other? Of these enough has been already seen. He instanced Acts of Virga. & Maryland which give a preference to their own Citizens in cases where the Citizens of other States are entitled to equality of privileges by the Articles of Confederation. He considered the emissions of paper money & other kindred measures as also aggressions. The States relatively to one another being each of them either Debtors or Creditor; The Creditor States must suffer unjustly from every emission by the debtor States. We have seen retaliating acts on this subject which threatened danger not to the harmony only, but the tranquility of the Union. The plan of Mr. Patterson, not giving even a negative on the Acts of the States, left them as much at liberty as ever to execute their unrighteous projects agst. each other.

4. Will it secure the internal tranquility of the States themselves? The insurrections in Massts. admonished all the States of the danger to which they were exposed. Yet the plan of Mr. P. contained no provisions for supplying the defect of the Confederation on this point. According to the Republican theory indeed, Right & power being both vested in the majority, are held to be synonimous. According to fact & experience, a minority may in an appeal to force be an overmatch for the majority. 1. If the minority happen to include all such as possess the skill & habits of military life, with such as possess the great pecuniary resources, one third may conquer the

remaining two thirds. 2. One third of those who participate in the choice of rulers may be rendered a majority by the accession of those whose poverty disqualifies them from a suffrage, & who for obvious reasons may be more ready to join the standard of sedition than that of the established Government. 3. Where slavery exists, the Republican Theory becomes still more fallacious.

5. Will it secure a good internal legislation & administration to the particular States? In developing the evils which vitiate the political system of the U.S. it is proper to take into view those which prevail within the States individually as well as those which affect them collectively: Since the former indirectly affect the whole; and there is great reason to believe that the pressure of them had a full share in the motives which produced the present Convention. Under this head he enumerated and animadverted on 1. the multiplicity of the laws passed by the several States. 2. the mutability of their laws. 3. the injustice of them. 4. the impotence of them: observing that Mr. Patterson's plan contained no remedy for this dreadful class of evils; and could not therefore be received as an adequate provision for the exigences of the Community.

6. Will it secure the Union agst. the influence of foreign powers over its members. He pretended not to say that any such influence had yet been tried: but it was naturally to be expected that occasions would produce it. As lessons which claimed particular attention, he cited the intrigues practised among the Amphyctionic Confederates first by the Kings of Persia, and afterwards fatally by Philip of Macedon: Among the Achæans, first by Macedon & afterwards no less fatally by Rome: Among the Swiss by Austria, France & the lesser neighbouring powers: among the members of the Germanic Body by France, England, Spain & Russia: And in the Belgic Republic, by all the great neighbouring powers. The plan of Mr. Patterson, not giving to the general Councils any negative on the will of the particular States, left the door open for the like pernicious machinations among ourselves.

7. He begged the smaller States which were most attached to Mr. Pattersons plan to consider the situation in which it would leave them. In the first place they would continue to bear the whole expence of maintaining their Delegates in

Congress. It ought not to be said that if they were willing to bear this burden, no others had a right to complain. As far as it led the small States to forbear keeping up a representation, by which the public business was delayed, it was evidently a matter of common concern. An examination of the minutes of Congress would satisfy every one that the public business had been frequently delayed by this cause; and that the States most frequently unrepresented in Congs. were not the larger States. He reminded the convention of another consequence of leaving on a small State the burden of maintaining a Representation in Congs. During a considerable period of the War, one of the Representatives of Delaware, in whom alone before the signing of the Confederation the entire vote of that State and after that event one half of its vote, frequently resided, was a Citizen & Resident of Pena. and held an office in his own State incompatible with an appointment from it to Congs. During another period, the same State was represented by three delegates two of whom were citizens of Penna. and the third a Citizen of New Jersey. These expedients must have been intended to avoid the burden of supporting delegates from their own State. But whatever might have been the cause, was not in effect the vote of one State doubled, and the influence of another increased by it? In the 2d. place the coercion, on which the efficacy of the plan depends, can never be exerted but on themselves. The larger States will be impregnable, the smaller only can feel the vengeance of it. He illustrated the position by the history of the Amphyctionic Confederates: and the ban of the German Empire. It was the cobweb wch. could entangle the weak, but would be the sport of the strong.

8. He begged them to consider the situation in which they would remain in case their pertinacious adherence to an inadmissible plan, should prevent the adoption of any plan. The contemplation of such an event was painful; but it would be prudent to submit to the task of examining it at a distance, that the means of escaping it might be the more readily embraced. Let the Union of the States be dissolved, and one of two consequences must happen. Either the States must remain individually independent & sovereign; or two or more Confederacies must be formed among them. In the first event

would the small States be more secure agst. the ambition & power of their larger neighbours, than they would be under a general Government pervading with equal energy every part of the Empire, and having an equal interest in protecting every part agst. every other part? In the second, can the smaller expect that their larger neighbours would confederate with them on the principle of the present confederacy, which gives to each member, an equal suffrage; or that they would exact less severe concessions from the smaller States, than are proposed in the scheme of Mr. Randolph?

The great difficulty lies in the affair of Representation; and if this could be adjusted, all others would be surmountable. It was admitted by both the gentlemen from N. Jersey, (Mr. Brearly and Mr. Patterson) that it would not be *just to allow Virga.* which was 16 times as large as Delaware an equal vote only. Their language was that it would not be *safe for Delaware* to allow Virga. 16 times as many votes. The expedient proposed by them was that all the States should be thrown into one mass and a new partition be made into 13 equal parts. Would such a scheme be practicable? The dissimilarities existing in the rules of property, as well as in the manners, habits and prejudices of the different States, amounted to a prohibition of the attempt. It had been found impossible for the power of one of the most absolute princes in Europe (K. of France), directed by the wisdom of one of the most enlightened and patriotic Ministers (Mr. Neckar) that any age has produced, to equalize in some points only the different usages & regulations of the different provinces. But admitting a general amalgamation and repartition of the States, to be practicable, and the danger apprehended by the smaller States from a proportional representation to be real; would not a particular and voluntary coalition of these with their neighbours, be less inconvenient to the whole community, and equally effectual for their own safety. If N. Jersey or Delaware conceived that an advantage would accrue to them from an equalization of the States, in which case they would necessaryly form a junction with their neighbours, why might not this end be attained by leaving them at liberty by the Constitution to form such a junction whenever they pleased? And why should they wish to obtrude a like arrangement on all the States, when it was, to say the least, extremely difficult, would be obnoxious to many of the States, and when neither the inconveniency, nor the benefit of the expedient to themselves, would be lessened, by confining it to themselves. The prospect of many new States to the Westward was another consideration of importance. If they should come into the Union at all, they would come when they contained but few inhabitants. If they shd. be entitled to vote according to their proportions of inhabitants, all would be right & safe. Let them have an equal vote, and a more objectionable minority than ever might give law to the whole.

June 19, 1787

Speech in the Federal Convention on the General and State Governments

Mr. Madison was of opinion that there was 1. less danger of encroachment from the Genl. Govt. than from the State Govts. 2. that the mischeif from encroachments would be less fatal if made by the former, than if made by the latter. 1. All the examples of other confederacies prove the greater tendency in such systems to anarchy than to tyranny; to a disobedience of the members than to usurpations of the federal head. Our own experience had fully illustrated this tendency. But it will be said that the proposed change in the principles & form of the Union will vary the tendency, that the genl. Govt. will have real & greater powers, and will be derived in one branch at least from the people, not from the Govts. of the States. To give full force to this objection, let it be supposed for a moment that indefinite power should be given to the Genl. Legislature, and the States reduced to corporations dependent on the Genl. Legislature; Why shd. it follow that the Genl. Govt. wd. take from the States any branch of their power as far as its operation was beneficial, and its continuance desireable to the people? In some of the States, particularly in Connecticut, all the Townships are incorporated, and have a certain limited jurisdiction. Have the Representatives of the people of the Townships in the Legislature of the State ever endeavored to despoil the Townships of any part of their local authority? As far as this local authority is convenient to the people they are attached to it; and their representatives chosen by & amenable to them naturally respect their attachment to this, as much as their attachment to any other right or interest. The relation of a general Govt. to State Govts. is parallel. 2. Guards were more necessary agst. encroachments of the State Govts. on the Genl. Govt. than of the latter on the former. The great objection made agst. an abolition of the State Govts. was that the Genl. Govt. could not extend its care to all the minute objects which fall under the cognizance of the local jurisdictions. The objection as stated lay not agst. the probable abuse of the general power, but agst. the imperfect use that could be made of it throughout so great an extent of Country, and over so great a variety of objects. As far as its operation would be practicable it could not in this view be improper; as far as it would be impracticable, the conveniency of the Genl. Govt. itself would concur with that of the people in the maintenance of subordinate Governments. Were it practicable for the genl. Govt. to extend its care to every requisite object without the cooperation of the State Govts. the people would not be less free as members of one great Republic than as members of thirteen small ones. A Citizen of Delaware was not more free than a Citizen of Virginia: nor would either be more free than a Citizen of America: supposing therefore a tendency in the genl. Government to absorb the State Govts. no fatal consequence could result. Taking the reverse of the supposition, that a tendency should be left in the State Govts. towards an independence on the General Govt. and the gloomy consequences need not be pointed out. The imagination of them, must have suggested to the States the experiment we are now making to prevent the calamity, and must have formed the cheif motive with those present to undertake the arduous task.

June 21, 1787

Speech in the Federal Convention on the Senate

MR. MADISON.   In order to judge of the form to be given to this institution, it will be proper to take a view of the ends to be served by it. These were first to protect the people agst. their rulers: secondly to protect the people agst. the transient impressions into which they themselves might be led. A people deliberating in a temperate moment, and with the experience of other nations before them, on the plan of Govt. most likely to secure their happiness, would first be aware, that those chargd. with the public happiness, might betray their trust. An obvious precaution agst. this danger wd. be to divide the trust between different bodies of men, who might watch & check each other. In this they wd. be governed by the same prudence which has prevailed in organizing the subordinate departments of Govt., where all business liable to abuses is made to pass thro' separate hands, the one being a check on the other. It wd. next occur to such a people, that they themselves were liable to temporary errors, thro' want of information as to their true interest, and that men chosen for a short term, & employed but a small portion of that in public affairs, might err from the same cause. This reflection wd. naturally suggest that the Govt. be so constituted, as that one of its branches might have an oppy. of acquiring a competent knowledge of the public interests. Another reflection equally becoming a people on such an occasion, wd. be that they themselves, as well as a numerous body of Representatives, were liable to err also, from fickleness and passion. A necessary fence agst. this danger would be to select a portion of enlightened citizens, whose limited number, and firmness might seasonably interpose agst. impetuous counsels. It ought finally to occur to a people deliberating on a Govt. for themselves, that as different interests necessarily result from the liberty meant to be secured, the major interest might under sudden impulses be tempted to commit injustice on the minority. In all civilized Countries the people fall into different classes havg. a real or supposed difference of interests. There will be creditors & debtors, farmers, merchts. & manufacturers. There will be particularly the distinction of rich & poor. It was true as had been observd. (by Mr. Pinkney) we had not among us those hereditary distinctions, of rank which were a great source of the contests in the ancient Govts. as well as the modern States of Europe, nor those extremes of wealth or poverty which characterize the latter. We cannot however be regarded even at this time, as one homogeneous mass, in which every thing that affects a part will affect in the same manner the whole. In framing a system which we wish to last for ages, we shd. not lose sight of the changes which ages will produce. An increase of population will of necessity increase the proportion of those who will labour under all the hardships of life, & secretly sigh for a more equal distribution of its blessings. These may in time outnumber those who are placed above the feelings of indigence. According to the equal laws of suffrage, the power will slide into the hands of the former. No agrarian attempts have yet been made in this Country, but symtoms, of a leveling spirit, as we have understood, have sufficiently appeared in a certain quarters to give notice of the future danger. How is this danger to be guarded agst. on republican principles? How is the danger in all cases of interested coalitions to oppress the minority to be guarded agst.? Among other means by the establishment of a body in the Govt. sufficiently respectable for its wisdom & virtue, to aid on such emergences, the preponderance of justice by throwing its weight into that scale. Such being the objects of the second branch in the proposed Govt. he thought a considerable duration ought to be given to it. He did not conceive that the term of nine years could threaten any real danger; but in pursuing his particular ideas on the subject, he should require that the long term allowed to the 2d. branch should not commence till such a period of life, as would render a perpetual disqualification to be re-elected little inconvenient either in a public or private view. He observed that as it was more than probable we were now digesting a plan which in its operation wd. decide for ever the fate of Republican Govt. we ought not only to provide every guard to liberty that its preservation cd. require, but be equally careful to supply the defects which our own experience had particularly pointed out.

June 26, 1787

Speech in the Federal Convention
on Relations Among the States

Mr. Madison sd. he was much disposed to concur in any expedient not inconsistent with fundamental principles, that could remove the difficulty concerning the rule of representation. But he could neither be convinced that the rule contended for was just, nor necessary for the safety of the small States agst. the large States. That it was not just, had been conceded by Mr. Breerly & Mr. Patterson themselves. The expedient proposed by them was a new partition of the territory of the U. States. The fallacy of the reasoning drawn from the equality of Sovereign States in the formation of compacts, lay in confounding mere Treaties, in which were specified certain duties to which the parties were to be bound, and certain rules by which their subjects were to be reciprocally governed in their intercourse, with a compact by which an authority was created paramount to the parties, & making laws for the government of them. If France, England & Spain were to enter into a Treaty for the regulation of commerce &c with the Prince of Monacho & 4 or 5 other of the smallest sovereigns of Europe, they would not hesitate to treat as equals, and to make the regulations perfectly reciprocal. Wd. the case be the same, if a Council were to be formed of deputies from each with authority and discretion, to raise money, levy troops, determine the value of coin &c? Would 30 or 40. million of people submit their fortunes into the hands, of a few thousands? If they did it would only prove that they expected more from the terror of their superior force, than they feared from the selfishness of their feeble associates. Why are Counties of the same states represented in proportion to their numbers? Is it because the representatives are chosen by the people themselves? So will be the representatives in the Nationl. Legislature. Is it because, the larger have more at stake than the smaller? The case will be the same with the larger & smaller States. Is it because the laws are to operate immediately on their persons & properties? The same is the case in some degree as the articles of confederation stand; the same will be the case in a far greater degree under the plan

proposed to be substituted. In the cases of captures, of piracies, and of offences in a federal army, the property & persons
of individuals depend on the laws of Congs. By the plan proposed a compleat power of taxation, the highest prerogative
of supremacy is proposed to be vested in the national Govt.
Many other powers are added which assimilate it to the Govt.
of individual States. The negative proposed on the State laws,
will make it an essential branch of the State Legislatures & of
course will require that it should be exercised by a body established on like principles with the other branches of those
Legislatures. That it is not necessary to secure the small States
agst. the large ones he conceived to be equally obvious: Was
a combination of the large ones dreaded? This must arise
either from some interest common to Va. Masts. & Pa. & distinguishing them from the other States or from the mere
circumstance of similarity of size. Did any such common interest exist? In point of situation they could not have been
more effectually separated from each other by the most jealous citizen of the most jealous State. In point of manners,
Religion, and the other circumstances which sometimes beget
affection between different communities, they were not more
assimilated than the other States. In point of the staple productions they were as dissimilar as any three other States in
the Union. The Staple of Masts. was *fish*, of Pa. *flower*, of Va.
Tobo. Was a Combination to be apprehended from the mere
circumstance of equality of size? Experience suggested no
such danger. The journals of Congs. did not present any peculiar association of these States in the votes recorded. It had
never been seen that different Counties in the same State,
conformable in extent, but disagreeing in other circumstances, betrayed a propensity to such combinations. Experience rather taught a contrary lesson. Among individuals of
superior eminence & weight in Society, rivalships were much
more frequent than coalitions. Among independent nations,
pre-eminent over their neighbours, the same remark was verified. Carthage & Rome tore one another to pieces instead of
uniting their forces to devour the weaker nations of the
Earth. The Houses of Austria & France were hostile as long
as they remained the greatest powers of Europe. England &
France have succeeded to the pre-eminence & to the enmity.

To this principle we owe perhaps our liberty. A coalition between those powers would have been fatal to us. Among the
principal members of antient & modern confederacies, we
find the same effect from the same cause. The contentions,
not the Coalitions of Sparta, Athens & Thebes, proved fatal
to the smaller members of the Amphyctionic Confederacy.
The contentions, not the combinations of Prussia & Austria,
have distracted & oppressed the Germanic empire. Were the
large States formidable *singly* to their smaller neighbours? On
this supposition the latter ought to wish for such a general
Govt. as will operate with equal energy on the former as on
themselves. The more lax the band, the more liberty the
larger will have to avail themselves of their superior force.
Here again Experience was an instructive monitor. What is
the situation of the weak compared with the strong in those
stages of Civilization in which the violence of individuals is
least controuled by an efficient Government? The Heroic period of antient Greece the feudal licentiousness of the middle
ages of Europe, the existing condition of the American
Savages, answer this question. What is the situation of the minor sovereigns in the great society of independent nations, in
which the more powerful are under no controul but the nominal authority of the law of Nations? Is not the danger to the
former exactly in proportion to their weakness. But there are
cases still more in point. What was the condition of the
weaker members of the Amphyctionic Confederacy. Plutarch
(life of Themistocles) will inform us that it happened but too
often that the strongest cities corrupted & awed the weaker,
and that Judgment went in favor of the more powerful party.
What is the condition of the lesser states in the German
Confederacy? We all know that they are exceedingly trampled
upon; and that they owe their safety as far as they enjoy it,
partly to their enlisting themselves, under the rival banners of
the pre-eminent members, partly to alliances with neighbouring Princes which the Constitution of the Empire does not
prohibit. What is the state of things in the lax system of the
Dutch Confederacy? Holland contains about 1/2 the People,
supplies about 1/2 of the money, and by her influence, silently
& indirectly governs the whole republic. In a word; the two
extremes before us are a perfect separation & a perfect incor-

poration, of the 13 States. In the first case they would be independent nations subject to no law, but the law of nations. In the last, they would be mere counties of one entire republic, subject to one common law. In the first case the smaller States would have every thing to fear from the larger. In the last they would have nothing to fear. The true policy of the small States therefore lies in promoting those principles & that form of Govt. which will most approximate the States to the condition of counties. Another consideration may be added. If the Genl Govt. be feeble, the large States distrusting its continuance, and foreseeing that their importance & security may depend on their own size & strength, will never submit to a partition. Give to the Genl. Govt. sufficient energy & permency, & you remove the objection. Gradual partitions of the large, & junctions of the small States will be facilitated, and time may effect that equalization, which is wished for by the small States now, but can never be accomplished at once.

June 28, 1787

Speech in the Federal Convention on the Danger of Dissolution

Mr. Madison agreed with Docr. Johnson, that the mixed nature of the Govt. ought to be kept in view; but thought too much stress was laid on the rank of the States as political societies. There was a gradation, he observed from the smallest corporation, with the most limited powers, to the largest empire with the most perfect sovereignty. He pointed out the limitations on the sovereignty of the States, as now confederated their laws in relation to the paramount law of the Confederacy were analogous to that of bye laws to the supreme law, within a State. Under the proposed Govt. the Powers of the States will be much farther reduced. According to the views of every member, the Genl. Govt will have powers far beyond those exercised by the British Parliament, when the states were part of the British Empire. It will in particular have the power, without the consent of the state Legislatures, to levy money directly on the people themselves; and therefore not to divest such *unequal* portions of the people as composed the several States, of an *equal* voice, would subject the system to the reproaches & evils which have resulted from the vicious representation in G.B.

He entreated the gentlemen representing the small States to renounce a principle wch. was confessedly unjust, which cd. never be admitted, & if admitted must infuse mortality into a Constitution which we wished to last for ever. He prayed them to ponder well the consequences of suffering the Confederacy to go to pieces. It had been sd. that the want of energy in the large states wd. be a security to the small. It was forgotten that this want of energy proceeded from the supposed security of the States agst. all external danger. Let each state depend on itself for its security, & let apprehensions arise of danger, from distant powers or from neighbouring states, & the languishing condition of all the states, large as well as small, wd. soon be transformed into vigorous & high toned Govts. His great fear was that their Govts. wd. then have too much energy, that these might not only be formidable in the large to the small States, but fatal to the internal liberty of all. The same causes which have rendered the old world the Theatre of incessant wars, & have banished liberty from the face of it, wd. soon produce the same effects here. The weakness & jealousy of the small States wd. quickly introduce some regular military force agst. sudden danger from their powerful neighbours. The example wd. be followed by others, and wd. soon become universal. In time of actual war, great discretionary powers are constantly given to the Executive Magistrate. Constant apprehension of war, has the same tendency to render the head too large for the body. A standing military force, with an overgrown Executive will not long be safe companions to liberty. The means of defence agst. foreign danger, have been always the instruments of tyranny at home. Among the Romans it was a standing maxim to excite a war, whenever a revolt was apprehended. Throughout all Europe, the armies kept up under the pretext of defending, have enslaved the people. It is perhaps questionable, whether the best concerted system of Absolute power in Europe cd.

maintain itself, in a situation, where no alarms of external danger cd. tame the people to the domestic yoke. The insular situation of G. Britain was the principal cause of her being an exception to the general fate of Europe. It has rendered less defence necessary, and admitted a kind of defence wch. cd. not be used for the purpose of oppression. These consequences he conceived ought to be apprehended whether the States should run into a total separation from each other, or shd. enter into partial confederacies. Either event wd. be truly deplorable; & those who might be accessary to either, could never be forgiven by their Country, nor by themselves.

June 29, 1787

Speech in the Federal Convention on Divisions Between the States

Mr. Madison did justice to the able & close reasoning of Mr. E. but must observe that it did not always accord with itself. On another occasion, the large States were described by him as the Aristocratic States, ready to oppress the small. Now the small are the House of Lords requiring a negative to defend them agst. the more numerous Commons. Mr. E. had also erred in saying that no instance had existed in which confederated States had not retained to themselves a perfect equality of suffrage. Passing over the German system in which the K. of Prussia has nine voices, he reminded Mr. E. of the Lycian confederacy, in which the component members had votes proportioned to their importance, and which Montesquieu recommends as the fittest model for that form of Government. Had the fact been as stated by Mr. E. it would have been of little avail to him, or rather would have strengthened the arguments agst. him; The History & fate of the several Confederacies modern as well as Antient, demonstrating some radical vice in their structure. In reply to the appeal of Mr. E. to the faith plighted in the existing federal compact, he remarked that the party claiming from others an adherence to a common engagement ought at least to be guiltless itself of

a violation. Of all the States however Connecticut was perhaps least able to urge this plea. Besides the various omissions
to perform the stipulated acts from which no State was free,
the Legislature of that State had by a pretty recent vote, *positively refused* to pass a law for complying with the Requisitions
of Congs. and had transmitted a copy of the vote to Congs.
It was urged, he said, continually that an equality of votes in
the 2d. branch was not only necessary to secure the small, but
would be perfectly safe to the large ones whose majority in
the 1st. branch was an effectual bulwark. But notwithstanding
this apparent defence, the Majority of States might still injure
the majority of people. 1. they could *obstruct* the wishes and
interests of the majority. 2. they could *extort* measures repugnant to the wishes & interest of the Majority. 3. they could
impose measures adverse thereto; as the 2d. branch will probly.
exercise some great powers, in which the 1st. will not participate. He admitted that every peculiar interest whether in any
class of Citizens, or any description of States, ought to be secured as far as possible. Wherever there is danger of attack
there ought be given a constitutional power of defence. But
he contended that the States were divided into different interests not by their difference of size, but by other circumstances; the most material of which resulted partly from
climate, but principally from the effects of their having or not
having slaves. These two causes concurred in forming the
great division of interests in the U. States. It did not lie between the large & small States: It lay between the Northern
& Southern. And if any defensive power were necessary, it
ought to be mutually given to these two interests. He was so
strongly impressed with this important truth that he had been
casting about in his mind for some expedient that would answer the purpose. The one which had occurred was that instead of proportioning the votes of the States in both
branches, to their respective numbers of inhabitants computing the slaves in the ratio of 5 to 3, they should be represented
in one branch according to the number of free inhabitants
only, and in the other according to the whole no. counting
the slaves as free. By this arrangement the southern Scale
would have the advantage in one House, and the Northern in
the other. He had been restrained from proposing this expe-

dient by two considerations; one was his unwillingness to urge any diversity of interests on an occasion where it is but too apt to arise of itself—the other was the inequality of powers that must be vested in the two branches, and which wd. destroy the equilibrium of interests.

June 30, 1787

Speech in the Federal Convention on the Proposed Compromise on State Representation

Mr. Madison could not regard the exclusive privilege of originating money bills as any concession on the side of the small States. Experience proved that it had no effect. If seven States in the upper branch wished a bill to be originated, they might surely find some member from some of the same States in the lower branch who would originate it. The restriction as to amendments was of as little consequence. Amendments could be handed privately by the Senate to members in the other house. Bills could be negatived that they might be sent up in the desired shape. If the Senate should yield to the obstinacy of the 1st. branch the use of that body as a check would be lost. If the 1st. branch should yield to that of the Senate, the privilege would be nugatory. Experience had also shewn both in G.B. and the States having a similar regulation that it was a source of frequent & obstinate altercations. These considerations had produced a rejection of a like motion on a former occasion when judged by its own merits. It could not therefore be deemed any concession on the present, and left in force all the objections which had prevailed agst. allowing each State an equal voice. He conceived that the Convention was reduced to the alternative of either departing from justice in order to conciliate the smaller States, and the minority of the people of the U.S. or of displeasing these by justly gratifying the larger States and the majority of the people. He could not himself hesitate as to the option he ought to make. The Convention with justice & the majority of the people on their side, had nothing to fear. With injustice and the minority on their side they had every thing to fear. It was in vain to purchase concord in the Convention on terms which would perpetuate discord among their Constituents. The Convention ought to pursue a plan which would bear the test of examination, which would be espoused & supported by the enlightened and impartial part of America, & which they could themselves vindicate and urge. It should be considered that altho' at first many may judge of the system recommended, by their opinion of the Convention, yet finally all will judge of the Convention by the System. The merits of the System alone can finally & effectually obtain the public suffrage. He was not apprehensive that the people of the small States would obstinately refuse to accede to a Govt. founded on just principles, and promising them substantial protection. He could not suspect that Delaware would brave the consequences of seeking her fortunes apart from the other States, rather than submit to such a Govt.: much less could he suspect that she would pursue the rash policy of courting foreign support, which the warmth of one of her representatives (Mr. Bedford) had suggested, or if she shd. that any foreign nation wd. be so rash as to hearken to the overture. As little could he suspect that the people of N. Jersey notwithstanding the decided tone of the gentlemen from that State, would choose rather to stand on their own legs, and bid defiance to events, than to acquiesce under an establishment founded on principles the justice of which they could not dispute, and absolutely necessary to redeem them from the exactions levied on them by the Commerce of the neighbouring States. A review of other States would prove that there was as little reason to apprehend an inflexible opposition elsewhere. Harmony in the Convention was no doubt much to be desired. Satisfaction to all the States, in the first instance still more so. But if the principal States comprehending a majority of the people of the U.S. should concur in a just & judicious Plan, he had the firmest hopes, that all the other States would by degrees accede to it.

July 5, 1787

Speech in the Federal Convention on Apportioning Representation

Mr. Madison was not a little surprised to hear this implicit confidence urged by a member who on all occasions, had inculcated so strongly, the political depravity of men, and the necessity of checking one vice and interest by opposing to them another vice & interest. If the Representatives of the people would be bound by the ties he had mentioned, what need was there of a Senate? What of a Revisionary power? But his reasoning was not only inconsistent with his former reasoning, but with itself. At the same time that he recommended this implicit confidence to the Southern States in the Northern Majority, he was still more zealous in exhorting all to a jealousy of the Western Majority. To reconcile the gentln. with himself, it must be imagined that he determined the human character by the points of the compass. The truth was that all men having power ought to be distrusted to a certain degree. The case of Pena. had been mentioned where it was admitted that those who were possessed of the power in the original settlement, never admitted the new settlemts. to a due share of it. England was a still more striking example. The power there had long been in the hands of the boroughs, of the minority; who had opposed & defeated every reform which had been attempted. Virga. was in a lesser degree another example. With regard to the Western States, he was clear & firm in opinion, that no unfavorable distinctions were admissible either in point of justice or policy. He thought also that the hope of contributions to the Treasy from them had been much underrated. Future contributions it seemed to be understood on all hands would be principally levied on imports & exports. The extent and fertility of the Western Soil would for a long time give to agriculture a preference over manufactures. Trials would be repeated till some articles could be raised from it that would bear a transportation to places where they could be exchanged for imported manufactures. Whenever the Mississpi. should be opened to them, which would of necessity be the case, as soon as their population would subject them to any considerable share of the Public burdin, imposts on their trade could be collected with less expence & greater certainty, than on that of the Atlantic States. In the mean time, as their supplies must pass thro' the *Atlantic States*, their contributions would be levied in the same manner with those of the Atlantic States. He could not agree that any substantial objection lay agst. fixing numbers for the perpetual standard of Representation. It was said that Representation & taxation were to go together; that taxation and wealth ought to go together, that population & wealth were not measures of each other. He admitted that in different climates, under different forms of Govt. and in different stages of civilization the inference was perfectly just. He would admit that in no situation, numbers of inhabitants were an accurate measure of wealth. He contended however that in the U. States it was sufficiently so for the object in contemplation. Altho' their climate varied considerably, yet as the Govts. the laws, and the manners of all were nearly the same, and the intercourse between different parts perfectly free, population, industry, arts, and the value of labour, would constantly tend to equalize themselves. The value of labour, might be considered as the principal criterion of wealth and ability to support taxes; and this would find its level in different places where the intercourse should be easy & free, with as much certainty as the value of money or any other thing. Wherever labour would yield most, people would resort, till the competition should destroy the inequality. Hence it is that the people are constantly swarming from the more to the less populous places—from Europe to Ama. from the Northn. & Middle parts of the U.S. to the Southern & Western. They go where land is cheaper, because there labour is dearer. If it be true that the same quantity of produce raised on the banks of the Ohio is of less value, than on the Delaware, it is also true that the same labor will raise twice or thrice, the quantity in the former, that it will raise in the latter situation.

July 11, 1787

Speech in the Federal Convention Opposing Equal Representation in the Senate

Mr Madison expressed his apprehensions that if the proper foundation of Governmt. was destroyed, by substituting an equal in place of a proportional Representation, no proper superstructure would be raised. If the small States really wish for a Government armed with the powers necessary to secure their liberties, and to enforce obedience on the larger members as well as on themselves he could not help thinking them extremely mistaken in their means. He reminded them of the consequences of laying the existing confederation on improper principles. All the principal parties to its compilation, joined immediately in mutilating & fettering the Governmt. in such a manner that it has disappointed every hope placed on it. He appealed to the doctrine & arguments used by themselves on a former occasion. It had been very properly observed by (Mr. Patterson) that Representation was an expedient by which the meeting of the people themselves was rendered unnecessary; and that the representatives ought therefore to bear a proportion to the votes which their constituents if convened, would respectively have. Was not this remark as applicable to one branch of the Representation as to the other? But it had been said that the Governt. would in its operation be partly federal, partly national; that altho' in the latter respect the Representatives of the people ought to be in proportion to the people: yet in the former it ought to be according to the number of States. If there was any solidity in this distinction he was ready to abide by it, if there was none it ought to be abandoned. In all cases where the Genl. Governmt. is to act on the people, let the people be represented and the votes be proportional. In all cases where the Governt. is to act on the States as such, in like manner as Congs. now act on them, let the States be represented & the votes be equal. This was the true ground of compromise if there was any ground at all. But he denied that there was any ground. He called for a single instance in which the Genl. Govt. was not to operate on the people individually. The practicability of making laws, with coercive sanctions, for the States as Political bodies, had been exploded on all hands. He observed that the people of the large States would in some way or other secure to themselves a weight proportioned to the importance accruing from their superior numbers. If they could not effect it by a proportional representation in the Govt. they would probably accede to no Govt. which did not in great measure depend for its efficacy on their voluntary cooperation, in which case they would indirectly secure their object. The existing confederacy proved that where the Acts of the Genl. Govt. were to be executed by the particular

Govts. the latter had a weight in proportion to their importance. No one would say that either in Congs. or out of Congs. Delaware had equal weight with Pensylva. If the latter was to supply ten times as much money as the former, and no compulsion could be used, it was of ten times more importance, that she should voluntarily furnish the supply. In the Dutch confederacy the votes of the Provinces were equal. But Holland, which supplies about half the money, governs the whole republic. He enumerated the objections agst. an equality of votes in the 2d. branch, notwithstanding the proportional representation in the first. 1 the minority could negative the will of the majority of the people. 2. they could extort measures by making them a condition of their assent to other necessary measures. 3. they could obtrude measures on the majority by virtue of the peculiar powers which would be vested in the Senate. 4. the evil instead of being cured by time, would increase with every new State that should be admitted, as they must all be admitted on the principle of equality. 5. the perpetuity it would give to the preponderance of the Northn. agst. the Southn. Scale was a serious consideration. It seemed now to be pretty well understood that the real difference of interests lay, not between the large & small but between the N. & Southn. States. The institution of slavery & its consequences formed the line of discrimination. There were 5 States on the South, 8 on the Northn. side of this line. Should a proportl. representation take place it was true, the N. side would still outnumber the other: but not in the same degree, at this time; and every day would tend towards an equilibrium.

July 14, 1787

Remarks in the Federal Convention on Electing the Executive

MR. MADISON.   If it be essential to the preservation of liberty that the Legisl: Execut: & Judiciary powers be separate, it is essential to a maintenance of the separation, that they should be independent of each other. The Executive could not be independent of the Legislure., if dependent on the pleasure of that branch for a re-appointment. Why was it determined that the Judges should not hold their places by such a tenure? Because they might be tempted to cultivate the Legislature, by an undue complaisance, and thus render the Legislature the virtual expositor, as well the maker of the laws. In like manner a dependence of the Executive on the Legislature, would render it the Executor as well as the maker of laws; & then according to the observation of Montesquieu, tyrannical laws may be made that they may be executed in a tyrannical manner. There was an analogy between the Executive & Judiciary departments in several respects. The latter executed the laws in certain cases as the former did in others. The former expounded & applied them for certain purposes, as the latter did for others. The difference between them seemed to consist chiefly in two circumstances—1. the collective interests & security were much more in the power belonging to the Executive than to the Judiciary department. 2. in the administration of the former much greater latitude is left to opinion and discretion than in the administration of the latter. But if the 2d. consideration proves that it will be more difficult to establish a rule sufficiently precise for trying the Execut: than the Judges, & forms an objection to the same tenure of office, both considerations prove that it might be more dangerous to suffer a Union between the Executive & Legisl: powers, than between the Judiciary & Legislative powers. He conceived it to be absolutely necessary to a well constituted Republic that the two first shd. be kept distinct & independent of each other. Whether the plan proposed by the motion was a proper one was another question, as it depended on the practicability of instituting a tribunal for impeachmts. as certain & as adequate in the one case as in the other. On the other hand, respect for the mover entitled his proposition to a fair hearing & discussion, until a less objectionable expedient should be applied for guarding agst. a dangerous union of the Legislative & Executive departments.

———

Mr. Madison was not apprehensive of being thought to favor any step towards monarchy. The real object with him was to prevent its introduction. Experience had proved a tendency in our governments to throw all power into the Legislative vortex. The Executives of the States are in general little more than Cyphers; the legislatures omnipotent. If no effectual check be devised for restraining the instability & encroachments of the latter, a revolution of some kind or other would be inevitable. The preservation of Republican Govt. therefore required some expedient for the purpose, but required evidently at the same time that in devising it, the genuine principles of that form should be kept in view.

July 17, 1787

Speech in the Federal Convention on Electing the Executive

MR. MADISON   If it be a fundamental principle of free Govt. that the Legislative, Executive & Judiciary powers should be *separately* exercised, it is equally so that they be *independently* exercised. There is the same & perhaps greater reason why the Executive shd. be independent of the Legislature, than why the Judiciary should: A coalition of the two former powers would be more immediately & certainly dangerous to public liberty. It is essential then that the appointment of the Executive should either be drawn from some source, or held by some tenure, that will give him a free agency with regard to the Legislature. This could not be if he was to be appointable from time to time by the Legislature. It was not clear that an appointment in the 1st. instance even with an ineligibility afterwards would not establish an improper connection between the two departments. Certain it was that the appointment would be attended with intrigues and contentions that ought not to be unnecessarily admitted. He was disposed for these reasons to refer the appointment to some other source. The people at large was in his opinion the fittest in itself. It would be as likely as any that could be devised to produce an Executive Magistrate of distinguished Character. The people generally could only know & vote for some Citizen whose merits had rendered him an object of general attention & esteem. There was one difficulty however of a serious nature attending an immediate choice by the people. The right of suffrage was much more diffusive in the Northern than the Southern States; and the latter could have no influence in the election on the score of the Negroes. The substitution of electors obviated this difficulty and seemed on the whole to be liable to fewest objections.

July 19, 1787

Speech in the Federal Convention on Impeachment

Mr. Madison thought it indispensable that some provision should be made for defending the Community agst the incapacity, negligence or perfidy of the chief Magistrate. The limitation of the period of his service, was not a sufficient security. He might lose his capacity after his appointment. He might pervert his administration into a scheme of peculation or oppression. He might betray his trust to foreign powers. The case of the Executive Magistracy was very distinguishable, from that of the Legislature or of any other public body, holding offices of limited duration. It could not be presumed that all or even a majority of the members of an Assembly would either lose their capacity for discharging, or be bribed to betray, their trust. Besides the restraints of their personal integrity & honor, the difficulty of acting in concert for purposes of corruption was a security to the public. And if one or a few members only should be seduced, the soundness of the remaining members, would maintain the integrity and fidelity of the body. In the case of the Executive Magistracy which was to be administered by a single man, loss of capacity or corruption was more within the compass of probable events, and either of them might be fatal to the Republic.

July 20, 1787

Speech in the Federal Convention on Ratification

Mr. Madison thought it clear that the Legislatures were incompetent to the proposed changes. These changes would make essential inroads on the State Constitutions, and it would be a novel & dangerous doctrine that a Legislature could change the constitution under which it held its existence. There might indeed be some Constitutions within the Union, which had given a power to the Legislature to concur in alterations of the federal Compact. But there were certainly some which had not; and in the case of these, a ratification must of necessity be obtained from the people. He considered the difference between a system founded on the Legislatures only, and one founded on the people, to be the true difference between a *league* or *treaty*, and a *Constitution*. The former in point of *moral obligation* might be as inviolable as the latter. In point of *political operation*, there were two important distinctions in favor of the latter. 1. A law violating a treaty ratified by a pre-existing law, might be respected by the Judges as a law, though an unwise or perfidious one. A law violating a constitution established by the people themselves, would be considered by the Judges as null & void. 2. The doctrine laid down by the law of Nations in the case of treaties is that a breach of any one article by any of the parties, frees the other parties from their engagements. In the case of a union of people under one Constitution, the nature of the pact has always been understood to exclude such an interpretation. Comparing the two modes in point of expediency he thought all the considerations which recommended this Convention in preference to Congress for proposing the reform were in favor of State Conventions in preference to the Legislatures for examining and adopting it.

July 23, 1787

Speech in the Federal Convention on Electing the Executive

MR. MADISON.   There are objections agst. every mode that has been, or perhaps can be proposed. The election must be made either by some existing authority under the Natil. or State Constitutions—or by some special authority derived from the people—or by the people themselves. The two Existing authorities under the Natl. Constitution wd. be the Legislative & Judiciary. The latter he presumed was out of the question. The former was in his Judgment liable to insuperable objections. Besides the general influence of that mode on the independence of the Executive, 1. the election of the Chief Magistrate would agitate & divide the legislature so much that the public interest would materially suffer by it. Public bodies are always apt to be thrown into contentions, but into more violent ones by such occasions than by any others. 2. the candidate would intrigue with the Legislature, would derive his appointment from the predominant faction, and be apt to render his administration subservient to its views. 3. The Ministers of foreign powers would have and make use of, the opportunity to mix their intrigues & influence with the Election. Limited as the powers of the Executive are, it will be an object of great moment with the great rival powers of Europe who have American possessions, to have at the head of our Governmt. a man attached to their respective politics & interests. No pains, nor perhaps expence, will be spared, to gain from the Legislature an appointmt. favorable to their wishes. Germany & Poland are witnesses of this danger. In the former, the election of the Head of the Empire, till it became in a manner hereditary, interested all Europe, and was much influenced by foreign interference. In the latter, altho' the elective Magistrate has very little real power, his election has at all times produced the most eager interference of foreign princes, and has in fact at length slid entirely into foreign hands. The existing authorities in the States are the Legislative, Executive & Judiciary. The appointment of the Natl. Executive by the first, was objectionable in many points of view, some of which had been already mentioned. He would mention one which of itself would decide his opinion. The Legislatures of the States had betrayed a strong propensity to a variety of pernicious measures. One object of the Natl. Legislre. was to controul this propensity. One object of the Natl. Executive, so far as it would have a negative on the laws, was to controul the Natl. Legislature, so far as it might be infected with a similar propensity. Refer the appointmt of the Natl. Executive to the State Legislatures, and this controuling purpose may be defeated. The Legislatures can & will act with some kind of regular plan, and will promote the appointmt. of a man who will not oppose himself to a favorite object. Should a majority of the Legislatures at the time of election have the same object, or different objects of the same kind, The Natl. Executive would be rendered subservient to them. An appointment by the State Executives, was liable among other objections to this insuperable one, that being standing bodies, they could & would be courted, and intrigued with by the Candidates, by their partizans, and by the Ministers of foreign powers. The State Judiciarys had not & he presumed wd. not be proposed as a proper source of appointment. The option before us then lay between an appointment by Electors chosen by the people— and an immediate appointment by the people. He thought the former mode free from many of the objections which had been urged agst. it, and greatly preferable to an appointment by the Natl. Legislature. As the electors would be chosen for the occasion, would meet at once, & proceed immediately to an appointment, there would be very little opportunity for cabal, or corruption. As a further precaution, it might be required that they should meet at some place, distinct from the seat of Govt. and even that no person within a certain distance of the place at the time shd. be eligible. This Mode however had been rejected, so recently & by so great a majority that it probably would not be proposed anew. The remaining mode was an election by the people or rather by the qualified part of them, at large. With all its imperfections he liked this best. He would not repeat either the general argumts. for or the objections agst. this mode. He would only take notice of two difficulties which he admitted to have weight. The first arose from the disposition in the people to prefer a Citizen of their own State, and the disadvantage this wd. throw on the smaller States. Great as this objection might be he did not think it equal to such as lay agst. every other mode which had been proposed. He thought too that some expedient might be hit upon that would obviate it. The second difficulty arose from the disproportion of qualified voters in the N. & S. States, and the disadvantages which this mode would throw on the latter. The answer to this objection was 1. that this disproportion would be continually decreasing under the influence of the Republican laws introduced in the S. States, and the more rapid increase of their population. 2. That local considerations must give way to the general interest. As an individual from the S. States he was willing to make the sacrifice.

July 25, 1787

Speech in the Federal Convention on Suffrage

MR. MADISON. The right of suffrage is certainly one of the fundamental articles of republican Government, and ought not to be left to be regulated by the Legislature. A gradual abridgment of this right has been the mode in which Aristocracies have been built on the ruins of popular forms. Whether the Constitutional qualification ought to be a freehold, would with him depend much on the probable reception such a change would meet with in States where the right was now exercised by every description of people. In several of the States a freehold was now the qualification. Viewing the subject in its merits alone, the freeholders of the Country would be the safest depositories of Republican liberty. In future times a great majority of the people will not only be without landed, but any other sort of, property. These will either combine under the influence of their common situation: in which case, the rights of property & the public liberty, will not be secure in their hands: or which is more probable, they will become the tools of opulence & ambition, in which case there will be equal danger on another side. The example of England had been misconceived (by Col Mason). A very small proportion of the Representatives are there chosen by freeholders. The greatest part are chosen by the Cities & boroughs, in many of which the qualification of suffrage is as low as it is in any one of the U.S. and it was in the boroughs & Cities rather than the Counties, that bribery most prevailed, & the influence of the Crown on elections was most dangerously exerted.

note to speech of J. M. in convention
of 1787, August 7th.

As appointments for the General Government here contemplated will, in part, be made by the State Govts: all the Citizens in States where the right of suffrage is not limited to the holders of property, will have an indirect share of representation in the General Government. But this does not satisfy the fundamental principle that men can not be justly bound by laws in making which they have no part. Persons & property being both essential objects of Government, the most that either can claim, is such a structure of it, as will leave a reasonable security for the other. And the most obvious provision, of this double character, seems to be that of confining to the holders of property the object deemed least secure in popular Govts., the right of suffrage for one of the two Legislative branches. This is not without example among us, as well as other constitutional modifications, favoring the influence of property in the Government. But the U.S. have not reached the Stage of Society in which conflicting feelings of the Class with, and the Class without property, have the operation natural to them in Countries fully peopled. The most difficult of all political arrangements is that of so adjusting the claims of the two Classes as to give security to each and to promote the welfare of all. The federal principle, which enlarges the sphere of Power without departing from the elective basis of it and controuls in various ways the propensity in small republics to rash measures & the facility of forming & executing them, will be found the best expedient yet tried for solving the problem.

August 7, 1787

Speech in the Federal Convention
on Control of Congressional Elections

MR. MADISON.   The necessity of a Genl. Govt. supposes that the State Legislatures will sometimes fail or refuse to consult the common interest at the expence of their local conveniency or prejudices. The policy of referring the appointment of the House of Representatives to the people and not to the Legislatures of the States, supposes that the result will be somewhat influenced by the mode. This view of the question seems to decide that the Legislatures of the States ought not to have the uncontrouled right of regulating the times places & manner of holding elections. These were words of great latitude. It was impossible to foresee all the abuses that might be made of the discretionary power. Whether the electors should vote by ballot or viva voce, should assemble at this place or that place; should be divided into districts or all meet at one place, shd. all vote for all the representatives; or all in a district vote for a number allotted to the district; these & many other points would depend on the Legislatures, and might materially affect the appointments. Whenever the State Legislatures had a favorite measure to carry, they would take care so to mould their regulations as to favor the candidates they wished to succeed. Besides, the inequality of the Representation in the Legislatures of particular States, would produce a like inequality in their representation in the Natl. Legislature, as it was presumable that the Counties having the power in the former case would secure it to themselves in the latter. What danger could there be in giving a controuling power to the Natl. Legislature? Of whom was it to consist? 1. of a Senate to be chosen by the State Legislatures. If the latter therefore could be trusted, their representatives could not be dangerous. 2. of Representatives elected by the same people who elect the State Legislatures; surely then if confidence is due to the latter, it must be due to the former. It seemed as improper in principle, though it might be less inconvenient in practice, to give to the State Legislatures this great authority over the election of Representatives of the people in the Genl. Legislature, as it would be to give to the latter a like power over the election of their Representatives in the State Legislatures.

August 9, 1787

To Thomas Jefferson

Dear Sir   Philada. Sepr. 6. 1787.

My last was intended for the Augst. Packet and put into the hands of Commodore Paul Jones. Some disappointments prevented his going, and as he did not know but its contents might be unfit for the ordinary conveyance, he retained it. The precaution was unnecessary. For the same reason the delay has been of little consequence. The rule of secresy in the Convention rendered that as it will this letter barren of those communications which might otherwise be made. As the Convention will shortly rise I should feel little scruple in disclosing what will be public here, before it could reach you, were it practicable for me to guard by Cypher against an intermediate discovery. But I am deprived of this resource by the shortness of the interval between the receipt of your letter of June 20. and the date of this. This is the first day which has been free from Committee service both before & after the hours of the House, and the last that is allowed me by the time advertised for the sailing of the Packet.

The Convention consists now as it has generally done of Eleven States. There has been no intermission of its Sessions since a house was formed; except an interval of about ten days allowed a Committee appointed to detail the general propositions agreed on in the House. The term of its dissolution cannot be more than one or two weeks distant. A Govermt. will probably be submitted to the *people of* the *states* consisting of a President *cloathed* with *executive power:* a *Senate chosen* by the *Legislatures:* and another *house chosen* by the *people of* the *states* jointly *possessing* the *legislative power* and a regular *judiciary* establishment. The mode of constituting the *executive* is among the few points not yet finally settled. The *Senate* will consist of two *members* from each *state* and *appointed sexennially:* The other, of *members appointed biennially* by the *people of* the *states* in proportion to their number. The Legislative power will *extend to taxation trade* and sundry other general matters. The powers of Congress will be *distributed* according to their *nature among the several departments.* The States will be *restricted from paper money* and in a *few other instances.* These are *the outlines.* The extent of them may perhaps surprize you. I hazard an opinion nevertheless that the *plan should* it *be adopted* will neither effectually *answer* its *national object* nor prevent the local *mischiefs* which every where *excite disgusts* agst the *state governments.* The grounds of this opinion will be the subject of a future letter.

I have written to a friend in Congs. intimating in a covert manner the necessity of deciding & notifying the intentions of Congs. with regard to their foreign Ministers after May next, and have dropped a hint on the communications of Dumas.

Congress have taken some measures for disposing of their public land, and have actually sold a considerable tract. Another bargain I learn is on foot for a further sale.

Nothing can exceed the universal anxiety for the event of the Meeting here. Reports and conjectures abound concerning the nature of the plan which is to be proposed. The public however is certainly in the dark with regard to it. The Convention is equally in the dark as to the reception wch. may be given to it on its publication. All the prepossessions are on the right side, but it may well be expected that certain characters will wage war against any reform whatever. My own idea is that the public mind will now or in a very little time receive any thing that promises stability to the public Councils & security to private rights, and that no regard ought to be had to local prejudices or temporary considerations. If the present moment be lost it is hard to say what may be our fate.

Our information from Virginia is far from being agreeable. In many parts of the Country the drouth has been extremely injurious to the Corn. I fear, tho' I have no certain information, that Orange & Albemarle share in the distress. The people also are said to be generally discontented. A paper emission is again a topic among them. So is an instalment of all debts in some places and the making property a tender in others. The taxes are another source of discontent. The weight of them is complained of, and the abuses in collecting them still more so. In several Counties the prisons & Court Houses & Clerks offices have been wilfully burnt. In Green Briar the course of Justice has been mutinously stopped, and associations entered into agst. the payment of taxes. No other County has yet followed the example. The approaching meeting of the Assembly will probably allay the discontents on one side by measures which will excite them on another.

Mr. Wythe has never returned to us. His lady whose illness carryed him away, died some time after he got home. The other deaths in Virga. are Col. A. Cary, and a few days ago, Mrs Harrison, wife of Benjn. Harrison Junr. & sister of J. F. Mercer. Wishing you all happiness I remain Dear Sir Yrs. Affectly.

To George Washington

Dear Sir   N York Sepr. 30 1787.
I found on my arrival here that certain ideas unfavorable to the Act of the Convention which had created difficulties in that body, had made their way into Congress. They were patronised cheifly by Mr. R. H. L. and Mr. Dane of Massts. It was first urged that as the new Constitution was more than an Alteration of the Articles of Confederation under which Congress acted, and even subverted these articles altogether, there was a Constitutional impropriety in their taking any positive agency in the work. The answer given was that the Resolution of Congress in Feby. had recommended the Convention as the best mean of obtaining a firm *national Government*; that as the powers of the Convention were defined by their Commissions in nearly the same terms with the powers of Congress given by the Confederation on the subject of alterations, Congress were not more restrained from acceding to the new plan, than the Convention were from proposing it. If the plan was within the powers of the Convention it was within those of Congress; if beyond those powers, the same necessity which justified the Convention would justify

Congress; and a failure of Congress to Concur in what was
done, would imply either that the Convention had done
wrong in exceeding their powers, or that the Government
proposed was in itself liable to insuperable objections; that
such an inference would be the more natural, as Congress had
never scrupled to recommend measures foreign to their
Constitutional functions, whenever the Public good seemed
to require it; and had in several instances, particularly in the
establishment of the new Western Governments, exercised assumed powers of a very high & delicate nature, under motives
infinitely less urgent than the present state of our affairs, if any
faith were due to the representations made by Congress
themselves, ecchoed by 12 States in the Union, and confirmed
by the general voice of the People. An attempt was made in
the next place by R. H. L. to amend the Act of the Convention before it should go forth from Congress. He proposed a
bill of Rights—provision for juries in civil cases & several
other things corresponding with the ideas of Col. M. He was
supported by Mr. Me—— Smith of this State. It was contended that Congress had an undoubted right to insert
amendments, and that it was their duty to make use of it in a
case where the essential guards of liberty had been omitted.
On the other side the right of Congress was not denied, but
the inexpediency of exerting it was urged on the following
grounds. 1. that every circumstance indicated that the introduction of Congress as a party to the reform, was intended by
the States merely as a matter of form and respect. 2. that it
was evident from the contradictory objections which had
been expressed by the different members who had animadverted on the plan, that a discussion of its merits would consume much time, without producing agreement even among
its adversaries. 3. that it was clearly the intention of the States
that the plan to be proposed should be the act of the
Convention with the assent of Congress, which could not be
the case, if alterations were made, the Convention being no
longer in existence to adopt them. 4. that as the Act of the
Convention, when altered would instantly become the mere
act of Congress, and must be proposed by them as such, and
of course be addressed to the Legislatures, not conventions of
the States, and require the ratification of thirteen instead of

nine States, and as the unaltered act would go forth to the States directly from the Convention under the auspices of that Body—Some States might ratify one & some the other of the plans, and confusion & disappointment be the least evils that could ensue. These difficulties which at one time threatened a serious division in Congs. and popular alterations with the yeas & nays on the journals, were at length fortunately terminated by the following Resolution—"Congress having recd. the Report of the Convention lately assembled in Philada., Resold. *unanimously* that the said Report, with the Resolutions & letter accompanying the same, be transmitted to the several Legislatures, in order to be submitted to a Convention of Delegates chosen in each State by the people thereof, in conformity to the Resolves of the Convention made & provided in that case." Eleven States were present, the absent ones R.I. & Maryland. A more direct approbation would have been of advantage in this & some other States, where stress will be laid on the agency of Congress in the matter, and a handle taken by adversaries of any ambiguity on the subject. With regard to Virginia & some other States, reserve on the part of Congress will do no injury. The circumstance of unaninimity must be favorable every where.

The general voice of this City seems to espouse the new Constitution. It is supposed nevertheless that the party in power is strongly opposed to it. The Country must finally decide, the sense of which is as yet wholly unknown. As far as Boston & Connecticut has been heard from, the first impression seems to be auspicious. I am waiting with anxiety for the eccho from Virginia but with very faint hopes of its corresponding with my wishes. With every sentiment of respect & esteem, & every wish for your health & happiness, I am Dear Sir, Your Obedient, humble servt.

P.S. A small packet of the size of 2 Vol. 8o. addressed to you, lately came to my hands with books of my own from France. Genl. Pinkney has been so good as to take charge of them. He set out yesterday for S. Carolina & means to call at Mount Vernon.

To George Washington

Dear Sir   N. York Octr. 18. 1787.

I have been this day honoured with your favor of the 10th. instant, under the same cover with which is a copy of Col. Mason's objections to the Work of the Convention. As he persists in the temper which produced his dissent it is no small satisfaction to find him reduced to such distress for a proper gloss on it; for no other consideration surely could have led him to dwell on an objection which he acknowledged to have been in some degree removed by the Convention themselves —on the paltry right of the Senate to propose alterations in money bills—on the appointment of the vice President, President of the Senate instead of making the President of the Senate the vice President, which seemed to be the alternative—and on the *possibility*, that the Congress may misconstrue their powers & betray their trust so far as to grant monopolies in trade &c. If I do not forget too some of his other reasons were either not at all or very faintly urged at the time when alone they ought to have been urged; such as the power of the Senate in the case of treaties & of impeachments; and their duration in office. With respect to the latter point I recollect well that he more than once disclaimed opposition to it. My memory fails me also if he did not acquiesce in if not vote for, the term allowed for the further importation of slaves; and the prohibition of duties on exports by the States. What he means by the dangerous tendency of the Judiciary I am at some loss to comprehend. It never was intended, nor can it be supposed that in ordinary cases the inferior tribunals will not have final jurisdiction in order to prevent the evils of which he complains. The great mass of suits in every State lie between Citizen & Citizen, and relate to matters not of federal cognizance. Notwithstanding the stress laid on the necessity of a Council to the President I strongly suspect, tho I was a friend to the thing, that if such an one as Col. Mason proposed, had been established, and the power of the Senate in appointments to offices transferred to it, that as great a clamour would have been heard from some quarters which in general eccho his Objections. What can he mean by saying that the Common law is not secured by the new constitution, though it has been adopted by the State Constitutions. The common law is nothing more than the unwritten law, and is left by all the constitutions equally liable to legislative alterations. I am not sure that any notice is particularly taken of it in the Constitutions of the States. If there is, nothing more is provided than a general declaration that it shall continue along with other branches of law to be in force till legally changed. The Constitution of Virga. drawn up by Col Mason himself, is absolutely silent on the subject. An *ordinance* passed during the same Session, declared the Common law as heretofore & all Statutes of prior date to the 4 of James I. to be still the law of the land, merely to obviate pretexts that the separation from G. Britain threw us into a State of nature, and abolished all civil rights and Obligations. Since the Revolution every State has made great inroads & with great propriety in many instances on this *monarchical* code. The "revisal of the laws" by a Committee of wch. Col. Mason was a member, though not an acting one, abounds with such innovations. The abolition of the *right of primo-geniture*, which I am sure Col. Mason does not disapprove, falls under this head. What could the Convention have done? If they had in general terms declared the Common law to be in force, they would have broken in upon the legal Code of every State in the most material points: they wd. have done more, they would have brought over from G.B. a thousand heterogeneous & antirepublican doctrines, and even the *ecclesiastical Hierarchy itself*, for that is a part of the Common law. If they had undertaken a discrimination, they must have formed a digest of laws, instead of a Constitution. This objection surely was not brought forward in the Convention, or it wd. have been placed in such a light that a repetition of it out of doors would scarcely have been hazarded. Were it allowed the weight which Col. M. may suppose it deserves, it would remain to be decided whether it be candid to arraign the Convention for omissions which were never suggested to them—or prudent to vindicate the dissent by reasons which either were not previously thought of, or must have been wilfully concealed. But I am running into a comment as prolix, as it is out of place.

I find by a letter from the Chancellor (Mr. Pendleton) that

he views the act of the Convention in its true light, and gives it his unequivocal approbation. His support will have great effect. The accounts we have here of some other respectable characters vary considerably. Much will depend on Mr. Henry, and I am glad to find by your letter that his favorable decision on the subject may yet be hoped for. The Newspapers here begin to teem with vehement & virulent calumniations of the proposed Govt. As they are cheifly borrowed from the Pensylvania papers, you see them of course. The reports however from different quarters continue to be rather flattering. With the highest respect & sincerest attachment I remain Dear Sir Yr. Obedt. & Affecte. Servant

To Thomas Jefferson

Dear Sir   New York Octr. 24. 1787.

My two last, though written for the two last Packets, have unluckily been delayed till this conveyance. The first of them was sent from Philada. to Commodore Jones in consequence of information that he was certainly to go by the Packet then about to sail. Being detained here by his business with Congress, and being unwilling to put the letter into the mail without my approbation which could not be obtained in time, he detained the letter also. The second was sent from Philada. to Col. Carrington, with a view that it might go by the last packet at all events in case Commodore Jones should meet with further detention here. By ill luck he was out of Town, and did not return till it was too late to make use of the opportunity. Neither of the letters were indeed of much consequence at the time, and are still less so now. I let them go forward nevertheless as they may mention some circumstances not at present in my recollection, and as they will prevent a chasm in my part of [   ] correspondence which I have so many motives to cherish by an exact punctuality.

Your favor of June 20. has been already acknowledged. The last Packet from France brought me that of August 2d. I have recd. also by the Mary Capt. Howland the three Boxes for W.H. B.F. and myself. The two first have been duly forwarded. The contents of the last are a valuable addition to former literary remittances and lay me under additional obligations, which I shall always feel more strongly than I express. The articles included for Congress have been delivered & those for the two Universities and for General Washington have been forwarded, as have been the various letters for your friends in Virginia and elsewhere. The parcel of rice referred to in your letter to the Delegates of S. Carolina has met with some accident. No account whatever can be gathered concerning it. It probably was not shipped from France. Ubbo's book I find was not omitted as you seem to have apprehended. The charge for it however is, which I must beg you to supply. The duplicate vol. of the Encyclopedie, I left in Virginia, and it is uncertain when I shall have an opportunity of returning it. Your Spanish duplicates will I fear be hardly vendible. I shall make a trial wherever a chance presents itself. A few days ago I recd. your favor of the 15 of Augst. via L'Orient & Boston. The letters inclosed along with it were immediately sent on to Virga.

You will herewith receive the result of the Convention, which continued its Session till the 17th. of September. I take the liberty of making some observations on the subject which will help to make up a letter, if they should answer no other purpose.

It appeared to be the sincere and unanimous wish of the Convention to cherish and preserve the Union of the States. No proposition was made, no suggestion was thrown out, in favor of a partition of the Empire into two or more Confederacies.

It was generally agreed that the objects of the Union could not be secured by any system founded on the principle of a confederation of sovereign States. A *voluntary* observance of the federal law by all the members, could never be hoped for. A *compulsive* one could evidently never be reduced to practice, and if it could, involved equal calamities to the innocent & the guilty, the necessity of a military force both obnoxious & dangerous, and in general, a scene resembling much more a civil war, than the administration of a regular Government.

Hence was embraced the alternative of a Government which instead of operating, on the States, should operate without their intervention on the individuals composing them: and hence the change in the principle and proportion of representation.

This ground-work being laid, the great objects which presented themselves were 1. to unite a proper energy in the Executive and a proper stability in the Legislative departments, with the essential characters of Republican Government. 2. to draw a line of demarkation which would give to the General Government every power requisite for general purposes, and leave to the States every power which might be most beneficially administered by them. 3. to provide for the different interests of different parts of the Union. 4. to adjust the clashing pretensions of the large and small States. Each of these objects was pregnant with difficulties. The whole of them together formed a task more difficult than can be well concieved by those who were not concerned in the execution of it. Adding to these considerations the natural diversity of human opinions on all new and complicated subjects, it is impossible to consider the degree of concord which ultimately prevailed as less than a miracle.

The first of these objects as it respects the Executive, was peculiarly embarrassing. On the question whether it should consist of a single person, or a plurality of co-ordinate members, on the mode of appointment, on the duration in office, on the degree of power, on the re-eligibility, tedious and reiterated discussions took place. The plurality of co-ordinate members had finally but few advocates. Governour Randolph was at the head of them. The modes of appointment proposed were various, as by the people at large—by electors chosen by the people—by the Executives of the States— by the Congress, some preferring a joint ballot of the two Houses—some a separate concurrent ballot allowing to each a negative on the other house—some a nomination of several candidates by one House, out of whom a choice should be made by the other. Several other modifications were started. The expedient at length adopted seemed to give pretty general satisfaction to the members. As to the duration in office, a few would have preferred a tenure during good behaviour— a considerable number would have done so, in case an easy & effectual removal by impeachment could be settled. It was much agitated whether a long term, seven years for example, with a subsequent & perpetual ineligibility, or a short term with a capacity to be re-elected, should be fixed. In favor of the first opinion were urged the danger of a gradual degeneracy of re-elections from time to time, into first a life and then a heriditary tenure, and the favorable effect of an incapacity to be reappointed, on the independent exercise of the Executive authority. On the other side it was contended that the prospect of necessary degradation, would discourage the most dignified characters from aspiring to the office, would take away the principal motive to the faithful discharge of its duties—the hope of being rewarded with a reappointment, would stimulate ambition to violent efforts for holding over the constitutional term—and instead of producing an independent administration, and a firmer defence of the constitutional rights of the department, would render the officer more indifferent to the importance of a place which he would soon be obliged to quit for ever, and more ready to yield to the incroachmts. of the Legislature of which he might again be a member. The questions concerning the degree of power turned chiefly on the appointment to offices, and the controul on the Legislature. An *absolute* appointment to all offices—to some offices—to no offices, formed the scale of opinions on the first point. On the second, some contended for an absolute negative, as the only possible mean of reducing to practice, the theory of a free Government which forbids a mixture of the Legislative & Executive powers. Others would be content with a revisionary power to be overruled by three fourths of both Houses. It was warmly urged that the judiciary department should be associated in the revision. The idea of some was that a separate revision should be given to the two departments—that if either objected two thirds; if both three fourths, should be necessary to overrule.

In forming the Senate, the great anchor of the Government, the questions as they came within the first object turned mostly on the mode of appointment, and the duration of it. The different modes proposed were, 1. by the House of Representatives 2. by the Executive, 3. by electors chosen by the people for the purpose. 4. by the State Legislatures. On the point of duration, the propositions descended from good-behavior to four years, through the intermediate terms of nine, seven, six, & five years. The election of the other branch was first determined to be triennial, and afterwards reduced to biennial.

The second object, the due partition of power, between the General & local Governments, was perhaps of all, the most nice and difficult. A few contended for an entire abolition of the States; some for indefinite power of Legislation in the Congress, with a negative on the laws of the States: some for such a power without a negative: some for a limited power of legislation, with such a negative: the majority finally for a limited power without the negative. The question with regard to the Negative underwent repeated discussions, and was finally rejected by a bare majority. As I formerly intimated to you my opinion in favor of this ingredient, I will take this occasion of explaining myself on the subject. Such a check on the States appears to me necessary 1. to prevent encroachments on the General authority. 2. to prevent instability and injustice in the legislation of the States.

1. Without such a check in the whole over the parts, our system involves the evil of imperia in imperio. If a compleat supremacy some where is not necessary in every Society, a controuling power at least is so, by which the general authority may be defended against encroachments of the subordinate authorities, and by which the latter may be restrained from encroachments on each other. If the supremacy of the British Parliament is not necessary as has been contended, for the harmony of that Empire; it is evident I think that without the royal negative or some equivalent controul, the unity of the system would be destroyed. The want of some such provision seems to have been mortal to the antient Confederacies, and to be the disease of the modern. Of the Lycian Confederacy little is known. That of the Amphyctions is well known to have been rendered of little use whilst it lasted, and in the end to have been destroyed by the predominance of the local over the federal authority. The same observation may be made, on the authority of Polybius, with regard to the Achæan League. The Helvetic System scarcely amounts to a Confederacy, and is distinguished by too many peculiarities, to be a ground of comparison. The case of the United

Netherlands is in point. The authority of a Statholder, the influence of a Standing army, the common interest in the conquered possessions, the pressure of surrounding danger, the guarantee of foreign powers, are not sufficient to secure the authority and interests of the generality, agst. the antifederal tendency of the provincial sovereignties. The German Empire is another example. A Hereditary chief with vast independent resources of wealth and power, a federal Diet, with ample parchment authority, a regular Judiciary establishment, the influence of the neighbourhood of great & formidable Nations, have been found unable either to maintain the subordination of the members, or to prevent their mutual contests & encroachments. Still more to the purpose is our own experience both during the war and since the peace. Encroachments of the States on the general authority, sacrifices of national to local interests, interferences of the measures of different States, form a great part of the history of our political system. It may be said that the new Constitution is founded on different principles, and will have a different operation. I admit the difference to be material. It presents the aspect rather of a feudal system of republics, if such a phrase may be used, than of a Confederacy of independent States. And what has been the progress and event of the feudal Constitutions? In all of them a continual struggle between the head and the inferior members, until a final victory has been gained in some instances by one, in others, by the other of them. In one respect indeed there is a remarkable variance between the two cases. In the feudal system the sovereign, though limited, was independent; and having no particular sympathy of interests with the great Barons, his ambition had as full play as theirs in the mutual projects of usurpation. In the American Constitution The general authority will be derived entirely from the subordinate authorities. The Senate will represent the States in their political capacity; the other House will represent the people of the States in their individual capacity. The former will be accountable to their constituents at moderate, the latter at short periods. The President also derives his appointment from the States, and is periodically accountable to them. This dependence of the General, on the local authorities, seems effectually to guard the latter against any dangerous encroachments of the former: Whilst the latter, within their respective limits, will be continually sensible of the abridgment of their power, and be stimulated by ambition to resume the surrendered portion of it. We find the representatives of Counties and corporations in the Legislatures of the States, much more disposed to sacrifice the aggregate interest, and even authority, to the local views of their Constituents: than the latter to the former. I mean not by these remarks to insinuate that an esprit de corps will not exist in the national Government or that opportunities may not occur, of extending its jurisdiction in some points. I mean only that the danger of encroachments is much greater from the other side, and that the impossibility of dividing powers of legislation, in such a manner, as to be free from different constructions by different interests, or even from ambiguity in the judgment of the impartial, requires some such expedient as I contend for. Many illustrations might be given of this impossibility. How long has it taken to fix, and how imperfectly is yet fixed the legislative power of corporations, though that power is subordinate in the most compleat manner? The line of distinction between the power of regulating trade and that of drawing revenue from it, which was once considered as the barrier of our liberties, was found on fair discussion, to be absolutely undefinable. No distinction seems to be more obvious than that between spiritual and temporal matters. Yet wherever they have been made objects of Legislation, they have clashed and contended with each other, till one or the other has gained the supremacy. Even the boundaries between the Executive, Legislative & Judiciary powers, though in general so strongly marked in themselves, consist in many instances of mere shades of difference. It may be said that the Judicial authority under our new system will keep the States within their proper limits, and supply the place of a negative on their laws. The answer is, that it is more convenient to prevent the passage of a law, than to declare it void after it is passed; that this will be particularly the case, where the law aggrieves individuals, who may be unable to support an appeal agst. a State to the supreme Judiciary; that a State which would violate the Legislative rights of the Union, would not be very ready to obey a Judicial decree in support of them, and that a recurrence to force, which in the event of disobedience would be necessary, is an evil which the new Constitution meant to exclude as far as possible.

2. A constitutional negative on the laws of the States seems equally necessary to secure individuals agst. encroachments on their rights. The mutability of the laws of the States is found to be a serious evil. The injustice of them has been so frequent and so flagrant as to alarm the most stedfast friends of Republicanism. I am persuaded I do not err in saying that the evils issuing from these sources contributed more to that uneasiness which produced the Convention, and prepared the public mind for a general reform, than those which accrued to our national character and interest from the inadequacy of the Confederation to its immediate objects. A reform therefore which does not make provision for private rights, must be materially defective. The restraints agst. paper emissions, and violations of contracts are not sufficient. Supposing them to be effectual as far as they go, they are short of the mark. Injustice may be effected by such an infinitude of legislative expedients, that where the disposition exists it can only be controuled by some provision which reaches all cases whatsoever. The partial provision made, supposes the disposition which will evade it. It may be asked how private rights will be more secure under the Guardianship of the General Government than under the State Governments, since they are both founded on the republican principle which refers the ultimate decision to the will of the majority, and are distinguished rather by the extent within which they will operate, than by any material difference in their structure. A full discussion of this question would, if I mistake not, unfold the true principles of Republican Government, and prove in contradiction to the concurrent opinions of theoretical writers, that this form of Government, in order to effect its purposes, must operate not within a small but an extensive sphere. I will state some of the ideas which have occurred to me on this subject. Those who contend for a simple Democracy, or a pure republic, actuated by the sense of the majority, and operating within narrow limits, assume or suppose a case which is altogether fictitious. They found their reasoning on the idea, that the people composing the Society, enjoy not only an equality

of political rights; but that they have all precisely the same interests, and the same feelings in every respect. Were this in reality the case, their reasoning would be conclusive. The interest of the majority would be that of the minority also; the decisions could only turn on mere opinion concerning the good of the whole, of which the major voice would be the safest criterion; and within a small sphere, this voice could be most easily collected, and the public affairs most accurately managed. We know however that no Society ever did or can consist of so homogeneous a mass of Citizens. In the savage State indeed, an approach is made towards it; but in that State little or no Government is necessary. In all civilized Societies, distinctions are various and unavoidable. A distinction of property results from that very protection which a free Government gives to unequal faculties of acquiring it. There will be rich and poor; creditors and debtors; a landed interest, a monied interest, a mercantile interest, a manufacturing interest. These classes may again be subdivided according to the different productions of different situations & soils, & according to different branches of commerce, and of manufactures. In addition to these natural distinctions, artificial ones will be founded, on accidental differences in political, religious or other opinions, or an attachment to the persons of leading individuals. However erroneous or ridiculous these grounds of dissention and faction, may appear to the enlightened Statesman, or the benevolent philosopher, the bulk of mankind who are neither Statesmen nor Philosophers, will continue to view them in a different light. It remains then to be enquired whether a majority having any common interest, or feeling any common passion, will find sufficient motives to restrain them from oppressing the minority. An individual is never allowed to be a judge or even a witness in his own cause. If two individuals are under the biass of interest or enmity agst. a third, the rights of the latter could never be safely referred to the majority of the three. Will two thousand individuals be less apt to oppress one thousand, or two hundred thousand, one hundred thousand? Three motives only can restrain in such cases. 1. a prudent regard to private or partial good, as essentially involved in the general and permanent good of the whole. This ought no doubt to be sufficient of itself. Experience however shews that it has little effect on individuals, and perhaps still less on a collection of individuals, and least of all on a majority with the public authority in their hands. If the former are ready to forget that honesty is the best policy; the last do more. They often proceed on the converse of the maxim: that whatever is politic is honest. 2. respect for character. This motive is not found sufficient to restrain individuals from injustice, and loses its efficacy in proportion to the number which is to divide the praise or the blame. Besides as it has reference to public opinion, which is that of the majority, the Standard is fixed by those whose conduct is to be measured by it. 3. Religion. The inefficacy of this restraint on individuals is well known. The conduct of every popular Assembly, acting on oath, the strongest of religious ties, shews that individuals join without remorse in acts agst. which their consciences would revolt, if proposed to them separately in their closets. When Indeed Religion is kindled into enthusiasm, its force like that of other passions is increased by the sympathy of a multitude. But enthusiasm is only a temporary state of Religion, and whilst it lasts will hardly be seen with pleasure at the helm. Even in its coolest state, it has been much oftener a motive to oppression than a restraint from it. If then there must be different interests and parties in Society; and a majority when united by a common interest or passion can not be restrained from oppressing the minority, what remedy can be found in a republican Government, where the majority must ultimately decide, but that of giving such an extent to its sphere, that no common interest or passion will be likely to unite a majority of the whole number in an unjust pursuit. In a large Society, the people are broken into so many interests and parties, that a common sentiment is less likely to be felt, and the requisite concert less likely to be formed, by a majority of the whole. The same security seems requisite for the civil as for the religious rights of individuals. If the same sect form a majority and have the power, other sects will be sure to be depressed. Divide et impera, the reprobated axiom of tyranny, is under certain qualifications, the only policy, by which a republic can be administered on just principles. It must be observed however that this doctrine can only hold within a sphere of a mean extent. As in too small a sphere oppressive combinations may be too easily formed agst. the weaker party; so in too extensive a one, a defensive concert may be rendered too difficult against the oppression of those entrusted with the administration. The great desideratum in Government is, so to modify the sovereignty as that it may be sufficiently neutral between different parts of the Society to controul one part from invading the rights of another, and at the same time sufficiently controuled itself, from setting up an interest adverse to that of the entire Society. In absolute monarchies, the Prince may be tolerably neutral towards different classes of his subjects, but may sacrifice the happiness of all to his personal ambition or avarice. In small republics, the sovereign will is controuled from such a sacrifice of the entire Society, but is not sufficiently neutral towards the parts composing it. In the extended Republic of the United States, The General Government would hold a pretty even balance between the parties of particular States, and be at the same time sufficiently restrained by its dependence on the community, from betraying its general interests.

Begging pardon for this immoderate digression I return to the third object abovementioned, the adjustment of the different interests of different parts of the Continent. Some contended for an unlimited power over trade including exports as well as imports, and over slaves as well as other imports; some for such a power, provided the concurrence of two thirds of both House were required; Some for such a qualification of the power, with an exemption of exports and slaves, others for an exemption of exports only. The result is seen in the Constitution. S. Carolina & Georgia were inflexible on the point of the slaves.

The remaining object created more embarrassment, and a greater alarm for the issue of the Convention than all the rest put together. The little States insisted on retaining their equality in both branches, unless a compleat abolition of the State Governments should take place; and made an equality in the Senate a sine qua non. The large States on the other hand urged that as the new Government was to be drawn principally from the people immediately and was to operate directly on them, not on the States; and consequently as the States wd. lose that importance which is now proportioned to the importance of their voluntary compliances with the requisitions of Congress, it was necessary that the representation in both Houses should be in proportion to their size. It ended in the compromise which you will see, but very much to the dissatisfaction of several members from the large States.

It will not escape you that three names only from Virginia are subscribed to the Act. Mr. Wythe did not return after the death of his lady. Docr. MClurg left the Convention some time before the adjournment. The Governour and Col. Mason refused to be parties to it. Mr. Gerry was the only other member who refused. The objections of the Govr. turn principally on the latitude of the general powers, and on the connection established between the President and the Senate. He wished that the plan should be proposed to the States with liberty to them to suggest alterations which should all be referred to another general Convention, to be incorporated into the plan as far as might be judged expedient. He was not inveterate in his opposition, and grounded his refusal to subscribe pretty much on his unwillingness to commit himself, so as not to be at liberty to be governed by further lights on the subject. Col. Mason left Philada. in an exceeding ill humour indeed. A number of little circumstances arising in part from the impatience which prevailed towards the close of the business, conspired to whet his acrimony. He returned to Virginia with a fixed disposition to prevent the adoption of the plan if possible. He considers the want of a Bill of Rights as a fatal objection. His other objections are to the substitution of the Senate in place of an Executive Council & to the powers vested in that body—to the powers of the Judiciary—to the vice President being made President of the Senate—to the smallness of the number of Representatives—to the restriction on the States with regard to ex post facto laws—and most of all probably to the power of regulating trade, by a majority only of each House. He has some other lesser objections. Being now under the necessity of justifying his refusal to sign, he will of course muster every possible one. His conduct has given great umbrage to the County of Fairfax, and particularly to the Town of Alexandria. He is already instructed to promote in the Assembly the calling a Convention, and will probably be either not deputed to the Convention, or be tied up by express instructions. He did not object in general to the powers vested in the National Government, so much as to the modification. In some respects he admitted that some further powers would have improved the system. He acknowledged in particular that a negative on the State laws, and the appointment of the State Executives ought to be ingredients; but supposed that the public mind would not now bear them, and that experience would hereafter produce these amendments.

The final reception which will be given by the people at large to the proposed System can not yet be decided. The Legislature of N. Hampshire was sitting when it reached that State and was well pleased with it. As far as the sense of the people there has been expressed, it is equally favorable. Boston is warm and almost unanimous in embracing it. The impression on the Country is not yet known. No symptoms of disapprobation have appeared. The Legislature of that State is now sitting, through which the sense of the people at large will soon be promulged with tolerable certainty. The paper money faction in Rh. Island is hostile. The other party zealously attached to it. Its passage through Connecticut is likely to be very smooth and easy. There seems to be less agitation in this State than any where. The discussion of the subject seems confined to the newspapers. The principal characters are known to be friendly. The Governour's party which has hitherto been the popular & most numerous one, is supposed to be on the opposite side; but considerable reserve is practised, of which he sets the example. N. Jersey takes the affirmative side of course. Meetings of the people are declaring their approbation, and instructing their representatives. Penna. will be divided. The City of Philada., the Republican party, the Quakers, and most of the Germans espouse the Constitution. Some of the Constitutional leaders, backed by the western Country will oppose. An unlucky ferment on the subject in their Assembly just before its late adjournment has irritated both sides, particularly the opposition, and by redoubling the exertions of that party may render the event doubtful. The voice of Maryland I understand from pretty good authority, is, as far as it has been declared, strongly in favor of the

Constitution. Mr. Chase is an enemy, but the Town of Baltimore which he now represents, is warmly attached to it, and will shackle him as far as they can. Mr. Paca will probably be, as usual, in the politics of Chase. My information from Virginia is as yet extremely imperfect. I have a letter from Genl. Washington which speaks favorably of the impression within a circle of some extent; and another from Chancellor Pendleton which expresses his full acceptance of the plan, and the popularity of it in his district. I am told also that Innis and Marshall are patrons of it. In the opposite scale are Mr. James Mercer, Mr. R. H. Lee, Docr. Lee and their connections of course, Mr. M. Page according to Report, and most of the Judges & Bar of the general Court. The part which Mr. Henry will take is unknown here. Much will depend on it. I had taken it for granted from a variety of circumstances that he wd. be in the opposition, and still think that will be the case. There are reports however which favor a contrary supposition. From the States South of Virginia nothing has been heard. As the deputation from S. Carolina consisted of some of its weightiest characters, who have returned unanimously zealous in favor of the Constitution, it is probable that State will readily embrace it. It is not less probable, that N. Carolina will follow the example unless that of Virginia should counterbalance it. Upon the whole, although, the public mind will not be fully known, nor finally settled for a considerable time, appearances at present augur a more prompt, and general adoption of the Plan than could have been well expected.

When the plan came before Congs. for their sanction, a very serious effort was made by R. H. Lee & Mr. Dane from Masts. to embarrass it. It was first contended that Congress could not properly give any positive countenance to a measure which had for its object the subversion of the Constitution under which they acted. This ground of attack failing, the former gentleman urged the expediency of sending out the plan with amendments, & proposed a number of them corresponding with the objections of Col. Mason. This experiment had still less effect. In order however to obtain unanimity it was necessary to couch the resolution in very moderate terms.

Mr. Adams has recd. permission to return, with thanks for

his Services. No provision is made for supplying his place, or keeping up any representation there. Your reappointment for three years will be notified from the Office of F. Affrs. It was *made without a negative eight states* being *present. Connecticut however put in a blank ticket* the *sense of* that *state having been declared against embassies. Massachusets betrayed some scruple* on *like ground.* Every *personal consideration* was *avowed & I believe with sincerity* to have *militated against these scruples.* It seems to be understood that letters to & from the foreign Ministers of the U.S. are not free of Postage: but that the charge is to be allowed in their accounts.

The exchange of our French for Dutch Creditors has not been countenanced either by Congress or the Treasury Board. The paragraph in your last letter to Mr. Jay, on the subject of applying a loan in Holland to the discharge of the pay due to the foreign Officers has been referred to the Board since my arrival here. No report has yet been made. But I have little idea that the proposition will be adopted. Such is the state & prospect of our fiscal department that any new loan however small, that should now be made, would probably subject us to the reproach of premeditated deception. The balance of Mr. Adams' last loan will be wanted for the interest due in Holland, and with all the income here, will, it is feared, not save our credit in Europe from further wounds. It may well be doubted whether the present Govt. can be kept alive thro' the ensuing year, or untill the new one may take its place.

Upwards of 100,000 Acres of the surveyed lands of the U.S. have been disposed of in open market. Five million of unsurveyed have been sold by private contract to a N. England Company, at ⅔ of a dollar per acre, payment to be made in the principal of the public securities. A negociation is nearly closed with a N. Jersey Company for two million more on like terms, and another commenced with a Company of this City for four million. Col. Carrington writes more fully on this subject.

You will receive herewith the desired information from Alderman Broome in the case of Mr. Burke. Also the Virga. Bill on crimes & punishments. Sundry alterations having been made in conformity to the sense of the House in its latter stages, it is less accurate & methodical than it ought to have been. To these papers I add a Speech of Mr. C. P. on the Missippi. business. It is printed under precautions of secrecy, but surely could not have been properly exposed to so much risk of publication. You will find also among the Pamplets & papers I send by Commodore Jones, another printed speech of the same Gentleman. The Musæum, Magazine, & Philada. Gazettes, will give you a tolerable idea of the objects of present attention.

The summer crops in the Eastern & Middle States have been extremely plentiful. Southward of Virga. They differ in different places. On the whole I do not know that they are bad in that region. In Virginia the drought has been unprecedented, particularly between the falls of the Rivers & the Mountains. The Crops of Corn are in general alarmingly short. In Orange I find there will be scarcely subsistence for the inhabitants. I have not heard from Albemarle. The crops of Tobo. are every where said to be pretty good in point of quantity; & the quality unusually fine. The crops of wheat were also in general excellent in quality & tolerable in quantity.

Novr. 1. Commodore Jones having preferred another vessel to the packet, has remained here till this time. The interval has produced little necessary to be added to the above. The Legislature of Massts. has it seems taken up the Act of the Convention, and have appointed or probably will appoint an early day for its State Convention. There are letters also from Georgia which denote a favorable disposition. I am informed from Richmond that the New Election-law from the Revised Code produced a pretty full House of Delegates, as well as a Senate, on the first day. It had previously had equal effect in producing full meetings of the freeholders for the County elections. A very decided majority of the Assembly is said to be zealous in favor of the New Constitution. The same is said of the Country at large. It appears however that individuals of great weight both within & without the Legislature are opposed to it. A letter I just have from Mr. A. Stuart, names Mr. Henry, Genl. Nelson, W. Nelson, the family of Cabels, St. George Tucker, John Taylor and the Judges of the Genl. Court except P. Carrington. The other opponents he describes as of too little note to be mentioned, which gives a negative information of the Characters on the other side. All are agreed that the plan must be submitted to a Convention.

We hear from Georgia that that State is threatened with a dangerous war with the Creek Indians. The alarm is of so serious a nature, that law-martial has been proclaimed, and they are proceeding to fortify even the Town of Savannah. The idea there, is that the Indians derive their motives as well as their means from their Spanish neighbours. Individuals complain also that their fugitive slaves are encouraged by East Florida. The policy of this is explained by supposing that it is considered as a discouragement to the Georgians to form settlements near the Spanish boundaries.

There are but few States on the spot here which will survive the expiration of the federal year; and it is extremely uncertain when a Congress will again be formed. We have not yet heard who are to be in the appointment of Virginia for the next year. With the most affectionate attachment I remain Dear Sr. Your Obed friend & servant

To George Washington

Dear Sir   New York Novr. 18. 1787.

Your favor of the 5th. instant found me in Philada. whither I had proceeded, under arrangements for proceeding to Virginia or returning to this place, as I might there decide. I did not acknowledge it in Philada. because I had nothing to communicate, which you would not receive more fully and correctly from the Mr. Morris's who were setting out for Virginia.

All my informations from Richmond concur in representing the enthusiasm in favor of the new Constitution as subsiding, and giving place to a spirit of criticism. I was fearful of such an event from the influence and co-operation of some of the adversaries. I do not learn however that the cause has lost its majority in the Legislature, and still less among the people at large.

I have nothing to add to the information heretofore given concerning the progress of the Constitution in other States.

Mr. Gerry has presented his objections to the Legislature in a letter addressed to them, and signified his readiness if desired to give the particular reasons on which they were founded. The Legislature it seems decline the explanation, either from a supposition that they have nothing further to do in the business, having handed it over to the Convention; or from an unwillingness to countenance Mr. Gerry's conduct; or from both these considerations. It is supposed that the promulgation of this letter will shake the confidence of some, and embolden the opposition of others in that State; but I cannot discover any ground for distrusting the prompt & decided concurrence of a large majority.

I inclose herewith the 7 first numbers of the federalist, a paper addressed to the people of this State. They relate entirely to the importance of the Union. If the whole plan should be executed, it will present to the public a full discussion of the merits of the proposed Constitution in all its relations. From the opinion I have formed of the views of a party in Virginia I am inclined to think that the observations on the first branch of the subject may not be superfluous antidotes in that State, any more than in this. If you concur with me, perhaps the papers may be put into the hand of some of your confidential correspondents at Richmond who would have them reprinted there. I will not conceal *from you* that I am likely to have such *a degree* of connection with the publication here, as to afford a restraint of delicacy from interesting myself directly in the republication elsewhere. You will recognize one of the pens concerned in the task. There are three in the whole. A fourth may possibly bear a part.

The intelligence by the packet as far as I have collected it, is contained in the gazette of yesterday.

Virginia is the only State represented as yet. When a Congress will be formed is altogether uncertain. It is not very improbable I think that the interregnum may continue throughout the winter. With every sentiment of respect & attachment I remain dear Sir Yr. Affect. & hble servant

The Federalist No. 10

Among the numerous advantages promised by a well constructed union, none deserves to be more accurately developed than its tendency to break and control the violence of faction. The friend of popular governments, never finds himself so much alarmed for their character and fate, as when he contemplates their propensity to this dangerous vice. He will not fail therefore to set a due value on any plan which, without violating the principles to which he is attached, provides a proper cure for it. The instability, injustice and confusion introduced into the public councils, have in truth been the mortal diseases under which popular governments have every where perished; as they continue to be the favorite and fruitful topics from which the adversaries to liberty derive their most specious declamations. The valuable improvements made by the American constitutions on the popular models, both antient and modern, cannot certainly be too much admired; but it would be an unwarrantable partiality, to contend that they have as effectually obviated the danger on this side as was wished and expected. Complaints are every where heard from our most considerate and virtuous citizens, equally the friends of public and private faith, and of public and personal liberty; that our governments are too unstable; that the public good is disregarded in the conflicts of rival parties; and that measures are too often decided, not according to the rules of justice, and the rights of the minor party; but by the superior force of an interested and over-bearing majority. However anxiously we may wish that these complaints had no foundation, the evidence of known facts will not permit us to deny that they are in some degree true. It will be found indeed, on a candid review of our situation, that some of the distresses under which we labour, have been erroneously charged on the operation of our governments; but it will be found at the same time, that other causes will not alone account for many of our heaviest misfortunes; and particularly, for that prevailing and increasing distrust of public engagements, and alarm for private rights, which are echoed from one end of the continent to the other. These must be chiefly, if not wholly, effects of the unsteadiness and injustice, with which a factious spirit has tainted our public administration.

By a faction I understand a number of citizens, whether amounting to a majority or minority of the whole, who are united and actuated by some common impulse of passion, or of interest, adverse to the rights of other citizens, or to the permanent and aggregate interests of the community.

There are two methods of curing the mischiefs of faction: The one, by removing its causes; the other, by controlling its effects.

There are again two methods of removing the causes of faction: The one by destroying the liberty which is essential to its existence; the other, by giving to every citizen the same opinions, the same passions, and the same interests.

It could never be more truly said than of the first remedy, that it is worse than the disease. Liberty is to faction, what air is to fire, an aliment without which it instantly expires. But it could not be a less folly to abolish liberty, which is essential to political life, because it nourishes faction, than it would be to wish the annihilation of air, which is essential to animal life because it imparts to fire its destructive agency.

The second expedient is as impracticable, as the first would be unwise. As long as the reason of man continues fallible, and he is at liberty to exercise it, different opinions will be formed. As long as the connection subsists between his reason and his self-love, his opinions and his passions will have a reciprocal influence on each other; and the former will be objects to which the latter will attach themselves. The diversity in the faculties of men from which the rights of property originate, is not less an insuperable obstacle to an uniformity of interests. The protection of these faculties is the first object of government. From the protection of different and unequal faculties of acquiring property, the possession of different degrees and kinds of property immediately results: And from the influence of these on the sentiments and views of the respective proprietors, ensues a division of the society into different interests and parties.

The latent causes of faction are thus sown in the nature of man; and we see them every where brought into different degrees of activity, according to the different circumstances of civil society. A zeal for different opinions concerning religion, concerning government, and many other points, as well of speculation as of practice; an attachment to different leaders ambitiously contending for pre-eminence and power; or to persons of other descriptions whose fortunes have been interesting to the human passions, have in turn divided mankind into parties, inflamed them with mutual animosity, and rendered them much more disposed to vex and oppress each other, than to co-operate for their common good. So strong is this propensity of mankind to fall into mutual animosities, that where no substantial occasion presents itself, the most frivolous and fanciful distinctions have been sufficient to kindle their unfriendly passions, and excite their most violent conflicts. But the most common and durable source of factions, has been the various and unequal distribution of property. Those who hold, and those who are without property, have ever formed distinct interests in society. Those who are creditors, and those who are debtors, fall under a like discrimination. A landed interest, a manufacturing interest, a mercantile interest, a monied interest, with many lesser interests, grow up of necessity in civilized nations, and divide them into different classes, actuated by different sentiments and views. The regulation of these various and interfering interests forms the principal task of modern legislation, and involves the spirit of party and faction in the necessary and ordinary operations of government.

No man is allowed to be a judge in his own cause; because his interest would certainly bias his judgment, and, not improbably, corrupt his integrity. With equal, nay with greater reason, a body of men, are unfit to be both judges and parties, at the same time; yet, what are many of the most important acts of legislation, but so many judicial determinations, not indeed concerning the rights of single persons, but concerning the rights of large bodies of citizens; and what are the different classes of legislators, but advocates and parties to the causes which they determine? Is a law proposed concerning private debts? It is a question to which the creditors are parties on one side, and the debtors on the other. Justice ought to hold the balance between them. Yet the parties are and must be themselves the judges; and the most numerous party, or, in other words, the most powerful faction must be expected to prevail. Shall domestic manufactures be encouraged, and in what degree, by restrictions on foreign manufactures? are questions which would be differently decided by the landed and the manufacturing classes; and probably by neither, with a sole regard to justice and the public good. The apportionment of taxes on the various descriptions of property, is an act which seems to require the most exact impartiality, yet there is perhaps no legislative act in which greater opportunity and temptation are given to a predominant party, to trample on the rules of justice. Every shilling with which they over-burden the inferior number, is a shilling saved to their own pockets.

It is in vain to say, that enlightened statesmen will be able to adjust these clashing interests, and render them all subservient to the public good. Enlightened statesmen will not always be at the helm: Nor, in many cases, can such an adjustment be made at all, without taking into view indirect and remote considerations, which will rarely prevail over the immediate interest which one party may find in disregarding the rights of another, or the good of the whole.

The inference to which we are brought, is, that the *causes* of faction cannot be removed; and that relief is only to be sought in the means of controlling its *effects.*

If a faction consists of less than a majority, relief is supplied by the republican principle, which enables the majority to defeat its sinister views by regular vote: It may clog the administration, it may convulse the society; but it will be unable to execute and mask its violence under the forms of the constitution. When a majority is included in a faction, the form of popular government on the other hand enables it to sacrifice to its ruling passion or interest, both the public good and the rights of other citizens. To secure the public good, and private rights against the danger of such a faction, and at the same time to preserve the spirit and the form of popular government, is then the great object to which our enquiries are directed. Let me add that it is the great desideratum, by which alone this form of government can be rescued from the opprobrium under which it has so long labored, and be recommended to the esteem and adoption of mankind.

By what means is this object attainable? Evidently by one of two only. Either the existence of the same passion or interest in a majority at the same time, must be prevented; or the majority, having such co-existent passion or interest, must be rendered, by their number and local situation, unable to concert and carry into effect schemes of oppression. If the impulse and the opportunity be suffered to coincide, we well know that neither moral nor religious motives can be relied on as an adequate control. They are not found to be such on the injustice and violence of individuals, and lose their efficacy in proportion to the number combined together; that is, in proportion as their efficacy becomes needful.

From this view of the subject, it may be concluded that a pure democracy, by which I mean a society, consisting of a small number of citizens, who assemble and administer the government in person, can admit of no cure for the mischiefs of faction. A common passion or interest will, in almost every case, be felt by a majority of the whole; a communication and concert results from the form of government itself; and there is nothing to check the inducements to sacrifice the weaker party, or an obnoxious individual. Hence it is, that such democracies have ever been spectacles of turbulence and contention; have ever been found incompatible with personal security, or the rights of property; and have in general been as short in their lives, as they have been violent in their deaths. Theoretic politicians, who have patronized this species of government, have erroneously supposed, that by reducing mankind to a perfect equality in their political rights, they would, at the same time, be perfectly equalized, and assimilated in their possessions, their opinions, and their passions.

A republic, by which I mean a government in which the scheme of representation takes place, opens a different prospect, and promises the cure for which we are seeking. Let us examine the points in which it varies from pure democracy, and we shall comprehend both the nature of the cure, and the efficacy which it must derive from the union.

The two great points of difference between a democracy and a republic, are first, the delegation of the government, in the latter, to a small number of citizens elected by the rest; secondly, the greater number of citizens, and greater sphere of country, over which the latter may be extended.

The effect of the first difference is, on the one hand, to refine and enlarge the public views, by passing them through the medium of a chosen body of citizens, whose wisdom may best discern the true interest of their country, and whose patriotism and love of justice, will be least likely to sacrifice it to temporary or partial considerations. Under such a regulation, it may well happen that the public voice pronounced by the representatives of the people, will be more consonant to the public good, than if pronounced by the people themselves convened for the purpose. On the other hand, the effect may be inverted. Men of factious tempers, of local prejudices, or of sinister designs, may by intrigue, by corruption, or by other means, first obtain the suffrages, and then betray the interests of the people. The question resulting is, whether small or extensive republics are most favourable to the election of proper guardians of the public weal; and it is clearly decided in favour of the latter by two obvious considerations.

In the first place it is to be remarked, that however small the republic may be, the representatives must be raised to a certain number, in order to guard against the cabals of a few; and that however large it may be, they must be limited to a certain number, in order to guard against the confusion of a multitude. Hence the number of representatives in the two cases not being in proportion to that of the constituents, and being proportionally greatest in the small republic, it follows, that if the proportion of fit characters be not less in the large than in the small republic, the former will present a greater option, and consequently a greater probability of a fit choice.

In the next place, as each representative will be chosen by a greater number of citizens in the large than in the small republic, it will be more difficult for unworthy candidates to practise with success the vicious arts, by which elections are too often carried; and the suffrages of the people being more free, will be more likely to centre on men who possess the most attractive merit, and the most diffusive and established characters.

It must be confessed, that in this, as in most other cases, there is a mean, on both sides of which inconveniencies will be found to lie. By enlarging too much the number of electors, you render the representative too little acquainted with all their local circumstances and lesser interests; as by reducing it too much, you render him unduly attached to these, and too little fit to comprehend and pursue great and national objects. The federal constitution forms a happy combination in this respect; the great and aggregate interests being referred to the national, the local and particular to the state legislatures.

The other point of difference is, the greater number of citizens and extent of territory which may be brought within the compass of republican, than of democratic government; and it is this circumstance principally which renders factious combinations less to be dreaded in the former, than in the latter. The smaller the society, the fewer probably will be the distinct parties and interests composing it; the fewer the distinct parties and interests, the more frequently will a majority be found of the same party; and the smaller the number of individuals composing a majority, and the smaller the compass within which they are placed, the more easily will they concert and execute their plans of oppression. Extend the sphere, and you take in a greater variety of parties and interests; you make it less probable that a majority of the whole will have a common motive to invade the rights of other citizens; or if such a common motive exists, it will be more difficult for all who feel it to discover their own strength, and to act in unison with each other. Besides other impediments, it may be remarked, that where there is a consciousness of unjust or dishonourable purposes, communication is always checked by distrust, in proportion to the number whose concurrence is necessary.

Hence it clearly appears, that the same advantage, which a republic has over a democracy, in controlling the effects of faction, is enjoyed by a large over a small republic—is enjoyed by the union over the states composing it. Does this advantage consist in the substitution of representatives, whose enlightened views and virtuous sentiments render them superior to local prejudices, and to schemes of injustice? It will not be denied, that the representation of the union will be most likely to possess these requisite endowments. Does it consist in the greater security afforded by a greater variety of parties, against the event of any one party being able to outnumber and oppress the rest? In an equal degree does the encreased variety of parties, comprised within the union, encrease this security. Does it, in fine, consist in the greater obstacles opposed to the concert and accomplishment of the secret wishes of an unjust and interested majority? Here, again, the extent of the union gives it the most palpable advantage.

The influence of factious leaders may kindle a flame within their particular states, but will be unable to spread a general conflagration through the other states: A religious sect, may degenerate into a political faction in a part of the confederacy; but the variety of sects dispersed over the entire face of it, must secure the national councils against any danger from that source: A rage for paper money, for an abolition of debts, for an equal division of property, or for any other improper or wicked project, will be less apt to pervade the whole body of the union, than a particular member of it; in the same proportion as such a malady is more likely to taint a particular county or district, than an entire state.

In the extent and proper structure of the union, therefore, we behold a republican remedy for the diseases most incident to republican government. And according to the degree of pleasure and pride, we feel in being republicans, ought to be our zeal in cherishing the spirit, and supporting the character of federalists.

November 22, 1787

The Federalist No. 14

We have seen the necessity of the union as our bulwark against foreign danger, as the conservator of peace among ourselves, as the guardian of our commerce and other common interests, as the only substitute for those military establishments which have subverted the liberties of the old world, and as the proper antidote for the diseases of faction, which have proved fatal to other popular governments, and of which alarming symptoms have been betrayed by our own. All that remains, within this branch of our enquiries, is to take notice of an objection, that may be drawn from the great extent of country which the union embraces. A few observations on this subject will be the more proper, as it is perceived that the adversaries of the new constitution are availing themselves of a prevailing prejudice, with regard to the practicable sphere of republican administration, in order to supply by imaginary difficulties, the want of those solid objections, which they endeavour in vain to find.

The error which limits republican government to a narrow district, has been unfolded and refuted in preceding papers. I remark here only, that it seems to owe its rise and prevalence chiefly to the confounding of a republic with a democracy: And applying to the former reasonings drawn from the nature of the latter. The true distinction between these forms was also adverted to on a former occasion. It is, that in a democracy, the people meet and exercise the government in person; in a republic they assemble and administer it by their representatives and agents. A democracy consequently must be confined to a small spot. A republic may be extended over a large region.

To this accidental source of the error may be added, the artifice of some celebrated authors, whose writings have had a great share in forming the modern standard of political opinions. Being subjects either of an absolute, or limited monarchy, they have endeavoured to heighten the advantages or palliate the evils of those forms; by placing in comparison with them, the vices and defects of the republican, and by citing as specimens of the latter, the turbulent democracies of ancient Greece, and modern Italy. Under the confusion of names, it has been an easy task to transfer to a republic, observations applicable to a democracy only, and among others, the observation that it can never be established but among a small number of people, living within a small compass of territory.

Such a fallacy may have been the less perceived, as most of the popular governments of antiquity were of the democratic species; and even in modern Europe, to which we owe the great principle of representation, no example is seen of a government wholly popular, and founded at the same time wholly on that principle. If Europe has the merit of discovering this great mechanical power in government, by the simple agency of which, the will of the largest political body may be concentred and its force directed to any object, which the public good requires: America can claim the merit of making the discovery the basis of unmixed and extensive republics. It is only to be lamented, that any of her citizens should wish to deprive her of the additional merit of displaying its full efficacy in the establishment of the comprehensive system now under her consideration.

As the natural limit of a democracy is that distance from the central point, which will just permit the most remote citizens to assemble as often as their public functions demand; and will include no greater number than can join in those functions; so the natural limit of a republic is that distance from the centre, which will barely allow the representatives of the people to meet as often as may be necessary for the administration of public affairs. Can it be said, that the limits of the United States exceed this distance? It will not be said by those who recollect that the Atlantic coast is the longest side of the union; that during the term of thirteen years, the representatives of the states have been almost continually assembled; and that the members from the most distant states are not chargeable with greater intermissions of attendance, than those from the states in the neighbourhood of Congress.

That we may form a juster estimate with regard to this interesting subject, let us resort to the actual dimensions of the union. The limits, as fixed by the treaty of peace are on the East the Atlantic, on the South the latitude of thirty one

degrees, on the West the Mississippi, and on the North an irregular line running in some instances beyond the forty-fifth
degree, in others falling as low as the forty-second. The
Southern shore of lake Erie lies below that latitude. Computing the distance between the thirty-first and forty-fifth degrees, it amounts to nine hundred and seventy three common
miles; computing it from thirty one to forty two degrees to
seven hundred, sixty four miles and an half. Taking the mean
for the distance, the amount will be eight hundred, sixty eight
miles and three fourths. The mean distance from the Atlantic
to the Mississippi, does not probably exceed seven hundred
and fifty miles. On a comparison of this extent, with that of
several countries in Europe, the practicability of rendering our
system commensurate to it, appears to be demonstrable. It is
not a great deal larger than Germany, where a diet, representing the whole empire is continually assembled; or than Poland
before the late dismemberment, where another national diet
was the depositary of the supreme power. Passing by France
and Spain, we find that in Great Britain, inferior as it may be
in size, the representatives of the Northern extremity of the
island, have as far to travel to the national council, as will be
required of those of the most remote parts of the union.

Favourable as this view of the subject may be, some observations remain which will place it in a light still more satisfactory.

In the first place it is to be remembered, that the general
government is not to be charged with the whole power of
making and administering laws. Its jurisdiction is limited to
certain enumerated objects, which concern all the members of
the republic, but which are not to be attained by the separate
provisions of any. The subordinate governments which can
extend their care to all those other objects, which can be separately provided for, will retain their due authority and activity. Were it proposed by the plan of the convention to abolish
the governments of the particular states, its adversaries would
have some ground for their objection, though it would not be
difficult to show that if they were abolished, the general government would be compelled by the principle of self preservation, to reinstate them in their proper jurisdiction.

A second observation to be made is, that the immediate

object of the federal constitution is to secure the union of the Thirteen primitive States, which we know to be practicable; and to add to them such other states, as may arise in their own bosoms, or in their neighbourhoods, which we cannot doubt to be equally practicable. The arrangements that may be necessary for those angles and fractions of our territory, which lie on our north-western frontier, must be left to those whom further discoveries and experience will render more equal to the task.

Let it be remarked in the third place, that the intercourse throughout the union will be daily facilitated by new improvements. Roads will every where be shortened, and kept in better order; accommodations for travellers will be multiplied and meliorated; an interior navigation on our eastern side will be opened throughout, or nearly throughout the whole extent of the Thirteen States. The communication between the Western and Atlantic districts, and between different parts of each, will be rendered more and more easy by those numerous canals with which the beneficence of nature has intersected our country, and which art finds it so little difficult to connect and complete.

A fourth and still more important consideration is, that as almost every state will on one side or other be a frontier, and will thus find in a regard to its safety, an inducement to make some sacrifices for the sake of the general protection; so the states which lie at the greatest distance from the heart of the union, and which of course may partake least of the ordinary circulation of its benefits, will be at the same time immediately contiguous to foreign nations, and will consequently stand on particular occasions, in greatest need of its strength and resources. It may be inconvenient for Georgia or the states forming our Western or North-Eastern borders, to send their representatives to the seat of government, but they would find it more so to struggle alone against an invading enemy, or even to support alone the whole expence of those precautions, which may be dictated by the neighbourhood of continual danger. If they should derive less benefit therefore from the union in some respects, than the less distant states, they will derive greater benefit from it in other respects, and thus the proper equilibrium will be maintained throughout.

I submit to you my fellow citizens, these considerations, in full confidence that the good sense which has so often marked your decisions, will allow them their due weight and effect; and that you will never suffer difficulties, however formidable in appearance or however fashionable the error on which they may be founded, to drive you into the gloomy and perilous scenes into which the advocates for disunion would conduct you. Hearken not to the unnatural voice which tells you that the people of America, knit together as they are by so many cords of affection, can no longer live together as members of the same family; can no longer continue the mutual guardians of their mutual happiness; can no longer be fellow citizens of one great respectable and flourishing empire. Hearken not to the voice which petulantly tells you that the form of govern-ment recommended for your adoption is a novelty in the po-litical world; that it has never yet had a place in the theories of the wildest projectors; that it rashly attempts what it is im-possible to accomplish. No my countrymen, shut your ears against this unhallowed language. Shut your hearts against the poison which it conveys; the kindred blood which flows in the veins of American citizens, the mingled blood which they have shed in defence of their sacred rights, consecrate their union, and excite horror at the idea of their becoming aliens, rivals, enemies. And if novelties are to be shunned, believe me the most alarming of all novelties, the most wild of all proj-ects, the most rash of all attempts, is that of rending us in pieces, in order to preserve our liberties and promote our happiness. But why is the experiment of an extended republic to be rejected merely because it may comprise what is new? Is it not the glory of the people of America, that whilst they have paid a decent regard to the opinions of former times and other nations, they have not suffered a blind veneration for antiquity, for custom, or for names, to overrule the sugges-tions of their own good sense, the knowledge of their own situation, and the lessons of their own experience? To this manly spirit, posterity will be indebted for the possession, and the world for the example of the numerous innovations dis-played on the American theatre, in favour of private rights and public happiness. Had no important step been taken by the leaders of the revolution for which a precedent could not be discovered, no government established of which an exact model did not present itself, the people of the United States might, at this moment, have been numbered among the melancholy victims of misguided councils, must at best have been labouring under the weight of some of those forms which have crushed the liberties of the rest of mankind. Happily for America, happily we trust for the whole human race, they pursued a new and more noble course. They accomplished a revolution which has no parallel in the annals of human society: They reared the fabrics of governments which have no model on the face of the globe. They formed the design of a great confederacy, which it is incumbent on their successors to improve and perpetuate. If their works betray imperfections, we wonder at the fewness of them. If they erred most in the structure of the union, this was the work most difficult to be executed, this is the work which has been new modelled by the act of your convention, and it is that act on which you are now to deliberate and to decide.

November 30, 1787

The Federalist No. 18

Among the confederacies of antiquity, the most consider-able was that of the Grecian republics associated under the Amphyctionic council. From the best accounts transmitted of this celebrated institution, it bore a very instructive analogy to the present confederation of the American states.

The members retained the character of independent and sovereign states, and had equal votes in the federal council. This council had a general authority to propose and resolve whatever it judged necessary for the common welfare of Greece—to declare and carry on war—to decide in the last re-sort all controversies between the members—to fine the ag-gressing party—to employ the whole force of the confederacy against the disobedient—to admit new members. The Am-phyctions were the guardians of religion, and of the immense riches belonging to the temple of Delphos, where they had the right of jurisdiction in controversies between the inhabi-tants and those who came to consult the oracle. As a further provision for the efficacy of the federal powers, they took an oath mutually to defend and protect the united cities, to pun-ish the violators of this oath, and to inflict vengeance on sac-rilegious despoilers of the temple.

In theory and upon paper, this apparatus of powers, seems amply sufficient for all general purposes. In several material in-stances, they exceed the powers enumerated in the articles of confederation. The Amphyctions had in their hands the su-perstition of the times, one of the principal engines by which government was then maintained; they had a declared author-ity to use coertion against refractory cities, and were bound by oath to exert this authority on the necessary occasions.

Very different nevertheless was the experiment from the theory. The powers, like those of the present congress, were administered by deputies appointed wholly by the cities in their political capacities; and exercised over them in the same capacities. Hence the weakness, the disorders, and finally the destruction of the confederacy. The more powerful members, instead of being kept in awe and subordination, tyrannized successively over all the rest. Athens, as we learn from Demosthenes, was the arbiter of Greece seventy-three years. The Lacedemonians next governed it twenty-nine years; at a subsequent period, after the battle of Leuctra, the Thebans had their turn of domination.

It happened but too often, according to Plutarch, that the deputies of the strongest cities, awed and corrupted those of the weaker, and that judgment went in favor of the most powerful party.

Even in the midst of defensive and dangerous wars with Persia and Macedon, the members never acted in concert, and were more or fewer of them, eternally the dupes, or the hirelings of the common enemy. The intervals of foreign war, were filled up by domestic vicissitudes, convulsions and carnage.

After the conclusion of the war with Xerxes, it appears that the Lacedemonians required that a number of the cities should be turned out of the confederacy for the unfaithful part they had acted. The Athenians finding that the Lacedemonians would lose fewer partizans by such a measure than themselves, and would become masters of the public deliberations, vigorously opposed and defeated the attempt. This piece of history proves at once the inefficiency of the union; the ambition and jealousy of its most powerful members, and the dependent and degraded condition of the rest. The smaller members, though entitled by the theory of their system, to revolve in equal pride and majesty around the common center, had become in fact satellites of the orbs of primary magnitude.

Had the Greeks, says the Abbé Milot, been as wise as they were courageous, they would have been admonished by experience of the necessity of a closer union, and would have availed themselves of the peace which followed their success against the Persian arms, to establish such a reformation. Instead of this obvious policy, Athens and Sparta, inflated with the victories and the glory they had acquired, became first rivals, and then enemies; and did each other infinitely more mischief, than they had suffered from Xerxes. Their mutual jealousies, fears, hatreds and injuries, ended in the celebrated Peloponnesian war; which itself ended in the ruin and slavery of the Athenians who had begun it.

As a weak government, when not at war, is ever agitated by internal dissentions; so these never fail to bring on fresh calamities from abroad. The Phocians having ploughed up some consecrated ground belonging to the temple of Apollo, the Amphyctionic council, according to the superstition of the age, imposed a fine on the sacrilegious offenders. The Phocians, being abetted by Athens and Sparta, refused to submit to the decree. The Thebans, with others of the cities, undertook to maintain the authority of the Amphyctions, and to avenge the violated god. The latter being the weaker party, invited the assistance of Philip of Macedon, who had secretly fostered the contest. Philip gladly seized the opportunity of executing the designs he had long planned against the liberties of Greece. By his intrigues and bribes he won over to his interests the popular leaders of several cities; by their influence and votes, gained admission into the Amphyctionic council; and by his arts and his arms, made himself master of the confederacy.

Such were the consequences of the fallacious principle, on which this interesting establishment was founded. Had Greece, says a judicious observer on her fate, been united by a stricter confederation, and persevered in her union, she would never have worn the chains of Macedon; and might have proved a barrier to the vast projects of Rome.

The Achæan league, as it is called, was another society of Grecian republics, which supplies us with valuable instruction.

The union here was far more intimate, and its organization much wiser, than in the preceding instance. It will accordingly appear, that though not exempt from a similar catastrophe, it by no means equally deserved it.

The cities composing this league, retained their municipal jurisdiction, appointed their own officers, and enjoyed a perfect equality. The senate in which they were represented, had the sole and exclusive right of peace and war—of sending and receiving ambassadors—of entering into treaties and alliances—of appointing a chief magistrate or pretor, as he was called, who commanded their armies; and who with the advice and consent of ten of the senators, not only administered the government in the recess of the senate, but had a great share in its deliberation, when assembled. According to the primitive constitution, there were two pretors associated in the administration, but on trial, a single one was preferred.

It appears that the cities had all the same laws and customs, the same weights and measures, and the same money. But how far this effect proceeded from the authority of the federal council, is left in uncertainty. It is said only, that the cities were in a manner compelled to receive the same laws and usages. When Lacedemon was brought into the league by Philopœmen, it was attended with an abolition of the institutions and laws of Lycurgus, and an adoption of those of the Achæans. The Amphyctionic confederacies, of which she had been a member, left her in the full exercise of her government and her legislation. This circumstance alone proves a very material difference in the genius of the two systems.

It is much to be regretted that such imperfect monuments remain of this curious political fabric. Could its interior structure and regular operation be ascertained, it is probable that more light would be thrown by it on the science of federal government, than by any of the like experiments with which we are acquainted.

One important fact seems to be witnessed by all the historians who take notice of Achæan affairs. It is, that as well after the renovation of the league by Aratus, as before its dissolution by the arts of Macedon, there was infinitely more of moderation and justice in the administration of its government, and less of violence and sedition in the people, than were to be found in any of the cities exercising *singly* all the prerogatives of sovereignty. The abbé Mably in his observations on Greece, says that the popular government, which was so tempestuous elsewhere, caused no disorders in the members of the Achæan republic, *because it was there tempered by the general authority and laws of the confederacy.*

We are not to conclude too hastily, however, that faction did not in a certain degree agitate the particular cities; much less, that a due subordination and harmony reigned in the general system. The contrary is sufficiently displayed in the vicissitudes and fate of the republic.

Whilst the Amphyctionic confederacy remained, that of the Achæans, which comprehended the less important cities only, made little figure on the theatre of Greece. When the former became a victim to Macedon, the latter was spared by the policy of Philip and Alexander. Under the successors of these princes, however, a different policy prevailed. The arts of division were practised among the Achæans; each city was seduced into a separate interest; the union was dissolved. Some of the cities fell under the tyranny of Macedonian garrisons; others under that of usurpers springing out of their own confusions. Shame and oppression ere long awakened their love of liberty. A few cities re-united. Their example was followed by others, as opportunities were found of cutting off their tyrants. The league soon embraced almost the whole Peloponnesus. Macedon saw its progress; but was hindered by internal dissentions from stopping it. All Greece caught the enthusiasm, and seemed ready to unite in one confederacy, when the jealousy and envy in Sparta and Athens, of the rising glory of the Achæans, threw a fatal damp on the enterprize. The dread of the Macedonian power induced the league to court the alliance of the kings of Egypt and Syria; who, as successors of Alexander were rivals of the king of Macedon. This policy was defeated by Cleomenes, king of Sparta, who was led by his ambition to make an unprovoked attack on his neighbours the Achæans; and who as an enemy to Macedon, had interest enough with the Egyptian and Syrian princes, to effect a breach of their engagements with the league. The Achæans were now reduced to the dilemma of submitting to Cleomenes, or of supplicating the aid of Macedon, its former oppressor. The latter expedient was adopted. The contest of the Greeks always afforded a pleasing opportunity to that powerful neighbour, of intermeddling in their affairs. A Macedonian army quickly appeared: Cleomenes was vanquished. The Achæans soon experienced, as often happens, that a victorious and powerful ally, is but another name for a master. All that their most abject compliances could obtain from him was a toleration of the exercise of their laws. Philip, who was now on the throne of Macedon, soon provoked, by his tyrannies, fresh combinations among the Greeks. The Achæans, though weakened by internal dissentions, and by the revolt of Messene one of its members, being joined by the Etolians and Athenians, erected the standard of opposition. Finding themselves, though thus sup-

ported unequal to the undertaking, they once more had recourse to the dangerous expedient of introducing the succour
of foreign arms. The Romans to whom the invitation was
made, eagerly embraced it. Philip was conquered: Macedon
subdued. A new crisis ensued to the league. Dissentions broke
out among its members. These the Romans fostered. Calli-
crates and other popular leaders, became mercenary instruments for inveigling their countrymen. The more effectually
to nourish discord and disorder, the Romans had, to the astonishment of those who confided in their sincerity, already
proclaimed universal liberty* throughout Greece. With the
same insidious views, they now seduced the members from
the league, by representing to their pride, the violation it
committed on their sovereignty. By these arts, this union, the
last hope of Greece, the last hope of antient liberty, was torn
into pieces; and such imbecility and distraction introduced,
that the arms of Rome found little difficulty in compleating
the ruin which their arts had commenced. The Achæans were
cut to pieces; and Achaia loaded with chains, under which it
is groaning at this hour.

I have thought it not superfluous to give the outlines of
this important portion of history; both because it teaches
more than one lesson; and because, as a supplement to the
outlines of the Achæan constitution, it emphatically illustrates
the tendency of federal bodies, rather to anarchy among the
members than to tyranny in the head.

*This was but another name more specious for the independence of the
members on the federal head.

December 7, 1787

The Federalist No. 19

The examples of antient confederacies, cited in my last paper, have not exhausted the source of experimental instruction on this subject. There are existing institutions, founded on a similar principle, which merit particular consideration. The first which presents itself is the Germanic body.

In the early ages of christianity Germany was occupied by seven distinct nations, who had no common chief. The Franks, one of the number, having conquered the Gauls, established the kingdom which has taken its name from them. In the ninth century, Charlemagne, its warlike monarch, carried his victorious arms in every direction; and Germany became a part of his vast dominions. On the dismemberment, which took place under his sons, this part was erected into a separate and independent empire. Charlemagne and his immediate descendants possessed the reality, as well as the ensigns and dignity of imperial power. But the principal vassals, whose fiefs had become hereditary, and who composed the national diets which Charlemagne had not abolished, gradually threw off the yoke, and advanced to sovereign jurisdiction and independence. The force of imperial sovereignty was insufficient to restrain such powerful dependents; or to preserve the unity and tranquility of the empire. The most furious private wars, accompanied with every species of calamity, were carried on between the different princes and states. The imperial authority, unable to maintain the public order, declined by degrees, till it was almost extinct in the anarchy, which agitated the long interval between the death of the last emperor of the Suabian, and the accession of the first emperor of the Austrian lines. In the eleventh century, the emperors enjoyed full sovereignty: In the fifteenth they had little more than the symbols and decorations of power.

Out of this feudal system, which has itself many of the important features of a confederacy, has grown the federal system, which constitutes the Germanic empire. Its powers are vested in a diet representing the component members of the confederacy; in the emperor who is the executive magistrate, with a negative on the decrees of the diet; and in the imperial chamber and aulic council, two judiciary tribunals having supreme jurisdiction in controversies which concern the empire, or which happen among its members.

The diet possesses the general power of legislating for the empire—of making war and peace—contracting alliances—assessing quotas of troops and money—constructing fortresses —regulating coin—admitting new members—and subjecting disobedient members to the ban of the empire, by which the party is degraded from his sovereign rights, and his possessions forfeited. The members of the confederacy are expressly restricted from entering into compacts, prejudicial to the empire, from imposing tolls and duties on their mutual intercourse, without the consent of the emperor and diet; from altering the value of money; from doing injustice to one another; or from affording assistance or retreat to disturbers of the public peace. And the ban is denounced against such as shall violate any of these restrictions. The members of the diet, as such, are subject in all cases to be judged by the emperor and diet, and in their private capacities, by the aulic council and imperial chamber.

The prerogatives of the emperor are numerous. The most important of them are, his exclusive right to make propositions to the diet—to negative its resolutions—to name ambassadors—to confer dignities and titles—to fill vacant electorates—to found universities—to grant privileges not injurious to the states of the empire—to receive and apply the public revenues—and generally to watch over the public safety. In certain cases, the electors form a council to him. In quality of emperor he possesses no territory within the empire; nor receives any revenue for his support. But his revenue and dominions, in other qualities, constitute him one of the most powerful princes in Europe.

From such a parade of constitutional powers, in the representatives and head of this confederacy, the natural supposition would be, that it must form an exception to the general character which belongs to its kindred systems. Nothing would be farther from the reality. The fundamental principle, on which it rests, that the empire is a community of sovereigns; that the diet is a representation of sovereigns; and that the laws are addressed to sovereigns; render the empire a nerveless body; incapable of regulating its own members; in-secure against external dangers; and agitated with unceasing fermentations in its own bowels.

The history of Germany is a history of wars between the emperor and the princes and states; of wars among the princes and states themselves; of the licentiousness of the strong, and the oppression of the weak; of foreign intrusions, and foreign intrigues; of requisitions of men and money, disregarded, or partially complied with; of attempts to enforce them, alto-gether abortive, or attended with slaughter and desolation, involving the innocent with the guilty; of general imbecility, confusion and misery.

In the sixteenth century, the emperor with one part of the empire on his side, was seen engaged against the other princes and states. In one of the conflicts, the emperor himself was put to flight, and very near being made prisoner by the elec-tor of Saxony. The late king of Prussia was more than once pitted against his imperial sovereign; and commonly proved an overmatch for him. Controversies and wars among the members themselves have been so common, that the German annals are crowded with the bloody pages which describe them. Previous to the peace of Westphalia, Germany was des-olated by a war of thirty years, in which the emperor, with one half of the empire was on one side; and Sweden with the other half on the opposite side. Peace was at length negoti-ated and dictated by foreign powers; and the articles of it, to which foreign powers are parties, made a fundamental part of the Germanic constitution.

If the nation happens, on any emergency, to be more united by the necessity of self defence; its situation is still de-plorable. Military preparations must be preceded by so many tedious discussions, arising from the jealousies, pride, separate views, and clashing pretensions, of sovereign bodies; that be-fore the diet can settle the arrangements, the enemy are in the field; and before the federal troops are ready to take it, are re-tiring into winter quarters.

The small body of national troops which has been judged necessary in time of peace, is defectively kept up, badly paid, infected with local prejudices, and supported by irregular and disproportionate contributions to the treasury.

The impossibility of maintaining order, and dispensing jus-tice among these sovereign subjects, produced the experiment of dividing the empire into nine or ten circles or districts; of giving them an interior organization; and of charging them with the military execution of the laws against delinquent and contumacious members. This experiment has only served to demonstrate more fully, the radical vice of the constitution. Each circle is the miniature picture of the deformities of this political monster. They either fail to execute their com-missions, or they do it with all the devastation and carnage of civil war. Sometimes whole circles are defaulters, and then they increase the mischief which they were instituted to remedy.

We may form some judgment of this scheme of military co-ertion, from a sample given by Thuanus. In Donawerth, a free and imperial city, of the circle of Suabia, the abbé de St. Croix enjoyed certain immunities which had been reserved to him. In the exercise of these, on some public occasion, out-rages were committed on him, by the people of the city. The consequence was, that the city was put under the ban of the empire; and the duke of Bavaria, though director of another circle, obtained an appointment to enforce it. He soon ap-peared before the city, with a corps of ten thousand troops and finding it a fit occasion, as he had secretly intended from the beginning, to revive an antiquated claim, on the pretext that his ancestors had suffered the place to be dismembered from his territory*; he took possession of it, in his own name; disarmed and punished the inhabitants, and re-annexed the city to his domains.

It may be asked perhaps what has so long kept this dis-jointed machine from falling entirely to pieces? The answer is obvious. The weakness of most of the members, who are un-willing to expose themselves to the mercy of foreign powers; the weakness of most of the principal members, compared with the formidable powers all around them; the vast weight and influence which the emperor derives from his separate and hereditary dominions; and the interest he feels in preserving a

---

*Pfeffel, Nouvel abreg. chronol. de l'hist. &c. d'Allemagne, says the pre-text was to indemnify himself for the expence of the expedition.

system, with which his family pride is connected, and which constitutes him the first prince in Europe; these causes support a feeble and precarious union; whilst the repellent quality, incident to the nature of sovereignty, and which time continually strengthens, prevents any reform whatever, founded on a proper consolidation. Nor is it to be imagined, if this obstacle could be surmounted, that the neighbouring powers would suffer a revolution to take place, which would give to the empire the force and pre-eminence to which it is entitled. Foreign nations have long considered themselves as interested in the changes made by events in this constitution; and have, on various occasions, betrayed their policy of perpetuating its anarchy and weakness.

If more direct examples were wanting, Poland as a government over local sovereigns, might not improperly be taken notice of. Nor could any proof more striking, be given of the calamities flowing from such institutions. Equally unfit for self government, and self defence, it has long been at the mercy of its powerful neighbours; who have lately had the mercy to disburden it of one third of its people and territories.

The connection among the Swiss cantons scarcely amounts to a confederacy; though it is sometimes cited as an instance of the stability of such institutions.

They have no common treasury—no common troops even in war—no common coin—no common judicatory, nor any other common mark of sovereignty.

They are kept together by the peculiarity of their topographical position, by their individual weakness and insignificancy; by the fear of powerful neighbours, to one of which they were formerly subject; by the few sources of contention among a people of such simple and homogeneous manners; by their joint interest in their dependent possessions; by the mutual aid they stand in need of, for suppressing insurrections and rebellions; an aid expressly stipulated, and often required and afforded; and by the necessity of some regular and permanent provision for accommodating disputes among the cantons. The provision is, that the parties at variance shall each chuse four judges out of the neutral cantons who in case of disagreement, chuse an umpire. This tribunal, under an oath of impartiality, pronounces definitive sentence; which all the cantons are bound to enforce. The competency of this regulation may be estimated, by a clause in their treaty of 1683, with Victor Amadeus of Savoy; in which he obliges himself to interpose as mediator in disputes between the cantons; and to employ force, if necessary, against the contumacious party.

As far as the peculiarity of their case will admit of comparison with that of the United States; it serves to confirm the principle intended to be established. Whatever efficacy the union may have had in ordinary cases, it appears that the moment a cause of difference sprang up, capable of trying its strength, it failed. The controversies on the subject of religion, which in three instances have kindled violent and bloody contests, may be said in fact to have severed the league. The Protestant and Catholic cantons have since had their separate diets; where all the most important concerns are adjusted, and which have left the general diet little other business than to take care of the common bailages.

That separation had another consequence which merits attention. It produced opposite alliances with foreign powers; of Bern as the head of the Protestant association, with the United Provinces; and of Luzerne, as the head of the Catholic association, with France.

December 8, 1787

The Federalist No. 20

The United Netherlands are a confederacy of republics, or rather of aristocracies, of a very remarkable texture; yet confirming all the lessons derived from those which we have already reviewed.

The union is composed of seven co-equal and sovereign states, and each state or province is a composition of equal and independent cities. In all important cases not only the provinces, but the cities must be unanimous.

The sovereignty of the union is represented by the states general, consisting usually of about fifty deputies appointed by the provinces. They hold their seats, some for life, some for six, three and one years. From two provinces they continue in appointment during pleasure.

The states general have authority to enter into treaties and alliances—to make war and peace—to raise armies and equip fleets—to ascertain quotas and demand contributions. In all these cases however, unanimity and the sanction of their constituents are requisite. They have authority to appoint and receive ambassadors—to execute treaties and alliances already formed—to provide for the collection of duties on imports and exports—to regulate the mint, with a saving to the provincial rights—to govern as sovereigns the dependent territories. The provinces are restrained, unless with the general consent, from entering into foreign treaties—from establishing imposts injurious to others, or charging their neighbours with higher duties than their own subjects. A council of state, a chamber of accounts, with five colleges of admiralty, aid and fortify the federal administration.

The executive magistrate of the union is the stadtholder, who is now a hereditary prince. His principal weight and influence in the republic are derived from his independent title; from his great patrimonial estates; from his family connections with some of the chief potentates of Europe; and more than all, perhaps, from his being stadtholder in the several provinces, as well as for the union, in which provincial quality, he has the appointment of town magistrates under certain regulations, executes provincial decrees, presides when he pleases in the provincial tribunals; and has throughout the power of pardon.

As stadtholder of the union, he has however considerable prerogatives.

In his political capacity he has authority to settle disputes between the provinces, when other methods fail—to assist at the deliberations of the states general, and at their particular conferences—to give audiences to foreign ambassadors, and to keep agents for his particular affairs at foreign courts.

In his military capacity, he commands the federal troops—provides for garrisons, and in general regulates military affairs—disposes of all appointments from colonels to ensigns, and of the governments and posts of fortified towns.

In his marine capacity, he is admiral general, and superintends and directs every thing relative to naval forces, and other naval affairs—presides in the admiralties in person or by proxy—appoints lieutenant admirals and other officers—and establishes councils of war, whose sentences are not executed till he approves them.

His revenue, exclusive of his private income, amounts to 300,000 florins. The standing army which he commands consists of about 40,000 men.

Such is the nature of the celebrated Belgic confederacy, as delineated on parchment. What are the characters which practice has stampt upon it? Imbecility in the government; discord among the provinces; foreign influence and indignities; a precarious existence in peace, and peculiar calamities from war.

It was long ago remarked by Grotius, that nothing but the hatred of his countrymen to the house of Austria, kept them from being ruined by the vices of their constitution.

The union of Utrecht, says another respectable writer, reposes an authority in the states general seemingly sufficient to secure harmony, but the jealousy in each province renders the practice very different from the theory.

The same instrument says another, obliges each province to levy certain contributions; but this article never could and probably never will be executed; because the inland provinces who have little commerce cannot pay an equal quota.

In matters of contribution, it is the practice to wave the articles of the constitution. The danger of delay obliges the consenting provinces to furnish their quotas, without waiting for the others; and then to obtain reimbursement from the others, by deputations, which are frequent, or otherwise as they can. The great wealth and influence of the province of Holland, enable her to effect both these purposes.

It has more than once happened that the deficiencies have been ultimately to be collected at the point of the bayonet; a thing practicable, though dreadful, in a confederacy, where one of the members exceeds in force all the rest; and where several of them are too small to meditate resistance: But utterly impracticable in one composed of members, several of which are equal to each other in strength and resources, and equal singly to a vigorous and persevering defence.

Foreign ministers, says Sir William Temple, who was himself a foreign minister, elude matters taken *ad referendum*, by tampering with the provinces and cities. In 1726, the treaty of Hanover was delayed by these means a whole year. Instances of a like nature are numerous and notorious.

In critical emergencies, the states general are often compelled to overleap their constitutional bounds. In 1688, they concluded a treaty of themselves at the risk of their heads. The treaty of Westphalia in 1648, by which their independence was formally and finally recognized, was concluded without the consent of Zealand. Even as recently as the last treaty of peace with Great-Britain, the constitutional principle of unanimity was departed from. A weak constitution must necessarily terminate in dissolution, for want of proper powers, or the usurpation of powers requisite for the public safety. Whether the usurpation, when once begun, will stop at the salutary point, or go forward to the dangerous extreme, must depend on the contingencies of the moment. Tyranny has perhaps oftener grown out of the assumptions of power, called for, on pressing exigencies, by a defective constitution, than out of the full exercise of the largest constitutional authorities.

Notwithstanding the calamities produced by the stadtholdership, it has been supposed, that without his influence in the individual provinces, the causes of anarchy manifest in the confederacy, would long ago have dissolved it. "Under such a government," says the abbé Mably, "the union could never have subsisted, if the provinces had not a spring within themselves, capable of quickening their tardiness, and compelling them to the same way of thinking. This spring is the stadtholder." It is remarked by Sir William Temple, "that in the intermissions of the stadtholdership, Holland by her riches and her authority which drew the others into a sort of dependence, supplied the place."

These are not the only circumstances which have controuled the tendency to anarchy and dissolution. The surrounding powers impose an absolute necessity of union to a certain degree, at the same time, that they nourish by their intrigues, the constitutional vices, which keep the republic in some degree always at their mercy.

The true patriots have long bewailed the fatal tendency of these vices and have made no less than four regular experiments, by *extraordinary assemblies*, convened for the special purpose, to apply a remedy: As many times, has their laudable zeal found it impossible to *unite the public councils* in reforming the known, the acknowledged, the fatal evils of the existing constitution. Let us pause my fellow citizens, for one moment, over this melancholy and monitory lesson of history; and with the tear that drops for the calamities brought on mankind by their adverse opinions and selfish passions; let our gratitude mingle an ejaculation to Heaven, for the propitious concord which has distinguished the consultations for our political happiness.

A design was also conceived of establishing a general tax to be administered by the federal authority. This also had its adversaries and failed.

This unhappy people seem to be now suffering from popular convulsions, from dissentions among the states and from the actual invasion of foreign arms, the crisis of their destiny. All nations have their eyes fixed on the awful spectacle. The first wish prompted by humanity is, that this severe trial may issue in such a revolution of their government, as will establish their union, and render it the parent of tranquility, freedom and happiness: The next, that the asylum under which, we trust, the enjoyment of these blessings, will speedily be secured in this country, may receive and console them for the catastrophe of their own.

I make no apology for having dwelt so long on the contemplation of these federal precedents. Experience is the oracle of truth; and where its responses are unequivocal, they ought to be conclusive and sacred. The important truth, which it unequivocally pronounces in the present case, is, that a sovereignty over sovereigns, a government over governments, a legislation for communities, as contradistinguished from individuals; as it is a solecism in theory; so in practice, it is subversive of the order and ends of civil polity, by substituting *violence* in place of *law*, or the destructive *coertion* of the *sword*, in place of the mild and salutary *coertion* of the *magistracy*.

December 11, 1787

To Edmund Randolph

My dear friend   N. York Jany. 10. 1788.

I have put off writing from day to day for some time past, in expectation of being able to give you the news from the packet, which has been looked for every hour. Both the French & English have overstaid their usual time ten or 15 days, and are neither of them yet arrived. We remain wholly in the dark with regard to the posture of things in Europe.

I received two days ago your favor of Decr. 27. inclosing a copy of your letter to the Assembly. I have read it with attention, and I can add with pleasure, because the spirit of it does as much honor to your candour, as the general reasoning does to your abilities. Nor can I believe that in this quarter the opponents to the Constitution will find encouragement in it. You are already aware that your objections are not viewed in the same decisive light by me as they are by you. I must own that I differ still more from your opinion, that a prosecution of the experiment of a second Convention will be favorable even in Virginia to the object which I am sure you have at heart. It is to me apparent that had your duty led you to throw your influence into the opposite scale, that it would have given it a decided and unalterable preponderancy; and that Mr. Henry would either have suppressed his enmity, or been baffled in the policy which it has dictated. It appears also that the ground taken by the opponents in different quarters, forbids any hope of concord among them. Nothing can be farther from your views than the principles of different setts of men, who have carried on their opposition under the respectability of your name. In this State the party adverse to the Constitution, notoriously meditate either a dissolution of the Union, or protracting it by patching up the Articles of Confederation. In Connecticut & Massachussetts, the opposition proceeds from that part of the people who have a repugnancy in general to good government, to any substantial abridgment of State powers, and a part of whom in Massts. are known to aim at confusion, and are suspected of wishing a reversal of the Revolution. The Minority in Pennsylva. as far as they are governed by any other views than an habitual & factious opposition, to their rivals, are manifestly averse to some essential ingredients in a national Government. You are better acquainted with Mr. Henry's politics that I can be, but I have for some time considered him as driving at a Southern Confederacy and as not farther concurring in the plan of amendments than as he hopes to render it subservient to his real designs. Viewing the matter in this light, the inference with me is unavoidable that were a second trial to be made, the friends of a good constitution for the Union would not only find themselves not a little differing from each other as to the proper amendments; but perplexed & frustrated by men who had objects totally different. A second Convention would of course be formed under the influence, and composed in great measure of the members of opposition in the several States. But were the first difficulties overcome, and the Constitution re-edited with amendments, the event would still be infinitely precarious. Whatever respect may be due to the rights of private judgment, and no man feels more of it than I do, there can be no doubt that there are subjects to which the capacities of the bulk of mankind are unequal, and on which they must and will be governed by those with whom they happen to have acquaintance and confidence. The proposed Constitution is of this description. The great body of those who are both for & against it, must follow the judgment of others not their own. Had the Constitution been framed & recommended by an obscure individual, instead of a body possessing public respect & confidence, there can not be a doubt, that altho' it would have stood in the identical words, it would have commanded little attention from most of those who now admire its wisdom. Had yourself, Col. Mason, Col. R. H. L. Mr. Henry & a few others, seen the Constitution in the same light with those who subscribed it, I have no doubt that Virginia would have been as zealous & unanimous as she is now divided on the subject. I infer from these considerations that if a Government be ever adopted in America, it must result from a fortunate coincidence of leading opinions, and a general confidence of the people in those who may recommend it. The very attempt at a second Convention strikes at the confidence in the first; and the existence of a second by opposing influence to influence, would in a manner destroy an effectual confidence in either, and give a loose to human opinions; which must be as various and irreconcileable concerning theories of Government, as doctrines of Religion; and give opportunities to designing men which it might be impossible to counteract.

The Connecticut Convention has probably come to a decision before this; but the event is not known here. It is understood that a great majority will adopt the Constitution. The accounts from Massts. vary extremely according to the channels through which they come. It is said that S. Adams who has hitherto been reserved, begins to make open declaration of his hostile views. His influence is not great, but this step argues an opinion that he can calculate on a considerable party. It is said here, and I believe on good ground that N. Carolina has postponed her Convention till July, in order to have the previous example of Virga. Should N. Carolina fall into Mr. H—y's politics which does not appear to me improbable, it will endanger the Union more than any other circumstance that could happen. My apprehensions of this danger increase every day. The multiplied inducements at this moment to the local sacrifices necessary to keep the States together, can never be expected to co-incide again, and they are counteracted by so many unpropitious circumstances, that their efficacy can with difficulty be confided in. I have no information from S. Carolina or Georgia, on which any certain opinion can be formed of the temper of those States. The prevailing idea has been that both of them would speedily & generally embrace the Constitution. It is impossible however that the example of Virga. & N. Carolina should not have an influence on their politics. I consider every thing therefore as problematical from Maryland Southward.

I am surprised that Col. H. Lee who is a well-wisher to the Constitution should have furnished Wilkinson with the alarm concerning the Mississippi, but the political connections of the latter in Pena. would account for his biass on the subject.

We have no Congress yet. The number of Sts on the Spot does not exceed five. It is probable that a quorum will now be soon made. A Delegate from N. Hampshire is expected which will make up a representation from that State. The termination of the Connecticut Convention will set her delegates at liberty. And the Meeting of the Assembly of this State, will fill the vacancy which has some time existed in her Delegation. I wish you every happiness, and am with the sincerest affection Yrs.

The Federalist No. 37

In reviewing the defects of the existing confederation, and shewing that they cannot be supplied by a government of less energy than that before the public, several of the most important principles of the latter fell of course under consideration. But as the ultimate object of these papers is to determine clearly and fully the merits of this constitution, and the expediency of adopting it, our plan cannot be compleated without taking a more critical and thorough survey of the work of the convention; without examining it on all its sides; comparing it in all its parts, and calculating its probable effects. That this remaining task may be executed under impressions conducive to a just and fair result, some reflections must in this place be indulged, which candour previously suggests. It is a misfortune, inseparable from human affairs, that public measures are rarely investigated with that spirit of moderation which is essential to a just estimate of their real tendency to advance or obstruct the public good; and that this spirit is more apt to be diminished than promoted, by those occasions which require an unusual exercise of it. To those who have been led by experience to attend to this consideration, it could not appear surprising, that the act of the convention which recommends so many important changes and innovations, which may be viewed in so many lights and relations, and which touches the springs of so many passions and interests, should find or excite dispositions unfriendly both on one side, and on the other, to a fair discussion and accurate judgment of its merits. In some, it has been too evident from their own publications, that they have scanned the proposed constitution, not only with a predisposition to censure; but with a predetermination to condemn: As the language held by others betrays an opposite predetermination or bias, which must render their opinions also of little moment in the question. In placing however, these different characters on a level, with respect to the weight of their opinions, I wish not to insinuate that there may not be a material difference in the purity of their intentions. It is but just to remark in favor of the latter description, that as our situation is universally admitted to be peculiarly critical, and to require indispensably, that something should be done for our relief, the predetermined patron of what has been actually done, may have taken his bias from the weight of these considerations, as well as from considerations of a sinister nature. The predetermined adversary on the other hand, can have been governed by no venial motive whatever. The intentions of the first may be upright, as they may on the contrary be culpable. The views of the last cannot be upright, and must be culpable. But the truth is, that these papers are not addressed to persons falling under either of these characters. They solicit the attention of those only, who add to a sincere zeal for the happiness of their country, a temper favorable to a just estimate of the means of promoting it.

Persons of this character will proceed to an examination of the plan submitted by the convention, not only without a disposition to find or to magnify faults; but will see the propriety of reflecting that a faultless plan was not to be expected. Nor will they barely make allowances for the errors which may be chargeable on the fallibility to which the convention, as a body of men, were liable; but will keep in mind that they themselves also are but men, and ought not to assume an infallibility in rejudging the fallible opinions of others.

With equal readiness will it be perceived, that besides these inducements to candour, many allowances ought to be made for the difficulties inherent in the very nature of the undertaking referred to the convention.

The novelty of the undertaking immediately strikes us. It has been shewn in the course of these papers, that the existing confederation is founded on principles which are fallacious; that we must consequently change this first foundation, and with it, the superstructure resting upon it. It has been shewn, that the other confederacies which could be consulted as precedents, have been viciated by the same erroneous principles, and can therefore furnish no other light than that of beacons, which give warning of the course to be shunned, without pointing out that which ought to be pursued. The most that the convention could do in such a situation, was to avoid the errors suggested by the past experience of other countries, as well as of our own; and to provide a convenient mode of rectifying their own errors, as future experience may unfold them.

Among the difficulties encountered by the convention, a very important one must have lain, in combining the requisite stability and energy in government with the inviolable attention due to liberty, and to the republican form. Without substantially accomplishing this part of their undertaking, they would have very imperfectly fulfilled the object of their appointment, or the expectation of the public: Yet, that it could not be easily accomplished, will be denied by no one, who is unwilling to betray his ignorance of the subject. Energy in government is essential to that security against external and internal danger, and to that prompt and salutary execution of the laws, which enter into the very definition of good government. Stability in government, is essential to national character, and to the advantages annexed to it, as well as to that repose and confidence in the minds of the people, which are among the chief blessings of civil society. An irregular and mutable legislation is not more an evil in itself, than it is odious to the people; and it may be pronounced with assurance, that the people of this country, enlightened as they are, with regard to the nature, and interested, as the great body of them are, in the effects of good government will never be satisfied, till some remedy be applied to the vicissitudes and uncertainties, which characterize the state administrations. On comparing, however these valuable ingredients with the vital principles of liberty, we must perceive at once, the difficulty of mingling them together in their due proportions. The genius of republican liberty, seems to demand on one side, not only, that all power should be derived from the people; but, that those entrusted with it should be kept in dependence on the people, by a short duration of their appointments; and, that, even during this short period, the trust should be placed not in a few, but in a number of hands. Stability, on the contrary, requires, that the hands, in which power is lodged, should continue for a length of time the same. A frequent change of men will result from a frequent return of electors, and a frequent change of measures, from a frequent change of men; whilst energy in government requires not only a certain duration of power, but the execution of it by a single hand. How far the convention may have succeeded in this part of their work, will better appear on a more accurate view of it. From the cursory view, here taken, it must clearly appear to have been an arduous part.

Not less arduous must have been the task of marking the proper line of partition, between the authority of the general, and that of the state governments. Every man will be sensible of this difficulty, in proportion as he has been accustomed to contemplate and discriminate objects, extensive and complicated in their nature. The faculties of the mind itself have never yet been distinguished and defined, with satisfactory precision, by all the efforts of the most acute and metaphysical philosophers. Sense, perception, judgment, desire, volition, memory, imagination, are found to be separated, by such delicate shades and minute gradations, that their boundaries have eluded the most subtle investigations, and remain a pregnant source of ingenious disquisition and controversy. The boundaries between the great kingdoms of nature, and still more, between the various provinces, and lesser portions, into which they are subdivided, afford another illustration of the same important truth. The most sagacious and laborious naturalists have never yet succeeded, in tracing with certainty, the line which separates the district of vegetable life from the neighbouring region of unorganized matter, or which marks the termination of the former and the commencement of the animal empire. A still greater obscurity lies in the distinctive characters, by which the objects in each of these great departments of nature have been arranged and assorted. When we pass from the works of nature, in which all the delineations are perfectly accurate, and appear to be otherwise only from the imperfection of the eye which surveys them, to the institutions of man, in which the obscurity arises as well from the object itself, as from the organ by which it is contemplated; we must perceive the necessity of moderating still farther our expectations and hopes from the efforts of human sagacity. Experience has instructed us that no skill in the science of government has yet been able to discriminate and define, with sufficient certainty, its three great provinces, the legislative, executive and judiciary; or even the privileges and powers of the different legislative branches. Questions daily occur in the

course of practice, which prove the obscurity which reigns in
these subjects, and which puzzles the greatest adepts in political science. The experience of ages, with the continued and
combined labors of the most enlightened legislators and jurists, have been equally unsuccessful in delineating the several
objects and limits of different codes of laws and different tribunals of justice. The precise extent of the common law, the
statute law, the maritime law, the ecclesiastical law, the law of
corporations and other local laws and customs, remain still to
be clearly and finally established in Great Britain, where accuracy in such subjects has been more industriously pursued
than in any other part of the world. The jurisdiction of her
several courts, general and local, of law, of equity, of admiralty, &c. is not less a source of frequent and intricate discussions, sufficiently denoting the indeterminate limits by which
they are respectively circumscribed. All new laws, though
penned with the greatest technical skill, and passed on the
fullest and most mature deliberation, are considered as more
or less obscure and equivocal, until their meaning be liquidated and ascertained by a series of particular discussions and
adjudications. Besides the obscurity arising from the complexity of objects, and the imperfection of the human faculties,
the medium through which the conceptions of men are conveyed to each other, adds a fresh embarrassment. The use of
words is to express ideas. Perspicuity therefore requires not
only that the ideas should be distinctly formed, but that they
should be expressed by words distinctly and exclusively appropriated to them. But no language is so copious as to supply words and phrases for every complex idea, or so correct as
not to include many equivocally denoting different ideas.
Hence it must happen, that however accurately objects may
be discriminated in themselves, and however accurately the
discrimination may be considered, the definition of them may
be rendered inaccurate by the inaccuracy of the terms in
which it is delivered. And this unavoidable inaccuracy must be
greater or less, according to the complexity and novelty of the
objects defined. When the Almighty himself condescends to
address mankind in their own language, his meaning lumi-
nous as it must be, is rendered dim and doubtful, by the

cloudy medium through which it is communicated. Here then are three sources of vague and incorrect definitions; indistinctness of the object, imperfection of the organ of conception, inadequateness of the vehicle of ideas. Any one of these must produce a certain degree of obscurity. The convention, in delineating the boundary between the federal and state jurisdictions, must have experienced the full effect of them all.

To the difficulties already mentioned, may be added the interfering pretensions of the larger and smaller states. We cannot err in supposing that the former would contend for a participation in the government, fully proportioned to their superior wealth and importance; and that the latter would not be less tenacious of the equality at present enjoyed by them. We may well suppose that neither side would entirely yield to the other, and consequently that the struggle could be terminated only by compromise. It is extremely probable also, that after the ratio of representation had been adjusted, this very compromise must have produced a fresh struggle between the same parties, to give such a turn to the organization of the government, and to the distribution of its powers, as would increase the importance of the branches, in forming which they had respectively obtained the greatest share of influence. There are features in the constitution which warrant each of these suppositions; and as far as either of them is well founded, it shews that the convention must have been compelled to sacrifice theoretical propriety to the force of extraneous considerations.

Nor could it have been the large and small states only which would marshal themselves in opposition to each other on various points. Other combinations, resulting from a difference of local position and policy, must have created additional difficulties. As every state may be divided into different districts, and its citizens into different classes, which give birth to contending interests and local jealousies; so the different parts of the United States are distinguished from each other, by a variety of circumstances, which produce a like effect on a larger scale. And although this variety of interests, for reasons sufficiently explained in a former paper, may have a salutary influence on the administration of the government when formed; yet every one must be sensible of the contrary influence which must have been experienced in the task of forming it.

Would it be wonderful if under the pressure of all these difficulties, the convention should have been forced into some deviations from that artificial structure and regular symmetry, which an abstract view of the subject might lead an ingenious theorist to bestow on a constitution planned in his closet or in his imagination? The real wonder is, that so many difficulties should have been surmounted; and surmounted with an unanimity almost as unprecedented as it must have been unexpected. It is impossible for any man of candor to reflect on this circumstance, without partaking of the astonishment. It is impossible for the man of pious reflection not to perceive in it, a finger of that Almighty Hand which has been so frequently and signally extended to our relief in the critical stages of the revolution. We had occasion in a former paper, to take notice of the repeated trials which have been unsuccessfully made in the United Netherlands, for reforming the baneful and notorious vices of their constitution. The history of almost all the great councils and consultations, held among mankind for reconciling their discordant opinions, assuaging their mutual jealousies, and adjusting their respective interests, is a history of factions, contentions and disappointments; and may be classed among the most dark and degrading pictures which display the infirmities and depravities of the human character. If, in a few scattered instances, a brighter aspect is presented, they serve only as exceptions to admonish us of the general truth; and by their lustre to darken the gloom of the adverse prospect to which they are contrasted. In revolving the causes from which these exceptions result, and applying them to the particular instance before us, we are necessarily led to two important conclusions. The first is, that the convention must have enjoyed in a very singular degree, an exemption from the pestilential influence of party animosities; the diseases most incident to deliberative bodies, and most apt to contaminate their proceedings. The second conclusion is, that all the deputations composing the convention, were either satisfactorily accommodated by the final act; or were induced to accede to it, by a deep conviction of the necessity of sacrificing private opinions and partial interests, to the public good, and by a despair of seeing this necessity diminished by delays or by new experiments.

January 11, 1788

The Federalist No. 38

It is not a little remarkable that in every case reported by antient history, in which government has been established with deliberation and consent, the task of framing it has not been committed to an assembly of men; but has been performed by some individual citizen of pre-eminent wisdom and approved integrity. Minos, we learn, was the primitive founder of the government of Crete; as Zaleucus was of that of the Locrians. Theseus first, and after him Draco and Solon, instituted the government of Athens. Lycurgus was the lawgiver of Sparta. The foundation of the original government of Rome was laid by Romulus; and the work compleated by two of his elective successors, Numa, and Tullus Hostilius. On the abolition of royalty, the consular administration was substituted by Brutus, who stepped forward with a project for such a reform, which he alledged had been prepared by Servius Tullius, and to which his address obtained the assent and ratification of the senate and people. This remark is applicable to confederate governments also. Amphyction, we are told, was the author of that which bore his name. The Achæan league received its first birth from Achæus, and its second from Aratus. What degree of agency these reputed lawgivers might have in their respective establishments, or how far they might be cloathed with the legitimate authority of the people, cannot in every instance be ascertained. In some, however, the proceeding was strictly regular. Draco appears to have been entrusted by the people of Athens, with indefinite powers to reform its government and laws. And Solon, according to Plutarch, was in a manner compelled by the universal suffrage of his fellow citizens, to take upon him the sole and absolute power of new modelling the constitution. The proceedings under Lycurgus were less regular; but as far as the advocates for a regular reform could prevail, they all turned their eyes towards the single efforts of that celebrated patriot and sage, instead of seeking to bring about a revolution, by the intervention of a deliberative body of citizens. Whence could it have proceeded that a people, jealous as the Greeks were of their liberty, should so far abandon the rules of caution, as to place their destiny in the hands of a single citizen? Whence could it have proceeded that the Athenians, a people who would not suffer an army to be commanded by fewer than ten generals, and who required no other proof of danger to their liberties than the illustrious merit of a fellow citizen, should consider one illustrious citizen as a more eligible depositary of the fortunes of themselves and their posterity, than a select body of citizens, from whose common deliberations more wisdom, as well as more safety, might have been expected? These questions cannot be fully answered without supposing that the fears of discord and disunion among a number of counsellors, exceeded the apprehension of treachery or incapacity in a single individual. History informs us likewise of the difficulties with which these celebrated reformers had to contend; as well as of the expedients which they were obliged to employ, in order to carry their reforms into effect. Solon, who seems to have indulged a more temporising policy, confessed that he had not given to his countrymen the government best suited to their happiness, but most tolerable to their prejudices. And Lycurgus, more true to his object, was under the necessity of mixing a portion of violence with the authority of superstition; and of securing his final success, by a voluntary renunciation, first of his country, and then of his life. If these lessons teach us, on one hand, to admire the improvement made by America on the ancient mode of preparing and establishing regular plans of government; they serve not less on the other, to admonish us of the hazards and difficulties incident to such experiments, and of the great imprudence of unnecessarily multiplying them.

Is it an unreasonable conjecture that the errors which may be contained in the plan of the convention are such as have resulted rather from the defect of antecedent experience on this complicated and difficult subject, than from a want of accuracy or care in the investigation of it; and consequently such as will not be ascertained until an actual trial shall have pointed them out? This conjecture is rendered probable not only by many considerations of a general nature, but by the particular case of the articles of confederation. It is observable that among the numerous objections and amendments suggested by the several states, when these articles were submitted for their ratification, not one is found which alludes to the great and radical error, which on actual trial has discovered itself. And if we except the observations which New-Jersey was led to make rather by her local situation than by her peculiar foresight, it may be questioned whether a single suggestion was of sufficient moment to justify a revision of the system. There is abundant reason nevertheless to suppose that immaterial as these objections were, they would have been adhered to with a very dangerous inflexibility in some states, had not a zeal for their opinions and supposed interests, been stifled by the more powerful sentiment of self-preservation. One state, we may remember, persisted for several years in refusing her concurrence, although the enemy remained the whole period at our gates, or rather in the very bowels of our country. Nor was her pliancy in the end effected by a less motive than the fear of being chargeable with protracting the public calamities, and endangering the event of the contest. Every candid reader will make the proper reflections on these important facts.

A patient who finds his disorder daily growing worse; and that an efficacious remedy can no longer be delayed without extreme danger; after coolly revolving his situation, and the characters of different physicians, selects and calls in such of them as he judges most capable of administering relief, and best entitled to his confidence. The physicians attend: The case of the patient is carefully examined: a consultation is held. They are unanimously agreed that the symptoms are critical, but that the case, with proper and timely relief, is so far from being desperate, that it may be made to issue in an improvement of his constitution. They are equally unanimous in prescribing the remedy by which this happy effect is to be produced. The prescription is no sooner made known however, than a number of persons interpose, and without denying the reality or danger of the disorder, assure the patient that the prescription will be poison to his constitution, and forbid him under pain of certain death to make use of it. Might not the patient reasonably demand before he ventured to follow this advice, that the authors of it should at least agree among themselves, on some other remedy to be substituted? And if he found them differing as much from one another, as from his first counsellors, would he not act prudently, in trying the experiment unanimously recommended by the latter, rather than in hearkening to those who could neither deny the necessity of a speedy remedy, nor agree in proposing one?

Such a patient, and in such a situation is America at this moment. She has been sensible of her malady. She has obtained a regular and unanimous advice from men of her own deliberate choice. And she is warned by others against following this advice, under pain of the most fatal consequences. Do the monitors deny the reality of her danger? No. Do they deny the necessity of some speedy and powerful remedy? No. Are they agreed, are any two of them agreed in their objections to the remedy proposed, or in the proper one to be substituted? Let them speak for themselves. This one tells us that the proposed constitution ought to be rejected, because it is not a confederation of the states, but a government over individuals. Another admits that it ought to be a government over individuals, to a certain extent, but by no means to the extent proposed. A third does not object to the government over individuals or to the extent proposed, but to the want of a bill of rights. A fourth concurs in the absolute necessity of a bill of rights, but contends that it ought to be declaratory not of the personal rights of individuals, but of the rights reserved to the states in their political capacity. A fifth is of opinion that a bill of rights of any sort would be superfluous and misplaced, and that the plan would be unexceptionable, but for the fatal power of regulating the times and places of election. An objector in a large state exclaims loudly against the unreasonable equality of representation in the senate. An objector in a small state is equally loud against the dangerous inequality in the house of representatives. From this quarter we are alarmed with the amazing expence from the number of persons who are to administer the new government. From another quarter, and sometimes from the same quarter, on another occasion, the cry is, that the congress will be but the shadow of a representation, and that the government would be far less objectionable, if the number and the expence were doubled. A patriot in a state that does not import or export, discerns insuperable objections against the power of direct taxation. The patriotic adversary in a state of great exports and imports, is not less dissatisfied that the whole burthen of taxes may be thrown on consumption. This politician discovers in the constitution a direct and irresistible tendency to monarchy. That is equally sure, it will end in aristocracy. Another is puzzled to say which of these shapes it will ultimately assume, but sees clearly it must be one or other of them. Whilst a fourth is not wanting, who with no less confidence affirms that the constitution is so far from having a bias towards either of these dangers, that the weight on that side will not be sufficient to keep it upright and firm against its opposite propensities. With another class of adversaries to the constitution, the language is that the legislative, executive and judiciary departments are intermixed in such a manner as to contradict all the ideas of regular government, and all the requisite precautions in favour of liberty. Whilst this objection circulates in vague and general expressions, there are not a few who lend their sanction to it. Let each one come forward with his particular explanation and scarce any two are exactly agreed on the subject. In the eyes of one the junction of the senate with the president in the responsible function of appointing to offices, instead of vesting this executive power in the executive, alone, is the vicious part of the organisation. To another, the exclusion of the house of representatives, whose numbers alone could be a due security against corruption and partiality in the exercise of such a power, is equally obnoxious. With another, the admission of the president into any share of a power which must ever be a dangerous engine in the hands of the executive magistrate, is an unpardonable violation of the maxims of republican jealousy. No part of the arrangement according to some is more admissible than the trial of impeachments by the senate, which is alternately a member both of the legislative and executive departments, when this power so evidently belonged to the judiciary department. We concur fully, reply others, in the objection to this part of the plan, but we can never agree that a reference of impeachments to the judiciary authority would be an amendment of the error. Our principal dislike to the organisation arises from the extensive powers already lodged in that department. Even among the zealous patrons of a council of state, the most irreconcilable variance is discovered concerning the mode in which it ought to be constituted. The demand of one gentleman is that the council should consist of a small number, to be appointed by the most numerous branch of the legislature. Another would prefer a larger number, and considers it as a fundamental condition that the appointment should be made by the president himself.

As it can give no umbrage to the writers against the plan of the federal constitution, let us suppose that as they are the most zealous, so they are also the most sagacious of those who think the late convention were unequal to the task assigned them, and that a wiser and better plan might and ought to be substituted. Let us further suppose that their country should concur both in this favourable opinion of their merits, and in their unfavourable opinion of the convention; and should accordingly proceed to form them into a second convention, with full powers and for the express purpose of revising and remoulding the work of the first. Were the experiment to be seriously made, though it requires some effort to view it seriously even in fiction, I leave it to be decided by the sample of opinions just exhibited, whether with all their enmity to their predecessors, they would in any one point depart so widely from their example, as in the discord and ferment that would mark their own deliberations; and whether the constitution, now before the public, would not stand as fair a chance for immortality, as Lycurgus gave to that of Sparta, by making its change to depend on his own return from exile and death, if it were to be immediately adopted, and were to continue in force, not until a BETTER, but until ANOTHER should be agreed upon by this new assembly of lawgivers.

It is a matter both of wonder and regret, that those who raise so many objections against the new constitution, should never call to mind the defects of that which is to be exchanged for it. It is not necessary that the former should be perfect; it is sufficient that the latter is more imperfect. No man would refuse to give brass for silver or gold, because the latter had some alloy in it. No man would refuse to quit a shattered and tottering habitation, for a firm and commodious building, because the latter had not a porch to it; or because some of the rooms might be a little larger or smaller, or the ceiling a little higher or lower than his fancy would have planned them. But waving illustrations of this sort, is it not manifest that most of the capital objections urged against the new system, lie with tenfold weight against the existing confederation? Is an indefinite power to raise money dangerous in the hands of a federal government? The present congress can make requisitions to any amount they please; and the states are constitutionally bound to furnish them; they can emit bills of credit as long as they will pay for the paper; they can borrow both abroad and at home, as long as a shilling will be lent. Is an indefinite power to raise troops dangerous? The confederation gives to congress that power also; and they have already begun to make use of it. Is it improper and unsafe to intermix the different powers of government in the same body of men? Congress, a single body of men, are the sole depository of all the federal powers. Is it particularly dangerous to give the keys of the treasury, and the command of the army, into the same hands? The confederation places them both in the hands of congress. Is a bill of rights essential to liberty? The confederation has no bill of rights. Is it an objection against the new constitution, that it empowers the senate with the concurrence of the executive to make treaties which are to be the laws of the land? The existing congress, without any such controul, can make treaties which they themselves have declared, and most of the states have recognized, to be the supreme law of the land. Is the importation of slaves permitted by the new constitution for twenty years? By the old, it is permitted for ever.

I shall be told that however dangerous this mixture of powers may be in theory, it is rendered harmless by the dependence of congress on the states for the means of carrying them into practice: That however large the mass of powers may be, it is in fact a lifeless mass. Then say I in the first place, that the confederation is chargeable with the still greater folly of declaring certain powers in the federal government to be absolutely necessary, and at the same time rendering them absolutely nugatory: And in the next place, that if the union is to continue, and no better government be substituted, effective powers must either be granted to or assumed by the existing congress, in either of which events the contrast just stated will hold good. But this is not all. Out of this lifeless mass has already grown an excrescent power, which tends to realize all the dangers that can be apprehended from a defective construction of the supreme government of the union. It is now no longer a point of speculation and hope that the western territory is a mine of vast wealth to the United States; and although it is not of such a nature as to extricate them from their present distresses, or for some time to come, to yield any regular supplies for the public expences, yet must it hereafter be able under proper management both to effect a gradual discharge of the domestic debt, and to furnish for a certain period, liberal tributes to the federal treasury. A very large proportion of this fund has been already surrendered by individual states; and it may with reason be expected, that the remaining states will not persist in withholding similar proofs of their equity and generosity. We may calculate therefore that a rich and fertile country, of an area equal to the inhabited extent of the United States, will soon become a national stock. Congress have assumed the administration of this stock. They have begun to render it productive. Congress have undertaken to do more, they have proceeded to form new states; to erect temporary governments; to appoint officers for them; and to prescribe the conditions on which such states shall be admitted into the confederacy. All this has been done; and done without the least colour of constitutional authority. Yet no blame has been whispered; no alarm has been sounded. A GREAT and INDEPENDENT fund of revenue is passing into the hands of a SINGLE BODY of men, who can RAISE TROOPS to an INDEFINITE NUMBER, and appropriate money to their support for an INDEFINITE PERIOD OF TIME. And yet there are men who have not only been silent spectators of this prospect; but who are advocates for the system which exhibits it; and at the same time urge against the new system the objections which we have heard. Would they not act with more consistency in urging the establishment of the latter, as no less necessary to guard the union against the future powers and resources of a body constructed like the existing congress, than to save it from the dangers threatened by the present impotency of that assembly?

I mean not by any thing here said to throw censure on the measures which have been pursued by congress. I am sensible they could not have done otherwise. The public interest, the necessity of the case, imposed upon them the task of over-leaping their constitutional limits. But is not the fact an alarming proof of the danger resulting from a government which does not possess regular powers commensurate to its objects? A dissolution or usurpation is the dreadful dilemma to which it is continually exposed.

January 12, 1788

The Federalist No. 39

The last paper having concluded the observations which were meant to introduce a candid survey of the plan of government reported by the convention, we now proceed to the execution of that part of our undertaking. The first question that offers itself is, whether the general form and aspect of the government be strictly republican? It is evident that no other form would be reconcileable with the genius of the people of America; with the fundamental principles of the revolution; or with that honorable determination, which animates every votary of freedom, to rest all our political experiments on the capacity of mankind for self-government. If the plan of the convention therefore be found to depart from the republican character, its advocates must abandon it as no longer defensible.

What then are the distinctive characters of the republican form? Were an answer to this question to be sought, not by recurring to principles, but in the application of the term by political writers, to the constitutions of different states, no satisfactory one would ever be found. Holland, in which no particle of the supreme authority is derived from the people, has passed almost universally under the denomination of a republic. The same title has been bestowed on Venice, where absolute power over the great body of the people, is exercised in the most absolute manner, by a small body of hereditary nobles. Poland, which is a mixture of aristocracy and of monarchy in their worst forms, has been dignified with the same appellation. The government of England, which has one republican branch only, combined with a hereditary aristocracy and monarchy, has with equal impropriety been frequently placed on the list of republics. These examples, which are nearly as dissimilar to each other as to a genuine republic, shew the extreme inaccuracy with which the term has been used in political disquisitions.

If we resort for a criterion, to the different principles on which different forms of government are established, we may define a republic to be, or at least may bestow that name on, a government which derives all its powers directly or

indirectly from the great body of the people; and is administered by persons holding their offices during pleasure, for a
limited period, or during good behaviour. It is *essential* to
such a government, that it be derived from the great body of
the society, not from an inconsiderable proportion, or a favored class of it; otherwise a handful of tyrannical nobles,
exercising their oppressions by a delegation of their powers,
might aspire to the rank of republicans, and claim for their
government the honorable title of republic. It is *sufficient* for
such a government, that the persons administering it be appointed, either directly or indirectly, by the people; and that
they hold their appointments by either of the tenures just
specified; otherwise every government in the United States, as
well as every other popular government that has been or can
be well organised or well executed, would be degraded from
the republican character. According to the constitution of
every state in the union, some or other of the officers of
government are appointed indirectly only by the people. According to most of them the chief magistrate himself is so appointed. And according to one, this mode of appointment is
extended to one of the co-ordinate branches of the legislature. According to all the constitutions also, the tenure of the
highest offices is extended to a definite period, and in many
instances, both within the legislative and executive departments, to a period of years. According to the provisions of
most of the constitutions, again, as well as according to the
most respectable and received opinions on the subject, the
members of the judiciary department are to retain their offices by the firm tenure of good behaviour.

On comparing the constitution planned by the convention,
with the standard here fixed, we perceive at once that it is in
the most rigid sense conformable to it. The house of representatives, like that of one branch at least of all the state legislatures, is elected immediately by the great body of the
people. The senate, like the present congress, and the senate
of Maryland, derives its appointment indirectly from the people. The president is indirectly derived from the choice of the
people, according to the example in most of the states. Even
the judges, with all other officers of the union, will, as in the
several states, be the choice, though a remote choice, of the

people themselves. The duration of the appointments is equally conformable to the republican standard, and to the model of the state constitutions. The house of representatives is periodically elective as in all the states; and for the period of two years as in the state of South Carolina. The senate is elective for the period of six years; which is but one year more than the period of the senate of Maryland; and but two more than that of the senates of New-York and Virginia. The president is to continue in office for the period of four years; as in New-York and Delaware, the chief magistrate is elected for three years, and in South Carolina for two years. In the other states the election is annual. In several of the states however, no explicit provision is made for the impeachment of the chief magistrate. And in Delaware and Virginia, he is not impeachable till out of office. The president of the United States is impeachable at any time during his continuance in office. The tenure by which the judges are to hold their places, is, as it unquestionably ought to be, that of good behaviour. The tenure of the ministerial offices generally will be a subject of legal regulation, conformably to the reason of the case, and the example of the state constitutions.

Could any further proof be required of the republican complexion of this system, the most decisive one might be found in its absolute prohibition of titles of nobility, both under the federal and the state governments; and in its express guarantee of the republican form to each of the latter.

But it was not sufficient, say the adversaries of the proposed constitution, for the convention to adhere to the republican form. They ought with equal care, to have preserved the *federal* form, which regards the union as a *confederacy* of sovereign states; instead of which, they have framed a *national* government, which regards the union as a *consolidation* of the states. And it is asked by what authority this bold and radical innovation was undertaken. The handle which has been made of this objection requires, that it should be examined with some precision.

Without enquiring into the accuracy of the distinction on which the objection is founded, it will be necessary to a just estimate of its force, first to ascertain the real character of the government in question; secondly, to enquire how far the convention were authorised to propose such a government; and thirdly, how far the duty they owed to their country, could supply any defect of regular authority.

First. In order to ascertain the real character of the government it may be considered in relation to the foundation on which it is to be established; to the sources from which its ordinary powers are to be drawn; to the operation of those powers; to the extent of them; and to the authority by which future changes in the government are to be introduced.

On examining the first relation, it appears on one hand that the constitution is to be founded on the assent and ratification of the people of America, given by deputies elected for the special purpose; but on the other that this assent and ratification is to be given by the people, not as individuals composing one entire nation; but as composing the distinct and independent states to which they respectively belong. It is to be the assent and ratification of the several states derived from the supreme authority in each state, the authority of the people themselves. The act therefore establishing the constitution, will not be a *national* but a *federal* act.

That it will be a federal and not a national act, as these terms are understood by the objectors, the act of the people as forming so many independent states, not as forming one aggregate nation is obvious from this single consideration, that it is to result neither from the decision of a *majority* of the people of the union, nor from that of a *majority* of the states. It must result from the *unanimous* assent of the several states that are parties to it, differing no other wise from their ordinary assent than in its being expressed, not by the legislative authority, but by that of the people themselves. Were the people regarded in this transaction as forming one nation, the will of the majority of the whole people of the United States, would bind the minority; in the same manner as the majority in each state must bind the minority; and the will of the majority must be determined either by a comparison of the individual votes; or by considering the will of the majority of the states, as evidence of the will of a majority of the people of the United States. Neither of these rules has been adopted. Each state in ratifying the constitution, is considered as a sovereign body independent of all others, and only to be bound by its own voluntary act. In this relation then the new constitution will, if established, be a *federal* and not a *national* constitution.

The next relation is to the sources from which the ordinary powers of government are to be derived. The house of representatives will derive its powers from the people of America, and the people will be represented in the same proportion, and on the same principle, as they are in the legislature of a particular state. So far the government is *national* not *federal.* The senate on the other hand will derive its powers from the states, as political and co-equal societies; and these will be represented on the principle of equality in the senate, as they now are in the existing congress. So far the government is *federal*, not *national.* The executive power will be derived from a very compound source. The immediate election of the president is to be made by the states in their political characters. The votes allotted to them, are in a compound ratio, which considers them partly as distinct and co-equal societies; partly as unequal members of the same society. The eventual election, again is to be made by that branch of the legislature which consists of the national representatives; but in this particular act, they are to be thrown into the form of individual delegations from so many distinct and co-equal bodies politic. From this aspect of the government, it appears to be of a mixed character, presenting at least as many *federal* as *national* features.

The difference between a federal and national government, as it relates to the *operation of the government*, is, by the adversaries of the plan of the convention, supposed to consist in this, that in the former, the powers operate on the political bodies composing the confederacy, in their political capacities; in the latter, on the individual citizens composing the nation, in their individual capacities. On trying the constitution by this criterion, it falls under the *national*, not the *federal* character; though perhaps not so compleatly as has been understood. In several cases, and particularly in the trial of controversies to which states may be parties, they must be viewed and proceeded against in their collective and political capacities only. But the operation of the government on the people in their individual capacities, in its ordinary and most essential proceedings, will on the whole, in the sense of its opponents, designate it in this relation, a *national* government.

But if the government be national with regard to the *operation* of its powers, it changes its aspect again when we contemplate it in relation to the *extent* of its powers. The idea of a national government involves in it, not only an authority over the individual citizens, but an indefinite supremacy over all persons and things, so far as they are objects of lawful government. Among a people consolidated into one nation, this supremacy is compleatly vested in the national legislature. Among communities united for particular purposes, it is vested partly in the general, and partly in the municipal legislatures. In the former case, all local authorities are subordinate to the supreme; and may be controuled, directed, or abolished by it at pleasure. In the latter, the local or municipal authorities form distinct and independent portions of the supremacy, no more subject within their respective spheres to the general authority, than the general authority is subject to them within its own sphere. In this relation then, the proposed government cannot be deemed a *national* one; since its jurisdiction extends to certain enumerated objects only, and leaves to the several states a residuary and inviolable sovereignty over all other objects. It is true that in controversies relating to the boundary between the two jurisdictions, the tribunal which is ultimately to decide, is to be established under the general government. But this does not change the principle of the case. The decision is to be impartially made, according to the rules of the constitution; and all the usual and most effectual precautions are taken to secure this impartiality. Some such tribunal is clearly essential to prevent an appeal to the sword, and a dissolution of the compact; and that it ought to be established under the general, rather than under the local governments; or to speak more properly, that it could be safely established under the first alone, is a position not likely to be combated.

If we try the constitution by its last relation, to the authority by which amendments are to be made, we find it neither wholly *national*, nor wholly *federal*. Were it wholly national, the supreme and ultimate authority would reside in the *majority* of the people of the union; and this authority would be competent at all times, like that of a majority of every national society, to alter or abolish its established government. Were it wholly federal on the other hand, the concurrence of each state in the union would be essential to every alteration that would be binding on all. The mode provided by the plan of the convention, is not founded on either of these principles. In requiring more than a majority, and particularly, in computing the proportion by *states*, not by *citizens*, it departs from the *national*, and advances towards the *federal* character: In rendering the concurrence of less than the whole number of states sufficient, it loses again the *federal*, and partakes of the *national* character.

The proposed constitution therefore, even when tested by the rules laid down by its antagonists, is in strictness, neither a national nor a federal constitution; but a composition of both. In its foundation it is federal, not national; in the sources from which the ordinary powers of the government are drawn, it is partly federal, and partly national; in the operation of these powers, it is national, not federal; in the extent of them again, it is federal, not national; and finally, in the authoritative mode of introducing amendments, it is neither wholly federal, nor wholly national.

January 16, 1788

The Federalist No. 40

The *second* point to be examined is, whether the convention were authorised to frame and propose this mixed constitution.

The powers of the convention ought in strictness to be determined by an inspection of the commissions given to the members by their respective constituents. As all of these however, had reference, either to the recommendation from the meeting at Annapolis in September, 1786, or to that from congress in February, 1787, it will be sufficient to recur to these particular acts.

The act from Annapolis recommends the "appointment of commissioners to take into consideration the situation of the United States, to devise *such further provisions* as shall appear to them necessary to render the constitution of the federal government *adequate to the exigencies of the union*; and to report such an act for that purpose, to the United States in congress assembled, as, when agreed to by them, and afterwards confirmed by the legislature of every state, will effectually provide for the same."

The recommendatory act of congress is in the words following: "Whereas there is provision in the articles of confederation and perpetual union, for making alterations therein, by the assent of a congress of the United States, and of the legislatures of the several states: And whereas experience hath evinced, that there are defects in the present confederation, as a mean to remedy which several of the states, and *particularly the state of New-York*, by express instructions to their delegates in congress, have suggested a convention for the purposes expressed in the following resolution; and such convention appearing to be the most probable mean of establishing in these states, *a firm national government*."

"Resolved, That in the opinion of congress, it is expedient, that on the 2d Monday in May next, a convention of delegates, who shall have been appointed by the several states, be held at Philadelphia, for the sole and express purpose *of revising the articles of confederation*, and reporting to congress and the several legislatures, such *alterations and provisions therein*, as shall, when agreed to in congress, and confirmed by the states, render the federal constitution *adequate to the exigencies of government and the preservation of the union.*"

From these two acts it appears, 1st. that the object of the convention was to establish in these states, *a firm national government*; 2d. that this government was to be such as would be *adequate to the exigencies of government* and *the preservation of the union*; 3d. that these purposes were to be effected by *alterations and provisions in the articles of confederation*, as it is expressed in the act of congress, or by *such further provisions as should appear necessary*, as it stands in the recommendatory act from Annapolis; 4th. that the alterations and provisions were to be reported to congress, and to the states, in order to be agreed to by the former, and confirmed by the latter.

From a comparison and fair construction of these several modes of expression, is to be deduced the authority under which the convention acted. They were to frame a *national government*, adequate to the *exigencies of government* and *of the union*, and to reduce the articles of confederation into such form as to accomplish these purposes.

There are two rules of construction dictated by plain reason, as well as founded on legal axioms. The one is, that every part of the expression ought, if possible, to be allowed some meaning, and be made to conspire to some common end. The other is, that where the several parts cannot be made to coincide, the less important should give way to the more important part; the means should be sacrificed to the end, rather than the end to the means.

Suppose then that the expressions defining the authority of the convention, were irreconcileably at variance with each other; that a *national* and *adequate government* could not possibly, in the judgment of the convention, be effected by *alterations* and *provisions* in the *articles of confederation*, which part of the definition ought to have been embraced, and which rejected? Which was the more important, which the less important part? Which the end, which the means? Let the most scrupulous expositors of delegated powers; let the most inveterate objectors against those exercised by the convention, answer these questions. Let them declare, whether it was of most importance to the happiness of the people of America, that the articles of confederation should be disregarded, and an adequate government be provided, and the union preserved; or that an adequate government should be omitted, and the articles of confederation preserved. Let them declare, whether the preservation of these articles was the end for securing which a reform of the government was to be introduced as the means; or whether the establishment of a government, adequate to the national happiness, was the end at which these articles themselves originally aimed, and to which they ought, as insufficient means, to have been sacrificed.

But is it necessary to suppose that these expressions are absolutely irreconcileable to each other; that no *alterations* or *provisions* in the *articles of the confederation*, could possibly mould them into a national and adequate government; into such a government as has been proposed by the convention?

No stress it is presumed will in this case be laid on the *title*, a change of that could never be deemed an exercise of ungranted power. *Alterations* in the body of the instrument, are expressly authorised. *New provisions* therein are also expressly authorised. Here then is a power to change the title; to insert new articles; to alter old ones. Must it of necessity be admitted that this power is infringed, so long as a part of the old articles remain? Those who maintain the affirmative, ought at least to mark the boundary between authorised and usurped innovations, between that degree of change which lies within the compass of *alterations and further provisions*; and that which amounts to a *transmutation* of the government. Will it be said that the alterations ought not to have touched the substance of the confederation? The states would never have appointed a convention with so much solemnity, nor described its objects with so much latitude, if some *substantial* reform had not been in contemplation. Will it be said that the *fundamental principles* of the confederation were not within the purview of the convention, and ought not to have been varied? I ask what are these principles? Do they require that in the establishment of the constitution, the states should be regarded as distinct and independent sovereigns? They are so regarded by the constitution proposed. Do they require that

the members of the government should derive their appointment from the legislatures, not from the people of the states?
One branch of the new government is to be appointed by
these legislatures; and under the confederation the delegates
to congress *may all* be appointed immediately by the people,
and in two states* are actually so appointed. Do they require
that the powers of the government should act on the states,
and not immediately on individuals? In some instances, as has
been shewn, the powers of the new government will act on
the states in their collective characters. In some instances also
those of the existing government act immediately on individuals: In cases of capture, of piracy, of the post-office, of coins,
weights and measures, of trade with the Indians, of claims under grants of land by different states, and above all, in the case
of trials by courts-martial in the army and navy, by which
death may be inflicted without the intervention of a jury, or
even of a civil magistrate; in all these cases the powers of the
confederation operate immediately on the persons and interests of individual citizens. Do these fundamental principles require particularly that no tax should be levied without the
intermediate agency of the states? The confederation itself authorises a direct tax to a certain extent on the post-office. The
power of coinage has been so construed by congress, as to
levy a tribute immediately from that source also. But preter-
mitting these instances, was it not an acknowledged object of
the convention, and the universal expectation of the people,
that the regulation of trade should be submitted to the general government in such a form as would render it an immediate source of general revenue? Had not congress repeatedly
recommended this measure as not inconsistent with the fundamental principles of the confederation? Had not every state
but one, had not New-York herself, so far complied with the
plan of congress, as to recognize the *principle* of the innovation? Do these principles in fine require that the powers of the
general government should be limited, and that beyond this
limit, the states should be left in possession of their sovereignty and independence? We have seen that in the new government as in the old, the general powers are limited, and

*Connecticut and Rhode-Island.

that the states, in all unenumerated cases, are left in the enjoyment of their sovereign and independent jurisdiction.

The truth is, that the great principles of the constitution proposed by the convention, may be considered less as absolutely new, than as the expansion of principles which are found in the articles of confederation. The misfortune under the latter system has been, that these principles are so feeble and confined as to justify all the charges of inefficiency which have been urged against it; and to require a degree of enlargement which gives to the new system, the aspect of an entire transformation of the old.

In one particular it is admitted that the convention have departed from the tenor of their commission. Instead of reporting a plan requiring the confirmation *of all the states*, they have reported a plan which is to be confirmed and may be carried into effect by *nine states only*. It is worthy of remark, that this objection, though the most plausible, has been the least urged in the publications which have swarmed against the convention. The forbearance can only have proceeded from an irresistible conviction of the absurdity of subjecting the fate of twelve states, to the perverseness or corruption of a thirteenth; from the example of inflexible opposition given by a *majority* of one sixtieth of the people of America, to a measure approved and called for by the voice of twelve states comprising fifty-nine sixtieths of the people; an example still fresh in the memory and indignation of every citizen who has felt for the wounded honor and prosperity of his country. As this objection therefore, has been in a manner waved by those who have criticised the powers of the convention, I dismiss it without further observation.

The *third* point to be enquired into is, how far considerations of duty arising out of the case itself, could have supplied any defect of regular authority.

In the preceding enquiries, the powers of the convention have been analyzed and tried with the same rigour, and by the same rules, as if they had been real and final powers, for the establishment of a constitution for the United States. We have seen, in what manner they have borne the trial, even on that supposition. It is time now to recollect, that the powers were merely advisory and recommendatory; that they were so meant by the states, and so understood by the convention; and that the latter have accordingly planned and proposed a constitution, which is to be of no more consequence than the paper on which it is written, unless it be stamped with the approbation of those to whom it is addressed. This reflection places the subject in a point of view altogether different, and will enable us to judge with propriety of the course taken by the convention.

Let us view the ground on which the convention stood. It may be collected from their proceedings, that they were deeply and unanimously impressed with the crisis which had led their country almost with one voice to make so singular and solemn an experiment, for correcting the errors of a system by which this crisis had been produced; that they were no less deeply and unanimously convinced, that such a reform as they have proposed, was absolutely necessary to effect the purposes of their appointment. It could not be unknown to them, that the hopes and expectations of the great body of citizens, throughout this great empire, were turned with the keenest anxiety, to the event of their deliberations. They had every reason to believe that the contrary sentiments agitated the minds and bosoms of every external and internal foe to the liberty and prosperity of the United States. They had seen in the origin and progress of the experiment, the alacrity with which the *proposition*, made by a single state (Virginia) towards a partial amendment of the confederation, had been attended to and promoted. They had seen the *liberty assumed* by a *very few* deputies, from a *very few* states, convened at Annapolis, of recommending a great and critical object, wholly foreign to their commission, not only justified by the public opinion, but actually carried into effect, by twelve out of the Thirteen States. They had seen in a variety of instances, assumptions by congress not only of recommendatory, but of operative powers, warranted in the public estimation, by occasions and objects infinitely less urgent than those by which their conduct was to be governed. They must have reflected, that in all great changes of established governments, forms ought to give way to substance; that a rigid adherence in such cases to the former, would render nominal and nugatory, the transcendent and precious right of the people to "abolish or alter their governments as to them shall seem most likely to effect their safety and happiness"*; since it is impossible for the people spontaneously and universally, to move in concert towards their object; and it is therefore essential, that such changes be instituted by some *informal and unauthorised propositions*, made by some patriotic and respectable citizen or number of citizens. They must have recollected that it was by this irregular and assumed privilege of proposing to the people plans for their safety and happiness, that the states were first united against the danger with which they were threatened by their antient government; that committees and congresses were formed for concentrating their efforts, and defending their rights; and that *conventions* were *elected* in *the several states*, for establishing the constitutions under which they are now governed; nor could it have been forgotten that no little ill-timed scruples, no zeal for adhering to ordinary forms were any where seen, except in those who wished to indulge under these masks, their secret enmity to the substance contended for. They must have borne in mind, that as the plan to be framed and proposed, was to be submitted to *the people themselves*, the disapprobation of this supreme authority would destroy it for ever; its approbation blot out all antecedent errors and irregularities. It might even have occurred to them, that where a disposition to cavil prevailed, their neglect to execute the degree of power vested in them, and still more their recommendation of any measure whatever not warranted by their commission, would not less excite animadversion, than a recommendation at once of a measure fully commensurate to the national exigencies.

Had the convention under all these impressions, and in the midst of all these considerations, instead of exercising a manly confidence in their country, by whose confidence they had been so peculiarly distinguished, and of pointing out a system capable in their judgment of securing its happiness, taken the cold and sullen resolution of disappointing its ardent hopes of sacrificing substance to forms, of committing the dearest interests of their country to the uncertainties of delay, and the hazard of events; let me ask the man, who can raise his mind

*Declaration of Independence.

to one elevated conception; who can awaken in his bosom, one patriotic emotion, what judgment ought to have been pronounced by the impartial world, by the friends of mankind, by every virtuous citizen, on the conduct and character of this assembly, or if there be a man whose propensity to condemn, is susceptible of no controul, let me then ask what sentence he has in reserve for the twelve states who *usurped the power of* sending deputies to the convention, a body utterly unknown to their constitutions; for congress, who recommended the appointment of this body, equally unknown to the confederation; and for the state of New-York in particular, who first urged, and then complied with this unauthorised interposition.

But that the objectors may be disarmed of every pretext, it shall be granted for a moment, that the convention were neither authorised by their commission, nor justified by circumstances, in proposing a constitution for their country: Does it follow that the constitution ought for that reason alone to be rejected? If according to the noble precept, it be lawful to accept good advice even from an enemy, shall we set the ignoble example of refusing such advice even when it is offered by our friends? The prudent enquiry in all cases, ought surely to be not so much *from whom* the advice comes, as whether the advice be *good*.

The sum of what has been here advanced and proved, is that the charge against the convention of exceeding their powers, except in one instance little urged by the objectors, has no foundation to support it; that if they had exceeded their powers, they were not only warranted but required, as the confidential servants of their country, by the circumstances in which they were placed, to exercise the liberty which they assumed, and that finally, if they had violated both their powers, and their obligations in proposing a constitution, this ought nevertheless to be embraced, if it be calculated to accomplish the views and happiness of the people of America. How far this character is due to the constitution, is the subject under investigation.

January 18, 1788

The Federalist No. 41

The constitution proposed by the convention may be considered under two general points of view. The FIRST relates to the sum or quantity of power which it vests in the government, including the restraints imposed on the states. The SECOND, to the particular structure of the government, and the distribution of this power, among its several branches.

Under the first view of the subject two important questions arise; 1. Whether any part of the powers transferred to the general government be unnecessary or improper? 2. Whether the entire mass of them be dangerous to the portion of jurisdiction left in the several states?

Is the aggregate power of the general government greater than ought to have been vested in it? This is the first question.

It cannot have escaped those who have attended with candour to the arguments employed against the extensive powers of the government, that the authors of them have very little considered how far these powers were necessary means of attaining a necessary end. They have chosen rather to dwell on the inconveniences which must be unavoidably blended with all political advantages; and on the possible abuses which must be incident to every power or trust of which a beneficial use can be made. This method of handling the subject cannot impose on the good sense of the people of America. It may display the subtlety of the writer; it may open a boundless field for rhetoric and declamation; it may inflame the passions of the unthinking, and may confirm the prejudices of the misthinking. But cool and candid people will at once reflect, that the purest of human blessings must have a portion of alloy in them; that the choice must always be made, if not of the lesser evil, at least of the GREATER, not the PERFECT good; and that in every political institution, a power to advance the public happiness involves a discretion which may be misapplied and abused. They will see therefore that in all cases, where power is to be conferred, the point first to be decided is whether such a power be necessary to the public good; as the next will be, in case of an affirmative decision, to guard as effectually as possible against a perversion of the power to the public detriment.

That we may form a correct judgment on this subject, it will be proper to review the several powers conferred on the government of the union; and that this may be the more conveniently done, they may be reduced into different classes as they relate to the following different objects; 1. Security against foreign danger; 2. Regulation of the intercourse with foreign nations; 3. Maintenance of harmony and proper intercourse among the states; 4. Certain miscellaneous objects of general utility; 5. Restraint of the states from certain injurious acts; 6. Provisions for giving due efficacy to all these powers.

The powers falling within the first class, are those of declaring war, and granting letters of marque; of providing armies and fleets; of regulating and calling forth the militia; of levying and borrowing money.

Security against foreign danger is one of the primitive objects of civil society. It is an avowed and essential object of the American union. The powers requisite for attaining it, must be effectually confided to the federal councils.

Is the power of declaring war necessary? No man will answer this question in the negative. It would be superfluous therefore to enter into a proof of the affirmative. The existing confederation establishes this power in the most ample form.

Is the power of raising armies, and equipping fleets necessary? This is involved in the foregoing power. It is involved in the power of self-defence.

But was it necessary to give an INDEFINITE POWER of raising TROOPS, as well as providing fleets; and of maintaining both in PEACE, as well as in WAR?

The answer to these questions has been too far anticipated, in another place, to admit an extensive discussion of them in this place. The answer indeed seems to be so obvious and conclusive as scarcely to justify such a discussion in any place. With what colour of propriety could the force necessary for defence, be limited by those who cannot limit the force of offence? If a federal constitution could chain the ambition, or set bounds to the exertions of all other nations, then indeed might it prudently chain the discretion of its own government, and set bounds to the exertions for its own safety.

How could a readiness for war in time of peace be safely prohibited, unless we could prohibit in like manner the preparations and establishments of every hostile nation? The means of security can only be regulated by the means and the danger of attack. They will in fact be ever determined by these rules, and by no others. It is in vain to oppose constitutional barriers to the impulse of self-preservation. It is worse than in vain; because it plants in the constitution itself necessary usurpations of power, every precedent of which is a germ of unnecessary and multiplied repetitions. If one nation maintains constantly a disciplined army ready for the service of ambition or revenge, it obliges the most pacific nations, who may be within the reach of its enterprizes, to take corresponding precautions. The fifteenth century was the unhappy epoch of military establishments in time of peace. They were introduced by Charles VII. of France. All Europe has followed, or been forced into the example. Had the example not been followed by other nations, all Europe must long ago have worn the chains of a universal monarch. Were every nation except France now to disband its peace establishment, the same event might follow. The veteran legions of Rome were an overmatch for the undisciplined valour of all other nations, and rendered her mistress of the world.

Not less true is it, that the liberties of Rome proved the final victim to her military triumphs, and that the liberties of Europe, as far as they ever existed, have, with few exceptions been the price of her military establishments. A standing force therefore is a dangerous, at the same time that it may be a necessary provision. On the smallest scale it has its inconveniences. On an extensive scale, its consequences may be fatal. On any scale, it is an object of laudable circumspection and precaution. A wise nation will combine all these considerations; and whilst it does not rashly preclude itself from any resource which may become essential to its safety, will exert all its prudence in diminishing both the necessity and the danger of resorting to one which may be inauspicious to its liberties.

The clearest marks of this prudence are stamped on the proposed constitution. The union itself which it cements and secures, destroys every pretext for a military establishment which could be dangerous. America, united with a handful of troops, or without a single soldier, exhibits a more forbidding posture to foreign ambition, than America disunited, with an

hundred thousand veterans ready for combat. It was remarked on a former occasion, that the want of this pretext
had saved the liberties of one nation in Europe. Being rendered by her insular situation and her maritime resources, impregnable to the armies of her neighbours, the rulers of
Great-Britain have never been able, by real or artificial dangers, to cheat the public into an extensive peace establishment. The distance of the United States from the powerful
nations of the world, gives them the same happy security. A
dangerous establishment can never be necessary or plausible,
so long as they continue a united people. But let it never for
a moment be forgotten, that they are indebted for this advantage to their union alone. The moment of its dissolution
will be the date of a new order of things. The fears of the
weaker or the ambition of the stronger states or confederacies, will set the same example in the new, as Charles VII. did
in the old world. The example will be followed here from the
same motives which produced universal imitation there.
Instead of deriving from our situation the precious advantage
which Great-Britain has derived from hers, the face of
America will be but a copy of that of the continent of Europe.
It will present liberty every where crushed between standing
armies and perpetual taxes. The fortunes of disunited America
will be even more disastrous than those of Europe. The
sources of evil in the latter are confined to her own limits. No
superior powers of another quarter of the globe intrigue
among her rival nations, inflame their mutual animosities, and
render them the instruments of foreign ambition, jealousy
and revenge. In America, the miseries springing from her internal jealousies, contentions and wars, would form a part
only of her lot. A plentiful addition of evils would have their
source in that relation in which Europe stands to this quarter
of the earth, and which no other quarter of the earth bears to
Europe. This picture of the consequences of disunion cannot
be too highly coloured, or too often exhibited. Every man
who loves peace, every man who loves his country, every man
who loves liberty, ought to have it ever before his eyes, that
he may cherish in his heart a due attachment to the union of
America, and be able to set a due value on the means of preserving it.

Next to the effectual establishment of the union, the best possible precaution against danger from standing armies, is a limitation of the term for which revenue may be appropriated to their support. This precaution the constitution has prudently added. I will not repeat here the observations, which I flatter myself have placed this subject in a just and satisfactory light. But it may not be improper to take notice of an argument against this part of the constitution, which has been drawn from the policy and practice of Great-Britain. It is said that the continuance of an army in that kingdom, requires an annual vote of the legislature; whereas the American constitution has lengthened this critical period to two years. This is the form in which the comparison is usually stated to the public: But is it a just form? Is it a fair comparison? Does the British constitution restrain the parliamentary discretion to one year? Does the American impose on the congress appropriations for two years? On the contrary, it cannot be unknown to the authors of the fallacy themselves, that the British constitution fixes no limit whatever to the discretion of the legislature, and that the American ties down the legislature to two years, as the longest admissible term.

Had the argument from the British example been truly stated, it would have stood thus: The term for which supplies may be appropriated to the army establishment, though unlimited by the British constitution, has nevertheless in practice been limited by parliamentary discretion, to a single year. Now if in Great-Britain, where the house of commons is elected for seven years; where so great a proportion of the members are elected by so small a proportion of the people; where the electors are so corrupted by the representatives, and the representatives so corrupted by the crown, the representative body can possess a power to make appropriations to the army for an indefinite term, without desiring, or without daring, to extend the term beyond a single year; ought not suspicion herself to blush in pretending that the representatives of the United States, elected FREELY, by the WHOLE BODY of the people, every SECOND YEAR, cannot be safely entrusted with a discretion over such appropriations, expressly limited to the short period of TWO YEARS?

A bad cause seldom fails to betray itself. Of this truth, the management of the opposition to the federal government is an unvaried exemplification. But among all the blunders which have been committed, none is more striking than the attempt to enlist on that side, the prudent jealousy entertained by the people, of standing armies. The attempt has awakened fully the public attention to that important subject; and has led to investigations which must terminate in a thorough and universal conviction, not only that the constitution has provided the most effectual guards against danger from that quarter, but that nothing short of a constitution fully adequate to the national defence, and the preservation of the union, can save America from as many standing armies as it may be split into states or confederacies; and from such a progressive augmentation of these establishments in each, as will render them as burdensome to the properties and ominous to the liberties of the people; as any establishment that can become necessary, under a united and efficient government, must be tolerable to the former, and safe to the latter.

The palpable necessity of the power to provide and maintain a navy has protected that part of the constitution against a spirit of censure, which has spared few other parts. It must indeed be numbered among the greatest blessings of America, that as her union will be the only source of her maritime strength, so this will be a principal source of her security against danger from abroad. In this respect our situation bears another likeness to the insular advantage of Great-Britain. The batteries most capable of repelling foreign enterprizes on our safety, are happily such as can never be turned by a perfidious government against our liberties.

The inhabitants of the Atlantic frontier are all of them deeply interested in this provision for naval protection, and if they have hitherto been suffered to sleep quietly in their beds; if their property has remained safe against the predatory spirit of licentious adventurers; if their maritime towns have not yet been compelled to ransom themselves from the terrors of a conflagration, by yielding to the exactions of daring and sudden invaders, these instances of good fortune are not to be ascribed to the capacity of the existing government for the protection of those from whom it claims allegiance, but to causes that are fugitive and fallacious. If we except perhaps

Virginia and Maryland, which are peculiarly vulnerable on their eastern frontiers, no part of the union ought to feel more anxiety on this subject than New-York. Her sea coast is extensive. The very important district of the state is an Island. The state itself is penetrated by a large navigable river for more than fifty leagues. The great emporium of its commerce, the great reservoir of its wealth, lies every moment at the mercy of events, and may almost be regarded as a hostage, for ignominious compliances with the dictates of a foreign enemy, or even with the rapacious demands of pirates and barbarians. Should a war be the result of the precarious situation of European affairs, and all the unruly passions attending it, be let loose on the ocean, our escape from insults and depredations, not only on that element but every part of the other bordering on it, will be truly miraculous. In the present condition of America, the states more immediately exposed to these calamities, have nothing to hope from the phantom of a general government which now exists; and if their single resources were equal to the task of fortifying themselves against the danger, the object to be protected would be almost consumed by the means of protecting them.

The power of regulating and calling forth the militia has been already sufficiently vindicated and explained.

The power of levying and borrowing money, being the sinew of that which is to be exerted in the national defence, is properly thrown into the same class with it. This power also has been examined already with much attention, and has I trust been clearly shewn to be necessary both in the extent and form given to it by the constitution. I will address one additional reflection only to those who contend that the power ought to have been restrained to external taxation, by which they mean taxes on articles imported from other countries. It cannot be doubted that this will always be a valuable source of revenue, that for a considerable time, it must be a principal source, that at this moment it is an essential one. But we may form very mistaken ideas on this subject, if we do not call to mind in our calculations, that the extent of revenue drawn from foreign commerce, must vary with the variations both in the extent and the kind of imports, and that these variations do not correspond with the progress of population, which must be the general measure of the public wants. As long as agriculture continues the sole field of labour, the importation of manufactures must increase as the consumers multiply. As soon as domestic manufactures are begun by the hands not called for by agriculture, the imported manufactures will decrease as the numbers of people increase. In a more remote stage, the imports may consist in considerable part of raw materials which will be wrought into articles for exportation, and will therefore require rather the encouragement of bounties, than to be loaded with discouraging duties. A system of government, meant for duration ought to contemplate these revolutions, and be able to accommodate itself to them.

Some who have not denied the necessity of the power of taxation, have grounded a very fierce attack against the constitution on the language in which it is defined. It has been urged and echoed, that the power "to lay and collect taxes, duties, imposts and excises, to pay the debts, and provide for the common defence and general welfare of the United States," amounts to an unlimited commission to exercise every power which may be alledged to be necessary for the common defence or general welfare. No stronger proof could be given of the distress under which these writers labour for objections, than their stooping to such a misconstruction.

Had no other enumeration or definition of the powers of the congress been found in the constitution, than the general expressions just cited, the authors of the objection might have had some colour for it; though it would have been difficult to find a reason for so awkward a form of describing an authority to legislate in all possible cases. A power to destroy the freedom of the press, the trial by jury or even to regulate the course of descents, or the forms of conveyances, must be very singularly expressed by the terms "to raise money for the general welfare."

But what colour can the objection have, when a specification of the objects alluded to by these general terms, immediately follows; and is not even separated by a longer pause than a semicolon. If the different parts of the same instrument ought to be so expounded as to give meaning to every part which will bear it; shall one part of the same sentence be excluded altogether from a share in the meaning; and shall the more doubtful and indefinite terms be retained in their full extent and the clear and precise expressions, be denied any signification whatsoever? For what purpose could the enumeration of particular powers be inserted, if these and all others were meant to be included in the preceding general power? Nothing is more natural or common than first to use a general phrase, and then to explain and qualify it by a recital of particulars. But the idea of an enumeration of particulars, which neither explain nor qualify the general meaning, and can have no other effect than to confound and mislead, is an absurdity which as we are reduced to the dilemma of charging either on the authors of the objection, or on the authors of the constitution, we must take the liberty of supposing, had not its origin with the latter.

The objection here is the more extraordinary, as it appears, that the language used by the convention is a copy from the articles of confederation. The objects of the union among the states as described in article 3d, are, "their common defence, security of their liberties, and mutual and general welfare." The terms of article 8th, are still more identical. "All charges of war, and all other expences, that shall be incurred for the common defence or general welfare, and allowed by the United States in congress shall be defrayed out of a common treasury, &c." A similar language again occurs in article 9. Construe either of these articles by the rules which would justify the construction put on the new constitution, and they vest in the existing Congress a power to legislate in all cases whatsoever. But what would have been thought of that assembly, if attaching themselves to these general expressions, and disregarding the specifications, which ascertain and limit their import, they had exercised an unlimited power of providing for the common defence and general welfare? I appeal to the objectors themselves, whether they would in that case have employed the same reasoning in justification of congress, as they now make use of against the convention. How difficult it is for error to escape its own condemnation.

January 19, 1788

The Federalist No. 42

The *second* class of powers lodged in the general government, consists of those which regulate the intercourse with foreign nations, to wit, to make treaties; to send and receive ambassadors, other public ministers and consuls; to define and punish piracies and felonies committed on the high seas, and offences against the law of nations; to regulate foreign commerce, including a power to prohibit after the year 1808, the importation of slaves, and to lay an intermediate duty of ten dollars per head, as a discouragement to such importations.

This class of powers forms an obvious and essential branch of the federal administration. If we are to be one nation in any respect, it clearly ought to be in respect to other nations.

The powers to make treaties and to send and receive ambassadors, speak their own propriety. Both of them are comprised in the articles of confederation; with this difference only, that the former is disembarrassed by the plan of the convention of an exception, under which treaties might be substantially frustrated by regulations of the states; and that a power of appointing and receiving "other public ministers and consuls," is expressly and very properly added to the former provision concerning ambassadors. The term ambassador, if taken strictly, as seems to be required by the second of the articles of confederation, comprehends the highest grade only of public ministers; and excludes the grades which the United States will be most likely to prefer where foreign embassies may be necessary. And under no latitude of construction will the term comprehend consuls. Yet it has been found expedient, and has been the practice of congress to employ the inferior grades of public ministers; and to send and receive consuls. It is true that where treaties of commerce stipulate for the mutual appointment of consuls, whose functions are connected with commerce, the admission of foreign consuls may fall within the power of making commercial treaties; and that where no such treaties exist, the mission of American consuls into foreign countries, may *perhaps* be covered under the authority given by the 9th article of the confederation, to appoint all such civil officers as may be

necessary for managing the general affairs of the United
States. But the admission of consuls into the United States,
where no previous treaty has stipulated it, seems to have been
no where provided for. A supply of the omission is one of the
lesser instances in which the convention have improved on
the model before them. But the most minute provisions become important when they tend to obviate the necessity or
the pretext for gradual and unobserved usurpations of power.
A list of the cases in which congress have been betrayed, or
forced by the defects of the confederation into violations of
their chartered authorities, would not a little surprise those
who have paid no attention to the subject; and would be no
inconsiderable argument in favor of the new constitution,
which seems to have provided no less studiously for the lesser,
than the more obvious and striking defects of the old.

The power to define and punish piracies and felonies committed on the high seas, and offences against the law of
nations, belongs with equal propriety to the general government; and is a still greater improvement on the articles of
confederation.

These articles contain no provision for the case of offences
against the law of nations; and consequently leave it in the
power of any indiscreet member to embroil the confederacy
with foreign nations.

The provision of the federal articles on the subject of piracies and felonies, extends no farther than to the establishment
of courts for the trial of these offences. The definition of piracies might perhaps, without inconveniency, be left to the law
of nations; though a legislative definition of them is found in
most municipal codes. A definition of felonies on the high
seas is evidently requisite. Felony is a term of loose signification even in the common law of England; and of various import in the statute law of that kingdom. But neither the
common, nor the statute law of that or of any other nation,
ought to be a standard for the proceedings of this, unless previously made its own by legislative adoption. The meaning of
the term as defined in the codes of the several states, would
be as impracticable as the former would be a dishonorable
and illegitimate guide. It is not precisely the same in any two
of the states; and varies in each with every revision of its crim-

inal laws. For the sake of certainty and uniformity therefore, the power of defining felonies in this case, was in every respect necessary and proper.

The regulation of foreign commerce, having fallen within several views which have been taken of this subject, has been too fully discussed to need additional proofs here of its being properly submitted to the federal administration.

It were doubtless to be wished that the power of prohibiting the importation of slaves, had not been postponed until the year 1808, or rather that it had been suffered to have immediate operation. But it is not difficult to account either for this restriction on the general government, or for the manner in which the whole clause is expressed. It ought to be considered as a great point gained in favor of humanity, that a period of twenty years may terminate for ever within these states, a traffic which has so long and so loudly upbraided the barbarism of modern policy; that within that period it will receive a considerable discouragement from the federal government, and may be totally abolished by a concurrence of the few states which continue the unnatural traffic, in the prohibitory example which has been given by so great a majority of the union. Happy would it be for the unfortunate Africans, if an equal prospect lay before them, of being redeemed from the oppressions of their European brethren!

Attempts have been made to pervert this clause into an objection against the constitution, by representing it on one side as a criminal toleration of an illicit practice, and on another, as calculated to prevent voluntary and beneficial emigrations from Europe to America. I mention these misconstructions, not with a view to give them an answer, for they deserve none; but as specimens of the manner and spirit in which some have thought fit to conduct their opposition to the proposed government.

The powers included in the *third* class, are those which provide for the harmony and proper intercourse among the states.

Under this head might be included the particular restraints imposed on the authority of the states, and certain powers of the judicial department; but the former are reserved for a distinct class, and the latter will be particularly examined when we arrive at the structure and organization of the government. I shall confine myself to a cursory review of the remaining powers comprehended under this third description, to wit, to regulate commerce among the several states and the Indian tribes; to coin money, regulate the value thereof and of foreign coin; to provide for the punishment of counterfeiting the current coin and securities of the United States; to fix the standard of weights and measures; to establish an uniform rule of naturalization, and uniform laws of bankruptcy; to prescribe the manner in which the public acts, records and judicial proceedings of each state shall be proved, and the effect they shall have in other states, and to establish post-offices and post-roads.

The defect of power in the existing confederacy, to regulate the commerce between its several members, is in the number of those which have been clearly pointed out by experience. To the proofs and remarks which former papers have brought into view on this subject, it may be added, that without this supplemental provision, the great and essential power of regulating foreign commerce, would have been incomplete, and ineffectual. A very material object of this power was the relief of the states which import and export through other states, from the improper contributions levied on them by the latter. Were these at liberty to regulate the trade between state and state, it must be foreseen that ways would be found out, to load the articles of import and export, during the passage through their jurisdiction, with duties which would fall on the makers of the latter, and the consumers of the former: We may be assured by past experience, that such a practice would be introduced by future contrivances; and both by that and a common knowledge of human affairs, that it would nourish unceasing animosities, and not improbably terminate in serious interruptions of the public tranquility. To those who do not view the question through the medium of passion or of interest, the desire of the commercial states to collect in any form, an indirect revenue from their uncommercial neighbours, must appear not less impolitic than it is unfair; since it would stimulate the injured party, by resentment as well as interest, to resort to less convenient channels for their foreign trade. But the mild voice of reason, pleading the cause of an enlarged and permanent interest, is but too often drowned before public bodies as well as individuals, by the clamours of an impatient avidity for immediate and immoderate gain.

The necessity of a superintending authority over the reciprocal trade of confederated states has been illustrated by other examples as well as our own. In Switzerland, where the union is so very slight, each canton is obliged to allow to merchandizes, a passage through its jurisdiction into other cantons, without an augmentation of the tolls. In Germany, it is a law of the empire, that the princes and states shall not lay tolls or customs on bridges, rivers, or passages, without the consent of the emperor and diet; though it appears from a quotation in an antecedent paper, that the practice in this as in many other instances in that confederacy, has not followed the law, and has produced there the mischiefs which have been foreseen here. Among the restraints imposed by the union of the Netherlands, on its members, one is, that they shall not establish imposts disadvantageous to their neighbours, without the general permission.

The regulation of commerce with the Indian tribes is very properly unfettered from two limitations in the articles of confederation, which render the provision obscure and contradictory. The power is there restrained to Indians, not members of any of the states, and is not to violate or infringe the legislative right of any state within its own limits. What description of Indians are to be deemed members of a state, is not yet settled; and has been a question of frequent perplexity and contention in the federal councils. And how the trade with Indians, though not members of a state, yet residing within its legislative jurisdiction, can be regulated by an external authority, without so far intruding on the internal rights of legislation, is absolutely incomprehensible. This is not the only case in which the articles of confederation have inconsiderately endeavoured to accomplish impossibilities; to reconcile a partial sovereignty in the union, with complete sovereignty in the states; to subvert a mathematical axiom, by taking away a part, and letting the whole remain.

All that need be remarked on the power to coin money, regulate the value thereof, and of foreign coin, is that by providing for this last case, the constitution has supplied a material omission in the articles of confederation. The authority of the existing congress is restrained to the regulation of coin *struck* by their own authority, or that of the respective states. It must be seen at once, that the proposed uniformity in the *value* of the current coin might be destroyed by subjecting that of foreign coin to the different regulations of the different states.

The punishment of counterfeiting the public securities as well as of the current coin, is submitted of course to that authority, which is to secure the value of both.

The regulation of weights and measures is transferred from the articles of confederation, and is founded on like considerations with the preceding power of regulating coin.

The dissimilarity in the rules of naturalization, has long been remarked as a fault in our system, and as laying a foundation for intricate and delicate questions. In the 4th article of the confederation, it is declared "that the *free inhabitants* of each of these states, paupers, vagabonds, and fugitives from justice excepted, shall be entitled to all privileges and immunities of *free citizens*, in the several states, and *the people* of each state, shall in every other, enjoy all the privileges of trade and commerce, &c." There is a confusion of language here, which is remarkable. Why the terms *free inhabitants*, are used in one part of the article; *free citizens* in another, and *people* in another, or what was meant by superadding "to all privileges and immunities of free citizens,"—"all the privileges of trade and commerce," cannot easily be determined. It seems to be a construction scarcely avoidable, however that those who come under the denomination of *free inhabitants* of a state, although not citizens of such state, are entitled in every other state to all the privileges of *free citizens* of the latter; that is, to greater privileges than they may be entitled to in their own state; so that it may be in the power of a particular state, or rather every state is laid under a necessity, not only to confer the rights of citizenship in other states upon any whom it may admit to such rights within itself; but upon any whom it may allow to become inhabitants within its jurisdiction. But were an exposition of the term "inhabitants" to be admitted, which would confine the stipulated privileges to citizens alone, the difficulty is diminished only, not removed. The very improper power would still be retained by each state, of naturalizing aliens in every other state. In one state residence for a short term confers all the rights of citizenship. In another qualifications of greater importance are required. An alien therefore legally incapacitated for certain rights in the latter, may by previous residence only in the former elude his incapacity; and thus the law of one state, be preposterously rendered paramount to the law of another within the jurisdiction of the other. We owe it to mere casualty, that very serious embarrassments on this subject have been hitherto escaped. By the laws of several states, certain descriptions of aliens who had rendered themselves obnoxious, were laid under interdicts inconsistent, not only with the rights of citizenship, but with the privileges of residence. What would have been the consequence, if such persons, by residence or otherwise, had acquired the character of citizens under the laws of another state, and then asserted their rights as such, both to residence and citizenship within the state proscribing them? Whatever the legal consequences might have been, other consequences would probably have resulted of too serious a nature, not to be provided against. The new constitution has accordingly with great propriety made provision against them, and all others proceeding from the defect of the confederation, on this head by authorising the general government to establish an uniform rule of naturalization throughout the United States.

The power of establishing uniform laws of bankruptcy, is so intimately connected with the regulation of commerce, and will prevent so many frauds where the parties or their property may lie or be removed into different states, that the expediency of it seems not likely to be drawn into question.

The power of prescribing by general laws the manner in which the public acts, records and judicial proceedings of each state shall be proved, and the effect they shall have in other states, is an evident and valuable improvement on the clause relating to this subject in the articles of confederation. The meaning of the latter is extremely indeterminate; and can be of little importance under any interpretation which it will bear. The power here established, may be rendered a very convenient instrument of justice, and be particularly beneficial on the borders of contiguous states, where the effects liable to justice, may be suddenly and secretly translated in any stage of the process, within a foreign jurisdiction.

The power of establishing post-roads, must in every view be a harmless power; and may perhaps, by judicious management, become productive of great public conveniency. Nothing which tends to facilitate the intercourse between the states, can be deemed unworthy of the public care.

January 22, 1788

The Federalist No. 43

The *fourth* class comprises the following miscellaneous powers:

1. A power to "promote the progress of science and useful arts, by securing for a limited time, to authors and inventors, the exclusive right to their respective writings and discoveries."

The utility of this power will scarcely be questioned. The copy right of authors has been solemnly adjudged in Great Britain, to be a right at common law. The right to useful inventions, seems with equal reason to belong to the inventors. The public good fully coincides in both cases, with the claims of individuals. The states cannot separately make effectual provision for either of the cases, and most of them have anticipated the decision of this point, by laws passed at the instance of congress.

2. "To exercise exclusive legislation in all cases whatsoever, over such district (not exceeding ten miles square) as may by cession of particular states, and the acceptance of congress, become the seat of the government of the United States; and to exercise like authority over all places purchased by the consent of the legislature of the states, in which the same shall be, for the erection of forts, magazines, arsenals, dock yards, and other needful buildings."

The indispensable necessity of compleat authority at the seat of government, carries its own evidence with it. It is a power exercised by every legislature of the union, I might say of the world, by virtue of its general supremacy. Without it, not only the public authority might be insulted and its proceedings be interrupted, with impunity; but a dependence of the members of the general government on the state, comprehending the seat of the government for protection in the exercise of their duty, might bring on the national councils an imputation of awe or influence, equally dishonorable to the government, and dissatisfactory to the other members of the confederacy. This consideration has the more weight as the gradual accumulation of public improvements at the stationary residence of the government, would be both too great a public pledge to be left in the hands of a single state; and would create so many obstacles to a removal of the government, as still further to abridge its necessary independence. The extent of this federal district is sufficiently circumscribed to satisfy every jealousy of an opposite nature. And as it is to be appropriated to this use with the consent of the state ceding it; as the state will no doubt provide in the compact for the rights, and the consent of the citizens inhabiting it; as the inhabitants will find sufficient inducements of interest to become willing parties to the cession; as they will have had their voice in the election of the government which is to exercise authority over them; as a municipal legislature for local purposes, derived from their own suffrages, will of course be allowed them; and as the authority of the legislature of the state, and of the inhabitants of the ceded part of it, to concur in the cession, will be derived from the whole people of the state, in their adoption of the constitution, every imaginable objection seems to be obviated.

The necessity of a like authority over forts, magazines, &c. established by the general government is not less evident. The public money expended on such places, and the public property deposited in them, require that they should be exempt from the authority of the particular state. Nor would it be proper for the places on which the security of the entire union may depend, to be in any degree dependent on a particular member of it. All objections and scruples are here also obviated by requiring the concurrence of the states concerned, in every such establishment.

3. "To declare the punishment of treason, but no attainder of treason shall work corruption of blood, or forfeiture, except during the life of the person attainted."

As treason may be committed against the United States, the authority of the United States ought to be enabled to punish it; but as new fangled and artificial treasons, have been the great engines, by which violent factions, the natural offspring of free governments, have usually wreaked their alternate malignity on each other, the convention have with great judgment opposed a barrier to this peculiar danger, by inserting a constitutional definition of the crime, fixing the proof necessary for conviction of it, and restraining the congress, even in punishing it, from extending the consequences of guilt beyond the person of its author.

4. "To admit new states into the union; but no new state shall be formed or erected within the jurisdiction of any other state; nor any state be formed by the junction of two or more states, or parts of states, without the consent of the legislatures of the states concerned, as well as of the congress."

In the articles of confederation no provision is found on this important subject. Canada was to be admitted of right on her joining in the measures of the United States; and the other *colonies*, by which were evidently meant, the other British colonies, at the discretion of nine states. The eventual establishment of *new states*, seems to have been overlooked by the compilers of that instrument. We have seen the inconvenience of this omission, and the assumption of power into which congress have been led by it. With great propriety therefore has the new system supplied the defect. The general precaution that no new states shall be formed without the concurrence of the federal authority and that of the states concerned, is consonant to the principles which ought to govern such transactions. The particular precaution against the erection of new states, by the partition of a state without its consent, quiets the jealousy of the larger states; as that of the smaller is quieted by a like precaution against a junction of states without their consent.

5. "To dispose of and make all needful rules and regulations respecting the territory or other property belonging to the United States, with a proviso that nothing in the constitution shall be so construed as to prejudice any claims of the United States, or of any particular state."

This is a power of very great importance, and required by considerations similar to those which shew the propriety of the former. The proviso annexed is proper in itself, and was probably rendered absolutely necessary, by jealousies and questions concerning the western territory, sufficiently known to the public.

6. "To guarantee to every state in the union a republican form of government; to protect each of them against invasion; and on application of the legislature, or of the executive

(when the legislature cannot be convened) against domestic violence."

In a confederacy founded on republican principles, and composed of republican members, the superintending government ought clearly to possess authority to defend the system against aristocratic or monarchical innovations. The more intimate the nature of such a union may be, the greater interest have the members in the political institutions of each other; and the greater right to insist that the forms of government under which the compact was entered into, should be *substantially* maintained. But a right implies a remedy; and where else could the remedy be deposited, than where it is deposited by the constitution? Governments of dissimilar principles and forms, have been found less adapted to a federal coalition of any sort, than those of a kindred nature. "As the confederate republic of Germany," says Montesquieu, "consists of free cities and petty states, subject to different princes, experience shews us that it is more imperfect than that of Holland and Switzerland." "Greece was undone," he adds, "as soon as the king of Macedon obtained a seat among the Amphyctions." In the latter case, no doubt, the disproportionate force, as well as the monarchical form of the new confederate, had its share of influence on the events. It may possibly be asked what need there could be of such a precaution, and whether it may not become a pretext for alterations in the state governments, without the concurrence of the states themselves. These questions admit of ready answers. If the interposition of the general government should not be needed, the provision for such an event will be a harmless superfluity only in the constitution. But who can say what experiments may be produced by the caprice of particular states, by the ambition of enterprizing leaders, or by the intrigues and influence of foreign powers? To the second question it may be answered, that if the general government should interpose by virtue of this constitutional authority, it will be of course bound to pursue the authority. But the authority extends no farther than to a *guaranty* of a republican form of government, which supposes a pre-existing government of the form which is to be guaranteed. As long therefore as the existing republican forms are continued by the states, they are guaranteed by the federal constitution. Whenever the states may chuse to substitute other republican forms, they have a right to do so, and to claim the federal guaranty for the latter. The only restriction imposed on them is, that they shall not exchange republican for anti-republican constitutions; a restriction which it is presumed will hardly be considered as a grievance.

A protection against invasion is due from every society to the parts composing it. The latitude of the expression here used, seems to secure each state not only against foreign hostility, but against ambitious or vindictive enterprizes of its more powerful neighbours. The history both of antient and modern confederacies, proves that the weaker members of the union ought not to be insensible to the policy of this article.

Protection against domestic violence is added with equal propriety. It has been remarked that even among the Swiss cantons, which properly speaking are not under one government, provision is made for this object; and the history of that league informs us, that mutual aid is frequently claimed and afforded; and as well by the most democratic, as the other cantons. A recent and well known event among ourselves, has warned us to be prepared for emergencies of a like nature.

At first view it might seem not to square with the republican theory, to suppose either that a majority have not the right, or that a minority will have the force to subvert a government; and consequently that the federal interposition can never be required but when it would be improper. But theoretic reasoning in this, as in most other cases, must be qualified by the lessons of practice. Why may not illicit combinations for purposes of violence be formed as well by a majority of a state, especially a small state, as by a majority of a county or a district of the same state; and if the authority of the state ought in the latter case to protect the local magistracy, ought not the federal authority in the former to support the state authority? Besides, there are certain parts of the state constitutions which are so interwoven with the federal constitution, that a violent blow cannot be given to the one without communicating the wound to the other. Insurrections in a state will rarely induce a federal interposition, unless the number concerned in them, bear some proportion to the friends of government. It will be much better that the violence in such cases should be repressed by the superintending power, than that the majority should be left to maintain their cause by a bloody and obstinate contest. The existence of a right to interpose will generally prevent the necessity of exerting it.

Is it true that force and right are necessarily on the same side in republican governments? May not the minor party possess such a superiority of pecuniary resources, of military talents and experience, or of secret succours from foreign powers, as will render it superior also in an appeal to the sword? May not a more compact and advantageous position turn the scale on the same side against a superior number so situated as to be less capable of a prompt and collected exertion of its strength? Nothing can be more chimerical than to imagine that in a trial of actual force, victory may be calculated by the rules which prevail in a census of the inhabitants, or which determine the event of an election! May it not happen in fine that the minority of *citizens* may become a majority of *persons*, by the accession of alien residents, of a casual concourse of adventurers, or of those whom the constitution of the state has not admitted to the rights of suffrage? I take no notice of an unhappy species of population abounding in some of the states, who during the calm of regular government are sunk below the level of men; but who in the tempestuous scenes of civil violence may emerge into the human character, and give a superiority of strength to any party with which they may associate themselves.

In cases where it may be doubtful on which side justice lies, what better umpires could be desired by two violent factions, flying to arms and tearing a state to pieces, than the representatives of confederate states not heated by the local flame? To the impartiality of judges they would unite the affection of friends. Happy would it be if such a remedy for its infirmities, could be enjoyed by all free governments; if a project equally effectual could be established for the universal peace of mankind.

Should it be asked what is to be the redress for an insurrection pervading all the states, and comprizing a superiority of the entire force, though not a constitutional right; the answer must be, that such a case, as it would be without the compass of human remedies, so it is fortunately not within the compass of human probability; and that it is a sufficient recommendation of the federal constitution, that it diminishes the risk of a calamity, for which no possible constitution can provide a cure.

Among the advantages of a confederate republic enumerated by Montesquieu, an important one is, "that should a popular insurrection happen in one of the states, the others are able to quell it. Should abuses creep into one part, they are reformed by those that remain sound."

7. "To consider all debts contracted and engagements entered into, before the adoption of this constitution, as being no less valid against the United States under this constitution, than under the confederation."

This can only be considered as a declaratory proposition; and may have been inserted, among other reasons, for the satisfaction of the foreign creditors of the United States, who cannot be strangers to the pretended doctrine that a change in the political form of civil society, has the magical effect of dissolving its moral obligations.

Among the lesser criticisms which have been exercised on the constitution, it has been remarked that the validity of engagements ought to have been asserted in favor of the United States, as well as against them; and in the spirit which usually characterises little critics, the omission has been transformed and magnified into a plot against the national rights. The authors of this discovery may be told, what few others need be informed of, that as engagements are in their nature reciprocal, an assertion of their validity on one side necessarily involves a validity on the other side; and that as the article is merely declaratory, the establishment of the principle in one case is sufficient for every case. They may be further told that every constitution must limit its precautions to dangers that are not altogether imaginary; and that no real danger can exist that the government would *dare*, with or even without this constitutional declaration before it, to remit the debts justly due to the public, on the pretext here condemned.

8. "To provide for amendments to be ratified by three-fourths of the states, under two exceptions only."

That useful alterations will be suggested by experience, could not but be foreseen. It was requisite therefore that a mode for introducing them should be provided. The mode preferred by the convention seems to be stamped with every mark of propriety. It guards equally against that extreme facility which would render the constitution too mutable; and that extreme difficulty which might perpetuate its discovered faults. It moreover equally enables the general and the state governments to originate the amendment of errors as they may be pointed out by the experience on one side or on the other. The exception in favor of the equality of suffrage in the senate was probably meant as a palladium to the residuary sovereignty of the states, implied and secured by that principle of representation in one branch of the legislature; and was probably insisted on by the states particularly attached to that equality. The other exception must have been admitted on the same considerations which produced the privilege defended by it.

9. "The ratification of the conventions of nine states shall be sufficient for the establishment of this constitution between the states ratifying the same."

This article speaks for itself. The express authority of the people alone could give due validity to the constitution. To have required the unanimous ratification of the thirteen states, would have subjected the essential interests of the whole to the caprice or corruption of a single member. It would have marked a want of foresight in the convention, which our own experience would have rendered inexcuseable.

Two questions of a very delicate nature present themselves on this occasion. 1. On what principle the confederation, which stands in the solemn form of a compact among the states, can be superceded without the unanimous consent of the parties to it? 2. What relation is to subsist between the nine or more states ratifying the constitution, and the remaining few who do not become parties to it.

The first question is answered at once by recurring to the absolute necessity of the case; to the great principle of self preservation; to the transcendent law of nature and of nature's God, which declares that the safety and happiness of society, are the objects at which all political institutions aim, and to which all such institutions must be sacrificed. *Perhaps* also an answer may be found without searching beyond the principles of the compact itself. It has been heretofore noted among the defects of the confederation, that in many of the states, it had received no higher sanction than a mere legislative ratification. The principle of reciprocality seems to require, that its obligation on the other states should be reduced to the same standard. A compact between independent sovereigns, founded on acts of legislative authority, can pretend to no higher validity than a league or treaty between the parties. It is an established doctrine on the subject of treaties that all the articles are mutually conditions of each other; that a breach of any one article is a breach of the whole treaty; and that a breach committed by either of the parties absolves the others; and authorises them, if they please, to pronounce the compact violated and void. Should it unhappily be necessary to appeal to these delicate truths for a justification for dispensing with the consent of particular states to a dissolution of the federal pact, will not the complaining parties find it a difficult task to answer the *multiplied* and *important* infractions with which they may be confronted? The time has been when it was incumbent on us all to veil the ideas which this paragraph exhibits. The scene is now changed and with it, the part which the same motives dictate.

The second question is not less delicate; and the flattering prospect of its being merely hypothetical, forbids an over-curious discussion of it. It is one of those cases which must be left to provide for itself. In general it may be observed, that although no political relation can subsist between the assenting and dissenting states, yet the moral relations will remain uncancelled. The claims of justice, both on one side and on the other, will be in force, and must be fulfilled; the rights of humanity must in all cases be duly and mutually respected; whilst considerations of a common interest, and above all the remembrance of the endearing scenes which are past, and the anticipation of a speedy triumph over the obstacles to reunion, will, it is hoped, not urge in vain *moderation* on one side, and *prudence* on the other.

January 23, 1788

The Federalist No. 44

A *Fifth* class of provisions in favor of the federal authority, consists of the following restrictions on the authority of the several states.

1. "No state shall enter into any treaty, alliance or confederation, grant letters of marque and reprisal, coin money, emit bills of credit, make any thing but gold and silver a legal tender in payment of debts; pass any bill of attainder, *ex post facto* law, or law impairing the obligation of contracts, or grant any title of nobility."

The prohibition against treaties, alliances and confederations, makes a part of the existing articles of union; and for reasons which need no explanation, is copied into the new constitution. The prohibition of letters of marque is another part of the old system, but is somewhat extended in the new. According to the former, letters of marque could be granted by the states, after a declaration of war. According to the latter, these licences must be obtained as well during war as previous to its declaration, from the government of the United States. This alteration is fully justified by the advantage of uniformity in all points which relate to foreign powers; and of immediate responsibility to the nation in all those, for whose conduct the nation itself is to be responsible.

The right of coining money, which is here taken from the states, was left in their hands by the confederation as a concurrent right with that of congress, under an exception in favor of the exclusive right of congress to regulate the alloy and value. In this instance also the new provision is an improvement on the old. Whilst the alloy and value depended on the general authority, a right of coinage in the particular states could have no other effect than to multiply expensive mints, and diversify the forms and weights of the circulating pieces. The latter inconveniency defeats one purpose for which the power was originally submitted to the federal head. And as far as the former might prevent an inconvenient remittance of gold and silver to the central mint for recoinage, the end can be as well attained by local mints established under the general authority.

The extension of the prohibition to bills of credit must give pleasure to every citizen in proportion to his love of justice, and his knowledge of the true springs of public prosperity. The loss which America has sustained since the peace, from the pestilent effects of paper money, on the necessary confidence between man and man; on the necessary confidence in the public councils; on the industry and morals of the people, and on the character of republican government, constitutes an enormous debt against the states chargeable with this unadvised measure, which must long remain unsatisfied; or rather an accumulation of guilt, which can be expiated no otherwise than by a voluntary sacrifice on the altar of justice, of the power which has been the instrument of it. In addition to these persuasive considerations, it may be observed that the same reasons which shew the necessity of denying to the states the power of regulating coin, prove with equal force that they ought not to be at liberty to substitute a paper medium in the place of coin. Had every state a right to regulate the value of its coin, there might be as many different currencies as states; and thus the intercourse among them would be impeded; retrospective alterations in its value might be made, and thus the citizens of other states be injured, and animosities be kindled among the states themselves. The subjects of foreign powers might suffer from the same cause, and hence the union be discredited and embroiled by the indiscretion of a single member. No one of these mischiefs is less incident to a power in the states to emit paper money, than to coin gold or silver. The power to make any thing but gold and silver a tender in payment of debts, is withdrawn from the states, on the same principle with that of striking of paper currency.

Bills of attainder, *ex post facto* laws, and laws impairing the obligation of contracts, are contrary to the first principles of the social compact, and to every principle of sound legislation. The two former are expressly prohibited by the declarations prefixed to some of the state constitutions, and all of them are prohibited by the spirit and scope of these fundamental charters. Our own experience has taught us nevertheless, that additional fences against these dangers ought not to be omitted. Very properly therefore have the convention added this constitutional bulwark in favor of personal security and private rights; and I am much deceived if they have not in so doing as faithfully consulted the genuine sentiments, as the undoubted interests of their constituents. The sober people of America are weary of the fluctuating policy which has directed the public councils. They have seen with regret and with indignation, that sudden changes and legislative interferences in cases affecting personal rights, become jobs in the hands of enterprizing and influential speculators; and snares to the more industrious and less informed part of the community. They have seen too, that one legislative interference is but the first link of a long chain of repetitions; every subsequent interference being naturally produced by the effects of the preceding. They very rightly infer, therefore, that some thorough reform is wanting which will banish speculations on public measures, inspire a general prudence and industry, and give a regular course to the business of society. The prohibition with respect to titles of nobility, is copied from the articles of confederation and needs no comment.

2. "No state shall, without the consent of the congress, lay any imposts or duties on imports or exports, except what may be absolutely necessary for executing its inspection laws, and the neat produce of all duties and imposts laid by any state on imports or exports, shall be for the use of the treasury of the United States; and all such laws shall be subject to the revision and controul of the congress. No state shall, without the consent of congress, lay any duty on tonnage, keep troops or ships of war in time of peace; enter into any agreement or compact with another state, or with a foreign power, or engage in war, unless actually invaded, or in such imminent danger as will not admit of delay."

The restraint on the power of the states over imports and exports is enforced by all the arguments which prove the necessity of submitting the regulation of trade to the federal councils. It is needless therefore to remark further on this head, than that the manner in which the restraint is qualified, seems well calculated at once to secure to the states a reasonable discretion in providing for the conveniency of their imports and exports, and to the United States a reasonable check against the abuse of this discretion. The remaining particulars of this clause, fall within reasonings which are either so obvious, or have been so fully developed, that they may be passed over without remark.

The sixth and last class consists of the several powers and provisions by which efficacy is given to all the rest.

1. "Of these the first is the power to make all laws which shall be necessary and proper for carrying into execution the foregoing powers, and all other powers vested by this constitution in the government of the United States."

Few parts of the constitution have been assailed with more intemperance than this; yet on a fair investigation of it, as has been elsewhere shewn, no part can appear more completely invulnerable. Without the *substance* of this power, the whole constitution would be a dead letter. Those who object to the article therefore as a part of the constitution, can only mean that the *form* of the provision is improper. But have they considered whether a better form could have been substituted?

There are four other possible methods which the convention might have taken on this subject. They might have copied the second article of the existing confederation which would have prohibited the exercise of any power not *expressly* delegated; they might have attempted a positive enumeration of the powers comprehended under the general terms "necessary and proper"; they might have attempted a negative enumeration of them, by specifying the powers excepted from the general definition: They might have been altogether silent on the subject; leaving these necessary and proper powers, to construction and inference.

Had the convention taken the first method of adopting the second article of confederation; it is evident that the new congress would be continually exposed as their predecessors have been, to the alternative of construing the term "*expressly*" with so much rigour as to disarm the government of all real authority whatever, or with so much latitude as to destroy altogether the force of the restriction. It would be easy to shew if it were necessary, that no important power, delegated by the articles of confederation, has been or can be executed by congress, without recurring more or less to the doctrine of *construction* or *implication*. As the powers delegated under the new system are more extensive, the government which is to administer it would find itself still more distressed with the alternative of betraying the public interest by doing nothing; or of violating the constitution by exercising powers indispensably necessary and proper; but at the same time, not *expressly* granted.

Had the convention attempted a positive enumeration of the powers necessary and proper for carrying their other powers into effect; the attempt would have involved a compleat digest of laws on every subject to which the constitution relates; accommodated too not only to the existing state of things, but to all the possible changes which futurity may produce: For in every new application of a general power, the *particular powers*, which are the means of attaining the *object* of the general power, must always necessarily vary with that object; and be often properly varied whilst the object remains the same.

Had they attempted to enumerate the particular powers or means, not necessary or proper for carrying the general powers into execution, the task would have been no less chimerical; and would have been liable to this further objection; that every defect in the enumeration, would have been equivalent to a positive grant of authority. If to avoid this consequence they had attempted a partial enumeration of the exceptions and described the residue by the general terms, *not necessary or proper*: It must have happened that the enumeration would comprehend a few of the excepted powers only; that these would be such as would be least likely to be assumed or tolerated because the enumeration would of course select such as would be least necessary or proper, and that the unnecessary and improper powers included in the residuum, would be less forcibly excepted, than if no partial enumeration had been made.

Had the constitution been silent on this head, there can be no doubt that all the particular powers, requisite as means of executing the general powers, would have resulted to the government, by unavoidable implication. No axiom is more clearly established in law, or in reason, than that wherever the end is required, the means are authorised; wherever a general power to do a thing is given, every particular power necessary for doing it, is included. Had this last method therefore been pursued by the convention, every objection now urged against their plan, would remain in all its plausibility; and the real inconveniency would be incurred, of not removing a pretext which may be seized on critical occasions for drawing into question the essential powers of the union.

If it be asked, what is to be the consequence, in case the congress shall misconstrue this part of the constitution, and exercise powers not warranted by its true meaning? I answer the same as if they should misconstrue or enlarge any other power vested in them, as if the general power had been reduced to particulars, and any one of these were to be violated; the same in short, as if the state legislatures should violate their respective constitutional authorities. In the first instance, the success of the usurpation will depend on the executive and judiciary departments, which are to expound and give effect to the legislative acts; and in the last resort, a remedy must be obtained from the people, who can by the election of more faithful representatives, annul the acts of the usurpers. The truth is, that this ultimate redress may be more confided in against unconstitutional acts of the federal than of the state legislatures, for this plain reason, that as every such act of the former, will be an invasion of the rights of the latter, these will be ever ready to mark the innovation, to sound the alarm to the people, and to exert their local influence in effecting a change of federal representatives. There being no such intermediate body between the state legislatures and the people, interested in watching the conduct of the former, violations of the state constitution are more likely to remain unnoticed and unredressed.

2. "This constitution and the laws of the United States which shall be made in pursuance thereof, and all treaties made, or which shall be made, under the authority of the United States, shall be the supreme law of the land, and the judges in every state shall be bound thereby, any thing in the constitution or laws of any state to the contrary notwithstanding."

The indiscreet zeal of the adversaries to the constitution, has betrayed them into an attack on this part of it also, without which it would have been evidently and radically defective. To be fully sensible of this we need only suppose for a moment, that the supremacy of the state constitutions had been left compleat by a saving clause in their favor.

In the first place, as these constitutions invest the state legislatures with absolute sovereignty, in all cases not excepted by the existing articles of confederation, all the authorities contained in the proposed constitution, so far as they exceed those enumerated in the confederation, would have been annulled, and the new congress would have been reduced to the same impotent condition with their predecessors.

In the next place, as the constitutions of some of the states do not even expressly and fully recognize the existing powers of the confederacy, an express saving of the supremacy of the former, would in such states have brought into question, every power contained in the proposed constitution.

In the third place, as the constitutions of the states differ much from each other, it might happen that a treaty or national law of great and equal importance to the states, would interfere with some and not with other constitutions, and would consequently be valid in some of the states at the same time that it would have no effect in others.

In fine, the world would have seen for the first time, a system of government founded on an inversion of the fundamental principles of all government; it would have seen the authority of the whole society every where subordinate to the authority of the parts; it would have seen a monster in which the head was under the direction of the members.

3. "The senators and representatives, and the members of the several state legislatures; and all executive and judicial officers, both of the United States, and the several states shall be bound by oath or affirmation, to support this constitution."

It has been asked, why it was thought necessary, that the state magistracy should be bound to support the federal constitution, and unnecessary that a like oath should be imposed on the officers of the United States in favour of the state constitutions?

Several reasons might be assigned for the distinctions. I content myself with one which is obvious and conclusive. The members of the federal government will have no agency in carrying the state constitutions into effect. The members and officers of the state governments, on the contrary, will have an essential agency in giving effect to the federal constitution. The election of the president and senate, will depend in all cases, on the legislatures of the several states. And the election of the house of representatives, will equally depend on the same authority in the first instance; and will probably, for ever be conducted by the officers and according to the laws of the states.

4. Among the provisions for giving efficacy to the federal powers, might be added, those which belong to the executive and judiciary departments: But as these are reserved for particular examination in another place, I pass them over in this.

We have now reviewed in detail all the articles composing the sum or quantity of power delegated by the proposed constitution to the federal government; and are brought to this undeniable conclusion, that no part of the power is unnecessary or improper for accomplishing the necessary objects of the union. The question therefore, whether this amount of power shall be granted or not, resolves itself into another question, whether or not a government commensurate to the exigencies of the union, shall be established; or in other words, whether the union itself shall be preserved.

January 25, 1788

The Federalist No. 45

Having shewn that no one of the powers transferred to the federal government is unnecessary or improper, the next question to be considered is whether the whole mass of them will be dangerous to the portion of authority left in the several states.

The adversaries to the plan of the convention instead of considering in the first place what degree of power was absolutely necessary for the purposes of the federal government, have exhausted themselves in a secondary enquiry into the possible consequences of the proposed degree of power, to the governments of the particular states. But if the union, as has been shewn, be essential, to the security of the people of America against foreign danger; if it be essential to their security against contentions and wars among the different states; if it be essential to guard them against those violent and oppressive factions which imbitter the blessings of liberty, and against those military establishments which must gradually poison its very fountain; if, in a word the union be essential to the happiness of the people of America, is it not preposterous, to urge as an objection to a government without which the objects of the union cannot be attained, that such a government may derogate from the importance of the governments of the individual states? Was then the American revolution effected, was the American confederacy formed, was the precious blood of thousands spilt, and the hard earned substance of millions lavished, not that the people of America should enjoy peace, liberty, and safety; but that the governments of the individual states, that particular municipal establishments might enjoy a certain extent of power, and be arrayed with certain dignities and attributes of sovereignty? We have heard of the impious doctrine in the old world that the people were made for kings, not kings for the people. Is the same doctrine to be revived in the new, in another shape, that the solid happiness of the people is to be sacrificed to the views of political institutions of a different form? It is too early for politicians to presume on our forgetting that the public good, the real welfare of the great body of the people is the supreme object to be pursued; and that no form of government whatever, has any other value, than as it may be fitted for the attainment of this object. Were the plan of the convention adverse to the public happiness, my voice would be, reject the plan. Were the union itself inconsistent with the public happiness, it would be, abolish the union. In like manner as far as the sovereignty of the states cannot be reconciled to the happiness of the people; the voice of every good citizen must be, let the former be sacrificed to the latter. How far the sacrifice is necessary, has been shewn. How far the unsacrificed residue will be endangered, is the question before us.

Several important considerations have been touched in the course of these papers, which discountenance the supposition that the operation of the federal government will by degrees prove fatal to the state governments. The more I revolve the subject the more fully I am persuaded that the balance is much more likely to be disturbed by the preponderancy of the last than of the first scale.

We have seen in all the examples of antient and modern confederacies, the strongest tendency continually betraying itself in the members to despoil the general government of its authorities, with a very ineffectual capacity in the latter to defend itself against the encroachments. Although in most of these examples, the system has been so dissimilar from that under consideration, as greatly to weaken any inference concerning the latter from the fate of the former; yet as the states will retain under the proposed constitution a very extensive portion of active sovereignty, the inference ought not to be wholly disregarded. In the Achæan league, it is probable that the federal head had a degree and species of power, which gave it a considerable likeness to the government framed by the convention. The Lycian confederacy, as far as its principles and form are transmitted, must have borne a still greater analogy to it. Yet history does not inform us that either of them ever degenerated or tended to degenerate into one consolidated government. On the contrary, we know that the ruin of one of them proceeded from the incapacity of the federal authority to prevent the dissentions, and finally the disunion of the subordinate authorities. These cases are the more worthy of our attention, as the external causes by which the component parts were pressed together, were much more numerous and powerful than in our case; and consequently, less powerful ligaments within, would be sufficient to bind the members to the head, and to each other.

In the feudal system we have seen a similar propensity exemplified. Notwithstanding the want of proper sympathy in every instance between the local sovereigns and the people, and the sympathy in some instances between the general sovereign and the latter; it usually happened that the local sovereigns prevailed in the rivalship for encroachments. Had no external dangers enforced internal harmony and subordination; and particularly had the local sovereigns possessed the affections of the people, the great kingdoms in Europe, would at this time consist of as many independent princes as there were formerly feudatory barons.

The state governments will have the advantage of the federal government, whether we compare them in respect to the immediate dependence of the one on the other; to the weight of personal influence which each side will possess; to the powers respectively vested in them; to the predilection and probable support of the people; to the disposition and faculty of resisting and frustrating the measures of each other.

The state governments may be regarded as constituent and essential parts of the federal government; whilst the latter is no wise essential to the operation or organisation of the former. Without the intervention of the state legislatures, the president of the United States cannot be elected at all. They must in all cases have a great share in his appointment, and will perhaps in most cases of themselves determine it. The senate will be elected absolutely and exclusively by the state legislatures. Even the house of representatives, though drawn immediately from the people, will be chosen very much under the influence of that class of men, whose influence over the people obtains for themselves an election into the state legislatures. Thus each of the principal branches of the federal government will owe its existence more or less to the favor of the state governments, and must consequently feel a dependence, which is much more likely to beget a disposition too obsequious, than too overbearing towards them. On the other side, the component parts of the state governments will in no instance be indebted for their appointment to the direct agency of the federal government, and very little if at all, to the local influence of its members.

The number of individuals employed under the constitution of the United States, will be much smaller, than the number employed under the particular states. There will consequently be less of personal influence on the side of the former, than of the latter. The members of the legislative, executive and judiciary departments of thirteen and more states; the justices of peace, officers of militia, ministerial officers of justice, with all the county corporation and town officers, for three millions and more of people, intermixed and having particular acquaintance with every class and circle of people, must exceed beyond all proportion, both in number and influence, those of every description who will be employed in the administration of the federal system. Compare the members of the three great departments, of the Thirteen States, excluding from the judiciary department the justices of peace, with the members of the corresponding departments of the single government of the union; compare the militia officers of three millions of people, with the military and marine officers of any establishment which is within the compass of probability, or I may add, of possibility, and in this view alone, we may pronounce the advantage of the states to be decisive. If the federal government is to have collectors of revenue, the state governments will have theirs also. And as those of the former will be principally on the sea-coast, and not very numerous; whilst those of the latter will be spread over the face of the country, and will be very numerous, the advantage in this view also lies on the same side. It is true that the confederacy is to possess, and may exercise, the power of collecting internal as well as external taxes throughout the states: But it is probable that this power will not be resorted to, except for supplemental purposes of revenue; that an option will then be given to the states to supply their quotas by previous collections of their own; and that the eventual collection under the immediate authority of the union, will generally be made by the officers, and according to the rules, appointed by the several states. Indeed it is extremely probable that in other instances, particularly in the organization of the judicial power,

the officers of the states will be cloathed with the correspondent authority of the union. Should it happen however that
separate collectors of internal revenue should be appointed
under the federal government, the influence of the whole
number would not be a comparison with that of the multitude of state-officers in the opposite scale. Within every district, to which a federal collector would be allotted, there
would not be less than thirty or forty or even more officers of
different descriptions and many of them persons of character
and weight, whose influence would lie on the side of the
state.

The powers delegated by the proposed constitution to the
federal government, are few and defined. Those which are to
remain in the state governments are numerous and indefinite.
The former will be exercised principally on external objects, as
war, peace, negociation, and foreign commerce; with which
last the power of taxation will for the most part be connected.
The powers reserved to the several states will extend to all the
objects, which, in the ordinary course of affairs, concern the
lives, liberties and properties of the people; and the internal
order, improvement and prosperity of the state.

The operations of the federal government will be most extensive and important in times of war and danger; those of
the state governments, in times of peace and security. As the
former periods will probably bear a small proportion to the
latter, the state governments will here enjoy another advantage over the federal government. The more adequate indeed
the federal powers may be rendered to the national defence,
the less frequent will be those scenes of danger which might
favour their ascendancy over the governments of the particular states.

If the new constitution be examined with accuracy and candour, it will be found that the change which it proposes, consists much less in the addition of NEW POWERS to the union,
than in the invigoration of its ORIGINAL POWERS. The regulation of commerce, it is true, is a new power; but that seems
to be an addition which few oppose, and from which no apprehensions are entertained. The powers relating to war and
peace, armies and fleets, treaties and finance, with the other
more considerable powers, are all vested in the existing con-

gress by the articles of confederation. The proposed change does not enlarge these powers; it only substitutes a more effectual mode of administering them. The change relating to taxation, may be regarded as the most important: and yet the present congress have as compleat authority to REQUIRE of the states indefinite supplies of money for the common defence and general welfare, as the future congress will have to require them of individual citizens; and the latter will be no more bound than the states themselves have been, to pay the quotas respectively taxed on them. Had the states complied punctually with the articles of confederation, or could their compliance have been enforced by as peaceable means as may be used with success towards single persons, our past experience is very far from countenancing an opinion that the state governments would have lost their constitutional powers, and have gradually undergone an entire consolidation. To maintain that such an event would have ensued, would be to say at once, that the existence of the state governments is incompatible with any system whatever that accomplishes the essential purposes of the union.

January 26, 1788

The Federalist No. 46

Resuming the subject of the last paper I proceed to enquire whether the federal government or the state governments will have the advantage with regard to the predilection and support of the people. Notwithstanding the different modes in which they are appointed, we must consider both of them, as substantially dependent on the great body of the citizens of the United States. I assume this position here as it respects the first, reserving the proofs for another place. The federal and state governments are in fact but different agents and trustees of the people, instituted with different powers, and designated for different purposes. The adversaries of the constitution seem to have lost sight of the people altogether in their reasonings on this subject; and to have viewed these different establishments, not only as mutual rivals and enemies, but as uncontrouled by any common superior in their efforts to usurp the authorities of each other. These gentlemen must here be reminded of their error. They must be told that the ultimate authority, wherever the derivative may be found, resides in the people alone; and that it will not depend merely on the comparative ambition or address of the different governments, whether either, or which of them, will be able to enlarge its sphere of jurisdiction at the expence of the other. Truth no less than decency requires, that the event in every case should be supposed to depend on the sentiments and sanction of their common constituents.

Many considerations, besides those suggested on a former occasion, seem to place it beyond doubt, that the first and most natural attachment of the people will be to the governments of their respective states. Into the administration of these, a greater number of individuals will expect to rise. From the gift of these, a greater number of offices and emoluments will flow. By the superintending care of these, all the more domestic and personal interests of the people will be regulated and provided for. With the affairs of these, the people will be more familiarly and minutely conversant. And with the members of these, will a greater proportion of the people have the ties of personal acquaintance and friendship, and of family and party attachments; on the side of these, therefore, the popular bias may well be expected most strongly to incline.

Experience speaks the same language in this case. The federal administration, though hitherto very defective, in comparison with what may be hoped under a better system, had during the war, and particularly, whilst the independent fund of paper emissions was in credit, an activity and importance as great as it can well have, in any future circumstances whatever. It was engaged too in a course of measures, which had for their object, the protection of every thing that was dear, and the acquisition of every thing that could be desirable to the people at large. It was nevertheless, invariably found, after the transient enthusiasm for the early congresses was over, that the attention and attachment of the people were turned anew to their own particular governments; that the federal council was at no time the idol of popular favor; and that opposition to proposed enlargements of its powers and importance, was the side usually taken by the men who wished to build their political consequence on the prepossessions of their fellow citizens.

If therefore, as has been elsewhere remarked, the people should in future become more partial to the federal than to the state governments, the change can only result from such manifest and irresistible proofs of a better administration, as will overcome all their antecedent propensities. And in that case, the people ought not surely to be precluded from giving most of their confidence where they may discover it to be most due: But even in that case, the state governments could have little to apprehend, because it is only within a certain sphere, that the federal power can, in the nature of things, be advantageously administered.

The remaining points on which I proposed to compare the federal and state governments, are the disposition, and the faculty they may respectively possess, to resist and frustrate the measures of each other.

It has been already proved, that the members of the federal will be more dependent on the members of the state governments, than the latter will be on the former. It has appeared also, that the prepossessions of the people on whom both will depend, will be more on the side of the state governments, than of the federal government. So far as the disposition of each, towards the other, may be influenced by these causes, the state governments must clearly have the advantage. But in a distinct and very important point of view, the advantage will lie on the same side. The prepossessions which the members themselves will carry into the federal government, will generally be favorable to the states; whilst it will rarely happen, that the members of the state governments will carry into the public councils, a bias in favor of the general government. A local spirit will infallibly prevail much more in the members of the congress, than a national spirit will prevail in the legislatures of the particular states. Every one knows that a great proportion of the errors committed by the state legislatures proceeds from the disposition of the members to sacrifice the comprehensive and permanent interests of the state, to the particular and separate views of the counties or districts in which they reside. And if they do not sufficiently enlarge their policy to embrace the collective welfare of their particular state, how can it be imagined, that they will make the aggregate prosperity of the union, and the dignity and respectability of its government, the objects of their affections and consultations? For the same reason, that the members of the state legislatures will be unlikely to attach themselves sufficiently to national objects, the members of the federal legislature will be likely to attach themselves too much to local objects. The states will be to the latter, what counties and towns are to the former. Measures will too often be decided according to their probable effect, not on the national prosperity and happiness, but on the prejudices, interests and pursuits of the governments and people of the individual states. What is the spirit that has in general characterized the proceedings of congress? A perusal of their journals as well as the candid acknowledgments of such as have had a seat in that assembly, will inform us, that the members have but too frequently displayed the character, rather of partizans of their respective states, than of impartial guardians of a common interest; that where, on one occasion, improper sacrifices have been made of local considerations to the aggrandizement of the federal government; the great interests of the nation have suffered on an hundred, from an undue attention to the local prejudices, interests and views of the particular states. I mean not by these reflections to insinuate, that the new federal government will not embrace a more enlarged plan of policy than the existing government may have pursued, much less that its views will be as confined as those of the state legislatures; but only that it will partake sufficiently of the spirit of both, to be disinclined to invade the rights of the individual states, or the prerogatives of their governments. The motives on the part of the state governments, to augment their prerogatives by defalcations from the federal government, will be over-ruled by no reciprocal predispositions in the members.

Were it admitted however that the federal government may feel an equal disposition with the state governments to extend its power beyond the due limits, the latter would still have the advantage in the means of defeating such encroachments. If an act of a particular state, though unfriendly to the national government, be generally popular in that state, and should not too grossly violate the oaths of the state officers, it is executed immediately, and of course, by means on the spot, and depending on the state alone. The opposition of the federal government, or the interposition of federal officers, would but inflame the zeal of all parties on the side of the state, and the evil could not be prevented or repaired, if at all, without the employment of means which must always be resorted to with reluctance and difficulty. On the other hand, should an unwarrantable measure of the federal government be unpopular in particular states, which would seldom fail to be the case, or even a warrantable measure be so, which may sometimes be the case, the means of opposition to it are powerful and at hand. The disquietude of the people, their repugnance and perhaps refusal to co-operate with the officers of the union, the frowns of the executive magistracy of the state, the embarrassments created by legislative devices, which would often be added on such occasions, would oppose in any state difficulties not to be despised; would form in a large state very serious impediments, and where the sentiments of several adjoining states happened to be in unison, would present obstructions which the federal government would hardly be willing to encounter.

But ambitious encroachments of the federal government, on the authority of the state governments, would not excite the opposition of a single state or of a few states only. They would be signals of general alarm. Every government would espouse the common cause. A correspondence would be opened. Plans of resistance would be concerted. One spirit would animate and conduct the whole. The same combination in short would result from an apprehension of the federal, as was produced by the dread of a foreign yoke; and unless the projected innovations should be voluntarily renounced, the same appeal to a trial of force would be made in the one case, as was made in the other. But what degree of madness could ever drive the federal government to such an extremity? In the contest with Great-Britain, one part of the empire was employed against the other. The more numerous part invaded the rights of the less numerous part. The attempt was unjust and unwise; but it was not in speculation absolutely chimerical. But what would be the contest in the case we are supposing? Who would be the parties? A few representatives of the people would be opposed to the people themselves; or rather one set of representatives would be contending against thirteen sets of representatives, with the whole body of their common constituents on the side of the latter.

The only refuge left for those who prophecy the downfall of the state governments, is the visionary supposition that the federal government may previously accumulate a military force for the projects of ambition. The reasonings contained in these papers must have been employed to little purpose indeed, if it could be necessary now to disprove the reality of this danger. That the people and the states should for a sufficient period of time elect an uninterrupted succession of men ready to betray both; that the traitors should throughout this period, uniformly and systematically pursue some fixed plan for the extension of the military establishment; that the governments and the people of the states should silently and patiently behold the gathering storm, and continue to supply the materials, until it should be prepared to burst on their own heads, must appear to every one more like the incoherent dreams of a delirious jealousy, or the misjudged exaggerations of a counterfeit zeal, than like the sober apprehensions of genuine patriotism. Extravagant as the supposition is, let it however be made. Let a regular army, fully equal to the resources of the country be formed; and let it be entirely at the devotion of the federal government; still it would not be going too far to say, that the state governments with the people on their side would be able to repel the danger. The highest number to which, according to the best computation, a standing army can be carried in any country, does not exceed one hundredth part of the whole number of souls; or one twenty-fifth part of the number able to bear arms. This proportion would not yield in the United States an army of more than twenty-five or thirty thousand men. To these would be opposed a militia amounting to near half a million of citizens with arms in their hands, officered by men chosen from among themselves, fighting for their common liberties, and united and conducted by governments possessing their affections and confidence. It may well be doubted whether a militia thus circumstanced could ever be conquered by such a proportion of regular troops. Those who are best acquainted with the late successful resistance of this country against the British arms will be most inclined to deny the possibility of it. Besides the advantage of being armed, which the Americans possess over the people of almost every other nation, the existence of subordinate governments to which the people are attached, and by which the militia officers are appointed, forms a barrier against the enterprizes of ambition, more insurmountable than any which a simple government of any form can admit of. Notwithstanding the military establishments in the several kingdoms of Europe, which are carried as far as the public resources will bear, the governments are afraid to trust the people with arms. And it is not certain that with this aid alone, they would not be able to shake off their yokes. But were the people to possess the additional advantages of local governments chosen by themselves, who could collect the national will, and direct the national force, and of officers appointed out of the militia, by these governments and attached both to them and to the militia, it may be affirmed with the greatest assurance that the throne of every tyranny in Europe would be speedily overturned, in spite of the legions which surround it. Let us not insult the free and gallant citizens of America with the suspicion that they would be less able to defend the rights of which they would be in actual possession, than the debased subjects of arbitrary power would be to rescue theirs from the hands of their oppressors. Let us rather no longer insult them with the supposition, that they can ever reduce themselves to the necessity of making the experiment, by a blind and tame submission to the long train of insidious measures, which must precede and produce it.

The argument under the present head may be put into a very concise form, which appears altogether conclusive. Either the mode in which the federal government is to be constructed will render it sufficiently dependent on the people, or it will not. On the first supposition, it will be restrained by that dependence from forming schemes obnoxious to their constituents. On the other supposition it will not possess the confidence of the people, and its schemes of usurpation will be easily defeated by the state governments; who will be supported by the people.

On summing up the considerations stated in this and the last paper, they seem to amount to the most convincing evidence, that the powers proposed to be lodged in the federal government, are as little formidable to those reserved to the individual states, as they are indispensably necessary to accomplish the purposes of the union; and that all those alarms which have been sounded, of a meditated and consequential annihilation of the state governments, must, on the most favorable interpretation, be ascribed to the chimerical fears of the authors of them.

January 29, 1788

The Federalist No. 47

Having reviewed the general form of the proposed government, and the general mass of power allotted to it; I proceed to examine the particular structure of this government, and the distribution of this mass of power among its constituent parts.

One of the principal objections inculcated by the more respectable adversaries to the constitution, is its supposed violation of the political maxim, that the legislative, executive and judiciary departments ought to be separate and distinct. In the structure of the federal government, no regard, it is said, seems to have been paid to this essential precaution in favor of liberty. The several departments of power are distributed and blended in such a manner, as at once to destroy all symmetry and beauty of form; and to expose some of the essential parts of the edifice to the danger of being crushed by the disproportionate weight of other parts.

No political truth is certainly of greater intrinsic value or is stamped with the authority of more enlightened patrons of liberty, than that on which the objection is founded. The accumulation of all powers legislative, executive and judiciary in the same hands, whether of one, a few or many, and whether hereditary, self appointed, or elective, may justly be pronounced the very definition of tyranny. Were the federal constitution therefore, really chargeable with this accumulation of power or with a mixture of powers, having a dangerous tendency to such an accumulation, no further arguments would be necessary to inspire a universal reprobation of the system. I persuade myself however, that it will be made apparent to every one, that the charge cannot be supported, and that the maxim on which it relies, has been totally misconceived and misapplied. In order to form correct ideas on this important subject, it will be proper to investigate the sense, in which the preservation of liberty requires, that the three great departments of power should be separate and distinct.

The oracle who is always consulted and cited on this subject, is the celebrated Montesquieu. If he be not the author of this invaluable precept in the science of politics, he has the

merit at least of displaying and recommending it most effectually to the attention of mankind. Let us endeavour in the
first place to ascertain his meaning on this point.

The British constitution was to Montesquieu, what Homer
has been to the didactic writers on epic poetry. As the latter
have considered the work of the immortal bard, as the perfect
model from which the principles and rules of the epic art were
to be drawn, and by which all similar works were to be
judged; so this great political critic appears to have viewed the
constitution of England as the standard, or to use his own
expression, as the mirror of political liberty; and to have delivered in the form of elementary truths, the several characteristic principles of that particular system. That we may be
sure then not to mistake his meaning in this case, let us recur
to the source from which the maxim was drawn.

On the slightest view of the British constitution we must
perceive, that the legislative, executive, and judiciary departments are by no means totally separate and distinct from each
other. The executive magistrate forms an integral part of the
legislative authority. He alone has the prerogative of making
treaties with foreign sovereigns, which when made, have,
under certain limitations, the force of legislative acts. All the
members of the judiciary department are appointed by him;
can be removed by him on the address of the two houses of
parliament, and form, when he pleases to consult them, one
of his constitutional councils. One branch of the legislative
department forms also, a great constitutional council to the
executive chief; as on another hand, it is the sole depositary of
judicial power in cases of impeachment, and is invested with
the supreme appellate jurisdiction, in all other cases. The
judges again are so far connected with the legislative department, as often to attend and participate in its deliberations,
though not admitted to a legislative vote.

From these facts by which Montesquieu was guided it may
clearly be inferred, that in saying, "there can be no liberty
where the legislative and executive powers are united in the
same person, or body of magistrates," or, "if the power of
judging be not separated from the legislative and executive
powers," he did not mean that these departments ought to
have no *partial agency* in, or no *control* over the acts of each

other. His meaning, as his own words import, and still more conclusively as illustrated by the example in his eye, can amount to no more than this, that where the *whole* power of one department is exercised by the same hands which possess the *whole* power of another department, the fundamental principles of a free constitution, are subverted. This would not have been the case in the constitution examined by him, if the king who is the sole executive magistrate, had possessed also the complete legislative power, or the supreme administration of justice; or if the entire legislative body, had possessed the supreme judiciary, or the supreme executive authority. This however is not among the vices of that constitution. The magistrate in whom the whole executive power resides cannot of himself make a law, though he can put a negative on every law, nor administer justice in person, though he has the appointment of those who do administer it. The judges can exercise no executive prerogative, though they are shoots from the executive stock, nor any legislative function, though they may be advised with by the legislative councils. The entire legislature, can perform no judiciary act; though by the joint act of two of its branches, the judges may be removed from their offices; and though one of its branches is possessed of the judicial power in the last resort. The entire legislature again can exercise no executive prerogative, though one of its branches* constitutes the supreme executive magistracy; and another, on the impeachment of a third, can try and condemn all the subordinate officers in the executive department.

The reasons on which Montesquieu grounds his maxim are a further demonstration of his meaning. "When the legislative and executive powers are united in the same person or body," says he, "there can be no liberty, because apprehensions may arise lest *the same* monarch or senate should *enact* tyrannical laws, to *execute* them in a tyrannical manner." Again "Were the power of judging joined with the legislative, the life and liberty of the subject would be exposed to arbitrary control, for *the judge* would then be *the legislator*. Were it joined to the executive power, *the judge* might behave with all the

*The King.

violence of *an oppressor*." Some of these reasons are more fully explained in other passages; but briefly stated as they are here, they sufficiently establish the meaning which we have put on this celebrated maxim of this celebrated author.

If we look into the constitutions of the several states, we find that notwithstanding the emphatical, and in some instances, the unqualified terms in which this axiom has been laid down, there is not a single instance in which the several departments of power have been kept absolutely separate and distinct. New-Hampshire, whose constitution was the last formed, seems to have been fully aware of the impossibility and inexpediency of avoiding any mixture whatever of these departments; and has qualified the doctrine by declaring "that the legislative, executive and judiciary powers ought to be kept as separate from, and independent of each other *as the nature of a free government will admit; or as is consistent with that chain of connection, that binds the whole fabric of the constitution in one indissoluble bond of unity and amity.*" Her constitution accordingly mixes these departments in several respects. The senate, which is a branch of the legislative department, is also a judicial tribunal for the trial of impeachments. The president who is the head of the executive department, is the presiding member also of the senate; and besides an equal vote in all cases, has a casting vote in case of a tie. The executive head is himself eventually elective every year by the legislative department; and his council is every year chosen by and from the members of the same department. Several of the officers of state are also appointed by the legislature. And the members of the judiciary department are appointed by the executive department.

The constitution of Massachusetts has observed a sufficient though less pointed caution in expressing this fundamental article of liberty. It declares, "that the legislative department shall never exercise the executive and judicial powers, or either of them: The executive shall never exercise the legislative and judicial powers, or either of them: The judicial shall never exercise the legislative and executive powers, or either of them." This declaration corresponds precisely with the doctrine of Montesquieu, as it has been explained, and is not in a single point violated by the plan of the convention. It goes no farther than to prohibit any one of the entire departments from exercising the powers of another department. In the very constitution to which it is prefixed, a partial mixture of powers has been admitted. The executive magistrate has a qualified negative on the legislative body; and the senate, which is a part of the legislature, is a court of impeachment for members both of the executive and judiciary departments. The members of the judiciary department again are appointable by the executive department, and removeable by the same authority, on the address of the two legislative branches. Lastly, a number of the officers of government are annually appointed by the legislative department. As the appointment to offices, particularly executive offices, is in its nature an executive function, the compilers of the constitution have in this last point at least, violated the rule established by themselves.

I pass over the constitutions of Rhode-Island and Connecticut, because they were formed prior to the revolution; and even before the principle under examination had become an object of political attention.

The constitution of New-York contains no declaration on this subject; but appears very clearly to have been framed with an eye to the danger of improperly blending the different departments. It gives nevertheless to the executive magistrate a partial controul over the legislative department; and what is more, gives a like controul to the judiciary department, and even blends the executive and judiciary departments in the exercise of this controul. In its council of appointment, members of the legislative are associated with the executive authority in the appointment of officers both executive and judiciary. And its court for the trial of impeachments and correction of errors, is to consist of one branch of the legislature and the principal members of the judiciary department.

The constitution of New-Jersey has blended the different powers of government more than any of the preceding. The governor, who is the executive magistrate, is appointed by the legislature; is chancellor and ordinary or surrogate of the state; is a member of the supreme court of appeals, and president with a casting vote, of one of the legislative branches. The same legislative branch acts again as executive council of the governor, and with him constitutes the court of appeals. The members of the judiciary department are appointed by the legislative department, and removeable by one branch of it, on the impeachment of the other.

According to the constitution of Pennsylvania, the president, who is head of the executive department, is annually elected by a vote in which the legislative department predominates. In conjunction with an executive council, he appoints the members of the judiciary department, and forms a court of impeachments for trial of all officers, judiciary as well as executive. The judges of the supreme court, and justices of the peace, seem also to be removeable by the legislature; and the executive power of pardoning in certain cases to be referred to the same department. The members of the executive council are made EX OFFICIO justices of peace throughout the state.

In Delaware, the chief executive magistrate is annually elected by the legislative department. The speakers of the two legislative branches are vice-presidents in the executive department. The executive chief, with six others, appointed three by each of the legislative branches, constitute the supreme court of appeals: He is joined with the legislative department in the appointment of the other judges. Throughout the states it appears that the members of the legislature may at the same time be justices of the peace. In this state, the members of one branch of it are EX OFFICIO justices of the peace; as are also the members of the executive council. The principal officers of the executive department are appointed by the legislative; and one branch of the latter forms a court of impeachments. All officers may be removed on address of the legislature.

Maryland has adopted the maxim in the most unqualified terms; declaring that the legislative, executive and judicial powers of government, ought to be forever separate and distinct from each other. Her constitution, notwithstanding makes the executive magistrate appointable by the legislative department; and the members of the judiciary, by the executive department.

The language of Virginia is still more pointed on this subject. Her constitution declares, "that the legislative, executive and judiciary departments, shall be separate and distinct; so that neither exercise the powers properly belonging to the other; nor shall any person exercise the powers of more than one of them at the same time; except that the justices of county courts shall be eligible to either house of assembly." Yet we find not only this express exception, with respect to the members of the inferior courts; but that the chief magistrate with his executive council are appointable by the legislature; that two members of the latter are triennially displaced at the pleasure of the legislature; and that all the principal officers, both executive and judiciary, are filled by the same department. The executive prerogative of pardoning, also is in one case vested in the legislative department.

The constitution of North-Carolina, which declares, "that the legislative, executive and supreme judicial powers of government, ought to be forever separate and distinct from each other," refers at the same time to the legislative department, the appointment not only of the executive chief, but all the principal officers within both that and the judiciary department.

In South-Carolina, the constitution makes the executive magistracy eligible by the legislative department. It gives to the latter also the appointment of the members of the judiciary department, including even justices of the peace and sheriffs; and the appointment of officers in the executive department, down to captains in the army and navy of the state.

In the constitution of Georgia, where it is declared, "that the legislative, executive and judiciary departments shall be separate and distinct, so that neither exercise the powers properly belonging to the other," we find that the executive department is to be filled by appointments of the legislature; and the executive prerogative of pardoning, to be finally exercised by the same authority. Even justices of the peace are to be appointed by the legislature.

In citing these cases in which the legislative, executive and judiciary departments have not been kept totally separate and distinct, I wish not to be regarded as an advocate for the particular organizations of the several state governments. I am fully aware that among the many excellent principles which they exemplify, they carry strong marks of the haste, and still stronger of the inexperience, under which they were framed. It is but too obvious that in some instances, the fundamental principle under consideration has been violated by too great a mixture, and even an actual consolidation of the different powers; and that in no instance has a competent provision been made for maintaining in practice the separation delineated on paper. What I have wished to evince is, that the charge brought against the proposed constitution, of violating a sacred maxim of free government, is warranted neither by the real meaning annexed to that maxim by its author; nor by the sense in which it has hitherto been understood in America. This interesting subject will be resumed in the ensuing paper.

January 30, 1788

The Federalist No. 48

It was shewn in the last paper, that the political apothegm there examined, does not require that the legislative, executive and judiciary departments should be wholly unconnected with each other. I shall undertake in the next place, to shew that unless these departments be so far connected and blended, as to give to each a constitutional controul over the others, the degree of separation which the maxim requires as essential to a free government, can never in practice be duly maintained.

It is agreed on all sides, that the powers properly belonging to one of the departments, ought not to be directly and compleatly administered by either of the other departments. It is equally evident, that neither of them ought to possess directly or indirectly, an over-ruling influence over the others in the administration of their respective powers. It will not be denied that power is of an encroaching nature, and that it ought to be effectually restrained from passing the limits, assigned to it. After discriminating therefore in theory, the several classes of power, as they may in their nature be legislative, executive or judiciary; the next and most difficult task, is to provide some practical security for each against the invasion of the others. What this security ought to be, is the great problem to be solved.

Will it be sufficient to mark with precision the boundaries of these departments in the constitution of the government, and to trust to these parchment barriers against the encroaching spirit of power? This is the security which appears to have been principally relied on by the compilers of most of the American constitutions. But experience assures us that the efficacy of the provision has been greatly over-rated; and that some more adequate defence is indispensably necessary for the more feeble, against the more powerful members of the government. The legislative department is every where extending the sphere of its activity, and drawing all power into its impetuous vortex.

The founders of our republics have so much merit for the wisdom which they have displayed, that no task can be less pleasing than that of pointing out the errors into which they have fallen. A respect for truth however obliges us to remark, that they seem never for a moment to have turned their eyes from the danger to liberty from the overgrown and all-grasping prerogative of an hereditary magistrate, supported and fortified by an hereditary branch of the legislative authority. They seem never to have recollected the danger from legislative usurpations, which by assembling all power in the same hands, must lead to the same tyranny as is threatened by executive usurpations.

In a government, where numerous and extensive prerogatives are placed in the hands of a hereditary monarch, the executive department is very justly regarded as the source of danger, and watched with all the jealousy which a zeal for liberty ought to inspire. In a democracy, where a multitude of people exercise in person the legislative functions, and are continually exposed by their incapacity for regular deliberation and concerted measures, to the ambitious intrigues of their executive magistrates, tyranny may well be apprehended on some favourable emergency, to start up in the same quarter. But in a representative republic, where the executive magistracy is carefully limited both in the extent and the duration of its power; and where the legislative power is exercised by an assembly, which is inspired by a supposed influence over the people with an intrepid confidence in its own strength; which is sufficiently numerous to feel all the passions which actuate a multitude; yet not so numerous as to be incapable of pursuing the objects of its passions, by means which reason prescribes; it is against the enterprising ambition of this department, that the people ought to indulge all their jealousy and exhaust all their precautions.

The legislative department derives a superiority in our governments from other circumstances. Its constitutional powers being at once more extensive and less susceptible of precise limits, it can with the greater facility, mask under complicated and indirect measures, the encroachments which it makes, on the co-ordinate departments. It is not unfrequently a question of real nicety in legislative bodies, whether the operation of a particular measure, will, or will not extend beyond the legislative sphere. On the other side, the executive power being restrained within a narrower compass, and being more simple in its nature; and the judiciary being described by land marks, still less uncertain, projects of usurpation by either of these departments, would immediately betray and defeat themselves. Nor is this all: As the legislative department alone has access to the pockets of the people, and has in some constitutions full discretion, and in all, a prevailing influence over the pecuniary rewards of those who fill the other departments, a dependence is thus created in the latter, which gives still greater facility to encroachments of the former.

I have appealed to our own experience for the truth of what I advance on this subject. Were it necessary to verify this experience by particular proofs, they might be multiplied without end. I might collect vouchers in abundance from the records and archives of every state in the union. But as a more concise and at the same time, equally satisfactory evidence I will refer to the example of two states, attested by two unexceptionable authorities.

The first example is that of Virginia, a state which, as we have seen, has expressly declared in its constitution, that the three great departments ought not to be intermixed. The authority in support of it is Mr. Jefferson, who, besides his other advantages for remarking the operation of the government, was himself the chief magistrate of it. In order to convey fully the ideas with which his experience had impressed him on this subject, it will be necessary to quote a passage of some length from his very interesting "Notes on the state of Virginia." (p. 195) "All the powers of government, legislative, executive and judiciary, result to the legislative body. The concentrating these in the same hands is precisely the definition of despotic government. It will be no alleviation that these powers will be exercised by a plurality of hands, and not by a single one. One hundred and seventy-three despots would surely be as oppressive as one. Let those who doubt it turn their eyes on the republic of Venice. As little will it avail us that they are chosen by ourselves. An *elective despotism* was not the government we fought for; but one which should not only be founded on free principles, but in which the powers of government should be so divided and balanced among several bodies of magistracy, as that no one could transcend their legal limits, without being effectually checked and restrained by the others. For this reason, that convention which passed the ordinance of government laid its foundation on this basis, that the legislative, executive and judiciary departments, should be separate and distinct, so that no person should exercise the powers of more than one of them at the same time. *But no barrier was provided between these several powers.* The judiciary and executive members were left dependent on the legislative for their subsistence in office, and some of them for their continuance in it. If therefore the legislature assumes executive and judiciary powers, no opposition is likely to be made; nor if made can be effectual; because in that case, they may put their proceeding into the form of an act of assembly, which will render them obligatory on the other branches. They have accordingly *in many* instances *decided rights* which should have been left to *judiciary controversy;* and *the direction of the executive, during the whole time of their session, is becoming habitual and familiar.*"

The other state which I shall have for an example, is Pennsylvania; and the other authority the council of censors which assembled in the years 1783 and 1784. A part of the duty of this body, as marked out by the constitution, was "to enquire whether the constitution had been preserved inviolate in every part; and whether the legislative and executive branches of government had performed their duty as guardians of the people, or assumed to themselves, or exercised other or greater powers than they are entitled to by the constitution." In the execution of this trust, the council were necessarily led to a comparison, of both the legislative and executive proceedings, with the constitutional powers of these departments; and from the facts enumerated, and to the truth of most of which, both sides in the council subscribed, it appears that the constitution had been flagrantly violated by the legislature in a variety of important instances.

A great number of laws had been passed violating without any apparent necessity, the rule requiring that all bills of a publick nature shall be previously printed for the consideration of the people; although this is one of the precautions chiefly relied on by the constitution, against improper acts of the legislature.

The constitutional trial by jury had been violated; and powers assumed, which had not been delegated by the constitution.

Executive powers had been usurped.

The salaries of the judges, which the constitution expressly requires to be fixed, had been occasionally varied; and cases belonging to the judiciary department, frequently drawn within legislative cognizance and determination.

Those who wish to see the several particulars falling under each of these heads, may consult the journals of the council which are in print. Some of them, it will be found may be imputable to peculiar circumstances connected with the war: But the greater part of them may be considered as the spontaneous shoots of an ill-constituted government.

It appears also, that the executive department had not been innocent of frequent breaches of the constitution. There are three observations however, which ought to be made on this head. *First.* A great proportion of the instances, were either immediately produced by the necessities of the war, or recommended by Congress or the commander in chief. *Second.* In most of the other instances, they conformed either to the declared or the known sentiments of the legislative department. *Third.* The executive department of Pennsylvania is distinguished from that of the other states, by the number of members composing it. In this respect it has as much affinity to a legislative assembly, as to an executive council. And being at once exempt from the restraint of an individual responsibility for the acts of the body, and deriving confidence from mutual example and joint influence; unauthorised measures would of course be more freely hazarded, than where the executive department is administered by a single hand or by a few hands.

The conclusion which I am warranted in drawing from these observations is, that a mere demarkation on parchment of the constitutional limits of the several departments, is not a sufficient guard against those encroachments which lead to a tyrannical concentration of all the powers of government in the same hands.

February 1, 1788

The Federalist No. 49

The author of the "Notes on the state of Virginia," quoted in the last paper, has subjoined to that valuable work, the draught of a constitution which had been prepared in order to be laid before a convention expected to be called in 1783, by the legislature, for the establishment of a constitution for that commonwealth. The plan, like every thing from the same pen, marks a turn of thinking original, comprehensive and accurate; and is the more worthy of attention, as it equally displays a fervent attachment to republican government, and an enlightened view of the dangerous propensities against which it ought to be guarded. One of the precautions which he proposes, and on which he appears ultimately to rely as a palladium to the weaker departments of power, against the invasions of the stronger, is perhaps altogether his own, and as it immediately relates to the subject of our present enquiry, ought not to be overlooked.

His proposition is, "that whenever any two of the three branches of government shall concur in opinion, each by the voices of two thirds of their whole number, that a convention is necessary for altering the constitution or *correcting breaches of it*, a convention shall be called for the purpose."

As the people are the only legitimate fountain of power, and it is from them that the constitutional charter, under which the several branches of government hold their power, is derived; it seems strictly consonant to the republican theory, to recur to the same original authority, not only whenever it may be necessary to enlarge, diminish, or new-model the powers of government; but also whenever any one of the departments may commit encroachments on the chartered authorities of the others. The several departments being perfectly co-ordinate by the terms of their common commission, neither of them, it is evident, can pretend to an exclusive or superior right of settling the boundaries between their respective powers; and how are the encroachments of the stronger to be prevented, or the wrongs of the weaker to be redressed, without an appeal to the people themselves; who, as the grantors of the commission, can alone declare its true meaning and enforce its observance?

There is certainly great force in this reasoning, and it must be allowed to prove, that a constitutional road to the decision of the people, ought to be marked out, and kept open, for certain great and extraordinary occasions. But there appear to be insuperable objections against the proposed recurrence to the people, as a provision in all cases for keeping the several departments of power within their constitutional limits.

In the first place, the provision does not reach the case of a combination of two of the departments against a third. If the legislative authority, which possesses so many means of operating on the motives of the other departments, should be able to gain to its interest either of the others, or even one third of its members, the remaining department could derive no advantage from this remedial provision. I do not dwell however, on this objection, because it may be thought to lie rather against the modification of the principle, than against the principle itself.

In the next place, it may be considered as an objection inherent in the principle, that as every appeal to the people would carry an implication of some defect in the government, frequent appeals would in great measure deprive the government of that veneration which time bestows on every thing, and without which perhaps the wisest and freest governments would not possess the requisite stability. If it be true that all governments rest on opinion, it is no less true that the strength of opinion in each individual, and its practical influence on his conduct, depend much on the number which he supposes to have entertained the same opinion. The reason of man, like man himself, is timid and cautious, when left alone; and acquires firmness and confidence, in proportion to the number with which it is associated. When the examples, which fortify opinion, are *antient* as well as *numerous*, they are known to have a double effect. In a nation of philosophers, this consideration ought to be disregarded. A reverence for the laws, would be sufficiently inculcated by the voice of an enlightened reason. But a nation of philosophers is as little to be expected as the philosophical race of kings wished for by Plato. And in every other nation, the most rational government will not find it a superfluous advantage to have the prejudices of the community on its side.

The danger of disturbing the public tranquility by interesting too strongly the public passions, is a still more serious objection against a frequent reference of constitutional questions, to the decision of the whole society. Notwithstanding the success which has attended the revisions of our established forms of government, and which does so much honor to the virtue and intelligence of the people of America, it must be confessed, that the experiments are of too ticklish a nature to be unnecessarily multiplied. We are to recollect that all the existing constitutions were formed in the midst of a danger which repressed the passions most unfriendly to order and concord; of an enthusiastic confidence of the people in their patriotic leaders, which stifled the ordinary diversity of opinions on great national questions; of a universal ardor for new and opposite forms, produced by a universal resentment and indignation against the antient government; and whilst no spirit of party, connected with the changes to be made, or the abuses to be reformed, could mingle its leaven in the operation. The future situations in which we must expect to be usually placed, do not present any equivalent security against the danger which is apprehended.

But the greatest objection of all is that the decisions which would probably result from such appeals, would not answer the purpose of maintaining the constitutional equilibrium of the government. We have seen that the tendency of republican governments is to an aggrandizement of the legislative, at the expence of the other departments. The appeals to the people therefore, would usually be made by the executive and judiciary departments. But whether made by one side or the other, would each side enjoy equal advantages on the trial? Let us view their different situations. The members of the executive and judiciary departments, are few in number, and can be personally known to a small part only of the people. The latter by the mode of their appointment, as well as by the nature and permanency of it, are too far removed from the people to share much in their prepossessions. The former are generally the objects of jealousy: and their administration is always liable to be discoloured and rendered unpopular. The members of the legislative department, on the other hand, are numerous. They are distributed and dwell among the people at large. Their connections of blood, of friendship and of acquaintance, embrace a great proportion of the most influential part of the society. The nature of their public trust implies a personal influence among the people, and that they are more immediately the confidential guardians of the rights and liberties of the people. With these advantages, it can hardly be supposed that the adverse party would have an equal chance for a favorable issue.

But the legislative party would not only be able to plead their cause most successfully with the people: They would probably be constituted themselves the judges. The same influence which had gained them an election into the legislature, would gain them a seat in the convention. If this should not be the case with all, it would probably be the case with many, and pretty certainly with those leading characters, on whom every thing depends in such bodies. The convention in short would be composed chiefly of men, who had been, who actually were, or who expected to be, members of the department whose conduct was arraigned. They would consequently be parties to the very question to be decided by them.

It might however sometimes happen, that appeals would be made under circumstances less adverse to the executive and judiciary departments. The usurpations of the legislature might be so flagrant and so sudden, as to admit of no specious colouring. A strong party among themselves might take side with the other branches. The executive power might be in the hands of a peculiar favorite of the people. In such a posture of things, the public decision might be less swayed by prepossessions in favor of the legislative party. But still it could never be expected to turn on the true merits of the question. It would inevitably be connected with the spirit of pre-existing parties, or of parties springing out of the question itself. It would be connected with persons of distinguished character and extensive influence in the community. It would be pronounced by the very men who had been agents in, or opponents of the measures, to which the decision would relate. The *passions* therefore not the *reason*, of the public, would sit in judgment.

But it is the reason of the public alone that ought to controul and regulate the government. The passions ought to be controuled and regulated by the government.

We found in the last paper that mere declarations in the written constitution, are not sufficient to restrain the several departments within their legal limits. It appears in this that occasional appeals to the people would be neither a proper nor an effectual provision, for that purpose. How far the provisions of a different nature contained in the plan above quoted, might be adequate, I do not examine. Some of them are unquestionably founded on sound political principles, and all of them are framed with singular ingenuity and precision.

February 2, 1788

The Federalist No. 50

It may be contended perhaps, that instead of *occasional* appeals to the people, which are liable to the objections urged against them, *periodical* appeals are the proper and adequate means of *preventing and correcting infractions of the constitution*.

It will be attended to, that in the examination of these expedients, I confine myself to their aptitude for *enforcing* the constitution by keeping the several departments of power within their due bounds, without particularly considering them, as provisions for *altering* the constitution itself. In the first view, appeals to the people at fixed periods, appear to be nearly as ineligible, as appeals on particular occasions as they emerge. If the periods be separated by short intervals, the measures to be reviewed and rectified, will have been of recent date, and will be connected with all the circumstances which tend to viciate and pervert the result of occasional revisions. If the periods be distant from each other, the same remark will be applicable to all recent measures, and in proportion as the remoteness of the others may favor a dispassionate review of them, this advantage is inseparable from inconveniences which seem to counterbalance it. In the first place, a distant prospect of public censure would be a very feeble restraint on power from those excesses, to which it might be urged by the force of present motives. Is it to be imagined, that a legislative assembly, consisting of a hundred or two hundred members, eagerly bent on some favorite object, and breaking through the restraints of the constitution in pursuit of it, would be arrested in their career, by considerations drawn from a censorial revision of their conduct at the future distance of ten, fifteen or twenty years? In the next place, the abuses would often have completed their mischievous effects, before the remedial provision would be applied. And in the last place, where this might not be the case, they would be of long standing, would have taken deep root, and would not easily be extirpated.

The scheme of revising the constitution in order to correct recent breaches of it, as well as for other purposes, has been actually tried in one of the states. One of the objects of the council of censors, which met in Pennsylvania, in 1783 and 1784, was, as we have seen, to enquire "whether the constitution had been violated, and whether the legislative and executive departments had encroached on each other." This important and novel experiment in politics, merits in several points of view, very particular attention. In some of them it may perhaps as a single experiment, made under circumstances somewhat peculiar, be thought to be not absolutely conclusive. But as applied to the case under consideration, it involves some facts which I venture to remark, as a complete and satisfactory illustration of the reasoning which I have employed.

First. It appears from the names of the gentlemen who composed the council, that some at least of its most active and leading members, had also been active and leading characters in the parties which pre-existed in the state.

Second. It appears that the same active and leading members of the council, had been active and influential members of the legislative and executive branches, within the period to be reviewed; and even patrons or opponents of the very measures to be thus brought to the test of the constitution. Two of the members had been vice-presidents of the state, and several others, members of the executive council within the seven preceding years. One of them had been speaker, and a number of others distinguished members of the legislative assembly, within the same period.

Third. Every page of their proceedings witnesses the effect of all these circumstances on the temper of their deliberations. Throughout the continuance of the council, it was split into two fixed and violent parties. The fact is acknowledged and lamented by themselves. Had this not been the case, the face of their proceedings exhibit a proof equally satisfactory. In all questions, however unimportant in themselves, or unconnected with each other, the same names stand invariably contrasted on the opposite columns. Every unbiassed observer, may infer without danger of mistake, and at the same time, without meaning to reflect on either party, or any individuals of either party, that unfortunately *passion*, not *reason*, must have presided over their decisions. When men exercise their reason coolly and freely, on a variety of distinct questions, they inevitably fall into different opinions on some of them.

When they are governed by a common passion, their opinions, if they are so to be called, will be the same.

Fourth. It is at least problematical, whether the decisions of this body do not, in several instances, misconstrue the limits prescribed for the legislative and executive departments, instead of reducing and limiting them within their constitutional places.

Fifth. I have never understood that the decisions of the council on constitutional questions, whether rightly or erroneously formed, have had any effect in varying the practice founded on legislative constructions. It even appears, if I mistake not, that in one instance, the cotemporary legislature denied the constructions of the council, and actually prevailed in the contest.

This censorial body, therefore, proves at the same time, by its researches, the existence of the disease; and by its example, the inefficacy of the remedy.

This conclusion cannot be invalidated by alledging that the state in which the experiment was made, was at that crisis, and had been for a long time before, violently heated and distracted by the rage of party. Is it to be presumed, that at any future septennial epoch, the same state will be free from parties? Is it to be presumed that any other state, at the same or any other given period, will be exempt from them? Such an event ought to be neither presumed nor desired; because an extinction of parties necessarily implies either a universal alarm for the public safety, or an absolute extinction of liberty.

Were the precaution taken of excluding from the assemblies elected by the people to revise the preceding administration of the government, all persons who should have been concerned in the government within the given period, the difficulties would not be obviated. The important task would probably devolve on men, who with inferior capacities, would in other respects be little better qualified. Although they might not have been personally concerned in the administration, and therefore not immediately agents in the measures to be examined; they would probably have been involved in the parties connected with these measures, and have been elected under their auspices.

February 5, 1788

The Federalist No. 51

To what expedient then shall we finally resort for maintaining in practice the necessary partition of power among the several departments, as laid down in the constitution? The only answer that can be given is, that as all these exterior provisions are found to be inadequate, the defect must be supplied, by so contriving the interior structure of the government, as that its several constituent parts may, by their mutual relations, be the means of keeping each other in their proper places. Without presuming to undertake a full developement of this important idea, I will hazard a few general observations, which may perhaps place it in a clearer light, and enable us to form a more correct judgment of the principles and structure of the government planned by the convention.

In order to lay a due foundation for that separate and distinct exercise of the different powers of government, which to a certain extent, is admitted on all hands to be essential to the preservation of liberty, it is evident that each department should have a will of its own; and consequently should be so constituted that the members of each should have as little agency as possible in the appointment of the members of the others. Were this principle rigorously adhered to, it would require that all the appointments for the supreme executive, legislative and judiciary magistracies should be drawn from the same fountain of authority, the people, through channels, having no communication whatever with one another. Perhaps such a plan of constructing the several departments would be less difficult in practice than it may in contemplation appear. Some difficulties however, and some additional expence, would attend the execution of it. Some deviations therefore from the principle must be admitted. In the constitution of the judiciary department in particular, it might be inexpedient to insist rigorously on the principle; first, because peculiar qualifications being essential in the members, the primary consideration ought to be to select that mode of choice, which best secures these qualifications; secondly, because the permanent tenure by which the appointments are held in that department, must soon destroy all sense of dependence on the authority conferring them.

It is equally evident that the members of each department should be as little dependent as possible on those of the others, for the emoluments annexed to their offices. Were the executive magistrate, or the judges, not independent of the legislature in this particular, their independence in every other, would be merely nominal.

But the great security against a gradual concentration of the several powers in the same department, consists in giving to those who administer each department, the necessary constitutional means, and personal motives, to resist encroachments of the others. The provision for defence must in this, as in all other cases, be made commensurate to the danger of attack. Ambition must be made to counteract ambition. The interest of the man must be connected with the constitutional rights of the place. It may be a reflection on human nature, that such devices should be necessary to control the abuses of government. But what is government itself but the greatest of all reflections on human nature? If men were angels, no government would be necessary. If angels were to govern men, neither external nor internal controls on government would be necessary. In framing a government which is to be administered by men over men, the great difficulty lies in this: You must first enable the government to control the governed; and in the next place, oblige it to control itself. A dependence on the people is no doubt the primary control on the government; but experience has taught mankind the necessity of auxiliary precautions.

This policy of supplying by opposite and rival interests, the defect of better motives, might be traced through the whole system of human affairs, private as well as public. We see it particularly displayed in all the subordinate distributions of power; where the constant aim is to divide and arrange the several offices in such a manner as that each may be a check on the other; that the private interest of every individual, may be a centinel over the public rights. These inventions of prudence cannot be less requisite in the distribution of the supreme powers of the state.

But it is not possible to give to each department an equal

power of self-defence. In republican government the legislative authority necessarily predominates. The remedy for this inconveniency is, to divide the legislature into different branches; and to render them by different modes of election, and different principles of action, as little connected with each other, as the nature of their common functions, and their common dependence on the society, will admit. It may even be necessary to guard against dangerous encroachments by still further precautions. As the weight of the legislative authority requires that it should be thus divided, the weakness of the executive may require, on the other hand, that it should be fortified. An absolute negative, on the legislature, appears at first view to be the natural defence with which the executive magistrate should be armed. But perhaps it would be neither altogether safe, nor alone sufficient. On ordinary occasions, it might not be exerted with the requisite firmness; and on extraordinary occasions, it might be perfidiously abused. May not this defect of an absolute negative be supplied by some qualified connection between this weaker department, and the weaker branch of the stronger department, by which the latter may be led to support the constitutional rights of the former, without being too much detached from the rights of its own department?

If the principles on which these observations are founded be just, as I persuade myself they are, and they be applied as a criterion to the several state constitutions, and to the federal constitution, it will be found, that if the latter does not perfectly correspond with them, the former are infinitely less able to bear such a test.

There are moreover two considerations particularly applicable to the federal system of America, which place that system in a very interesting point of view.

First. In a single republic, all the power surrendered by the people, is submitted to the administration of a single government; and the usurpations are guarded against by a division of the government into distinct and separate departments. In the compound republic of America, the power surrendered by the people, is first divided between two distinct governments, and then the portion allotted to each, subdivided among distinct and separate departments. Hence a double security arises to the rights of the people. The different governments will control each other; at the same time that each will be controled by itself.

Second. It is of great importance in a republic, not only to guard the society against the oppression of its rulers; but to guard one part of the society against the injustice of the other part. Different interests necessarily exist in different classes of citizens. If a majority be united by a common interest, the rights of the minority will be insecure. There are but two methods of providing against this evil: The one by creating a will in the community independent of the majority, that is, of the society itself; the other by comprehending in the society so many separate descriptions of citizens, as will render an unjust combination of a majority of the whole very improbable, if not impracticable. The first method prevails in all governments possessing an hereditary or self-appointed authority. This at best is but a precarious security; because a power independent of the society may as well espouse the unjust views of the major, as the rightful interests of the minor party, and may possibly be turned against both parties. The second method will be exemplified in the federal republic of the United States. Whilst all authority in it will be derived from, and dependent on the society, the society itself will be broken into so many parts, interests and classes of citizens, that the rights of individuals or of the minority, will be in little danger from interested combinations of the majority. In a free government, the security for civil rights must be the same as that for religious rights. It consists in the one case in the multiplicity of interests, and in the other, in the multiplicity of sects. The degree of security in both cases will depend on the number of interests and sects; and this may be presumed to depend on the extent of country and number of people comprehended under the same government. This view of the subject must particularly recommend a proper federal system to all the sincere and considerate friends of republican government: Since it shews that in exact proportion as the territory of the union may be formed into more circumscribed confederacies or states, oppressive combinations of a majority will be facilitated, the best security under the republican form, for the rights of every class of citizens, will be diminished; and consequently, the stability and independence of some member of the government, the only other security must be proportionally increased. Justice is the end of government. It is the end of civil society. It ever has been, and ever will be pursued, until it be obtained, or until liberty be lost in the pursuit. In a society under the forms of which the stronger faction can readily unite and oppress the weaker, anarchy may as truly be said to reign, as in a state of nature where the weaker individual is not secured against the violence of the stronger: And as in the latter state even the stronger individuals are prompted by the uncertainty of their condition, to submit to a government which may protect the weak as well as themselves: So in the former state, will the more powerful factions or parties be gradually induced by a like motive, to wish for a government which will protect all parties, the weaker as well as the more powerful. It can be little doubted, that if the state of Rhode-Island was separated from the confederacy, and left to itself, the insecurity of rights under the popular form of government within such narrow limits, would be displayed by such reiterated oppressions of factious majorities, that some power altogether independent of the people would soon be called for by the voice of the very factions whose misrule had proved the necessity of it. In the extended republic of the United States, and among the great variety of interests, parties and sects which it embraces, a coalition of a majority of the whole society could seldom take place upon any other principles than those of justice and the general good: Whilst there being thus less danger to a minor from the will of the major party, there must be less pretext also, to provide for the security of the former, by introducing into the government a will not dependent on the latter; or in other words, a will independent of the society itself. It is no less certain than it is important, notwithstanding the contrary opinions which have been entertained, that the larger the society, provided it lie within a practicable sphere, the more duly capable it will be of self government. And happily for the *republican cause*, the practicable sphere may be carried to a very great extent, by a judicious modification and mixture of the *federal principle*.

February 6, 1788

The Federalist No. 52

From the more general enquiries pursued in the four last papers, I pass on to a more particular examination of the several parts of the government. I shall begin with the house of representatives.

The first view to be taken of this part of the government, relates to the qualifications of the electors and the elected. Those of the former are to be the same with those of the electors of the most numerous branch of the state legislatures. The definition of the right of suffrage is very justly regarded as a fundamental article of republican government. It was incumbent on the convention, therefore, to define and establish this right in the constitution. To have left it open for the occasional regulation of the congress, would have been improper for the reason just mentioned. To have submitted it to the legislative discretion of the states, would have been improper for the same reason; and for the additional reason, that it would have rendered too dependent on the state governments, that branch of the federal government, which ought to be dependent on the people alone. To have reduced the different qualifications in the different states to one uniform rule, would probably have been as dissatisfactory to some of the states, as it would have been difficult to the convention. The provision made by the convention appears therefore, to be the best that lay within their option. It must be satisfactory to every state; because it is conformable to the standard already established, or which may be established by the state itself. It will be safe to the United States; because, being fixed by the state constitutions, it is not alterable by the state governments, and it cannot be feared that the people of the states will alter this part of their constitutions, in such a manner as to abridge the rights secured to them by the federal constitution.

The qualifications of the elected being less carefully and properly defined by the state constitutions, and being at the same time more susceptible of uniformity, have been very properly considered and regulated by the convention. A representative of the United States must be of the age of twenty-five years; must have been seven years a citizen of the United

States; must at the time of his election, be an inhabitant of the state he is to represent, and during the time of his service must be in no office under the United States. Under these reasonable limitations, the door of this part of the federal government is open to merit of every description, whether native or adoptive, whether young or old, and without regard to poverty or wealth, or to any particular profession of religious faith.

The term for which the representatives are to be elected, falls under a second view which may be taken of this branch. In order to decide on the propriety of this article, two questions must be considered; first, whether biennial elections will, in this case, be safe; secondly, whether they be necessary or useful.

First. As it is essential to liberty, that the government in general should have a common interest with the people; so it is particularly essential that the branch of it under consideration should have an immediate dependence on, and an intimate sympathy with the people. Frequent elections are unquestionably the only policy by which this dependence and sympathy can be effectually secured. But what particular degree of frequency may be absolutely necessary for the purpose, does not appear to be susceptible of any precise calculation: And must depend on a variety of circumstances with which it may be connected. Let us consult experience, the guide that ought always to be followed, whenever it can be found.

The scheme of representation, as a substitute for a meeting of the citizens in person, being at most but very imperfectly known to antient polity; it is in more modern times only, that we are to expect instructive examples. And even here, in order to avoid a research too vague and diffusive, it will be proper to confine ourselves to the few examples which are best known, and which bear the greatest analogy to our particular case. The first to which this character ought to be applied, is the house of commons in Great-Britain. The history of this branch of the English constitution, anterior to the date of Magna Charta, is too obscure to yield instruction. The very existence of it has been made a question among political antiquaries. The earliest records of subsequent date prove, that parliaments were to *sit* only, every year; not that they were to be *elected* every year. And even these annual sessions were left so much at the discretion of the monarch, that under various pretexts, very long and dangerous intermissions were often contrived by royal ambition. To remedy this grievance, it was provided by a statute in the reign of Charles IId. that the intermissions, should not be protracted beyond a period of three years. On the accession of William IIId, when a revolution took place in the government, the subject was still more seriously resumed, and it was declared to be among the fundamental rights of the people, that parliaments ought to be held *frequently*. By another statute which passed a few years later in the same reign, the term "frequently" which had alluded to the triennial period settled in the time of Charles IId. is reduced to a precise meaning, it being expressly enacted that a new parliament shall be called within three years after the determination of the former. The last change from three to seven years is well known to have been introduced pretty early in the present century, under an alarm for the Hanoverian succession. From these facts it appears, that the greatest frequency of elections which has been deemed necessary in that kingdom, for binding the representatives to their constituents, does not exceed a triennial return of them. And if we may argue from the degree of liberty retained even under septennial elections, and all the other vicious ingredients in the parliamentary constitution, we cannot doubt that a reduction of the period from seven to three years, with the other necessary reforms, would so far extend the influence of the people over their representatives as to satisfy us, that biennial elections under the federal system, cannot possibly be dangerous to the requisite dependence of the house of representatives on their constituents.

Elections in Ireland, till of late, were regulated entirely by the discretion of the crown, and were seldom repeated except on the accession of a new prince, or some other contingent event. The parliament which commenced with George IId. was continued throughout his whole reign, a period of about thirty-five years. The only dependence of the representatives on the people, consisted in the right of the latter to supply occasional vacancies, by the election of new members, and in the chance of some event which might produce a general new election. The ability also of the Irish parliament to maintain the rights of their constituents, so far as the disposition might exist, was extremely shackled by the control of the crown over the subjects of their deliberation. Of late these shackles, if I mistake not, have been broken; and octennial parliaments have besides been established. What effect may be produced by this partial reform, must be left to further experience. The example of Ireland, from this view of it, can throw but little light on the subject. As far as we can draw any conclusion from it, it must be, that if the people of that country have been able, under all these disadvantages, to retain any liberty whatever, the advantage of biennial elections would secure to them every degree of liberty which might depend on a due connection between their representatives and themselves.

Let us bring our enquiries nearer home. The example of these states when British colonies, claims particular attention; at the same time that it is so well known, as to require little to be said on it. The principle of representation, in one branch of the legislature at least, was established in all of them. But the periods of election were different. They varied from one to seven years. Have we any reason to infer from the spirit and conduct of the representatives of the people, prior to the revolution, that biennial elections would have been dangerous to the public liberties? The spirit which every where displayed itself at the commencement of the struggle; and which vanquished the obstacles to independence, is the best of proofs that a sufficient portion of liberty had been every where enjoyed to inspire both a sense of its worth, and a zeal for its proper enlargement. This remark holds good as well with regard to the then colonies, whose elections were least frequent, as to those whose elections were most frequent. Virginia was the colony which stood first in resisting the parliamentary usurpations of Great-Britain; it was the first also in espousing by public act, the resolution of independence. In Virginia, nevertheless, if I have not been misinformed, elections under the former government were septennial. This particular example is brought into view, not as a proof of any peculiar merit, for the priority in those instances, was probably accidental; and still less of any advantage in *septennial* elections, for when compared with a greater frequency they are inadmissible; but merely as a proof, and I conceive it to be a very substantial proof, that the liberties of the people can be in no danger from *biennial* elections.

The conclusion resulting from these examples will be not a little strengthened by recollecting three circumstances. The first is, that the federal legislature will possess a part only of that supreme legislative authority which is vested completely in the British parliament, and which, with a few exceptions, was exercised by the colonial assemblies and the Irish legislature. It is a received and well founded maxim, that, where no other circumstances affect the case, the greater the power is, the shorter ought to be its duration; and conversely, the smaller the power, the more safely may its duration be protracted. In the second place, it has, on another occasion, been shewn that the federal legislature will not only be restrained by its dependence on the people, as other legislative bodies are; but that it will be moreover watched and controled by the several collateral legislatures, which other legislative bodies are not. And in the third place, no comparison can be made between the means that will be possessed by the more permanent branches of the federal government for seducing, if they should be disposed to seduce, the house of representatives from their duty to the people; and the means of influence over the popular branch, possessed by the other branches of the governments above cited. With less power therefore to abuse, the federal representatives can be less tempted on one side, and will be doubly watched on the other.

February 8, 1788

The Federalist No. 53

I shall here perhaps be reminded of a current observation, "that where annual elections end, tyranny begins." If it be true, as has often been remarked, that sayings which become proverbial, are generally founded in reason, it is not less true that when once established, they are often applied to cases to which the reason of them does not extend. I need not look for a proof beyond the case before us. What is the reason on which this proverbial observation is founded? No man will subject himself to the ridicule of pretending that any natural connection subsists between the sun or the seasons, and the period within which human virtue can bear the temptations of power. Happily for mankind, liberty is not in this respect confined to any single point of time; but lies within extremes, which afford sufficient latitude for all the variations which may be required by the various situations and circumstances of civil society. The election of magistrates might be, if it were found expedient, as in some instances it actually has been, daily, weekly, or monthly, as well as annual; and if circumstances may require a deviation from the rule on one side, why not also on the other side? Turning our attention to the periods established among ourselves, for the election of the most numerous branches of the state legislatures, we find them by no means coinciding any more in this instance, than in the elections of other civil magistrates. In Connecticut and Rhode-Island, the periods are half-yearly. In the other states, South-Carolina excepted, they are annual. In South-Carolina, they are biennial; as is proposed in the federal government. Here is a difference, as four to one, between the longest and the shortest periods; and yet it would be not easy to shew that Connecticut or Rhode-Island is better governed, or enjoys a greater share of rational liberty than South-Carolina; or that either the one or the other of these states are distinguished in these respects, and by these causes, from the states whose elections are different from both.

In searching for the grounds of this doctrine, I can discover but one, and that is wholly inapplicable to our case. The important distinction so well understood in America between a constitution established by the people, and unalterable by the government; and a law established by the government, and alterable by the government, seems to have been little understood and less observed in any other country. Wherever the supreme power of legislation has resided, has been supposed to reside also, a full power to change the form of the government. Even in Great Britain, where the principles of political and civil liberty have been most discussed, and where we hear most of the rights of the constitution, it is maintained that the authority of the parliament is transcendent and uncontrolable, as well with regard to the constitution, as the ordinary objects of legislative provision. They have accordingly, in several instances, actually changed, by legislative acts, some of the most fundamental articles of the government. They have in particular, on several occasions, changed the period of election; and on the last occasion, not only introduced septennial, in place of triennial elections; but by the same act continued themselves in place four years beyond the term for which they were elected by the people. An attention to these dangerous practices has produced a very natural alarm in the votaries of free government, of which frequency of elections is the corner stone; and has led them to seek for some security to liberty against the danger to which it is exposed. Where no constitution paramount to the government, either existed or could be obtained, no constitutional security similar to that established in the United States, was to be attempted. Some other security therefore was to be sought for; and what better security would the case admit, than that of selecting and appealing to some simple and familiar portion of time, as a standard for measuring the danger of innovations, for fixing the national sentiment, and for uniting the patriotic exertions. The most simple and familiar portion of time, applicable to the subject, was that of a year; and hence the doctrine has been inculcated by a laudable zeal to erect some barrier against the gradual innovations of an unlimited government, that the advance towards tyranny was to be calculated by the distance of departure from the fixed point of annual elections. But what necessity can there be of applying this expedient to a government, limited as the federal government will be, by the authority of a paramount constitution? Or who will pretend that the liberties of the people of America will not be more secure under biennial elections, unalterably fixed by such a constitution, than those of any other nation would be, where elections were annual or even more frequent, but subject to alterations by the ordinary power of the government?

The second question stated is, whether biennial elections be necessary or useful? The propriety of answering this question in the affirmative will appear from several very obvious considerations.

No man can be a competent legislator who does not add to an upright intention and a sound judgment, a certain degree of knowledge of the subjects on which he is to legislate. A part of this knowledge may be acquired by means of information which lie within the compass of men in private as well as public stations. Another part can only be attained, or at least thoroughly attained, by actual experience in the station which requires the use of it. The period of service ought therefore in all such cases to bear some proportion to the extent of practical knowledge, requisite to the due performance of the service. The period of legislative service established in most of the states for the more numerous branch is, as we have seen, one year. The question then may be put into this simple form; does the period of two years bear no greater proportion to the knowledge requisite for federal legislation, than one year does to the knowledge requisite for state legislation? The very statement of the question in this form, suggests the answer that ought to be given to it.

In a single state, the requisite knowledge relates to the existing laws which are uniform throughout the state, and with which all the citizens are more or less conversant; and to the general affairs of the state, which lie within a small compass, are not very diversified and occupy much of the attention and conversation of every class of people. The great theatre of the United States presents a very different scene. The laws are so far from being uniform, that they vary in every state; whilst the public affairs of the union are spread throughout a very extensive region, and are extremely diversified by the local affairs connected with them, and can with difficulty be correctly learnt in any other place, than in the central councils, to which a knowledge of them will be brought by the representatives of every part of the empire. Yet some knowledge of the affairs, and even of the laws of all the states, ought to be possessed by the members from each of the states. How can foreign trade be properly regulated by uniform laws, without some acquaintance with the commerce, the ports, the usages, and the regulations of the different states? How can the trade between the different states be duly regulated without some knowledge of their relative situations in these and other points? How can taxes be judiciously imposed, and effectually collected, if they be not accommodated to the different laws and local circumstances relating to these objects in the different states? How can uniform regulations for the militia be duly provided without a similar knowledge of some internal circumstances by which the states are distinguished from each other? These are the principal objects of federal legislation, and suggest most forceably, the extensive information which the representatives ought to acquire. The other inferior objects will require a proportional degree of information with regard to them.

It is true that all these difficulties will by degrees be very much diminished. The most laborious task will be the proper inauguration of the government, and the primeval formation of a federal code. Improvements on the first draught will every year become both easier and fewer. Past transactions of the government will be a ready and accurate source of information to new members. The affairs of the union will become more and more objects of curiosity and conversation among the citizens at large. And the increased intercourse among those of different states will contribute not a little to diffuse a mutual knowledge of their affairs, as this again will contribute to a general assimilation of their manners and laws. But with all these abatements the business of federal legislation must continue so far to exceed both in novelty and difficulty the legislative business of a single state, as to justify the longer period of service assigned to those who are to transact it.

A branch of knowledge which belongs to the acquirements of a federal representative, and which has not been mentioned, is that of foreign affairs. In regulating our own commerce, he ought to be not only acquainted with the treaties between the United States and other nations, but also with the commercial policy and laws of other nations. He ought not be altogether ignorant of the law of nations, for that as far as it is a proper object of municipal legislation is submitted to the federal government. And although the house of representatives is not immediately to participate in foreign negociations and arrangements, yet from the necessary connection between the several branches of public affairs, those particular branches will frequently deserve attention in the ordinary course of legislation, and will sometimes demand particular legislative sanction and cooperation. Some portion of this knowledge may no doubt be acquired in a man's closet; but some of it also can only be derived from the public sources of information; and all of it will be acquired to best effect by a practical attention to the subject during the period of actual service in the legislature.

There are other considerations of less importance perhaps, but which are not unworthy of notice. The distance which many of the representatives will be obliged to travel, and the arrangements rendered necessary by that circumstance, might be much more serious objections with fit men to this service if limited to a single year, than if extended to two years. No argument can be drawn on this subject from the case of the delegates to the existing congress. They are elected annually it is true; but their re-election is considered by the legislative assemblies almost as a matter of course. The election of the representatives by the people would not be governed by the same principle.

A few of the members, as happens in all such assemblies, will possess superior talents; will, by frequent re-elections, become members of long standing; will be thoroughly masters of the public business, and perhaps not unwilling to avail themselves of those advantages. The greater the proportion of new members, and the less the information of the bulk of the members, the more apt will they be to fall into the snares that may be laid for them. This remark is no less applicable to the relation which will subsist between the house of representatives and the senate.

It is an inconvenience mingled with the advantages of our frequent elections, even in single states, where they are large and hold but one legislative session in the year, that spurious elections cannot be investigated and annulled in time for the decision to have its due effect. If a return can be obtained, no matter by what unlawful means, the irregular member, who takes his seat of course, is sure of holding it a sufficient time to answer his purposes. Hence a very pernicious encouragement is given to the use of unlawful means for obtaining irregular returns. Were elections for the federal legislature to be annual, this practice might become a very serious abuse; particularly in the more distant states. Each house is, as it necessarily must be, the judge of the elections, qualifications and returns of its members, and whatever improvements may be suggested by experience for simplifying and accelerating the process in disputed cases, so great a portion of a year would unavoidably elapse, before an illegitimate member could be dispossessed of his seat, that the prospect of such an event would be little check to unfair and illicit means of obtaining a seat.

All these considerations taken together warrant us in affirming that biennial elections will be as useful to the affairs of the public, as we have seen that they will be safe to the liberties of the people.

February 9, 1788

The Federalist No. 54

The next view which I shall take of the house of representatives, relates to the apportionment of its members to the several states, which is to be determined by the same rule with that of direct taxes.

It is not contended that the number of people in each state ought not to be the standard for regulating the proportion of those who are to represent the people of each state. The establishment of the same rule for the apportionment of taxes, will probably be as little contested; though the rule itself in this case, is by no means founded on the same principle. In the former case, the rule is understood to refer to the personal rights of the people, with which it has a natural and universal connection. In the latter, it has reference to the proportion of wealth, of which it is in no case a precise measure, and in ordinary cases, a very unfit one. But notwithstanding the imperfection of the rule as applied to the relative wealth and contributions of the states, it is evidently the least exceptionable among the practicable rules; and had too recently obtained the general sanction of America, not to have found a ready preference with the convention.

All this is admitted, it will perhaps be said: But does it follow from an admission of numbers for the measure of representation, or of slaves combined with free citizens, as a ratio of taxation, that slaves ought to be included in the numerical rule of representation? Slaves are considered as property, not as persons. They ought therefore to be comprehended in estimates of taxation which are founded on property, and to be excluded from representation which is regulated by a census of persons. This is the objection, as I understand it, stated in its full force. I shall be equally candid in stating the reasoning which may be offered on the opposite side.

We subscribe to the doctrine, might one of our southern brethren observe, that representation relates more immediately to persons, and taxation more immediately to property, and we join in the application of this distinction to the case of our slaves. But we must deny the fact that slaves are considered merely as property, and in no respect whatever as persons. The true state of the case is, that they partake of both these qualities; being considered by our laws, in some respects, as persons, and in other respects, as property. In being compelled to labor not for himself, but for a master; in being vendible by one master to another master; and in being subject at all times to be restrained in his liberty, and chastised in his body, by the capricious will of another, the slave may appear to be degraded from the human rank, and classed with those irrational animals, which fall under the legal denomination of property. In being protected on the other hand in his life and in his limbs, against the violence of all others, even the master of his labour and his liberty; and in being punishable himself for all violence committed against others; the slave is no less evidently regarded by the law as a member of the society; not as a part of the irrational creation; as a moral person, not as a mere article of property. The federal constitution therefore, decides with great propriety on the case of our slaves, when it views them in the mixt character of persons and of property. This is in fact their true character. It is the character bestowed on them by the laws under which they live; and it will not be denied that these are the proper criterion; because it is only under the pretext that the laws have transformed the negroes into subjects of property, that a place is disputed them in the computation of numbers; and it is admitted that if the laws were to restore the rights which have been taken away, the negroes could no longer be refused an equal share of representation with the other inhabitants.

This question may be placed in another light. It is agreed on all sides, that numbers are the best scale of wealth and taxation, as they are the only proper scale of representation. Would the Convention have been impartial or consistent, if they had rejected the slaves from the list of inhabitants when the shares of representation were to be calculated; and inserted them on the lists when the tariff of contributions was to be adjusted? Could it be reasonably expected that the southern states would concur in a system which considered their slaves in some degree as men, when burdens were to be imposed, but refused to consider them in the same light when advantages were to be conferred? Might not some surprize also be expressed that those who reproach the southern states with the barbarous policy of considering as property, a part of their human brethren, should themselves contend that the government to which all the states are to be parties, ought to consider this unfortunate race more compleatly in the unnatural light of property, than the very laws of which they complain?

It may be replied perhaps that slaves are not included in the estimate of representatives in any of the states possessing them. They neither vote themselves, nor increase the votes of their masters. Upon what principle then ought they to be taken into the federal estimate of representation? In rejecting them altogether, the constitution would in this respect, have followed the very laws which have been appealed to, as the proper guide.

This objection is repelled by a single observation. It is a fundamental principle of the proposed constitution, that as the aggregate number of representatives allotted to the several states is to be determined by a federal rule founded on the aggregate number of inhabitants, so the right of choosing this allotted number in each state is to be exercised by such part of the inhabitants, as the state itself may designate. The qualifications on which the right of suffrage depend, are not perhaps the same in any two states. In some of the states the difference is very material. In every state a certain proportion of inhabitants are deprived of this right by the constitution of the state, who will be included in the census by which the federal constitution apportions the representatives. In this point of view, the southern states might retort the complaint, by insisting, that the principle laid down by the convention required that no regard should be had to the policy of particular states towards their own inhabitants; and consequently, that the slaves as inhabitants should have been admitted into the census according to their full number, in like manner with other inhabitants, who by the policy of other states, are not admitted to all the rights of citizens. A rigorous adherence however, to this principle, is waved by those who would be gainers by it. All that they ask is, that equal moderation be shewn on the other side. Let the case of the slaves be considered, as it is in truth a peculiar one. Let the compromising expedient of the constitution be mutually adopted, which regards them as inhabitants, but as debased by servitude below the equal level of free inhabitants, which regards the *slave* as divested of two fifths of the *man*.

After all, may not another ground be taken on which this article of the constitution will admit of a still more ready defence? We have hitherto proceeded on the idea that representation related to persons only, and not at all to property. But is it a just idea? Government is instituted no less for protection of the property, than of the persons of individuals. The one as well as the other, therefore, may be considered as represented by those who are charged with the government. Upon this principle it is, that in several of the states, and particularly in the state of New-York, one branch of the government is intended more especially to be the guardian of property, and is accordingly elected by that part of the society which is most interested in this object of government. In the federal constitution this policy does not prevail. The rights of property are committed into the same hands with the personal rights. Some attention ought therefore to be paid to property in the choice of those hands.

For another reason the votes allowed in the federal legislature to the people of each state, ought to bear some proportion to the comparative wealth of the states. States have not, like individuals, an influence over each other arising from superior advantages of fortune. If the law allows an opulent citizen but a single vote in the choice of his representative, the respect and consequence which he derives from his fortunate situation, very frequently guide the votes of others to the objects of his choice; and through this imperceptible channel the rights of property are conveyed into the public representation. A state possesses no such influence over other states. It is not probable that the richest state in the confederacy will ever influence the choice of a single representative in any other state. Nor will the representatives of the larger and richer states, possess any other advantage in the federal legislature over the representatives of other states, than what may result from their superior number alone; as far therefore as their superior wealth and weight may justly entitle them to any advantage, it ought to be secured to them by a superior share of representation. The new constitution is in this respect materially different from the existing confederation, as well as from that of the United Netherlands, and other similar confederacies. In each of the latter, the efficacy of the federal resolutions depends on the subsequent and voluntary resolutions of the states composing the union. Hence the states, though possessing an equal vote in the public councils, have an unequal influence, corresponding with the unequal importance of these subsequent and voluntary resolutions. Under the proposed constitution, the federal acts will take effect without the necessary intervention of the individual states. They will depend merely on the majority of votes in the federal legislature, and consequently each vote, whether proceeding from a larger or smaller state, or a state more or less wealthy or powerful, will have an equal weight and efficacy; in the same manner as the votes individually given in a state legislature, by the representatives of unequal counties or other districts, have each a precise equality of value and effect; or if there be any difference in the case, it proceeds from the difference in the personal character of the individual representative, rather than from any regard to the extent of the district from which he comes.

Such is the reasoning which an advocate for the southern interests might employ on this subject: And although it may appear to be a little strained in some points, yet on the whole, I must confess, that it fully reconciles me to the scale of representation, which the convention have established.

In one respect the establishment of a common measure for representation and taxation will have a very salutary effect. As the accuracy of the census to be obtained by the congress, will necessarily depend in a considerable degree on the disposition, if not the co-operation of the states, it is of great importance that the states should feel as little bias as possible to swell or to reduce the amount of their numbers. Were their share of representation alone to be governed by this rule, they would have an interest in exaggerating their inhabitants. Were the rule to decide their share of taxation alone, a contrary temptation would prevail. By extending the rule to both objects, the states will have opposite interests, which will control and balance each other; and produce the requisite impartiality.

February 12, 1788

The Federalist No. 55

The number of which the house of representatives is to consist, forms another, and a very interesting point of view under which this branch of the federal legislature may be contemplated. Scarce any article indeed in the whole constitution seems to be rendered more worthy of attention, by the weight of character and the apparent force of argument, with which it has been assailed. The charges exhibited against it are, first, that so small a number of representatives will be an unsafe depositary of the public interests; secondly that they will not possess a proper knowledge of the local circumstances of their numerous constituents; thirdly, that they will be taken from that class of citizens which will sympathize least with the feelings of the mass of the people, and be most likely to aim at a permanent elevation of the few on the depression of the many; fourthly, that defective as the number will be in the first instance, it will be more and more disproportionate, by the increase of the people, and the obstacles which will prevent a correspondent increase of the representatives.

In general it may be remarked on this subject, that no political problem is less susceptible of a precise solution, than that which relates to the number most convenient for a representative legislature; nor is there any point on which the policy of the several states is more at variance; whether we compare their legislative assemblies directly with each other, or consider the proportions which they respectively bear to the number of their constituents. Passing over the difference between the smallest and largest states, as Delaware, whose most numerous branch consists of twenty-one representatives, and Massachusetts, where it amounts to between three and four hundred; a very considerable difference is observable among states nearly equal in population. The number of representatives in Pennsylvania is not more than one fifth of that in the state last mentioned. New-York, whose population is to that of South-Carolina as six to five, has little more than one third of the number of representatives. As great a disparity prevails between the states of Georgia and Delaware, or Rhode-Island. In Pennsylvania the representatives do not bear a greater proportion to their constituents than of one for every four or five thousand. In Rhode-Island, they bear a proportion of at least one for every thousand. And according to the constitution of Georgia, the proportion may be carried to one for every ten electors; and must unavoidably far exceed the proportion in any of the other states.

Another general remark to be made is, that the ratio between the representatives and the people, ought not to be the same where the latter are very numerous, as where they are very few. Were the representatives in Virginia to be regulated by the standard in Rhode-Island, they would at this time amount to between four and five hundred; and twenty or thirty years hence, to a thousand. On the other hand, the ratio of Pennsylvania, if applied to the state of Delaware, would reduce the representative assembly of the latter to seven or eight members. Nothing can be more fallacious than to found our political calculations on arithmetical principles. Sixty or seventy men, may be more properly trusted with a given degree of power than six or seven. But it does not follow, that six or seven hundred would be proportionally a better depositary. And if we carry on the supposition to six or seven thousand, the whole reasoning ought to be reversed. The truth is, that in all cases a certain number at least seems to be necessary to secure the benefits of free consultation and discussion, and to guard against too easy a combination for improper purposes: As on the other hand, the number ought at most to be kept within a certain limit, in order to avoid the confusion and intemperance of a multitude. In all very numerous assemblies, of whatever characters composed, passion never fails to wrest the sceptre from reason. Had every Athenian citizen been a Socrates, every Athenian assembly would still have been a mob.

It is necessary also to recollect here the observations which were applied to the case of biennial elections. For the same reason that the limited powers of the congress and the control of the state legislatures, justify less frequent elections than the public safety might otherwise require; the members of the congress need be less numerous than if they possessed the whole power of legislation, and were under no other than the ordinary restraints of other legislative bodies.

With these general ideas in our minds, let us weigh the objections which have been stated against the number of members proposed for the house of representatives. It is said in the first place, that so small a number cannot be safely trusted with so much power.

The number of which this branch of the legislature is to consist at the outset of the government, will be sixty-five. Within three years a census is to be taken, when the number may be augmented to one for every thirty thousand inhabitants; and within every successive period of ten years, the census is to be renewed, and augmentations may continue to be made under the above limitation. It will not be thought an extravagant conjecture, that the first census will, at the rate of one for every thirty thousand, raise the number of representatives to at least one hundred. Estimating the negroes in the proportion of three-fifths, it can scarcely be doubted that the population of the United States will by that time, if it does not already, amount to three millions. At the expiration of twenty-five years, according to the computed rate of increase, the number of representatives will amount to two hundred; and of fifty years to four hundred. This is a number which I presume will put an end to all fears arising from the smallness of the body. I take for granted here what I shall in answering the fourth objection hereafter shew, that the number of representatives will be augmented from time to time in the manner provided by the constitution. On a contrary supposition, I should admit the objection to have very great weight indeed.

The true question to be decided then is, whether the smallness of the number as a temporary regulation, be dangerous to the public liberty: Whether sixty-five members for a few years, and a hundred or two hundred for a few more, be a safe depositary for a limited and well guarded power of legislating for the United States? I must own that I could not give a negative answer to this question, without first obliterating every impression which I have received with regard to the present genius of the people of America, the spirit which actuates the state legislatures, and the principles which are incorporated with the political character of every class of citizens. I am unable to conceive that the people of America in their present temper, or under any circumstances which can speedily happen, will chuse, and every second year repeat the choice of sixty-five or an hundred men, who would be disposed to form and pursue a scheme of tyranny or treachery. I am unable to conceive that the state legislatures which must feel so many motives to watch, and which possess so many means of counteracting the federal legislature, would fail either to detect or to defeat a conspiracy of the latter against the liberties of their common constituents. I am equally unable to conceive that there are at this time, or can be in any short time, in the United States, any sixty-five or an hundred men capable of recommending themselves to the choice of the people at large, who would either desire or dare within the short space of two years, to betray the solemn trust committed to them. What change of circumstances time and a fuller population of our country may produce, requires a prophetic spirit to declare, which makes no part of my pretensions. But judging from the circumstances now before us, and from the probable state of them within a moderate period of time, I must pronounce that the liberties of America cannot be unsafe in the number of hands proposed by the federal constitution.

From what quarter can the danger proceed? Are we afraid of foreign gold? If foreign gold could so easily corrupt our federal rulers, and enable them to ensnare and betray their constituents, how has it happened that we are at this time a free and independent nation? The congress which conducted us through the revolution were a less numerous body than their successors will be; they were not chosen by nor responsible to their fellow citizens at large; though appointed from year to year, and recallable at pleasure, they were generally continued for three years; and prior to the ratification of the federal articles, for a still longer term; they held their consultations always under the veil of secrecy; they had the sole transaction of our affairs with foreign nations; through the whole course of the war, they had the fate of their country more in their hands, than it is to be hoped will ever be the case with our future representatives; and from the greatness of the prize at stake and the eagerness of the party which lost it, it may well be supposed, that the use of other means than force would not have been scrupled: Yet we know by happy experience that the public trust was not betrayed; nor has the purity of our public councils in this particular ever suffered even from the whispers of calumny.

Is the danger apprehended from the other branches of the federal government? But where are the means to be found by the president or the senate, or both? Their emoluments of office it is to be presumed will not, and without a previous corruption of the house of representatives cannot, more than suffice for very different purposes: Their private fortunes, as they must all be American citizens, cannot possibly be sources of danger. The only means then which they can possess, will be in the dispensation of appointments. Is it here that suspicion rests her charge? Sometimes we are told that this fund of corruption is to be exhausted by the president in subduing the virtue of the senate. Now the fidelity of the other house is to be the victim. The improbability of such a mercenary and perfidious combination of the several members of government standing on as different foundations as republican principles will well admit, and at the same time accountable to the society over which they are placed, ought alone to quiet this apprehension. But fortunately the constitution has provided a still further safeguard. The members of the congress are rendered ineligible to any civil offices that may be created or of which the emoluments may be increased, during the term of their election. No offices therefore can be dealt out to the existing members, but such as may become vacant by ordinary casualties; and to suppose that these would be sufficient to purchase the guardians of the people, selected by the people themselves, is to renounce every rule by which events ought to be calculated, and to substitute an indiscriminate and unbounded jealousy, with which all reasoning must be vain. The sincere friends of liberty who give themselves up to the extravagancies of this passion are not aware of the injury they do their own cause. As there is a degree of depravity in mankind which requires a certain degree of circumspection and distrust: So there are other qualities in human nature, which justify a certain portion of esteem and confidence. Republican government presupposes the existence of these qualities in a higher degree than any other form. Were the pictures which have been drawn by the political jealousy of some among us, faithful likenesses of the human character, the inference would be that there is not sufficient virtue among men for self-government; and that nothing less than the chains of despotism can restrain them from destroying and devouring one another.

February 13, 1788

The Federalist No. 56

The *second* charge against the house of representatives is, that it will be too small to possess a due knowledge of the interests of its constituents.

As this objection evidently proceeds from a comparison of the proposed number of representatives, with the great extent of the United States, the number of their inhabitants, and the diversity of their interests, without taking into view at the same time the circumstances which will distinguish the congress from other legislative bodies, the best answer that can be given to it, will be a brief explanation of these peculiarities.

It is a sound and important principle, that the representative ought to be acquainted with the interests and circumstances of his constituents. But this principle can extend no farther than to those circumstances and interests to which the authority and care of the representative relate. An ignorance of a variety of minute and particular objects, which do not lie within the compass of legislation, is consistent with every attribute necessary to a due performance of the legislative trust. In determining the extent of information required in the exercise of a particular authority, recourse then must be had to the objects within the purview of that authority.

What are to be the objects of federal legislation? Those which are of most importance, and which seem most to require local knowledge, are commerce, taxation and the militia.

A proper regulation of commerce requires much information, as has been elsewhere remarked; but as far as this information relates to the laws and local situation of each individual state, a very few representatives would be very sufficient vehicles of it to the federal councils.

Taxation will consist in great measure, of duties which will be involved in the regulation of commerce. So far the preceding remark is applicable to this object. As far as it may consist of internal collections, a more diffusive knowledge of the circumstances of the state may be necessary. But will not this also be possessed in sufficient degree by a very few intelligent men, diffusively elected within the state. Divide the largest state into ten or twelve districts, and it will be found that there will be no peculiar local interest in either, which will not be within the knowledge of the representative of the district. Besides this source of information, the laws of the state framed by representatives from every part of it, will be almost of themselves a sufficient guide. In every state there have been made, and must continue to be made, regulations on this subject, which will in many cases leave little more to be done by the federal legislature, than to review the different laws, and reduce them into one general act. A skilful individual in his closet, with all the local codes before him, might compile a law on some subjects of taxation for the whole union, without any aid from oral information; and it may be expected, that whenever internal taxes may be necessary, and particularly in cases requiring uniformity throughout the states, the more simple objects will be preferred. To be fully sensible of the facility which will be given to this branch of federal legislation, by the assistance of the state codes, we need only suppose for a moment, that this or any other state were divided into a number of parts, each having and exercising within itself a power of local legislation. Is it not evident that a degree of local information and preparatory labour would be found in the several volumes of their proceedings, which would very much shorten the labours of the general legislature, and render a much smaller number of members sufficient for it? The federal councils will derive great advantage from another circumstance. The representatives of each state will not only bring with them a considerable knowledge of its laws, and a local knowledge of their respective districts; but will probably in all cases have been members, and may even at the very time be members of the state legislature, where all the local information and interests of the state are assembled, and from whence they may easily be conveyed by a very few hands into the legislature of the United States.

With regard to the regulation of the militia, there are scarcely any circumstances in reference to which local knowledge can be said to be necessary. The general face of the country, whether mountainous or level, most fit for the operations of infantry or cavalry, is almost the only consideration of this nature that can occur. The art of war teaches general principles of organization, movement and discipline, which apply universally.

The attentive reader will discern that the reasoning here used to prove the sufficiency of a moderate number of representatives, does not in any respect contradict what was urged on another occasion with regard to the extensive information which the representatives ought to possess, and the time that might be necessary for acquiring it. This information, so far as it may relate to local objects, is rendered necessary and difficult, not by a difference of laws and local circumstances within a single state, but of those among different states. Taking each state by itself, its laws are the same, and its interests but little diversified. A few men therefore will possess all the knowledge requisite for a proper representation of them. Were the interests and affairs of each individual state, perfectly simple and uniform, a knowledge of them in one part would involve a knowledge of them in every other, and the whole state might be competently represented, by a single member taken from any part of it. On a comparison of the different states together, we find a great dissimilarity in their laws, and in many other circumstances connected with the objects of federal legislation, with all of which the federal representatives ought to have some acquaintance. Whilst a few representatives therefore from each state may bring with them a due knowledge of their own state, every representative will have much information to acquire concerning all the other states. The changes of time, as was formerly remarked, on the comparative situation of the different states, will have an assimilating effect. The effect of time on the internal affairs of the states taken singly, will be just the contrary. At present some of the states are little more than a society of husbandmen. Few of them have made much progress in those branches of industry, which give a variety and complexity to the affairs of a nation. These however will in all of them be the fruits of a more advanced population; and will require on the part of each state a fuller representation. The foresight of the convention has accordingly taken care that the progress of population may be accompanied with a proper increase of the representative branch of the government.

The experience of Great Britain which presents to mankind

so many political lessons, both of the monitory and exemplary kind, and which has been frequently consulted in the course of these enquiries, corroborates the result of the reflections which we have just made. The number of inhabitants in the two kingdoms of England and Scotland, cannot be stated at less than eight millions. The representatives of these eight millions in the house of commons, amount to five hundred fifty eight. Of this number one ninth are elected by three hundred and sixty four persons, and one half by five thousand seven hundred and twenty three persons.* It cannot be supposed that the half thus elected, and who do not even reside among the people at large, can add any thing either to the security of the people against the government, or to the knowledge of their circumstances and interests, in the legislative councils. On the contrary it is notorious that they are more frequently the representatives and instruments of the executive magistrate, than the guardians and advocates of the popular rights. They might therefore with great propriety be considered as something more than a mere deduction from the real representatives of the nation. We will however consider them, in this light alone, and will not extend the deduction, to a considerable number of others, who do not reside among their constituents, are very faintly connected with them, and have very little particular knowledge of their affairs. With all these concessions two hundred and seventy nine persons only will be the depositary of the safety, interest and happiness of eight millions; that is to say; there will be one representative only to maintain the rights and explain the situation *of twenty-eight thousand six hundred and seventy* constituents, in an assembly exposed to the whole force of executive influence, and extending its authority to every object of legislation within a nation whose affairs are in the highest degree diversified and complicated. Yet it is very certain not only that a valuable portion of freedom has been preserved under all these circumstances, but that the defects in the British code are chargeable in a very small proportion, on the ignorance of the legislature concerning the circumstances of the people. Allowing to this case the weight which is due

*Burgh's Political Disquisitions.

to it; and comparing it with that of the house of representatives as above explained, it seems to give the fullest assurance that a representative for every *thirty thousand inhabitants* will render the latter both a safe and competent guardian of the interests which will be confided to it.

February 16, 1788

The Federalist No. 57

The *third* charge against the house of representatives is, that it will be taken from that class of citizens which will have least sympathy with the mass of the people, and be most likely to aim at an ambitious sacrifice of the many to the aggrandizement of the few.

Of all the objections which have been framed against the federal constitution, this is perhaps the most extraordinary. Whilst the objection itself is levelled against a pretended oligarchy, the principle of it strikes at the very root of republican government.

The aim of every political constitution is, or ought to be, first, to obtain for rulers men who possess most wisdom to discern, and most virtue to pursue the common good of the society; and in the next place, to take the most effectual precautions for keeping them virtuous, whilst they continue to hold their public trust. The elective mode of obtaining rulers is the characteristic policy of republican government. The means relied on in this form of government for preventing their degeneracy, are numerous and various. The most effectual one is such a limitation of the term of appointments, as will maintain a proper responsibility to the people.

Let me now ask what circumstance there is in the constitution of the house of representatives, that violates the principles of republican government; or favors the elevation of the few on the ruins of the many? Let me ask whether every circumstance is not, on the contrary, strictly conformable to these principles; and scrupulously impartial to the rights and pretensions of every class and description of citizens?

Who are to be the electors of the federal representatives? Not the rich more than the poor; not the learned more than the ignorant; not the haughty heirs of distinguished names, more than the humble sons of obscure and unpropitious fortune. The electors are to be the great body of the people of the United States. They are to be the same who exercise the right in every state of electing the correspondent branch of the legislature of the state.

Who are to be the objects of popular choice? Every citizen

whose merit may recommend him to the esteem and confidence of his country. No qualification of wealth, of birth, of religious faith, or of civil profession, is permitted to fetter the judgment or disappoint the inclination of the people.

If we consider the situation of the men on whom the free suffrages of their fellow citizens may confer the representative trust, we shall find it involving every security which can be devised or desired for their fidelity to their constituents.

In the first place, as they will have been distinguished by the preference of their fellow citizens, we are to presume, that in general, they will be somewhat distinguished also, by those qualities which entitle them to it, and which promise a sincere and scrupulous regard to the nature of their engagements.

In the second place, they will enter into the public service under circumstances which cannot fail to produce a temporary affection at least to their constituents. There is in every breast a sensibility to marks of honour, of favour, of esteem, and of confidence, which, apart from all considerations of interest, is some pledge for grateful and benevolent returns. Ingratitude is a common topic of declamation against human nature; and it must be confessed, that instances of it are but too frequent and flagrant both in public and in private life. But the universal and extreme indignation which it inspires, is itself a proof of the energy and prevalence of the contrary sentiment.

In the third place, those ties which bind the representative to his constituents are strengthened by motives of a more selfish nature. His pride and vanity attach him to a form of government which favors his pretensions, and gives him a share in its honors and distinctions. Whatever hopes or projects might be entertained by a few aspiring characters, it must generally happen that a great proportion of the men deriving their advancement from their influence with the people, would have more to hope from a preservation of the favor, than from innovations in the government subversive of the authority of the people.

All these securities however would be found very insufficient without the restraint of frequent elections. Hence, in the fourth place, the house of representatives is so constituted as to support in the members an habitual recollection of their dependence on the people. Before the sentiments impressed on their minds by the mode of their elevation, can be effaced by the exercise of power, they will be compelled to anticipate the moment when their power is to cease, when their exercise of it is to be reviewed, and when they must descend to the level from which they were raised; there forever to remain, unless a faithful discharge of their trust shall have established their title to a renewal of it.

I will add as a fifth circumstance in the situation of the house of representatives, restraining them from oppressive measures, that they can make no law which will not have its full operation on themselves and their friends, as well as on the great mass of the society. This has always been deemed one of the strongest bonds by which human policy can connect the rulers and the people together. It creates between them that communion of interest and sympathy of sentiments of which few governments have furnished examples; but without which every government degenerates into tyranny. If it be asked what is to restrain the house of representatives from making legal discriminations in favor of themselves and a particular class of the society? I answer, the genius of the whole system, the nature of just and constitutional laws, and above all the vigilant and manly spirit which actuates the people of America, a spirit which nourishes freedom, and in return is nourished by it.

If this spirit shall ever be so far debased as to tolerate a law not obligatory on the legislature as well as on the people, the people will be prepared to tolerate any thing but liberty.

Such will be the relation between the house of representatives and their constituents. Duty, gratitude, interest, ambition itself, are the cords by which they will be bound to fidelity and sympathy with the great mass of the people. It is possible that these may all be insufficient to control the caprice and wickedness of men. But are they not all that government will admit, and that human prudence can devise? Are they not the genuine and the characteristic means by which republican government provides for the liberty and happiness of the people? Are they not the identical means on which every state government in the union, relies for the attainment of these important ends? What then are we to understand by the objection which this paper has combated? What are we to say to the men who profess the most flaming zeal for republican government, yet boldly impeach the fundamental principle of it; who pretend to be champions for the right and the capacity of the people to chuse their own rulers, yet maintain that they will prefer those only who will immediately and infallibly betray the trust committed to them?

Were the objection to be read by one who had not seen the mode prescribed by the constitution for the choice of representatives, he could suppose nothing less than that some unreasonable qualification of property was annexed to the right of suffrage; or that the right of eligibility was limited to persons of particular families or fortunes; or at least that the mode prescribed by the state constitutions was in some respect or other very grossly departed from. We have seen how far such a supposition would err as to the two first points. Nor would it in fact be less erroneous as to the last. The only difference discoverable between the two cases is, that each representative of the United States will be elected by five or six thousand citizens; whilst in the individual states the election of a representative is left to about as many hundred. Will it be pretended that this difference is sufficient to justify an attachment to the state governments and an abhorrence to the federal government? If this be the point on which the objection turns, it deserves to be examined.

Is it supported by *reason*? This cannot be said, without maintaining that five or six thousand citizens are less capable of chusing a fit representative, or more liable to be corrupted by an unfit one, than five or six hundred. Reason, on the contrary assures us, that as in so great a number, a fit representative would be most likely to be found, so the choice would be less likely to be diverted from him, by the intrigues of the ambitious, or the bribes of the rich.

Is the *consequence* from this doctrine admissible? If we say that five or six hundred citizens are as many as can jointly exercise their right of suffrage, must we not deprive the people of the immediate choice of their public servants in every instance where the administration of the government does not require as many of them as will amount to one for that number of citizens?

Is the doctrine warranted by *facts?* It was shewn in the last paper, that the real representation in the British house of commons very little exceeds the proportion of one for every thirty thousand inhabitants. Besides a variety of powerful causes, not existing here and which favor in that country, the pretensions of rank and wealth, no person is eligible as a representative of a county, unless he possess real estate of the clear value of six hundred pounds sterling per year; nor of a city or borough, unless he possess a like estate of half that annual value. To this qualification on the part of the county representatives, is added another on the part of the county electors, which restrains the right of suffrage to persons having a freehold estate of the annual value of more than twenty pounds sterling, according to the present rate of money. Notwithstanding these unfavourable circumstances, and notwithstanding some very unequal laws in the British code, it cannot be said that the representatives of the nation have elevated the few on the ruins of the many.

But we need not resort to foreign experience on this subject. Our own is explicit and decisive. The districts in New-Hampshire in which the senators are chosen immediately by the people, are nearly as large as will be necessary for her representatives in the congress. Those of Massachusetts are larger than will be necessary for that purpose. And those of New-York still more so. In the last state the members of assembly, for the cities and counties of New-York and Albany, are elected by very nearly as many voters as will be entitled to a representative in the congress, calculating on the number of sixty-five representatives only. It makes no difference that in these senatorial districts and counties, a number of representatives are voted for by each elector at the same time. If the same electors, at the same time, are capable of choosing four or five representatives, they cannot be incapable of choosing one. Pennsylvania is an additional example. Some of her counties which elect her state representatives, are almost as large as her districts will be by which her federal representatives will be elected. The city of Philadelphia is supposed to contain between fifty and sixty thousand souls. It will therefore form nearly two districts for the choice of federal representatives. It forms however but one county, in which every elector votes for each of its representatives in the state legislature. And what may appear to be still more directly to our purpose, the whole city actually elects a *single member* for the executive council. This is the case in all the other counties of the state.

Are not these facts the most satisfactory proofs of the fallacy which has been employed against the branch of the federal government under consideration? Has it appeared on trial that the senators of New-Hampshire, Massachusetts and New-York; or the executive council of Pennsylvania; or the members of the assembly in the two last states, have betrayed any peculiar disposition to sacrifice the many to the few; or are in any respect less worthy of their places than the representatives and magistrates appointed in other states, by very small divisions of the people?

But there are cases of a stronger complexion than any which I have yet quoted. One branch of the legislature of Connecticut is so constituted that each member of it is elected by the whole state. So is the governor of that state, of Massachusetts, and of this state, and the president of New Hampshire. I leave every man to decide whether the result of any one of these experiments can be said to countenance a suspicion that a diffusive mode of chusing representatives of the people tends to elevate traitors, and to undermine the public liberty.

February 19, 1788

The Federalist No. 58

The remaining charge against the house of representatives which I am to examine, is grounded on a supposition that the number of members will not be augmented from time to time, as the progress of population may demand.

It has been admitted that this objection, if well supported, would have great weight. The following observations will shew that like most other objections against the constitution, it can only proceed from a partial view of the subject; or from a jealousy which discolours and disfigures every object which is beheld.

1. Those who urge the objection seem not to have recollected that the federal constitution will not suffer by a comparison with the state constitutions, in the security provided for a gradual augmentation of the number of representatives. The number which is to prevail in the first instance is declared to be temporary. Its duration is limited to the short term of three years.

Within every successive term of ten years, a census of inhabitants is to be repeated. The unequivocal objects of these regulations are, first, to re-adjust from time to time the apportionment of representatives to the number of inhabitants; under the single exception that each state shall have one representative at least: Secondly, to augment the number of representatives at the same periods; under the sole limitation, that the whole number shall not exceed one for every thirty thousand inhabitants. If we review the constitutions of the several states, we shall find that some of them contain no determinate regulations on this subject; that others correspond pretty much on this point with the federal constitution; and that the most effectual security in any of them is resolvable into a mere directory provision.

2. As far as experience has taken place on this subject, a gradual increase of representatives under the state constitutions, has at least kept pace with that of the constituents; and it appears that the former have been as ready to concur in such measures, as the latter have been to call for them.

3. There is a peculiarity in the federal constitution which

ensures a watchful attention in a majority both of the people and of their representatives, to a constitutional augmentation of the latter. The peculiarity lies in this, that one branch of the legislature is a representation of citizens; the other of the states: In the former, consequently the larger states will have most weight; in the latter, the advantage will be in favor of the smaller states. From this circumstance it may with certainty be inferred, that the larger states will be strenuous advocates for increasing the number and weight of that part of the legislature in which their influence predominates. And it so happens that four only of the largest, will have a majority of the whole votes in the house of representatives. Should the representatives or people therefore of the smaller states oppose at any time a reasonable addition of members, a coalition of a very few states will be sufficient to overrule the opposition; a coalition, which notwithstanding the rivalship and local prejudices which might prevent it on ordinary occasions, would not fail to take place, when not merely prompted by common interest but justified by equity and the principles of the constitution.

It may be alledged, perhaps, that the senate would be prompted by like motives to an adverse coalition; and as their concurrence would be indispensable, the just and constitutional views of the other branch might be defeated. This is the difficulty which has probably created the most serious apprehensions in the jealous friends of a numerous representation. Fortunately it is among the difficulties which, existing only in appearance, vanish on a close and accurate inspection. The following reflections will, if I mistake not, be admitted to be conclusive and satisfactory on this point.

Notwithstanding the equal authority which will subsist between the two houses on all legislative subjects, except the originating of money bills, it cannot be doubted that the house composed of the greater number of members, when supported by the more powerful states, and speaking the known and determined sense of a majority of the people, will have no small advantage in a question depending on the comparative firmness of the two houses.

This advantage must be increased by the consciousness felt by the same side, of being supported in its demands, by right, by reason, and by the constitution; and the consciousness on the opposite side, of contending against the force of all these solemn considerations.

It is farther to be considered that in the gradation between the smallest and largest states, there are several which, though most likely in general to arrange themselves among the former, are too little removed in extent and population from the latter, to second an opposition to their just and legitimate pretensions. Hence it is by no means certain that a majority of votes, even in the senate, would be unfriendly to proper augmentations in the number of representatives.

It will not be looking too far to add, that the senators from all the new states may be gained over to the just views of the house of representatives, by an expedient too obvious to be overlooked. As these states will for a great length of time advance in population with peculiar rapidity, they will be interested in frequent re-apportionments of the representatives to the number of inhabitants. The large states therefore, who will prevail in the house of representatives, will have nothing to do, but to make reapportionments and augmentations mutually conditions of each other; and the senators from all the most growing states will be bound to contend for the latter, by the interest which their states will feel in the former.

These considerations seem to afford ample security on this subject; and ought alone to satisfy all the doubts and fears which have been indulged with regard to it. Admitting however, that they should all be insufficient to subdue the unjust policy of the smaller states, or their predominant influence in the councils of the senate; a constitutional and infallible resource still remains with the larger states, by which they will be able at all times to accomplish their just purposes. The house of representatives can not only refuse, but they alone can propose the supplies requisite for the support of government. They in a word hold the purse; that powerful instrument by which we behold in the history of the British constitution, an infant and humble representation of the people, gradually enlarging the sphere of its activity and importance, and finally reducing, as far as it seems to have wished, all the overgrown prerogatives of the other branches of the government. This power over the purse, may in fact be regarded as the most compleat and effectual weapon with which any constitution can arm the immediate representatives of the people, for obtaining a redress of every grievance, and for carrying into effect every just and salutary measure.

But will not the house of representatives be as much interested as the senate in maintaining the government in its proper functions, and will they not therefore be unwilling to stake its existence or its reputation on the pliancy of the senate? Or if such a trial of firmness between the two branches were hazarded, would not the one be as likely first to yield as the other? These questions will create no difficulty with those who reflect, that in all cases the smaller the number and the more permanent and conspicuous the station of men in power, the stronger must be the interest which they will individually feel in whatever concerns the government. Those who represent the dignity of their country in the eyes of other nations, will be particularly sensible to every prospect of public danger or of a dishonorable stagnation in public affairs. To those causes we are to ascribe the continual triumph of the British house of commons over the other branches of the government, whenever the engine of a money bill has been employed. An absolute inflexibility on the side of the latter, although it could not have failed to involve every department of the state in the general confusion, has neither been apprehended nor experienced. The utmost degree of firmness that can be displayed by the federal senate or president will not be more than equal to a resistance in which they will be supported by constitutional and patriotic principles.

In this review of the constitution of the house of representatives, I have passed over the circumstance of economy, which in the present state of affairs might have had some effect in lessening the temporary number of representatives; and a disregard of which would probably have been as rich a theme of declamation against the constitution as has been furnished by the smallness of the number proposed. I omit also any remarks on the difficulty which might be found, under present circumstances, in engaging in the federal service, a large number of such characters as the people will probably elect. One observation however, I must be permitted to add on this subject, as claiming in my judgment a very serious

attention. It is, that in all legislative assemblies, the greater
the number composing them may be, the fewer will be the
men who will in fact direct their proceedings. In the first
place, the more numerous any assembly may be, of whatever
characters composed, the greater is known to be the ascendancy of passion over reason. In the next place, the larger the
number, the greater will be the proportion of members of
limited information and of weak capacities. Now it is precisely
on characters of this description that the eloquence and address of the few are known to act with all their force. In the
antient republics, where the whole body of the people assembled in person, a single orator, or an artful statesman, was
generally seen to rule with as compleat a sway, as if a sceptre
had been placed in his single hands. On the same principle
the more multitudinous a representative assembly may be rendered, the more it will partake of the infirmities incident to
collective meetings of the people. Ignorance will be the dupe
of cunning; and passion the slave of sophistry and declamation. The people can never err more than in supposing that by
multiplying their representatives beyond a certain limit, they
strengthen the barrier against the government of a few.
Experience will forever admonish them that on the contrary,
*after securing a sufficient number for the purposes of safety, of
local information, and of diffusive sympathy with the whole society*, they will counteract their own views by every addition
to their representatives. The countenance of the government
may become more democratic; but the soul that animates it
will be more oligarchic. The machine will be enlarged, but
the fewer, and often the more secret, will be the springs by
which its motions are directed.

As connected with the objection against the number of representatives, may properly be here noticed, that which has
been suggested against the number made competent for legislative business. It has been said that more than a majority
ought to have been required for a quorum, and in particular
cases, if not in all, more than a majority of a quorum for a decision. That some advantages might have resulted from such a
precaution, cannot be denied. It might have been an additional shield to some particular interests, and another obstacle
generally to hasty and partial measures. But these considera-

tions are outweighed by the inconveniencies in the opposite scale. In all cases where justice or the general good might require new laws to be passed, or active measures to be pursued, the fundamental principle of free government would be reversed. It would be no longer the majority that would rule; the power would be transferred to the minority. Were the defensive privilege limited to particular cases, an interested minority might take advantage of it to screen themselves from equitable sacrifices to the general weal, or in particular emergencies to extort unreasonable indulgences. Lastly, it would facilitate and foster the baneful practice of secessions; a practice which has shewn itself even in states where a majority only is required; a practice subversive of all the principles of order and regular government; a practice which leads more directly to public convulsions, and the ruin of popular governments, than any other which has yet been displayed among us.

February 20, 1788

The Federalist No. 62

Having examined the constitution of the house of representatives, and answered such of the objections against it as seemed to merit notice, I enter next on the examination of the senate. The heads into which this member of the government may be considered, are—I. the qualifications of senators —II. the appointment of them by the state legislatures—III. the equality of representation in the senate—IV. the number of senators, and the term for which they are to be elected— V. the powers vested in the senate.

I. The qualifications proposed for senators, as distinguished from those of representatives, consist in a more advanced age, and a longer period of citizenship. A senator must be thirty years of age at least; as a representative, must be twenty-five. And the former must have been a citizen nine years; as seven years are required for the latter. The propriety of these distinctions is explained by the nature of the senatorial trust; which requiring greater extent of information and stability of character, requires at the same time that the senator should have reached a period of life most likely to supply these advantages; and which participating immediately in transactions with foreign nations, ought to be exercised by none who are not thoroughly weaned from the prepossessions and habits incident to foreign birth and education. The term of nine years appears to be a prudent mediocrity between a total exclusion of adopted citizens, whose merit and talents may claim a share in the public confidence; and an indiscriminate and hasty admission of them, which might create a channel for foreign influence on the national councils.

II. It is equally unnecessary to dilate on the appointment of senators by the state legislatures. Among the various modes which might have been devised for constituting this branch of the government, that which has been proposed by the convention is probably the most congenial with the public opinion. It is recommended by the double advantage of favoring a select appointment, and of giving to the state governments such an agency in the formation of the federal government, as must secure the authority of the former, and may form a convenient link between the two systems.

III. The equality of representation in the senate is another point, which, being evidently the result of compromise between the opposite pretensions of the large and the small states, does not call for much discussion. If indeed it be right that among a people thoroughly incorporated into one nation, every district ought to have a *proportional* share in the government; and that among independent and sovereign states bound together by a simple league, the parties however unequal in size, ought to have an *equal* share in the common councils, it does not appear to be without some reason, that in a compound republic partaking both of the national and federal character, the government ought to be founded on a mixture of the principles of proportional and equal representation. But it is superfluous to try by the standard of theory, a part of the constitution which is allowed on all hands to be the result not of theory, but "of a spirit of amity, and that mutual deference and concession which the peculiarity of our political situation rendered indispensable." A common government, with powers equal to its objects, is called for by the voice, and still more loudly by the political situation of America. A government founded on principles more consonant to the wishes of the larger states, is not likely to be obtained from the smaller states. The only option then for the former lies between the proposed government and a government still more objectionable. Under this alternative the advice of prudence must be, to embrace the lesser evil; and instead of indulging a fruitless anticipation of the possible mischiefs which may ensue, to contemplate rather the advantageous consequences which may qualify the sacrifice.

In this spirit it may be remarked, that the equal vote allowed to each state, is at once a constitutional recognition of the portion of sovereignty remaining in the individual states, and an instrument for preserving that residuary sovereignty. So far the equality ought to be no less acceptable to the large than to the small states; since they are not less solicitous to guard by every possible expedient against an improper consolidation of the states into one simple republic.

Another advantage accruing from this ingredient in the

constitution of the senate, is the additional impediment it must prove against improper acts of legislation. No law or resolution can now be passed without the concurrence first of a majority of the people, and then of a majority of the states. It must be acknowledged that this complicated check on legislation may in some instances be injurious as well as beneficial; and that the peculiar defence which it involves in favor of the smaller states would be more rational, if any interests common to them, and distinct from those of the other states, would otherwise be exposed to peculiar danger. But as the larger states will always be able by their power over the supplies, to defeat unreasonable exertions of this prerogative of the lesser states; and as the facility and excess of law making seem to be the diseases to which our governments are most liable, it is not impossible that this part of the constitution may be more convenient in practice than it appears to many in contemplation.

IV. The number of senators and the duration of their appointment come next to be considered. In order to form an accurate judgment on both these points, it will be proper to enquire into the purposes which are to be answered by a senate; and in order to ascertain these it will be necessary to review the inconveniencies which a republic must suffer from the want of such an institution.

First. It is a misfortune incident to republican government, though in a less degree than to other governments, that those who administer it, may forget their obligations to their constituents, and prove unfaithful to their important trust. In this point of view, a senate, as a second branch of the legislative assembly, distinct from, and dividing the power with, a first, must be in all cases a salutary check on the government. It doubles the security to the people, by requiring the concurrence of two distinct bodies in schemes of usurpation or perfidy, where the ambition or corruption of one, would otherwise be sufficient. This is a precaution founded on such clear principles, and now so well understood in the United States, that it would be more than superfluous to enlarge on it. I will barely remark that as the improbability of sinister combinations will be in proportion to the dissimilarity in the genius of the two bodies; it must be politic to distinguish them from each other by every circumstance which will consist with a due harmony in all proper measures, and with the genuine principles of republican government.

Second. The necessity of a senate is not less indicated by the propensity of all single and numerous assemblies, to yield to the impulse of sudden and violent passions, and to be seduced by factious leaders into intemperate and pernicious resolutions. Examples on this subject might be cited without number; and from proceedings within the United States, as well as from the history of other nations. But a position that will not be contradicted need not be proved. All that need be remarked is that a body which is to correct this infirmity ought itself be free from it, and consequently ought to be less numerous. It ought moreover to possess great firmness, and consequently ought to hold its authority by a tenure of considerable duration.

Third. Another defect to be supplied by a senate lies in a want of due acquaintance with the objects and principles of legislation. It is not possible that an assembly of men called for the most part from pursuits of a private nature, continued in appointment for a short time, and led by no permanent motive to devote the intervals of public occupation to a study of the laws, the affairs and the comprehensive interests of their country, should, if left wholly to themselves, escape a variety of important errors in the exercise of their legislative trust. It may be affirmed, on the best grounds, that no small share of the present embarrassments of America is to be charged on the blunders of our governments; and that these have proceeded from the heads rather than the hearts of most of the authors of them. What indeed are all the repealing, explaining and amending laws, which fill and disgrace our voluminous codes, but so many monuments of deficient wisdom; so many impeachments exhibited by each succeeding, against each preceding session; so many admonitions to the people of the value of those aids which may be expected from a well constituted senate?

A good government implies two things; first, fidelity to the object of government, which is the happiness of the people; secondly, a knowledge of the means by which that object can be best attained. Some governments are deficient in both these qualities: Most governments are deficient in the first. I scruple not to assert that in the American governments, too little attention has been paid to the last. The federal constitution avoids this error; and what merits particular notice, it provides for the last in a mode which increases the security for the first.

Fourth. The mutability in the public councils, arising from a rapid succession of new members, however qualified they may be, points out in the strongest manner, the necessity of some stable institution in the government. Every new election in the states, is found to change one half of the representatives. From this change of men must proceed a change of opinions; and from a change of opinions, a change of measures. But a continual change even of good measures is inconsistent with every rule of prudence, and every prospect of success. The remark is verified in private life, and becomes more just as well as more important, in national transactions.

To trace the mischievous effects of a mutable government would fill a volume. I will hint a few only, each of which will be perceived to be a source of innumerable others.

In the first place it forfeits the respect and confidence of other nations, and all the advantages connected with national character. An individual who is observed to be inconstant to his plans, or perhaps to carry on his affairs without any plan at all, is marked at once by all prudent people, as a speedy victim to his own unsteadiness and folly. His more friendly neighbours may pity him; but all will decline to connect their fortunes with his; and not a few will seize the opportunity of making their fortunes out of his. One nation is to another what one individual is to another; with this melancholy distinction perhaps, that the former with fewer of the benevolent emotions than the latter, are under fewer restraints also from taking undue advantage of the indiscretions of each other. Every nation consequently, whose affairs betray a want of wisdom and stability, may calculate on every loss which can be sustained from the more systematic policy of its wiser neighbours. But the best instruction on this subject is unhappily conveyed to America by the example of her own situation. She finds that she is held in no respect by her friends; that she is the derision of her enemies; and that she is a prey to every nation which has an interest in speculating on her fluctuating councils and embarrassed affairs.

The internal effects of a mutable policy are still more calamitous. It poisons the blessings of liberty itself. It will be of little avail to the people that the laws are made by men of their own choice, if the laws be so voluminous that they cannot be read, or so incoherent that they cannot be understood; if they be repealed or revised before they are promulged, or undergo such incessant changes that no man who knows what the law is today can guess what it will be to-morrow. Law is defined to be a rule of action; but how can that be a rule, which is little known and less fixed?

Another effect of public instability is the unreasonable advantage it gives to the sagacious, the enterprising and the moneyed few, over the industrious and uninformed mass of the people. Every new regulation concerning commerce or revenue; or in any manner affecting the value of the different species of property, presents a new harvest to those who watch the change and can trace its consequences; a harvest reared not by themselves but by the toils and cares of the great body of their fellow citizens. This is a state of things in which it may be said with some truth that laws are made for the *few* not for the *many.*

In another point of view great injury results from an unstable government. The want of confidence in the public councils damps every useful undertaking; the success and profit of which may depend on a continuance of existing arrangements. What prudent merchant will hazard his fortunes in any new branch of commerce, when he knows not but that his plans may be rendered unlawful before they can be executed? What farmer or manufacturer will lay himself out for the encouragement given to any particular cultivation or establishment, when he can have no assurance that his preparatory labours and advances will not render him a victim to an inconstant government? In a word, no great improvement or laudable enterprise can go forward, which requires the auspices of a steady system of national policy.

But the most deplorable effect of all is that diminution of attachment and reverence which steals into the hearts of the people, towards a political system which betrays so many marks of infirmity, and disappoints so many of their flattering hopes. No government any more than an individual will long be respected, without being truly respectable, nor be truly respectable without possessing a certain portion of order and stability.

February 27, 1788

The Federalist No. 63

A fifth desideratum illustrating the utility of a senate, is the want of a due sense of national character. Without a select and stable member of the government, the esteem of foreign powers will not only be forfeited by an unenlightened and variable policy, proceeding from the causes already mentioned; but the national councils will not possess that sensibility to the opinion of the world, which is perhaps not less necessary in order to merit, than it is to obtain, its respect and confidence.

An attention to the judgment of other nations is important to every government for two reasons: The one is, that independently of the merits of any particular plan or measure, it is desirable on various accounts, that it should appear to other nations as the offspring of a wise and honorable policy: The second is, that in doubtful cases, particularly where the national councils may be warped by some strong passion, or momentary interest, the presumed or known opinion of the impartial world, may be the best guide that can be followed. What has not America lost by her want of character with foreign nations? And how many errors and follies would she not have avoided, if the justice and propriety of her measures had in every instance been previously tried by the light in which they would probably appear to the unbiassed part of mankind.

Yet however requisite a sense of national character may be, it is evident that it can never be sufficiently possessed by a numerous and changeable body. It can only be found in a number so small, that a sensible degree of the praise and blame of public measures may be the portion of each individual; or in an assembly so durably invested with public trust, that the pride and consequence of its members may be sensibly incorporated with the reputation and prosperity of the community. The half-yearly representatives of Rhode-Island, would probably have been little affected in their deliberations on the iniquitous measures of that state, by arguments drawn from the light in which such measures would be viewed by foreign nations, or even by the sister states; whilst it can scarcely be doubted, that if the concurrence of a select and stable body had been necessary, a regard to national character alone, would have prevented the calamities under which that misguided people is now labouring.

I add as a *sixth* defect, the want in some important cases of a due responsibility in the government to the people, arising from that frequency of elections, which in other cases produces this responsibility. The remark will perhaps appear not only new but paradoxical. It must nevertheless be acknowledged, when explained, to be as undeniable as it is important.

Responsibility in order to be reasonable must be limited to objects within the power of the responsible party; and in order to be effectual, must relate to operations of that power, of which a ready and proper judgment can be formed by the constituents. The objects of government may be divided into two general classes; the one depending on measures which have singly an immediate and sensible operation; the other depending on a succession of well chosen and well connected measures, which have a gradual and perhaps unobserved operation. The importance of the latter description to the collective and permanent welfare of every country needs no explanation. And yet it is evident, that an assembly elected for so short a term as to be unable to provide more than one or two links in a chain of measures, on which the general welfare may essentially depend, ought not to be answerable for the final result, any more than a steward or tenant, engaged for one year, could be justly made to answer for places or improvements, which could not be accomplished in less than half a dozen years. Nor is it possible for the people to estimate the *share* of influence which their annual assemblies may respectively have on events resulting from the mixed transactions of several years. It is sufficiently difficult, at any rate, to preserve a personal responsibility in the members of a *numerous* body, for such acts of the body as have an immediate, detached and palpable operation on its constituents.

The proper remedy for this defect must be an additional body in the legislative department, which having sufficient permanency to provide for such objects as require a continued attention, and a train of measures, may be justly and effectually answerable for the attainment of those objects.

Thus far I have considered the circumstances which point out the necessity of a well constructed senate, only as they relate to the representatives of the people. To a people as little blinded by prejudice, or corrupted by flattery, as those whom I address, I shall not scruple to add, that such an institution may be sometimes necessary, as a defence to the people against their own temporary errors and delusions. As the cool and deliberate sense of the community ought in all governments, and actually will in all free governments ultimately prevail over the views of its rulers; so there are particular moments in public affairs, when the people stimulated by some irregular passion, or some illicit advantage, or misled by the artful misrepresentations of interested men, may call for measures which they themselves will afterwards be the most ready to lament and condemn. In these critical moments, how salutary will be the interference of some temperate and respectable body of citizens, in order to check the misguided career, and to suspend the blow meditated by the people against themselves, until reason, justice and truth, can regain their authority over the public mind? What bitter anguish would not the people of Athens have often escaped, if their government had contained so provident a safeguard against the tyranny of their own passions? Popular liberty might then have escaped the indelible reproach of decreeing to the same citizens, the hemlock on one day, and statues on the next.

It may be suggested that a people spread over an extensive region, cannot like the crouded inhabitants of a small district, be subject to the infection of violent passions; or to the danger of combining in the pursuit of unjust measures. I am far from denying that this is a distinction of peculiar importance. I have on the contrary endeavoured in a former paper to shew that it is one of the principal recommendations of a confederated republic. At the same time this advantage ought not to be considered as superseding the use of auxiliary precautions. It may even be remarked that the same extended situation which will exempt the people of America from some of the dangers incident to lesser republics, will expose them to the inconveniency of remaining for a longer time, under the influence of those misrepresentations which the combined industry of interested men may succeed in distributing among them.

It adds no small weight to all these considerations, to recollect, that history informs us of no long lived republic which had not a senate. Sparta, Rome and Carthage are in fact the only states to whom that character can be applied. In each of the two first there was a senate for life. The constitution of the senate in the last, is less known. Circumstantial evidence makes it probable that it was not different in this particular from the two others. It is at least certain that it had some quality or other which rendered it an anchor against popular fluctuations; and that a smaller council drawn out of the senate was appointed not only for life, but filled up vacancies itself. These examples, though as unfit for the imitation as they are repugnant to the genius of America, are notwithstanding, when compared with the fugitive and turbulent existence of other antient republics, very instructive proofs of the necessity of some institution that will blend stability with liberty. I am not unaware of the circumstances which distinguish the American from other popular governments, as well antient as modern; and which render extreme circumspection necessary in reasoning from the one case to the other. But after allowing due weight to this consideration, it may still be maintained that there are many points of similitude which render these examples not unworthy of our attention. Many of the defects as we have seen, which can only be supplied by a senatorial institution, are common to a numerous assembly frequently elected by the people, and to the people themselves. There are others peculiar to the former, which require the controul of such an institution. The people can never wilfully betray their own interests: but they may possibly be betrayed by the representatives of the people; and the danger will be evidently greater where the whole legislative trust is lodged in the hands of one body of men, than where the concurrence of separate and dissimilar bodies is required in every public act.

The difference most relied on between the American and other republics, consists in the principle of representation, which is the pivot on which the former move, and which is supposed to have been unknown to the latter, or at least to the antient part of them. The use which has been made of this difference, in reasonings contained in former papers, will have shewn that I am disposed neither to deny its existence nor to undervalue its importance. I feel the less restraint therefore in observing that the position concerning the ignorance of the antient governments on the subject of representation is by no means precisely true in the latitude commonly given to it. Without entering into a disquisition which here would be misplaced, I will refer to a few known facts in support of what I advance.

In the most pure democracies of Greece, many of the executive functions were performed not by the people themselves, but by officers elected by the people, and *representing* the people in their *executive* capacity.

Prior to the reform of Solon, Athens was governed by nine archons, annually *elected by the people at large*. The degree of power delegated to them seems to be left in great obscurity. Subsequent to that period, we find an assembly first of four and afterwards of six hundred members, annually *elected by the people*; and *partially* representing them in their *legislative* capacity, since they were not only associated with the people in the function of making laws; but had the exclusive right of originating legislative propositions to the people. The senate of Carthage also, whatever might be its power or the duration of its appointment, appears to have been elective by the suffrages of the people. Similar instances might be traced in most if not all the popular governments of antiquity.

Lastly in Sparta, we meet with the Ephori, and in Rome with the tribunes; two bodies, small indeed in number, but annually *elected by the whole body of the people*, and considered as the *representatives* of the people, almost in their *plenipotentiary* capacity. The Cosmi of Crete were also annually *elected by the people*: and have been considered by some authors as an institution analogous to those of Sparta and Rome, with this difference only, that in the election of that representative body the right of suffrage was communicated to a part only of the people.

From these facts, to which many others might be added, it is clear that the principle of representation was neither unknown to the ancients, nor wholly overlooked in their political constitutions. The true distinction between these and the

American governments lies *in the total exclusion of the people in their collective capacity* from any share in the *latter*, and not in the *total exclusion of representatives of the people*, from the administration of the *former*. The distinction however thus qualified must be admitted to leave a most advantageous superiority in favour of the United States. But to ensure to this advantage its full effect, we must be careful not to separate it from the other advantage, of an extensive territory. For it cannot be believed that any form of representative government, could have succeeded within the narrow limits occupied by the democracies of Greece.

In answer to all these arguments, suggested by reason, illustrated by examples, and enforced by our own experience, the jealous adversary of the constitution will probably content himself with repeating, that a senate appointed not immediately by the people, and for the term of six years, must gradually acquire a dangerous pre-eminence in the government, and finally transform it into a tyrannical aristocracy.

To this general answer the general reply ought to be sufficient; that liberty may be endangered by the abuses of liberty, as well as by the abuses of power; that there are numerous instances of the former as well as of the latter; and that the former rather than the latter is apparently most to be apprehended by the United States. But a more particular reply may be given.

Before such a revolution can be effected, the senate, it is to be observed, must in the first place corrupt itself; must next corrupt the state legislatures, must then corrupt the house of representatives, and must finally corrupt the people at large. It is evident that the senate must be first corrupted, before it can attempt an establishment of tyranny. Without corrupting the legislatures, it cannot prosecute the attempt, because the periodical change of members would otherwise regenerate the whole body. Without exerting the means of corruption with equal success on the house of representatives, the opposition of that co-equal branch of the government would inevitably defeat the attempt; and without corrupting the people themselves, a succession of new representatives would speedily restore all things to their pristine order. Is there any man who can seriously persuade himself that the proposed senate can, by any possible means within the compass of human address, arrive at the object of a lawless ambition, through all these obstructions?

If reason condemns the suspicion, the same sentence is pronounced by experience. The constitution of Maryland furnishes the most apposite example. The senate of that state is elected, as the federal senate will be, indirectly by the people; and for a term less by one year only, than the federal senate. It is distinguished also by the remarkable prerogative of filling up its own vacancies within the term of its appointment; and at the same time, is not under the control of any such rotation, as is provided for the federal senate. There are some other lesser distinctions, which would expose the former to colorable objections that do not lie against the latter. If the federal senate therefore really contained the danger which has been so loudly proclaimed, some symptoms at least of a like danger ought by this time to have been betrayed by the senate of Maryland; but no such symptoms have appeared. On the contrary the jealousies at first entertained by men of the same description with those who view with terror the correspondent part of the federal constitution, have been gradually extinguished by the progress of the experiment; and the Maryland constitution is daily deriving from the salutary operations of this part of it, a reputation in which it will probably not be rivalled by that of any state in the union.

But if any thing could silence the jealousies on this subject, it ought to be the British example. The senate there, instead of being elected for a term of six years, and of being unconfined to particular families or fortunes, is an hereditary assembly of opulent nobles. The house of representatives, instead of being elected for two years, and by the whole body of the people, is elected for seven years; and in very great proportion, by a very small proportion of the people. Here unquestionably ought to be seen in full display, the aristocratic usurpations and tyranny, which are at some future period to be exemplified in the United States. Unfortunately however for the antifederal argument, the British history informs us, that this hereditary assembly has not even been able to defend itself against the continual encroachments of the house of representatives; and that it no sooner lost the support of the monarch, than it was actually crushed by the weight of the popular branch.

As far as antiquity can instruct us on this subject, its examples support the reasoning which we have employed. In Sparta the Ephori, the annual representatives of the people, were found an overmatch for the senate for life, continually gained on its authority, and finally drew all power into their own hands. The tribunes of Rome, who were the representatives of the people, prevailed, it is well known, in almost every contest with the senate for life, and in the end gained the most complete triumph over it. This fact is the more remarkable, as unanimity was required in every act of the tribunes, even after their number was augmented to ten. It proves the irresistible force possessed by that branch of a free government, which has the people on its side. To these examples might be added that of Carthage, whose senate, according to the testimony of Polybius, instead of drawing all power into its vortex, had at the commencement of the second punic war, lost almost the whole of its original portion.

Besides the conclusive evidence resulting from this assemblage of facts, that the federal senate will never be able to transform itself, by gradual usurpations, into an independent and aristocratic body; we are warranted in believing that if such a revolution should ever happen from causes which the foresight of man cannot guard against, the house of representatives with the people on their side will at all times be able to bring back the constitution to its primitive form and principles. Against the force of the immediate representatives of the people, nothing will be able to maintain even the constitutional authority of the senate, but such a display of enlightened policy, and attachment to the public good, as will divide with that branch of the legislature, the affections and support of the entire body of the people themselves.

March 1, 1788

To Eliza House Trist

Orange March 25. The badness of the roads & some other delays retarded the completion of my journey till the day before yesterday. I called at Col Syms in Alexanda. but had not the pleasure of seeing either him or his lady. He was not at home though in Town and I was so hurried that I could halt a few minutes only; and she was confined to her chamber by indisposition. I had the satisfaction to find all my friends well on my arrival; and the chagrin to find the County filled with the most absurd and groundless prejudices against the fœderal Constitution. I was therefore obliged at the election which succeeded the day of my arrival to mount for the first time in my life, the rostrum before a large body of the people, and to launch into a harangue of some length in the open air and on a very windy day. What the effect might be I cannot say, but either from that experiment or the exertion of the fœderalists or perhaps both, the misconceptions of the Government were so far corrected that two federalists one of them myself were elected by a majority of nearly 4 to one. It is very probable that a very different event would have taken place as to myself if the efforts of my friends had not been seconded by my presence. The elections as yet are not sufficiently known to authorize any judgment on the probable complexion of the Convention. As far as I have heard of them they are not discouraging; but I have heard little from the great district of Country which is said to be most tainted with antifederalism. I am so taken up with company that I cannot at present add more than my sincerest wishes for your happiness. Adieu.

March 25, 1788

Speech in the Virginia Ratifying Convention in Defense of the Constitution

Mr. *Madison* then arose—(but he spoke so low that his exordium could not be heard distinctly). I shall not attempt to make impressions by any ardent professions of zeal for the public welfare: we know the principles of every man will, and ought to be judged, not by his professions and declarations, but by his conduct; by that criterion I mean in common with every other member to be judged; and should it prove unfavourable to my reputation, yet it is a criterion, from which I will by no means depart. Comparisons have been made between the friends of this constitution, and those who oppose it: although I disapprove of such comparisons, I trust, that in points of truth, honor, candor, and rectitude of motives, the friends of this system, here, and in other states, are not inferior to its opponents. But professions of attachment to the public good, and comparisons of parties, ought not to govern or influence us now. We ought, sir, to examine the constitution on its own merits solely: we are to enquire whether it will promote the public happiness: its aptitude to produce this desirable object, ought to be the exclusive subject of our present researches. In this pursuit, we ought not to address our arguments to the feelings and passions, but to those understandings and judgments which were selected by the people of this country, to decide this great question, by a calm and rational investigation. I hope that gentlemen, in displaying their abilities, on this occasion, instead of giving opinions, and making assertions, will condescend to prove and demonstrate, by a fair and regular discussion. It gives me pain to hear gentlemen continually distorting the natural construction of language; for, it is sufficient if any human production can stand a fair discussion. Before I proceed to make some additions to the reasons which have been adduced by my honorable friend over the way, I must take the liberty to make some observations on what was said by another gentleman, (Mr. *Henry*). He told us, that this constitution ought to be rejected, because it endangered the public liberty, in his opinion, in many instances. Give me leave to make one answer to that observation—let the dangers which this system is supposed to be re-plete with, be clearly pointed out. If any dangerous and un-necessary powers be given to the general legislature, let them be plainly demonstrated, and let us not rest satisfied with gen-eral assertions of dangers, without examination. If powers be necessary, apparent danger is not a sufficient reason against conceding them. He has suggested, that licentiousness has seldom produced the loss of liberty; but that the tyranny of rulers has almost always effected it. Since the general civiliza-tion of mankind, I believe there are more instances of the abridgment of the freedom of the people, by gradual and silent encroachments of those in power, than by violent and sudden usurpations: but on a candid examination of history, we shall find that turbulence, violence and abuse of power, by the majority trampling on the rights of the minority, have produced factions and commotions, which, in republics, have more frequently than any other cause, produced despotism. If we go over the whole history of ancient and modern re-publics, we shall find their destruction to have generally re-sulted from those causes. If we consider the peculiar situation of the United States, and what are the sources of that diver-sity of sentiments which pervades its inhabitants, we shall find great danger to fear, that the same causes may terminate here, in the same fatal effects, which they produced in those re-publics. This danger ought to be wisely guarded against. Perhaps in the progress of this discussion it will appear, that the only possible remedy for those evils, and means of pre-serving and protecting the principles of republicanism, will be found in that very system which is now exclaimed against as the parent of oppression. I must confess, I have not been able to find his usual consistency, in the gentleman's arguments on this occasion: he informs us that the people of this country are at perfect repose; that every man enjoys the fruits of his labor, peaceably and securely, and that every thing is in per-fect tranquility and safety. I wish sincerely, sir, this were true. If this be their happy situation, why has every state acknowl-edged the contrary? Why were deputies from all the states sent to the general convention? Why have complaints of na-tional and individual distresses been echoed and re-echoed throughout the continent? Why has our general government been so shamefully disgraced, and our constitution violated? Wherefore have laws been made to authorise a change, and wherefore are we now assembled here? A federal government is formed for the protection of its individual members. Ours was attacked itself with impunity. Its authority has been disobeyed and despised. I think I perceive a glaring inconsistency in another of his arguments. He complains of this constitution, because it requires the consent of at least three-fourths of the states to introduce amendments which shall be necessary for the happiness of the people. The assent of so many, he urges as too great an obstacle, to the admission of salutary amendments; which he strongly insists, ought to be at the will of a bare majority—we hear this argument, at the very moment we are called upon to assign reasons for proposing a constitution, which puts it in the power of nine states to abolish the present inadequate, unsafe, and pernicious confederation! In the first case he asserts, that a majority ought to have the power of altering the government, when found to be inadequate to the security of public happiness. In the last case, he affirms, that even three-fourths of the community have not a right to alter a government, which experience has proved to be subversive of national felicity! Nay, that the most necessary and urgent alterations, cannot be made without the absolute unanimity of all the states. Does not the thirteenth article of the confederation expressly require, that no alteration shall be made without the unanimous consent of all the states? Could any thing in theory, be more perniciously improvident and injudicious, than this submission of the will of the majority to the most trifling minority? Have not experience and practice actually manifested this theoretical inconvenience to be extremely impolitic? Let me mention one fact, which I conceive must carry conviction to the mind of any one—the smallest state in the union has obstructed every attempt to reform the government—that little member has repeatedly disobeyed and counteracted the general authority; nay, has even supplied the enemies of its country with provisions. Twelve states had agreed to certain improvements which were proposed, being thought absolutely necessary to preserve the existence of the general government; but as these improvements, though really indispensible, could not by the confederation be introduced into it without the consent of every state; the refractory dissent of that little state prevented their adoption. The inconveniences resulting from this requisition, of unanimous concurrence in alterations in the confederation, must be known to every member in this convention; 'tis therefore needless to remind them of them. Is it not self-evident, that a trifling minority ought not to bind the majority? Would not foreign influence be exerted with facility over a small minority? Would the honorable gentleman agree to continue the most radical defects in the old system, because the petty state of Rhode Island would not agree to remove them?

He next objects to the exclusive legislation over the district where the seat of the government may be fixed. Would he submit that the representatives of this state should carry on their deliberations under the control of any one member of the union? If any state had the power of legislation over the place where congress should fix the general government; this would impair the dignity, and hazard the safety of congress. If the safety of the union were under the control of any particular state, would not foreign corruption probably prevail in such a state, to induce it to exert its controling influence over the members of the general government? Gentlemen cannot have forgotten the disgraceful insult which congress received some years ago. When we also reflect, that the previous cession of particular states is necessary, before congress can legislate exclusively any where, we must, instead of being alarmed at this part, heartily approve of it.

But the honorable member sees great danger in the provision concerning the militia: this I conceive to be an additional security to our liberty, without diminishing the power of the states, in any considerable degree—it appears to me so highly expedient, that I should imagine it would have found advocates even in the warmest friends of the present system: the authority of training the militia, and appointing the officers, is reserved to the states. Congress ought to have the power of establishing an uniform discipline throughout the states; and to provide for the execution of the laws, suppress insurrections and repel invasions: these are the only cases wherein they can interfere with the militia; and the obvious necessity of their having power over them in these cases, must convince any reflecting mind. Without uniformity of discipline, military bodies would be incapable of action: without a general controlling power to call forth the strength of the union, to repel invasions, the country might be over-run, and conquered by foreign enemies. Without such a power to suppress insurrections, our liberties might be destroyed by domestic faction, and domestic tyranny be established.

The honorable member then told us, that there was no instance of power once transferred, being voluntarily renounced. Not to produce European examples, which may probably be done before the rising of this convention; have we not seen already in seven states (and probably in an eighth state) legislatures surrendering some of the most important powers they possessed? But, sir, by this government, powers are not given to any particular set of men—they are in the hands of the people—delegated to their representatives chosen for short terms—to representatives responsible to the people, and whose situation is perfectly similar to their own: as long as this is the case we have no danger to apprehend. When the gentleman called our recollection to the usual effects of the concession of powers, and imputed the loss of liberty generally to open tyranny, I wish he had gone on further. Upon a review of history he would have found, that the loss of liberty very often resulted from factions and divisions; from local considerations, which eternally lead to quarrels—he would have found internal dissentions to have more frequently demolished civil liberty, than a tenacious disposition in rulers to retain any stipulated powers.

(Here Mr. *Madison* enumerated the various means whereby nations had lost their liberties.)

The power of raising and supporting armies is exclaimed against, as dangerous and unnecessary. I wish there were no necessity of vesting this power in the general government. But suppose a foreign nation to declare war against the United States, must not the general legislature have the power of defending the United States? Ought it to be known to foreign nations, that the general government of the United States of America has no power to raise or support an army, even in the utmost danger, when attacked by external ene-

mies? Would not their knowledge of such a circumstance
stimulate them to fall upon us. If, sir, congress be not invested with this power, any powerful nation, prompted by
ambition or avarice, will be invited, by our weakness, to attack
us; and such an attack, by disciplined veterans, would certainly be attended with success, when only opposed by irregular, undisciplined militia. Whoever considers the peculiar
situation of this country; the multiplicity of its excellent inlets
and harbours, and the uncommon facility of attacking it,
however much he may regret the necessity of such a power,
cannot hesitate a moment in granting it. One fact may elucidate this argument. In the course of the late war, when the
weak parts of the union were exposed, and many states were
in the most deplorable situation, by the enemy's ravages; the
assistance of foreign nations was thought so urgently necessary for our protection, that the relinquishment of territorial
advantages was not deemed too great a sacrifice for the acquisition of one ally. This expedient was admitted with great
reluctance even by those states who expected most advantages
from it. The crisis however at length arrived when it was
judged necessary for the salvation of this country, to make
certain cessions to Spain; whether wisely, or otherwise, is not
for me to say; but the fact was, that instructions were sent to
our representative at the court of Spain, to empower him to
enter into negociations for that purpose. How it terminated is
well known. This fact shews the extremities to which nations
will recur in cases of imminent danger, and demonstrates the
necessity of making ourselves more respectable. The necessity
of making dangerous cessions, and of applying to foreign aid,
ought to be excluded.

   The honorable member then told us, that there are heart-
burnings in the adopting states, and that Virginia may, if she
does not come into the measure, continue in amicable confederacy with the adopting states. I wish as seldom as possible
to contradict the assertions of gentlemen, but I can venture
to affirm, without danger of being in an error, that there is
the most satisfactory evidence, that the satisfaction of those
states is increasing every day, and that in that state where it
was adopted only by a majority of nineteen, there is not one-
fifth of the people dissatisfied. There are some reasons which

induce us to conclude, that the grounds of proselytism extend every where—its principles begin to be better understood—and the inflammatory violence, wherewith it was opposed by designing, illiberal, and unthinking minds, begins to subside. I will not enumerate the causes from which, in my conception, the heart-burnings of a majority of its opposers have originated. Suffice it to say, that in all they were founded on a misconception of its nature and tendency. Had it been candidly examined and fairly discussed, I believe, sir, that but a very inconsiderable minority of the people of the United States would have opposed it. With respect to the Swiss, which the honorable gentleman has proposed for our example, as far as historical authority may be relied upon, we shall find their government quite unworthy of our imitation. I am sure if the honorable member had adverted to their history and government, he never would have quoted their example here: he would have found that instead of respecting the rights of mankind, their government (at least of several of their cantons) is one of the vilest aristocracies that ever was instituted: the peasants of some of their cantons are more oppressed and degraded, than the subjects of any monarch in Europe: nay, almost as much so, as those of any eastern despot. It is a novelty in politics, that from the worst of systems the happiest consequences should ensue. Their aristocratical rigor, and the peculiarity of their situation, have so long supported their union: without the closest alliance and amity, dismemberment might follow: their powerful and ambitious neighbours would immediately avail themselves of their least jarrings. As we are not circumstanced like them, no conclusive precedent can be drawn from their situation. I trust, the gentleman does not carry his idea so far as to recommend a separation from the adopting states. This government may secure our happiness; this is at least as probable, as that it shall be oppressive. If eight states have, from a persuasion of its policy and utility, adopted it, shall Virginia shrink from it, without a full conviction of its danger and inutility? I hope she will never shrink from any duty: I trust she will not determine without the most serious reflection and deliberation.

I confess to you, sir, were uniformity of religion to be introduced by this system, it would, in my opinion, be ineligible; but I have no reason to conclude, that uniformity of government will produce that of religion. This subject is, for the honor of America, perfectly free and unshackled. The government has no jurisdiction over it—the least reflection will convince us, there is no danger to be feared on this ground.

But we are flattered with the probability of obtaining previous amendments. This calls for the most serious attention of this house. If amendments are to be proposed by one state, other states have the same right, and will also propose alterations. These cannot but be dissimilar, and opposite in their nature. I beg leave to remark, that the governments of the different states are in many respects dissimilar in their structure—their legislative bodies are not similar—their executives are more different. In several of the states the first magistrate is elected by the people at large—in others, by joint ballot of the members of both branches of the legislature—and in others, in other different manners. This dissimilarity has occasioned a diversity of opinion on the theory of government, which will, without many reciprocal concessions, render a concurrence impossible. Although the appointment of an executive magistrate, has not been thought destructive to the principles of democracy in any of the states, yet, in the course of the debate, we find objections made to the federal executive: it is urged that the president will degenerate into a tyrant. I intended, in compliance with the call of the honorable member, to explain the reasons of proposing this constitution, and develop its principles; but I shall postpone my remarks, till we hear the supplement which he has informed us, he intends to add to what he has already said.

Give me leave to say something of the nature of the government, and to shew that it is safe and just to vest it with the power of taxation. There are a number of opinions; but the principal question is, whether it be a federal or consolidated government: in order to judge properly of the question before us, we must consider it minutely in its principal parts. I conceive myself, that it is of a mixed nature: it is in a manner unprecedented: we cannot find one express example in the experience of the world: it stands by itself. In some respects, it is a government of a federal nature; in others it is of a consolidated nature. Even if we attend to the manner in which the constitution is investigated, ratified, and made the act of the people of America, I can say, notwithstanding what the honorable gentleman has alledged, that this government is not completely consolidated, nor is it entirely federal. Who are parties to it? The people—but not the people as composing one great body—but the people as composing thirteen sovereignties: were it as the gentleman asserts, a consolidated government, the assent of a majority of the people would be sufficient for its establishment, and as a majority have adopted it already, the remaining states would be bound by the act of the majority, even if they unanimously reprobated it: were it such a government as it is suggested, it would be now binding on the people of this state, without having had the priviledge of deliberating upon it: but, sir, no state is bound by it, as it is, without its own consent. Should all the states adopt it, it will be then a government established by the thirteen states of America, not through the intervention of the legislatures, but by the people at large. In this particular respect the distinction between the existing and proposed governments is very material. The existing system has been derived from the dependent derivative authority of the legislatures of the states; whereas this is derived from the superior power of the people. If we look at the manner in which alterations are to be made in it, the same idea is in some degree attended to. By the new system a majority of the states cannot introduce amendments; nor are all the states required for that purpose; three-fourths of them must concur in alterations; in this there is a departure from the federal idea. The members to the national house of representatives are to be chosen by the people at large, in proportion to the numbers in the respective districts. When we come to the senate, its members are elected by the states in their equal and political capacity; but had the government been completely consolidated, the senate would have been chosen by the people in their individual capacity, in the same manner as the members of the other house. Thus it is of a complicated nature, and this complication, I trust, will be found to exclude the evils of absolute consolidation, as well as of a mere confederacy. If Virginia were separated from all the states, her power and authority would extend to all cases: in like manner were all powers vested in the general government, it would be a consolidated government: but the powers of the federal government are enumerated; it can only operate in certain cases: it has legislative powers on defined and limited objects, beyond which it cannot extend its jurisdiction.

But the honorable member has satirized with peculiar acrimony, the powers given to the general government by this constitution. I conceive that the first question on this subject is, whether these powers be necessary; if they be, we are reduced to the dilemma of either submitting to the inconvenience, or, losing the union. Let us consider the most important of these reprobated powers; that of direct taxation is most generally objected to. With respect to the exigencies of government, there is no question but the most easy mode of providing for them will be adopted. When therefore direct taxes are not necessary, they will not be recurred to. It can be of little advantage to those in power, to raise money in a manner oppressive to the people. To consult the conveniences of the people, will cost them nothing, and in many respects will be advantageous to them. Direct taxes will only be recurred to for great purposes. What has brought on other nations those immense debts, under the pressure of which many of them labour? Not the expenses of the governments, but war. If this country should be engaged in war (and I conceive we ought to provide for the possibility of such a case) how would it be carried on? By the usual means provided from year to year? As our imports will be necessary for the expences of government, and other common exigencies, how are we to carry on the means of defence? How is it possible a war could be supported without money or credit? And would it be possible for a government to have credit, without having the power of raising money? No, it would be impossible for any government in such a case to defend itself. Then, I say, sir, that it is necessary to establish funds for extraordinary exigencies, and give this power to the general government—for the utter inutility of previous requisitions on the states is too well known. Would it be possible for those countries whose finances and revenues are carried to the highest perfection, to carry on the operations of government on great emergencies, such as the maintenance of a war, without an uncontrolled power of raising money? Has it not been necessary for Great-Britain, notwithstanding the facility of the collection of her taxes, to have recourse very often to this and other extraordinary methods of procuring money? Would not her public credit have been ruined, if it was known that her power to raise money was limitted? Has not France been obliged on great occasions to use unusual means to raise funds? It has been the case in many countries, and no government can exist, unless its powers extend to make provisions for every contingency. If we were actually attacked by a powerful nation, and our general government had not the power of raising money, but depended solely on requisitions, our condition would be truly deplorable: if the revenue of this commonwealth were to depend on twenty distinct authorities, it would be impossible for it to carry on its operations. This must be obvious to every member here: I think therefore, that it is necessary for the preservation of the union, that this power should be given to the general government.

But it is urged, that its consolidated nature, joined to the power of direct taxation, will give it a tendency to destroy all subordinate authority; that its increasing influence will speedily enable it to absorb the state governments. I cannot think this will be the case. If the general government were wholly independent of the governments of the particular states, then indeed usurpation might be expected to the fullest extent: but, sir, on whom does this general government depend? It derives its authority from these governments, and from the same sources from which their authority is derived. The members of the federal government are taken from the same men from whom those of the state legislatures are taken. If we consider the mode in which the federal representatives will be chosen, we shall be convinced, that the general will never destroy the individual governments; and this conviction must be strengthened by an attention to the construction of the senate. The representatives will be chosen, probably under the influence of the members of the state legislatures: but there is not the least probability that the election of the latter will be influenced by the former. One hundred and sixty members represent this commonwealth in one branch of the legislature, are drawn from the people at large, and must ever possess more influence than the few men who will be elected to the general legislature. The reasons offered on this subject, by a gentleman on the same side (Mr. *Nicholas*) were unanswerable, and have been so full, that I shall add but little more on the subject. Those who wish to become federal representatives, must depend on their credit with that class of men who will be the most popular in their counties, who generally represent the people in the state governments: they can, therefore, never succeed in any measure contrary to the wishes of those on whom they depend. It is almost certain, therefore, that the deliberations of the members of the federal house of representatives, will be directed to the interests of the people of America. As to the other branch, the senators will be appointed by the legislatures, and though elected for six years, I do not conceive they will so soon forget the source from whence they derive their political existence. This election of one branch of the federal, by the state legislatures, secures an absolute dependence of the former on the latter. The biennial exclusion of one-third, will lessen the facility of a combination, and may put a stop to intrigues. I appeal to our past experience, whether they will attend to the interests of their constituent states. Have not those gentlemen who have been honored with seats in congress, *often signalized themselves by their attachment* to their states? I wish this government may answer the expectation of its friends, and foil the apprehensions of its enemies. I hope the patriotism of the people will continue, and be a sufficient guard to their liberties. I believe its tendency will be, that the state governments will counteract the general interest, and ultimately prevail. The number of the representatives is yet sufficient for our safety, and will gradually increase—and if we consider their different sources of information, the number will not appear too small.

June 6, 1788

Speech in the Virginia Ratifying Convention on Direct Taxation

MR. MADISON. Mr. Chairman—It was my purpose to resume before now, what I had left unfinished, concerning the necessity of a radical change of our system. The intermission which has taken place, has discontinued the progress of the argument, and has given opportunity to others to advance arguments on different parts of the plan. I hope we shall steer our course in a different manner from what we have hitherto done. I presume that vague discourses and mere sports of fancy, not relative to the subject at all, are very improper on this interesting occasion. I hope these will be no longer attempted, but that we shall come to the point. I trust we shall not go out of order, but confine ourselves to the clause under consideration. I beg gentlemen would observe this rule. I shall endeavour not to depart from it myself.

The subject of direct taxation is perhaps one of the most important that can possibly engage our attention, or that can be involved in the discussion of this question. If it be to be judged by the comments made upon it, by the opposers and favorers of the proposed system, it requires a most clear and critical investigation. The objections against the exercise of this power by the general government as far as I am able to comprehend them, are founded upon the supposition of its being unnecessary, impracticable, unsafe and accumulative of expence. I shall therefore consider, 1st, how far it may be necessary; 2dly, how far it may be practicable; 3dly, how far it may be safe, as well with respect to the public liberty at large, as to the state legislatures; and 4thly, with respect to œconomy. First then, is it necessary? I must acknowledge that I concur in opinion with those gentlemen who told you that this branch of revenue was essential to the salvation of the union. It appears to me necessary, in order to secure that punctuality which is necessary in revenue matters. Without punctuality individuals will give it no confidence; without which it cannot get resources. I beg gentlemen to consider the situation of this country, if unhappily the government were to be deprived of this power. Let us suppose for a moment that one of those powers which may be unfriendly to us, should take advantage of our weakness, which they will be more ready to do when they know the want of this resource in our government. Suppose it should attack us, what forces could we oppose to it? Could we find safety in such forces as we could call out? Could we call forth a sufficient number, either by draughts, or any other way, to repel a powerful enemy? The inability of the government to raise and support regular troops, would compel us to depend on militia. It would be then necessary to give this power to the government, or run the risk of national annihilation. It is my firm belief, that if a hostile attack were made this moment on the United States, it would flash conviction on the minds of the citizens of the United States, of the necessity of vesting the government with this power, which alone can enable it to protect the community. I do not wish to frighten the members of this convention into a concession of this power, but to bring to their minds those considerations which demonstrate its necessity. If we were secured from the possibility, or the probability of danger, it might be unnecessary. I shall not review that concourse of dangers which may probably arise at remote periods of futurity, nor all those which we have immediately to apprehend, for this would lead me beyond the bounds which I prescribed myself. But I will mention one single consideration, drawn from fact itself. I hope to have your attention.

By the treaty between the United States and his most Christian majesty, among other things it is stipulated, that the great principle on which the armed neutrality in Europe was founded, should prevail in case of future wars. The principle is this, that free ships shall make free goods, and that vessels and goods shall be both free from condemnation. Great-Britain did not recognize it. While all Europe was against her, she held out without acceding to it. It has been considered for some time past, that the flames of war already kindled, would spread, and that France and England were likely to draw those swords which were so recently put up. This is judged probable. We should not be surprised in a short time, to consider ourselves as a neutral nation—France on one side, and Great-Britain on the other. What is the situation of America? She is remote from Europe, and ought not to engage in her politics or wars. The American vessels, if they can do it with advantage, may carry on the commerce of the contending nations. It is a source of wealth which we ought not to deny to our citizens. But, sir, is there not infinite danger, that in despite of all our caution we shall be drawn into the war? If American vessels have French property on board, Great-Britain will seize them. By this means we shall be obliged to relinquish the advantage of a neutral nation, or be engaged in a war. A neutral nation ought to be respectable, or else it will be insulted and attacked. America in her present impotent situation would run the risk of being drawn in as a party in the war, and lose the advantage of being neutral. Should it happen that the British fleet should be superior, have we not reason to conclude, from the spirit displayed by that nation to us and to all the world, that we should be insulted in our own ports, and our vessels seized? But if we be in a respectable situation—if it be known that our government can command the whole resources of the union, we shall be suffered to enjoy the great advantages of carrying on the commerce of the nations at war; for none of them would be willing to add us to the number of their enemies. I shall say no more on this point, there being others which merit your consideration.

The expedient proposed by the gentlemen opposed to this clause, is, that requisitions shall be made, and if not complied with in a certain time, that then taxation shall be recurred to. I am clearly convinced, that whenever requisitions shall be made, they will disappoint those who put their trust in them. One reason to prevent the concurrent exertions of all the states, will arise from the suspicion, in some states, of delinquency in others. States will be governed by the motives that actuate individuals.

When a tax law is in operation in a particular state, every citizen, if he knows of the energy of the laws to enforce payment, and that every other citizen is performing his duty, will chearfully discharge his duty; but were it known that the citizens of one district were not performing their duty, and that it was left to the policy of the government to make them come up with it, the citizens of the other districts would be very supine and careless in making provisions for payment. Our own experience makes the illustration more natural. If requi-

sitions be made on thirteen different states, when one delib-
erates on the subject, she will know that all the rest will deliberate upon it also. This, sir, has been a principal cause of the
inefficacy of requisitions heretofore, and will hereafter produce the same evil. If the legislatures are to deliberate on this
subject, (and the honorable gentleman opposed to this clause,
thinks their deliberation necessary) is it not presumable, that
they will consider peculiar local circumstances? In the general
council, on the contrary, the sense of all America would be
drawn to a single point. The collective interest of the union at
large, will be known and pursued. No local views will be permitted to operate against the general welfare. But when
propositions would come before a particular state, there is
every reason to believe, that qualifications of the requisitions
would be proposed—compliance might be promised, and
some instant remittances might be made. This will cause delays, which in the first instance will produce disappointment.
This also will make failures every where else. This I hope will
be considered with the attention it deserves. The public creditors will be disappointed, and more pressing. Requisitions
will be made for purposes equally pervading all America; but
the exertions to make compliances, will probably be not uniform in the states. If requisitions be made for future occasions; for putting the states in a state of military defence, or to
repel an invasion, will the exertions be uniform and equal in
all the states? Some parts of the United States are more exposed than others. Will the least exposed states exert themselves equally? We know that the most exposed will be more
immediately interested, and will make less sacrifices in making
exertions. I beg gentlemen to consider that this argument will
apply with most effect to the states which are most defenceless
and exposed. The southern states are most exposed, whether
we consider their situation, or the smallness of their population. And there are other circumstances which render them
still more vulnerable, which do not apply to the northern
states. They are therefore more interested in giving the government a power to command the whole strength of the
union in cases of emergency. Do not gentlemen conceive that
this mode of obtaining supplies from the states, will keep alive
animosities between the general government and particular

states? Where the chances of failures are so numerous as thirteen, by the thirteen states, disappointment in the first place, and consequent animosity must inevitably take place.

Let us consider the alternatives proposed by gentlemen instead of the power of laying direct taxes. After the states shall have refused to comply, weigh the consequences of the exercise of this power by congress. When it comes in the form of a punishment, great clamours will be raised among the people against the government; hatred will be excited against it. It will be considered as an ignominious stigma on the state. It will be considered at least in this light by the state where the failure is made, and these sentiments will no doubt be diffused through the other states. Now let us consider the effect, if collectors are sent where the state governments refuse to comply with requisitions. It is too much the disposition of mankind not to stop at one violation of duty. I conceive that every requisition that will be made on any part of America, will kindle a contention between the delinquent member, and the general government. Is there no reason to suppose divisions in the government (for seldom does any thing pass with unanimity) on the subject of requisitions? The parts least exposed will oppose those measures which may be adopted for the defence of the weakest parts. Is there no reason to presume, that the representatives from the delinquent state will be more likely to foster disobedience to the requisitions of the government, than study to recommend them to the public?

There is, in my opinion, another point of view in which this alternative will produce great evil. I will suppose, what is very probable, that partial compliances will be made. A difficulty here arises which fully demonstrates its impolicy. If a part be paid, and the rest withheld, how is the general government to proceed? They are to impose a tax, but how shall it be done in this case? Are they to impose it by way of punishment, on those who have paid, as well as those who have not? All these considerations taken in view (for they are not visionary or fanciful speculations) will, perhaps, produce this consequence. The general government to avoid those disappointments which I first described, and to avoid the contentions and embarrassments which I last described, will, in all probability, throw the public burdens on those branches of revenue which will be more in their power. They will be continually necessitated to augment the imposts. If we throw a disproportion of the burdens on that side, shall we not discourage commerce, and suffer many political evils? Shall we not increase that disproportion on the southern states, which for some time will operate against us? The southern states, from having fewer manufacturers, will import and consume more. They will therefore pay more of the imposts. The more commerce is burdened, the more the disproportion will operate against them. If direct taxation be mixed with other taxes, it will be in the power of the general government to lessen that inequality. But this inequality will be increased to the utmost extent, if the general government have not this power. There is another point of view in which this subject affords us instruction. The imports will decrease in time of war. The honorable gentleman who spoke yesterday, said, that the imposts would be so productive, that there would be no occasion of laying taxes. I will submit two observations to him and the committee. First: in time of war the imposts will be less; and as I hope we are considering a government for a perpetual duration, we ought to provide for every future contingency. At present our importations bear a full proportion to the full amount of our sales, and to the number of our inhabitants; but when we have inhabitants enough, our imports will decrease; and as the national demands will increase with our population, our resources will increase as our wants increase. The other consideration which I will submit on this part of the subject is this: I believe that it will be found in practice, that those who fix the public burthens, will feel a greater degree of responsibility when they are to impose them on the citizens immediately, than if they were to say what sum should be paid by the states. If they exceed the limits of propriety, universal discontent and clamour will arise. Let us suppose they were to collect the taxes from the citizens of America—would they not consider their circumstances? Would they not attentively consider what could be done by the citizens at large? Were they to exceed in their demands, what were reasonable burdens, the people would impute it to the right source, and look on the imposers as odious.

When I consider the nature of the various objections brought against this clause, I should be led to think, that the difficulties were such that gentlemen would not be able to get over them, and that the power, as defined in the plan of the convention, was impracticable. I shall trouble them with a few observations on that point.

It has been said that ten men deputed from this state, and others in proportion from other states, will not be able to adjust direct taxes so as to accommodate the various citizens in thirteen states.

I confess I do not see the force of this observation. Could not ten intelligent men, chosen from ten districts from this state, lay direct taxes on a few objects in the most judicious manner? It is to be conceived, that they would be acquainted with the situation of the different citizens of this country. Can any one divide this state into any ten districts so as not to contain men of sufficient information? Could not one man of knowledge be found in a district? When thus selected, will they not be able to carry their knowledge into the general council? I may say with great propriety, that the experience of our own legislature demonstrates the competency of congress to lay taxes wisely. Our assembly consists of considerably more than a hundred, yet from the nature of the business, it devolves on a much smaller number. It is through their sanction, approved of by all the others. It will be found that there are seldom more than ten men who rise to high information on this subject. Our federal representatives, as has been said by the gentleman (Mr. *Marshall*) who entered into the subject with a great deal of ability, will get information from the state governments. They will be perfectly well informed of the circumstances of the people of the different states, and the mode of taxation that would be most convenient for them, from the laws of the states. In laying taxes, they may even refer to the state systems of taxation. Let it not be forgotten, that there is a probability, that that ignorance which is complained of in some parts of America, will be continually diminishing. Let us compare the degree of knowledge which the people had in time past, to their present information. Does not our own experience teach us, that the people are better informed than they were a few years ago? The citizen of Georgia knows more now of the affairs of New-Hampshire, than he did before the revolution, of those of South-Carolina. When the representatives from the different states are collected together, to consider this subject, they will interchange their knowledge with one another, and will have the laws of each state on the table. Besides this, the intercourse of the states will be continually increasing. It is now much greater than before the revolution. My honorable friend over the way, (Mr. *Monroe*) yesterday, seemed to conceive, as an insuperable objection, that if land were made the particular object of taxation, it would be unjust, as it would exonerate the commercial part of the community—that if it were laid on trade, it would be unjust in discharging the landholders; and that any exclusive selection would be unequal and unfair. It the general government were tied down to one object, I confess the objection would have some force in it. But if this be not the case, it can have no weight. If it should have a general power of taxation, they could select the most proper objects, and distribute the taxes in such a manner, as that they should fall in a due degree on every member of the community. They will be limited to fix the proportion of each state, and they must raise it in the most convenient and satisfactory manner to the public.

The honorable member considered it as another insuperable objection, that uniform laws could not be made for thirteen states, and that dissonance would produce inconvenience and oppression. Perhaps it may not be found, on due enquiry, to be so impracticable as he supposes. But were it so, where is the evil of different laws operating in different states, to raise money for the general government? Where is the evil of such laws? There are instances in other countries, of different laws operating in different parts of the country, without producing any kind of oppression. The revenue-laws are different in England and Scotland in several respects. Their laws relating to custom, excises, and trade, are similar; but those respecting direct taxation are dissimilar. There is a land-tax in England, and a land-tax in Scotland, but the laws concerning them are not the same. It is much heavier in proportion in the former than in the latter. The mode of collection is different—yet this is not productive of any national inconvenience. Were we to conclude from the objections against the proposed plan, this dissimilarity, in that point alone, would have involved those kingdoms in difficulties. In England itself, there is a variety of different laws operating differently in different places.

I will make another observation on the objection of my honorable friend. He seemed to conclude, that concurrent collections under different authorities, were not reducible to practice. I agree that were they independent of the people, the argument would be good. But they must serve one common master. They must act in concert, or the defaulting party must bring on itself the resentment of the people. If the general government be so constructed, that it will not dare to impose such burdens, as will distress the people, where is the evil of its having a power of taxation concurrent with the states? The people would not support it, were it to impose oppressive burdens. Let me make one more comparison of the state governments to this plan. Do not the states impose taxes for local purposes? Does the concurrent collection of taxes, imposed by the legislatures for general purposes, and of levies laid by the counties for parochial and county purposes, produce any inconvenience or oppression? The collection of these taxes is perfectly practicable, and consistent with the views of both parties. The people at large are the common superior of the state governments, and the general government. It is reasonable to conclude, that they will avoid interferences for two causes—to avoid public oppression, and to render the collections more productive. I conceive they will be more likely to produce disputes, in rendering it convenient for the people, than run into interfering regulations.

In the third place I shall consider, whether the power of taxation to be given the general government be safe: and first, whether it be safe as to the public liberty in general. It would be sufficient to remark, that they are, because, I conceive, the point has been clearly established by more than one gentleman who has spoken on the same side of the question. In the decision of this question, it is of importance to examine, whether elections of representatives by great districts of freeholders be favorable to fidelity in representatives. The greatest degree of treachery in representatives, is to be apprehended where they are chosen by the least number of electors; because there is a greater facility of using undue influence, and because the electors must be less independent. This position is verified in the most unanswerable manner, in that country to which appeals are so often made, and sometimes instructively. Who are the most corrupt members in parliament? Are they not the inhabitants of small towns and districts? The supporters of liberty are from the great counties. Have we not seen that the representatives of the city of London, who are chosen by such thousands of voters, have continually studied and supported the liberties of the people, and opposed the corruption of the crown? We have seen continually that most of the members in the ministerial majority are drawn from small circumscribed districts. We may therefore conclude, that our representatives being chosen by such extensive districts, will be upright and independent. In proportion as we have security against corruption in representatives, we have security against corruption from every other quarter whatsoever.

I shall take a view of certain subjects which will lead to some reflections, to quiet the minds of those gentlemen who think that the individual governments will be swallowed up by the general government. In order to effect this, it is proper to compare the state governments to the general government with respect to reciprocal dependence, and with respect to the means they have of supporting themselves, or of encroaching on one another. At the first comparison we must be struck with these remarkable facts. The general government has not the appointment of a single branch of the individual governments, or of any officers within the states, to execute their laws. Are not the states integral parts of the general government? Is not the president chosen under the influence of the state legislatures? May we not suppose that he will be complaisant to those from whom he has his appointment, and from whom he must have his re-appointment? The senators are appointed altogether by the legislatures.

My honorable friend apprehended a coalition between the president, senate, and house of representatives, against the states. This could be supposed only from a similarity of the component parts.

A coalition is not likely to take place, because its component parts are heterogeneous in their nature. The house of representatives is not chosen by the state governments, but

under the influence of those who compose the state legislature. Let us suppose ten men appointed to carry the government into effect; there is every degree of certainty, that they
would be indebted for their re-election, to the members of
the legislatures. If they derive their appointment from them,
will they not execute their duty to them? Besides this, will not
the people (whose predominant interest will ultimately prevail) feel great attachment to the state legislatures? They have
the care of all local interests—those familiar domestic objects,
for which men have the strongest predilection. The general
government on the contrary, has the preservation of the
aggregate interests of the union—objects, which being less
familiar, and more remote from men's notice, have a less
powerful influence on their minds. Do we not see great and
natural attachments arising from local considerations? This
will be the case in a much stronger degree in the state governments, than in the general government. The people will be
attached to their state legislatures from a thousand causes; and
into whatever scale the people at large will throw themselves,
that scale will preponderate. Did we not perceive in the early
stages of the war, when congress was the idol of America, and
when in pursuit of the object most dear to America, that they
were attached to their states? Afterwards the whole current of
their affection was to the states, and would be still the case,
were it not for the alarming situation of America.

At one period of the congressional history, they had power
to trample on the states. When they had that fund of paper
money in their hands, and could carry on all their measures
without any dependence on the states, was there any disposition to debase the state governments? All that municipal authority which was necessary to carry on the administration of
the government, they still retained unimpaired. There was no
attempt to diminish it.

I am led by what fell from my honorable friend yesterday to
take this supposed combination in another view. Is it supposed, that the influence of the general government will facilitate a combination between the members? Is it supposed,
that it will preponderate against that of the state governments? The means of influence consist in having the disposal
of gifts and emoluments, and in the number of persons em-

ployed by, and dependent upon a government. Will any gentleman compare the number of persons, which will be employed in the general government, with the number of those which will be in the state governments? The number of dependants upon the state governments will be infinitely greater than those on the general government. I may say with truth, that there never was a more œconomical government in any age or country; nor which will require fewer hands, or give less influence.

Let us compare the members composing the legislative, executive and judicial powers in the general government, with those in the states, and let us take into view the vast number of persons employed in the states; from the chief officers to the lowest, we will find the scale preponderating so much in favor of the states, that while so many persons are attached to them, it will be impossible to turn the balance against them. There will be an irresistible bias towards the state governments. Consider the number of militia officers, the number of justices of the peace, the number of the members of the legislatures, and all the various officers for districts, towns and corporations, all intermixing with, and residing among the people at large. While this part of the community retains their affection to the state governments, I conceive that the fact will be, that the state governments, and not the general government, will preponderate. It cannot be contradicted that they have more extensive means of influence. I have my fears as well as the honorable gentleman—but my fears are on the other side. Experience, I think, will prove (though there be no infallible proof of it here) that the powerful and prevailing influence of the states, will produce such attention to local considerations as will be inconsistent with the advancement of the interests of the union. But I choose rather to indulge my hopes than fears, because I flatter myself, if inconveniences should result from it, that the clause which provides amendments will remedy them. The combination of powers vested in those persons, would seem conclusive in favor of the states.

The powers of the general government relate to external objects, and are but few. But the powers in the states relate to those great objects which immediately concern the prosperity of the people. Let us observe also, that the powers in the general government are those which will be exercised mostly in time of war, while those of the state governments will be exercised in time of peace. But I hope the time of war will be little compared to that of peace. I should not complete the view which ought to be taken of this subject, without making this additional remark, that the powers vested in the proposed government, are not so much an augmentation of powers in the general government, as a change rendered necessary, for the purpose of giving efficacy to those which were vested in it before. It cannot escape any gentleman, that this power in theory, exists in the confederation as fully as in this constitution. The only difference is this, that now they tax states, and by this plan they will tax individuals. There is no theoretic difference between the two. But in practice there will be an infinite difference between them. The one is an ineffectual power: the other is adequate to the purpose for which it is given. This change was necessary for the public safety.

Let us suppose for a moment, that the acts of congress requiring money from the states, had been as effectual as the paper on the table—suppose all the laws of congress had had complete compliance, will any gentleman say, that as far as we can judge from past experience, that the state governments would have been debased, and all consolidated and incorporated in one system? My imagination cannot reach it. I conceive, that had those acts that effect which all laws ought to have, the states would have retained their sovereignty.

It seems to be supposed, that it will introduce new expences and burdens on the people. I believe it is not necessary here to make a comparison between the expences of the present and of the proposed government. All agree that the general government ought to have power for the regulation of commerce. I will venture to say, that very great improvements, and very œconomical regulations will be made. It will be a principal object to guard against smuggling, and such other attacks on the revenue as other nations are subject to. We are now obliged to defend against those lawless attempts, but from the interfering regulations of different states, with little success. There are regulations in different states which are unfavorable to the inhabitants of other states, and which militate against the revenue. New-York levies money from

New-Jersey by her imposts. In New-Jersey, instead of co-operating with New-York, the legislature favors violations on her regulations. This will not be the case when uniform regulations will be made.

Requisitions though ineffectual are unfriendly to œconomy. When requisitions are submitted to the states, there are near 2500 or 2000 persons deliberating on the mode of payment. All these, during their deliberation, receive public pay. A great proportion of every session, in every state, is employed to consider whether they will pay at all, and in what mode. Let us suppose 1500 persons are deliberating on this subject. Let any one make a calculation—it will be found that a very few days of their deliberation will consume more of the public money, than one year of that of the general legislature. This is not all, Mr. Chairman. When general powers will be vested in the general government, there will be less of that mutability which is seen in the legislation of the states. The consequence will be a great saving of expence and time. There is another great advantage which I will but barely mention. The greatest calamity to which the United States can be subject, is a vicissitude of laws, and continual shifting and changing from one object to another, which must expose the people to various inconveniences. This has a certain effect, of which sagacious men always have, and always will make an advantage. From whom is advantage made? From the industrious farmers and tradesmen, who are ignorant of the means of making such advantages. The people will not be exposed to these inconveniences under an uniform and steady course of legislation. But they have been so heretofore. The history of taxation of this country is so fully and well known to every member of this committee, that I shall say no more of it.

We have hitherto discussed the subject very irregularly. I dare not dictate to any gentleman, but I hope we shall pursue that mode of going through the business, which the house resolved. With respect to a great variety of arguments made use of, I mean to take notice of them when we come to those parts of the constitution to which they apply. If we exchange this mode, for the regular way of proceeding, we can finish it better in one week than in one month.

June 11, 1778

Speech in the Virginia Ratifying Convention on Taxation, a Bill of Rights, and the Mississippi

MR. MADISON. Mr. Chairman, Pardon me for making a few remarks on what fell from the honorable gentleman last up. I am sorry to follow the example of gentlemen in deviating from the rule of the house: But as they have taken the utmost latitude in their objections, it is necessary that those who favor the government should answer them. But I wish as soon as possible to take up the subject regularly. I will therefore take the liberty to answer some observations which have been irregularly made, though they might be more properly answered when we came to discuss those parts of the constitution to which they respectively refer. I will, however, postpone answering some others till then. If there be that terror in direct taxation, that the states would comply with requisitions to guard against the federal legislature; and if, as gentlemen say, this state will always have it in her power to make her collections speedily and fully, the people will be compelled to pay the same amount as quickly and punctually as if raised by the general government.

It has been amply proved, that the general government can lay taxes as conveniently to the people as the state governments, by imitating the state systems of taxation. If the general government have not the power of collecting its own revenues, in the first instance, it will be still dependent on the state governments in some measure; and the exercise of this power after refusal, will be inevitably productive of injustice and confusion, if partial compliances be made before it is driven to assume it. Thus, sir, without relieving the people in the smallest degree, the alternative proposed will impair the efficacy of the government, and will perpetually endanger the tranquillity of the union.

The honorable member's objection with respect to requisitions of troops will be fully obviated at another time. Let it suffice now to say, that it is altogether unwarrantable, and founded upon a misconception of the paper before you. But the honorable member in order to influence our decision, has mentioned the opinion of a citizen who is an ornament to this state. When the name of this distinguished character was introduced, I was much surprised. Is it come to this then, that we are not to follow our own reason? Is it proper to introduce the opinions of respectable men not within these walls? If the opinion of an important character were to weigh on this occasion, could we not adduce a character equally great on our side? Are we who (in the honorable gentleman's opinion) are not to be governed by an *erring world*, now to submit to the opinion of a citizen beyond the Atlantic? I believe that were that gentleman now on this floor, he would be *for* the adoption of this constitution. I wish his name had never been mentioned. I wish every thing spoken here relative to his opinion may be suppressed if our debates should be published. I know that the delicacy of his feelings will be wounded when he will see in print what has and may be said, concerning him on this occasion. I am in some measure acquainted with his sentiments on this subject. It is not right for me to unfold what he has informed me. But I will venture to assert, that the clause now discussed, is not objected to by Mr. Jefferson. He approves of it, because it enables the government to carry on its operations. He admires several parts of it, which have been reprobated with vehemence in this house. He is captivated with the equality of suffrage in the senate, which the honorable gentleman (Mr. *Henry*) calls the rotten part of this constitution. But whatever be the opinion of that illustrious citizen, considerations of personal delicacy should dissuade us from introducing it here.

The honorable member has introduced the subject of religion. Religion is not guarded—there is no bill of rights declaring that religion should be secure. Is a bill of rights a security for religion? Would the bill of rights in this state exempt the people from paying for the support of one particular sect, if such sect were exclusively established by law? If there were a majority of one sect, a bill of rights would be a poor protection for liberty. Happily for the states, they enjoy the utmost freedom of religion. This freedom arises from that multiplicity of sects, which pervades America, and which is the best and only security for religious liberty in any society.

For where there is such a variety of sects, there cannot be a majority of any one sect to oppress and persecute the rest. Fortunately for this commonwealth, a majority of the people are decidedly against any exclusive establishment—I believe it to be so in the other states. There is not a shadow of right in the general government to intermeddle with religion. Its least interference with it would be a most flagrant usurpation. I can appeal to my uniform conduct on this subject, that I have warmly supported religious freedom. It is better that this security should be depended upon from the general legislature, than from one particular state. A particular state might concur in one religious project. But the United States abound in such a variety of sects, that it is a strong security against religious persecution, and is sufficient to authorise a conclusion, that no one sect will ever be able to out-number or depress the rest.

I will not travel over that extensive tract, which the honorable member has traversed. I shall not now take notice of all his desultory objections. As occasions arise, I shall answer them.

It is worthy of observation on this occasion, that the honorable gentleman himself, seldom fails to contradict the arguments of gentlemen on that side of the question. For example, he strongly complains that the federal government from the number of its members will make an addition to the public expence, too formidable to be borne; and yet he and other gentlemen on the same side, object that the number of representatives is too small, though ten men are more than we are entitled to under the existing system! How can these contradictions be reconciled? If we are to adopt any efficient government at all, how can we discover or establish such a system, if it be thus attacked? Will it be possible to form a rational conclusion upon contradictory principles? If arguments of a contradictory nature were to be brought against the wisest and most admirable system, to the formation of which human intelligence is competent, it never could stand them.

He has acrimoniously inveighed against the government, because such transactions as congress think require secrecy, may be concealed—and particularly those which relate to treaties. He admits that when a treaty is forming, secrecy is proper; but urges that when actually made, the public ought to be made acquainted with every circumstance relative to it. The policy of not divulging the most important transactions, and negociations of nations, such as those which relate to warlike arrangements and treaties, is universally admitted. The congressional proceedings are to be occasionally published, including *all receipts and expenditures* of public money, of which no part can be used, but in consequence of appropriations made by law. This is a security which we do not enjoy under the existing system. That part which authorises the government to withhold from the public knowledge what in their judgment may require secrecy, is imitated from the confederation—that very system which the gentleman advocates.

No treaty has been formed, and I will undertake to say, that none *will* be formed under the old system, which will secure to us the actual enjoyment of the navigation of the Mississippi. Our weakness precludes us from it. We *are* entitled to it. But it is not under an inefficient government that we shall be able to avail ourselves fully of that right. I most conscientiously believe, that it will be far better secured under the new government, than the old, as we will be more able to enforce our right. The people of Kentucky will have an additional safe-guard from the change of system. The strength and respectability of the union will secure them in the enjoyment of that right, till that country becomes sufficiently populous. When this happens, they will be able to retain it in spite of every opposition.

I never can admit that seven states are disposed to surrender that navigation. Indeed it never was the case. Some of their most distinguished characters are decidedly opposed to its relinquishment. When its cession was proposed by the southern states, the northern states opposed it. They still oppose it. New-Jersey directed her delegates to oppose it, and is strenuously against it. The same sentiments pervade Pennsylvania: At least I am warranted to say so, from the best information which I have. Those states, added to the southern states, would be a majority against it.

The honorable gentleman, to obviate the force of my observations with respect to concurrent collections of taxes under different authorities, said, that there was no interference between the concurrent collections of parochial, county and state taxes, because they all irradiated from the same centre; but that this was not the case with the general government. To make use of the gentleman's own term, the concurrent collections under the authorities of the general government and state governments, all irradiate from the people at large. The people is their common superior. The sense of the people at large is to be the predominant spring of their actions. This is a sufficient security against interference.

Our attention was called to our commercial interest, and at the same time the landed interest was said to be in danger. If those ten men who were to be chosen, be elected by landed men, and have land themselves, can the electors have any thing to apprehend? If the commercial interest be in danger, why are we alarmed about the carrying trade? Why is it said, that the carrying states will preponderate, if commerce be in danger? With respect to speculation, I will remark that stock-jobbing has more or less prevailed in all countries, and ever will in some degree, notwithstanding any exertions to prevent it. If you judge from what has happened under the existing system, any change would render a melioration probable.

June 12, 1788

Speech in the Virginia Ratifying Convention on the Militia

MR. MADISON. Mr. Chairman—The honorable gentleman has laid much stress on the maxim, that the purse and sword ought not to be put in the same hands; with a view of pointing out the impropriety of vesting this power in the general government. But it is totally inapplicable to this question. What is the meaning of this maxim? Does it mean that the sword and purse ought not to be trusted in the hands of the same government? This cannot be the meaning. For there never was, and I can say there never will be, an efficient government, in which both are not vested. The only rational meaning, is, that the sword and purse are not to be given to the same member. Apply it to the British government, which has been mentioned. The sword is in the hands of the British king. The purse in the hands of the parliament. It is so in America, as far as any analogy can exist. Would the honorable member say, that the sword ought to be put in the hands of the representatives of the people, or in other hands independent of the government altogether? If he says so, it will violate the meaning of that maxim. This would be a novelty hitherto unprecedented. The purse is in the hands of the representatives of the people. They have the appropriation of all monies. They have the direction and regulation of land and naval forces. They are to *provide* for calling forth the militia—and the president is to have the command; and, in conjunction with the senate, to appoint the officers. The means ought to be commensurate to the end. The end is general protection. This cannot be effected without a general power to use the strength of the union.

We are told that both sides are distinguished by these great traits, *confidence* and *distrust*. Perhaps there may be a less or greater tincture of suspicion on one side, than the other. But give me leave to say, that where power can be safely lodged, if it be necessary, reason commands its cession. In such case it is imprudent and unsafe to withhold it. It is universally admitted that it must be lodged in some hands or other. The question then is, in what part of the government it ought to be placed; and not whether any other political body independent of the government should have it or not. I profess myself to have had an uniform zeal for a republican government. If the honorable member, or any other person, conceives that my attachment to this system arises from a different source, he is greatly mistaken. From the first moment that my mind was capable of contemplating political subjects, I never, till this moment, ceased wishing success to a well regulated republican government. The establishment of such in America was my most ardent desire. I have considered attentively (and my consideration has been aided by experience) the tendency of a relaxation of laws, and licentiousness of manners.

If we review the history of all republics, we are justified by the supposition, that if the bands of the government be relaxed, confusion will ensue. Anarchy ever has, and I fear ever will, produce despotism. What was the state of things that preceded the wars and revolutions in Germany? Faction and confusion. What produced the disorders and commotions of Holland? The like causes. In this commonwealth, and every state in the union, the relaxed operation of the government has been sufficient to alarm the friends of their country. The rapid increase of population in every state is an additional reason to check dissipation and licentiousness. Does it not strongly call for the friends of republican government to endeavor to establish a republican organization? A change is absolutely necessary. I can see no danger in submitting to practice an experiment which seems to be founded on the best theoretic principles.

But the honorable member tells us, there is not an equal responsibility delineated on that paper, to that which is in the English government. Calculations have been made here, that when you strike off those entirely elected by the influence of the crown, the other part does not bear a greater proportion to the number of their people, than the number fixed in that paper, bears to the number of inhabitants in the United States. If it were otherwise, there is still more responsibility in this government. Our representatives are chosen for two years. In Great-Britain they are chosen for seven years. Any citizen may be elected here. In Great-Britain no one can be elected to represent a county, without having an estate of the

value of £.600 sterling, a year; nor to represent a corporation
without an annual estate of £.300. Yet we are told, there is no
sympathy or fellow-feeling between the people here, and their
representatives; but that in England they have both. A just
comparison will shew, that if confidence be due to the government there, it is due ten-fold here. (Mr. *Madison* made
many other observations, but spoke so very low that he could
not be distinctly heard.)

June 14, 1788

Speech in the Virginia Ratifying Convention on Control of the Military

MR. MADISON.   Mr. Chairman—I will endeavor to follow the rule of the house; but must pay due attention to the observations which fell from the gentleman. I should conclude, from abstracted reasoning, that they were ill founded. I should think, that if there were any object, which the general government ought to command, it would be the direction of the national forces. And as the force which lies in militia is most safe, the direction of that part ought to be submitted to, in order to render another force unnecessary. The power objected to is necessary, because it is to be employed for national purposes. It is necessary to be given to every government. This is not opinion, but fact. The highest authority may be given: That the want of such authority in the government protracted the late war, and prolonged its calamities.

He says, that one ground of complaint at the beginning of the revolution, was, that a standing army was quartered upon us. This was not the whole complaint. We complained because it was done without the local authority of this country—without the consent of the people of America. As to the exclusion of standing armies in the bills of rights of the states, we shall find, that though in one or two of them, there is something like a prohibition, yet in most of them it is only provided, that no armies shall be kept up without the legislative authority; that is, without the consent of the community itself. Where is the impropriety of saying we shall have an army, if necessary? Does not the notoriety of this constitute security? If inimical nations were to fall upon us when defenceless, what would be the consequence? Would it be wise to say, that we should have no defence? Give me leave to say that the only possible way to provide against standing armies, is, to make them unnecessary. The way to do this, is to organize and discipline our militia, so as to render them capable of defending the country against external invasions, and internal insurrections. But it is urged, that abuses may happen. How is it possible to answer objections against possibility of abuses? It must strike every logical reasoner, that these cannot be entirely provided against. I really thought that the objection to the militia was at an end. Was there ever a constitution, in which, if authority was vested, it must not have been executed by force, if resisted? Was it not in the contemplation of this state, when contemptuous proceedings were expected, to recur to something of this kind? How is it possible to have a more proper resource than this? That the laws of every country ought to be executed, cannot be denied. That force must be used if necessary, cannot be denied. Can any government be established, that will answer any purpose whatever, unless force be provided for executing its laws? The constitution does not say that a standing army shall be called out to execute the laws. Is not this a more proper way? The militia ought to be called forth to suppress smugglers. Will this be denied? The case actually happened at Alexandria. There were a number of smugglers, who were too formidable for the civil power to overcome. The militia quelled the sailors, who, otherwise, would have perpetrated their intentions. Should a number of smugglers have a number of ships, the militia ought to be called forth to quell them. We do not know but what there may be combinations of smugglers in Virginia hereafter. We all know the use made of the Isle of Man. It was a general depositary of contraband goods. The parliament found the evil so great, as to render it necessary to wrest it out of the hands of its possessor.

The honorable gentleman says, it is a government of force. If he means *military* force, the clause under consideration proves the contrary. There never was a government without force. What is the meaning of government? An institution to make people do their duty. A government leaving it to a man to do his duty, or not, as he pleases, would be a new species of government, or rather no government at all. The ingenuity of the gentleman is remarkable, in introducing the riot-act of Great Britain. That act has no connection, or analogy, to any regulation of the militia: Nor is there any thing in the constitution to warrant the general government to make such an act. It never was a complaint in Great-Britain, that the militia could be called forth. If riots should happen, the militia are proper to quell it, to prevent a resort to another mode. As to the infliction of ignominious punishments, we have no ground of alarm, if we consider the circumstances of the people at large. There will be no punishments so ignominious as have been inflicted already. The militia law of every state to the north of Maryland, is less rigorous than the particular law of this state. If a change be necessary to be made by the general government, it will be in our favor. I think that the people of those states would not agree to be subjected to a more harsh punishment than their own militia laws inflict. An observation fell from a gentleman, on the same side with myself, which deserves to be attended to. If we be dissatisfied with the national government—if we should choose to renounce it, this is an additional safe-guard to our defence. I conceive that we are peculiarly interested in giving the general government as extensive means as possible to protect us. If there be a particular discrimination between places in America, the southern states are, from their situation and circumstances, most interested in giving the national government the power of protecting its members. (Here Mr. *Madison* made some other observations; but spoke so very low, that his meaning could not be comprehended.) An act passed a few years ago, in this state, to enable the government to call forth the militia to enforce the laws, when a powerful combination should take place to oppose them. This is the same power which the constitution is to have. There is a great deal of difference between calling forth the militia, when a combination is formed to prevent the execution of the laws, and the sheriff or constable carrying with him a body of militia to execute them in the first instance; which is a construction not warranted by the clause. There is an act also in this state, empowering the officers of the customs to summon *any* persons to assist them when they meet with obstruction in executing their duty. This shews the necessity of giving the government power to call forth the militia when the laws are resisted. It is a power vested in every legislature in the union, and which is necessary to every government.

June 16, 1788

Speech in the Virginia Ratifying Convention on the Slave Trade Clause

MR. MADISON. Mr. Chairman—I should conceive this clause to be impolitic, if it were one of those things which could be excluded without encountering greater evils. The southern states would not have entered into the union of America, without the temporary permission of that trade. And if they were excluded from the union, the consequences might be dreadful to them and to us. We are not in a worse situation than before. That traffic is prohibited by our laws, and we may continue the prohibition. The union in general is not in a worse situation. Under the articles of confederation, it might be continued forever: But by this clause an end may be put to it after twenty years. There is therefore an amelioration of our circumstances. A tax may be laid in the mean time; but it is limited, otherwise congress might lay such a tax as would amount to a prohibition. From the mode of representation and taxation, congress cannot lay such a tax on slaves as will amount to manumission. Another clause secures us that property which we now possess. At present, if any slave elopes to any of those states where slaves are free, he becomes emancipated by their laws. For the laws of the states are uncharitable to one another in this respect. But in this constitution, "no person held to service, or labor, in one state, under the laws thereof, escaping into another, shall in consequence of any law or regulation therein, be discharged from such service or labor; but shall be delivered up on claim of the party to whom such service or labor may be due." This clause was expressly inserted to enable owners of slaves to reclaim them. This is a better security than any that now exists. No power is given to the general government to interpose with respect to the property in slaves now held by the states. The taxation of this state being equal only to its representation, such a tax cannot be laid as he supposes. They cannot prevent the importation of slaves for twenty years; but after that period they can. The gentlemen from South-Carolina and Georgia argued in this manner: "We have now liberty to import this species of property, and much of the property now possessed, has been purchased, or otherwise acquired, in contemplation of improving it by the assistance of imported slaves. What would be the consequence of hindering us from it? The slaves of Virginia would rise in value, and we would be obliged to go to your markets." I need not expatiate on this subject. Great as the evil is, a dismemberment of the union would be worse. If those states should disunite from the other states, for not indulging them in the temporary continuance of this traffic, they might solicit and obtain aid from foreign powers.

June 17, 1788

Speech in the Virginia Ratifying Convention on the Judicial Power

MR. MADISON.   Mr. Chairman—Permit me to make a few observations which may place this part in a more favorable light than the gentleman placed it in yesterday. It may be proper to remark, that the organization of the general government for the United States, was, in all its parts, very difficult. There was a peculiar difficulty in that of the Executive. Every thing incident to it, must have participated of that difficulty. That mode which was judged most expedient was adopted, till experience should point out one more eligible. This part was also attended with difficulties. It claims the indulgence of a fair and liberal interpretation. I will not deny that, according to my view of the subject, a more accurate attention might place it in terms which would exclude some of the objections now made to it. But if we take a liberal construction, I think we shall find nothing dangerous or inadmissible in it. In compositions of this kind, it is difficult to avoid technical terms which have the same meaning. An attention to this may satisfy gentlemen, that precision was not so easily obtained as may be imagined. I will illustrate this by one thing in the constitution. There is a general power to provide courts to try felonies and piracies committed on the high seas. *Piracy* is a word which may be considered as a term of the law of nations. Felony is a word unknown to the law of nations, and is to be found in the British laws, and from thence adopted in the laws of these states. It was thought dishonorable to have recourse to that standard. A technical term of the law of nations is therefore used, that we should find ourselves authorised to introduce it into the laws of the United States. The first question which I shall consider, is, whether the subjects of its cognizance be proper subjects of a federal jurisdiction. The second will be, whether the provisions respecting it be consistent with safety and propriety, will answer the purposes intended, and suit local circumstances. The first class of cases to which its jurisdiction extends, are those which may arise under the constitution; and this is to extend to equity as well as law. It may be a misfortune that in organizing any government, the explication of its authority should be left to any of its co-ordinate branches. There is no example in any country where it is otherwise. There is a new policy in submitting it to the judiciary of the United States. That causes of a federal nature will arise, will be obvious to every gentleman, who will recollect that the states are laid under restrictions; and that the rights of the union are secured by these restrictions. They may involve equitable as well as legal controversies. With respect to the laws of the union, it is so necessary and expedient that the judicial power should correspond with the legislative, that it has not been objected to. With respect to treaties, there is a peculiar propriety in the judiciary expounding them. These may involve us in controversies with foreign nations. It is necessary therefore, that they should be determined in the courts of the general government. There are strong reasons why there should be a supreme court to decide such disputes. If in any case uniformity be necessary, it must be in the exposition of treaties. The establishment of one revisionary superintending power, can alone secure such uniformity. The same principles hold with respect to cases affecting ambassadors, and foreign ministers. To the same principles may also be referred their cognizance in admiralty and maritime cases. As our intercourse with foreign nations will be affected by decisions of this kind, they ought to be uniform. This can only be done by giving the federal judiciary exclusive jurisdiction. Controversies affecting the interest of the United States ought to be determined by their own judiciary, and not be left to partial local tribunals.

The next case, where two or more states are the parties, is not objected to. Provision is made for this by the existing articles of confederation; and there can be no impropriety in referring such disputes to this tribunal.

Its jurisdiction in controversies between a state and citizens of another state, is much objected to, and perhaps without reason. It is not in the power of individuals to call any state into court. The only operation it can have, is, that if a state should wish to bring suit against a citizen, it must be brought before the federal court. This will give satisfaction to individuals, as it will prevent citizens on whom a state may have a claim, being dissatisfied with the state courts. It is a case which cannot often happen, and if it should be found improper, it will be altered. But it may be attended with good effects. This may be illustrated by other cases. It is provided, that citizens of different states may be carried to the federal court. But this will not go beyond the cases where they may be parties. A *feme covert* may be a citizen of another state, but cannot be a party in this court. A subject of a foreign power having a dispute with a citizen of this state, may carry it to the federal court; but an alien enemy cannot bring suit at all. It appears to me, that this can have no operation but this—to give a citizen a right to be heard in the federal court; and if a state should condescend to be a party, this court may take cognizance of it.

As to its cognizance of disputes between citizens of different states, I will not say it is a matter of such importance. Perhaps it might be left to the state courts. But I sincerely believe this provision will be rather salutary, than otherwise. It may happen that a strong prejudice may arise in some states, against the citizens of others, who may have claims against them. We know what tardy, and even defective administration of justice, has happened in some states. A citizen of another state might not chance to get justice in a state court, and at all events he might think himself injured.

To the next clause there is no objection.

The next case provides for disputes between a foreign state, and one of our states, should such a case ever arise; and between a citizen and a foreign citizen or subject. I do not conceive that any controversy can ever be decided in these courts, between an American state and a foreign state, without the consent of the parties. If they consent, provision is here made. The disputes ought to be tried by the national tribunal. This is consonant to the law of nations. Could there be a more favorable or eligible provision to avoid controversies with foreign powers? Ought it to be put in the power of a member of the union to drag the whole community into war? As the national tribunal is to decide, justice will be done. It appears to me from this review, that, though on some of the subjects of this jurisdiction, it may seldom or never operate, and though others be of inferior consideration, yet they are mostly of great importance, and indispensably necessary.

The second question which I proposed to consider, was, whether such organization be made as would be safe and convenient for the states and the people at large. Let us suppose that the subjects of its jurisdiction had been only enumerated, and power given to the general legislature to establish such courts as might be judged necessary and expedient; I do not think that in that case any rational objection could be made to it, any more than would be made to a general power of legislation in certain enumerated cases. If that would be safe, this appears to me better and more restrictive, so far as it might be abused by an extension of power. The most material part is the discrimination of superior and inferior jurisdiction, and the arrangement of its powers; as, *where* it shall have original, and where appellate cognizance. Where it speaks of appellate jurisdiction, it expressly provides, that such regulations will be made as will accommodate every citizen, so far as is practicable in any government. The principal criticism which has been made, was against the appellate cognizance, as well of fact as law. I am happy that the honorable member who presides, and who is familiarly acquainted with the subject does not think it involves any thing unnecessarily dangerous. I think that the distinction of fact as well as law, may be satisfied by the discrimination of the civil and common law. But if gentlemen should contend, that appeals as to fact can be extended to jury cases, I contend, that by the word *regulations*, it is in the power of congress to prevent it, or prescribe such a mode as will secure the privilege of jury trial. They may make a regulation to prevent such appeals entirely: Or they may remand the fact, or send it to an inferior contiguous court, to be tried; or otherwise preserve that ancient and important trial.

Let me observe, that so far as the judicial power may extend to controversies between citizens of different states, and so far as it gives them power to correct by another trial, a verdict obtained by local prejudices, it is favorable to those states who carry on commerce. There are a number of commercial states, who carry on trade for other states. Should the states in debt to them make unjust regulations, the justice that would be obtained by the creditors, might be merely imaginary and nominal. It might be either entirely denied, or partially granted. This is no imaginary evil. Before the war, New-York was to a great amount a creditor of Connecticut: While it depended on the laws and regulations of Connecticut, she might withhold payment. If I be not misinformed, there were reasons to complain. These illiberal regulations and causes of complaint, obstruct commerce. So far as this power may be exercised, Virginia will be benefited by it. It appears to me from the most correct view, that by the word *regulations*, authority is given them to provide against all inconveniences; and so far as it is exceptionable, they can remedy it. This they will do if they be worthy of the trust we put in them. I think them worthy of that confidence which that paper puts in them. Were I to select a power which might be given with confidence, it would be judicial power. This power cannot be abused, without raising the indignation of all the people of the states. I cannot conceive that they would encounter this odium. Leaving behind them their characters and friends, and carrying with them local prejudices, I cannot think they would run such a risk. That men should be brought from all parts of the union to the seat of government, on trivial occasions, cannot reasonably be supposed. It is a species of possibility; but there is every degree of probability against it. I would as soon believe, that by virtue of the power of collecting taxes or customs, they would compel every man to go and pay the money for his taxes with his own hands to the federal treasurer, as I would believe this. If they would not do the one, they would not the other.

I am of opinion, and my reasoning and conclusions are drawn from facts, that as far as the power of congress can extend, the judicial power will be accommodated to every part of America. Under this conviction, I conclude, that the legislature, instead of making the supreme federal court absolutely stationary, will fix it in different parts of the continent, to render it more convenient. I think this idea perfectly warrantable. There is an example within our knowledge which illustrates it. By the confederation, congress have an exclusive right of establishing rules for deciding in all cases, what captures should be legal, and establishing courts for determining such cases finally. A court was established for that purpose, which was at first stationary. Experience, and the desire of accommodating the decisions of this court to the convenience of the citizens of the different parts of America, had this effect—it soon became a regulation, that this court should be held in different parts of America, and was held so accordingly. If such a regulation was made, when only the interest of the small number of people who are concerned with captures was affected, will not the public convenience be consulted, when that of a very considerable proportion of the people of America will be concerned? It will be also in the power of congress to vest this power in the state courts, both inferior and superior. This they will do, when they find the tribunals of the states established on a good footing. Another example will illustrate this subject further. By the confederation, congress are authorised to establish courts for trying piracies and felonies committed on the high seas. Did they multiply courts unnecessarily in this case? No, sir, they invested the admiralty courts of each state with this jurisdiction. Now, sir, if there will be as much sympathy between congress and the people, as now, we may fairly conclude, that the federal cognizance will be vested in the local tribunals.

I have observed, that gentlemen suppose, that the general legislature will do every mischief they possibly can, and that they will omit to do every thing good which they are authorised to do. If this were a reasonable supposition, their objections would be good. I consider it reasonable to conclude, that they will as readily do their duty, as deviate from it: Nor do I go on the grounds mentioned by gentlemen on the other side—that we are to place unlimited confidence in them, and expect nothing but the most exalted integrity and sublime virtue. But I go on this great republican principle, that the people will have virtue and intelligence to select men of virtue and wisdom. Is there no virtue among us? If there be not, we are in a wretched situation. No theoretical checks—no form of government can render us secure. To suppose that any form of government will secure liberty or happiness without any virtue in the people, is a chimerical idea. If there be sufficient virtue and intelligence in the community, it will be exercised in the selection of these men. So that we do not depend on their virtue, or put confidence in our rulers, but in the people who are to choose them.

Having taken this general view of the subject, I will now advert to what has fallen from the honorable gentleman who presides. His criticism is, that the judiciary has not been guarded from an increase of the salary of the judges. I wished myself, to insert a restraint on the augmentation as well as diminution of their compensation; and supported it in the convention. But I was over-ruled. I must state the reasons which were urged. They had great weight. The business must increase. If there was no power to increase their pay, according to the increase of business, during the life of the judges, it might happen, that there would be such an accumulation of business, as would reduce the pay to a most trivial consideration. This reason does not hold as to the president. For in the short period which he presides, this cannot happen. His salary ought not therefore to be increased. It was objected yesterday, that there was no provision for a jury from the vicinage. If it could have been done with safety, it would not have been opposed. It might so happen, that a trial would be impracticable in the county. Suppose a rebellion in a whole district, would it not be impossible to get a jury? The trial by jury is held as sacred in England as in America. There are deviations of it in England: yet greater deviations have happened here since we established our independence, than have taken place there for a long time, though it be left to the legislative discretion. It is a misfortune in any case that this trial should be departed from, yet in some cases it is necessary. It must be therefore left to the discretion of the legislature to modify it according to circumstances. This is a complete and satisfactory answer.

It was objected, that this jurisdiction would extend to all cases, and annihilate the state courts. At this moment of time it might happen, that there are many disputes between citizens of different states. But in the ordinary state of things I believe that any gentleman will think, that the far greater number of causes—ninety-nine out of an hundred, will remain with the state judiciaries. All controversies directly between citizen and citizen, will still remain with the local courts. The number of cases within the jurisdiction of these courts are very small when compared to those in which the local tribunals will have cognizance. No accurate calculation

can be made, but I think that any gentleman who will contemplate the subject at all, must be struck with this truth.
(Here Mr. *Madison* spoke too low to be understood.)

As to vexatious appeals, they can be remedied by congress.
It would seldom happen that mere wantonness would produce such an appeal, or induce a man to sue unjustly. If the
courts were on a good footing in the states, what can induce
them to take so much trouble? I have frequently in the discussion of this subject, been struck with one remark. It has
been urged, that this would be oppressive to those who by
imprudence, or otherwise, are under the denomination of
debtors. I know not how this can be conceived. I will venture
one observation. If this system should have the effect of establishing universal justice, and accelerating it throughout
America, it will be one of the most fortunate circumstances
that could happen for those men. With respect to that class of
citizens, compassion is their due. To those, however, who are
involved in such incumbrances, relief cannot be granted.
Industry and œconomy are their only resources. It is in vain
to wait for money, or temporise. The great desiderata are
public and private confidence. No country in the world can
do without them. Let the influx of money be ever so great, if
there be no confidence, property will sink in value, and there
will be no inducements or emulation to industry. The circulation of confidence is better than the circulation of money.
Compare the situation of nations in Europe, where justice is
administered with celerity, to that of those where it is refused,
or administered tardily. Confidence produces the best effects
in the former. The establishment of confidence will raise the
value of property, and relieve those who are so unhappy as to
be involved in debts. If this be maturely considered, I think it
will be found, that as far as it will establish uniformity of justice, it will be of real advantage to such persons. I will not
enter into those considerations which the honorable gentleman added. I hope some other gentleman will undertake to
answer him.

June 20, 1788

Speech in the Virginia Ratifying Convention on Ratification and Amendments

MR. MADISON. Mr. Chairman—Nothing has excited more admiration in the world, than the manner in which free governments have been established in America. For it was the first instance from the creation of the world to the American revolution, that the free inhabitants have been seen deliberating on a form of government, and selecting such of their citizens as possessed their confidence, to determine upon, and give effect to it. But why has this excited so much wonder and applause? Because it is of so much magnitude, and because it is liable to be frustrated by so many accidents. If it has excited so much wonder, that the United States have in the middle of war and confusion, formed free systems of government, how much more astonishment and admiration will be excited, should they be able, peaceably, freely and satisfactorily, to establish one general government, when there is such a diversity of opinions, and interests, when not cemented or stimulated by any common danger? How vast must be the difficulty of concentrating in one government, the interests, and conciliating the opinions of so many different heterogeneous bodies? How have the confederacies of ancient and modern times been formed? As far as ancient history describes the former to us, they were brought about by the wisdom of some eminent sage. How was the imperfect union of the Swiss Cantons formed? By danger—how was the confederacy of the United Netherlands formed? By the same. They are surrounded by dangers. By these and one influential character, they were stimulated to unite. How was the Germanic system formed? By danger, in some degree, but principally by the over-ruling influence of individuals. When we consider this government, we ought to make great allowances. We must calculate the impossibility that every state should be gratified in its wishes, and much less that every individual should receive this gratification. It has never been denied by the friends of the paper on the table, that it has defects. But they do not think that it contains any real danger. They conceive that they will in all probability be removed when experience will shew it to be necessary. I beg that gentlemen in deliberating on this subject, would consider the alternative. Either nine states shall have ratified it, or they will not. If nine states will adopt it, can it be reasonably presumed or required, that nine states having freely and fully considered the subject, and come to an affirmative decision, will, upon the demand of a single state, agree that they acted wrong, and could not see its defects—tread back the steps which they have taken, and come forward and reduce it to uncertainty, whether a general system shall be adopted or not? Virginia has always heretofore spoken the language of respect to the other states, and she has always been attended to. Will it be that language, to call on a great majority of the states to acknowledge that they have done wrong? Is it the language of confidence to say, that we do not believe that amendments for the preservation of the common liberty and general interest of the states, will be consented to by them? This is neither the language of confidence nor respect. Virginia, when she speaks respectfully, will be as much attended to, as she has hitherto been, when speaking this language. It is a most awful thing that depends on our decision—no less than whether the thirteen states shall unite freely, peaceably, and unanimously, for the security of their common happiness and liberty, or whether every thing is to be put in confusion and disorder! Are we to embark in this dangerous enterprize, uniting various opinions to contrary interests, with the vain hopes of coming to an amicable concurrence?

It is worthy of our consideration, that those who prepared the paper on the table, found difficulties not to be described, in its formation—mutual deference and concession were absolutely necessary. Had they been inflexibly tenacious of their individual opinions, they would never have concurred. Under what circumstances was it formed? When no party was formed, or particular proposition made, and men's minds were calm and dispassionate. Yet under these circumstances, it was difficult, extremely difficult to agree to any general system.

Suppose eight states only should ratify it, and Virginia should propose certain alterations, as the previous condition of her accession. If they should be disposed to accede to her proposition, which is the most favorable conclusion, the difficulty attending it will be immense. Every state, which has decided it, must take up the subject again. They must not only have the mortification of acknowledging that they had done wrong, but the difficulty of having a re-consideration of it among the people, and appointing new conventions to deliberate upon it. They must attend to *all* the amendments, which may be dictated by as great a diversity of political opinions, as there are local attachments. When brought together in one assembly they must go through, and accede to every one of the amendments. The gentlemen who within this house have thought proper to propose previous amendments, have brought no less than forty amendments—a bill of rights which contains twenty amendments, and twenty other alterations, some of which are improper and inadmissible. Will not every state think herself equally entitled to propose as many amendments? And suppose them to be contradictory, I leave it to this convention, whether it be probable that they can agree, or agree to any thing but the plan on the table; or whether greater difficulties will not be encountered, than were experienced in the progress of the formation of this constitution.

I have said that there was a great contrariety of opinions among the gentlemen in the opposition. It has been heard in every stage of their opposition. I can see from their amendments, that very great sacrifices have been made by some of them. Some gentlemen think that it contains too much state influence; others, that it is a complete consolidation, and a variety of other things. Some of them think that the equality in the senate, is not a defect; others, that it is the bane of all good governments. I might, if there were time, shew a variety of other cases, where their opinions are contradictory. If there be this contrariety of opinions in this house, what contrariety may not be expected, when we take into view, thirteen conventions equally or more numerous? Besides, it is notorious from the debates which have been published, that there is no sort of uniformity in the grounds of the opposition.

The state of New-York has been adduced. Many in that state are opposed to it from local views. The two who opposed it in the general convention from that state, are in the state convention. Every step of this system was opposed by those two gentlemen. They were unwilling to part with the old confederation. Can it be presumed then, sir, that gentlemen in this state, who admit the necessity of changing, should ever be able to unite in sentiments with those who are totally averse to any change.

I have revolved this question in my mind, with as much serious attention, and called to my aid as much information as I could, yet I can see no reason for the apprehensions of gentlemen; but I think that the most happy effects for this country would result from adoption, and if Virginia will agree to ratify this system, I shall look upon it as one of the most fortunate events that ever happened, for human nature. I cannot, therefore, without the most excruciating apprehensions, see a possibility of losing its blessings—It gives me infinite pain to reflect, that all the earnest endeavours of the warmest friends of their country, to introduce a system promotive of our happiness, may be blasted by a rejection, for which I think with my honorable friend, that previous amendments are but another name. The gentlemen in opposition seem to insist on those previous amendments, as if they were all necessary for the liberty and happiness of the people. Were I to hazard an opinion on the subject, I would declare it infinitely more safe in its present form, than it would be after introducing into it that long train of alterations which they call amendments.

With respect to the proposition of the honorable gentleman to my left (Mr. *Wythe*) gentlemen apprehend, that by enumerating three rights, it implied there were no more. The observations made by a gentleman lately up, on that subject, correspond precisely with my opinion. That resolution declares, that the powers granted by the proposed constitution, are the gift of the people, and may be resumed by them when perverted to their oppression, and every power not granted thereby, remains with the people, and at their will. It adds likewise, that *no right of any denomination*, can be cancelled, abridged, restrained or modified, by the general government, or any of its officers, except in those instances in which power is given by the constitution for these purposes. There cannot be a more positive and unequivocal declaration of the principles of the adoption—that every thing not granted, is reserved. This is obviously and self-evidently the case, without the declaration. Can the general government exercise any power not delegated? If an enumeration be made of our rights, will it not be implied, that every thing omitted, is given to the general government? Has not the honorable gentleman himself, admitted, that an imperfect enumeration is dangerous? Does the constitution say that they shall not alter the law of descents, or do these things which would subvert the whole system of the state laws? If it did, what was not excepted, would be granted. Does it follow from the omission of such restrictions, that they can exercise powers not delegated? The reverse of the proposition holds. The delegation alone warrants the exercise of any power. With respect to the amendments, proposed by the honorable gentleman, it ought to be considered how far they are good. As far as they are palpably and insuperably objectionable, they ought to be opposed. One amendment he proposes, is, that any army which shall be necessary, shall be raised by the consent of two-thirds of the states. I most devoutly wish, that there may never be an occasion of having a single regiment. There can be no harm in declaring, that standing armies in time of peace, are dangerous to liberty, and ought to be avoided, as far as it may be consistent with the protection of the community. But when we come to say, that the national security shall depend, not on a majority of the people of America, but that it may be frustrated by less than one-third of the people of America; I ask if this be a safe or proper mode? What part of the United States are most likely to stand in need of this protection? The weak parts, which are the southern states. Will it be safe to leave the United States at the mercy of *one-third* of the states, a number, which may comprise a very small proportion of the American people? They may all be in that part of America which is least exposed to danger. As far as a remote situation from danger, would render exertions for public defence less active, so far the southern states would be endangered.

The regulation of commerce, he further proposes, should depend on two-thirds of both houses. I wish I could recollect the history of this matter, but I cannot call it to mind with sufficient exactness. But I well recollect the reasoning of some gentlemen on that subject. It was said, and I believe with truth, that every part of America, does not stand in equal need of security. It was observed, that the northern states were most competent to their own safety. Was it reasonable, asked they, that they should bind themselves to the defence of the southern states; and still be left at the mercy of the minority for commercial advantages? Should it be in the power of the minority to deprive them of this and other advantages, when they were bound to defend the whole union, it might be a disadvantage for them to confederate. These were their arguments. This policy of guarding against political inconveniences, by enabling a small part of the community to oppose the government, and subjecting the majority to a small minority is fallacious. In some cases it may be good; in others it may be fatal. In all cases it puts it in the power of the minority to decide a question which concerns the majority.

I was struck with surprise when I heard him express himself alarmed with respect to the emancipation of slaves. Let me ask, if they should even attempt it, if it will not be an usurpation of power? There is no power to warrant it, in that paper. If there be, I know it not. But why should it be done? Says the honorable gentleman, for the general welfare—it will infuse strength into our system. Can any member of this committee suppose, that it will increase our strength? Can any one believe, that the American councils will come into a measure which will strip them of their property, discourage, and alienate the affections of five-thirteenths of the union. Why was nothing of this sort aimed at before? I believe such an idea never entered into any American breast, nor do I believe it ever will, unless it will enter into the heads of those gentlemen who substitute unsupported suspicions for reasons.

I am persuaded that the gentlemen who contend for previous amendments, are not aware of the dangers which must result. Virginia after having made opposition, will be obliged to recede from it. Might not the nine states say with a great deal of propriety—"it is not proper, decent, or right in you, to demand that we should reverse what we have done. Do as we have done—place confidence in us, as we have done in one another—and then we shall freely, fairly and dispassionately consider and investigate your propositions, and endeavour to gratify your wishes: But if you do not do this, it is more reasonable that you should yield to us, than we to you. You cannot exist without us—you must be a member of the union."

The case of Maryland, instanced by the gentleman, does not hold. She would not agree to confederate, because the other states would not assent to her claims of the western lands. Was she gratified? No—She put herself like the rest. Nor has she since been gratified. The lands are in the common stock of the union.

As far as his amendments are not objectionable, or unsafe, so far they may be subsequently recommended. Not because they are necessary but because they can produce no possible danger, and may gratify some gentlemen's wishes. But I never can consent to his previous amendments, because they are pregnant with dreadful dangers.

June 24, 1788

To Alexander Hamilton

My Dear Sir   Richd. June 27.
    This day put an end to the existence of our Convention. The inclosed is a copy of the Act of Ratification. It has been followed by a number of recommendatory alterations; many of them highly objectionable. One of the most so is an article prohibiting direct taxes where effectual laws shall be passed by the States for the purpose. It was impossible to prevent this error. The minority will sign an address to the people. The genesis of it is unknown to me. It is announced as an exhortation to acquiescence in the result of the Convention. Notwithstanding the fair professions made by some, I am so uncharitable as to suspect that the ill will to the Constitution will produce [   ] every peaceable effort to disgrace & destroy it. Mr. H—y declared previous to the final question that although he should submit as a quiet citizen, he should wait with impatience for the favorable moment of regaining in a *constitutional way*, the lost liberties of his country. My conjecture is that exertions will be made to engage ⅔ds of the

Legislatures in the task of regularly undermining the government. This hint may not be unworthy of your attention. Yrs. Affecly.

June 27, 1788

To Alexander Hamilton

My Dear Sir   N. York Sunday Evening
    Yours of yesterday is this instant come to hand & I have but a few minutes to answer it. I am sorry that your situation obliges you to listen to propositions of the nature you describe. My opinion is that a reservation of a right to withdraw if amendments be not decided on under the form of the Constitution within a certain time, is a *conditional* ratification, that it does not make N. York a member of the New Union, and consequently that she could not be received on that plan. Compacts must be reciprocal, this principle would not in such a case be preserved. The Constitution requires an adoption *in toto*, and *for ever*. It has been so adopted by the other States. An adoption for a limited time would be as defective as an adoption of some of the articles only. In short any *condition* whatever must viciate the ratification. What the New Congress by virtue of the power to admit new States, may be *able* & disposed to do in such case, I do not enquire as I suppose that is not the material point at present. I have not a moment to add more than my fervent wishes for your success & happiness

This idea of reserving right to withdraw was started at Richmd. & considered as a conditional ratification which was itself considered as worse than a rejection.

July 20, 1788

Observations on the "Draught of a Constitution for Virginia"

Senate. The term of two years is too short. Six years are not more than sufficient. A Senate is to withstand the occasional impetuosities of the more numerous branch. The members ought therefore to derive a firmness from the tenure of their places. It ought to supply the defect of knowledge and experience incident to the other branch, there ought to be time given therefore for attaining the qualifications necessary for that purpose. It ought finally to maintain that system and steadiness in public affairs without which no Government can prosper or be respectable. This cannot be done by a body undergoing a frequent change of its members. A Senate for six years will not be dangerous to liberty. On the contrary it will be one of its best guardians. By correcting the infirmities of popular Government, it will prevent that disgust agst. that form which may otherwise produce a sudden transition to some very different one. It is no secret to any attentive & dispassionate observer of the pol: Situation of the U. S. that the real danger to republican liberty has lurked in that cause.

The appointment of Senators by districts seems to be objectionable. A spirit of *locality* is inseparable from that mode. The evil is fully displayed in the County representations; the members of which are every where observed to lose sight of the aggregate interests of the Community, and even to sacrifice them to the interests or prejudices of their respective constituents. In general these local interests are miscalculated. But it is not impossible for a measure to be accomodated to the particular interests of every County or district, when considered by itself, and not so, when considered in relation to each other and to the whole State; in the same manner as the interests of individuals may be very different in a State of nature and in a Political Union. The most effectual remedy for the local biass is to impress on the minds of the Senators an attention to the interest of the whole Society by making them the choice of the whole Society, each citizen voting for every Senator. The objection here is that the fittest characters would not be sufficiently known to the people at large. But in free

Governments, merit and notoriety of character are rarely separated, and such a regulation would connect them more and more together. Should this mode of election be on the whole not approved, that established in Maryland presents a valuable alternative. The latter affords perhaps a greater security for the selection of merit. The inconveniences chargeable on it are two: first that the Council of electors favors cabal. Against this the shortness of its existence is a good antidote. Secondly that in a large State the meeting of the Electors must be expensive if they be paid, or badly attended if the service be onerous. To this it may be answered that in a case of such vast importance, the expence which could not be great, ought to be disregarded. Whichever of these modes may be preferred, it cannot be amiss so far to admit the plan of districts as to restrain the choice to persons residing in different parts of the State. Such a regulation will produce a diffusive confidence in the Body, which is not less necessary than the other means of rendering it useful. In a State having large towns which can easily unite their votes the precaution would be essential to an immediate choice by the people at large. In Maryland no regard is paid to residence. And what is remarkable vacancies are filled by the Senate itself. This last is an obnoxious expedient and cannot in any point of view have much effect. It was probably meant to obviate the trouble of occasional meetings of the Electors. But the purpose might have been otherwise answered by allowing the unsuccessful candidates to supply vacancies according to the order of their standing on the list of votes, or by requiring provisional appointments to be made along with the positive ones. If an election by districts be unavoidable and the ideas here suggested be sound, the evil will be diminished in proportion to the extent given to the districts, taking two or more Senators from each district.

Electors. The first question arising here is how far property ought to be made a qualification. There is a middle way to be taken which corresponds at once with the Theory of free government and the lessons of experience. A freehold or equivalent of a certain value may be annexed to the right of voting for Senators, & the right left more at large in the election of the other House. Examples of this distinction may be found

in the Constitutions of several States, particularly if I mistake
not, of North Carolina & N. York. This middle mode reconciles and secures the two cardinal objects of Government, the
rights of persons, and the rights of property. The former will
be sufficiently guarded by one branch, the latter more particularly by the other. Give all power to property; and the indigent will be oppressed. Give it to the latter and the effect
may be transposed. Give a defensive share to each and each
will be secure. The necessity of thus guarding the rights of
property was for obvious reasons unattended to in the commencement of the Revolution. In all the Governments which
were considered as beacons to republican patriots & lawgivers, the rights of persons were subjected to those of property. The poor were sacrificed to the rich. In the existing state
of American population, & American property, the two
classes of rights were so little discriminated that a provision
for the rights of persons was supposed to include of itself
those of property, and it was natural to infer from the tendency of republican laws, that these different interests would
be more and more identified. Experience and investigation
have however produced more correct ideas on this subject. It
is now observed that in all populous countries, the smaller
part only can be interested in preserving the rights of property. It must be foreseen that America, and Kentucky itself
will by degrees arrive at this State of Society; that in some
parts of the Union a very great advance is already made towards it. It is well understood that interest leads to injustice
as well when the opportunity is presented to bodies of men,
as to individuals; to an interested majority in a republic, as to
the interested minority of any other form of Government.
The time to guard agst. this danger is at the first forming of
the Constitution, and in the present state of population when
the bulk of the people have a sufficient interest in possession
or in prospect to be attached to the rights of property, without being insufficiently attached to the rights of persons.
Liberty not less than justice pleads for the policy here recommended. If *all* power be suffered to slide into hands not
interested in the rights of property which must be the case
whenever a majority fall under that description, one of two
things cannot fail to happen; either they will unite against

the other description and become the dupes & instruments of ambition, or their poverty & independence will render them the mercenary instruments of wealth. In either case liberty will be subverted; in the first by a despotism growing out of anarchy, in the second, by an oligarchy founded on corruption.

The second question under this head is whether the ballot be not a better mode than that of voting viva voce. The comparative experience of the States pursuing the different modes is in favor of the first. It is found less difficult to guard against fraud in that, than against bribery in the other.

Exclusions. Does not the exclusion of Ministers of the Gospel as such violate a fundamental principle of liberty by punishing a religious profession with the privation of a civil right? Does it not violate another article of the plan itself which exempts religion from the cognizance of Civil power? Does it not violate justice by at once taking away a right and prohibiting a compensation for it. And does it not in fine violate impartiality by shutting the door agst the Ministers of one religion and leaving it open for those of every other.

The re-eligibility of members after accepting offices of profit is so much opposed to the present way of thinking in America that any discussion of the subject would probably be a waste of time.

Limits of power. It is at least questionable whether death ought to be confined to "Treason and murder." It would not therefore be prudent to tie the hands of Government in the manner here proposed. The prohibition of pardon, however specious in theory would have practical consequences, which render it inadmissible. A single instance is a sufficient proof. The crime of treason is generally shared by a number, and often a very great number. It would be politically if not morally wrong to take away the lives of all, even if every individual were equally guilty. What name would be given to a severity which made no distinction between the legal & the moral offence—between the deluded multitude, and their wicked leaders. A second trial would not avoid the difficulty; because the oaths of the jury would not permit them to hearken to any voice but the inexorable voice of the law.

The power of the Legislature to appoint any other than their own officers departs too far from the Theory which requires a separation of the great Depts of Government. One of the best securities against the creation of unnecessary offices or tyrannical powers, is an exclusion of the authors from all share in filling the one, or influence in the execution of the others. The proper mode of appointing to offices will fall under another head.

Executive Governour. An election by the Legislature is liable to insuperable objections. It not only tends to faction intrigue and corruption, but leaves the Executive under the influence of an improper obligation to that department. An election by the people at large, as in this & several other States—or by Electors as in the appointment of the Senate in Maryland, or indeed by the people through any other channel than their legislative representatives, seems to be far preferable. The ineligibility a second time, though not perhaps without advantages, is also liable to a variety of strong objections. It takes away one powerful motive to a faithful & useful administration, the desire of acquiring that title to a re-appointment. By rendering a periodical change of men necessary, it discourages beneficial undertakings which require perseverance and system, or, as frequently happened in the Roman Consulate, either precipitates or prevents the execution of them. It may inspire desperate enterprizes for the attainment of what is not attainable by legitimate means. It fetters the judgment and inclination of the Community; and in critical moments would either produce a violation of the Constitution, or exclude a choice which might be essential to the public safety. Add to the whole, that by putting the Executive Magistrate in the situation of the tenant of an unrenewable lease, it would tempt him to neglect the constitutional rights of his department, and to connive at usurpations by the Legislative department, with which he may connect his future ambition or interest.

The clause restraining the first Magistrate from the immediate command of the military force would be made better by excepting cases in which he should receive the sanction of the two branches of the Legislature.

Council of State. The following variations are suggested. 1. The election to be made by the people immediately, or thro' some other medium than the Legislature. 2. A distributive choice should perhaps be secured as in the case of the Senate. 3 instead of an ineligibility a second time, a rotation as in the federal Senate, with an abrdgmt. of the term to be substituted.

The appointment to offices is, of all the functions of Republican & perhaps every other form of Government, the most difficult to guard against abuse. Give it to a numerous body, and you at once destroy all responsibility, and create a perpetual source of faction and corruption. Give it to the Executive wholly, and it may be made an engine of improper influence and favoritism. Suppose the power were divided thus: let the Executive alone make all the subordinate appointments; and the Govr. and Senate as in the Fedl. Constn:, those of the superior order. It seems particularly fit that the Judges, who are to form a distinct department should owe their offices partly to each of the other departments rather than wholly to either.

Judiciary. Much detail ought to be avoided in the constitutional regulation of this department, that there may be room for changes which may be demanded by the progressive changes in the state of our population. It is at least doubtful whether the number of Courts, the number of Judges, or even the boundaries of Jurisdiction ought to be made unalterable but by a revisal of the Constitution. The precaution seems no otherwise necessary than as it may prevent sudden modifications of the establishment, or addition of obsequious Judges, for the purpose of evadg. the checks of the Constn. & giving effect to some sinister policy of the Legisre. But might not the same object be otherwise attained? By prohibiting, for example, any innovations in those particulars without the consent of that department: or without the annual sanction of two or three successive assemblies; over & above the other pre-requisites to the passage of a law.

The model here proposed for a Court of Appeals is not recommended by experience. It is found as might well be presumed that the members are always warped in their appellate decisions by an attachment to the principles and jurisdiction of their respective Courts & still more so by the previous decision on the case removed by appeal. The only effectual cure for the evil, is to form a Court of Appeals, of distinct and select Judges. The expence ought not be admitted as an objection. 1. because the proper administration of Justice is of too essential a nature to be sacrificed to that consideration. 2. The number of inferior Judges might in that case be lessened. 3. The whole department may be made to support itself by a judicious tax on law proceedings.

The excuse for non-attendance would be a more proper subject of enquiry some where else than in the Court to which the party belonged. Delicacy, mutual connivance &c. would soon reduce the regulation to mere form; or if not, it might become a disagreeable source of little irritations among the members. A certificate from the local Court or some other local authority where the party might reside or happen to be detained from his duty, expressing the cause of absence as well as that it was judged to be satisfactory, might be safely substituted. Few Judges would improperly claim their wages, if such a formality stood in the way. These observations are applicable to the Council of State.

A Court of Impeachments is among the most puzzling articles of a republican Constitution; and it is far more easy to point out defects in any plan, than to supply a cure for them. The diversified expedients adopted in the Constitutions of the several States prove how much the compilers were embarrassed on this subject. The plan here proposed varies from all of them; and is perhaps not less than any a proof of the difficulties which pressed the ingenuity of its author. The remarks arising on it are 1. that it seems not to square with reason, that the right to impeach should be united to that of trying the impeachment, & consequently in a proportional degree, to that of sharing in the appointment of, or influence on the Tribunal to which the trial may belong. 2. As the Executive & Judiciary would form a majority of the Court, and either have a right to impeach, too much might depend on a combination of these departments. This objection would be still stronger, if the members of the Assembly were capable as proposed of holding offices, and were amenable in that capacity to the Court. 3. The H. of Delegates and either of those departments could appt. a majority of the Court. Here is another danger of combination, and the more to be apprehended as that branch of the Legisl: wd. also have the right to impeach, a right in their hands of itself sufficiently weighty; and as the power of the Court wd. extend to the head of the Ex. by whose independence the constitutil. rights of that department are to be secured agst. Legislative usurpations. 4. The dangers in the two last cases would be still more formidable; as the power extends not only to deprivation; but to future incapacity of office. In the case of all officers of sufficient importance to be objects of factious persecution, the latter branch of power is in every view of a delicate nature. In that of the Cheif Magistrate, it seems inadmissible, if he be chosen by the Legislature; and much more so, if immediately by the people themselves. A temporary incapacitation is the most that cd. be properly authorised.

The 2 great desiderata in a Court of impeachts. are 1. impartiality. 2. respectability—the first in order to a right—the second in order to a satisfactory decision. These characteristics are arrived at in the following modification—Let the Senate be denied the right to impeach. Let ⅓ of the members be struck out, by alternate nominations of the prosecutors & party impeached; the remaining ⅔ to be the *Stamen* of the Court. When the H: of Del: impeach, let the Judges or a certain proportion of them—and the Council of State be associated in the trial. When the Govr. or Council impeaches, let the Judges only be associated: When the Judges impeach let the Council only be associated. But if the party impeached by the H. of Dels. be a member of the Ex. or Judicy. let that of which he is a member not be associated. If the party impeached belong to one & be impeached by the other of these branches, let neither of them be associated, the decision being in this case left with the Senate alone or if that be thought exceptionable, a few members might be added by the H. of Ds. ⅔ of the Court should in all cases be necessary to a conviction, & the cheif Magistrate *at least* should be exempt from a

sentence of perpetual if not of temporary incapacity. It is extremely probable that a critical discussion of this outline may
discover objections which do not occur. Some do occur; but
appear not to be greater than are incident to any different
modification of the Tribunal.

The establishment of trials by Jury & viva voce testimony in
all cases and in *all* Courts, is to say the least a delicate experiment; and would most probably be either violated, or be
found inconvenient.

Council of Revision. A revisionary power is meant as a
check to precipitate, to unjust, and to unconstitutional laws.
These important ends would it is conceived be more effectually secured, without disarming the Legislature of its requisite
authority, by requiring bills to be separately communicated to
the Exec: & Judicy. depts. If either of these object, let ⅔, if
both ¾ of each House be necessary to overrule the objection;
and if either or both protest agst. a bill as violating the
Constitution, let it moreover be suspended, notwithstanding
the overruling proportion of the Assembly, until there shall
have been a subsequent election of the H. of Ds. and a repas-
sage of the bill by ⅔ or ¾ of both Houses, as the case may be.
It sd. not be allowed the Judges or the Ex to pronounce a law
thus enacted, unconstitul. & invalid.

In the State Constitutions & indeed in the Fedl. one also,
no provision is made for the case of a disagreement in expounding them; and as the Courts are generally the last in
making their decision, it results to them, by refusing or not
refusing to execute a law, to stamp it with its final character.
This makes the Judiciary Dept paramount in fact to the Legislature, which was never intended, and can never be proper.

The extension of the Habs. Corps. to the cases in which it
has been usually suspended, merits consideration at least. If
there be emergences which call for such a suspension, it can
have no effect to prohibit it, because the prohibition will assuredly give way to the impulse of the moment; or rather it
will have the bad effect of facilitating other violations that
may be less necessary. The Exemption of the press from liability in every case for *true facts*, is also an innovation and as
such ought to be well considered. This essential branch of

liberty is perhaps in more danger of being interrupted by local tumults, or the silent awe of a predominant party, than by any direct attacks of Power.

c. October 15, 1788

To Thomas Jefferson

Dear Sir　　　　　　　　　　　　　　New York Oct. 17, 1788

I have written a number of letters to you since my return here, and shall add this by another casual opportunity just notified to me by Mr St. John. Your favor of July 31. came to hand the day before yesterday. The pamphlets of the Marquis Condorcet & Mr. Dupont referred to in it have also been received. Your other letters inclosed to the Delegation have been and will be disposed of as you wish; particularly those to Mr. Eppes & Col. Lewis.

Nothing has been done on the subject of the *outfit*: there not having been a Congress of nine States for some time, nor even of seven for the last week. It is pretty certain that there will not again be a quorum of either number within the present year; and by no means certain that there will be one at all under the old Confederation. The Committee finding that nothing could be done have neglected to make a report as yet. I have spoken with a member of it in order to get one made, that the case may fall of course and in a favorable shape within the attention of the new Government. The fear of a precedent will probably lead to an allowance for a limited time, of the *salary as enjoyed originally* by *foreign ministers* in *preference to a separate allowance for outfit*. One of the *members of the treasury board* who ought, if certain facts have *not escaped his memory to witness the reasonableness of your* calculations, *takes occasion I find to impress a contrary idea*. Fortunately *his influence will* not *be a very formidable obstacle to right*.

The States which have adopted the new Constitution are all proceeding to the arrangements for putting it into action in March next. Pennsylva. alone has as yet actually appointed deputies, & that only for the Senate. My last mentioned that these were Mr. R. Morris & a Mr. McClay. How the other elections there & elsewhere will run is matter of uncertainty. The Presidency alone unites the conjectures of the public. The vice president is not at all marked out by the general voice. As the President will be from a Southern State, it falls almost of course for the other part of the Continent to supply the next in rank. South Carolina may however think of Mr. Rutlidge unless it should be previously discovered that votes will be wasted on him. The only candidates in the Northern States brought forward with their known consent are *Hancock and Adams* and *between these it seems probable the question will lie*. Both of them *are objectionable and would I think be postponed* by the *general suffrage to several others* if they *would accept the place. Hancock* is *weak ambitious a courtier of popularity given to low intrigue* and *lately reunited by a factious friendship with S. Adams—J. Adams* has made *himself obnoxious to many* particularly in the *Southern states by the political principles avowed in his book*. Others *recollecting his cabal during the war against General Washington* knowing *his extravagant self importance* and *considering his preference of an unprofitable dignity to* some *place of emolument* better *adapted to private fortune as a proof of his* having *an eye to the presidency conclude* that *he would not be a very cordial second to the general* and that *an impatient ambition* might *even intrigue for a premature advancement*. The *danger would be the greater if* particular *factious characters* as may be the case, *should get into the public councils. Adams* it appears, is *not unaware of* some *of the obstacles to his wish*: and *thro a letter to Smith* has *thrown out popular sentiments as to the proposed president.*

The little pamphlet herewith inclosed will give you a collective view of the alterations which have been proposed for the new Constitution. Various and numerous as they appear they certainly omit many of the true grounds of opposition. The articles relating to Treaties—to paper money, and to contracts, created more enemies than all the errors in the System positive & negative put together. It is true nevertheless that not a few, particularly in Virginia have contended for the proposed alterations from the most honorable & patriotic motives; and that among the advocates for the Constitution, there are some who wish for further guards to public liberty & individual rights. As far as these may consist of a constitutional declaration of the most essential rights, it is probable they will be added; though there are many who think such addition unnecessary, and not a few who think it misplaced in such a Constitution. There is scarce any point on which the party in opposition is so much divided as to its importance and its propriety. My own opinion has always been in favor of a bill of rights; provided it be so framed as not to imply powers not meant to be included in the enumeration. At the same time I have never thought the omission a material defect, nor been anxious to supply it even by *subsequent* amendment, for any other reason than that it is anxiously desired by others. I have favored it because I supposed it might be of use, and if properly executed could not be of disservice. I have not viewed it in an important light 1. because I conceive that in a certain degree, though not in the extent argued by Mr. Wilson, the rights in question are reserved by the manner in which the federal powers are granted. 2 because there is great reason to fear that a positive declaration of some of the most essential rights could not be obtained in the requisite latitude. I am sure that the rights of Conscience in particular, if submitted to public definition would be narrowed much more than they are likely ever to be by an assumed power. One of the objections in New England was that the Constitution by prohibiting religious tests opened a door for Jews Turks & infidels. 3. because the limited powers of the federal Government and the jealousy of the subordinate Governments, afford a security which has not existed in the case of the State Governments, and exists in no other. 4 because experience proves the inefficacy of a bill of rights on those occasions when its controul is most needed. Repeated violations of these parchment barriers have been committed by overbearing majorities in every State. In Virginia I have seen the bill of rights violated in every instance where it has been opposed to a popular current. Notwithstanding the explicit provision contained in that instrument for the rights of Conscience it is well known that a religious establishment wd. have taken place in that State, if the legislative majority had found as they expected, a majority of the people in favor of the measure;

and I am persuaded that if a majority of the people were now of one sect, the measure would still take place and on narrower ground than was then proposed, notwithstanding the additional obstacle which the law has since created. Wherever the real power in a Government lies, there is the danger of oppression. In our Governments the real power lies in the majority of the Community, and the invasion of private rights is *cheifly* to be apprehended, not from acts of Government contrary to the sense of its constituents, but from acts in which the Government is the mere instrument of the major number of the constituents. This is a truth of great importance, but not yet sufficiently attended to: and is probably more strongly impressed on my mind by facts, and reflections suggested by them, than on yours which has contemplated abuses of power issuing from a very different quarter. Wherever there is an interest and power to do wrong, wrong will generally be done, and not less readily by a powerful & interested party than by a powerful and interested prince. The difference, so far as it relates to the superiority of republics over monarchies, lies in the less degree of probability that interest may prompt abuses of power in the former than in the latter; and in the security in the former agst. oppression of more than the smaller part of the society, whereas in the former it may be extended in a manner to the whole. The difference so far as it relates to the point in question—the efficacy of a bill of rights in controuling abuses of power—lies in this, that in a monarchy the latent force of the nation is superior to that of the sovereign, and a solemn charter of popular rights must have a great effect, as a standard for trying the validity of public acts, and a signal for rousing & uniting the superior force of the community; whereas in a popular Government, the political and physical power may be considered as vested in the same hands, that is in a majority of the people, and consequently the tyrannical will of the sovereign is not to be controuled by the dread of an appeal to any other force within the community. What use then it may be asked can a bill of rights serve in popular Governments? I answer the two following which though less essential than in other Governments, sufficiently recommend the precaution. 1. The political truths declared in that solemn manner acquire by degrees the character of fundamental maxims of free Government, and as they become incorporated with the national sentiment, counteract the impulses of interest and passion. 2. Altho' it be generally true as above stated that the danger of oppression lies in the interested majorities of the people rather than in usurped acts of the Government, yet there may be occasions on which the evil may spring from the latter sources; and on such, a bill of rights will be a good ground for an appeal to the sense of the community. Perhaps too there may be a certain degree of danger, that a succession of artful and ambitious rulers, may by gradual & well-timed advances, finally erect an independent Government on the subversion of liberty. Should this danger exist at all, it is prudent to guard agst. it, especially when the precaution can do no injury. At the same time I must own that I see no tendency in our governments to danger on that side. It has been remarked that there is a tendency in all Governments to an augmentation of power at the expence of liberty. But the remark as usually understood does not appear to me well founded. Power when it has attained a certain degree of energy and independence goes on generally to further degrees. But when below that degree, the direct tendency is to further degrees of relaxation, until the abuses of liberty beget a sudden transition to an undue degree of power. With this explanation the remark may be true; and in the latter sense only is it in my opinion applicable to the Governments in America. It is a melancholy reflection that liberty should be equally exposed to danger whether the Government have too much or too little power, and that the line which divides these extremes should be so inaccurately defined by experience.

Supposing a bill of rights to be proper the articles which ought to compose it, admit of much discussion. I am inclined to think that *absolute* restrictions in cases that are doubtful, or where emergencies may overrule them, ought to be avoided. The restrictions however strongly marked on paper will never be regarded when opposed to the decided sense of the public; and after repeated violations in extraordinary cases, they will lose even their ordinary efficacy. Should a Rebellion or insurrection alarm the people as well as the Government, and a suspension of the Hab. Corp. be dictated by the alarm, no written prohibitions on earth would prevent the measure. Should an army in time of peace be gradually established in our neighbourhood by Britn: or Spain, declarations on paper would have as little effect in preventing a standing force for the public safety. The best security agst. these evils is to remove the pretext for them. With regard to monopolies they are justly classed among the greatest nusances in Government. But is it clear that as encouragements to literary works and ingenious discoveries, they are not too valuable to be wholly renounced? Would it not suffice to reserve in all cases a right to the Public to abolish the privilege at a price to be specified in the grant of it? Is there not also infinitely less danger of this abuse in our Governments, than in most others? Monopolies are sacrifices of the many to the few. Where the power is in the few it is natural for them to sacrifice the many to their own partialities and corruptions. Where the power, as with us, is in the many not in the few, the danger can not be very great that the few will be thus favored. It is much more to be dreaded that the few will be unnecessarily sacrificed to the many.

I inclose a paper containing the late proceedings in Kentucky. I wish the ensuing Convention may take no step injurious to the character of the district, and favorable to the views of those who wish ill to the U. States. One of my late letters communicated some circumstances which will not fail to occur on perusing the objects of the proposed Convention in next month. Perhaps however there may be less connection between the two cases than at first one is ready to conjecture. I am Dr Sir with the sincerst esteem & Affectn Yours

To Edmund Randolph

My Dear Friend   N York Novr. 2, 1788
I recd. yesterday your favor of the 23d. Ult. The first countenance of the Assembly corresponds with the picture which my imagination had formed of it. The views of the greater part of the opposition to the federal Government, and particularly of its principal leader, have ever since the Convention,

been regarded by me as permanently hostile, and likely to produce every effort that might endanger or embarrass it. The defects which drew forth objections from many quarters, were evidently of little consequence in the eye of Mr H.ry. His own arguments proved it. His enmity was levelled, as he did not scruple to insinuate agst the *whole System*; and the destruction of the whole System, I take to be still the secret wish of his heart, and the real object of his pursuit. If temperate and rational alterations only were his plan, is it conceivable that his coalition and patronage would be extended to men whose particular ideas on the subject must differ more from his own than those of others who share most liberally in his hatred?

My last letter with Col. Carrington's communications to which it referred, will have sufficiently explained my sentiments with regard to the Legislative service under the new Constitution. My first wish is to see the Government put into quiet and successful operation; and to afford any service, that may be acceptable from me, for that purpose. My second wish if that were to be consulted would prefer, for reasons formerly hinted, an opportunity of contributing that service in the House of Reps. rather than in the Senate; provided the opportunity be attainable from the spontaneous suffrage of the Constituents: Should the real friends to the Constitution think this preference inconsistent with my primary object, as Col. Carrington tells me is the case with some who are entitled to peculiar respect; and view my renouncing it as of any material consequence, I shall not hesitate to comply. You will not infer from the freedom with which these observations are made, that I am in the least unaware of the probability that whatever my inclinations or those of my friends may be, they are likely to be of little avail in the present case. I take it for certain that a clear majority of the Assembly are enemies to the Govt. and I have no reason to suppose that I can be less obnoxious than others on the opposite side. An election into the Senate therefore can hardly come into question. I know also that a good deal will depend on the arrangements for the election of the other branch; and that much may depend moreover on steps to be taken by the Candidates which will not be taken by me. Here again therefore there must be great uncertainty, if not improbability of my election. With these circumstances in view, it is impossible that I can be the dupe of false calculations, even if I were in other cases disposed to indulge them. I trust it is equally impossible for the result whatever it may be, to rob me of any reflections which enter into the internal fund of comfort & happiness. Popular favor or disfavor, is no criterion of the character maintained with those whose esteem an honorable ambition must court. Much less can it be a criterion of that maintained with ones self. And when the spirit of party directs the public voice, it must be a little mind indeed that can suffer in its own estimation, or apprehend danger of suffering of that of others.

The Sepr. British Packet arrived yesterday, but I do not find that she makes any addition to the Stock of European intelligence. The change in the French Ministry is the only event of late date of much consequence; and that had arrived through several other channels. I do not know that it is even yet authenticated; but it seems to be doubted by no one, particularly among those who can best decide on its credibility. With the utmost affection I am my dear Sir Yrs. Sincerely

To Edmund Randolph

My Dear Friend   Philada. Novr. 23. 1788
    Your two favors of the 5th. & 10th instant have been duly recd. The appointments for the Senate communicated in the latter, answer to the calculations I had formed, notwithstanding the contrary appearances on which the former was founded. My only surprize is that in the present temper and disproportionate number of the antifederal part of the Assembly, my name should have been honored with so great a vote as it received. When this circumstance is combined with that of the characters which I have reason to believe concurred in it, I should be justly chargeable with a very mistaken ambition, if I did not consider the event in the light which you anticipated. I shall not be surprized if the attempt should be equally successful to shut the door of the other House agst. me, which was the real object of my preference as well

for the reason formerly suggested to you, as for the additional one that it will less require a stile of life with which my circumstances do not square, & for which an inadequate provision only will probably be made by the public. Being not yet acquainted with the allotment of Orange in the districts, I can form no estimate of the reception that will be given to an offer of my services. The district in which I am told it is likely to be thrown, for the choice of an Elector, is a very monitory sample of what may & probably will be done in that way.

My present situation embarrasses me somewhat. When I left N. York, I not only expected that the Choice for the Senate would be as it is, but was apprehensive that the spirit of party might chuse to add the supposed mortification of dropping my name from the deputation to Congress for the fraction of a year remaining. I accordingly left that place under arrangements which did not require my return. At the same time, I had it in view, if left entirely to my option, to pass the Winter or part of it there; being desirous of employing some of the time in matters which need access to the papers of Congress, & supposing moreover that I should be there master more of my time than in Virginia. The opportunity of executing my plan is given me I find by one of the votes of the Assembly. On the other hand I am now pressed by some of my friends to repair to Virginia as a requisite expedient for counteracting the machinations agst. my election into the H. of Reps. To this again I am extremely disinclined for reasons additional to the one above mentioned. It will have an electioneering appearance which I always despised and wish to shun. And as I should shew myself in Orange only, where there will probably be little difficulty, my presence could have no very favorable effect: Whilst it is very possible that such a mark of solicitude strengthened by my not declining a reappointment to Congress, and now declining to serve in it, might by a dextrous misinterpretation, be made to operate on the other side. These considerations are strong inducements to join my colleagues at N. York, and leave things to their own course in Virginia. If Orange should fall into a federal district it is probable I shall not be opposed; if otherwise a successful opposition seems unavoidable. My decision however is not finally taken.

Mr. Dawson arrived here this morning. He took Anapolis in his way, where he tells me the disputed election of Baltimore engages the whole attention at present.

Will you be good eno' to enable me to answer the inclosed paper. I do not chuse to trust my recollection of the law on the subject. The enquiry comes from the French Consul at N. York.

You may continue to address yr. letters to N. York till I give other notice as they will not be lost whatever direction I may take, and will be highly grateful if I should return thither. Yrs. most affectly.

To George Eve

Sir,   January 2d. 1789

Being informed that reports prevail not only that I am opposed to any amendments whatever to the new federal Constitution; but that I have ceased to be a friend to the rights of Conscience; and inferring from a conversation with my brother William, that you are disposed to contradict such reports as far as your knowledge of my sentiments may justify, I am led to trouble you with this communication of them. As a private Citizen it could not be my wish that erroneous opinions should be entertained, with respect to either of those points, particularly, with respect to religious liberty. But having been induced to offer my services to this district as its representative in the federal Legislature, considerations of a public nature make it proper that, with respect to both, my principles and views should be rightly understood.

I freely own that I have never seen in the Constitution as it now stands those serious dangers which have alarmed many respectable Citizens. Accordingly whilst it remained unratified, and it was necessary to unite the States in some one plan, I opposed all previous alterations as calculated to throw the States into dangerous contentions, and to furnish the secret enemies of the Union with an opportunity of promoting its dissolution. Circumstances are now changed: The Constitution is established on the ratifications of eleven States and a very great majority of the people of America; and amendments, if pursued with a proper moderation and in a proper mode, will be not only safe, but may serve the double purpose of satisfying the minds of well meaning opponents, and of providing additional guards in favour of liberty. Under this change of circumstances, it is my sincere opinion that the Constitution ought to be revised, and that the first Congress meeting under it, ought to prepare and recommend to the States for ratification, the most satisfactory provisions for all essential rights, particularly the rights of Conscience in the fullest latitude, the freedom of the press, trials by jury, security against general warrants &c. I think it will be proper also to provide expressly in the Constitution, for the periodical increase of the number of Representatives until the amount shall be entirely satisfactory; and to put the judiciary department into such a form as will render vexatious appeals impossible. There are sundry other alterations which are either eligible in themselves, or being at least safe, are recommended by the respect due to such as wish for them.

I have intimated that the amendments ought to be proposed by the first Congress. I prefer this mode to that of a General Convention, 1st. because it is the most expeditious mode. A convention must be delayed, until ⅔ of the State Legislatures shall have applied for one; and afterwards the amendments must be submitted to the States; whereas if the business be undertaken by Congress the amendments may be prepared and submitted in March next. 2dly. because it is the most certain mode. There are not a few States who will absolutely reject the proposal of a Convention, and yet not be averse to amendmends in the other mode. Lastly, it is the safest mode. The Congress, who will be appointed to execute as well as to amend the Government, will probably be careful not to destroy or endanger it. A convention, on the other hand, meeting in the present ferment of parties, and containing perhaps insidious characters from different parts of America, would at least spread a general alarm, and be but too likely to turn every thing into confusion and uncertainty. It is to be observed however that the question concerning a General Convention, will not belong to the federal Legislature. If ⅔ of the States apply for one, Congress can not refuse to call it: if not, the other mode of amendments must be pursued. I am Sir with due respect your friend & Obedt. servant

To Edmund Randolph

My dear friend   Alexandria March 1st. 1789
    This is the first convenient opportunity I have had for dropping you a line since I last came into the State. Your sanction to my remaining in N. York during the crisis of the elections, conveyed through Col: Carrington, never came to hand till I had arrived in Orange. It coincided so fully with my inclination, and indeed with my judgment, that had it been received in due time, I do not know, but I should have disregarded all the pressing exhortations which stood opposed to your opinion. I am persuaded however that my appearance in the district was more necessary to my election than you then calculated. In truth it has been evinced by the experiment, that my absence would have left a room for the calumnies of antifederal partizans which would have defeated much better pretensions than mine. In Culpeper which was the critical County, a continued attention was necessary to repel the multiplied falsehoods which circulated. Whether I ought to be satisfied or displeased with my success, I shall hereafter be more able to judge. My present anticipations are not flattering. I see on the lists of Representatives a very scanty proportion who will share in the drudgery of business. And I foresee contentions first between federal & antifederal parties, and then between Northern & Southern parties, which give additional disagreeableness to the prospect. Shoud the State-Elections give an antifederal colour to the Legislatures, which from causes not antifederal in the people, may well happen, difficulties will again start up in this quarter, which may have a still more serious aspect on the Congressional proceedings.
    In my last or one of my last letters was inclosed a Quere from Mr. St. John the French Consul at New York, relating to the law here which regulates the recording of deeds &c. As I

shall on my return be applied to for an answer, I will thank you for the proper one as soon as your leisure will allow.

I shall go on from this tomorrow. On my arrival I shall attend as far as I can, to whatever may deserve your perusal. Besides the private satisfaction, which I shall have in the Continuance of our correspondence, I promise myself the benefit of your suggestions on public subjects. Present me respectfully to Mrs. R. and rely on the Affection with which I remain Yrs truly

CONGRESS AND THE
REPUBLICAN OPPOSITION
1789–1801

Speech in Congress on Presidential Titles

Mr. Madison.   I may be well disposed to concur in opinion with gentlemen that we ought not to recede from our former vote on this subject, yet at the same time I may wish to proceed with due respect to the Senate, and give dignity and weight to our own opinion so far as it contradicts theirs by the deliberate and decent manner in which we decide. For my part, Mr. Speaker, I do not conceive titles to be so pregnant with danger as some gentlemen apprehend. I believe a President of the United States cloathed with all the powers given in the constitution would not be a dangerous person to the liberties of America, if you were to load him with all the titles of Europe or Asia. We have seen superb and august titles given without conferring power and influence or without even obtaining respect; one of the most impotent sovereigns in Europe has assumed a title as high as human invention can devise; for example, what words can imply a greater magnitude of power and strength than that of high mightiness; this title seems to border almost upon impiety; it is assuming the pre-eminence and omnipotency of the deity; yet this title and many others cast in the same mould have obtained a long time in Europe, but have they conferred power? Does experience sanctify such opinion? Look at the republic I have alluded to and say if their present state warrants the idea.

I am not afraid of titles because I fear the danger of any power they could confer, but I am against them because they are not very reconcilable with the nature of our government, or the genius of the people; even if they were proper in themselves, they are not so at this juncture of time. But my strongest objection is founded in principle; instead of encreasing they diminish the true dignity and importance of a republic, and would in particular, on this occasion, diminish the true dignity of the first magistrate himself. If we give titles, we must either borrow or invent them—if we have recourse to the fertile fields of luxuriant fancy, and deck out an airy being of our own creation, it is a great chance but its fantastic properties renders the empty fantom ridiculous and absurd. If we borrow, the servile imitation will be odious, not to say ridiculous also—we must copy from the pompous sovereigns of the east, or follow the inferior potentates of Europe; in either case, the splendid tinsel or gorgeous robe would disgrace the manly shoulders of our Chief. The more truly honorable shall we be, by shewing a total neglect and disregard to things of this nature; the more simple, the more republican we are in our manners, the more rational dignity we acquire; therefore I am better pleased with the report adopted by the house, than I should have been with any other whatsoever.

The Senate, no doubt, entertain different sentiments on this subject. I would wish therefore to treat their opinion with respect and attention. I would desire to justify the reasonable and republican decision of this house to the other branch of Congress, in order to prevent a misunderstanding. But that the motion of my worthy colleague, (Mr. Parker) has possession of the house, I would move a more temperate proposition, and I think it deserves some pains to bring about that good will and urbanity, which for the dispatch of public business, ought to be kept up between the two houses. I do not think it would be a sacrifice of dignity to appoint a committee of conference, but imagine it would tend to cement that harmony which has hitherto been preserved between the Senate and this House—therefore, while I concur with the gentlemen who express in such decided terms, their disapprobation of bestowing titles, I concur also, with those who are for the appointment of a committee of conference, not apprehending they will depart from the principles adopted and acted upon by the House.

May 11, 1789

Speech in Congress on the Removal Power

MR. MADISON. I look upon every constitutional question, whatever its nature may be, of great importance; I look upon the present to be doubly so, because its nature is of the highest moment to the well being of the government. I have listened with attention to the objections which have been stated, and to the replies that have been made; and I think the investigation of the meaning of the constitution, has supported the doctrine I brought forward. If you consult the expediency, it will be greatly against the doctrine advanced by gentlemen on the other side of the question. See to what inconsistency gentlemen drive themselves, by their construction of the constitution. The gentleman from South-Carolina, (Mr. Smith) in order to bring to conviction and punishment an offender in any of the principal offices, must have recourse to a breach of the common law, and yet he may there be found guilty, and maintain his office, because he is fixed by the constitution. It has been said, we may guard against the inconveniency of that construction, by limiting the duration of the office, to a term of years, but during that term, there is no way of getting rid of a bad officer, but by impeachment. During the time this is depending, the person may continue to commit those crimes for which he is impeached, because if his construction of the constitution is right, the president can have no more power to suspend than he has to remove.

What fell from one of my colleagues (Mr. Bland) appears to have more weight, than any thing hitherto suggested. The constitution at the first view, may seem to favor his opinion; but that must be the case only at the first view, for if we examine it, we shall find his construction incompatible with the spirit and principles, contained in that instrument.

It is said, that it comports with the nature of things, that those who appoint, should have the power of removal, but I cannot conceive that this sentiment is warranted by the constitution; I believe it would be found very inconvenient in practice. It is one of the most prominent features of the constitution, a principle that pervades the whole system, that there should be the highest possible degree of responsibility in all the executive officers thereof; any thing therefore which tends to lessen this responsibility is contrary to its spirit and intention, and unless it is saddled upon us expressly by the letter of that work, I shall oppose the admission of it into any act of the legislature. Now, if the heads of the executive departments are subjected to removal by the president alone, we have in him security for the good behaviour of the officer: If he does not conform to the judgment of the president, in doing the executive duties of his office, he can be displaced; this makes him responsible to the great executive power, and makes the president responsible to the public for the conduct of the person he has nominated and appointed to aid him in the administration of his department; but if the president shall join in a collusion with this officer, and continue a bad man in office, the case of impeachment will reach the culprit, and drag him forth to punishment. But if you take the other construction, and say, he shall not be displaced, but by and with the advice and consent of the senate, the president is no longer answerable for the conduct of the officer; all will depend upon the senate. You here destroy a real responsibility without obtaining even the shadow; for no gentleman will pretend to say, the responsibility of the senate can be of such a nature as to afford substantial security. But why, it may be asked, was the senate joined with the president in appointing to office, if they have no responsibility? I answer, merely for the sake of advising, being supposed, from their nature, better acquainted with the characters of the candidates than an individual; yet even here the president is held to the responsibility he nominates, and with their consent appoints; no person can be forced upon him as an assistant by any other branch of the government.

There is another objection to this construction, which I consider of some weight, and shall therefore mention to the committee. Perhaps there was no argument urged with more success, or more plausibly grounded, against the constitution, under which we are now deliberating, than that founded on the mingling of the executive and legislative branches of the government in one body. It has been objected, that the senate have too much of the executive power even, by having a controul over the president in the appointment to office. Now, shall we extend this connection between the legislative and executive departments, which will strengthen the objection, and diminish the responsibility we have in the head of the executive? I cannot but believe, if gentlemen weigh well these considerations, they will think it safe and expedient to adopt the clause.

May 19, 1789

Speech in Congress Proposing Constitutional Amendments

Mr. Madison. The gentleman from Georgia (Mr. Jackson) is certainly right in his opposition to my motion for going into a committee of the whole, because he is unfriendly to the object I have in contemplation; but I cannot see that the gentlemen, who wish for amendments being proposed at the present session, stand on good ground when they object to the house going into committee on this business.

When I first hinted to the house my intention of calling their deliberations to this object, I mentioned the pressure of other important subjects, and submitted the propriety of postponing this till the more urgent business was dispatched; but finding that business not dispatched, when the order of the day for considering amendments arrived, I thought it a good reason for a farther delay, I moved the postponement accordingly. I am sorry the same reason still exists in some degree; but operates with less force when it is considered, that it is not now proposed to enter into a full and minute discussion of every part of the subject, but merely to bring it before the house, that our constituents may see we pay a proper attention to a subject they have much at heart; and if it does not give that full gratification which is to be wished, they will discover that it proceeds from the urgency of business of a very important nature. But if we continue to postpone from time to time, and refuse to let the subject come into view, it may occasion suspicions, which, though not well founded, may tend to inflame or prejudice the public mind, against our decisions: they may think we are not sincere in our desire to incorporate such amendments in the constitution as will secure those rights, which they consider as not sufficiently guarded. The applications for amendments come from a very respectable number of our constituents, and it is certainly proper for congress to consider the subject, in order to quiet that anxiety which prevails in the public mind: Indeed I think it would have been of advantage to the government, if it had been practicable to have made some propositions for amendments the first business we entered upon; it would stifle the voice of complaint, and make friends of many who doubted its merits. Our future measures would then have been more universally agreeable and better supported; but the justifiable anxiety to put the government in operation prevented that; it therefore remains for us to take it up as soon as possible. I wish then to commence the consideration at the present moment; I hold it to be my duty to unfold my ideas, and explain myself to the house in some form or other without delay. I only wish to introduce the great work, and as I said before I do not expect it will be decided immediately; but if some step is taken in the business it will give reason to believe that we may come at a final result. This will inspire a reasonable hope in the advocates for amendments, that full justice will be done to the important subject; and I have reason to believe their expectation will not be defeated. I hope the house will not decline my motion for going into a committee.

———

MR. MADISON.   I am sorry to be accessary to the loss of a single moment of time by the house. If I had been indulged in my motion, and we had gone into a committee of the whole, I think we might have rose, and resumed the consideration of other business before this time; that is, so far as it depended on what I proposed to bring forward. As that mode seems not to give satisfaction, I will withdraw the motion, and move you, sir, that a select committee be appointed to consider and report such amendments as are proper for Congress to propose to the legislatures of the several States, conformably to the 5th article of the constitution. I will state my reasons why I think it proper to propose amendments; and state the amendments themselves, so far as I think they ought to be proposed. If I thought I could fulfil the duty which I owe to myself and my constituents, to let the subject pass over in silence, I most certainly should not trespass upon the indulgence of this house. But I cannot do this; and am therefore compelled to beg a patient hearing to what I have to lay before you. And I do most sincerely believe that if congress will devote but one day to this subject, so far as to satisfy the public that we do not disregard their wishes, it will have a salutary influence on the public councils, and prepare the way for a favorable reception of our future measures. It appears to me that this house is bound by every motive of prudence, not to let the first session pass over without proposing to the state legislatures some things to be incorporated into the constitution, as will render it as acceptable to the whole people of the United States, as it has been found acceptable to a majority of them. I wish, among other reasons why something should be done, that those who have been friendly to the adoption of this constitution, may have the opportunity of proving to those who were opposed to it, that they were as sincerely devoted to liberty and a republican government, as those who charged them with wishing the adoption of this constitution in order to lay the foundation of an aristocracy or despotism. It will be a desirable thing to extinguish from the bosom of every member of the community any apprehensions, that there are those among his countrymen who wish to deprive them of the liberty for which they valiantly fought and honorably bled. And if there are amendments desired, of such a nature as will not injure the constitution, and they can be ingrafted so as to give satisfaction to the doubting part of our fellow citizens; the friends of the federal government will evince that spirit of deference and concession for which they have hitherto been distinguished.

It cannot be a secret to the gentlemen in this house, that, notwithstanding the ratification of this system of government by eleven of the thirteen United States, in some cases unanimously, in others by large majorities; yet still there is a great number of our constituents who are dissatisfied with it; among whom are many respectable for their talents, their patriotism, and respectable for the jealousy they have for their liberty, which, though mistaken in its object, is laudable in its motive. There is a great body of the people falling under this description, who at present feel much inclined to join their support to the cause of federalism, if they were satisfied in this one point: We ought not to disregard their inclination, but, on principles of amity and moderation, conform to their wishes, and expressly declare the great rights of mankind secured under this constitution. The acquiescence which our fellow citizens shew under the government, calls upon us for a like return of moderation. But perhaps there is a stronger motive than this for our going into a consideration of the subject; it is to provide those securities for liberty which are required by a part of the community. I allude in a particular manner to those two states who have not thought fit to throw themselves into the bosom of the confederacy: it is a desirable thing, on our part as well as theirs, that a re-union should take place as soon as possible. I have no doubt, if we proceed to take those steps which would be prudent and requisite at this juncture, that in a short time we should see that disposition prevailing in those states that are not come in, that we have seen prevailing in those states which are.

But I will candidly acknowledge, that, over and above all these considerations, I do conceive that the constitution may be amended; that is to say, if all power is subject to abuse, that then it is possible the abuse of the powers of the general government may be guarded against in a more secure manner than is now done, while no one advantage, arising from the exercise of that power, shall be damaged or endangered by it. We have in this way something to gain, and, if we proceed with caution, nothing to lose; and in this case it is necessary to proceed with caution; for while we feel all these inducements to go into a revisal of the constitution, we must feel for the constitution itself, and make that revisal a moderate one. I should be unwilling to see a door opened for a re-consideration of the whole structure of the government, for a re-consideration of the principles and the substance of the powers given; because I doubt, if such a door was opened, if we should be very likely to stop at that point which would be safe to the government itself: But I do wish to see a door opened to consider, so far as to incorporate those provisions for the security of rights, against which I believe no serious objection has been made by any class of our constituents, such as would be likely to meet with the concurrence of two-thirds of both houses, and the approbation of three-fourths of the state legislatures. I will not propose a single alteration which I do not wish to see take place, as intrinsically proper in itself, or proper because it is wished for by a respectable number of my fellow citizens; and therefore I shall not propose a single alteration but is likely to meet the concurrence required by the constitution.

There have been objections of various kinds made against the constitution: Some were levelled against its structure, because the president was without a council; because the senate, which is a legislative body, had judicial powers in trials on impeachments; and because the powers of that body were compounded in other respects, in a manner that did not correspond with a particular theory; because it grants more power than is supposed to be necessary for every good purpose; and controuls the ordinary powers of the state governments. I know some respectable characters who opposed this government on these grounds; but I believe that the great mass of the people who opposed it, disliked it because it did not contain effectual provision against encroachments on particular rights, and those safeguards which they have been long accustomed to have interposed between them and the magistrate who exercised the sovereign power: nor ought we to consider them safe, while a great number of our fellow citizens think these securities necessary.

It has been a fortunate thing that the objection to the government has been made on the ground I stated; because it will be practicable on that ground to obviate the objection, so far as to satisfy the public mind that their liberties will be perpetual, and this without endangering any part of the constitution, which is considered as essential to the existence of the government by those who promoted its adoption.

The amendments which have occurred to me, proper to be recommended by congress to the state legislatures, are these:

First. That there be prefixed to the constitution a declaration—That all power is originally vested in, and consequently derived from the people.

That government is instituted, and ought to be exercised for the benefit of the people; which consists in the enjoyment of life and liberty, with the right of acquiring and using property, and generally of pursuing and obtaining happiness and safety.

That the people have an indubitable, unalienable, and indefeasible right to reform or change their government, whenever it be found adverse or inadequate to the purposes of its institution.

Secondly. That in article 1st. section 2, clause 3, these words be struck out, to wit, "The number of representatives shall not exceed one for every thirty thousand, but each state shall have at least one representative, and until such enumeration shall be made." And that in place thereof be inserted these words, to wit, "After the first actual enumeration, there shall be one representative for every thirty thousand, until the number amount to   after which the proportion shall be so regulated by congress, that the number shall never be less than   nor more than   but each state shall after the first enumeration, have at least two representatives; and prior thereto."

Thirdly. That in article 1st, section 6, clause 1, there be added to the end of the first sentence, these words, to wit, "But no law varying the compensation last ascertained shall operate before the next ensuing election of representatives."

Fourthly. That in article 1st, section 9, between clauses 3 and 4, be inserted these clauses, to wit, The civil rights of none shall be abridged on account of religious belief or worship, nor shall any national religion be established, nor shall the full and equal rights of conscience be in any manner, or on any pretext infringed.

The people shall not be deprived or abridged of their right to speak, to write, or to publish their sentiments; and the freedom of the press, as one of the great bulwarks of liberty, shall be inviolable.

The people shall not be restrained from peaceably assembling and consulting for their common good; nor from applying to the legislature by petitions, or remonstrances for redress of their grievances.

The right of the people to keep and bear arms shall not be infringed; a well armed, and well regulated militia being the best security of a free country: but no person religiously scrupulous of bearing arms, shall be compelled to render military service in person.

No soldier shall in time of peace be quartered in any house without the consent of the owner; nor at any time, but in a manner warranted by law.

No person shall be subject, except in cases of impeachment, to more than one punishment, or one trial for the same offence; nor shall be compelled to be a witness against himself;

nor be deprived of life, liberty, or property without due process of law; nor be obliged to relinquish his property, where it may be necessary for public use, without a just compensation.

Excessive bail shall not be required, nor excessive fines imposed, nor cruel and unusual punishments inflicted.

The rights of the people to be secured in their persons, their houses, their papers, and their other property from all unreasonable searches and seizures, shall not be violated by warrants issued without probable cause, supported by oath or affirmation, or not particularly describing the places to be searched, or the persons or things to be seized.

In all criminal prosecutions, the accused shall enjoy the right to a speedy and public trial, to be informed of the cause and nature of the accusation, to be confronted with his accusers, and the witnesses against him; to have a compulsory process for obtaining witnesses in his favor; and to have the assistance of counsel for his defence.

The exceptions here or elsewhere in the constitution, made in favor of particular rights, shall not be so construed as to diminish the just importance of other rights retained by the people; or as to enlarge the powers delegated by the constitution; but either as actual limitations of such powers, or as inserted merely for greater caution.

Fifthly. That in article 1st, section 10, between clauses 1 and 2, be inserted this clause, to wit:

No state shall violate the equal rights of conscience, or the freedom of the press, or the trial by jury in criminal cases.

Sixthly. That article 3d, section 2, be annexed to the end of clause 2d, these words to wit: but no appeal to such court shall be allowed where the value in controversy shall not amount to   dollars: nor shall any fact triable by jury, according to the course of common law, be otherwise re-examinable than may consist with the principles of common law.

Seventhly. That in article 3d, section 2, the third clause be struck out, and in its place be inserted the clauses following, to wit:

The trial of all crimes (except in cases of impeachments, and cases arising in the land or naval forces, or the militia when on actual service in time of war or public danger) shall be by an impartial jury of freeholders of the vicinage, with the requisite of unanimity for conviction, of the right of challenge, and other accustomed requisites; and in all crimes punishable with loss of life or member, presentment or indictment by a grand jury, shall be an essential preliminary, provided that in cases of crimes committed within any county which may be in possession of an enemy, or in which a general insurrection may prevail, the trial may by law be authorised in some other county of the same state, as near as may be to the seat of the offence.

In cases of crimes committed not within any county, the trial may by law be in such county as the laws shall have prescribed. In suits at common law, between man and man, the trial by jury, as one of the best securities to the rights of the people, ought to remain inviolate.

Eighthly. That immediately after article 6th, be inserted, as article 7th, the clauses following, to wit:

The powers delegated by this constitution, are appropriated to the departments to which they are respectively distributed: so that the legislative department shall never exercise the powers vested in the executive or judicial; nor the executive exercise the powers vested in the legislative or judicial; nor the judicial exercise the powers vested in the legislative or executive departments.

The powers not delegated by this constitution, nor prohibited by it to the states, are reserved to the States respectively.

Ninthly. That article 7th, be numbered as article 8th.

The first of these amendments, relates to what may be called a bill of rights; I will own that I never considered this provision so essential to the federal constitution, as to make it improper to ratify it, until such an amendment was added; at the same time, I always conceived, that in a certain form and to a certain extent, such a provision was neither improper nor altogether useless. I am aware, that a great number of the most respectable friends to the government and champions for republican liberty, have thought such a provision, not only unnecessary, but even improper, nay, I believe some have gone so far as to think it even dangerous. Some policy has been made use of perhaps by gentlemen on both sides of the question: I acknowledge the ingenuity of those arguments which were drawn against the constitution, by a comparison with the policy of Great-Britain, in establishing a declaration of rights; but there is too great a difference in the case to warrant the comparison: therefore the arguments drawn from that source, were in a great measure inapplicable. In the declaration of rights which that country has established, the truth is, they have gone no farther, than to raise a barrier against the power of the crown; the power of the legislature is left altogether indefinite. Altho' I know whenever the great rights, the trial by jury, freedom of the press, or liberty of conscience, came in question in that body, the invasion of them is resisted by able advocates, yet their Magna Charta does not contain any one provision for the security of those rights, respecting which, the people of America are most alarmed. The freedom of the press and rights of conscience, those choicest privileges of the people, are unguarded in the British constitution.

But altho' the case may be widely different, and it may not be thought necessary to provide limits for the legislative power in that country, yet a different opinion prevails in the United States. The people of many states, have thought it necessary to raise barriers against power in all forms and departments of government, and I am inclined to believe, if once bills of rights are established in all the states as well as the federal constitution, we shall find that altho' some of them are rather unimportant, yet, upon the whole, they will have a salutary tendency.

It may be said, in some instances they do no more than state the perfect equality of mankind; this to be sure is an absolute truth, yet it is not absolutely necessary to be inserted at the head of a constitution.

In some instances they assert those rights which are exercised by the people in forming and establishing a plan of government. In other instances, they specify those rights which are retained when particular powers are given up to be exercised by the legislature. In other instances, they specify positive rights, which may seem to result from the nature of the compact. Trial by jury cannot be considered as a natural right, but a right resulting from the social compact which regulates the action of the community, but is as essential to secure the liberty of the people as any one of the pre-existent rights of nature. In other instances they lay down dogmatic maxims with respect to the construction of the government; declaring, that the legislative, executive, and judicial branches shall be kept separate and distinct: Perhaps the best way of securing this in practice is to provide such checks, as will prevent the encroachment of the one upon the other.

But whatever may be the form which the several states have adopted in making declarations in favor of particular rights, the great object in view is to limit and qualify the powers of government, by excepting out of the grant of power those cases in which the government ought not to act, or to act only in a particular mode. They point these exceptions sometimes against the abuse of the executive power, sometimes against the legislative, and, in some cases, against the community itself; or, in other words, against the majority in favor of the minority.

In our government it is, perhaps, less necessary to guard against the abuse in the executive department than any other; because it is not the stronger branch of the system, but the weaker: It therefore must be levelled against the legislative, for it is the most powerful, and most likely to be abused, because it is under the least controul; hence, so far as a declaration of rights can tend to prevent the exercise of undue power, it cannot be doubted but such declaration is proper. But I confess that I do conceive, that in a government modified like this of the United States, the great danger lies rather in the abuse of the community than in the legislative body. The prescriptions in favor of liberty, ought to be levelled against that quarter where the greatest danger lies, namely, that which possesses the highest prerogative of power: But this is not found in either the executive or legislative departments of government, but in the body of the people, operating by the majority against the minority.

It may be thought all paper barriers against the power of the community, are too weak to be worthy of attention. I am sensible they are not so strong as to satisfy gentlemen of every description who have seen and examined thoroughly the texture of such a defence; yet, as they have a tendency to impress some degree of respect for them, to establish the public opinion in their favor, and rouse the attention of the whole community, it may be one mean to controul the majority from those acts to which they might be otherwise inclined.

It has been said by way of objection to a bill of rights, by many respectable gentlemen out of doors, and I find opposition on the same principles likely to be made by gentlemen on this floor, that they are unnecessary articles of a republican government, upon the presumption that the people have those rights in their own hands, and that is the proper place for them to rest. It would be a sufficient answer to say that this objection lies against such provisions under the state governments as well as under the general government; and there are, I believe, but few gentlemen who are inclined to push their theory so far as to say that a declaration of rights in those cases is either ineffectual or improper. It has been said that in the federal government they are unnecessary, because the powers are enumerated, and it follows that all that are not granted by the constitution are retained: that the constitution is a bill of powers, the great residuum being the rights of the people; and therefore a bill of rights cannot be so necessary as if the residuum was thrown into the hands of the government. I admit that these arguments are not entirely without foundation; but they are not conclusive to the extent which has been supposed. It is true the powers of the general government are circumscribed; they are directed to particular objects; but even if government keeps within those limits, it has certain discretionary powers with respect to the means, which may admit of abuse to a certain extent, in the same manner as the powers of the state governments under their constitutions may to an indefinite extent; because in the constitution of the United States there is a clause granting to Congress the power to make all laws which shall be necessary and proper for carrying into execution all the powers vested in the government of the United States, or in any department or officer thereof; this enables them to fulfil every purpose for which the government was established. Now, may not laws be considered necessary and proper by Congress, for it is them who are to judge of the necessity and propriety to accomplish those special purposes which they may have in contemplation, which laws in themselves are neither necessary or proper; as well as improper laws could be enacted by the state legislatures, for fulfilling the more extended objects of those governments. I will state an instance which I think in point, and proves that this might be the case. The general government has a right to pass all laws which shall be necessary to collect its revenue; the means for enforcing the collection are within the direction of the legislature: may not general warrants be considered necessary for this purpose, as well as for some purposes which it was supposed at the framing of their constitutions the state governments had in view. If there was reason for restraining the state governments from exercising this power, there is like reason for restraining the federal government.

It may be said, because it has been said, that a bill of rights is not necessary, because the establishment of this government has not repealed those declarations of rights which are added to the several state constitutions: that those rights of the people, which had been established by the most solemn act, could not be annihilated by a subsequent act of that people, who meant, and declared at the head of the instrument, that they ordained and established a new system, for the express purpose of securing to themselves and posterity the liberties they had gained by an arduous conflict.

I admit the force of this observation, but I do not look upon it to be conclusive. In the first place, it is too uncertain ground to leave this provision upon, if a provision is at all necessary to secure rights so important as many of those I have mentioned are conceived to be, by the public in general, as well as those in particular who opposed the adoption of this constitution. Beside some states have no bills of rights, there are others provided with very defective ones, and there are others whose bills of rights are not only defective, but absolutely improper; instead of securing some in the full extent which republican principles would require, they limit them too much to agree with the common ideas of liberty.

It has been objected also against a bill of rights, that, by enumerating particular exceptions to the grant of power, it would disparage those rights which were not placed in that enumeration, and it might follow by implication, that those rights which were not singled out, were intended to be assigned into the hands of the general government, and were consequently insecure. This is one of the most plausible arguments I have ever heard urged against the admission of a bill of rights into this system; but, I conceive, that may be guarded against. I have attempted it, as gentlemen may see by turning to the last clause of the 4th resolution.

It has been said, that it is unnecessary to load the constitution with this provision, because it was not found effectual in the constitution of the particular states. It is true, there are a few particular states in which some of the most valuable articles have not, at one time or other, been violated; but does it not follow but they may have, to a certain degree, a salutary effect against the abuse of power. If they are incorporated into the constitution, independent tribunals of justice will consider themselves in a peculiar manner the guardians of those rights; they will be an impenetrable bulwark against every assumption of power in the legislative or executive; they will be naturally led to resist every encroachment upon rights expressly stipulated for in the constitution by the declaration of rights. Beside this security, there is a great probability that such a declaration in the federal system would be inforced; because the state legislatures will jealously and closely watch the operations of this government, and be able to resist with more effect every assumption of power than any other power on earth can do; and the greatest opponents to a federal government admit the state legislatures to be sure guardians of the people's liberty. I conclude from this view of the subject, that it will be proper in itself, and highly politic, for the tranquility of the public mind, and the stability of the government, that we should offer something, in the form I have proposed, to be incorporated in the system of government, as a declaration of the rights of the people.

In the next place I wish to see that part of the constitution revised which declares, that the number of representatives shall not exceed the proportion of one for every thirty thousand persons, and allows one representative to every state which rates below that proportion. If we attend to the discussion of this subject, which has taken place in the state conventions, and even in the opinion of the friends to the constitution, an alteration here is proper. It is the sense of the people of America, that the number of representatives ought to be encreased, but particularly that it should not be left in the discretion of the government to diminish them, below that proportion which certainly is in the power of the legislature as the constitution now stands; and they may, as the population of the country encreases, increase the house of representatives to a very unwieldy degree. I confess I always thought this part of the constitution defective, though not dangerous; and that it ought to be particularly attended to whenever congress should go into the consideration of amendments.

There are several lesser cases enumerated in my proposition, in which I wish also to see some alteration take place. That article which leaves it in the power of the legislature to ascertain its own emolument is one to which I allude. I do not believe this is a power which, in the ordinary course of government, is likely to be abused, perhaps of all the powers granted, it is least likely to abuse; but there is a seeming impropriety in leaving any set of men without controul to put their hand into the public coffers, to take out money to put in their pockets; there is a seeming indecorum in such power, which leads me to propose a change. We have a guide to this alteration in several of the amendments which the different conventions have proposed. I have gone therefore so far as to fix it, that no law, varying the compensation, shall operate until there is a change in the legislature; in which case it cannot be for the particular benefit of those who are concerned in determining the value of the service.

I wish also, in revising the constitution, we may throw into that section, which interdicts the abuse of certain powers in the state legislatures, some other provisions of equal if not greater importance than those already made. The words, "No state shall pass any bill of attainder, ex post facto law, &c." were wise and proper restrictions in the constitution. I think there is more danger of those powers being abused by the state governments than by the government of the United States. The same may be said of other powers which they possess, if not controuled by the general principle, that laws are unconstitutional which infringe the rights of the community. I should therefore wish to extend this interdiction, and add, as I have stated in the 5th resolution, that no state shall violate the equal right of conscience, freedom of the press, or trial by jury in criminal cases; because it is proper that every government should be disarmed of powers which trench upon those particular rights. I know in some of the state constitutions the power of the government is controuled by such a declaration, but others are not. I cannot see any reason against obtaining even a double security on those points; and nothing can give a more sincere proof of the attachment of those who opposed this constitution to these great and important rights, than to see them join in obtaining the security I have now proposed; because it must be admitted, on all hands, that the state governments are as liable to attack these invaluable privileges as the general government is, and therefore ought to be as cautiously guarded against.

I think it will be proper, with respect to the judiciary powers, to satisfy the public mind on those points which I have mentioned. Great inconvenience has been apprehended to suitors from the distance they would be dragged to obtain justice in the supreme court of the United States, upon an appeal on an action for a small debt. To remedy this, declare, that no appeal shall be made unless the matter in controversy amounts to a particular sum: This, with the regulations respecting jury trials in criminal cases, and suits at common law, it is to be hoped will quiet and reconcile the minds of the people to that part of the constitution.

I find, from looking into the amendments proposed by the state conventions, that several are particularly anxious that it should be declared in the constitution, that the powers not therein delegated, should be reserved to the several states. Perhaps words which may define this more precisely, than the whole of the instrument now does, may be considered as superfluous. I admit they may be deemed unnecessary; but there can be no harm in making such a declaration, if gentlemen will allow that the fact is as stated. I am sure I understand it so, and do therefore propose it.

These are the points on which I wish to see a revision of the constitution take place. How far they will accord with the sense of this body, I cannot take upon me absolutely to determine; but I believe every gentleman will readily admit that nothing is in contemplation, so far as I have mentioned, that can endanger the beauty of the government in any one important feature, even in the eyes of its most sanguine admirers. I have proposed nothing that does not appear to me as proper in itself, or eligible as patronised by a respectable number of our fellow citizens; and if we can make the constitution better in the opinion of those who are opposed to it, without weakening its frame, or abridging its usefulness, in the judgment of those who are attached to it, we act the part of wise and liberal men to make such alterations as shall produce that effect.

Having done what I conceived was my duty, in bringing before this house the subject of amendments, and also stated such as I wish for and approve, and offered the reasons which occurred to me in their support; I shall content myself for the present with moving, that a committee be appointed to consider of and report such amendments as ought to be proposed by congress to the legislatures of the states, to become, if ratified by three-fourths thereof, part of the constitution of the United States. By agreeing to this motion, the subject may be going on in the committee, while other important business is proceeding to a conclusion in the house. I should advocate greater dispatch in the business of amendments, if I was not convinced of the absolute necessity there is of pursuing the organization of the government; because I think we should obtain the confidence of our fellow citizens, in proportion as we fortify the rights of the people against the encroachments of the government.

June 8, 1789

Speech in Congress on
Presidential Removal Power

MR. MADISON. If the construction of the constitution is to be left to its natural course with respect to the executive powers of this government, I own that the insertion of this sentiment in law may not be of material importance, though if it is nothing more than a mere declaration of a clear grant made by the constitution, it can do no harm; but if it relates to a doubtful part of the constitution, I suppose an exposition of the constitution may come with as much propriety from the legislature as any other department of government. If the power naturally belongs to the government, and the constitution is undecided as to the body which is to exercise it, it is likely that it is submitted to the discretion of the legislature, and the question will depend upon its own merits.

I am clearly of opinion with the gentleman from South-Carolina (Mr. Smith,) that we ought in this and every other case to adhere to the constitution, so far as it will serve as a guide to us, and that we ought not to be swayed in our decisions by the splendor of the character of the present chief magistrate, but to consider it with respect to the merit of men who, in the ordinary course of things, may be supposed to fill the chair. I believe the power here declared is a high one, and in some respects a dangerous one; but in order to come to a right decision on this point, we must consider both sides of the question. The possible abuses which may spring from the single will of the first magistrate, and the abuse which may spring from the combined will of the executive and the senatorial qualification.

When we consider that the first magistrate is to be appointed at present by the suffrages of three millions of people, and in all human probability in a few years time by double that number, it is not to be presumed that a vicious or bad character will be selected. If the government of any country on the face of the earth was ever effectually guarded against the election of ambitious or designing characters to the first office of the state, I think it may with truth be said to be the case under the constitution of the United States. With all the

infirmities incident to a popular election, corrected by the
particular mode of conducting it, as directed under the present system, I think we may fairly calculate, that the instances
will be very rare in which an unworthy man will receive that
mark of the public confidence which is required to designate
the president of the United States. Where the people are disposed to give so great an elevation to one of their fellow citizens, I own that I am not afraid to place my confidence in
him; especially when I know he is impeachable for any crime
or misdemeanor, before the senate, at all times; and that at all
events he is impeachable before the community at large every
four years, and liable to be displaced if his conduct shall have
given umbrage during the time he has been in office. Under
these circumstances, although the trust is a high one, and in
some degree perhaps a dangerous one, I am not sure but it
will be safer here than placed where some gentlemen suppose
it ought to be.

It is evidently the intention of the constitution that the first
magistrate should be responsible for the executive department; so far therefore as we do not make the officers who are
to aid him in the duties of that department responsible to
him, he is not responsible to his country. Again, is there no
danger that an officer when he is appointed by the concurrence of the senate, and has friends in that body, may chuse
rather to risk his establishment on the favor of that branch,
than rest it upon the discharge of his duties to the satisfaction
to the executive branch, which is constitutionally authorised
to inspect and controul his conduct? And if it should happen
that the officers connect themselves with the senate, they may
mutually support each other, and for want of efficacy reduce
the power of the president to a mere vapor, in which case his
responsibility would be annihilated, and the expectation of it
unjust. The high executive officers, joined in cabal with the
senate, would lay the foundation of discord, and end in an assumption of the executive power, only to be removed by a
revolution in the government. I believe no principle is more
clearly laid down in the constitution than that of responsibility. After premising this, I will proceed to an investigation of
the merits of the question upon constitutional ground.

I have since the subject was last before the house, examined the constitution with attention, and I acknowledge that it does not perfectly correspond with the ideas I entertained of it from the first glance. I am inclined to think that a free and systematic interpretation of the plan of government, will leave us less at liberty to abate the responsibility than gentlemen imagine. I have already acknowledged, that the powers of the government must remain as apportioned by the constitution. But it may be contended, that where the constitution is silent it becomes a subject of legislative discretion; perhaps, in the opinion of some, an argument in favor of the clause may be successfully brought forward on this ground: I however leave it for the present untouched.

By a strict examination of the constitution on what appears to be its true principles, and considering the great departments of the government in the relation they have to each other, I have my doubts whether we are not absolutely tied down to the construction declared in the bill. In the first section of the 1st article, it is said, that all legislative powers herein granted shall be vested in a congress of the United States. In the second article it is affirmed, that the executive power shall be vested in a president of the United States of America. In the third article it is declared, that the judicial power of the United States shall be vested in one supreme court, and in such inferior courts as congress may from time to time ordain and establish. I suppose it will be readily admitted, that so far as the constitution has separated the powers of these great departments, it would be improper to combine them together, and so far as it has left any particular department in the entire possession of the powers incident to that department, I conceive we ought not to qualify them farther than they are qualified by the constitution. The legislative powers are vested in congress, and are to be exercised by them uncontrolled by any other department, except the constitution has qualified it otherwise. The constitution has qualified the legislative power by authorising the president to object to any act it may pass, requiring, in this case two-thirds of both houses to concur in making a law; but still the absolute legislative power is vested in the congress with this qualification alone.

The constitution affirms, that the executive power shall be

vested in the president: Are there exceptions to this proposition? Yes there are. The constitution says that, in appointing to office, the senate shall be associated with the president, unless in the case of inferior officers, when the law shall otherwise direct. Have we a right to extend this exception? I believe not. If the constitution has invested all executive power in the president, I venture to assert, that the legislature has no right to diminish or modify his executive authority.

The question now resolves itself into this, Is the power of displacing an executive power? I conceive that if any power whatsoever is in its nature executive it is the power of appointing, overseeing, and controlling those who execute the laws. If the constitution had not qualified the power of the president in appointing to office, by associating the senate with him in that business, would it not be clear that he would have the right by virtue of his executive power to make such appointment? Should we be authorised, in defiance of that clause in the constitution—"The executive power shall be vested in a president," to unite the senate with the president in the appointment to office? I conceive not. If it is admitted we should not be authorised to do this, I think it may be disputed whether we have a right to associate them in removing persons from office, the one power being as much of an executive nature as the other, and the first only is authorised by being excepted out of the general rule established by the constitution, in these words, "the executive power shall be vested in the president."

The judicial power is vested in a supreme court, but will gentlemen say the judicial power can be placed elsewhere, unless the constitution has made an exception? The constitution justifies the senate in exercising a judiciary power in determining on impeachments: But can the judicial power be farther blended with the powers of that body? They cannot. I therefore say it is incontrovertible, if neither the legislative nor judicial powers are subjected to qualifications, other than those demanded in the constitution, that the executive powers are equally unabateable as either of the other; and inasmuch as the power of removal is of an executive nature, and not affected by any constitutional exception, it is beyond the reach of the legislative body.

If this is the true construction of this instrument, the clause in the bill is nothing more than explanatory of the meaning of the constitution, and therefore not liable to any particular objection on that account. If the constitution is silent, and it is a power the legislature have a right to confer, it will appear to the world, if we strike out the clause, as if we doubted the propriety of vesting it in the president of the United States. I therefore think it best to retain it in the bill.

June 16, 1789

———

MR. MADISON.   However various the opinions which exist upon the point now before us, it seems agreed on all sides, that it demands a careful investigation and full discussion. I feel the importance of the question, and know that our decision will involve the decision of all similar cases. The decision that is at this time made will become the permanent exposition of the constitution; and on a permanent exposition of the constitution will depend the genius and character of the whole government. It will depend, perhaps, on this decision, whether the government shall retain that equilibrium which the constitution intended, or take a direction toward aristocracy, or anarchy among the members of the government. Hence how careful ought we to be to give a true direction to a power so critically circumstanced. It is incumbent on us to weigh with particular attention the arguments which have been advanced in support of the various opinions with cautious deliberation. I own to you, Mr. Chairman, that I feel great anxiety upon this question; I feel an anxiety, because I am called upon to give a decision in a case that may affect the fundamental principles of the government under which we act, and liberty itself. But all that I can do on such an occasion is to weigh well every thing advanced on both sides, with the purest desire to find out the true meaning of the constitution, and to be guided by that, and an attachment to the true spirit of liberty, whose influence I believe strongly predominates here.

Several constructions have been put upon the constitution relative to the point in question. The gentleman from Connecticut (Mr. Sherman) has advanced a doctrine which was not touched upon before. He seems to think (if I understood him right), that the power of displacing from office is subject to legislative discretion; because it having a right to create, it may limit or modify as is thought proper. I shall not say but at first view this doctrine may seem to have some plausibility: But when I consider, that the constitution clearly intended to maintain a marked distinction between the legislative, executive, and judicial powers of government; and when I consider, that if the legislature has a power, such as contended for, they may subject, and transfer at discretion, powers from one department of government to another; they may, on that principle, exclude the president altogether from exercising any authority in the removal of officers; they may give it to the senate alone, or the president and senate combined; they may vest it in the whole congress, or they may reserve it to be exercised by this house. When I consider the consequences of this doctrine, and compare them with the true principles of the constitution, I own that I cannot subscribe to it.

Another doctrine which has found very respectable friends, has been particularly advocated by the gentleman from South-Carolina (Mr. Smith). It is this; when an officer is appointed by the president and senate, he can only be displaced from malfeasance in his office by impeachment: I think this would give a stability to the executive department so far as it may be described by the heads of departments, which is more incompatible with the genius of republican government in general, and this constitution in particular, than any doctrine which has yet been proposed. The danger to liberty, the danger of mal-administration has not yet been found to lay so much in the facility of introducing improper persons into office, as in the difficulty of displacing those who are unworthy of the public trust. If it is said that an officer once appointed shall not be displaced without the formality required by impeachment, I shall be glad to know what security we have for the faithful administration of the government. Every individual in the long chain which extends from the highest to the lowest link of the executive magistracy, would find a security in his situation which would relax his fidelity and promptitude in the discharge of his duty.

The doctrine, however, which seems to stand most in opposition to the principles I contend for, is that the power to annul an appointment is in the nature of things incidental to the power which makes the appointment. I agree that if nothing more was said in the constitution than that the president, by and with the advice and consent of the senate, should appoint to office, there would be great force in saying that the power of removal resulted by a natural implication from the power of appointing. But there is another part of the constitution no less explicit than the one on which the gentleman's doctrine is founded, it is that part which declares, that the executive power shall be vested in a president of the United States. The association of the senate with the president in exercising that particular function, is an exception to this general rule; and exceptions to general rules, I conceive, are ever to be taken strictly. But there is another part of the constitution which inclines in my judgment, to favor the construction I put upon it; the president is required to take care that the laws be faithfully executed. If the duty to see the laws faithfully executed be required at the hands of the executive magistrate, it would seem that it was generally intended he should have that species of power which is necessary to accomplish that end. Now if the officer when once appointed, is not to depend upon the president for his official existence, but upon a distinct body (for where there are two negatives required either can prevent the removal), I confess I do not see how the president can take care that the laws be faithfully executed. It is true by a circuitous operation, he may obtain an impeachment, and even without this it is possible he may obtain the concurrence of the senate for the purpose of displacing an officer; but would this give that species of control to the executive magistrate which seems to be required by the constitution? I own if my opinion was not contrary to that entertained by what I suppose to be the minority on this question, I should be doubtful of being mistaken, when I discovered how inconsistent that construction would make the constitution with itself. I can hardly bring myself to imagine the wisdom of the convention who framed the constitution, contemplated such incongruity.

There is another maxim which ought to direct us in expounding the constitution, and is of great importance. It is laid down in most of the constitutions or bills of rights in the republics of America, it is to be found in the political writings of the most celebrated civilians, and is every where held as essential to the preservation of liberty, That the three great departments of government be kept separate and distinct; and if in any case they are blended, it is in order to admit a partial qualification in order more effectually to guard against an entire consolidation. I think, therefore, when we review the several parts of this constitution, when it says that the legislative powers shall be vested in a Congress of the United States under certain exceptions, and the executive power vested in the president with certain exceptions, we must suppose they were intended to be kept separate in all cases in which they are not blended, and ought consequently to expound the constitution so as to blend them as little as possible.

Every thing relative to the merits of the question as distinguished from a constitutional question, seems to turn on the danger of such a power vested in the president alone. But when I consider the checks under which he lies in the exercise of this power, I own to you I feel no apprehensions but what arise from the dangers incidental to the power itself; for dangers will be incidental to it, vest it where you please. I will not reiterate what was said before with respect to the mode of election, and the extreme improbability that any citizen will be selected from the mass of citizens who is not highly distinguished by his abilities and worth; in this alone we have no small security for the faithful exercise of this power. But, throwing that out of the question, let us consider the restraints he will feel after he is placed in that elevated station. It is to be remarked that the power in this case will not consist so much in continuing a bad man in office, as in the danger of displacing a good one. Perhaps the great danger, as has been observed, of abuse in the executive power, lies in the improper continuance of bad men in office. But the power we contend for will not enable him to do this; for if an unworthy man be continued in office by an unworthy president, the house of representatives can at any time impeach him, and the senate can remove him, whether the president chuses or not. The danger then consists merely in this: the president can displace from office a man whose merits require that he should be continued in it. What will be the motives which the president can feel for such abuse of his power, and the restraints that operate to prevent it? In the first place, he will be impeachable by this house, before the senate, for such an act of mal-administration; for I contend that the wanton removal of meritorious officers would subject him to impeachment and removal from his own high trust. But what can be his motives for displacing a worthy man? It must be that he may fill the place with an unworthy creature of his own. Can he accomplish this end? No; he can place no man in the vacancy whom the senate shall not approve; and if he could fill the vacancy with the man he might chuse, I am sure he would have little inducement to make an improper removal. Let us consider the consequences. The injured man will be supported by the popular opinion; the community will take side with him against the president; it will facilitate those combinations, and give success to those exertions which will be pursued to prevent his re-election. To displace a man of high merit, and who from his station may be supposed a man of extensive influence, are considerations which will excite serious reflections beforehand in the mind of any man who may fill the presidential chair; the friends of those individuals, and the public sympathy will be against him. If this should not produce his impeachment before the senate, it will amount to an impeachment before the community, who will have the power of punishment by refusing to re-elect him. But suppose this persecuted individual, cannot obtain revenge in this mode; there are other modes in which he could make the situation of the president very inconvenient, if you suppose him resolutely bent on executing the dictates of resentment. If he had not influence enough to direct the vengeance of the whole community, he may probably be able to obtain an appointment in one or other branch of the legislature; and being a man of weight, talents and influence in either case, he may prove to the president troublesome indeed. We have seen examples in the history of other nations, which justifies the remark I now have made. Though the prerogatives of the British king are great as his rank, and it is unquestionably known that he has a positive influence over both branches of the legislative body, yet there have been examples in which the appointment and removal of ministers has been found to be dictated by one or other of those branches. Now if this is the case with an hereditary monarch, possessed of those high prerogatives and furnished with so many means of influence; can we suppose a president elected for four years only dependent upon the popular voice impeachable by the legislature? Little if at all distinguished for wealth, personal talents, or influence from the head of the department himself; I say, will he bid defiance to all these considerations, and wantonly dismiss a meritorious and virtuous officer? Such abuse of power exceeds my conception: If any thing takes place in the ordinary course of business of this kind, my imagination cannot extend to it on any rational principle. But let us not consider the question on one side only; there are dangers to be contemplated on the other. Vest this power in the senate jointly with the president, and you abolish at once that great principle of unity and responsibility in the executive department, which was intended for the security of liberty and the public good. If the president should possess alone the power of removal from office, those who are employed in the execution of the law will be in their proper situation, and the chain of dependence be preserved; the lowest officers, the middle grade, and the highest, will depend, as they ought, on the president, and the president on the community. The chain of dependence therefore terminates in the supreme body, namely, in the people; who will possess besides, in aid of their original power, the decisive engine of impeachment. Take the other supposition, that the power should be vested in the senate, on the principle that the power to displace is necessarily connected with the power to appoint. It is declared by the constitution, that we may by law vest the appointment of inferior officers, in the heads of departments, the power of removal being incidental, as stated by some gentlemen. Where does this terminate? If you begin with the subordinate officers, they are dependent on their superior, he on the next superior, and he on whom?—on the senate, a permanent body; a body, by its particular mode of election, in reality existing for ever; a body possessing that proportion of aristocratic power which the constitution no doubt thought wise to be established in the system, but which some have strongly excepted against: And let me ask gentlemen, is there equal security in this case as in the other? Shall we trust the senate, responsible to individual legislatures, rather than the person who is responsible to the whole community? It is true the senate do not hold their offices for life, like aristocracies recorded in the historic page; yet the fact is they will not possess that responsibility for the exercise of executive powers which would render it safe for us to vest such powers in them. But what an aspect will this give to the executive? Instead of keeping the departments of government distinct, you make an executive out of one branch of the legislature; you make the executive a two-headed monster, to use the expression of the gentleman from New-Hampshire (Mr. Livermore); you destroy the great principle of responsibility, and perhaps have the creature divided in its will, defeating the very purposes for which an unity in the executive was instituted. These objections do not lie against such an arrangement as the bill establishes. I conceive that the president is sufficiently accountable to the community; and if this power is vested in him, it will be vested where its nature requires it should be vested; if any thing in its nature is executive it must be that power which is employed in superintending and seeing that the laws are faithfully executed; the laws cannot be executed but by officers appointed for that purpose; therefore those who are over such officers naturally possess the executive power. If any other doctrine be admitted, what is the consequence? You may set the senate at the head of the executive department, or you may require that the officers hold their places during the pleasure of this branch of the legislature, if you cannot go so far as to say we shall appoint them; and by this means you link together two branches of the government which the preservation of liberty requires to be constantly separated.

Another species of argument has been urged against this clause. It is said, that it is improper, or at least unnecessary to come to any decision on this subject. It has been said by one gentleman, that it would be officious in this branch of the legislature to expound the constitution, so far as it relates to the division of power between the president and senate; it is incontrovertably of as much importance to this branch of the government as to any other, that the constitution should be preserved entire. It is our duty, so far as it depends upon us, to take care that the powers of the constitution be preserved entire to every department of government; the breach of the constitution in one point, will facilitate the breach in another; a breach in this point may destroy that equilibrium by which the house retains its consequence and share of power; therefore we are not chargeable with an officious interference; besides, the bill, before it can have effect, must be submitted to both those branches who are particularly interested in it; the senate may negative, or the president may object if he thinks it unconstitutional.

But the great objection drawn from the source to which the last arguments would lead us is, that the legislature itself has no right to expound the constitution; that wherever its meaning is doubtful, you must leave it to take its course, until the judiciary is called upon to declare its meaning. I acknowledge, in the ordinary course of government, that the exposition of the laws and constitution devolves upon the judicial. But, I beg to know, upon what principle it can be contended, that any one department draws from the constitution greater powers than another, in marking out the limits of the powers of the several departments. The constitution is the charter of the people to the government; it specifies certain great powers as absolutely granted, and marks out the departments to exercise them. If the constitutional boundary of either be brought into question, I do not see that any one of these independent departments has more right than another to declare their sentiments on that point.

Perhaps this is an omitted case. There is not one government on the face of the earth, so far as I recollect, there is not one in the United States, in which provision is made for a particular authority to determine the limits of the constitutional division of power between the branches of the government. In all systems there are points which must be adjusted by the departments themselves, to which no one of them is competent. If it cannot be determined in this way, there is no resource left but the will of the community, to be collected in some mode to be provided by the constitution, or one dictated by the necessity of the case. It is therefore a fair question, whether this great point may not as well be decided, at least by the whole legislature, as by a part, by us as well as by the executive or judicial? As I think it will be equally constitutional, I cannot imagine it will be less safe, that the exposition should issue from the legislative authority than any other; and the more so, because it involves in the decision the opinions of both those departments whose powers are supposed to be affected by it. Beside, I do not see in what way this question could come before the judges, to obtain a fair and solemn decision; but even if it were the case that it could, I should suppose, at least while the government is not led by passion, disturbed by faction, or deceived by any discoloured medium of light; but while there is a desire in all to see, and be guided by the benignant ray of truth, that the decision may be made with the most advantage by the legislature itself.

My conclusion from these reflections is, that it will be constitutional to retain the clause; that it expresses the meaning of the constitution as must be established by fair construction, and a construction which, upon the whole, not only consists with liberty, but is more favorable to it than any one of the interpretations that have been proposed.

June 17, 1789

To Edmund Pendleton

Dear Sir   N. York June 21. 1789.

The last favor for which I am to thank you is of June 9th. For some time past I have been obliged to content myself with inclosing you the Newspapers. In general they give, tho' frequently erroneous and sometimes perverted, yet on the whole, fuller accounts of what is going forward than could be put into a letter. The papers now covered contain a sketch of a very interesting discussion which consumed great part of the past week. The Constitution has omitted to declare expressly by what authority removals from office are to be made. Out of this silence four constructive doctrines have arisen 1. that the power of removal may be disposed of by the Legislative discretion. To this it is objected that the Legislature might then confer it on themselves, or even on the House of

Reps. which could not possibly have been intended by the Constitution. 2. that the power of removal can only be exercised in the mode of impeachment. To this the objection is that it would make officers of every description hold their places during good behavior, which could have still less been intended. 3. that the power of removal is incident to the power of appointment. To this the objections are that it would require the constant Session of the Senate, that it extends the mixture of Legislative & Executive power, that it destroys the responsibility of the President, by enabling a subordinate Executive officer to intrench himself behind a party in the Senate, and destroys the utility of the Senate in their legislative and Judicial characters, by involving them too much in the heats and cabals inseparable from questions of a personal nature; in fine that it transfers the trust in fact from the President who being at all times impeachable as well as every 4th. year eligible by the people at large, may be deemed the most responsible member of the Government, to the Senate who from the nature of that institution, is and was meant after the Judiciary & in some respects witht. that exception to be the most unresponsible branch of the Government. 4 that the Executive power being in general terms vested in the President, all power of an Executive nature, not particularly taken away must belong to that department, that the power of appointment only being expressly taken away, the power of Removal, so far as it is of an Executive nature must be reserved. In support of this construction it is urged that exceptions to general positions are to be taken strictly, and that the axiom relating to the separation of the Legislative & Executive functions ought to be favored. To this are objected the principle on which the 3d. construction is founded, & the danger of creating too much influence in the Executive Magistrate.

The last opinion has prevailed, but is subject to various modifications, by the power of the Legislature to limit the duration of laws creating offices, or the duration of the appointments for filling them, and by the power over the salaries and appropriations. In truth the Legislative power is of such a nature that it scarcely can be restrained either by the Constitution or by itself. And if the federal Government should lose its proper equilibrium within itself, I am persuaded that the effect will proceed from the Encroachments of the Legislative department. If the possibility of encroachments on the part of the Ex. or the Senate were to be compared, I should pronounce the danger to lie rather in the latter than the former. The mixture of Legislative Executive & Judiciary authorities lodged in that body, justifies such an inference; At the same time I am fully in the opinion, that the numerous and immediate representatives of the people, composing the other House, will decidedly predominate in the Government.

Mr. Page tells me he has forwarded to you a copy of the amendments lately submitted to the H. of Reps. They are restrained to points on which least difficulty was apprehended. Nothing of a controvertible nature ought to be hazarded by those who are sincere in wishing for the approbation of ⅔ of each House, and ¾ of the State Legislatures. I am Dr. Sir mo: affetly Yrs.

The President has been ill—but is now in a good way.

Remarks in Congress on Proposed Constitutional Amendments

MR. MADISON Said he apprehended the meaning of the words to be, that congress should not establish a religion, and enforce the legal observation of it by law, nor compel men to worship God in any manner contrary to their conscience; whether the words were necessary or not he did not mean to say, but they had been required by some of the state conventions, who seemed to entertain an opinion that under the clause of the constitution, which gave power to congress to make all laws necessary and proper to carry into execution the constitution, and the laws made under it, enabled them to make laws of such a nature as might infringe the rights of conscience, or establish a national religion. To prevent these effects he presumed the amendment was intended, and he thought it as well expressed as the nature of the language would admit.

Mr. Madison. I think the committee acted prudently in omitting to insert these words in the report they have brought forward; if unfortunately the attempt of proposing amendments should prove abortive, it will not arise from the want of a disposition in the friends of the constitution to do what is right with respect to securing the rights and privileges of the people of America; but from the difficulties arising from discussing and proposing abstract propositions, of which the judgment may not be convinced. I venture to say that if we confine ourselves to an enumeration of simple acknowledged principles, the ratification will meet with but little difficulty. Amendments of a doubtful nature will have a tendency to prejudice the whole system; the proposition now suggested, partakes highly of this nature; it is doubted by many gentlemen here; it has been objected to in intelligent publications throughout the union; it is doubted by many members of the state legislatures: In one sense this declaration is true; in many others it is certainly not true; in the sense in which it is true, we have asserted the right sufficiently in what we have done; if we mean nothing more than this, that the people have a right to express and communicate their sentiments and wishes, we have provided for it already. The right of freedom of speech is secured; the liberty of the press is expressly declared to be beyond the reach of this government; the people may therefore publicly address their representatives; may privately advise them, or declare their sentiments by petition to the whole body; in all these ways they may communicate their will. If gentlemen mean to go further, and to say that the people have a right to instruct their representatives in such a sense as that the delegates were obliged to conform to those instructions, the declaration is not true. Suppose they instruct a representative by his vote to violate the constitution, is he at liberty to obey such instructions? Suppose he is instructed to patronize certain measures, and from circumstances known to him, but not to his constituents, he is convinced that they will endanger the public good, is he obliged to sacrifice his own judgment to them? Is he absolutely bound to perform what he is instructed to do? Suppose he refuses, will his vote be the less valid, or the community be disengaged from that obedience which is due from the laws of the union? If his vote must inevitably have the same effect, what sort of a right is this in the constitution to instruct a representative who has a right to disregard the order, if he pleases? In this sense the right does not exist, in the other sense it does exist, and is provided largely for.

The honorable gentleman from Massachusetts, asks if the sovereignty is not with the people at large; does he infer that the people can, in detached bodies, contravene an act established by the whole people? My idea of the sovereignty of the people is, that the people can change the constitution if they please, but while the constitution exists, they must conform themselves to its dictates: But I do not believe that the inhabitants of any district can speak the voice of the people; so far from it, their ideas may contradict the sense of the whole people; hence the consequence that instructions are binding on the representative is of a doubtful, if not of a dangerous nature. I do not conceive, therefore, that it is necessary to agree to the proposition now made; so far as any real good is to arise from it, so far that real good is provided for; so far as it is of a doubtful nature, so far it obliges us to run the risk of losing the whole system.

————

MR. MADISON Was unwilling to take up any more of the time of the committee, but on the other hand, he was not willing to be silent after the charges that had been brought against the committee, and the gentleman who introduced the amendments, by the honorable members on each side of him, (Mr. Sumpter and Mr. Burke). Those gentlemen say that we are precipitating the business, and insinuate that we are not acting with candor; I appeal to the gentlemen who have heard the voice of their country, to those who have attended the debates of the state conventions, whether the amendments now proposed, are not those most strenuously required by the opponents to the constitution? It was wished that some security should be given for those great and essential rights which they had been taught to believe were in danger. I concurred, in the convention of Virginia, with those gentlemen, so far as to agree to a declaration of those rights which corresponded with my own judgment, and the other alterations which I had the honor to bring forward before the present congress. I appeal to the gentlemen on this floor who are desirous of amending the constitution, whether these proposed are not compatible with what are required by our constituents; have not the people been told that the rights of conscience, the freedom of speech, the liberty of the press, and trial by jury, were in jeopardy; that they ought not to adopt the constitution until those important rights were secured to them.

But while I approve of these amendments, I should oppose the consideration at this time, of such as are likely to change the principles of the government, or that are of a doubtful nature; because I apprehend there is little prospect of obtaining the consent of two-thirds of both houses of congress, and three-fourths of the state legislatures, to ratify propositions of this kind; therefore, as a friend to what is attainable, I would limit it to the plain, simple, and important security that has been required. If I was inclined to make no alteration in the constitution I would bring forward such amendments as were of a dubious cast, in order to have the whole rejected.

August 15, 1789

Remarks in Congress on the "Most Valuable Amendment"

MR. MADISON Conceived this to be the most valuable amendment on the whole list; if there was any reason to restrain the government of the United States from infringing upon these essential rights, it was equally necessary that they should be secured against the state governments; he thought that if they provided against the one, it was as necessary to provide against the other, and was satisfied that it would be equally grateful to the people.

August 17, 1789

To Richard Peters

Dear Sir   N. York Aug: 19. 1789
    I have been much delighted with the extract from your col-
lection of fables, and should have told you so sooner, were I
less incumbered with a number of involuntary corresponden-
cies, which stand in the way of those which my inclination
would cherish. May I hope that "The wise Cooks & foolish
Guests" is but a sample of the treat you meditate for your
friends, out of the "Aunciente & connynge balladdes." It will
be criminally selfish to keep so delicious and precious a dona-
tion of the Muses wholly for your own entertainment.
    The papers inclosed will shew that the nauseous project of
amendments has not yet been either dismissed or despatched.
We are so deep in them now, that right or wrong some thing
must be done. I say this not by way of apology, for to be sincere I think no apology requisite. 1. because a constitutional
provision in favr. of essential rights is a thing not improper in
itself and was always viewed in that light by myself. It may be
less necessary in a republic, than a Monarchy, & in a fedl.
Govt. than the former, but it is in some degree rational in
every Govt., since in every Govt. power may oppress, and
declarations on paper, tho' not an effectual restraint, are not
without some influence. 2. In many States the Constn. was
adopted under a tacit compact in favr. of some subsequent
provisions on this head. In Virga. It would have been *certainly* rejected, had no assurances been given by its advocates
that such provisions would be pursued. As an honest man *I
feel* my self bound by this consideration. 3. If the Candidates
in Virga. for the House of Reps. had not taken this conciliary
ground at the election, that State would have been represented almost wholly by disaffected characters, instead of the
federal reps. now in Congs. 4. If amendts. had not been proposed from the federal side of the House, the proposition
would have come *within three days*, from the adverse side. It
is certainly best that they should appear to be the free gift of
the friends of the Constitution rather than to be extorted by
the address & weight of its enemies. 5. It will kill the opposition every where, and by putting an end to the disaffection to
the Govt. itself, enable the administration to venture on

measures not otherwise safe. Those who hate the Govt. will always join the party disaffected to measures of the administration, and such a party will be created by every important measure. 6. If no amendts. be proposed the language of anti-fedl. leaders to the people, will be, we advised you not to adopt the Constn. witht. previous amendts—You listened to those who told you that subsequent securities for your rights would be most easily obtained—We urged you to insist on a Convention as the only effectual mode of obtaining these—You yielded to the assurances of those who told you that a Convention was unecessary, that Congs. wd. be the proper channel for getting what was wanted. &c &c. Here are fine texts for popular declaimers who wish to revive the antifedl. cause, and at the fall session of the Legislares. to blow the trumpet for a second Convention. In Virga. a majority of the Legislature last elected, is bitterly opposed to the Govt. and will be joined, if no amends. be proposed, by great nos. of the other side who will complain of being deceived. 7. Some amendts. are necssy for N. Carola. I am so informed by the best authorities in that State. I set out with an apology for not writing sooner, I must conclude with one, for writing so much, & still more for writing so scurvily. Yrs truly

Memorandum on Colonizing Freed Slaves

Without enquiring into the practicability or the most proper means of establishing a Settlement of freed blacks on the Coast of Africa, it may be remarked as one motive to the benevolent experiment that if such an asylum was provided, it might prove a great encouragement to manumission in the Southern parts of the U. S. and even afford the best hope yet presented of putting an end to the slavery in which not less than 600,000 unhappy negroes are now involved.

In all the Southern States of N. America, the laws permit masters, under certain precautions to manumit their slaves. But the continuance of such a permission in some of the States is rendered precarious by the ill effects suffered from freedmen who retain the vices and habits of slaves. The same consideration becomes an objection with many humane masters agst. an exertion of their legal right of freeing their slaves. It is found in fact that neither the good of the Society, nor the happiness of the individuals restored to freedom is promoted by such a change in their condition.

In order to render this change eligible as well to the Society as to the Slaves, it would be necessary that a compleat incorporation of the latter into the former should result from the act of manumission. This is rendered impossible by the prejudices of the Whites, prejudices which proceeding principally from the difference of colour must be considered as permanent and insuperable.

It only remains then that some proper external receptacle be provided for the slaves who obtain their liberty. The interior wilderness of America, and the Coast of Africa seem to present the most obvious alternative. The former is liable to great if not invincible objections. If the settlement were attempted at a considerable distance from the White frontier, it would be destroyed by the Savages who have a peculiar antipathy to the blacks: If the attempt were made in the neighbourhood of the White Settlements, peace would not long be expected to remain between Societies, distinguished by such characteristic marks, and retaining the feelings inspired by their former relation of oppressors & oppressed. The result then is that an experiment for providing such an external establishment for the blacks as might induce the humanity of Masters, and by degrees both the humanity & policy of the Governments, to forward the abolition of slavery in America, ought to be pursued on the Coast of Africa or in some other foreign situation.

c. October 20, 1789

To Thomas Jefferson

Dear Sir   New York Feby 4. 1790
Your favor of the 9th. of Jany. inclosing one of Sepr. last did not get to hand till a few days ago. The idea which the latter evolves is a great one, and suggests many interesting

reflections to legislators; particularly when contracting and providing for public debts. Whether it can be received in the extent your reasonings give it, is a question which I ought to turn more in my thoughts than I have yet been able to do, before I should be justified in making up a full opinion on it. My first thoughts though coinciding with many of yours, lead me to view the doctrine as not in *all* respects compatible with the course of human affairs. I will endeavor to sketch the grounds of my skepticism.

> "As the earth belongs to the living, not to the dead, a living generation can bind itself only: In every society the will of the majority binds the whole: According to the laws of mortality, a majority of those ripe at any moment for the exercise of their will do not live beyond nineteen years: To that term then is limited the validity of *every* act of the Society: Nor within that limitation, can any declaration of the public will be valid which is not *express*."

This I understand to be the outline of the argument.

The Acts of a political Society may be divided into three classes.

1. The fundamental Constitution of the Government.
2. Laws involving stipulations which render them irrevocable at the will of the Legislature
3. Laws involving no such irrevocable quality.

However applicable in Theory the doctrine may be to a Constitution, it seems liable in practice to some very powerful objections. Would not a Government so often revised become too mutable to retain those prejudices in its favor which antiquity inspires, and which are perhaps a salutary aid to the most rational Government in the most enlightened age? Would not such a periodical revision engender pernicious factions that might not otherwise come into existence? Would not, in fine, a Government depending for its existence beyond a fixed date, on some positive and authentic intervention of the Society itself, be too subject to the casualty and consequences of an actual interregnum?

In the 2d. class, exceptions at least to the doctrine seem to be requisite both in Theory and practice.

If the earth be the gift of nature to the living their title can extend to the earth in its natural State only. The *improvements* made by the dead form a charge against the living who take the benefit of them. This charge can no otherwise be satisfyed than by executing the will of the dead accompanying the improvements.

Debts may be incurred for purposes which interest the unborn, as well as the living: such are debts for repelling a conquest, the evils of which descend through many generations. Debts may even be incurred principally for the benifit of posterity: such perhaps is the present debt of the U. States, which far exceeds any burdens which the present generation could well apprehend for itself. The term of 19 years might not be sufficient for discharging the debts in either of these cases.

There seems then to be a foundation in the nature of things, in the relation which one generation bears to another, for the *descent* of obligations from one to another. Equity requires it. Mutual good is promoted by it. All that is indispensable in adjusting the account between the dead & the living is to see that the debits against the latter do not exceed the advances made by the former. Few of the incumbrances entailed on Nations would bear a liquidation even on this principle.

The objections to the doctrine as applied to the 3d. class of acts may perhaps be merely practical. But in that view they appear to be of great force.

Unless such laws should be kept in force by new acts regularly anticipating the end of the term, all the rights depending on positive laws, that is, most of the rights of property would become absolutely defunct; and the most violent struggles be generated between those interested in reviving and those interested in new-modelling the former State of property. Nor would events of this kind be improbable. The obstacles to the passage of laws which render a power to repeal inferior to an opportunity of rejecting, as a security agst. oppression, would here render an opportunity of rejecting, an insecure provision agst. anarchy. Add, that the possibility of an event so hazardous to the rights of property could not fail to depreciate its value; that the approach of the crisis would increase this effect; that the frequent return of periods superseding all the obligations depending on antecedent laws & usages, must by weakening the reverence for those obligations, co-operate with motives to licentiousness already too powerful; and that the uncertainty incident to such a state of things would on one side discourage the steady exertions of industry produced by permanent laws, and on the other, give a disproportionate advantage to the more, over the less, sagacious and interprizing part of the Society.

I find no relief from these consequences, but in the received doctrine that a tacit assent may be given to established Constitutions and laws, and that this assent may be inferred, where no positive dissent appears. It seems less impracticable to remedy, by wise plans of Government, the dangerous operation of this doctrine, than to find a remedy for the difficulties inseparable from the other.

May it not be questioned whether it be possible to exclude wholly the idea of tacit assent, without subverting the foundation of civil Society? On what principle does the voice of the majority bind the minority? It does not result I conceive from the law of nature, but from compact founded on conveniency. A greater proportion might be required by the fundamental constitution of a Society, if it were judged eligible. Prior then to the establishment of this principle, *unanimity* was necessary; and strict Theory at all times presupposes the assent of every member to the establishment of the rule itself. If this assent can not be given tacitly, or be not implied where no positive evidence forbids, persons born in Society would not on attaining ripe age be bound by acts of the Majority; and either a *unanimous* repetition of every law would be necessary on the accession of new members, or an express assent must be obtained from these to the rule by which the voice of the Majority is made the voice of the whole.

If the observations I have hazarded be not misapplied, it follows that a limitation of the validity of national acts to the computed life of a nation, is in some instances not required by Theory, and in others cannot be accomodated to practice. The observations are not meant however to impeach either the utility of the principle in some particular cases; or the general importance of it in the eye of the philosophical Legislator. On the contrary it would give me singular pleasure to see it first announced in the proceedings of the U. States, and always kept in their view, as a salutary curb on the living generation from imposing unjust or unnecessary burdens on their successors. But this is a pleasure which I have little hope of enjoying. The spirit of philosophical legislation has never reached some parts of the Union, and is by no means the fashion here, either within or without Congress. The evils suffered & feared from weakness in Government, and licentiousness in the people, have turned the attention more towards the means of strengthening the former, than of narrowing its extent in the minds of the latter. Besides this, it is so much easier to espy the little difficulties immediately incident to every great plan, than to comprehend its general and remote benefits, that our hemisphere must be still more enlightened before many of the sublime truths which are seen thro' the medium of Philosophy, become visible to the naked eye of the ordinary Politician.

I have nothing to add at present but that I remain always and most affectly. Yours

To Benjamin Rush

Dear Sir   N. York March 20. 1790
I recd. your favor of the 10th. instant some days ago. Altho' I feel the force of many of your remarks, I can not embrace the idea to which they lead. It would not be consistent with the view I have taken of the subject; nor indeed promise any chance of success agst. the present politics of the House.

The Petitions on the subject of Slavery have employed more than a week, and are still before a Committee of the whole. The Gentlemen from S. Carolina & Georgia are intemperate beyond all example and even all decorum. They are not content with palliating slavery as a deep-rooted abuse, but plead for the lawfulness of the African trade itself—nor with protesting agst. the object of the Memorials, but lavish the most virulent language on the authors of them. If this folly did not reproach the public councils, it ought to excite no regret in the patrons of Humanity & freedom. Nothing could hasten more the progress of those reflections & sentiments which are secretly undermining the institution which this mistaken zeal is laboring to secure agst. the most distant approach of danger.

A British Packet arrived a day or two ago, but I do not find that she throws much light on the affairs of Europe. Those of France do not go backward, but they go forward so slowly as to beget apprehensions for the event. I am Dear Sir Yrs. very respectfully,

Remarks in Congress During Debate on Militia Bill

Mr. Madison thought it an important principle, and one that ought in general to be attended to—That all laws should be made to operate as much on the law makers as upon the people; the greatest security for the preservation of liberty, is for the government to have a sympathy with those on whom the laws act, and a real participation and communication of all their burthens and grievances. Whenever it is necessary to exempt any part of the government from sharing in these common burthens, that necessity ought not only to be palpable, but should on no account be exceeded. He thought the amendment, together with the constitution, provided on this occasion for all that was necessary, and that the clause as it stood at present, went beyond that necessity.

December 16, 1790

Speech in Congress on Religious Exemptions from Militia Duty

Mr. Madison did not mean to object to the amendment under consideration, though he thought it too far, in making exceptions in favour of the members of Congress. But as the committee of the whole had decided that point against him by a respectable majority, he should not now renew the question. But there is a question of great magnitude, which I am desirous of having determined. I shall therefore take the liberty of moving it: That we add to the end of the amendment, the words, "and persons conscientiously scrupulous of bearing arms." I agree with the gentleman who was last up, that is the glory of this country, the boast of the revolution, and the pride of the present constitution, that here the rights of mankind are known and established on a basis more certain, and I trust, more durable, than any heretofore recorded in history, or existing in any other part of this globe; but above all, it is the particular glory of this country, to have secured the rights of conscience which in other nations are least understood or most strangely violated. In my opinion, were these things less clear, it would be a sufficient motive to indulge these men in the exercise of their religious sentiments—that they have evinced by an uniform conduct of moderation, their merit, and deserving of the high privilege; they knew its value, and generously extended it to all men, even when possessing the plentitude of legislative power, they are the only people in America who have not abused the rights of conscience, except the Roman Catholics, who anticipated them by an earlier settlement, in establishing a toleration of all religions in their governments in the United States. Their honorable example has procured them a merit with this country, which ought not to be disregarded—and could I reach to them this exemption, from the performance of what they conceive to be criminal, with justice to the other sects in the community, or if the other sects were willing to withdraw their plea for an equivalent, my own opinion would be, to grant them privilege on terms perfectly gratuitous.

It has been said, by a gentleman from Georgia, (Mr. Jackson) that if this privilege is extended to this class of citizens, all other denominations will be induced to secure it to themselves by counterfeiting their principles. I am persuaded, the gentleman indulged his imagination more than his judgment, when he predicted this effect. He cannot consult his own heart, nor the disposition of his fellow citizens, nor human nature itself, when he supposes either himself or the people of America, or of any nation, would apostatize from their

God for reasons so inconsiderable. Would any man consent to put on the mask of hypocrisy in order to avoid a duty which is honorable? I cannot believe that one out of a thousand, nay not a single citizen will be found throughout the United States, who will usurp this privilege by hypocritical pretensions. But it will be in vain to attempt to force them into the field, by such an attempt we shall only expose the imbecility of the government: Compulsion being out of the question, we must, therefore, from necessity, exempt them; if we are actuated by no more generous motive. Let us make a virtue of this necessity, and grant the exemption. By penalties we may oppress them, but by no means hitherto discovered, can you make them undertake the defence of this nation. My view, at this time is, to bring the question fairly before the house. I am not, therefore, tenacious of the words or mode of the amendment, but beg attention only to the principle.

December 22, 1790

Speech in Congress
Opposing the National Bank

Mr. Madison began with a general review of the advantages and disadvantages of banks. The former he stated to consist in, first, the aids they afford to merchants who can thereby push their mercantile operations farther with the same capital. 2d. The aids to merchants in paying punctually the customs. 3d. Aids to the government in complying punctually with its engagements, when deficiencies or delays happen in the revenue. 4th. In diminishing usury. 5th. In saving the wear of the gold and silver kept in the vaults, and represented by notes. 6th. In facilitating occasional remittances from different places where notes happen to circulate. The effect of the proposed bank, in raising the value of stock, he thought, had been greatly overrated. It would no doubt raise that of the stock subscribed into the bank; but could have little effect on stock in general, as the interest on it would remain the same, and the quantity taken out of the market would be replaced by bank stock.

The principal disadvantages consisted in, 1st. banishing the precious metals, by substituting another medium to perform their office: This effect was inevitable. It was admitted by the most enlightened patrons of banks, particularly by Smith on the Wealth of Nations. The common answer to the objection was, that the money banished was only an exchange for something equally valuable that would be imported in return. He admitted the weight of this observation in general, but doubted whether, in the present habits of this country, the returns would not be in articles of no permanent use to it. 2d. Exposing the public and individuals to all the evils of a run on the bank, which would be particularly calamitous in so great a country as this, and might happen from various causes, as false rumours, bad management of the institution, an unfavorable balance of trade from short crops, &c.

It was proper to be considered also, that the most important of the advantages would be better obtained by several banks properly distributed, than by a single one. The aids to commerce could only be afforded at or very near the seat of the bank. The same was true of aids to merchants in the payment of customs. Anticipations of the government would also be most convenient at the different places where the interest of the debt was to be paid. The case in America was different from that in England: the interest there was all due at one place, and the genius of the monarchy favored the concentration of wealth and influence at the metropolis.

He thought the plan liable to other objections: It did not make so good a bargain for the public as was due to its interests. The charter to the bank of England had been granted for 11 years only, and was paid for by a loan to the government on terms better than could be elsewhere got. Every renewal of the charter had in like manner been purchased; in some instances, at a very high price. The same had been done by the banks of Genoa, Naples, and other like banks of circulation. The plan was unequal to the public creditors—it gave an undue preference to the holders of a particular denomination of the public debt, and to those at and within reach of the seat of government. If the subscriptions should be rapid, the distant holders of paper would be excluded altogether.

In making these remarks on the merits of the bill, he had reserved to himself, he said, the right to deny the authority of Congress to pass it. He had entertained this opinion from the date of the constitution. His impression might perhaps be the stronger, because he well recollected that a power to grant charters of incorporation had been proposed in the general convention and rejected.

Is the power of establishing an *incorporated bank* among the powers vested by the constitution in the legislature of the United States? This is the question to be examined.

After some general remarks on the limitations of all political power, he took notice of the peculiar manner in which the federal government is limited. It is not a general grant, out of which particular powers are excepted—it is a grant of particular powers only, leaving the general mass in other hands. So it had been understood by its friends and its foes, and so it was to be interpreted.

As preliminaries to a right interpretation, he laid down the following rules:

An interpretation that destroys the very characteristic of the government cannot be just.

Where a meaning is clear, the consequences, whatever they may be, are to be admitted—where doubtful, it is fairly triable by its consequences.

In controverted cases, the meaning of the parties to the instrument, if to be collected by reasonable evidence, is a proper guide.

Contemporary and concurrent expositions are a reasonable evidence of the meaning of the parties.

In admitting or rejecting a constructive authority, not only the degree of its incidentality to an express authority, is to be regarded, but the degree of its importance also; since on this will depend the probability or improbability of its being left to construction.

Reviewing the constitution with an eye to these positions, it was not possible to discover in it the power to incorporate a Bank. The only clauses under which such a power could be pretended, are either—

1. The power to lay and collect taxes to pay the debts, and provide for the common defence and general welfare: Or,

2. The power to borrow money on the credit of the United States: Or,

3. The power to pass all laws necessary and proper to carry into execution those powers.

The bill did not come within the first power. It laid no tax to pay the debts, or provide for the general welfare. It laid no tax whatever. It was altogether foreign to the subject.

No argument could be drawn from the terms "common defence, and general welfare." The power as to these general purposes, was limited to acts laying taxes for them; and the general purposes themselves were limited and explained by the particular enumeration subjoined. To understand these terms in any sense, that would justify the power in question, would give to Congress an unlimited power; would render nugatory the enumeration of particular powers; would supercede all the powers reserved to the state governments. These terms are copied from the articles of confederation; had it ever been pretended, that they were to be understood otherwise than as here explained?

It had been said that "general welfare" meant cases in which a general power might be exercised by Congress, without interfering with the powers of the States; and that the establishment of a National Bank was of this sort. There were, he said, several answers to this novel doctrine.

1. The proposed Bank would interfere so as indirectly to defeat a State Bank at the same place. 2. It would directly interfere with the rights of the States, *to prohibit* as well as to establish Banks, and the circulation of Bank Notes. He mentioned a law of Virginia, actually prohibiting the circulation of notes payable to bearer. 3. Interference with the power of the States was no constitutional criterion of the power of Congress. If the power was not given, Congress could not exercise it; if given, they might exercise it, altho it should interfere with the laws, or even the constitution of the States. 4. If Congress could incorporate a Bank, merely because the act would leave the States free to establish Banks also; any other incorporations might be made by Congress. They could incorporate companies of manufacturers, or companies for

cutting canals, or even religious societies, leaving similar incorporations by the States, like State Banks to themselves:
Congress might even establish religious teachers in every
parish, and pay them out of the Treasury of the United States,
leaving other teachers unmolested in their functions. These
inadmissible consequences condemned the controverted
principle.

The case of the Bank established by the former Congress,
had been cited as a precedent. This was known, he said, to
have been the child of necessity. It never could be justified by
the regular powers of the articles of confederation. Congress
betrayed a consciousness of this in recommending to the
States to incorporate the Bank also. They did not attempt to
protect the Bank Notes by penalties against counterfeiters.
These were reserved wholly to the authority of the States.

The second clause to be examined is that, which empowers
Congress to borrow money.

Is this a bill to borrow money? It does not borrow a
shilling. Is there any fair construction by which the bill can be
deemed an exercise of the power to borrow money? The obvious meaning of the power to borrow money, is that of accepting it from, and stipulating payment to those who are
able and *willing* to lend.

To say that the power to borrow involves a power of creating the ability, where there may be the will, to lend, is not
only establishing a dangerous principle, as will be immediately
shewn, but is as forced a construction, as to say that it involves the power of compelling the will, where there may be
the ability, to lend.

The *third* clause is that which gives the power to pass all
laws necessary and proper to execute the specified powers.

Whatever meaning this clause may have, none can be admitted, that would give an unlimited discretion to Congress.

Its meaning must, according to the natural and obvious
force of the terms and the context, be limited to means *necessary* to the *end*, and *incident* to the *nature* of the specified
powers.

The clause is in fact merely declaratory of what would have
resulted by unavoidable implication, as the appropriate, and as
it were, technical means of executing those powers. In this

sense it had been explained by the friends of the constitution, and ratified by the state conventions.

The essential characteristic of the government, as composed of limited and enumerated powers, would be destroyed: If instead of direct and incidental means, any means could be used, which in the language of the preamble to the bill, 'might be conceived to be conducive to the successful conducting of the finances; or might be *conceived* to *tend* to give *facility* to the obtaining of loans.' He urged an attention to the diffuse and ductile terms which had been found requisite to cover the stretch of power contained in the bill. He compared them with the terms *necessary* and *proper*, used in the Constitution, and asked whether it was possible to view the two descriptions as synonimous, or the one as a fair and safe commentary on the other.

If, proceeded he, Congress, by virtue of the power to borrow, can create the means of lending, and in pursuance of these means, can incorporate a Bank, they may do any thing whatever creative of like means.

The East-India company has been a lender to the British government, as well as the Bank, and the South-Sea company is a greater creditor than either. Congress then may incorporate similar companies in the United States, and that too not under the idea of regulating trade, but under that of borrowing money.

Private capitals are the chief resources for loans to the British government. Whatever then may be conceived to favor the accumulation of capitals may be done by Congress. They may incorporate manufacturers. They may give monopolies in every branch of domestic industry.

If, again, Congress by virtue of the power to borrow money, can create the ability to lend, they may by virtue of the power to levy money, create the ability to pay it. The ability to pay taxes depends on the general wealth of the society, and this, on the general prosperity of agriculture, manufactures and commerce. Congress then may give bounties and make regulations on all of these objects.

The States have, it is allowed on all hands, a concurrent right to lay and collect taxes. This power is secured to them not by its being expressly reserved, but by its not being ceded by the constitution. The reasons for the bill cannot be admitted, because they would invalidate that right; why may it not be *conceived* by Congress, that an uniform and exclusive imposition of taxes, would not less than the proposed Banks 'be *conducive* to the successful conducting of the national finances, and *tend* to *give facility* to the obtaining of revenue, for the use of the government?'

The doctrine of implication is always a tender one. The danger of it has been felt in other governments. The delicacy was felt in the adoption of our own; the danger may also be felt, if we do not keep close to our chartered authorities.

Mark the reasoning on which the validity of the bill depends. To borrow money is made the *end* and the accumulation of capitals, *implied* as the *means*. The accumulation of capitals is then the *end*, and a bank *implied* as the *means*. The bank is then the *end*, and a charter of incorporation, a monopoly, capital punishments, &c. *implied* as the *means*.

If implications, thus remote and thus multiplied, can be linked together, a chain may be formed that will reach every object of legislation, every object within the whole compass of political economy.

The latitude of interpretation required by the bill is condemned by the rule furnished by the constitution itself.

Congress have power "to regulate the value of money"; yet it is expressly added not left to be implied, that counterfeitors may be punished.

They have the power "to declare war," to which armies are more incident, than incorporated Banks, to borrowing; yet is expressly added, the power "to raise and support armies"; and to this again, the express power "to make rules and regulations for the government of armies"; a like remark is applicable to the powers as to a navy.

The regulation and calling out of the militia are more appurtenant to war, than the proposed bank, to borrowing; yet the former is not left to construction.

The very power to borrow money is a less remote implication from the power of war, than an incorporated monopoly bank, from the power of borrowing—yet the power to borrow is not left to implication.

It is not pretended that every insertion or omission in the

constitution is the effect of systematic attention. This is not the character of any human work, particularly the work of a body of men. The examples cited, with others that might be added, sufficiently inculcate nevertheless a rule of interpretation, very different from that on which the bill rests. They condemn the exercise of any power, particularly a great and important power, which is not evidently and necessarily involved in an express power.

It cannot be denied that the power proposed to be exercised is an important power.

As a charter of incorporation the bill creates an artificial person previously not existing in law. It confers important civil rights and attributes, which could not otherwise be claimed. It is, though not precisely similar, at least equivalent, to the naturalization of an alien, by which certain new civil characters are acquired by him. Would Congress have had the power to naturalize, if it had not been expressly given?

In the power to make bye laws, the bill delegated a sort of legislative power, which is unquestionably an act of a high and important nature. He took notice of the only restraint on the bye laws, that they were not to be contrary to the law and the constitution of the bank; and asked what law was intended; if the law of the United States, the scantiness of their code would give a power, never before given to a corporation—and obnoxious to the States, whose laws would then be superceded not only by the laws of Congress, but by the bye laws of a corporation within their own jurisdiction. If the law intended, was the law of the State, then the State might make laws that would destroy an institution of the United States.

The bill gives a power to purchase and hold lands; Congress themselves could not purchase lands within a State "without the consent of its legislature." How could they delegate a power to others which they did not possess themselves?

It takes from our successors, who have equal rights with ourselves, and with the aid of experience will be more capable of deciding on the subject, an opportunity of exercising that right, for an immoderate term.

It takes from our constituents the opportunity of deliberating on the untried measure, although their hands are also to be tied by it for the same term.

It involves a monopoly, which affects the equal rights of every citizen.

It leads to a penal regulation, perhaps capital punishments, one of the most solemn acts of sovereign authority.

From this view of the power of incorporation exercised in the bill, it could never be deemed an accessary or subaltern power, to be deduced by implication, as a means of executing another power; it was in its nature a distinct, an independent and substantive prerogative, which not being enumerated in the constitution could never have been meant to be included in it, and not being included could never be rightfully exercised.

He here adverted to a distinction, which he said had not been sufficiently kept in view, between a power necessary and proper for the government or union, and a power necessary and proper for executing the enumerated powers. In the latter case, the powers included in each of the enumerated powers were not expressed, but to be drawn from the nature of each. In the former, the powers composing the government were expressly enumerated. This constituted the peculiar nature of the government, no power therefore not enumerated, could be inferred from the general nature of government. Had the power of making treaties, for example, been omitted, however necessary it might have been, the defect could only have been lamented, or supplied by an amendment of the constitution.

But the proposed bank could not even be called necessary to the government; at most it could be but convenient. Its uses to the government could be supplied by keeping the taxes a little in advance—by loans from individuals—by the other banks, over which the government would have equal command; nay greater, as it may grant or refuse to these the privilege, made a free and irrevocable gift to the proposed bank, of using their notes in the federal revenue.

He proceeded next to the contemporary expositions given to the constitution.

The defence against the charge founded on the want of a bill of rights, presupposed, he said, that the powers not given were retained; and that those given were not to be extended by remote implications. On any other supposition, the power of Congress to abridge the freedom of the press, or the rights of conscience, &c. could not have been disproved.

The explanations in the state conventions all turned on the same fundamental principle, and on the principle that the terms necessary and proper gave no additional powers to those enumerated. (Here he read sundry passages from the debates of the Pennsylvania, Virginia and North-Carolina conventions, shewing the grounds on which the constitution had been vindicated by its principal advocates, against a dangerous latitude of its powers, charged on it by its opponents.) He did not undertake to vouch for the accuracy or authenticity of the publications which he quoted—he thought it probable that the sentiments delivered might in many instances have been mistaken, or imperfectly noted; but the complexion of the whole, with what he himself and many others must recollect, fully justified the use he had made of them.

The explanatory declarations and amendments accompanying the ratifications of the several states formed a striking evidence, wearing the same complexion. He referred those who might doubt on the subject, to the several acts of ratification.

The explanatory amendments proposed by Congress themselves, at least, would be good authority with them; all these renunciations of power proceeded on a rule of construction, excluding the latitude now contended for. These explanations were the more to be respected, as they had not only been proposed by Congress, but ratified by nearly three-fourths of the states. He read several of the articles proposed, remarking particularly on the 11th. and 12th. the former, as guarding against a latitude of interpretation—the latter, as excluding every source of power not within the constitution itself.

With all this evidence of the sense in which the constitution was understood and adopted, will it not be said, if the bill should pass, that its adoption was brought about by one set of arguments, and that it is now administered under the influence of another set; and this reproach will have the keener sting, because it is applicable to so many individuals concerned in both the adoption and administration.

In fine, if the power were in the constitution, the immediate exercise of it cannot be essential—if not there, the exercise of it involves the guilt of usurpation, and establishes a precedent of interpretation, levelling all the barriers which limit the powers of the general government, and protect those of the state governments. If the point be doubtful only, respect for ourselves, who ought to shun the appearance of precipitancy and ambition; respect for our successors, who ought not lightly to be deprived of the opportunity of exercising the rights of legislation; respect for our constituents who have had no opportunity of making known their sentiments, and who are themselves to be bound down to the measure for so long a period; all these considerations require that the irrevocable decision should at least be suspended until another session.

It appeared on the whole, he concluded, that the power exercised by the bill was condemned by the silence of the constitution; was condemned by the rule of interpretation arising out of the constitution; was condemned by its tendency to destroy the main characteristic of the constitution; was condemned by the expositions of the friends of the constitution, whilst depending before the public; was condemned by the apparent intention of the parties which ratified the constitution; was condemned by the explanatory amendments proposed by Congress themselves to the Constitution; and he hoped it would receive its final condemnation, by the vote of this house.

February 2, 1791

To Thomas Jefferson

Dear Sir　　　　　　　　　　　　N. York May 12. 1791.

Your favor of the 9th. was recd. last evening. To my thanks for the several inclosures I must add a request that the letter to Baynton which came in one of them may be handed to him by one of your servants. The directory will point out his habitation.

I had seen Payne's pamphlet with the preface of the Philada. Editor. It immediately occurred that you were brought into the Frontispiece in the manner you explain. But I had not foreseen the particular use made of it by the British partizans.

Mr. Adams can least of all complain. Under a mock defence of the Republican Constitutions of this Country, he attacked them with all the force he possessed, and this in a book with his name to it whilst he was the Representative of his Country at a foreign Court. Since he has been the 2d. Magistrate in the new Republic, his pen has constantly been at work in the same cause; and tho' his name has not been prefixed to his antirepublican discourses, the author has been as well known as if that formality had been observed. Surely if it be innocent & decent in one servant of the public thus to write attacks agst its Government, it can not be very criminal or indecent in another to patronize a written defence of the principles on which that Govt. is founded. The sensibility of H. & B. to the indignity to the Brit: Court is truly ridiculous. If offence cd. be justly taken in that quarter, what would France have a right to say to Burke's pamphlet and the Countenance given to it & its author, particularly by the King himself? What in fact might not the U. S. say, whose revolution & democratic Governments come in for a large share of the scurrility lavished on those of France.

I do not foresee any objection to the route you propose. I had conversed with Beckley on a trip to Boston &c and still have that in view; but the time in view for starting from this place, will leave room for the previous excursion. Health recreation & curiousity being my objects, I can never be out of my way.

Not a word of news here. My letters from Virginia say little more than those you had recd. Carrington says the returns have come in pretty thickly of late and warrant the estimate founded on the Counties named to me some time ago. As well as I recollect, these averaged upwards of 8000 souls, and were considered by him as under the general average. Yrs. Affecly.

Population and Emigration

Both in the vegetable and animal kingdoms, every species derives from nature, a reproductive faculty beyond the demand for merely keeping up its stock: the seed of a single plant is sufficient to multiply it one hundred or a thousand fold. The animal offspring is never limited to the number of its parents.*

This ordinance of nature is calculated, in both instances, for a double purpose. In both, it ensures the life of the species, which, if the generative principle had not a multiplying energy, would be reduced in number by every premature destruction of individuals, and by degrees would be extinguished altogether. In the vegetable species, the surplus answers, moreover, the essential purpose of sustaining the herbivorous tribes of animals; as in the animal, the surplus serves the like purpose of sustenance to the carnivorous tribes. A crop of wheat may be reproduced by one tenth of itself. The remaining nine tenths can be spared for the animals which feed on it. A flock of sheep may be continued by a certain proportion of its annual increase. The residue is the bounty of nature to the animals which prey on that species.

Man who preys both on the vegetable and animal species, is himself a prey to neither. He too possesses the reproductive principle far beyond the degree requisite for the bare continuance of his species. What becomes of the surplus of human life to which this principle is competent?

It is either, 1st. destroyed by infanticide, as among the Chinese and Lacedemonians; or 2d. it is stifled or starved, as among other nations whose population is commensurate to its food; or 3d. it is consumed by wars and endemic diseases; or 4th. it overflows, by emigration, to places where a surplus of food is attainable.

*The multiplying power in some instances, animal as well as vegetable, is astonishing. An annual plant of two seeds produces in 20 years, 1,048,576; and there are plants which bear more than 40,000 seeds. The roe of a Codfish is said to contain a million of eggs; mites will multiply to a thousand in a day; and there are viviparous flies which produce 2000 at once. See Stillingfleet and Bradley's philosophical account of nature.

What may be the greatest ratio of increase of which the human species is susceptible, is a problem difficult to be solved; as well because precise experiments have never been made, as because the result would vary with the circumstances distinguishing different situations. It has been computed that under the most favorable circumstances possible, a given number would double itself in ten years. What has actually happened in this country is a proof, that nature would require for the purpose, a less period than twenty years. We shall be safe in averaging the surplus at five per cent.*

According to this computation, Great Britain and Ireland, which contain about ten millions of people, are capable of producing annually for emigration, no less than five hundred thousand; France, whose population amounts to twenty five millions, no less than one million two hundred and fifty thousand; and all Europe, stating its numbers at one hundred and fifty millions, no less than seven and a half millions.

It is not meant that such a surplus could, under any revolution of circumstances, suddenly take place: yet no reason occurs why an annual supply of human, as well as other animal life, to any amount not exceeding the multiplying faculty, would not be produced in one country, by a regular and commensurate demand of another. Nor is it meant that if such a redundancy of population were to happen in any particular country, an influx of it beyond a certain degree ought to be desired by any other, though within that degree, it ought to be invited by a country greatly deficient in its population. The calculation may serve, nevertheless, by placing an important principle in a striking view, to prepare the way for the following positions and remarks.

First. Every country, whose population is full, may annually spare a portion of its inhabitants, like a hive of bees its swarm, without any diminution of its number: nay, a certain portion

*Emigrants from Europe, *enjoying freedom* in a climate similar to their own, increase at the rate of five per cent a year. Among Africans *suffering or* (in the language of some) *enjoying slavery* in a climate similar to their own, human life has been *consumed* in an equal ratio. Under all the mitigations latterly applied in the British West-Indies, it is admitted that an annual *decrease* of one per cent. has taken place. What a comment on the African trade!

must, necessarily, be either spared, or destroyed, or kept out of existence.*

Secondly. It follows, moreover, from this multiplying faculty of human nature, that in a nation, sparing or losing more than its proper surplus, the level must soon be restored by the internal resources of life.

Thirdly. Emigrations may even augment the population of the country permitting them. The commercial nations of Europe, parting with emigrants, to America, are examples. The articles of consumption demanded from the former, have created employment for an additional number of manufacturers. The produce remitted from the latter, in the form of raw materials, has had the same effect—whilst the imports and exports of every kind, have multiplied European merchants and mariners. Where the settlers have doubled every twenty or twenty-five years, as in the United States, the encrease of products and consumption in the new country, and consequently of employment and people in the old, has had a corresponding rapidity.

Of the people of the United States, nearly three millions are of British descent.† The British population has notwithstanding increased within the period of our establishment. It was the opinion of the famous Sir Josiah Child, that every man in the British colonies found employment, and of course, subsistence, for four persons at home. According to this estimate, as more than half a million of the adult males in the United States equally contribute employment at this time to British subjects, there must at this time be more than two millions of British subjects subsisting on the fruits of British emigrations. This result, however, seems to be beyond the real proportion. Let us attempt a less vague calculation.

The value of British imports into the United States including British freight, may be stated at about fifteen millions of dol-

---

*The most remarkable instances of the swarms of people that have been spared without diminishing the parent stock, are the colonies and colonies of colonies among the antient Greeks. Miletum, which was itself a colony, is reported by Pliny, to have established no less than *eighty* colonies, on the Hellespont, the Propontis, and the Euxine. Other facts of a like kind are to be found in the Greek historians.

†Irish is meant to be included.

lars, Deduct two millions for foreign articles coming through British hands; there remain thirteen millions. About half our exports, valued at ten millions of dollars, are remitted to that nation. From the nature of the articles, the freight cannot be less than three millions of dollars; of which about one fifth* being the share of the United States, there is to be added to the former remainder; two millions four hundred thousand. The profit accruing from the articles as materials or auxiliaries for manufactures, is probably at least fifty per cent, or five millions of dollars.† The three sums make twenty millions four hundred thousand dollars; call them in round numbers twenty millions. The expence of supporting a labouring family in Great-Britain, as computed by Sir John Sinclair, on six families containing thirty-four persons, averages £:4:12:10½ sterling, or about twenty dollars a head. As his families were of the poorer class, and the subsistence a bare competency, let twenty-five per cent. be added, making the expence about twenty five dollars a head, dividing twenty millions by this sum, we have eight hundred thousand for the number of British persons whose subsistence may be traced to emigration for its source: or allowing eight shillings sterling a week, for the support of a working man, we have two hundred sixteen thousand three hundred forty-five of that class, for the number derived from the same source.

---

*This is stated as the fact is, not as it ought to be. The United States are reasonably entitled to half the freight, if, under regulations *perfectly reciprocal in every channel of navigation*, they could acquire that share. According to Lord Sheffield, indeed, the United States are well off, compared with other nations; the tonnage employed in the trade with the whole of them, previous to the American Revolution, having belonged to British subjects, in the proportion of more than eleven twelfths. In the year 1660, other nations owned about ¼; in 1700 less than ⅙; In 1725 ⅟19; in 1750 ⅟12; in 1774, less than that proportion. What the proportion is now, is not known. If such has been the operation of the British navigation law on other nations, it is our duty, with enquiring into their acquiescence in its monopolizing tendency, to defend ourselves against it, by all the fair and prudent means in our power.

†This is admitted to be a very vague estimate. The proportion of our exports which are either necessaries of life, or have some profitable connection with manufactures, might be pretty easily computed. The actual profit drawn from that proportion is a more difficult task; but if tolerably ascertained and compared with the proportion of such of our imports as are not for mere consumption, would present one very interesting view of the commerce of the United States.

This lesson of fact, which merits the notice, of every commercial nation, may be enforced by a more general view of the subject.

The present imports of the United States, adding to the first cost, &c. one half the freight as the reasonable share of foreign nations, may be stated at twenty-five millions of dollars. Deducting five millions on account of East-India articles, there remain in favour of Europe, twenty millions of dollars. The foreign labour incorporated with such part of our exports as are subjects or ingredients for manufactures, together with half the export freight, is probably not of less value than fifteen millions of dollars. The two sums together make thirty-five millions of dollars, capable of supporting two hundred thirty-three thousand three hundred thirty-three families of six persons in each: or three hundred seventy-eight thousand six hundred and five men, living on eight shillings sterling a week.

The share of this benefit, which each nation is to enjoy, will be determined by many circumstances. One that must have a certain and material influence, will be, the taste excited here for their respective products and fabrics. This influence has been felt in all its force by the commerce of Great-Britain, as the advantage originated in the emigrations from that country to this; among the means of retaining it, will not be numbered a restraint on emigrations. Other nations, who have to acquire their share in our commerce, are still more interested in aiding their other efforts, by permitting, and even promoting emigrations to this country, as fast as it may be disposed to welcome them. The space left by every ten or twenty thousand emigrants will be speedily filled by a surplus of life that would otherwise be lost. The twenty thousand in their new country, calling for the manufactures and productions required by their habits, will employ and sustain ten thousand persons in their former country, as a clear addition to its stock. In twenty or twenty-five years, the number, so employed and added, will be twenty thousand. And in the mean time, example and information will be diffusing the same taste among other inhabitants here, and proportionally extending employment and population there.

Fourthly. Freedom of emigration is due to the general interests of humanity. The course of emigrations being always, from places where living is more difficult, to places where it is less difficult, the happiness of the emigrant is promoted by the change: and as a more numerous progeny is another effect of the same cause, human life is at once made a greater blessing, and more individuals are created to partake of it.

The annual expence of supporting the poor in England amounts to more than one million and a half sterling.* The number of persons, subsisting themselves not more than six months in the year, is computed at one million two hundred sixty eight thousand, and the number of beggars at forty eight thousand. In France, it has been computed that seven millions of men women and children live one with another, on twenty-five livres, which is less than five dollars a year. Every benevolent reader will make his own reflections.

Fifthly. It may not be superfluous to add, that freedom of emigration is favorable to morals. A great proportion of the vices which distinguish crouded from thin settlements, are known to have their rise in the facility of illicit intercourse between the sexes, on one hand, and the difficulty of maintaining a family, on the other. Provide an outlet for the surplus of population, and marriages will be increased in proportion. Every four or five emigrants will be the fruit of a legitimate union which would not otherwise have taken place.

Sixthly. The remarks which have been made, though in many respects little applicable to the internal situation of the United States, may be of use as far as they tend to prevent mistaken and narrow ideas on an important subject. Our country being populated in different degrees in different parts of it, removals from the more compact to the more spare or vacant districts are continually going forward—The object of these removals is evidently to exchange a less easy for a more easy subsistence. The effect of them must therefore be to quicken the aggregate population of our country. Con-

*From Easter 1775 to Easter 1776, was expended the sum of £.1,556,804:6–3 sterling. See Anderson vol. 5. p. 275. This well informed writer conjectures the annual expence to be near £.2,000,000 sterling. It is to be regretted that the number and expence of the poor in the United States cannot be contrasted with such statements. The subject well merits research, and would produce the truest eulogium on our country.

sidering the progress made in some situations towards their natural complement of inhabitants, and the fertility of others, which have made little or no progress, the probable difference in their respective rates of increase is not less than as three in the former to five in the latter. Instead of lamenting then a loss of *three* human beings to Connecticut, Rhode-Island, or New-Jersey, the *Philanthropist*, will rejoice that *five* will be gained to New-York, Vermont or Kentucky; and the *patriot* will be not less pleased that *two* will be added to *the citizens of the United States*.

National Gazette, November 21, 1791

Consolidation

Much has been said, and not without reason, against a consolidation of the States into one government. Omitting lesser objections, two consequences would probably flow from such a change in our political system, which justify the cautions used against it. *First*, it would be impossible to avoid the dilemma, of either relinquishing the present energy and responsibility of a *single* executive magistrate, for some *plural* substitute, which by dividing so great a trust might lessen the danger of it; or suffering so great an accumulation of powers in the hands of that officer, as might by degrees transform him into a monarch. The incompetency of one Legislature to regulate all the various objects belonging to the local governments, would evidently force a transfer of many of them to the executive department; whilst the encreasing splendour and number of its prerogatives supplied by this source, might prove excitements to ambition too powerful for a sober execution of the elective plan, and consequently strengthen the pretexts for an hereditary designation of the magistrate. *Second*, were the state governments abolished, the same space of country that would produce an undue growth of the executive power, would prevent that controul on the Legislative body, which is essential to a faithful discharge of its trust, neither the voice nor the sense of ten or twenty millions of people, spread through so many latitudes as are comprehended within the United States, could ever be combined or called into effect, if deprived of those local organs, through which both can now be conveyed. In such a state of things, the impossibility of acting together, might be succeeded by the inefficacy of partial expressions of the public mind, and this at length, by a universal silence and insensibility, leaving the whole government to that *self directed course*, which, it must be owned, is the natural propensity of every government.

But if a consolidation of the states into one government be an event so justly to be avoided, it is not less to be desired, on the other hand, that a consolidation should prevail in their interests and affections; and this too, as it fortunately happens, for the very reasons, among others, which lie against a governmental consolidation. For, in the first place, in proportion as uniformity is found to prevail in the interests and sentiments of the several states, will be the practicability of accommodating *Legislative* regulations to them, and thereby of withholding new and dangerous prerogatives from the executive. Again, the greater the mutual confidence and affection of all parts of the Union, the more likely they will be to concur amicably, or to differ with moderation, in the elective designation of the chief magistrate; and by such examples, to guard and adorn the vital principle of our republican constitution. Lastly, the less the supposed difference of interests, and the greater the concord and confidence throughout the great body of the people, the more readily must they sympathize with each other, the more seasonably can they interpose a common manifestation of their sentiments, the more certainly will they take the alarm at usurpation or oppression, and the more effectually will they *consolidate* their defence of the public liberty.

Here then is a proper object presented, both to those who are most jealously attached to the separate authority reserved to the states, and to those who may be more inclined to contemplate the people of America in the light of one nation. Let the former continue to watch against every encroachment, which might lead to a gradual consolidation of the states into one government. Let the latter employ their utmost zeal, by eradicating local prejudices and mistaken rivalships, to consolidate the affairs of the states into one harmonious interest;

and let it be the patriotic study of all, to maintain the various authorities established by our complicated system, each in its respective constitutional sphere; and to erect over the whole, one paramount Empire of reason, benevolence and brotherly affection.

National Gazette, December 5, 1791

Dependent Territories

Are of two kinds. *First*—Such as yield to the superior state at once a monopoly of their useful productions, and a market for its superfluities. These, by exciting and employing industry, might be a source of beneficial riches, if an unfavorable balance were not created by the charge of keeping such possessions. The *West Indies* are an example. *Second*—those, which, though yielding also a monopoly and a market, are principally lucrative, by means of the wealth which they heap on individuals, who transport and dissipate it within the superior state. This wealth is not only like the former, overbalanced by the cost of maintaining its sources, but resembles that drawn, not from industry, but from mines, and is productive of similar effects. The *East-Indies* are an example.

All dependent countries are to the superior state, not in the relation of children and parent, according to the common phrase, but in that of slave and master, and have a like influence on character. By rendering the labour of the one, the property of the other, they cherish pride, luxury, and vanity on one side; on the other, vice and servility, or hatred and revolt.

National Gazette, December 12, 1791

Public Opinion

Public opinion sets bounds to every government, and is the real sovereign in every free one.

As there are cases where the public opinion must be obeyed by the government; so there are cases, where not being fixed, it may be influenced by the government. This distinction, if kept in view, would prevent or decide many debates on the respect due from the government to the sentiments of the people.

In proportion as government is influenced by opinion, it must be so, by whatever influences opinion. This decides the question concerning a *Constitutional Declaration of Rights*, which requires an influence on government, by becoming a part of the public opinion.

The larger a country, the less easy for its real opinion to be ascertained, and the less difficult to be counterfeited; when ascertained or presumed, the more respectable it is in the eyes of individuals. This is favorable to the authority of government. For the same reason, the more extensive a country, the more insignificant is each individual in his own eyes. This may be unfavorable to liberty.

Whatever facilitates a general intercourse of sentiments, as good roads, domestic commerce, a free press, and particularly a *circulation of newspapers through the entire body of the people*, and *Representatives going from, and returning among every part of them*, is equivalent to a contraction of territorial limits, and is favorable to liberty, where these may be too extensive.

National Gazette, December 19, 1791

Government

In monarchies there is a two fold danger—1st, That the eyes of a good prince cannot see all that he ought to know—2d, That the hands of a bad one will not be tied by the fear of combinations against him. Both these evils increase with the extent of dominion; and prove, contrary to the received opinion, that monarchy is even more unfit for a great state, than for a small one, notwithstanding the greater tendency in the former to that species of government.

Aristocracies, on the other hand, are generally seen in small states: where a concentration of the public will is required by external danger, and that degree of concentration is found sufficient. The *many*, in such cases, cannot govern on account

of emergencies which require the promptitude and precautions of a *few*; whilst the few themselves, resist the usurpations
of a *single* tyrant. In Thessaly, a country intersected by mountainous barriers into a number of small cantons, the governments, according to Thucydides, were in most instances,
oligarchical. Switzerland furnishes similar examples. The
smaller the state, the less intolerable is this form of government, its rigors being tempered by the facility and the fear of
combinations among the people.

A republic involves the idea of popular rights. A representative republic *chuses* the wisdom, of which hereditary aristocracy has the *chance*; whilst it excludes the oppression of that
form. And a confederated republic attains the force of monarchy, whilst it equally avoids the ignorance of a good prince,
and the oppression of a bad one. To secure all the advantages
of such a system, every good citizen will be at once a centinel
over the rights of the people; over the authorities of the confederal government; and over both the rights and the authorities of the intermediate governments.

National Gazette, January 2, 1792

Charters

In Europe, charters of liberty have been granted by power.
America has set the example and France has followed it, of
charters of power granted by liberty. This revolution in the
practice of the world, may, with an honest praise, be pronounced the most triumphant epoch of its history, and the
most consoling presage of its happiness. We look back, already, with astonishment, at the daring outrages committed
by despotism, on the reason and the rights of man; We look
forward with joy, to the period, when it shall be despoiled of
all its usurpations, and bound for ever in the chains, with
which it had loaded its miserable victims.

In proportion to the value of this revolution; in proportion
to the importance of instruments, every word of which decides a question between power and liberty; in proportion to
the solemnity of acts, proclaiming the will, and authenticated

by the seal of the people, the only earthly source of authority, ought to be the vigilance with which they are guarded by every citizen in private life, and the circumspection with which they are executed by every citizen in public trust.

As compacts, charters of government are superior in obligation to all others, because they give effect to all others. As trusts, none can be more sacred, because they are bound on the conscience by the religious sanctions of an oath. As metes and bounds of government, they transcend all other landmarks, because every public usurpation is an encroachment on the private right, not of one, but of all.

The citizens of the United States have peculiar motives to support the energy of their constitutional charters.

Having originated the experiment, their merit will be estimated by its success.

The complicated form of their political system, arising from the partition of government between the states and the union, and from the separations and subdivisions of the several departments in each, requires a more than common reverence for the authority which is to preserve order thro' the whole.

Being republicans, they must be anxious to establish the efficacy of popular charters, in defending liberty against power, and power against licentiousness: and in keeping every portion of power within its proper limits; by this means discomfiting the partizans of anti-republican contrivances for the purpose.

All power has been traced up to opinion. The stability of all governments and security of all rights may be traced to the same source. The most arbitrary government is controuled where the public opinion is fixed. The despot of Constantinople dares not lay a new tax, because every slave thinks he ought not. The most systematic governments are turned by the slightest impulse from their regular path, when the public opinion no longer holds them in it. We see at this moment the *executive* magistrate of Great-Britain, exercising under the authority of the representatives of the *people*, a *legislative* power over the West-India commerce.

How devoutly is it to be wished, then, that the public opinion of the United States should be enlightened; that it should attach itself to their governments as delineated in the *great charters*, derived not from the usurped power of kings, but from the legitimate authority of the people; and that it should guarantee, with a holy zeal, these political scriptures from every attempt to add to or diminish from them. Liberty and order will never be *perfectly* safe, until a trespass on the constitutional provisions for either, shall be felt with the same keenness that resents an invasion of the dearest rights; until every citizen shall be an ARGUS to espy, and an ÆGEON to avenge, the unhallowed deed.

National Gazette, January 19, 1792

Parties

In every political society, parties are unavoidable. A difference of interests, real or supposed, is the most natural and fruitful source of them. The great object should be to combat the evil: 1. By establishing a political equality among all. 2. By withholding *unnecessary* opportunities from a few, to increase the inequality of property, by an immoderate, and especially an unmerited, accumulation of riches. 3. By the silent operation of laws, which, without violating the rights of property, reduce extreme wealth towards a state of mediocrity, and raise extreme indigence towards a state of comfort. 4. By abstaining from measures which operate differently on different interests, and particularly such as favor one interest at the expence of another. 5. By making one party a check on the other, so far as the existence of parties cannot be prevented, nor their views accommodated. If this is not the language of reason, it is that of republicanism.

In all political societies, different interests and parties arise out of the nature of things, and the great art of politicians lies in making them checks and balances to each other. Let us then increase these *natural distinctions* by favoring an inequality of property; and let us add to them *artificial distinctions*, by establishing *kings*, and *nobles*, and *plebeians*. We shall then have the more checks to oppose to each other: we shall then have the more scales and the more weights to perfect and maintain the equilibrium. This is as little the voice of reason, as it is that of republicanism.

From the expediency, in politics, of making natural parties, mutual checks on each other, to infer the propriety of creating artificial parties, in order to form them into mutual checks, is not less absurd than it would be in ethics, to say, that new vices ought to be promoted, where they would counteract each other, because this use may be made of existing vices.

National Gazette, January 23, 1792

Universal Peace

Among the various reforms which have been offered to the world, the projects for universal peace have done the greatest honor to the hearts, though they seem to have done very little to the heads of their authors. Rousseau, the most distinguished of these philanthropists, has recommended a confederation of sovereigns, under a council of deputies, for the double purpose of arbitrating external controversies among nations, and of guaranteeing their respective governments against internal revolutions. He was aware, neither of the impossibility of executing his pacific plan among governments which feel so many allurements to war, nor, what is more extraordinary, of the tendency of his plan to perpetuate arbitrary power wherever it existed; and, by extinguishing the hope of one day seeing an end of oppression, to cut off the only source of consolation remaining to the oppressed.

A universal and perpetual peace, it is to be feared, is in the catalogue of events, which will never exist but in the imaginations of visionary philosophers, or in the breasts of benevolent enthusiasts. It is still however true, that war contains so much folly, as well as wickedness, that much is to be hoped from the progress of reason; and if any thing is to be hoped, every thing ought to be tried.

Wars may be divided into two classes; one flowing from the mere will of the government, the other according with the will of the society itself.

Those of the first class can no otherwise be prevented than by such a reformation of the government, as may identify its will with the will of the society. The project of Rousseau was, consequently, as preposterous as it was impotent. Instead of beginning with an external application, and even precluding internal remedies, he ought to have commenced with, and chiefly relied on the latter prescription.

He should have said, whilst war is to depend on those whose ambition, whose revenge, whose avidity, or whose caprice may contradict the sentiment of the community, and yet be uncontrouled by it; whilst war is to be declared by those who are to spend the public money, not by those who are to pay it; by those who are to direct the public forces, not by those who are to support them; by those whose power is to be raised, not by those whose chains may be riveted the disease must continue to be *hereditary* like the government of which it is the offspring. As the first step towards a cure, the government itself must be regenerated. Its will must be made subordinate to, or rather the same with, the will of the community.

Had Rousseau lived to see the constitutions of the United States and of France, his judgment might have escaped the censure to which his project has exposed it.

The other class of wars, corresponding with the public will, are less susceptible of remedy. There are antidotes, nevertheless, which may not be without their efficacy. As wars of the first class were to be prevented by subjecting the will of the government to the will of the society, those of the second, can only be controuled by subjecting the will of the society to the reason of the society; by establishing permanent and constitutional maxims of conduct, which may prevail over occasional impressions, and inconsiderate pursuits.

Here our republican philosopher might have proposed as a model to lawgivers, that war should not only be declared by the authority of the people, whose toils and treasures are to support its burdens, instead of the government which is to reap its fruits: but that each generation should be made to bear the burden of its own wars, instead of carrying them on, at the expence of other generations. And to give the fullest energy to his plan, he might have added, that each generation should not only bear its own burdens, but that the taxes composing them, should include a due proportion of such as by their direct operation keep the people awake, along with those, which being wrapped up in other payments, may leave them asleep, to misapplications of their money.

To the objection, if started, that where the benefits of war descend to succeeding generations, the burdens ought also to descend, he might have answered: that the exceptions could not be easily made; that, if attempted, they must be made by one only of the parties interested; that in the alternative of sacrificing exceptions to general rules, or of converting exceptions into general rules, the former is the lesser evil; that the expense of *necessary* wars, will never exceed the resources of an *entire* generation; that, in fine, the objection vanishes before the *fact*, that in every nation which has drawn on posterity for the support of its wars, *the accumulated interest* of its perpetual debts, has soon become more than *a sufficient principal*, for all its exigencies.

Were a nation to impose such restraints on itself, avarice would be sure to calculate the expences of ambition; in the equipoise of these passions, reason would be free to decide for the public good; and an ample reward would accrue to the state, first, from the avoidance of all its wars of folly, secondly, from the vigor of its unwasted resources for wars of necessity and defence. Were all nations to follow the example, the reward would be doubled to each; and the temple of Janus might be shut, never to be opened more.

Had Rousseau lived to see the rapid progress of reason and reformation, which the present day exhibits, the philanthropy which dictated his project would find a rich enjoyment in the scene before him: And after tracing the past frequency of wars to a will in the government independent of the will of the people; to the practice by each generation of taxing the principal of its debts on future generations; and to the facility with which each generation is seduced into assumptions of the interest, by the deceptive species of taxes which pay it; he would contemplate, in a reform of every government subjecting its will to that of the people, in a subjection of each generation to the payment of its own debts, and in a substitution of a more palpable, in place of an imperceptible mode of paying them, the only hope of UNIVERSAL AND PERPETUAL PEACE.

National Gazette, February 2, 1792

Government of the United States

Power being found by universal experience liable to abuses, a distribution of it into separate departments, has become a first principle of free governments. By this contrivance, the portion entrusted to the same hands being less, there is less room to abuse what is granted; and the different hands being interested, each in maintaining its own, there is less opportunity to usurp what is not granted. Hence the merited praise of governments modelled on a partition of their powers into legislative, executive, and judiciary, and a repartition of the legislative into different houses.

The political system of the United States claims still higher praise. The power delegated by the people is first divided between the general government and the state governments; each of which is then subdivided into legislative, executive, and judiciary departments. And as in a single government these departments are to be kept separate and safe, by a defensive armour for each; so, it is to be hoped, do the two governments possess each the means of preventing or correcting unconstitutional encroachments of the other.

Should this improvement on the theory of free government not be marred in the execution, it may prove the best legacy ever left by lawgivers to their country, and the best lesson ever given to the world by its benefactors. If a security against power lies in the division of it into parts mutually controuling each other, the security must increase with the increase of the parts into which the whole can be conveniently formed.

It must not be denied that the task of forming and maintaining a division of power between different governments, is greater than among different departments of the same government; because it may be more easy (though sufficiently difficult) to separate, by proper definitions, the legislative, executive, and judiciary powers, which are more distinct in their nature, than to discriminate, by precise enumerations, one class of legislative powers from another class, one class of executive from another class, and one class of judiciary from another class; where the powers being of a more kindred nature, their boundaries are more obscure and run more into each other.

If the task be difficult, however, it must by no means be abandoned. Those who would pronounce it impossible, offer no alternative to their country but schism, or consolidation; both of them bad, but the latter the worst, since it is the high road to monarchy, than which nothing worse, in the eye of republicans, could result from the anarchy implied in the former.

Those who love their country, its repose, and its republicanism, will therefore study to avoid the alternative, by elucidating and guarding the limits which define the two governments; by inculcating moderation in the exercise of the powers of both, and particularly a mutual abstinence from such as might nurse present jealousies, or engender greater.

In bestowing the eulogies due to the partitions and internal checks of power, it ought not the less to be remembered, that they are neither the sole nor the chief palladium of constitutional liberty. The people who are the authors of this blessing, must also be its guardians. Their eyes must be ever ready to mark, their voice to pronounce, and their arm to repel or repair aggressions on the authority of their constitutions; the highest authority next to their own, because the immediate work of their own, and the most sacred part of their property, as recognising and recording the title to every other.

National Gazette, February 6, 1792

Spirit of Governments

No Government is perhaps reducible to a sole principle of operation. Where the theory approaches nearest to this character, different and often heterogeneous principles mingle their influence in the administration. It is useful nevertheless

to analyse the several kinds of government, and to characterize them by the spirit which predominates in each.

Montesquieu has resolved the great operative principles of
government into fear, honor, and virtue, applying the first to
pure despotisms, the second to regular monarchies, and the
third to republics. The portion of truth blended with the
ingenuity of this system, sufficiently justifies the admiration
bestowed on its author. Its accuracy however can never be
defended against the criticisms which it has encountered.
Montesquieu was in politics not a Newton or a Locke, who
established immortal systems, the one in matter, the other in
mind. He was in his particular science what Bacon was in universal science: He lifted the veil from the venerable errors
which enslaved opinion, and pointed the way to those lumi-
nous truths of which he had but a glimpse himself.

May not governments be properly divided, according to
their predominant spirit and principles into three species of
which the following are examples?

First. A government operating by a permanent military
force, which at once maintains the government, and is maintained by it; which is at once the cause of burdens on the people, and of submission in the people to their burdens. Such
have been the governments under which human nature has
groaned through every age. Such are the governments which
still oppress it in almost every country of Europe, the quarter
of the globe which calls itself the pattern of civilization, and
the pride of humanity.

Secondly. A government operating by corrupt influence;
substituting the motive of private interest in place of public
duty; converting its pecuniary dispensations into bounties to
favorites, or bribes to opponents; accommodating its measures to the avidity of a part of the nation instead of the benefit of the whole: in a word, enlisting an army of interested
partizans, whose tongues, whose pens, whose intrigues, and
whose active combinations, by supplying the terror of the
sword, may support a real domination of the few, under an
apparent liberty of the many. Such a government, wherever to
be found, is an imposter. It is happy for the new world that it
is not on the west side of the Atlantic. It will be both happy
and honorable for the United States, if they never descend to

mimic the costly pageantry of its form, nor betray themselves into the venal spirit of its administration.

Thirdly. A government, deriving its energy from the will of the society, and operating by the reason of its measures, on the understanding and interest of the society. Such is the government for which philosophy has been searching, and humanity been sighing, from the most remote ages. Such are the republican governments which it is the glory of America to have invented, and her unrivalled happiness to possess. May her glory be compleated by every improvement on the theory which experience may teach; and her happiness be perpetuated by a system of administration corresponding with the purity of the theory.

National Gazette, February 20, 1792

Republican Distribution of Citizens

A perfect theory on this subject would be useful, not because it could be reduced to practice by any plan of legislation, or ought to be attempted by violence on the will or property of individuals: but because it would be a monition against empirical experiments by power, and a model to which the free choice of occupations by the people, might gradually approximate the order of society.

The best distribution is that which would most favor *health, virtue, intelligence* and *competency* in the *greatest number* of citizens. It is needless to add to these objects, *liberty* and *safety.* The first is presupposed by them. The last must result from them.

The life of the husbandman is pre-eminently suited to the comfort and happiness of the individual. *Health,* the first of blessings, is an appurtenance of his property and his employment. *Virtue,* the health of the soul, is another part of his patrimony, and no less favored by his situation. *Intelligence* may be cultivated in this as well as in any other walk of life. If the mind be less susceptible of polish in retirement than in a croud, it is more capable of profound and comprehensive efforts. Is it more ignorant of some things? It has a compensation in its ignorance of others. *Competency* is more universally the lot of those who dwell in the country, when liberty is at the same time their lot. The extremes both of want and of waste have other abodes. 'Tis not the country that peoples either the Bridewells or the Bedlams. These mansions of wretchedness are tenanted from the distresses and vices of overgrown cities.

The condition, to which the blessings of life are most denied is that of the sailor. His health is continually assailed and his span shortened by the stormy element to which he belongs. His virtue, at no time aided, is occasionally exposed to every scene that can poison it. His mind, like his body, is imprisoned within the bark that transports him. Though traversing and circumnavigating the globe, he sees nothing but the same vague objects of nature, the same monotonous occurrences in ports and docks; and at home in his vessel, what new ideas can shoot from the unvaried use of the ropes and the rudder, or from the society of comrades as ignorant as himself. In the supply of his wants he often feels a scarcity, seldom more than a bare sustenance; and if his ultimate prospects do not embitter the present moment, it is because he never looks beyond it. How unfortunate, that in the intercourse, by which nations are enlightened and refined, and their means of safety extended, the immediate agents should be distinguished by the hardest condition of humanity.

The great interval between the two extremes, is, with a few exceptions, filled by those who work the materials furnished by the earth in its natural or cultivated state.

It is fortunate in general, and particularly for this country, that so much of the ordinary and most essential consumption, takes place in fabrics which can be prepared in every family, and which constitute indeed the natural ally of agriculture. The former is the work within doors, as the latter is without; and each being done by hands or at times, that can be spared from the other, the most is made of every thing.

The class of citizens who provide at once their own food and their own raiment, may be viewed as the most truly independent and happy. They are more: they are the best basis of public liberty, and the strongest bulwark of public safety. It follows, that the greater the proportion of this class to the whole society, the more free, the more independent, and the more happy must be the society itself.

In appreciating the regular branches of manufacturing and mechanical industry, their tendency must be compared with the principles laid down, and their merits graduated accordingly. Whatever is least favorable to vigor of body, to the faculties of the mind, or to the virtues or the utilities of life, instead of being forced or fostered by public authority, ought to be seen with regret as long as occupations more friendly to human happiness, lie vacant.

The several professions of more elevated pretensions, the merchant, the lawyer, the physician, the philosopher, the divine, form a certain proportion of every civilized society, and readily adjust their numbers to its demands, and its circumstances.

National Gazette, March 5, 1792

Fashion

An humble address has been lately presented to the Prince of Wales by the BUCKLE MANUFACTURERS of Birmingham, Wassal, Wolverhampton, and their environs, stating that the BUCKLE TRADE gives employment to more than TWENTY THOUSAND persons, numbers of whom, in consequence of the prevailing fashion of SHOESTRINGS & SLIPPERS, are at present without employ, almost destitute of bread, and exposed to the horrors of want at the most inclement season; that to the manufactures of BUCKLES and BUTTONS, Birmingham owes its important figure on the map of England; that it is to no purpose to address FASHION herself, she being void of feeling and deaf to argument, but fortunately accustomed to listen to his voice, and to obey his commands: and finally, IMPLORING his Royal Highness to consider the deplorable condition of their trade, which is in danger of being ruined by the *mutability of fashion*, and to give that direction to the *public taste*, which will insure the lasting gratitude of the petitioners.

Several important reflections are suggested by this address.

I. The most precarious of all occupations which give bread to the industrious, are those depending on mere fashion, which generally changes so suddenly, and often so considerably, as to throw whole bodies of people out of employment.

II. Of all occupations those are the least desirable in a free state, which produce the most servile dependence of one class of citizens on another class. This dependence must increase as the *mutuality* of wants is diminished. Where the wants on one side are the absolute necessaries; and on the other are neither absolute necessaries, nor result from the habitual œconomy of life, but are the mere caprices of fancy, the evil is in its extreme; or if not,

III. The extremity of the evil must be in the case before us, where the absolute necessaries depend on the caprices of fancy, and the caprice of a single fancy directs the fashion of the community. Here the dependence sinks to the lowest point of servility. We see a proof of it in the *spirit* of the address. *Twenty thousand* persons are to get or go without their bread, as a wanton youth, may fancy to wear his shoes with or without straps, or to fasten his straps with strings or with buckles. Can any despotism be more cruel than a situation, in which the existence of thousands depends on one will, and that will on the most slight and fickle of all motives, a mere whim of the imagination.

IV. What a contrast is here to the independent situation and manly sentiments of American citizens, who live on their own soil, or whose labour is necessary to its cultivation, or who were occupied in supplying wants, which being founded in solid utility, in comfortable accommodation, or in settled habits, produce a reciprocity of dependence, at once ensuring subsistence, and inspiring a dignified sense of social rights.

V. The condition of those who receive employment and bread from the precarious source of fashion and superfluity, is a lesson to nations, as well as to individuals. In proportion as a nation consists of that description of citizens, and depends on external commerce, it is dependent on the consumption and caprice of other nations. If the laws of propriety did not forbid, the manufacturers of Birmingham, Wassal, and Wolverhampton, had as real an interest in supplicating the arbiters of fashion in America, as the patron they have addressed. The dependence in the case of nations is even greater than among individuals of the same nation: for besides the *mutability of fashion* which is the same in both, the *mutability of policy* is another source of danger in the former.

National Gazette, March 22, 1792

Property

This term in its particular application means "that dominion which one man claims and exercises over the external things of the world, in exclusion of every other individual."

In its larger and juster meaning, it embraces every thing to which a man may attach a value and have a right; and *which leaves to every one else the like advantage.*

In the former sense, a man's land, or merchandize, or money is called his property.

In the latter sense, a man has a property in his opinions and the free communication of them.

He has a property of peculiar value in his religious opinions, and in the profession and practice dictated by them.

He has a property very dear to him in the safety and liberty of his person.

He has an equal property in the free use of his faculties and free choice of the objects on which to employ them.

In a word, as a man is said to have a right to his property, he may be equally said to have a property in his rights.

Where an excess of power prevails, property of no sort is duly respected. No man is safe in his opinions, his person, his faculties, or his possessions.

Where there is an excess of liberty, the effect is the same, tho' from an opposite cause.

Government is instituted to protect property of every sort; as well that which lies in the various rights of individuals, as that which the term particularly expresses. This being the end of government, that alone is a *just* government, which *impartially* secures to every man, whatever is his *own*.

According to this standard of merit, the praise of affording a just security to property, should be sparingly bestowed on a

government which, however scrupulously guarding the possessions of individuals, does not protect them in the enjoyment and communication of their opinions, in which they
have an equal, and in the estimation of some, a more valuable
property.

More sparingly should this praise be allowed to a government, where a man's religious rights are violated by penalties,
or fettered by tests, or taxed by a hierarchy. Conscience is the
most sacred of all property; other property depending in part
on positive law, the exercise of that, being a natural and unalienable right. To guard a man's house as his castle, to pay
public and enforce private debts with the most exact faith, can
give no title to invade a man's conscience which is more sacred than his castle, or to withhold from it that debt of protection, for which the public faith is pledged, by the very
nature and original conditions of the social pact.

That is not a just government, nor is property secure under
it, where the property which a man has in his personal safety
and personal liberty, is violated by arbitrary seizures of one
class of citizens for the service of the rest. A magistrate issuing his warrants to a press gang, would be in his proper functions in Turkey or Indostan, under appellations proverbial of
the most compleat despotism.

That is not a just government, nor is property secure under
it, where arbitrary restrictions, exemptions, and monopolies
deny to part of its citizens that free use of their faculties, and
free choice of their occupations, which not only constitute
their property in the general sense of the word; but are the
means of acquiring property strictly so called. What must be
the spirit of legislation where a manufacturer of linen cloth is
forbidden to bury his own child in a linen shroud, in order to
favour his neighbour who manufactures woolen cloth; where
the manufacturer and wearer of woolen cloth are again forbidden the œconomical use of buttons of that material, in
favor of the manufacturer of buttons of other materials!

A just security to property is not afforded by that government, under which unequal taxes oppress one species of property and reward another species: where arbitrary taxes invade
the domestic sanctuaries of the rich, and excessive taxes grind
the faces of the poor; where the keenness and competitions of

want are deemed an insufficient spur to labor, and taxes are again applied, by an unfeeling policy, as another spur; in violation of that sacred property, which Heaven, in decreeing man to earn his bread by the sweat of his brow, kindly reserved to him, in the small repose that could be spared from the supply of his necessities.

If there be a government then which prides itself in maintaining the inviolability of property; which provides that none shall be taken *directly* even for public use without indemnification to the owner, and yet *directly* violates the property which individuals have in their opinions, their religion, their persons, and their faculties; nay more, which *indirectly* violates their property, in their actual possessions, in the labor that acquires their daily subsistence, and in the hallowed remnant of time which ought to relieve their fatigues and soothe their cares, the influence will have been anticipated, that such a government is not a pattern for the United States.

If the United States mean to obtain or deserve the full praise due to wise and just governments, they will equally respect the rights of property, and the property in rights: they will rival the government that most sacredly guards the former; and by repelling its example in violating the latter, will make themselves a pattern to that and all other governments.

National Gazette, March 29, 1792

The Union: Who Are Its Real Friends?

Not those who charge others with not being its friends, whilst their own conduct is wantonly multiplying its enemies.

Not those who favor measures, which by pampering the spirit of speculation within and without the government, disgust the best friends of the Union.

Not those who promote unnecessary accumulations of the debt of the Union, instead of the best means of discharging it as fast as possible; thereby encreasing the causes of corruption in the government, and the pretexts for new taxes under its authority, the former undermining the confidence, the latter alienating the affection of the people.

Not those who study, by arbitrary interpretations and insidious precedents, to pervert the limited government of the Union, into a government of unlimited discretion, contrary to the will and subversive of the authority of the people.

Not those who avow or betray principles of monarchy and aristocracy, in opposition to the republican principles of the Union, and the republican spirit of the people; or who espouse a system of measures more accommodated to the depraved examples of those hereditary forms, than to the true genius of our own.

Not those, in a word, who would force on the people the melancholy duty of chusing between the loss of the Union, and the loss of what the union was meant to secure.

The real FRIENDS *to the Union are those,*

Who are friends to the authority of the people, the sole foundation on which the Union rests.

Who are friends to liberty, the great end, for which the Union was formed.

Who are friends to the limited and republican system of government, the means provided by that authority, for the attainment of that end.

Who are enemies to every public measure that might smooth the way to hereditary government; for resisting the tyrannies of which the Union was first planned, and for more effectually excluding which, it was put into its present form.

Who considering a public debt as injurious to the interests of the people, and baneful to the virtue of the government, are enemies to every contrivance for *unnecessarily* increasing its amount, or protracting its duration, or extending its influence.

In a word, those are the real friends to the Union, who are friends to the republican policy throughout, which is the only *cement* for the Union of a republican people; in opposition to a spirit of usurpation and monarchy, which is the *menstruum* most capable of dissolving it.

National Gazette, April 2, 1792

Memorandum on Washington's Retirement

Substance of a Conversation with the President
5th. May. 1792.

In consequence of a note this morning from the President requesting me to call on him I did so; when he opened the conversation by observing that having some time ago communicated to me his intention of retiring from public life on the expiration of his four years, he wished to advise with me on the *mode* and *time* most proper for making known that intention. He had he said spoken with no one yet on those particular points, and took this opportunity of mentioning them to me, that I might consider the matter, and give him my opinion, before the adjournment of congress, or my departure from Philadelphia. He had he said forborne to communicate his intention to any other persons whatever, but Mr. Jefferson, Col. Hamilton, General Knox & myself, and of late to Mr. Randolph. Col: Hamilton & Genl. Knox he observed were extremely importunate that he should relinquish his purpose, and had made pressing representations to induce him to it. Mr. Jefferson had expressed his wishes to the like effect. He had not however persuaded himself that his continuance in public life could be of so much necessity or importance as was conceived, and his disinclination to it, was becoming every day more & more fixed; so that he wished to make up his mind as soon as possible on the points he had mentioned. What he desired was to prefer that mode which would be most remote from the appearance of arrogantly presuming on his re-election in case he should not withdraw himself, and such a time as would be most convenient to the public in making the choice of his successor. It had, he said, at first occurred to him, that the commencement of the ensuing Session of Congress, would furnish him with an apt occasion for introducing the intimation, but besides the lateness of the day, he was apprehensive that it might possibly produce some notice in the reply of Congress that might entangle him in further explanations.

I replied that I would revolve the subject as he desired and communicate the result before my leaving Philada.; but that I could not but yet hope there would be no necessity at this time for his decision on the two points he had stated. I told him that when he did me the honor to mention the resolution he had taken, I had forborne to do more than briefly express my apprehensions that it would give a surprize and shock to the public mind, being restrained from enlarging on the subject by an unwillingness to express sentiments sufficiently known to him; or to urge objections to a determination, which if absolute, it might look like affectation to oppose; that the aspect which things had been latterly assuming, seemed however to impose the task on all who had the opportunity, of urging a continuance of his public services; and that under such an impression I held it a duty, not indeed to express my wishes which would be superfluous, but to offer my opinion that his retiring at the present juncture, might have effects that ought not to be hazarded; that I was not unaware of the urgency of his inclination; or of the peculiar motives he might feel to withdraw himself from a situation into which it was so well known to myself he had entered with a scrupulous reluctance; that I well recollected the embarrassments under which his mind labored in deciding the question, on which he had consulted me, whether it could be his duty to accept his present station after having taken a final leave of public life; and that it was particularly in my recollection, that I then entertained & intimated a wish that his acceptance, which appeared to be indispensable, might be known hereafter to have been in no degree the effect of any motive which strangers to his character might suppose, but of the severe sacrifice which his friends knew, he made of his inclinations as a man, to his obligations as a citizen; that I owned I had at that time contemplated, & I believed, suggested as the most unequivocal tho' not the only proof of his real motives, a voluntary return to private life as soon as the state of the Government would permit, trusting that if any premature casualty should unhappily cut off the possibility of this proof, the evidence known to his friends would in some way or other be saved from oblivion and do justice to his character; that I was not less anxious on the same point now than I was then; and if I did not conceive that reasons of a like kind to those which required him to undertake, still required him to retain for some time longer, his present station;

or did not presume that the purity of his motives would be sufficiently vindicated, I should be the last of his friends to press, or even to wish such a determination.

He then entered on a more explicit disclosure of the state of his mind; observing that he could not believe or conceive himself anywise necessary to the successful administration of the Government; that on the contrary he had from the beginning found himself deficient in many of the essential qualifications, owing to his inexperience in the forms of public business, his unfitness to judge of legal questions, and questions arising out of the Constitution; that others more conversant in such matters would be better able to execute the trust; that he found himself also in the decline of life, his health becoming sensibly more infirm, & perhaps his faculties also; that the fatigues & disagreeableness of his situation were in fact scarcely tolerable to him; that he only uttered his real sentiments when he declared that his inclination would lead him rather to go to his farm, take his spade in his hand, and work for his bread, than remain in his present situation; that it was evident moreover that a spirit of party in the Government was becoming a fresh source of difficulty, and he was afraid was dividing some (alluding to the Secretary of State & Secry. of the Treasury) more particularly connected with him in the administration; that there were discontents among the people which were also shewing themselves more & more, & that altho' the various attacks against public men & measures had not in general been pointed at him, yet in some instances it had been visible that he was the indirect object, and it was probable the evidence would grow stronger and stronger that his return to private life was consistent with every public consideration, and consequently that he was justified in giving way to his inclination for it.

I was led by this explanation to remark to him, that however novel or difficult the business might have been to him, it could not be doubted that with the aid of the official opinions & informations within his command, his judgment must have been as competent in all cases, as that of any one who could have been put in his place, and in many cases certainly more so; that in the great point of conciliating and uniting all parties under a Govt. which had excited such violent contro-

versies & divisions, it was well known that his services had
been in a manner essential; that with respect to the spirit of
party that was taking place under the operations of the Govt.
I was sensible of its existence but considered that as an argument for his remaining, rather than retiring, until the public
opinion, the character of the Govt. and the course of its administration shd. be better decided, which could not fail to
happen in a short time, especially under his auspices; that the
existing parties did not appear to be so formidable to the
Govt as some had represented; that in one party there might
be a few who retaining their original disaffection to the Govt.
might still wish to destroy it, but that they would lose their
weight with their associates, by betraying any such hostile
purposes; that altho' it was pretty certain that the other were
in general unfriendly to republican Govt. and probably aimed
at a gradual approximation of ours to a mixt monarchy, yet
the public sentiment was so strongly opposed to their views,
and so rapidly manifesting itself, that the party could not long
be expected to retain a dangerous influence; that it might reasonably be hoped therefore that the conciliating influence of
a temperate & wise administration, would before another
term of four years should run out, give such a tone & firmness to the Government as would secure it against danger
from either of these descriptions of enemies; that altho' I
would not allow myself to believe but that the Govt. would
be safely administered by any successor elected by the people,
yet it was not to be denied that in the present unsettled condition of our young Government, it was to be feared that no
successor would answer all the purposes to be expected from
the continuance of the present chief magistrate; that the option evidently lay between a few characters; Mr. Adams, Mr.
Jay & Mr Jefferson were most likely to be brought into view;
that with respect to Mr Jefferson, his extreme repugnance to
public life & anxiety to exchange it for his farm & his philosophy, made it doubtful with his friends whether it would be
possible to obtain his own consent; and if obtained, whether
local prejudices in the Northern States, with the views of
Pennsylvania in relation to the seat of Govt. would not be a
bar to his appointment. With respect to Mr. Adams, his
monarchical principles, which he had not concealed, with his

late conduct on the representation-bill had produced such a settled dislike among republicans every where, & particularly in the Southern States, that he seemed to be out of the question. It would not be in the power of those who might be friendly to his private character, & willing to trust him in a public one, notwithstanding his political principles, to make head against the torrent. With respect to Mr. Jay his election would be extremely dissatisfactory on several accounts. By many he was believed to entertain the same obnoxious principles with Mr. Adams, & at the same time would be less open and therefore more successful in propagating them. By others (a pretty numerous class) he was disliked & distrusted, as being thought to have espoused the claims of British Creditors at the expence of the reasonable pretensions of his fellow Citizens in debt to them. Among the western people, to whom his negociations for ceding the Mississippi to Spain were generally known, he was considered as their most dangerous enemy & held in peculiar distrust & disesteem. In this state of our prospects, which was rendered more striking by a variety of temporary circumstances, I could not forbear thinking that altho' his retirement might not be fatal to the public good, yet a postponement of it was another sacrifice exacted by his patriotism.

Without appearing to be any wise satisfied with what I had urged, he turned the conversation to other subjects; & when I was withdrawing repeated his request that I would think of the points he had mentioned to me, & let him have my ideas on them before the adjournment. I told him I would do so: but still hoped his decision on the main question, would supersede for the present all such incidental questions.

Wednesday Evening May 9. 1792

Understanding that the President was to set out the ensuing morning for Mount Vernon, I called on him to let him know that as far as I had formed an opinion on the subject he had mentioned to me, it was in favor of a direct address of notification to the public in time for its proper effect on the election, which I thought might be put into such a form as would avoid every appearance of presumption or indelicacy, and seemed to be absolutely required by his situation. I observed that no other mode deserving consideration had occurred, except the one he had thought of & rejected, which seemed to me liable to the objections that had weighed with him. I added that if on further reflection I shd. view the subject in any new lights, I would make it the subject of a letter tho' I retained my hopes that it would not yet be necessary for him to come to any opinion on it. He begged that I would do so, and also suggest any matters that might occur as proper to be included in what he might say to Congs. at the opening of their next Session; passing over the idea of his relinquishing his purpose of retiring, in a manner that did not indicate the slightest assent to it.

Friday May 25. 1792

I met the President on the road returning from Mount Vernon to Philada., when he handed me the letter dated at the latter place on the 20th. of May, the copy of the answer to which on the 21st. of June is annexed.

To George Washington

Dear Sir   Orange June 20th. 1792
    Having been left to myself, for some days past, I have made use of the opportunity for bestowing on your letter of the 20 Ult: handed to me on the road, the attention which its important contents claimed. The questions which it presents for consideration, are 1. at which time a notification of your purpose to retire will be most convenient. 2 what mode will be most eligible. 3 whether a valedictory address will be proper and adviseable. 4 If both, whether it would be more properly annexed to the notification, or postponed to your actual retirement.
    The answer to the 1st. question involves two points, first the expediency of delaying the notification; secondly the propriety of making it before the choice of electors takes place, that the people may make their choice with an eye to the circumstances under which the trust is to be executed. On the first point, the reasons for as much delay as possible are too

obvious to need recital. The second, depending on the times fixed in the several States, which must be within thirty four days preceding the first wednesday in December, requires that the notification should be in time to pervade every part of the Union by the beginning of November. Allowing six weeks for this purpose, the middle of September or perhaps a little earlier, would seem a convenient date for the act.

2. With regard to the mode, none better occurs than a simple publication in the newspapers. If it were proper to address it through the medium of the general Legislature, there will be no opportunity. Nor does the change of situation seem to admit a recurrence to the State Governments which were the channels used for the former valedictory address. A direct address to the people who are your only constituents, can be made I think most properly through the independent channel of the press, through which they are, as a constituent body usually addressed.

3. On the third question I think there can be no doubt, that such an address is rendered *proper* in itself, by the peculiarity and importance of the circumstances which mark your situation; and *adviseable*, by the salutary and operative lessons of which it may be made the vehicle. The precedent at your military exit, might also subject an omission now to conjectures and interpretations, which it would not be well to leave room for.

4. The remaining question is less easily decided. Advantages and objections lie on both sides of the alternative. The occasion on which you are *necessarily* addressing the people, evidently introduces most easily and most delicately any *voluntary* observations that are meditated. In another view a farewell address, before the final moment of departure, is liable to the appearance of being premature and awkward. On the opposite side of the alternative, however, a postponement will beget a dryness, and an abridgment in the first address, little corresponding with the feelings which the occasion would naturally produce both in the author and the objects; and though not liable to the above objection, would require a resumption of the subject apparently more forced; and on which, the impressions having been anticipated & familiarized, and the public mind diverted perhaps to other scenes, a

second address would be received with less sensibility and effect, than if incorporated with the impressions incident to the original one. It is possible too, that previous to the close of the term, circumstances might intervene in relation to public affairs or the succession to the Presidency, which would be more embarrassing, if existing at the time of a valedictory appeal to the public, than if subsequent to that delicate measure.

On the whole my judgment leans to the propriety of blending together the notifying and valedictory address; and the more so as the crisis which will terminate your public career may still afford an opportunity, if any intermediate contingency should call for a supplement to your farewell observations. But as more correct views of the subject may produce a different result in your mind, I have endeavored to fit the draught inclosed to either determination. You will readily observe that in executing it I have aimed at that plainness & modesty of language which you had in view, and which indeed are so peculiarly becoming the character and the occasion; and that I have had little more to do, as to the matter, than to follow the just and comprehensive outline which you had sketched. I flatter myself however that in every thing which has depended on me, much improvement will be made, before so interesting a paper shall have taken its last form.

Having thus, Sir, complied with your wishes, by proceeding on a supposition that the idea of retiring from public life is to be carried into execution, I must now gratify my own by hoping that a reconsideration of the measure in all its circumstances and consequences, will have produced an acquiescence in one more sacrifice, severe as it may be, to the desires and interests of your country. I forbear to enter into the arguments which in my view plead for it; because it would be only repeating what I have already taken the liberty of fully explaining: But I could not conclude such a letter as the present without a repetition of my anxious wishes & hopes, that our country may not, in this important conjuncture, be deprived of the inestimable advantage of having you at the head of its councils. With every sentiment of respect & affectionate attachment, I am, Dear Sir, your most Obedt. friend & Servant,

———

The period which will close the appointment with which my fellow citizens have honoured me, being not very distant, and the time actually arrived, at which their thoughts must be designating the citizen who is to administer the Executive Government of the United States during the ensuing term, it may conduce to a more distinct expression of the public voice, that I should apprize such of my fellow citizens as may retain their partiality towards me, that I am not to be numbered among those out of whom a choice is to be made.

I beg them to be assured that the Resolution which dictates this intimation has not been taken without the strictest regard to the relation which as a dutiful citizen I bear to my country; and that in withdrawing that tender of my service, which silence in my situation might imply, I am not influenced by the smallest deficiency of zeal for its future interests, or of grateful respect for its past kindness; but by the fullest persuasion that such a step is compatible with both.

The impressions under which I entered on the present arduous trust were explained on the proper occasion. In discharge of this trust I can only say that I have contributed towards the organization and administration of the Government the best exertions of which a very fallible judgment was capable. For any errors which may have flowed from this source, I feel all the regret which an anxiety for the public good can excite; not without the double consolation, however, arising from a consciousness of their being involuntary, and an experience of the candor which will interpret them. If there were any circumstances that could give value to my inferior qualifications for the trust, these circumstances must have been temporary. In this light was the undertaking viewed when I ventured on it. Being, moreover still farther advanced into the decline of life, I am every day more sensible that the increasing weight of years, renders the private walks of it in the shade of retirement, as necessary as they will be acceptable to me. May I be allowed to add, that it will be among the highest as well as purest enjoyments that can sweeten the remnant of my days, to partake, in a private station in the midst of my fellow citizens, of that benign influence of good laws under a free Government, which has been the ultimate object of all our wishes, and in which I confide as the happy reward of our cares and labours. May I be allowed further to add, as a consideration far more important, that an early example of rotation in an office of so high and delicate a nature, may equally accord with the republican spirit of our constitution, and the ideas of liberty and safety entertained by the people.

(If a farewell address is to be added at the expiration of the term, the following paragraph may conclude the present)

Under these circumstances a return to my private station according to the purpose with which I quitted it, is the part which duty as well as inclination assigns me. In executing it I shall carry with me every tender recollection which gratitude to my fellow citizens can awaken; and a sensibility to the permanent happiness of my Country, which will render it the object of my unceasing vows and most fervent supplications.

(Should no further address be intended, the preceding paragraph being omitted, the present address may go on as follows)

In contemplating the moment at which the curtain is to drop for ever on the public scenes of my life, my sensations anticipate and do not permit me to suspend, the deep acknowledgments required by that debt of gratitude which I owe to my beloved country for the many honors it has conferred on me, for the distinguished confidence it has reposed in me, and for the opportunities I have thus enjoyed of testifying my inviolable attachment by the most steadfast services which my faculties could render. All the returns I have now to make will be in those vows which I shall carry with me to my retirement and to my grave, that Heaven may continue to favor the people of the United States with the choicest tokens of its beneficence; that their Union and brotherly affection may be perpetual; that the free constitution which is the work of their own hands, may be sacredly maintained; that its administration in every department, may be stamped with wisdom and with virtue; and that this character may be ensured to it, by that watchfulness over public servants and public measures, which on one hand will be necessary to prevent or correct a degeneracy; and that forbearance, on the other, from unfounded or indiscriminate jealousies which would deprive the public of the best services, by depriving a conscious integrity of one of the noblest incitements to perform them; that in fine, the happiness of the people of America, under the auspices of liberty, may be made complete, by so careful a preservation, and so prudent a use of this blessing, as will acquire them the glorious satisfaction of recommending it to the affection, the praise, and the adoption of every nation which is yet a stranger to it.

And may we not dwell with well grounded hopes on this flattering prospect; when we reflect on the many ties by which the people of America are bound together, and the many proofs they have given of an enlightened judgment and a magnanimous patriotism.

We may all be considered as the children of one common country. We have all been embarked in one common cause. We have all had our share in common sufferings and common successes. The portion of the Earth allotted for the theatre of our fortunes, fulfils our most sanguine desires. All its essential interests are the same; whilst its diversities arising from climate from soil and from other local & lesser peculiarities, will naturally form a mutual relation of the parts, that may give to the whole a more entire independence than has perhaps fallen to the lot of any other nation.

To confirm these motives to an affectionate and permanent Union, and to secure the great objects of it, we have established a common Government, which being free in its principles, being founded in our own choice, being intended as the guardian of our common rights and the patron of our common interests, and wisely containing within itself a provision for its own amendment, as experience may point out its errors, seems to promise every thing that can be expected from such an institution; and if supported by wise councils, by virtuous conduct, and by mutual and friendly allowances, must approach as near to perfection as any human work can aspire, and nearer than any which the annals of mankind have recorded.

With these wishes and hopes I shall make my exit from civil life; & I have taken the same liberty of expressing them, which I formerly used in offering the sentiments which were suggested by my exit from military life. If, in either instance, I have presumed more than I ought, on the indulgence of my fellow citizens, they will be too generous to ascribe it to any other cause than the extreme solicitude which I am bound to feel, and which I can never cease to feel, for their liberty, their prosperity and their happiness.

A Candid State of Parties

As it is the business of the contemplative statesman to trace the history of parties in a free country, so it is the duty of the citizen at all times to understand the actual state of them. Whenever this duty is omitted, an opportunity is given to designing men, by the use of artificial or nominal distinctions, to oppose and balance against each other those who never differed as to the end to be pursued, and may no longer differ as to the means of attaining it. The most interesting state of parties in the United States may be referred to three periods: Those who espoused the cause of independence and those who adhered to the British claims, formed the parties of the first period; if, indeed, the disaffected class were considerable enough to deserve the name of a party. This state of things was superseded by the treaty of peace in 1783. From 1783 to 1787 there were parties in abundance, but being rather local than general, they are not within the present review.

The Federal Constitution, proposed in the latter year, gave birth to a second and most interesting division of the people. Every one remembers it, because every one was involved in it.

Among those who embraced the constitution, the great body were unquestionably friends to republican liberty; tho' there were, no doubt, some who were openly or secretly attached to monarchy and aristocracy; and hoped to make the constitution a cradle for these hereditary establishments.

Among those who opposed the constitution, the great

body were certainly well affected to the union and to good government, tho' there might be a few who had a leaning unfavourable to both. This state of parties was terminated by the regular and effectual establishment of the federal government in 1788; out of the administration of which, however, has arisen a third division, which being natural to most political societies, is likely to be of some duration in ours.

One of the divisions consists of those, who from particular interest, from natural temper, or from the habits of life, are more partial to the opulent than to the other classes of society; and having debauched themselves into a persuasion that mankind are incapable of governing themselves, it follows with them, of course, that government can be carried on only by the pageantry of rank, the influence of money and emoluments, and the terror of military force. Men of those sentiments must naturally wish to point the measures of government less to the interest of the many than of a few, and less to the reason of the many than to their weaknesses; hoping perhaps in proportion to the ardor of their zeal, that by giving such a turn to the administration, the government itself may by degrees be narrowed into fewer hands, and approximated to an hereditary form.

The other division consists of those who believing in the doctrine that mankind are capable of governing themselves, and hating hereditary power as an insult to the reason and an outrage to the rights of man, are naturally offended at every public measure that does not appeal to the understanding and to the general interest of the community, or that is not strictly conformable to the principles, and conducive to the preservation of republican government.

This being the real state of parties among us, an experienced and dispassionate observer will be at no loss to decide on the probable conduct of each.

The antirepublican party, as it may be called, being the weaker in point of numbers, will be induced by the most obvious motives to strengthen themselves with the men of influence, particularly of moneyed, which is the most active and insinuating influence. It will be equally their true policy to weaken their opponents by reviving exploded parties, and taking advantage of all prejudices, local, political, and occupational, that may prevent or disturb a general coalition of sentiments.

The Republican party, as it may be termed, conscious that the mass of people in every part of the union, in every state, and of every occupation must at bottom be with them, both in interest and sentiment, will naturally find their account in burying all antecedent questions, in banishing every other distinction than that between enemies and friends to republican government, and in promoting a general harmony among the latter, wherever residing, or however employed.

Whether the republican or the rival party will ultimately establish its ascendance, is a problem which may be contemplated now; but which time alone can solve. On one hand experience shews that in politics as in war, stratagem is often an overmatch for numbers: and among more happy characteristics of our political situation, it is now well understood that there are peculiarities, some temporary, others more durable, which may favour that side in the contest. On the republican side, again, the superiority of numbers is so great, their sentiments are so decided, and the practice of making a common cause, where there is a common sentiment and common interest, in spight of circumstancial and artificial distinctions, is so well understood, that no temperate observer of human affairs will be surprised if the issue in the present instance should be reversed, and the government be administered in the spirit and form approved by the great body of the people.

National Gazette, September 26, 1792

Who Are the Best Keepers of the People's Liberties?

Republican.—The people themselves. The sacred trust can be no where so safe as in the hands most interested in preserving it.

Anti-republican.—The people are stupid, suspicious, licentious. They cannot safely trust themselves. When they have established government they should think of nothing but obedience, leaving the care of their liberties to their wiser rulers.

Republican.—Although all men are born free, and all nations might be so, yet too true it is, that slavery has been the general lot of the human race. Ignorant—they have been cheated; asleep—they have been surprized; divided—the yoke has been forced upon them. But what is the lesson? That because the people *may* betray themselves, they ought to give themselves up, blindfold, to those who have an interest in betraying them? Rather conclude that the people ought to be enlightened, to be awakened, to be united, that after establishing a government they should watch over it, as well as obey it.

Anti-republican.—You look at the surface only, where errors float, instead of fathoming the depths where truth lies hid. It is not the government that is disposed to fly off from the people; but the people that are ever ready to fly off from the government. Rather say then, enlighten the government, warn it to be vigilant, enrich it with influence, arm it with force, and to the people never pronounce but two words—*Submission* and *Confidence.*

Republican.—The centrifugal tendency then is in the people, not in the government, and the secret art lies in restraining the tendency, by augmenting the attractive principle of the government with all the weight that can be added to it. What a perversion of the natural order of things! to make *power* the primary and central object of the social system, and *Liberty* but its satellite.

Anti-republican.—The science of the stars can never instruct you in the mysteries of government. Wonderful as it may seem, the more you increase the attractive force of power, the more you enlarge the sphere of liberty; the more you make government independent and hostile towards the people, the better security you provide for their rights and interests. Hence the wisdom of the theory, which, after limiting the share of the people to a third of the government, and lessening the influence of that share by the mode and term of delegating it, establishes two grand hereditary orders, with feelings, habits, interests, and prerogatives all inveterately hostile to the rights and interests of the people, yet by a *mysterious* operation all combining to fortify the people in both.

Republican.—Mysterious indeed! But mysteries belong to religion, not to government; to the ways of the Almighty, not to the works of man. And in religion itself there is nothing mysterious to its author; the mystery lies in the dimness of the human sight. So in the institutions of man let there be no mystery, unless for those inferior beings endowed with a ray perhaps of the twilight vouchsafed to the first order of terrestrial creation.

Anti-republican.—You are destitute, I perceive, of every quality of a good citizen, or rather of a good *subject*. You have neither the light of faith nor the spirit of obedience. I denounce you to the government as an accomplice of atheism and anarchy.

Republican.—And I forbear to denounce you to the people, though a blasphemer of their rights and an idolater of tyranny. Liberty disdains to persecute.

National Gazette, December 22, 1792

To Thomas Jefferson

My dear Sir   Orange June 13. 93.

My last was of the 27 May. It inclosed among other things a letter to the French Ministre de l'Interieur, in answer to one inclosing a Decree of the Nat: Assemb. On the propriety of the answer I wished your freest judgment; and as the sending one at all may be rendered by events improper, I must request the favor of you not to forward the letter, if intelligence should confirm such to be the State of things that it would be totally mal-apropos *there*. Provided it be proper there, and consequently proper in itself, I shall not trouble myself about any comments which the publication attending all such things, may produce here. The letter preceding my last as well as the last, contained some other papers which I wish to know have been reced.

Your two last favors were of May 27. & June 2. The latter confirms the apostacy of Dumourier, but relieves us from the more alarming account of his being supported in it by the army. Still however much is to be dreaded from the general posture of things. Should they take a turn decidedly wrong, I fear little regard will be paid to the limited object avowed by the Austrian General in his first proclamation. In fact if the plan of Dumourier had succeeded, it is probable that under the clause of the Proclamation relating to an amendment of imperfections in the Constitution of 1791 the form of the national sanction would have been obtained, as in the Restoration of Charles II, to whatever establishment military despotism might please to dictate. The only hope of France, next to the success of her own efforts, seems to lie in the number of discordant views of her combined enemies.

I observe that the Newspapers continue to criticise the President's proclamation; and I find that some of the criticisms excite the attention of dispassionate & judicious individuals here. I have heard it remarked by such with some surprise that the P. should have declared the U. S. to be neutral in the unqualified terms used, when we were so notoriously & unequivocally under *eventual engagements* to defend the American possessions of F. I have heard it remarked also that the impartiality enjoined on the people was as little reconciliable with their moral obligations, as the unconditional neutrality proclaimed by the Government is with the express articles of the Treaty. It has been asked also whether the Authority of the Executive extended by any part of the Constitution to a declaration of the *Disposition* of the U. S. on the subject of war & peace? I have been mortified that on these points I could offer no bona fide explanations that ought to be satisfactory. On the last point I must own my surprise that such a prerogative should have been exercised. Perhaps I may have not attended to some part of the Constitution with sufficient care, or may have misapprehended its meaning: But, as I have always supposed & still conceive, a proclamation on the subject could not properly go beyond a declaration of the fact that the U. S. were at war or peace, and an enjunction of a suitable conduct on the Citizens. The right to decide the question whether the duty & interest of the U. S. require war or peace under any given circumstances, and whether their disposition be towards the one or the other

seems to be essentially & exclusively involved in the right
vested in the Legislature, of declaring war in time of peace;
and in the P. & S. of making peace in time of war. Did no
such view of the subject present itself in the discussions of the
Cabinet? I am extremely afraid that the P. may not be sufficiently aware of the snares that may be laid for his good intentions by men whose politics at bottom are very different
from his own. An assumption of prerogatives not clearly
found in the Constitution & having the appearance of being
copied from a Monarchical model, will beget animadversion
equally mortifying to him, & disadvantageous to the Government. Whilst animadversions of this sort can be plausibly
ascribed to the spirit of party, the force of them may not be
felt. But all his real friends will be anxious that his public conduct may bear the strictest scrutiny of future times as well as
of the present day: and all such friends of the Constitution
will be doubly pained at infractions of it under auspices that
may consecrate the evil till it be incurable.

It will not be in my power to take the step with the Friend
of our Friend, which you recommend. It is probable too that
it would be either unnecessary or without effect. If the complexion of the former be such as is presumed, he will fairly
state the truth & that alone is wanted. If, as I deem not impossible, his complexion be a little different from the general
belief, there would be more harm than good in the attempt.
The great danger of misconstruing the sentiment of Virginia
with regard to Liberty & France is from the heretical tone of
conversation in the Towns on the post-road. The voice of the
Country is universally and warmly right. If the popular disposition could be collected & carried into effect, a most important use might be made of it in obtaining contributions of the
necessaries called for by the danger of famine in France.
Unfortunately the disaffection of the Towns which alone
could give effect to a plan for the purpose, locks up the public gratitude & beneficence.

Our fine prospects in the wheat fields have been severely injured by the weather for some time past. A warm & moist
spring had pushed the wheat into rather a luxuriant state. It
had got safe into the head however, and with tolerable
weather would have ripened into a most exuberant crop. Just

as the grain was in a milky state, the weather became wetter than ever, and has continued raining or cloudy almost constantly since. This has brought on a little of the rust, and pretty universally in this quarter a decay of the ear called the Rot. Should the weather be ever so favorable henceforward, a considerable proportion will be lost: And if unfavorable, the loss may be almost entire. We are at this moment both excessively wet & hot. The forwardest wheat is turning fast & may be nearly safe. The generality is not sufficiently advanced to be out of danger of future or beyond the effect of past causes.

The (Kentucky) Coffee Trees in this Neighbourhood are all too young to bear for some years. I will do all I can to get the seed for Bartram from Kentucky as soon as possible. Adieu.

"Helvidius" No. 1

Several pieces with the signature of PACIFICUS were lately published, which have been read with singular pleasure and applause, by the foreigners and degenerate citizens among us, who hate our republican government, and the French revolution; whilst the publication seems to have been too little regarded, or too much despised by the steady friends to both.

Had the doctrines inculcated by the writer, with the natural consequences from them, been nakedly presented to the public, this treatment might have been proper. Their true character would then have struck every eye, and been rejected by the feelings of every heart. But they offer themselves to the reader in the dress of an elaborate dissertation; they are mingled with a few truths that may serve them as a passport to credulity; and they are introduced with professions of anxiety for the preservation of peace, for the welfare of the government, and for the respect due to the present head of the executive, that may prove a snare to patriotism.

In these disguises they have appeared to claim the attention I propose to bestow on them; with a view to shew, from the publication itself, that under colour of vindicating an important public act, of a chief magistrate, who enjoys the confidence and love of his country, principles are advanced which strike at the vitals of its constitution, as well as at its honor and true interest.

As it is not improbable that attempts may be made to apply insinuations which are seldom spared when particular purposes are to be answered, to the author of the ensuing observations, it may not be improper to premise, that he is a friend to the constitution, that he wishes for the preservation of peace, and that the present chief magistrate has not a fellow-citizen, who is penetrated with deeper respect for his merits, or feels a purer solicitude for his glory.

This declaration is made with no view of courting a more favorable ear to what may be said than it deserves. The sole purpose of it is, to obviate imputations which might weaken the impressions of truth; and which are the more likely to be resorted to, in proportion as solid and fair arguments may be wanting.

The substance of the first piece, sifted from its inconsistencies and its vague expressions, may be thrown into the following propositions:

That the powers of declaring war and making treaties are, in their nature, executive powers:

That being particularly vested by the constitution in other departments, they are to be considered as exceptions out of the general grant to the executive department:

That being, as exceptions, to be construed strictly, the powers not strictly within them, remain with the executive:

That the executive consequently, as the organ of intercourse with foreign nations, and the interpreter and executor of treaties, and the law of nations, is authorised, to expound all articles of treaties, those involving questions of war and peace, as well as others; to judge of the obligations of the United States to make war or not, under any casus federis or eventual operation of the contract, relating to war; and, to pronounce the state of things resulting from the obligations of the United States, as understood by the executive:

That in particular the executive had authority to judge whether in the case of the mutual guaranty between the United States and France, the former were bound by it to engage in the war:

That the executive has, in pursuance of that authority, decided that the United States are not bound: And,

That its proclamation of the 22d of April last, is to be taken as the effect and expression of that decision.

The basis of the reasoning is, we perceive, the extraordinary doctrine, that the powers of making war and treaties, are in their nature executive; and therefore comprehended in the general grant of executive power, where not specially and strictly excepted out of the grant.

Let us examine this doctrine; and that we may avoid the possibility of mistating the writer, it shall be laid down in his own words: a precaution the more necessary, as scarce any thing else could outweigh the improbability, that so extravagant a tenet should be hazarded, at so early a day, in the face of the public.

His words are—"Two of these (exceptions and qualifications to the executive powers) have been already noticed—the participation of the Senate in the *appointment of officers*, and the *making of treaties*. A *third* remains to be mentioned—the right of the legislature to *declare war, and grant letters of marque and reprisal*."

Again—"It deserves to be remarked, that as the participation of the Senate in the *making treaties*, and the power of the legislature to *declare war*, are *exceptions* out of the general *executive power*, vested in the President, they are to be construed *strictly*, and ought to be extended no farther than is essential to their execution."

If there be any countenance to these positions, it must be found either 1st, in the writers, of authority, on public law; or 2d, in the quality and operation of the powers to make war and treaties; or 3d, in the constitution of the United States.

It would be of little use to enter far into the first source of information, not only because our own reason and our own constitution, are the best guides; but because a just analysis and discrimination of the powers of government, according to their executive, legislative and judiciary qualities are not to be expected in the works of the most received jurists, who wrote before a critical attention was paid to those objects, and with their eyes too much on monarchical governments, where all powers are confounded in the sovereignty of the prince. It will be found however, I believe, that all of them, particularly Wolfius, Burlamaqui and Vattel, speak of the powers to declare war, to conclude peace, and to form alliances, as among the highest acts of the sovereignty; of which the legislative power must at least be an integral and preeminent part.

Writers, such as Locke and Montesquieu, who have discussed more particularly the principles of liberty and the structure of government, lie under the same disadvantage, of having written before these subjects were illuminated by the events and discussions which distinguish a very recent period. Both of them too are evidently warped by a regard to the particular government of England, to which one of them owed allegiance;* and the other professed an admiration bordering on idolatry. Montesquieu, however, has rather distinguished himself by enforcing the reasons and the importance of avoiding a confusion of the several powers of government, than by enumerating and defining the powers which belong to each particular class. And Locke, notwithstanding the early date of his work on civil government, and the example of his own government before his eyes, admits that the particular powers in question, which, after some of the writers on public law he calls *federative*, are really *distinct* from the *executive*, though almost always united with it, and *hardly to be separated into distinct hands*. Had he not lived under a monarchy, in which these powers were united; or had he written by the lamp which truth now presents to lawgivers, the last observation would probably never have dropt from his pen. But let us quit a field of research which is more likely to perplex than to decide, and bring the question to other tests of which it will be more easy to judge.

2. If we consult for a moment, the nature and operation of the two powers to declare war and make treaties, it will be impossible not to see that they can never fall within a proper definition of executive powers. The natural province of the executive magistrate is to execute laws, as that of the legisla-

---

*The chapter on prerogative, shews how much the reason of the philosopher was clouded by the royalism of the Englishman.

ture is to make laws. All his acts therefore, properly executive, must pre-suppose the existence of the laws to be executed. A treaty is not an execution of laws: it does not pre-suppose the existence of laws. It is, on the contrary, to have itself the force of a *law*, and to be carried into *execution*, like all *other laws*, by the *executive magistrate*. To say then that the power of making treaties which are confessedly laws, belongs naturally to the department which is to execute laws, is to say, that the executive department naturally includes a legislative power. In theory, this is an absurdity—in practice a tyranny.

The power to declare war is subject to similar reasoning. A declaration that there shall be war, is not an execution of laws: it does not suppose pre-existing laws to be executed: it is not in any respect, an act merely executive. It is, on the contrary, one of the most deliberative acts that can be performed; and when performed, has the effect of *repealing* all the *laws* operating in a state of peace, so far as they are inconsistent with a state of war: and of *enacting* as *a rule for the executive*, a *new code* adapted to the relation between the society and its foreign enemy. In like manner a conclusion of peace *annuls* all the *laws* peculiar to a state of war, and *revives* the general *laws* incident to a state of peace.

These remarks will be strengthened by adding that treaties, particularly treaties of peace, have sometimes the effect of changing not only the external laws of the society, but operate also on the internal code, which is purely municipal, and to which the legislative authority of the country is of itself competent and compleat.

From this view of the subject it must be evident, that although the executive may be a convenient organ of preliminary communications with foreign governments, on the subjects of treaty or war; and the proper agent for carrying into execution the final determinations of the competent authority; yet it can have no pretensions from the nature of the powers in question compared with the nature of the executive trust, to that essential agency which gives validity to such determinations.

It must be further evident that, if these powers be not in their nature purely legislative, they partake so much more of that, than of any other quality, that under a constitution leaving them to result to their most natural department, the legislature would be without a rival in its claim.

Another important inference to be noted is, that the powers of making war and treaty being substantially of a legislative, not an executive nature, the rule of interpreting exceptions strictly, must narrow instead of enlarging executive pretensions on those subjects.

3. It remains to be enquired whether there be any thing in the constitution itself which shews that the powers of making war and peace are considered as of an executive nature, and as comprehended within a general grant of executive power.

It will not be pretended that this appears from any *direct* position to be found in the instrument.

If it were *deducible* from any particular expressions it may be presumed that the publication would have saved us the trouble of the research.

Does the doctrine then result from the actual distribution of powers among the several branches of the government? Or from any fair analogy between the powers of war and treaty and the enumerated powers vested in the executive alone?

Let us examine.

In the general distribution of powers, we find that of declaring war expressly vested in the Congress, where every other legislative power is declared to be vested, and without any other qualification than what is common to every other legislative act. The constitutional idea of this power would seem then clearly to be, that it is of a legislative and not an executive nature.

This conclusion becomes irresistible, when it is recollected, that the constitution cannot be supposed to have placed either any power legislative in its nature, entirely among executive powers, or any power executive in its nature, entirely among legislative powers, without charging the constitution, with that kind of intermixture and consolidation of different powers, which would violate a fundamental principle in the organization of free governments. If it were not unnecessary to enlarge on this topic here, it could be shewn, that the constitution was originally vindicated, and has been constantly expounded, with a disavowal of any such intermixture.

The power of treaties is vested jointly in the President and in the Senate, which is a branch of the legislature. From this arrangement merely, there can be no inference that would necessarily exclude the power from the executive class: since the senate is joined with the President in another power, that of appointing to offices, which as far as relate to executive offices at least, is considered as of an executive nature. Yet on the other hand, there are sufficient indications that the power of treaties is regarded by the constitution as materially different from mere executive power, and as having more affinity to the legislative than to the executive character.

One circumstance indicating this, is the constitutional regulation under which the senate give their consent in the case of treaties. In all other cases the consent of the body is expressed by a majority of voices. In this particular case, a concurrence of two thirds at least is made necessary, as a substitute or compensation for the other branch of the legislature, which on certain occasions, could not be conveniently a party to the transaction.

But the conclusive circumstance is, that treaties when formed according to the constitutional mode, are confessedly to have the force and operation of *laws*, and are to be a rule for the courts in controversies between man and man, as much as any *other laws*. They are even emphatically declared by the constitution to be "the supreme law of the land."

So far the argument from the constitution is precisely in opposition to the doctrine. As little will be gained in its favour from a comparison of the two powers, with those particularly vested in the President alone.

As there are but few it will be most satisfactory to review them one by one.

"The President shall be commander in chief of the army and navy of the United States, and of the militia when called into the actual service of the United States."

There can be no relation worth examining between this power and the general power of making treaties. And instead of being analogous to the power of declaring war, it affords a striking illustration of the incompatibility of the two powers in the same hands. Those who are to *conduct a war* cannot in the nature of things, be proper or safe judges, whether *a war ought* to be *commenced*, *continued*, or *concluded*. They are barred from the latter functions by a great principle in free government, analogous to that which separates the sword from the purse, or the power of executing from the power of enacting laws.

"He may require the opinion in writing of the principal officers in each of the executive departments upon any subject relating to the duties of their respective offices; and he shall have power to grant reprieves and pardons for offences against the United States, except in case of impeachment." These powers can have nothing to do with the subject.

"The President shall have power to fill up vacancies that may happen during the recess of the senate, by granting commissions which shall expire at the end of the next session." The same remark is applicable to this power, as also to that of "receiving ambassadors, other public ministers and consuls." The particular use attempted to be made of this last power will be considered in another place.

"He shall take care that the laws shall be faithfully executed and shall commission all officers of the United States." To see the laws faithfully executed constitutes the essence of the executive authority. But what relation has it to the power of making treaties and war, that is, of determining what the *laws shall be* with regard to other nations? No other certainly than what subsists between the powers of executing and enacting laws; no other consequently, than what forbids a coalition of the powers in the same department.

I pass over the few other specified functions assigned to the President, such as that of convening of the legislature, &c. &c. which cannot be drawn into the present question.

It may be proper however to take notice of the power of removal from office, which appears to have been adjudged to the President by the laws establishing the executive departments; and which the writer has endeavoured to press into his service. To justify any favourable inference from this case, it must be shewn, that the powers of war and treaties are of a kindred nature to the power of removal, or at least are equally within a grant of executive power. Nothing of this sort has been attempted, nor probably will be attempted. Nothing can in truth be clearer, than that no analogy, or shade of analogy, can be traced between a power in the supreme officer respon-

sible for the faithful execution of the laws, to displace a subaltern officer employed in the execution of the laws; and a
power to make treaties, and to declare war, such as these have
been found to be in their nature, their operation, and their
consequences.

Thus it appears that by whatever standard we try this doctrine, it must be condemned as no less vicious in theory than
it would be dangerous in practice. It is countenanced neither
by the writers on law; nor by the nature of the powers themselves; nor by any general arrangements or particular expressions, or plausible analogies, to be found in the constitution.

Whence then can the writer have borrowed it?

There is but one answer to this question.

The power of making treaties and the power of declaring
war, are *royal prerogatives* in the *British government*, and are
accordingly treated as Executive prerogatives by *British commentators.*

We shall be the more confirmed in the necessity of this solution of the problem, by looking back to the æra of the constitution, and satisfying ourselves that the writer could not
have been misled by the doctrines maintained by our own
commentators on our own government. That I may not ram-
ble beyond prescribed limits, I shall content myself with an
extract from a work which entered into a systematic explanation and defence of the constitution, and to which there has
frequently been ascribed some influence in conciliating the
public assent to the government in the form proposed. Three
circumstances conspire in giving weight to this cotemporary
exposition. It was made at a time when no application to *persons* or *measures* could bias: The opinion given was not tran-
siently mentioned, but formally and critically elucidated: It
related to a point in the constitution which must consequently have been viewed as of importance in the public
mind. The passage relates to the power of making treaties;
that of declaring war, being arranged with such obvious propriety among the legislative powers, as to be passed over without particular discussion.

"Tho' several writers on the subject of government place
that power (*of making treaties*) in the class of *Executive authorities*, yet this is *evidently* an *arbitrary disposition*. For if we

attend *carefully*, to its operation, it will be found to partake *more* of the *legislative* than of the *executive* character, though it does not seem strictly to fall within the definition of either of them. The essence of the legislative authority, is to enact laws; or in other words, to prescribe rules for the regulation of the society. While the execution of the laws and the employment of the common strength, either for this purpose, or for the common defence, seem to comprize *all* the functions of the *Executive magistrate*. The power of making treaties is *plainly* neither the one nor the other. It relates neither to the execution of the subsisting laws, nor to the enaction of new ones, and still less to an exertion of the common strength. Its objects are contracts with foreign nations, which have the *force of law*, but derive it from the obligations of good faith. They are not rules prescribed by the sovereign to the subject, but agreements between sovereign and sovereign. The power in question seems therefore to form a distinct department, and to belong properly neither to the legislative nor to the executive. The qualities elsewhere detailed as indispensable in the management of foreign *negociations*, point out the executive as the most fit agent in those transactions: whilst the vast importance of the trust, and the operation of treaties *as Laws*, plead strongly for the participation of the whole or a part of the *legislative body* in the office of making them." Federalist vol. 2. p. 273.

It will not fail to be remarked on this commentary, that whatever doubts may be started as to the correctness of its reasoning against the legislative nature of the power to make treaties: it is *clear, consistent* and *confident*, in deciding that the power is *plainly* and *evidently* not an *executive power*.

August 24, 1793

To Thomas Jefferson

Dear Sir   Sepr. 2d. 1793
I dropped you a few lines this morning by the servant going to George Town with your horse. I had not time, without detaining him to say more than that I had your two favors of

the 11th. Ult: by Mr. D. R. and of the 18th. by post. The former was communicated to Monroe, as shall be the latter in
case of opportunity. The conduct of Genèt as developed in
these, and in his proceedings as exhibited in the newspapers,
is as unaccountable as it is distressing. The effect is beginning
to be strongly felt here in the surprize and disgust of those
who are attached to the French cause, and viewed this minister as the instrument for cementing instead of alienating the
two Republics. These sensations are powerfully reinforced by
the general and habitual veneration for the President. The
Anglican party is busy as you may suppose in making the
worst of every thing, and in turning the public feelings
against France, and thence, in favor of England. The only antidote for their poison, is to distinguish between the nation &
its Agent, between principles and events; and to impress the
well meaning with the fact that the enemies of France & of
Liberty are at work to lead them from their honorable connection with these, into the arms and ultimately into the
Government of G. B. If the genuine sense of the people could
be collected on the several points comprehended in the occasion, the calamity would be greatly alleviated if not absolutely
controuled. But this is scarcely possible. The Country is too
much uninformed, and too inert to speak for itself; and the
language of the towns which are generally directed by an adverse interest will insidiously inflame the evil. It is however of
such infinite importance to our own Government as well as to
that of France, that the real sentiments of the people here
should be understood, that something ought to be attempted
on that head. I inclose a copy of a train of ideas sketched on
the first rumour of the war between the Ex. & Genet, and
particularly suggested by the Richmond Resolutions, as a
groundwork for those who might take the lead in county
meetings. It was intended that they should be modified in
every particular according to the state of information and the
particular temper of the place. A copy has been sent to
Caroline with a hope that Mr. P. might find it not improper
to step forward. Another is gone to the District Court at
Staunton in the hands of Monroe, who carried a letter
from me on the subject to A. Stuart; and a third will be for
consideration at the District Ct. at Charlottesville. If these

examples should be set, there may be a chance of like proceedings elsewhere: and in themselves they will be respectable
specimens of the principles and sensations of the Agricultural,
which is the commanding part of the Society. I am not sanguine however that the effort will succeed. If it does not, the
State Legislatures, and the federal also if possible, must be induced to take up the matter in its true point of view. Monroe
& myself read with attention your despatch by D. R. and had
much conversation on what passed between you & the P. It
appd. to both of us that a real anxiety was marked to retain
you in office, that over & above other motives, it was felt that
your presence and implied sanction might be a necessary
shield against certain criticisms from certain quarters; that the
departure of the only counsellor possessing the confidence of
the Republicans would be a signal for new & perhaps very
disagreeable attacks; that in this point of view, the respectful
& conciliatory language of the P. is worthy of particular attention; and that it affords a better hope than has existed of
your being able to command attention, and to moderate the
predominant tone. We agreed in opinion also that whilst this
end is pursued, it would be wise to make as few concessions
as possible that might embarrass the free pursuit of measures
which may be dictated by Repubn. principles & required by
the public good. In a word we think you ought to make the
most of the value we perceive to be placed on your participation in the Ex: Counsels. I am extremely glad to find that you
are to remain another quarter. The season will be more apro-
pos in several respects; and it will prevent any co-operation
which a successor might be disposed to make towards a final
breach with France. I have little hope that you will have one
whose policy will have the same healing tendency with yours.
I foresee, I think, that it will be either King, if Johnson is put
at the Treasy: or E. Rutlege, if Walcot should be put there. I
am glad the President rightly infers my determination from
antecedent circumstances, so as to free me from imputations
in his mind connected with the present state of things.
Monroe is particularly solicitous that you should take the view
of your present position & opportunities above suggested.
He sees so forcibly the difficulty of keeping the feelings of
the people as to Genèt distinct from those due to his Con-

stituents, that he can hardly prevail on himself absolutely, and *openly*, to abandon him. I concur with him that it ought to be done no further than is forced upon us, that in general silence is better than open denunciation and crimination; and that it is not unfair to admit the apologetic influence of the errors in our own Government which may have inflamed the passions which now discolor every object to his eye: such as the refusal in the outset of the Government to favor the commerce of F. more than that of G. B—the unfortunate appt. of G. M. to the former: the language of the proclamation—the attempts of Pacificus to explain away & dissolve the Treaty, the notoriety of the Author, and the appearance of its being an informal manifestation of the views of the Ex. &c.

I paid a short visit to Mr. W. N. as I proposed. He talks like a sound Republican, and sincere friend to the French cause in every respect. I collected from him that E. R. had admitted to him that he drew the Procln., that he had been attacked on it at Chatham by Mr. Jos: Jones, that he reprobated the comment of Pac–f–s–&c. W. N observed that H. had taken the Ex. in by gaining phrases of which he could make the use he has done. The circumstances which derogate from full confidence in W. N. are 1st. his being embarked in a variety of projects which call for money, and keep him in intercourse with the merchts. of Richd. 2d. his communication & intimacy with Marshal of whose *disinterestedness* as well as understanding he has the highest opinion. It is said, that Marshal who is at the head of the great purchase from Fairfax, has lately obtained pecuniary aids from the Bank or people connected with it. I think it certain that he must have felt, in the moment of the purchase an absolute dependence on the monied interest, which will explain him to every one that reflects, in the active character he is assuming. I have been obliged to write this in great haste, the bearer impatiently waiting the whole time.

I hope you have rcd. the five Nos. of Hel–v–d–s. I must resume the task I suppose, in relation to the *Treaty*—& *Gratitude*. I feel however so much awkwardness under the new posture of things, that I shall deliberate whether a considerable postponement at least may not be adviseable. I found also on my return a House full of particular friends who will stay some weeks and receive & return visits from which I can not decently exclude myself. If I sd. perceive it impossible or improper to continue the publication so as to avail myself the channel used to the press, I shall suspend it till I see & talk with you on the whole matter. Adieu.

To Dolley Payne Todd

Orange Aug: 18. 94. I recd. some days ago your precious favor from Fredg. I can not express, but hope you will conceive the joy it gave me: The delay in hearing of your leaving Hanover which I regarded as the only satisfactory proof of your recovery, had filled me with extreme [   ] disquietude, and the communication of the welcome event was endeared to me by the *stile* in which it was conveyed. I hope you will never have another *deliberation*, on that subject. If the sentiments of my heart can guarantee those of yours, they assure me there can never be a cause for it. Is it not cruel that I should be obliged to mingle with the delicious [   ] your letter the pain [   ]

[   ] I cannot dismiss my fears that his illness may at least be prolonged. On the most favorable supposition, I can not venture to expect that he will be able to travel in less than 10 or 12 days. I should not hesitate to set out without him, tho' in several respects inconvenient were it not forbidden by his utter ignorance of our language, and my being the only person here who knows a word of his; so that in case his illness should continue his distress as well as that of those around him would be inexpressible; to say nothing of the difficulty of following me in the event of his getting well. This adverse incident is the more mortifying as I had spared no efforts and made some sacrifices, to meet you at [   ] than I hoped when we parted. I limited [   ]

[   ] set out. If he so far recovers that I can leave him, without being able in a few days, according to appearances, to travel, I shall then endeavor to proceed without him, and let him make his way after me as well as he can: In the mean time, allow me to hope that this unavoidable delay, will not

extend its influence to the epoch most [   ] and to repeat
the claim which I apprised [   ]

Speech in Congress on
"Self-Created Societies"

Mr. Madison—said he entirely agreed with those gentlemen who had observed that the house should not have advanced into this discussion, if it could have been avoided
—but having proceeded thus far it was indispensably necessary to finish it.

Much delicacy had been thrown into the discussion, in consequence of the chief magistrate; he always regretted the circumstance, when this was the case.

This he observed, was not the first instance of difference in
opinion between the President and this house. It may be recollected that the President dissented both from the Senate
and this House on a particular law (he referred to that apportioning the representatives)—on that occasion he thought
the President right. On the present question, supposing the
President really to entertain the opinion ascribed to him, it
affords no conclusive reason for the House to sacrifice its
own judgment.

It appeared to him, as it did to the gentleman from
Georgia, that there was an innovation in the mode of procedure adopted, on this occasion. The house are on different
ground from that usually taken—members seem to think that
in cases not cognizable by law, there is room for the interposition of the House. He conceived it to be a sound principle
that an action innocent in the eye of the law, could not be the
object of censure to a legislative body. When the people have
formed a constitution, they retain those rights which they
have not expressly delegated. It is a question whether what is
thus retained can be legislated upon. Opinions are not the
objects of legislation. You animadvert on the *abuse* of reserved rights—how far will this go? It may extend to the liberty of speech and of the press.

It is in vain to say that this indiscriminate censure is no

punishment. If it falls on classes or individuals it will be a severe punishment. He wished it to be considered how extremely guarded the constitution was in respect to cases not within its limits. Murder or treason cannot be noticed by the legislature. Is not this proposition, if voted, a vote of attainder? To consider a principle, we must try its nature, and see how far it will go; in the present case he considered the effects of the principle contended for, would be pernicious. If we advert to the nature of republican government, we shall find that the censorial power is in the people over the government, and not in the government over the people.

As he had confidence in the good sense and patriotism of the people, he did not anticipate any lasting evil to result from the publications of these societies; they will stand or fall by the public opinion; no line can be drawn in this case. The law is the only rule of right; what is consistent with that is not punishable; what is not contrary to that, is innocent, or at least not censurable by the legislative body.

With respect to the body of the people, (whether the outrages have proceeded from weakness or wickedness) what has been done, and will be done by the Legislature will have a due effect. If the *proceedings* of the government should not have an effect, will this declaration produce it? The people at large are possessed of proper sentiments on the subject of the insurrection—the whole continent reprobates the conduct of the insurgents, it is not therefore necessary to take the extra step. The press he believed would not be able to shake the confidence of the people in the government. In a republic, light will prevail over darkness, truth over error—he had undoubted confidence in this principle. If it be admitted that the law cannot animadvert on a particular case, neither can we do it. Governments are administered by men—the same degree of purity does not always exist. Honesty of motives may at present prevail—but this affords no assurance that it will always be the case—at a future period a Legislature may exist of a very different complexion from the present; in this view, we ought not by any vote of ours to give support to measures which now we do not hesitate to reprobate. The gentleman from Georgia had anticipated him in several remarks—no such inference can fairly be drawn as that we abandon the

President, should we pass over the whole business. The vote passed this morning for raising a force to compleat the good work of peace order and tranquility begun by the executive, speaks quite a different language from that which has been used to induce an adoption of the principle contended for.

Mr. Madison adverted to precedents—none parallel to the subject before us existed. The inquiry into the failure of the expedition under St. Clair was not in point. In that case the house appointed a Committee of enquiry into the conduct of an individual in the public service—the democratic societies are not. He knew of nothing in the proceedings of the Legislature which warrants the house in saying that institutions, confessedly not illegal, were subjects of legislative censure.

November 27, 1794

To James Monroe

Dear Sir   Philada. Decr. 20. 1795

The last of your favors come to hand bears date Sepr. 8. 1795, of which a duplicate has also been received. The others which it may be proper to acknowledge or reacknowledge, are of Novr. 30th. 1794. which was opened at Halifax, & forwarded to me in that state. Decr. 18. 1794. covering a copy of one of same date to Mr. *Randolph*—Feby. 18. 1795. covering a copy of one of Feby. 12. to the same. Feby. 25 covering a duplicate of ditto. June 13. inclosing a copy of a letter of May 4. from Mr. Short. June 3—28—30. July 26. covering the correspondence with *Jay*—and August 15. As I cannot now give minute answers to each of these letters, & the necessity of them as to most has been superseded, I shall proceed to the object most immediately interesting to you, towit the posture of things here resulting from the embassy of Mr. Jay. The Treaty concluded by him did not arrive till a few days after the 3d. of March which put an end to the last Session of Congs. According to a previous notification to the Senators that branch assembled on the 28th. of June, the contents of the Treaty being in the mean time impenetrably concealed. I understand that it was even witheld from the Secretaries at war & the Treasury, that is Pickering & Wolcot. The Senate after a few week's consultation, ratified the Treaty as you have seen. The injunction of secresy was then dissolved, by a full House, and quickly after restored sub modo, in a thin one. Mr. Mason disregarding the latter vote sent the Treaty to the press, from whence it flew with an electric velocity to every part of the Union. The first impression was universally & simultaneously against it. Even the mercantile body, with an exception of Foreigners & demi-Americans, joined in the general condemnation. Addresses to the P. agst. his ratification, swarmed from all quarters, and without a possibility of preconcert, or party influence. In short it appeared for a while that the latent party in favor of the Treaty, were struck dumb, by the voice of the nation. At length however, doubts began to be thrown out in New York, whether the Treaty was as bad as was represented. The Chamber of commerce proceeded to an address to the P. in which they hinted at war as the tendency of rejecting of rejecting of the Treaty, but rested the decision with the Constituted authorities. The Boston Chamber of Commerce followed the example, as did a few inland villages. For all the details on this subject I refer to the Gazettes which I presume you continue to receive from the Department of State. It appears that the struggle in the public mind was anxiously contemplated by the President, who had bound himself first not to disclose the Treaty till it should be submitted to the Senate, and in the next place, not to refuse his sanction if it should receive that of the Senate. On the receipt here, however of the predatory orders renewed by G. B, the President as we gather from Mr. R's pamphlet was advised not to ratify the Treaty, unless they should be revoked and adhered to this resolution, from the adjournment of the Senate about the last of June till the middle of August. At the latter epoch Mr. Fauchet's intercepted letter became known to him, and as no other circumstance on which a conjecture can be founded has been hinted to the public, his change of opinion, has been referred to some impression made by that letter, or by comments upon it; altho' it cannot easily be explained how the merits of the Treaty, or the demerits of the provision-order could be affected by the one or the other. As soon as it was known that the P. had yielded his ratification, the *British party* were *reinforced* by *those who bowed to* the *name of constituted authorities* and *those who are implicitly devoted to the president*. The principal *merchants of Philadelphia* with *others amounting to about four hundred* took the *lead in an address of approbation*. There is good reason to believe that *many subscriptions* were *obtained by the banks whose directors solicited them* and *by the influence of British capitalists*. In *Baltimore Charlestown* & the *other commercial towns* except *Philadelphia New York and Boston* no similar *proceeding* has *been attainable. Acquiescence has been* inculcated with *more success* by *exaggerated pictures of the public prosperity* an *appeal to the popular feeling for the president* and *the bugbear of war*. Still *however there is* little *doubt that the real sentiment of the mass of the community is hostile to the treaty*. How *far it may prove* im*pregnable* must be left *to events*. A good deal will *depend on the result of the session* & more than *ought on external contingencies*. You will see how the Session opened, in the President's Speech & the answer to it. That you may judge the better on the subject, I add in the margin of the latter, the clause expunged as not true in itself; and as squinting too favorably at the Treaty. This is the only form in which the pulse of the House has been felt. It is *pretty certain that a majority disapprove the treaty* but it is not *yet possible to ascertain their ultimate object* as *matters now lie*. The *speech of the president* was *well adapted to his* view. The *answer* was from a *committee consisting of myself Sedgwick & Seagrove* in the first *instance* with the addition of *two other members* on *the recommitment*. In the first *committee my two colleagues* were *of the treaty party*. And in the *second there was a* willingness to *say all* that *truth would permit*. This explanation will assist you in comprehending the transaction. Since the *answer passed* & was *presented nothing* has been said or *done in relation to the treaty*. It is much to be *feared that the majority against the treaty* will be *broken to pieces* by *lesser & collateral differences*. Some *will say it is too* soon *to take up the* subject *before it is officially presented in its finished form*: Others *will then say it is too late*. The opportunity of *declaring the sense of the House* in the *answer to the speech* was *sacrificed to the* opinion of *some from whom more decision* was expected than will be *experienced*, towards an *immediate consideration of the subject by itself.* The truest *policy seems to be to take up the business as soon as a majority* can be *ascertained but not to risk that* even *on a preliminary question.* What the *real state of opinions is is* now *under enquiry. I am* not *sanguine* as to *the result.* There is a clear *majority who disapprove the treaty* but it *will dwindle* under the *influence of causes well known to* you; more *especially as the states* instead of *backing the wavering* are themselves *rather giving way. Virginia* has indeed *set a firm example* but *Maryland North Carolina* & *New Hampshire* have *counteracted it* & *New York* will soon *follow with some strong proceeding* on *the same* side.

I am glad to find *by your letters that France notwithstanding the late treaty* continues *to be friendly.* A magnanimous conduct will *conduce to her interest as well as ours.* It must *ultimately baffle the* in*sidious projects* for *bartering our honour* and our *trade to British pride* & *British monopoly.* The *fifteenth article of the treaty* is evidently meant to *put Britain* on *a better foot than France* & *prevent a* further *treaty with the latter* since it secures to *Britain gratuitously all privileges* that *may be granted to others for an equivalent* and of *course obliges France* at *her sole expence to include the* interest of *Britain in her future treaties with us.* But if the *treaty should take effect* this *abominable part* will be of *short duration* and in the mean time, something may perhaps *be done toward disconcerting the mischief in some degree.* You will *observe a navigation act is* always *in our power.* The *article relating to the Missisipi* being *permanent* may be *more embarrassing;* yet possibly not *without some antidote for its poison.* I intended to go on in Cypher, but the tediousness obliges me to conclude the present letter, in order to seize a conveyance just known to me. Mr. R's pamphlet is just out. Mr. Tazewell will send that & several other things collected for you, by this conveyance. Pickering is Secretary of State—Chs. Lee Attorney Genl—no Secy. at War. The Senate have negatived Rutledge as chief Justice. Mr. Jones keeps you informed of your private affairs. He & Mr. Jefferson are well. I have just recd. your two favors of Octr. 23 & 24, with the accompaniments, by Mr. Murray. The articles have probably not arrived in the same ship—as Mr. Yard has no information from N. Y. thereon. Accept from Mrs. M. &

myself ten thousand thanks for your & Mrs. Monroe's good-ness—which will, as generally happens probably draw more trouble on you. Mr. Yard & Mrs. Y. well. Your friends at N. Y. so too.

Speech in Congress on the Jay Treaty

Mr. Madison said that the direct proposition before the House, had been so absorbed by the incidental question which had grown out of it, concerning the constitutional authority of Congress in the case of Treaties, that he should confine his present observations to the latter.

On some points there could be no difference of opinion; and there need not, consequently, be any discussion. All are agreed that the sovereignty resides in the people: that the Constitution, as the expression of their will, is the guide & the rule, to the Government; that the distribution of powers made by the Constitution, ought to be sacredly observed by the respective Departments: that the House of Representatives ought to be equally careful to avoid encroachments on the authority given to other departments, and to guard their own authority against encroachments from the other departments: These principles are as evident as they are vital & essential to our political system.

The true question, therefore, before the Committee, was not, whether the will of the people expressed in the Constitution was to be obeyed; but how that will was to be understood; in what manner it had actually divided the powers delegated to the Government; and what construction would best reconcile the several parts of the instrument with each other, and be most consistent with its general spirit & object.

On comparing the several passages in the Constitution, which had been already cited to the Committee, it appeared, that if taken literally and without limit, they must necessarily clash with each other. Certain powers to regulate commerce, to declare war, to raise armies, to borrow money &c &c, are first specifically vested in Congress. The power of making Treaties, which may relate to the same subjects, is afterwards vested in the President and two thirds of the Senate. And it is declared in another place that the Constitution, and the laws of the U. States made in pursuance thereof, and Treaties made or to be made under the authority of the U. States shall be the supreme law of the land: and the judges, in every State, shall be bound thereby, any thing in the Constitution or laws of any State, to the contrary notwithstanding.

The term *supreme*, as applied to Treaties evidently meant a supremacy over the State Constitutions and laws, and not over the Constitution & laws of the U. States. And it was observable that the Judicial authority & the existing laws, alone of the States, fell within the supremacy expressly enjoined. The injunction was not extended to the Legislative authority of the States or to laws requisite to be passed by the States, for giving effect to Treaties; and it might be a problem worthy of the consideration, though not needing the decision of the Committee, in what manner the requisite provisions were to be obtained from the States.

It was to be regretted, he observed, that on a question of such magnitude as the present, there should be any apparent inconsistency or inexplicitness in the Constitution, that could leave room for different constructions. As the case however had happened, all that could be done was to examine the different constructions with accuracy & fairness, according to the rules established therefor, and to adhere to that which should be found most rational, consistent, and satisfactory.

He stated the five following, as all the constructions worthy of notice, that had either been contended for, or were likely to occur.

I. The Treaty-power, and the Congressional power, might be regarded as moving in such separate orbits, and operating on such separate objects, as to be incapable of interfering with, or touching each other.

II. As concurrent powers relating to the same objects; and operating like the power of Congress, & the power of the State Legislatures, in relation to taxes on the same articles.

III As each of them supreme over the other, as it may be the last exercised; like the different assemblies of the people, under the Roman Government, in the form of Centuries, & in the form of Tribes.

IV The Treaty power may be viewed, according to the doctrine maintained by the opponents of the proposition before the Committee, as both unlimited in its objects, and compleatly paramount in its authority.

V. The Congressional power may be viewed as co-operative with the Treaty-power, on the Legislative subjects submitted to Congress by the Constitution; in the manner explained by the member from Pennsylvania (Mr. Galatin) and exemplified in the British Government.

The objection to the *First* construction is, that it would narrow too much the Treaty-power, to exclude from Treaties altogether, the enumerated subjects submitted to the power of Congress; some or other of this class of regulations being generally comprized in the important compacts which take place between nations.

The objection to the *Second* is, that a concurrent exercise of the Treaty, & Legislative powers, on the same objects, would be evidently impracticable. In the case of taxes laid both by Congress and by the State Legislatures on the same articles, the Constitution presumed that the concurrent authorities might be exercised with such prudence and moderation as would avoid an interference between their respective regulations. But it was manifest that such an interference would be unavoidable between the Treaty power & the power of Congress. A Treaty of commerce for example, would rarely be made, that would not trench on existing legal regulations, as well as be a bar to future ones.

To the *Third*, the objection was equally fatal; that it involved the absurdity of an Imperium in imperio; of two powers both of them supreme, yet each of them liable to be superseded by the other. There was indeed an instance of this kind found in the Government of Ancient Rome, where the two Authorities of the Comitia Curiata, or meetings by Centuries and the Comitia tributa or meetings by tribes, were each possessed of the supreme Legislative power, and could each annul the proceedings of the other: For altho the people composed the body of the meetings in both cases, yet as they voted in one according to wealth, and in the other according to numbers, the organizations were so distinct as to create in fact, two distinct authorities. But it was not necessary to dwell on this political phenomenon, which had been celebrated as a subject of curious speculation only, and not as a model for the institutions of any other Country.

The *Fourth* construction is that which is contended for by the opponents of the proposition depending; and which gives to the Treaty-power all the latitude which is not necessarily prohibited by a regard to the general form & fundamental principles of the Constitution.

In order to smooth the way for this doctrine, it had been Said, that the power to make treaties was laid down in the most indefinite terms; & that the power to make laws, was no limitation to it, because the two powers were essentially different in their nature. If there was ingenuity in this distinction, it was all the merit it could have: for it must be obvious that it could neither be reduced to practice, nor be reconciled to principles. Treaties and laws, whatever the nature of them may be, must in their operation, be often the same. Regulations by Treaty, if carried into effect, are laws. If Congress pass acts relating to provisions in a Treaty, so as to become incorporated with the Treaty, they are not the less laws on that account. A legislative act is the same whether performed by this or that body, or whether it be grounded on the consideration that a foreign nation agrees to pass a like act, or on any other consideration.

It must be objected to this construction therefore that it extends the Power of the President & Senate too far, and cramps the powers of Congress too much.

He did not admit, that the term "Treaty" had the extensive and unlimited meaning which some seemed to claim for it. It was to be considered as a Technical term, and its meaning was to be sought for in the use of it, particularly in Governments which bore most analogy to our own. In absolute Governments, where the whole power of the Nation is usurped by the Government, and all the Departments of power are united in the same person, the Treaty power has no bounds, because the power of the Sovereign to execute it has none. In limited Governments, the case is different. The Treaty power, if undefined is not understood to be unlimited. In Great Britain it is positively restrained on the subjects of money, and dismembering the Empire. Nor could the Executive there, if his recollection was right, make an Alien a subject by means of a Treaty.

But the question immediately under consideration, and which the context & spirit of the Constitution must decide, turned on the extent of the Treaty-power in relation to the objects *specifically & expressly* submitted to the *Legislative power of Congress.*

It was an important, & appeared to him to be a decisive view of the subject, that if the Treaty-power alone could perform any one act for which the authority of Congress is required by the Constitution, it may perform every act for which the authority of that part of the Government is required. Congress have power to regulate trade, to declare war, to raise armies, to levy, borrow, and appropriate money, &c. If by Treaty therefore, as paramount to the Legislative power, the President & Senate can regulate Trade; they can also declare war; they can raise armies to carry on war; and they can procure money to support armies. These powers, however different in their nature or importance, are on the same footing in the Constitution, and must share the same fate. A member from Connecticut (Mr. Griswold) had admitted that the power of war, was exclusively vested in Congress; but he had not attempted, nor did it seem possible, to draw any line between that, & the other enumerated powers. If any line could be drawn, it ought to be presented to the Committee; and he should, for one, be ready to give it the most impartial consideration. He had not, however, any expectation that such an attempt could succeed: and therefore should submit to the serious consideration of the Committee, that although the Constitution had carefully & jealously lodged the power of war, of armies, of the purse &c. in Congress, of which the immediate representatives of the people, formed an integral part; yet, according to the construction maintained on the other side, The President & Senate by means of a Treaty of alliance with a nation at war, might make the United States parties in the war: they might stipulate subsidies, and even borrow money to pay them: they might furnish Troops, to be carried to Europe, Asia or Africa: they might even undertake to keep up a standing army in time of peace, for the purpose of co-operating, on given contingences, with an Ally, for mutual safety or other common objects. Under this aspect, the Treaty power would be tremendous indeed.

The force of this reasoning is not obviated by saying that the P. & Senate would only pledge the public faith & that the agency of Congress would be necessary to carry it into operation. For, what difference does this make, if the obligation imposed be as is alledged, a *constitutional* one; if Congress have no will but to obey, & if to *disobey* be *Treason* & *rebellion* against the Constituted Authorities. Under a constitutional Obligation, with such sanctions to it, Congress, in case the P. & S. should enter into an alliance for war, would be nothing more than the mere heralds for proclaiming it. In fact it had been said that they must obey the injunctions of a Treaty as implicitly as a subordinate officer in the Executive line was bound to obey the chief Magistrate; or as the Judges are bound, to decide according to the laws.

As a further objection to the doctrine contended for, he called the attention of the Committee to another very serious consequence from it. The specific powers, as vested in Congress by the Constitution, are qualified by sundry exceptions deemed of great importance to the safe exercise of them. These restrictions are contained in §IX of the Constitution, and in the articles of amendment which have been added to it. Thus "the migration or importation of such persons as any of the States shall think proper to admit, shall not be prohibited *by Congress.*" He referred to several of the other restrictive paragraphs which followed, particularly the 5th. which says that no tax shall be laid on exports, & no preference given to ports of one State over those of another &c. It was *Congress* also he observed which was to make no law respecting an establishment of Religion, or prohibiting the free exercise thereof, or abridging the freedom of speech, or of the press; or the right of the people peaceably to assemble, &c &c. Now if the legislative powers specifically vested in Congress, are to be no limitation or check to the Treaty power, it was evident that the exceptions to those powers, could be no limitation or check to the Treaty power.

Returning to the powers particularly lodged in Congress, he took notice of those relating to war & money, or the sword & the purse as requiring a few additional observations, in order to shew that the Treaty power could not be paramount over them.

It was well known that with respect to the regulation of Commerce, it had long remained under the jurisdiction of the

States; and that in the establishment of the present Government the question was, whether & how far it should be transferred to the general jurisdiction. But with respect to the power of making war, it had, from the commencement of the Revolution, been judged & exercised as a branch of the General Authority, essential to the public safety. The only question therefore that could arise, was whether the power should be lodged in this or in that Department of the Federal Government. And we find it expressly vested in the Legislative, and not in the Executive Department; with a view, no doubt, to guard it against the abuses which might be apprehended from placing the power of declaring war, in those hands which would conduct it when declared, and which therefore in the ordinary course of things would be most tempted to go into war. But according to the doctrine now maintained, the United States, by means of an Alliance with a foreign power, might be driven into a State of war, by the President & Senate, contrary both to the sense of the Legislature, & to the letter & spirit of the Constitution.

On the subject also of appropriating money, particularly to a military establishment, the provision of the Constitution demanded the most severe attention. To prevent the continuance of a Military force for a longer term than might be indispensable, it is expressly declared that no appropriation for the support of armies shall be made for more than two years: so that at the end of every two years, the question whether a military force ought to be continued or not, must be open for consideration, and can be decided in the negative by either the House of Representatives, or the Senate's refusing to concur in the requisite appropriations. This is a most important check & security agst. the danger of standing armies, & against the prosecution of a war beyond its rational objects; and the efficacy of the precaution is the greater, as at the end of every two years, a re-election of the House of Representatives gives the people an opportunity of judging on the occasion for themselves. But if, as is contended, the House of Represents. have no right to *deliberate* on appropriations pledged by the President & Senate, and cannot refuse them, without a breach of the Constitution and of their oaths, the case is precisely the same, and the same effects would follow, as if the appropriation were not limited to two years, but made for the whole period contemplated at once. Where would be the check of a biennial appropriation for a military establishment raised for four years, if at the expiration of two years, the appropriation was to be continued by a constitutional necessity for two years more? It is evident that no real difference can exist between an appropriation for four years at once, & two appropriations for two years each, the second of which the two Houses would be *constitutionally obliged* to make.

It has been said that in all cases a law must either be repealed, or its execution provided for. Whatever respect might be due to this principle in general he denied that it could be applicable to the case in question. By the provision of the Constitution limiting appropriations to two years, it was clearly intended to enable *either branch* of the Legislature to *discontinue* a military force at the end of every two years. If the law establishing it, must be necessarily repealed, before an appropriation could be witheld, it would be in the power of *either* Branch to *keep up* an establishment by refusing to concur in a repeal. The construction and reasoning therefore opposed to the rights of the House, would evidently defeat an essential provision of the Constitution.

The Constitution of the U. States is a Constitution of limitations and checks. The powers given up by the people for the purposes of Government, had been divided into two great classes. One of these, formed the State Governments, the other the Federal Government. The powers of the Government had been further divided into three great Departments; and the Legislative department again subdivided into two independent branches. Around each of these portions of power, were seen also, exceptions and qualifications, as additional guards against the abuses to which power is liable. With a view to this policy of the Constitution, it could not be unreasonable, if the clauses under discussion were thought doubtful, to lean towards a construction that would limit & controul the Treaty-making power, rather than towards one that would make it omnipotent.

He came next to the *Fifth* Construction which left with the President & Senate the power of making Treaties, but

required at the same time the Legislative sanction & co-operation, in those cases where the Constitution had given express
& specific powers to the Legislature. It was to be presumed
that in all such cases, the Legislature would excise its authority with discretion, allowing due weight to the reasons which
led to the Treaty, and to the circumstance of the existence of
the Treaty. Still, however, this House in its Legislative capacity, must exercise its reason; it must deliberate; for deliberation is implied in Legislation. If it *must*, carry all Treaties into
effect, it would no longer exercise a legislative power: it
would be the mere instrument of the will of another Department, and would have no will of its own. Where the
Constitution contains a specific & peremptory injunction on
Congress to do a particular act, Congress must of course do
the act, because the Constitution, which is paramount over all
the Departments, has *expressly taken away* the Legislative discretion of Congress. The case is essentially different where the
act of one Department of Government interferes with a
power expressly vested in another and no where expressly
taken away. Here the latter power must be exercised according to its nature; and if it be a Legislative power, it must be
exercised with that deliberation & discretion which is essential
to the nature of Legislative power.

It was said yesterday that a Treaty was paramount to all
other Acts of Government, because all power resided in the
people, and the President & Senate, in making a Treaty, being the Constitutional organs of the people for that purpose,
a Treaty when made was the act of the people. The argument
was as strong the other way. Congress are as much the organs
of the people, in making laws, as the President & Senate can
be in making Treaties; and laws, when made are as much the
acts of the people, as any acts whatever can be.

It had been objected, that the Treaty-power would be in
fact frustrated, if Treaties were to depend in any degree on
the Legislature. He thought there was no such danger. The
several powers vested in the several Departments form but
one Government; and the will of the nation may be expressed
thro' one Government, operating under certain checks, on
the subject of Treaties, as well as under other checks on other

subjects. The objection would have weight if the voluntary cooperation of the different States was to be obtained.

Another objection was that no Treaty could be made at all, if the agency of Congress were to concur, because Congress could not Treat, and their Agency would not be of a Treaty nature. He would not stop to enquire how far a loan of money from a foreign Government, under a law of Congress, was or was not of the nature of a public Contract or Treaty. It was more proper to observe, that the practice in G. Britain was an evidence that a Legislative Agency did not viciate a Treaty. Nay, if the Objection were solid, it was evident that the Treaty lately entered into with that Nation, could never be binding on this; because, it had been laid before the Parliament for its Legislative agency as necessary to effectuate the Treaty; and if that agency was to viciate & destroy the nature of the Treaty on that side, the obligation, on the principle of all contracts, would be dissolved on both sides.

He did not see the utility in this case of urging, as had been done, a particular distrust of the House of Representatives. He thought the President & Senate would be as likely to make a bad Treaty, as this Branch of the Government would be to throw obstructions in the way of a good one, after it was made.

No construction he said might be perfectly free from difficulties. That which he had espoused, was subject to the least; as it gave signification to every part of the Constitution, was most consistent with its general spirit, and was most likely in practice to promote the great object of it, the public good. The construction which made the Treaty power in a manner omnipotent he thought utterly inadmissible, in a Constitution marked throughout with limitations & checks.

He should not at present he said, enter any further into the subject. It had been brought before the House rather earlier than he had expected or than was perhaps necessary; and his observations therefore might not have been as full or as well digested, as they ought to have been; such as they were he submitted them to the candid attention of the Committee.

March 10, 1796

Speech in Congress on the Jay Treaty

When the message was first proposed to be committed, the proposition had been treated by some gentlemen not only with levity, but with ridicule. He persuaded himself that the subject would appear in a very different light to the committee; and he hoped that it would be discussed on both sides, without either levity, intemperance or illiberality.

If there were any question which could make a serious appeal to the dispassionate judgement, it must be one which respected the meaning of the constitution; and if any constitutional question could, make the appeal with peculiar solemnity, it must be in a case like the present, where two of the constituted authorities interpreted differently the extent of their respective powers.

It was a consolation however, of which every member would be sensible, to reflect on the happy difference of our situation, on such occurrences, from that of governments, in which the constituent members possessed independent and hereditary prerogatives. In such governments, the parties having a personal interest in their public stations, and being not amenable to the national will, disputes concerning the limits of their respective authorities, might be productive of the most fatal consequences. With us, on the contrary, although disputes of that kind are always to be regretted, there were three most precious resources, against the evil tendency of them. In the first place, the responsibility which every department feels to the public will, under the forms of the constitution, may be expected to prevent the excesses incident to conflicts between rival and unresponsible authorities. In the next place, if the difference cannot be adjusted by friendly conference and mutual concession, the sense of the constituent body, brought into the government through the ordinary elective channels, may supply a remedy. And if this resource should fail, there remains in the third and last place, that provident article in the constitution itself, by which an avenue is always open to the sovereignty of the People for explanations or amendments as they might be found indispensable.

If, in the present instance, it was to be particularly regretted, that the existing difference of opinion had arisen; every motive to the regret, was a motive to calmness, to candor, and the most respectful delicacy towards the other constituted authority. On the other hand, the duty which the House of Representatives must feel to themselves and to their constituents, required that they should examine the subject with accuracy, as well as with candor, and decide on it with firmness, as well as with moderation.

In this temper he should proceed to make some observations on the message before the committee, and on the reasons contained in it.

The message related to two points: first, the application made for the papers; secondly the constitutional rights of Congress and of the House of Representatives, on the subject of treaties.

On the first point, he observed that the right of the house to apply for any information they might want, had been admitted by a number in the minority, who had opposed the exercise of the right in this particular case. He thought it clear that the house must have a right, in all cases, to ask for information, which might assist their deliberations on subjects submitted to them by the constitution; being responsible nevertheless for the propriety of the measure. He was as ready to admit, that the executive had a right under a due responsibility also, to withhold information, when of a nature that did not permit a disclosure of it at the time. And if the refusal of the President had been founded simply on a representation, that the state of the business within his department, and the contents of the Papers asked for, required it, although he might have regretted the refusal, he should have been little disposed to criticize it. But the message had contested what appeared to him a clear and important right of the house; and stated reasons for refusing the papers, which, with all the respect he could feel for the executive, he could not regard as satisfactory or proper.

One of the reasons, was, that it did not occur to the

executive that the papers could be relative to any purpose under the cognizance, and in the contemplation of the house:
The other was, that the purpose for which they were wanted,
was not expressed in the resolution of the house.

With respect to the first, it implied that the executive was
not only to judge of the proper objects and functions of the
executive department; but also of the objects and functions of
the house. He was not only to decide how far the executive
trust would permit a disclosure of information; but how far
the legislative trust could derive advantage from it. It belonged, he said, to each department to judge for itself.

If the executive conceived that in relation to his own department, papers could not be safely communicated, he might
on that ground refuse them, because he was the competent
though a responsible judge within his own department. If the
papers could be communicated, without injury to the objects
of his department, he ought not to refuse them as irrelative
to the objects of the House of Representatives, because the
House was in such cases the only proper judge of its own
objects.

The other reason of refusal was, that the use which the
house meant to make of the papers, was not expressed in the
resolution.

As far as he could recollect, no precedent could be found in
the records of the house, or elsewhere, in which the particular object in calling for information was expressed in the call.
It was not only contrary to right to require this; but it would
often be improper in the house, to express the object. In the
particular case of an impeachment referred to in the message
it might be evidently improper to state that to be the object
of information which might possibly lead to it, because it
would involve the preposterous idea of first determining to
impeach, and then enquiring whether an impeachment ought
to take place. Even the holding out an impeachment as a contemplated or contingent result of the information called for,
might be extremely disagreeable in practice, as it might inflict
a temporary pain on an individual, whom an investigation of
facts might prove to be innocent, and perhaps meritorious.

From this view of the subject he could not forbear wishing
that, if the papers were to be refused, other reasons had been

assigned for it. He thought the resolutions offered by the gentleman from North Carolina, one of which related to this subject, ought to stand on the Journal along with the message which had been entered there. Both the resolutions were penned with moderation and propriety. They went no farther than to assert the rights of the house; they courted no reply; and it ought not to be supposed they could give any offence.

The second object to which the message related, was the constitutional power of the house on the subject of treaties.

Here again he hoped it might be allowable to wish, that it had not been deemed necessary to take up, in so solemn a manner, a great constitutional question, which was not contained in the resolution presented by the house, which had been incidental only to the discussion of that resolution and which could only have been brought into view through the inauthentic medium of the newspapers. This however, would well account for the misconception which had taken place as to the doctrine maintained by the majority in the late question. It had been understood by the executive, that the house asserted its assent to be necessary to the validity of treaties. This was not the doctrine maintained by them. It was, he believed, fairly laid down in the resolution proposed, which limited the power of the house over treaties, to cases where treaties embraced legislative subjects, submitted by the constitution, to the power of the house.

Mr. M. did not mean to go into the general merits of this question as discussed when the former resolution was before the committee. The message did not require it; having drawn none of its reasoning from the text of the constitution. It had merely affirmed that the power of making treaties is exclusively vested by the constitution in the President, by and with the consent of the Senate. Nothing more was necessary on this point, than to observe that the constitution had, as expressly and exclusively vested in Congress, the power of making laws, as it had vested in the President and Senate the power of making treaties.

He proceeded to review the several topics on which the message relied: First, the intentions of the body which framed the constitution; Secondly, the opinions of the state conventions who adopted it; Thirdly, the peculiar rights and interests of the smaller states; Fourthly, the manner in which the constitution had been understood by the executive and the foreign nations, with which treaties had been formed; Fifthly, the acquiescence and acts of the house on former occasions.

1. When the members on the floor, who were members of the general convention, particularly a member from Georgia and himself, were called on in a former debate, for the sense of that body on the constitutional question, it was a matter of some surprize; which was much increased by the peculiar stress laid on the information expected. He acknowledged his surprise also at seeing the message of the executive appealing to the same proceedings in the general convention, as a clue to the meaning of the constitution.

It had been his purpose during the late debate to make some observations on what had fallen from the gentlemen from Connecticut and Maryland, if the sudden termination of the debate had not cut him off, from the opportunity. He should have reminded them, that this was the ninth year, since the convention executed their trust, and that he had not a single note in this place, to assist his memory. He should have remarked that neither himself nor the other members who had belonged to the federal convention, could be under any particular obligation to rise in answer to a few gentlemen, with information not merely of their own ideas at that period, but of the intention of the whole body: many members of which too had probably never entered into the discussions of the subject. He might have further remarked that there would be the more delicacy in the undertaking, as it appeared that a sense had been put on the constitution by some who were members of the convention, different from that which must have been entertained by others, who had concurred in ratifying the treaty. After taking notice of the doctrine (of Judge Wilson, who was a member of the federal convention, as quoted by Mr. Gallatin) from the Pennsylvania debates; he proceeded to mention that three gentlemen who had been members of the convention were parties to the proceedings in Charleston, S.C. which among other objections to the treaty, represented it as violating the constitution. That the very respectable citizen, who presided at the meeting in Wilmington, whose resolutions made a similar complaint, had also been a

distinguished member of the body that formed the constitution. It would have been proper for him also to have recollected what had, on a former occasion, happened to himself
during a debate in the house of representatives. When the bill
for establishing a national bank was under consideration, he
had opposed it as not warranted by the constitution, and in-
cidentally remarked that his impression might be stronger, as
he remembered that in the convention, a motion was made
and negatived for giving Congress a power to grant charters
of incorporation. This slight reference to the convention, he
said was animadverted on by several in the course of the debate, and particularly by a gentleman from Massachusetts,
who had himself been a member of the convention, and
whose remarks were not unworthy the attention of the committee. Here Mr. M. read a paragraph in Mr. Gerry's speech,
from the Gazette of the United States, p. 814, protesting in
strong terms, against arguments drawn from that source.

Mr. M. said he did not believe a single instance could be
cited in which the sense of the convention had been required
or admitted as material, in any constitutional question. In the
case of the bank, the committee had seen how a glance at that
authority had been treated in this house. When the question
on the suability of the states was depending on the supreme
court, he asked whether it had ever been understood that the
members of the bench who had been members of the convention, were called on for the meaning of the convention on
that very important point; although no constitutional question would be presumed more susceptible of elucidation from
that source.

He then adverted to that part of the message which contained an extract from the journal of the convention, shewing
that a proposition "that no treaty should be binding on the
United States, which was not ratified by law," was explicitly
rejected. He allowed this to be much more precise than any
evidence drawn from the debates in the convention, or resting on the memory of individuals. But admitting the case to
be as stated, of which he had no doubt, altho' he had no recollection of it; and admitting the record of the convention to
be the oracle that ought to decide the true meaning of the
constitution, what did this abstract vote amount to? Did it

condemn the doctrine of the majority? So far from it, that as he understood their doctrine, they must have voted as the convention did: For they do not contend that *no* treaty shall be operative without a law to sanction it; on the contrary they admit that *some* treaties will operate without this sanction; and that it is no further applicable in any case, than where legislative objects are embraced by treaties. The term *ratify* also deserved some attention, for altho' of loose signification in general, it had a technical meaning different from the agency claimed by the house on the subject of treaties.

But, after all, whatever veneration might be entertained for the body of men who formed our constitution, the sense of that body could never be regarded as the oracular guide in the expounding the constitution. As the instrument came from them, it was nothing more than the draught of a plan, nothing but a dead letter, until life and validity were breathed into it, by the voice of the people, speaking through the several state conventions. If we were to look therefore, for the meaning of the instrument, beyond the face of the instrument, we must look for it not in the general convention, which proposed, but in the state conventions, which accepted and ratified the constitution. To these also the message had referred, and it would be proper to follow it.

2. The debates of the conventions in three states, Pennsylvania, Virginia, and N. Carolina, had been before introduced into the discussion of this subject, and were he believed the only publications of the sort which contained any lights with respect to it. He would not fatigue the committee with a repetition of the passages then read to them. He would only appeal to the committee to decide whether it did not appear from a candid and collected view of the debates in those conventions, and particularly in that of Virginia that the treaty making power was a limited power; and that the powers in our constitution, on this subject, bore an analogy to the powers on the same subject, in the government of G. Britain. He wished as little as any member could, to extend the analogies between the two governments. But it was clear that the constituent parts of two governments might be perfectly heterogenous, and yet the powers be similar. At once to illustrate his meaning, and give a brief reply to some arguments on the

other side, which had heretofore been urged with ingenuity and learning, he would mention as an example, the power of pardoning offences. This power was vested in the President. It was a prerogative also of the British king. And in order to ascertain the extent of the compound and technical term "pardon" in our constitution; it would not be irregular to search into the meaning and exercise of the power in Great Britain; yet where is the general analogy between an hereditary sovereign, not accountable for his conduct, and a magistrate, like the President of the United States, elected for four years, with limited powers, and liable to impeachment for the abuse of them.

In referring to the debates of the state conventions as published, he wished not to be understood as putting entire confidence in the accuracy of them. Even those of Virginia which had been probably taken down by the most skilful hand, (whose merit he wished by no means to disparage) contained internal evidences in abundance of chasms, and misconceptions of what was said.

The amendments proposed by the several conventions, were better authority and would be found on a general view to favour the sense of the constitution which had prevailed in this house. But even here it would not be reasonable to expect a perfect precision and system in all their votes and proceedings. The agitations of the public mind on that occasion, with the hurry and compromise which generally prevailed in settling the amendments to be proposed, would at once explain and apologize for the several apparent inconsistencies which might be discovered. He would not undertake to say that the particular amendment referred to in the message by which two states required that "no commercial treaty should be ratified without the consent of two thirds of *the whole number* of Senators; and that no territorial rights &c. should be ceded without the consent of *three fourths* of the members of both houses" was digested with an accurate attention to the whole subject. On the other hand it was no proof that those particular conventions in annexing these guards to the treaty power understood it as different from that espoused by the majority of the house. They might consider Congress as having the power contended for over treaties stipulating on

Legislative subjects, and still very consistently wish for the amendment they proposed. They might not consider the territorial rights and other objects for which they required the concurrence of three fourths of the members of both houses, as coming within any of the enumerated powers of Congress, and therefore as not protected by that control over treaties. And although they might be sensible that commercial treaties were under that controul, yet as they would always come before Congress with great weight after they passed through the regular forms and sanctions of the treaty department, it might be deemed of real importance that the authority should be better guarded which was to give that weight to them. He asked whether it might not happen, even in the progress of a treaty through the treaty department, that each succeeding sanction might be given, more on account of preceding sanctions than of any positive approbation? And no one could doubt therefore that a treaty which had received all these sanctions would be controuled with great reluctance by the Legislature; and consequently that it might be desirable to strengthen the barriers against making improper treaties, rather than trust too much to the Legislative controul over carrying them into effect.

But said Mr. M. it will be proper to attend to other amendments proposed by the ratifying conventions, which may throw light on their opinions and intentions on the subject in question. He then read from the Declaration of Rights proposed by Virginia to be prefixed to the constitution, the 7th article as follows.

"That *all* power of suspending laws, or the execution of laws by *any* authority without the consent of the *Representatives* of the people in the *Legislature*, is injurious to their rights, and ought not to be exercised."

The convention of North Carolina, as he shewed, had laid down the same principle in the same words. And it was to be observed that in both conventions, the article was under the head of a DECLARATION OF RIGHTS, "asserting and securing from encroachment the essential and inalienable rights of the people" according to the language of the Virginia convention; and "asserting and securing from encroachment the great principles of civil and religious liberty, and the inalienable rights of the people" as expressed by the convention of North Carolina. It must follow, that these two conventions considered it as a fundamental and inviolable and universal principle in free governments, that no power could supercede a law without the consent of the Representatives of the people in the Legislature.

In the Maryland convention also, it was among the amendments proposed, tho' he believed not decided on, "that no power of suspending laws, or the execution of laws, unless derived from the Legislature, ought to be exercised or allowed."

The convention of North Carolina had further explained themselves on this point, by their 23d amendment proposed to the constitution, in the following words, "That no treaties which shall be directly opposed to the existing laws of the United States in Congress assembled, shall be valid until such laws shall be repealed, or made conformable to such treaty; nor shall any treaty be valid which is contradictory to the constitution of the United States."

The latter part of the amendment, was an evidence that the amendment was intended to ascertain, rather than to alter the meaning of the constitution; as it could not be supposed to have been the real intention of the constitution that a treaty contrary to it should be valid.

He proceeded to read the following amendments accompanying the ratifications of state conventions.

The N. York convention had proposed,

"That no standing army or regular troops shall be raised or kept up in time of peace without the consent of *two thirds* of the Senators and Representatives in each house."

"That no money be borrowed on the credit of the United States without the assent of *two thirds* of the Senators and Representatives in each house."

"That the Congress shall not declare war without the concurrence of *two thirds* of the Senators and Representatives present in each house."

The N. Hampshire convention had proposed,

"That no standing army shall be kept up in time of peace unless with the consent of *three quarters* of the members of each branch of Congress." In the Maryland convention a proposition was made in the same words.

The Virginia convention had proposed,

"That no navigation law, or law regulating commerce shall be passed without the consent of *two thirds* of the members present in both houses."

"That no standing army or regular troops shall be raised or kept up in time of peace, without the consent of *two thirds* of the members present in both houses."

"That no soldier shall be enlisted for any longer term than four years, except in time of war, and then for no longer term than the continuance of the war."

The convention of N. Carolina had proposed the same three amendments in the same words.

On a review of these proceedings may not, said he, the question be fairly asked, whether it ought to be supposed that the several conventions, who shewed so much jealousy with respect to the powers of commerce, of the sword, and of the purse, as to require for the exercise of them, in some cases *two thirds*, in others *three fourths*, of both branches of the Legislature, could have understood that by the treaty clauses in the constitution they had given to the President and Senate, without any controul whatever from the House of Representatives, an absolute and unlimited power over all those great objects?

3. It was with great reluctance, he said, that he should touch on the third topic, the alledged interest of the smaller states in the present question. He was the more unwilling to enter into this delicate part of the discussion, as he happened to be from a state which was in one of the extremes in point of size. He should limit himself therefore to two observations. The first was, that if the spirit of amity and mutual concession from which the constitution resulted, was to be consulted on expounding it, that construction ought to be favoured, which would preserve the mutual controul between the Senate and the House of Representatives, rather than that which gave powers to the Senate not controulable by, and paramount over those of the House of Representatives, whilst the House of Representatives could in no instance exercise their powers without the participation and controul of the Senate. The second observation was that whatever jealousy might have unhappily prevailed between the smaller and larger states, as

they had most weight in one or other branch of the government, it was a fact, for which he appealed to the journals of the old congress from its birth to its dissolution, and to those of the Congress under the present government, that in no instance would it appear from the yeas and nays, that a question had been decided by a division of the votes according to the size of the States. He considered this truth as worthy of the most pleasing and consoling reflection, and as one that ought to have the most conciliating and happy influence on the temper of all the states.

4. A fourth argument in the message was drawn from the manner by which the treaty power had been understood in both parties in the negociations with foreign powers. "In all the treaties made *we* have declared and *they* have believed, &c." By *we*, he remarked, was to be understood, the executive alone who had made the declaration, and in no respect, the House of Representatives. It was certainly to be regretted as had often been expressed that different branches of the government should disagree in the construction of their powers; but when this could not be avoided, each branch must judge for itself; and the judgment of the executive could in this case be no more an authority overruling the judgment of the house, than the judgment of the house, could be an authority overruling that of the executive. It was also to be regretted, that any foreign nation should at any time proceed under a misconception of the meaning of our constitution. But no principle was better established in the law of nations, as well as in common reason, than that one nation is not to be the interpreter of the constitution of another. Each nation must adjust the forms and operation of its own government: and all others are bound to understand them accordingly. It had before been remarked, and it would be proper to repeat here, that of all nations Great Britain would be least likely to object to this principle, because the construction given to our government, was particularly exemplified in her own.

5. In the fifth and last place, he had to take notice of the suggestion that every House of Representatives had concurred in the construction of the treaty power, now maintained by the Executive; from which it followed, that the House could not now consistently act under a different construction. On

this point it might be sufficient to remark, that this was the first instance in which a foreign treaty had been made, since the establishment of the constitution; and that this was the first time the treaty making power had come under formal and accurate discussion. Precedents therefore, would readily be seen to lose much of their weight. But whether the precedents found in the proceedings preparatory to the Algerine treaty, or in the provisions relative to the Indian treaties, were inconsistent with the right which had been contended for in behalf of the House, he should leave to be decided by the committee. A view of these precedents had been pretty fully presented to them by a gentleman from New York (Mr. Livingston) with all the observations which the subject seemed to require.

On the whole, it appeared that the rights of the House on two great constitutional points, had been denied by a high authority in the message before the committee. This message was entered on the journals of the House. If nothing was entered in opposition thereto; it would be inferred that the reasons in the message had changed the opinion of the House, and that their claims on those great points were relinquished. It was proper therefore that the questions, brought fairly before the committee in the propositions of the gentleman (Mr. Blount) from North Carolina, should be examined and formally decided. If the reasoning of the message should be deemed satisfactory, it would be the duty of this branch of the government to reject the propositions, and thus accede to the doctrines asserted by the Executive: If on the other hand this reasoning should not be satisfactory, it would be equally the duty of the House, in some such firm, but very decent terms, as are proposed, to enter their opinions on record. In either way, the meaning of the constitution would be established, as far as depends on a vote of the House of Representatives.

April 6, 1796

To Thomas Jefferson

Dear Sir
                                              Philada. Decr. 19. 1796
   The returns from N. Hampshire, Vermont, S. C. &
Georga. are still to come in, & leave the event of the Election
in some remaining uncertainty. It is but barely possible that
Adams may fail of the highest number. It is highly probable,
tho' not absolutely certain, that Pinkney will be third only on
the list. You must prepare yourself therefore to be summoned
to the place Mr. Adams now fills. I am aware of the objections
arising from the inadequateness of the importance of the
place to the sacrifices you would be willing to make to a
greater prospect of fulfilling the patriotic wishes of your
friends; and from the irksomeness of being at the head of a
body whose sentiments are at present so little in unison with
your own. But it is expected that as you had made up your
mind to obey the call of your Country, you will let it decide
on the particular place where your services are to be rendered.
It may even be said, that as you submitted to the election
knowing the contingency involved in it, you are bound to
abide by the event whatever it may be. On the whole it seems
essential that you should not refuse the station which is likely
to be your lot. There is reason to believe also that your neighbourhood to *Adams* may *have a valuable effect on his councils*
particularly in *relation to our external system.* You know that
his feelings will not *enslave him to the* example of *his predecessor.* It is certain that his *censures of our paper systems* & the
intrigues at *New York for setting P. above him* have fixed an *enmity with the British faction.* Nor should it pass for nothing,
that the true *interest of New England* particularly requires
reconciliation with France as the road to her commerce. *Add
to the whole that he* is said to speak of *you now in friendly terms*
and will no doubt be *soothed by your acceptance of a place subordinate to him.* It must be confessed however that all these
calculations, are qualified by *his political principles* and *prejudices.* But they add weight to the *obligation from which you
must not withdraw yourself.*
   You will see in the answer to the P.s speech, much *room
for criticism.* You must, for the present, be *content to know
that it resulted from a choice of evils. His reply to the* foreign

paragraph indicates a good effect *on his mind.* Indeed *he cannot but wish to avoid entailing a war on his successor.* The *danger lies in the* fetters *he has put on himself* & *in the irritation* & *distrust of the French government.*

To Thomas Jefferson

Dear Sir   Philada. Jany. 15. 1797.

The last mail brought me your favor of Jany. 1. inclosing an unsealed one for Mr. A. & submitting to my discretion the eligibility of delivering it. In exercising this delicate trust I have felt no small anxiety, arising by no means however from an apprehension that a free exercise of it could be in collision with your real purpose, but from a want of confidence in myself, & the importance of a wrong judgment in the case. After the best consideration I have been able to bestow, I have been led to suspend the delivery of the letter, till you should have an opportunity of deciding on the sufficiency or insufficiency of the following reasons. 1. It is certain that Mr. Adams, on his coming to this place, expressed to different persons a respectful cordiality towards you, & manifested a sensibility to the candid manner in which your friends had in general conducted the opposition to him. And it is equally known that your sentiments towards him personally have found their way to him in the most conciliating form. This being the state of things between you, it deserves to be considered whether the idea of bettering it is not outweighed by the possibility of changing it for the worse. 2. There is perhaps a general air on the letter which betrays the difficulty of your situation in writing it, and it is uncertain what the impression might be resulting from this appearance. 3 It is certain that Mr. A. is fully apprized of the trick aimed at by his pseudo-friends of N. Y: and there may be danger of his suspecting in memento's on that subject, a wish to make his resentment an instrument for avenging that of others. A hint of this kind was some time ago dropped by a judicious & sound man who lives under the same roof, with a wish that even the Newspapers might be silent on that point. 4. May not what is said of "the sublime delights of riding in the storm &c." be misconstrued into a reflexion on those who have no distaste to the helm at the present crisis? You know the temper of Mr. A. better than I do: but I have always conceived it to be rather a ticklish one. 5. The tenderness due to the zealous & active promoters of your election, makes it doubtful whether, their anxieties & exertions ought to be depreciated by any thing implying the unreasonableness of them. I know that some individuals who have deeply committed themselves, & probably incurred the political enmity at least of the P. elect, are already sore on this head. 6. Considering the probability that Mr. A.s course of administration may force an opposition to it from the Republican quarter, & the general uncertainty of the posture which our affairs may take, there may be real embarrassments from giving written possession to him, of the degree of compliment & confidence which your personal delicacy & friendship have suggested.

I have ventured to make these observations, because I am sure you will equally appreciate the motive & the matter of them; and because I do not view them as inconsistent with the duty & policy of cultivating Mr. Adam's favorable dispositions, and giving a fair start to his Executive career. As you have, no doubt, retained a copy of the letter I do not send it back as you request. It occurs however that, if the subject should not be changed in your view of it, by the reasons which influence mine, & the delivery of the letter be accordingly judged expedient, it may not be amiss to alter the date of it; either by writing the whole over again, or authorizing me to correct that part of it.

The special communication is still unmade. It is I am told to be extremely voluminous. I hope, under the sanction of the P.'s reply to our address, that it will be calculated rather to heal than irritate the wounded friendship of the two countries. Yet, I cannot look around at the men who counsel him, or look back at the snares into which he has hitherto been drawn without great apprehensions on this subject. Nothing from France subsequent to the arrival of Pinkney. The negociations for peace you will see are suspended. The accession of Spain to the war enforces the probability that its calamities are not likely yet to be terminated. The late News from the Rhine

& from Italy are on the whole favorable to the French. The last battle was on the 27 Ocr. in the Hunspruck, and ended in a victory on their side. The House of Rep: are on direct taxes, which seem to be so much nauseated & feared by those who have created both the necessity & odium of them, that the project will miscarry. Hamilton, you will recollect assured the farmers that all the purposes of the Govt. could be answered without resorting to lands Houses or stock on farms. This deceptive statement with other devices of his administration, is rising up in judgment agst. him & will very probably soon blast the prospects which his ambition & intrigues have contemplated. It is certain that he has lost ground in N. Y. of late; & his treachery to Adams, will open the eyes of N. England.

To Thomas Jefferson

Dear Sir

Since my last I have recd. yours of Feby. 8. with a continuation of the Gazettes down to that date, with the exception only mentioned already, of the gazette of Jany. 23. I am glad to find the public opinion to be taking the turn you describe on the subject of arming. For the public opinion alone can now save us from the rash measures of our hot-heated Executive; it being evident from some late votes of the House of Reps. particularly in the choice of Managers for the Impeachment, that a majority there as well as in the Senate are ready to go as far as the controul of their Constituents will permit. There never was perhaps a greater contrast between two characters, than between those of the present President & of his predecessor, altho' it is the boast & prop of the latter, that he treads in the steps of the former: The one cold considerate & cautious, the other headlong & kindled into flame by every spark that lights on his passions: the one ever scrutinizing into the public opinion, and ready to follow where he could not lead it: the other insulting it by the most adverse sentiments & pursuits: W. a hero in the field, yet overweighing every danger in the Cabinet—A. without a single pretension to the character of Soldier, a perfect Quixotte as a Statesman: the former cheif Magistrate pursuing peace every where with sincerity, tho' mistaking the means: the latter taking as much pains to get into war, as the former took to keep out of it. The contrast might be pursued into a variety of other particulars—the policy of the one in shunning connections with the arrangements of Europe, of the other in holding out the U. S. as a makeweight in its Balances of power: the avowed exultation of W. in the progress of liberty every where, & his eulogy on the Revolution & people of France posterior even to the bloody reign & fate of Robespierre—the open denunciations by Adams of the smallest disturbance of the antient discipline order & tranquility of Despotism, &c &c &c. The affair of Lyon & Griswold is bad eno' every way; but worst of all in becoming a topic of tedious & disgraceful debates in Congress. There certainly could be no necessity for removing it from the decision of the parties themselves before that tribunal, & its removal was evidently a sacrifice of the dignity of the latter, to the party-manœuvres of ruining a man whose popularity & activity were feared. If the state of the House suspended its rules in general, it was under no obligation to see any irregularity which did not force itself into public notice—and if Griswold be a man of the sword, he shd. not have permitted the step to be taken; if not he does not deserve to be avenged by the House. No man ought to reproach another with cowardice, who is not ready to give proof of his own courage. I have taken some pains but in vain to find out a person who will engage to carry the Mail from Fredg to Charlottesville. When I was in the neighbourhood of the latter I suggested the propriety of an effort there for the purpose, but do not know that it will be more successful. Our Winter has continued without snow & rather dry, and our Wheat-fields wear the most discouraging aspect. Adieu

c. February 18, 1798

To Thomas Jefferson

Dear Sir   April 2d. 1797

Since my last I am in debt for your two favors of the 15th. & 22, the Gazettes of the 3. 6 7 & 8 Ulto, with a regular continuation to the 22d—two statements from the Treasury Department, and Payne's letter to the French people & armies. The President's message is only a further developement to the public, of the violent passions, & heretical politics, which have been long privately known to govern him. It is to be hoped however that the H. of Reps. will not hastily eccho them. At least it may be expected that before war measures are instituted, they will recollect the principle asserted by 62 vs. 37. in the case of the Treaty, and insist on a full communication of the intelligence on which such measures are recommended. The present is a plainer, if it be not a stronger case, and if there has been sufficient defection to destroy the majority which was then so great & so decided, it is the worst symptom that has yet appeared in our Councils. The constitution supposes, what the History of all Govts. demonstrates, that the Ex. is the branch of power most interested in war, & most prone to it. It has accordingly with studied care, vested the question of war in the Legisl: But the Doctrines lately advanced strike at the root of all these provisions, and will deposit the peace of the Country in that Department which the Constitution distrusts as most ready without cause to renounce it. For if the opinion of the P. not the facts & proofs themselves are to sway the judgment of Congress in declaring war, and if the President in the recess of Congress create a foreign mission, appt. the minister, & negociate a War Treaty, without the possibility of a check even from the Senate, untill the measures present alternatives overruling the freedom of its judgment; if again a Treaty when made obliges the Legis: to declare war contrary to its judgment, and in pursuance of the same doctrine, a law declaring war, imposes a like moral obligation, to grant the requisite supplies, until it be formally repealed with the consent of the P. & Senate, it is evident that the people are cheated out of the best ingredients in their Govt. the safeguards of peace which is the greatest of their blessings. I like both your suggestions in the present crisis.

Congress ought clearly to prohibit arming, & the P. ought to be brought to declare on what ground he undertook to grant an indirect licence to arm. The first instructions were no otherwise legal than as they were in pursuance of the law of Nations, & consequently in execution of the law of the land. The revocation of the instructions is a virtual change of the law, & consequently a Usurpation by the Ex. of a legislative power. It will not avail to say that the law of Nations leaves this point undecided, & that every nation is free to decide it for itself. If this be the case, the regulation being a Legislative not an Executive one, belongs to the former, not the latter Authority; and comes expressly within the power to "define the law of Nations" given to Congress by the Constitution. I do not expect however that the Constitutional party in the H. of R. is strong eno' to do what ought to be done in the present instance. Your 2d idea that an adjournment for the purpose of consulting the Constituents on the subject of war, is more practicable because it can be effected by that branch alone if it pleases, & because an opposition to such a measure, will be more striking to the public eye. The expedient is the more desirable as it will be utterly impossible to call forth the sense of the people generally before the season will be over, especially as the Towns &c. where there can be most despatch in such an operation are on the wrong side; and it is to be feared that a partial expression of the public voice, may be misconstrued or miscalled, an evidence in favor of the war party. On what do you ground the idea that a decln. of war requires ⅔ of the Legislature? The force of your remark however is not diminished by this mistake, for it remains true, that measures are taking or may be taken by the Ex. that will end in war, contrary to the wish of the Body which alone can declare it.

April 2, 1798

To Thomas Jefferson

Dear Sir   May 13. 1798

I have recd. your favor of the 3d. instant. My last acknowl-edged your preceding one. The successful use of the Despatches in kindling a flame among the people, and of the flame in extending taxes armies & prerogative, are solemn lessons which I hope will have their proper effect when the in-fatuation of the moment is over. The management of foreign relations appears to be the most susceptible of abuse, of all the trusts committed to a Government, because they can be con-cealed or disclosed, or disclosed in such parts & at such times as will best suit particular views; and because the body of the people are less capable of judging & are more under the in-fluence of prejudices, on that branch of their affairs, than of any other. Perhaps it is a universal truth that the loss of liberty at home is to be charged to provisions agst. danger real or pretended from abroad. The credit given to Mr. A. for a spirit of conciliation towards France is wonderful, when we advert to the history of his irritations from the first name in the Envoyship, down to his last answer to the addressers. If he finds it thus easy to play on the prepossessions of the people for their own Govt. agst. a foreign, we ought not to be disap-pointed if the same game should have equal success in the hands of the Directory. We have had little or no rain for a month, and the evil has been increased by much windy & cold weather. The Thermr. yesterday morning was at 38°. and the frost such as to kill the leaves of tender trees in low situations. I hope now you will soon be released from the thorny seat in which you are placed, and that I shall not be disappointed of the pleasure of seeing you on your way. You must so arrange your time as to be able to ride a mile while with me to see a Threshing machine I have lately built on Martins plan. It is worked & attended by five or six hands at most, and I think promises more for general use than all the other modifica-tions. I shall not describe it, because your own inspection will so soon give you a more perfect idea of it. Yrs. always & affey

I recd. no paper by last mail but Fenno's. I hope the bridle is not yet put on the press.

Virginia Resolutions Against the Alien and Sedition Acts

In the House of Delegates

Friday Decr. 21st. 1798.

RESOLVED, that the General Assembly of Virginia doth unequivocally express a firm resolution to maintain and defend the constitution of the United States, and the Constitution of this state, against every aggression, either foreign or domestic, and that they will support the government of the United States in all measures, warranted by the former.

That this Assembly most solemnly declares a warm attachment to the Union of the States, to maintain which, it pledges all its powers; and that for this end, it is their duty, to watch over and oppose every infraction of those principles, which constitute the only basis of that union, because a faithful observance of them, can alone secure its existence, and the public happiness.

That this Assembly doth explicitly and peremptorily declare, that it views the powers of the federal government, as resulting from the compact to which the states are parties; as limited by the plain sense and intention of the instrument constituting that compact; as no farther valid than they are authorised by the grants enumerated in that compact, and that in case of a deliberate, palpable and dangerous exercise of other powers not granted by the said compact, the states who are parties thereto have the right, and are in duty bound, to interpose for arresting the progress of the evil, and for maintaining within their respective limits, the authorities, rights and liberties appertaining to them.

That the General Assembly doth also express its deep regret that a spirit has in sundry instances, been manifested by the federal government, to enlarge its powers by forced constructions of the constitutional charter which defines them; and that indications have appeared of a design to expound certain general phrases (which having been copied from the very limited grant of powers in the former articles of confederation were the less liable to be misconstrued) so as to destroy the meaning and effect of the particular enumeration, which

589

necessarily explains and limits the general phrases; and so as to consolidate the states by degrees into one sovereignty, the obvious tendency and inevitable consequence of which would be, to transform the present republican system of the United States, into an absolute, or at best a mixed monarchy.

That the General Assembly doth particularly protest against the palpable and alarming infractions of the constitution, in the two late cases of the "alien and sedition acts," passed at the last session of Congress; the first of which exercises a power no where delegated to the federal government; and which by uniting legislative and judicial powers, to those of executive, subverts the general principles of free government, as well as the particular organization and positive provisions of the federal constitution: and the other of which acts, exercises in like manner a power not delegated by the constitution, but on the contrary expressly and positively forbidden by one of the amendments thereto; a power which more than any other ought to produce universal alarm, because it is levelled against that right of freely examining public characters and measures, and of free communication among the people thereon, which has ever been justly deemed, the only effectual guardian of every other right.

That this State having by its convention which ratified the federal constitution, expressly declared, "that among other essential rights, the liberty of conscience and of the press cannot be cancelled, abridged, restrained or modified by any authority of the United States" and from its extreme anxiety to guard these rights from every possible attack of sophistry or ambition, having with other states recommended an amendment for that purpose, which amendment was in due time annexed to the Constitution, it would mark a reproachful inconsistency and criminal degeneracy, if an indifference were now shewn to the most palpable violation of one of the rights thus declared and secured, and to the establishment of a precedent which may be fatal to the other.

That the good people of this Commonwealth having ever felt and continuing to feel the most sincere affection for their bretheren of the other states, the truest anxiety for establishing and perpetuating the union of all, and the most scrupulous fidelity to that Constitution which is the pledge of mutual friendship, and the instrument of mutual happiness, the General Assembly doth solemnly appeal to the like dispositions of the other States, in confidence that they will concur with this Commonwealth in declaring, as it does hereby declare, that the acts aforesaid are unconstitutional, and that the necessary and proper measures will be taken by each, for cooperating with this State in maintaining unimpaired the authorities, rights, and liberties, reserved to the States respectively, or to the people.

That the Governor be desired to transmit a copy of the foregoing resolutions to the Executive authority of each of the other States, with a request, that the same may be communicated to the Legislature thereof.

And that a copy be furnished to each of the Senators and Representatives, representing this State in the Congress of the United States.

To Thomas Jefferson

Dear Sir   Decr. 29. 1798

I inclose a draught on Genl. Moylan out of which you will be pleased to pay yourself the price of the Nails £48–11.3. Va. Cy. to let Barnes have as much as will discharge the balance I owe him, & to let what may remain lie till I write you again.

The P.'s speech corresponds pretty much with the idea of it which was preconceived. It is the old song with no other variation of the tune than the spirit of the moment was thought to exact. It is evident also that he rises in his pitch as the Ecchoes of the S. & H. of R. embolden him, & particularly that he seizes with avidity that of the latter flattering his vigilance & firmness agst. illusory attempts on him, without noticing, as he was equally invited, the allusion to his pacific professions. The Senate as usual perform their part with alacrity in counteracting peace by dextrous provocations to the pride & irritability of the French Govt. It is pretty clear that their answer was cooked in the same shop, with the Speech. The finesse of the former calculated to impose on the public mind here, & the virulence of the latter still more calculated to draw from France the war, which can not be safely declared on this side, taste strongly of the genius of that subtle partizan of England who has contributed so much to the public misfortunes. It is not difficult to see how A. could be made a puppet thro' the instrumentality of creatures around him, nor how the Senate could be managed by similar artifice. I have not seen the Result of the discussions at Richmond on the Alien & Sedition laws. It is to be feared their zeal may forget some considerations which ought to temper their proceedings. Have you ever considered thoroughly the distinction between the power of the *State*, & that of *the Legislature*, on questions relating to the federal pact. On the supposition that the former is clearly the ultimate Judge of infractions, it does not follow that the latter is the legitimate organ especially as a Convention was the organ by which the Compact was made. This was a reason of great weight for using general expressions that would leave to other States a choice of all the modes possible of concurring in the substance, and would shield the Genl. Assembly agst. the charge of Usurpation in the very act of protesting agst the usurpations of Congress. I have not forgot my promise of McGeehee's prices, but cd. not conveniently copy them for the present mail. Always affly. Yrs.

Foreign Influence

The public attention has been much employed for some time, on the danger of foreign influence, and of divisions between the government and the people. The jealousy which has been awakened on these subjects, has however, been exclusively directed towards one foreign nation. To be honorable to our character, and adequate to our safety, it ought to be pointed to every quarter where danger lurks, and most awake to that, from which danger is most to be feared.

The two important questions that offer themselves to a mind in every respect *American*, are; *first*, whether there be greater danger of the government being separated from the people, by its own ambition, and by foreign intrigues; or of the people being separated from the government, by such intrigues and by its proneness to anarchy and sedition: *Secondly*, from what foreign quarter the greatest danger of influence is to be apprehended?

The first question being rendered peculiarly delicate by known causes, is left for hands better qualified to manage it: excepting, indeed, so far as light may be thrown on it from an examination of the second.

On this question I have bestowed much thought, and perhaps, with as much impartiality as is felt by those who profess the most of it. The conclusion with me, is, that Great Britain, above all other nations, ought to be dreaded and watched, as most likely to gain an undue and pernicious ascendency in our country.

I think so, because her *motives* are *stronger*, and her *means, greater*.

HER MOTIVES.

1. The pride of regaining by address—the benefits she formerly held by authority. That she is making at this crisis, every effort for the purpose, is seen by every eye that is not wilfully shut to facts.

2. Her spirit, and system of monopoly, must make her particularly dread the policy and prosperity of the United States, in the three great articles of which she is most jealous—to wit, *manufactures, commerce, navigation.*

The United States are the greatest and best market for her manufactures. To keep out those of other nations, and to keep down those of our own, is the grand object to which her efforts have ever been directed. It is well understood, that one of our manufactures has been strangled in its birth, by a dextrous operation from that quarter.

On the subject of commerce, she has the same feelings, the same interest, and the same system. To be our merchant as well as manufacturer, is the game she will most certainly play, in time to come as in time past, however differently her cards may be shuffled. The eastern states ought to know this better than any other part of the continent. It was known and felt both, at Boston, soon after the close of the war. The sentinels that proclaimed the alarm, then, where are they now?

With respect to *navigation*, all the world knows, the greater part of it by severe experience, that the most jealous lover never guarded an inconstant mistress with a more watchful eye. The United States, in their materials for ship building, and their bulky articles for transportation, possess resources more important to her, if she can force or *influence* us out of them, and presenting a more formidable rivalship to her, if she cannot, than any other nation whatever. Hence her rigid and compulsive monopoly, whilst we were colonies. Hence the obstinacy of her exertions, during the revolutionary war, this monopoly to retain. Hence her vigilance and activity, to regain it by her parliamentary regulations, and orders of council, before we had a general government, that could counteract them. Hence her address in seizing the moment of our humiliation, which gave her the British treaty. Hence the impatient and rigorous use made of that treaty in her "countervailing act," which cuts the throat of the American navigation, and transfuses the vital blood of it into her own.

3. But the most powerful, perhaps, of all her motives, is her *hatred and fear* of the *republican example* of our governments. The others are motives of *national* interest only; this is enlivened by the strong feeling, also, of a *governmental* and *personal* interest. This feeling shewed itself in many features of the revolutionary war. It shewed itself in the indignant treatment of the first minister from the United States, and in the distance and dislike displayed for a long period thereafter: It shewed itself by the strongest marks, in the *undisguised wishes* and hopes, that our union would be speedily dissolved, that our popular governments would tumble into anarchy and convulsions; and that the general wreck, would exhibit a spectacle of misery and horror, that would forever disgrace the republican principle, and add new braces to the monarchial fabric. The same acute and predominant feeling has shewed itself in an increased aversion to the smallest improvement of the British government in its *representative* branch; and has displayed itself, with all its force, in its instant alarm at the propagation of republican principles into France, and the unparalleled rage and inveteracy of the war pursued against them; a war in which every calculation of *national* advantage was sacrificed to the *monarchial* policy and passions of the government.

Whilst the abhorrence of the British government to republicanism in Europe is thus implacable, it must be proportionably so to the danger of the example elsewhere. If she has changed her course therefore towards this country, it is not that she has changed her sentiments, or is better reconciled to our political principles and institutions; but that she now hopes to attain her ends better in another way. The truth is, Great Britain, as a monarchy, containing a republican ingredient, of which (at all times, but in the present state of the world more particularly) the danger of a fermentation & expansion, fills her with distressing apprehensions, must view with a malignant eye the United States, as the real source of the present revolutionary state of the world, and as an example of republicanism more likely than any other, for very obvious reasons, to convey its contagion to her. In a word, the *British Monarchy* must, as it assuredly does, hate the *American Republic*; and this hatred must be in proportion to its fear; and this fear must be in proportion to the practical success of the Republican theory. It will consequently spare no pains to defeat this success, by drawing our Republic into foreign wars, by dividing the people among themselves, *by separating the government from the people*, by establishing a faction of its own in the country, by magnifying the importance of characters among us known to think more highly of the British government, than of their own, or of such as are ready to play any part that it may dictate to them; with a systematic view, on one hand of disgracing the Republican principle, and on the other, of swelling and shaping our government towards the pattern of its own.

This pursuit of the British government, is highly criminal, because at variance with right principles, yet it is so congenial with its situation and its interest, that it excites less indignation than the conduct of those who clandestinely favor the plan, or wilfully shut their own eyes, and endeavour to shut the eyes of others to it. For it is not possible that a government in which a few are cloathed with prerogatives and dignities almost divine, whilst many are suppressed to a condition scarcely human; and where a civil list, a military, and naval establishment, and a hierarchy (passing by the frightful mass of debts incurred by unnecessary wars) load the people with an annual burden of more than a hundred million of dollars—and where, besides, corruption is confessedly the vital principle that pervades the whole system; it is not possible, that such a government can see another, founded on the just rights of mankind, virtuously administered, at the small expence of a few hundred thousand dollars, and enjoying peace, order, tranquillity, and happiness without comparisons and reflections, leading to the idea that the example of the latter government must be dangerous to the former, if the *influence* of the former cannot in some way destroy the force of the example.

The MEANS of this influence are as obvious as the *motives*.

The British government has a more ready and ample command of money than any other government in the world.

Being an *absolute monarchy* in its *executive department*, it can distribute its money for *secret* services with every advantage of safety and success.

It is the long and systematic practice of effectuating its purposes both at home and abroad by means of money. The sum for *secret services* has been vastly augmented of late years. Great Britain expends more money annually, under that head, than is appropriated to support the government of the United States.

A British Ambassador and his suite, having the peculiar advantage of the same language, the same usages & the same manners, with our citizens, can more easily than any other foreigners, associate intimately and extensively with them, can write with less danger of detection, for our newspapers, and can intrigue, with less difficulty, with our government, if unhappily any department, should ever become susceptible of it. Nor is it to be overlooked, that there is not a state or district in the union, that does not present to them *countrymen* ready to second their views, if not execute their instructions.

There are among us not less than fifty or sixty thousand native subjects of the British Empire. Striking out the very respectable proportion of them who are Americans not only in allegiance, but in *principles* and *attachment*, the number remaining who are truly British in one or all their characteristics, constitutes a fund of foreign influence, that merits very serious attention, in the present estimate. The influence from this class of persons is the greater, as they are in no small degree scattered over the whole face of the country, and mingled (in some parts of America more than in others) in almost every neighbourhood, some of them possessed of wealth, others of friendly dispositions, and engaging manners; but all not the less foreigners in their principles and affections, and using all the influence of their conciliating qualities on the side of their native country, in every question which puts her interests in competition with ours. The universal and uniform ardour of this description of persons for war, in preference to peace with France, stands for a thousand proofs of the fact, that they are Britons, not Americans in their hearts.

In elections, the means of British influence are often no less visible, mixing among the people without any badge of their *alienism* in their language, dress, or appearance; British foreigners are frequently among the busiest canvassers, and most successful retailers of tickets.

In other meetings of the people, the same circumstances open the way for the same influence. How many British subjects, or natives of British principles, were there among the petitioners of this city in favor of the British Treaty? How many in the Chamber of Commerce of New-York? How many indeed every where among the eager partizans of that ill-omened measure?

This leads us to the great flood-gate of British influence *British Commerce*. The capital in the American trade amounts to thirty or forty millions of dollars. Three fourths of this is British capital; of this proportion three fourths is in British hands. The residue in the hands of Americans, has more effect in Anglicizing them, than in Americanizing the influence it gives. Individual exceptions are admitted and might be named. But it is of equal certainty that the American merchants generally who *value* on *British capital and credit*, are those who feel most powerfully the capitulating influence.

More than one volume would be necessary to trace in its details this species of British influence. The copious fountain is in Britain, principally in London. Every shipment, every consignment, every commission, is a channel in which a portion of it flows. It may be said to make a part of every cargo. Our Sea-port towns are the reservoirs into which it is collected. From these, issue a thousand streams to the inland towns, and country stores: which, in aid of the influence inherent in British trade and British credit, not unfrequently receive from the political zeal of the importing merchants, a stock of British ideas and sentiments proper to be retailed to the people. Thus it is, that our country is penetrated to its remotest corners with a foreign poison vitiating the American sentiment, recolonizing the American character, and duping us into the politics of a foreign nation. And thus it is, that the more the injuries and insults of Britain thicken upon us, the greater the apathy and silence respecting them. Her arbitrary edicts against our neutral rights; her daring perseverance in impressing our seamen, (even from our public armed ships) by which she levies on us a *tribute of men*, and equally tramples on our national independence and our neutrality; the intrigues of her ambassador to draw us into a war with a friendly power, at the risk perhaps of a part of our union; the establishment under the eyes of our government of a foreign newspaper, conducted by a British subject, avowing his allegiance to his King, glorying in his foreign attachments and monarchical principles, and villifying with the most unparalleled audacity, the revolution which obtained our Independence, and the republican principles which are the basis of our constitution: not to repeat the deadly blow which she has levelled at our navigation; why has so little been heard on all these topics? Because a spell has in this case been laid on the trumpet, which has blown unceasing alarms against the injuries and insults offered us from another foreign quarter.

Money in all its shapes is influence; our monied institutions consequently form another great engine of British influence. Our Bank is a powerful one. Their capital belongs in great part to Britons, or to proprietors interested in British connections. The proprietors chuse the Directors. The Directors dispense the credits and favours of the Banks. Every dependant on these therefore is a kind of vassal, owing homage to his pecuniary superiors, on pain of bankruptcy and ruin. Say ye citizens of Philadelphia, have ye not all felt or seen this influence, whenever Bank-Directors have been canvassers for votes or subscriptions? and has this influence ever been exerted but on the side espoused by the agents of Britain in this country?

As a vehicle of influence, the press, though the last to be named, must be allowed all its importance. How deplorable that this guardian of public rights, this organ of necessary truths, should be tainted with partiality at all. How bitter the reflection, that it should be subject to a foreign taint. So however is the fact. It cannot be denied. It hardly needs to be explained. The inland papers it is well known copy from the city papers; this city more particularly, as the centre of politics and news. The city papers are supported by advertisements. The advertisements for the most part, relate to articles of trade, and are furnished by merchants and traders. In this manner British influence steals into our newspapers, and circulates under their passport. Every printer, whether an exception to the remark or not, knows the fact to be as here stated. There are presses whose original independence, subsequent apostacies, occcasional conversions, speedy relapses, and final prostration to advertising customers, point them out as conspicuous examples.

To conclude: Great Britain feels every motive that a foreign power can feel to pinch our growth, and undermine our government; and enjoys greater means of influence for these purposes than ever were possessed by one nation towards another. On Great Britain then our eye at least will be constantly fixt by every real

ENEMY TO FOREIGN INFLUENCE.

Aurora General Advertiser, January 23, 1799

Political Reflections

There was never a time when it was more requisite for the public to be truly acquainted with foreign transactions than at the present; nor one at which this information was more difficult. With every thing that regards the French Republic, it is of peculiar importance that it should be accurately and fully understood, because that is the Foreign Power, with which our relations have become more interesting than with any other. It happens at the same time, that it is the very power, concerning whose affairs more than those of any other, it is difficult to gain the exact and authentic information which ought to regulate the opinion and direct the proceedings of the United States.

The French Revolution has produced such a ferment and agitation in the world, and has divided it, according to the different turns given to men's minds by temper, by interest, and by political principles, into such violent parties, that nothing depending on opinion, nor much even on facts, is received without a strong tincture from the channel through which it passes.

To this general consideration must be added some powerful obstacles of a more particular nature.

The publications in France are said to be under such influence and restraints from the Government, that little confidence can be put in them beyond the official documents which they sometimes contain. The publications indeed of any sort, from that quarter, arrive now so sparingly in this country, that they scarcely serve the purpose of assisting truth by those comparisons with other doubtful accounts by which it is sometimes approached.

In the next place, the mass of information relating to France is brought to this Country chiefly from England and Germany, and is consequently adulterated with all the exaggerations & perversions which the most raging hostility can infuse.

To these foreign sources of uncertainty is to be added, in the third place, the opposite dispositions under which our own presses make their extracts and comments; whereby the imperfect lights received from abroad are still further refracted and obscured.

Nor is any remedy to be derived in the present case, from the correspondence of American citizens in Europe. For besides that the letters ascribed to them are often the most palpable forgeries, dictated by the extravagant zeal of party, it is not to be denied that such as are genuine breathe an obvious spirit of partiality that turns away the ear of every discerning enquirer after truth.

For these reasons it is most prudent and safe to indulge a considerable measure of doubt as to a variety of scenes passing in the old world, particularly in France; and to wait for full and satisfactory information, till it shall be furnished by the course of facts and events properly authenticated.

In the mean time, however, it may be useful to reflect on the nature of some of the allegations and reproaches under which a country has fallen, that of late was so interesting to us by the ties of friendship, and that is still so by the relation of her revolution to ours, and by her form of government; as well as by the nature of her markets, by her power, and by her political views, whether amicable or otherwise towards this country. These allegations, if well founded, afford lessons too instructive to be unheeded; and even if unfounded, present an occasion for reflections well adapted to the present posture of our affairs. Our attention will be limited to two articles much dwelt on in the charge against the French Republic.

The *first* is, that the government has entirely separated itself from the people, and erected itself into a Tyranny, actuated by its own ambitious views, in opposition to the sentiments and interests of the nation.

It is not proposed to examine in what degree this charge is strictly true. If on one hand there be symptoms which favor it, it is not improbable, that some mitigating pleas at least might be urged on the other. It may be recollected that similar imputations were constantly thrown on the congress during our own revolution, tho' well known to be without foundation. Taking the fact however in the form in which it is stated, it certainly offers very serious admonitions to a people living under a representative government.

The French Republic, like ours, is founded on the principles of representation and responsibility. The members of its legislature are chosen by the people. They become at short periods amenable to their constituents, by the frequent return of elections. And as a further security, they are divided into two branches, as checks the one on the other. If it be true, as alledged, that under these circumstances, a tyrannical usurpation has already taken place in that government, is not here an example in point against the doctrine so ardently propagated by many, that in a republic the people ought to consider the whole of their political duty as discharged when they have chosen their representatives; that it is impossible in fact and ought never to be presumed, that men chosen by the people, and having a common interest with the people, can pursue an interest different from that of the people; and consequently that the people ought at all times to place an unlimited confidence in rulers so chosen, applauding the wisdom of public measures where they can see it and assuring themselves that it is equally the foundation of all others, where nothing but folly or mischief may appear on the face of them.

Nothing can be more contradictory than this reasoning, to the alledged usurpations of the French government, and yet, however curious it may be, many who proclaim these usurpations with most energy, are the same who with no less energy preach an unlimited confidence in representative government as incapable of them.

The inconsistency is not done away by pleading the extraordinary means employed by the French Government in their illegitimate pursuits, such as the expulsion and banishment of part of their own body, controuling the election of successors, &c. &c. The observation always recurs, that such means were in fact employed, in such pursuits, by elective and responsible agents; and consequently that such agents are not incapable of violating the trust committed to them.

It must not be permitted however, either to the friend of liberty in despair, or to its enemy in disguise, to turn this inference against the merit and competency of the Representative principle. The true lesson it teaches is, that in no case ought the eyes of the people to be shut on the conduct of those entrusted with power; nor their tongues tied from a just wholesome censure on it, any more than from merited commendations. If neither gratitude for the honor of the trust, nor responsibility for the use of it, be sufficient to curb the unruly passions of public functionaries, add new bits to the bridle rather than to take it off altogether. This is the precept of common sense illustrated and enforced by experience—uncontrouled power, ever has been, and ever will be administered by the passions more than by reason. The exceptions are too few to have the smallest weight with sober and sensible people. There is no possible state of things, therefore, where a remedy against the abuses of power ought to be sought for in a renewal of the checks on it.

The *second* charge against the French Republic is, that the

Directory has gained an omnipotent ascendancy over the Legislature, and makes use of its authority to sanction and disguise all the projects of its own ambition and rapacity.

The prompt and uniform concurrence of the two Departments, said to prevail in all the public measures, is a strong indication either that both are governed by the voice of the nation, or that one is extremely compliant with the will of the other. The first supposition being rejected, the inference from appearances certainly is that the Executive rules the Legislature, rather than that the Legislature rules the Executive.

Taking this for the fact, what a subject does it present for the meditation of free nations.

The French Directory it will be recollected, is not only an elective and responsible body, but is elected by, and in a certain degree responsible to the legislative body; yet in the short period that has passed, since that government was established, we are told that the power, and influence of the Executive Department, have rendered it the absolute masters of its creators and constituents. This surely is another example that does not favor the fashionable doctrine of the present day, that elective and responsible rulers ought never to be deemed capable of abusing their trust, much less does it favor the still more fashionable doctrine, that *executive influence* in a *representative* government is *a mere phantom* created by the imaginations of the credulous, or *the arts of the hypocritical friends of liberty*; and that all true patriots will ever unite their efforts *in strengthening the executive force*, by stifling every jealousy of its hostile misapplication.

But in order to comprehend this subject fully, and to draw from it all the instruction which it offers, the question must be asked, under what circumstances, and by what means, this Executive omnipotence has been brought about?

The answer to this question, one of the most important that could invite the public attention, will be best given by a simple view of facts.

The French Republic has been, and still is, in a state of war and danger, and this state of war and danger, have given to the Executive an immense army to command, innumerable offices to bestow, a mighty mass of money to deal out, a control over the freedom of speech and of the press; together with all the use that can be made of foreign relations, and internal alarms, for leading the counsels of the legislature, for crying down the opponents of its measures, and for imposing silence, if not satisfaction on the people.

An army such as that of France, which does not bear a *less proportion* to the whole nation, than *fifty thousand men* would do to the people of the United States, must be formidable at home as well as abroad; whilst a revenue and laws, &c. corresponding with the *proportion of twenty or thirty millions of dollars* to the United States, to be distributed in emoluments to officers and dependants beyond number, of every kind, and of every grade, must add an *influence*, equal to the power of the military establishment itself.

What other resources would a Walpole or a Mazarine desire for drawing all the corruption and all the weakness in the society into their views, and for building up a gigantic Executive on the ruins of every collateral department of power. Or if other resources were desired, might they not be found in an *unbounded license to applaud, without the privilege of censuring their movements*; and in that fund of influence enjoyed, by the prerogative that superintends all foreign dangers and designs, and that can exhibit and vary the pictures of them, at its pleasure.

Under circumstances like these, the Directory are models of virtue, if ambition has not somewhat yielded to the means of gratifying it; the legislative body more pure, than is probable, if the avarice of many of its members has not overpowered their duty; and the people more firm and enlightened than ought to be expected, if they are not in some measure awed or duped into a tacit acquiescence under oppression.

The usurped sway ascribed to the Directory, with the causes which must have led to it, cannot then be too much pondered and contemplated by Americans who love their country, and are sensible of the blessings of its free constitution. They ought most generously to reflect on the evils of a state of war, not only as it destroys the lives of the people, wastes their treasure, *and* corrupts their morals; but on the other, evils which lurk under its dreadful tendency, to destroy the equilibrium of the departments of power, by throwing improper weights into the Executive scale, and to betray the people into the snares which ambition may lay for their liberties.

When a state of war becomes absolutely and clearly necessary, all good citizens will submit with alacrity to the calamities inseparable from it. But wars are so often the result of causes which prudence and a love of peace might obviate, that it is equally the duty and the characteristic of good citizens to keep a watchful, tho' not censorious eye, over that branch of the government which derives the greatest accession of power and importance from the armies, offices, and expences, which compose the equipage of war. In spite of all the claims and examples of patriotism, which ought by no means to be undervalued, the testimony of all ages forces us to admit, that war is among the most dangerous of all enemies to liberty; and that the executive is the most favored by it, of all the branches of power. The charge brought against the French Directory adds a new fact to the evidence which will be allowed by all to have very great weight and to meet the particular attention of the United States.

It deserves to be well considered also, that actual war is not the only state which may supply the means of usurpation. The real or pretended apprehensions of it, are, sometimes of equal avail to the projects of ambition. Hence the propagation and management of alarms has grown into a kind of system. Its origin however is not of recent or even moderate date. The Roman Senate, and Athenian demagogues understood it as well as Mr. Pitt or any of the mimics of his policy. Nor ought it to be doubted, that the stratagem will readily occur to every government that can with impunity and without animadversion, indulge that "unlimited passion," which the frankness of our President has declared to be an attribute of human nature.

An alarm is proclaimed—Troops are raised—Taxes are imposed—Officers military and civil are created. The danger is repelled or disappears. But in the army, remains a real force, in the taxes pecuniary measures, and in the offices a political influence, all at hand for the internal interprizes of ambition. But should no other pretext present itself, one may possibly be found in the jealousies, discontents, and murmurs excited by the very danger which threatens.

Report on the Alien and Sedition Acts

Whatever room might be found in the proceedings of some of the states, who have disapproved of the resolutions of the General Assembly of this commonwealth, passed on the 21st day of December, 1798, for painful remarks on the spirit and manner of those proceedings, it appears to the committee, most consistent with the duty, as well as dignity of the General Assembly, to hasten an oblivion of every circumstance, which might be construed into a diminution of mutual respect, confidence and affection, among the members of the union.

The committee have deemed it a more useful task, to revise with a critical eye, the resolutions which have met with this disapprobation; to examine fully the several objections and arguments which have appeared against them; and to enquire, whether there be any errors of fact, of principle, or of reasoning, which the candour of the General Assembly ought to acknowledge and correct.

The first of the resolutions is in the words following:

Resolved, that the General Assembly of Virginia, doth unequivocally express a firm resolution to maintain and defend the Constitution of the United States, and the Constitution of this state, against every aggression either foreign or domestic, and that they will support the government of the United States in all measures warranted by the former.

No unfavorable comment can have been made on the sentiments here expressed. To maintain and defend the Constitution of the United States, and of their own state, against every aggression both foreign and domestic, and to support the government of the United States in all measures warranted by their constitution, are duties, which the General Assembly ought always to feel, and to which on such an occasion, it was evidently proper to express their sincere and firm adherence.

In their next resolution—*The General Assembly most solemnly declares a warm attachment to the union of the states, to maintain which, it pledges all its powers; and that for this end, it is their duty to watch over and oppose every infraction of those principles, which constitute the only basis of that union, be-*

cause a faithful observance of them, can alone secure its existence and the public happiness.

The observation just made is equally applicable to this solemn declaration, of warm attachment to the union, and this solemn pledge to maintain it: nor can any question arise among enlightened friends of the union, as to the duty of watching over and opposing every infraction of those principles which constitute its basis, and a faithful observance of which, can alone secure its existence, and the public happiness thereon depending.

The third resolution is in the words following:

That this Assembly doth explicitly and peremptorily declare, that it views the powers of the Federal Government, as resulting from the compact, to which the states are parties, as limited by the plain sense and intention of the instrument constituting that compact; as no farther valid than they are authorized by the grants enumerated in that compact; and that in case of a deliberate, palpable and dangerous exercise of other powers, not granted by the said compact, the states who are parties thereto, have the right, and are in duty bound, to interpose, for arresting the progress of the evil, and for maintaining within their respective limits, the authorities, rights and liberties appertaining to them.

On this resolution, the committee have bestowed all the attention which its importance merits: They have scanned it not merely with a strict, but with a severe eye; and they feel confidence in pronouncing, that in its just and fair construction, it is unexceptionably true in its several positions, as well as constitutional and conclusive in its inferences.

The resolution declares, *first*, that "it views the powers of the Federal Government, as resulting from the compact to which the states are parties," in other words, that the federal powers are derived from the Constitution, and that the Constitution is a compact to which the states are parties.

Clear as the position must seem, that the federal powers are derived from the Constitution, and from that alone, the committee are not unapprized of a late doctrine which opens another source of federal powers, not less extensive and important, than it is new and unexpected. The examination of this doctrine will be most conveniently connected with a review of a succeeding resolution. The committee satisfy themselves here with briefly remarking, that in all the co-temporary discussions and comments, which the Constitution underwent, it was constantly justified and recommended on the ground, that the powers not given to the government, were withheld from it; and that if any doubt could have existed on this subject, under the original text of the Constitution, it is removed as far as words could remove it, by the 12th amendment, now a part of the Constitution, which expressly declares, "that the powers not delegated to the United States, by the Constitution, nor prohibited by it to the states, are reserved to the states respectively, or to the people."

The other position involved in this branch of the resolution, namely, "that the states are parties to the Constitution or compact," is in the judgment of the committee, equally free from objection. It is indeed true that the term "States," is sometimes used in a vague sense, and sometimes in different senses, according to the subject to which it is applied. Thus it sometimes means the separate sections of territory occupied by the political societies within each; sometimes the particular governments, established by those societies; sometimes those societies as organized into those particular governments; and lastly, it means the people composing those political societies, in their highest sovereign capacity. Although it might be wished that the perfection of language admitted less diversity in the signification of the same words, yet little inconveniency is produced by it, where the true sense can be collected with certainty from the different applications. In the present instance whatever different constructions of the term "States," in the resolution may have been entertained, all will at least concur in that last mentioned; because in that sense, the Constitution was submitted to the "States": In that sense the "States" ratified it; and in that sense of the term "States," they are consequently parties to the compact from which the powers of the Federal Government result.

The next position is, that the General Assembly views the powers of the Federal Government, "as limited by the plain sense and intention of the instrument constituting that compact," and "as no farther valid than they are authorized by the grants therein enumerated." It does not seem possible that any just objection can lie against either of these clauses. The first amounts merely to a declaration that the compact ought to have the interpretation, plainly intended by the parties to it; the other, to a declaration, that it ought to have the execution and effect intended by them. If the powers granted, be valid, it is solely because they are granted; and if the granted powers are valid, because granted, all other powers not granted, must not be valid.

The resolution having taken this view of the federal compact, proceeds to infer, "that in case of a deliberate, palpable, and dangerous exercise of other powers not granted by the said compact, the states who are parties thereto, have the right, and are in duty bound to interpose for arresting the progress of the evil, and for maintaining within their respective limits, the authorities, rights and liberties appertaining to them."

It appears to your committee to be a plain principle, founded in common sense, illustrated by common practice, and essential to the nature of compacts; that where resort can be had to no tribunal superior to the authority of the parties, the parties themselves must be the rightful judges in the last resort, whether the bargain made, has been pursued or violated. The constitution of the United States was formed by the sanction of the states, given by each in its sovereign capacity. It adds to the stability and dignity, as well as to the authority of the constitution, that it rests on this legitimate and solid foundation. The states then being the parties to the constitutional compact, and in their sovereign capacity, it follows of necessity, that there can be no tribunal above their authority, to decide in the last resort, whether the compact made by them be violated; and consequently that as the parties to it, they must themselves decide in the last resort, such questions as may be of sufficient magnitude to require their interposition.

It does not follow, however, that because the states as sovereign parties to their constitutional compact, must ultimately decide whether it has been violated, that such a decision ought to be interposed either in a hasty manner, or on doubtful and inferior occasions. Even in the case of ordinary conventions between different nations, where, by the strict rule of interpretation, a breach of a part may be deemed a breach of the whole; every part being deemed a condition of every other part, and of the whole, it is always laid down that the breach must be both wilful and material to justify an application of the rule. But in the case of an intimate and constitutional union, like that of the United States, it is evident that the interposition of the parties, in their sovereign capacity, can be called for by occasions only, deeply and essentially affecting the vital principles of their political system.

The resolution has accordingly guarded against any misapprehension of its object, by expressly requiring for such an interposition "the case of a *deliberate, palpable* and *dangerous* breach of the constitution, by the exercise of *powers not granted* by it." It must be a case, not of a light and transient nature, but of a nature *dangerous* to the great purposes for which the constitution was established. It must be a case moreover not obscure or doubtful in its construction, but plain and *palpable*. Lastly, it must be a case not resulting from a partial consideration, or hasty determination; but a case stampt with a final consideration and *deliberate* adherence. It is not necessary because the resolution does not require, that the question should be discussed, how far the exercise of any particular power, ungranted by the constitution, would justify the interposition of the parties to it. As cases might easily be stated, which none would contend, ought to fall within that description: Cases, on the other hand, might, with equal ease, be stated, so flagrant and so fatal as to unite every opinion in placing them within the description.

But the resolution has done more than guard against misconstruction, by expressly referring to cases of a *deliberate, palapable* and *dangerous* nature. It specifies the object of the interposition which it contemplates, to be solely that of arresting the progress of the *evil* of usurpation, and of maintaining the authorities, rights and liberties appertaining to the states, as parties to the constitution.

From this view of the resolution, it would seem inconceivable that it can incur any just disapprobation from those, who laying aside all momentary impressions, and recollecting the genuine source and object of the federal constitution, shall candidly and accurately interpret the meaning of the General

Assembly. If the deliberate exercise, of dangerous powers, palpably withheld by the constitution, could not justify the parties to it, in interposing even so far as to arrest the progress of the evil, and thereby to preserve the constitution itself as well as to provide for the safety of the parties to it; there would be an end to all relief from usurped power, and a direct subversion of the rights specified or recognized under all the state constitutions, as well as a plain denial of the fundamental principle on which our independence itself was declared.

But it is objected that the judicial authority is to be regarded as the sole expositor of the constitution, in the last resort; and it may be asked for what reason, the declaration by the General Assembly, supposing it to be theoretically true, could be required at the present day and in so solemn a manner.

On this objection it might be observed *first*, that there may be instances of usurped power, which the forms of the constitution would never draw within the controul of the judicial department: secondly, that if the decision of the judiciary be raised above the authority of the sovereign parties to the constitution, the decisions of the other departments, not carried by the forms of the constitution before the judiciary, must be equally authoritative and final with the decisions of that department. But the proper answer to the objection is, that the resolution of the General Assembly relates to those great and extraordinary cases, in which all the forms of the constitution may prove ineffectual against infractions dangerous to the essential rights of the parties to it. The resolution supposes that dangerous powers not delegated, may not only be usurped and executed by the other departments, but that the Judicial Department also may exercise or sanction dangerous powers beyond the grant of the constitution; and consequently that the ultimate right of the parties to the constitution, to judge whether the compact has been dangerously violated, must extend to violations by one delegated authority, as well as by another; by the judiciary, as well as by the executive, or the legislature.

However true therefore it may be that the Judicial Department, is, in all questions submitted to it by the forms of the constitution, to decide in the last resort, this resort

must necessarily be deemed the last in relation to the authorities of the other departments of the government; not in relation to the rights of the parties to the constitutional compact,
from which the judicial as well as the other departments hold
their delegated trusts. On any other hypothesis, the delegation of judicial power, would annul the authority delegating
it; and the concurrence of this department with the others
in usurped powers, might subvert forever, and beyond the
possible reach of any rightful remedy, the very constitution,
which all were instituted to preserve.

The truth declared in the resolution being established, the
expediency of making the declaration at the present day, may
safely be left to the temperate consideration and candid judgment of the American public. It will be remembered that a
frequent recurrence to fundamental principles is solemnly enjoined by most of the state constitutions, and particularly by
our own, as a necessary safeguard against the danger of degeneracy to which republics are liable, as well as other governments, though in a less degree than others. And a fair
comparison of the political doctrines not unfrequent at the
present day, with those which characterized the epoch of our
revolution, and which form the basis of our republican constitutions, will best determine whether the declaratory recurrence here made to those principles ought to be viewed as
unseasonable and improper, or as a vigilant discharge of an
important duty. The authority of constitutions over governments, and of the sovereignty of the people over constitutions, are truths which are at all times necessary to be kept
in mind; and at no time perhaps more necessary than at the
present.

The fourth resolution stands as follows:—

*That the General Assembly doth also express its deep regret,
that a spirit has in sundry instances, been manifested by the
Federal Government, to enlarge its powers by forced constructions of the Constitutional charter which defines them; and that
indications have appeared of a design to expound certain general phrases, (which, having been copied from the very limited
grant of powers in the former articles of confederation were the
less liable to be misconstrued) so as to destroy the meaning and
effect, of the particular enumeration which necessarily explains,*

and limits the general phrases; and so as to consolidate the states by degrees, into one sovereignty, the obvious tendency and inevitable result of which would be, to transform the present Republican system of the United States, into an absolute, or at best a mixed monarchy.

The *first* question here to be considered is, whether a spirit has in sundry instances been manifested by the Federal Government to enlarge its powers by forced constructions of the Constitutional charter.

The General Assembly having declared their opinion merely by regreting in general terms that forced constructions for enlarging the federal powers have taken place, it does not appear to the committee necessary to go into a specification of every instance to which the resolution may allude. The alien and Sedition acts being particularly named in a succeeding resolution are of course to be understood as included in the allusion. Omitting others which have less occupied public attention, or been less extensively regarded as unconstitutional, the resolution may be presumed to refer particularly to the bank law, which from the circumstances of its passage as well as the latitude of construction on which it is founded, strikes the attention with singular force; and the carriage tax, distinguished also by circumstances in its history having a similar tendency. Those instances alone, if resulting· from forced construction and calculated to enlarge the powers of the Federal government, as the committee cannot but conceive to be the case, sufficiently warrant this part of the resolution. The committee have not thought it incumbent on them to extend their attention to laws which have been objected to, rather as varying the Constitutional distribution of powers in the Federal government, than as an absolute enlargement of them; because instances of this sort however important in their principles and tendencies, do not appear to fall strictly within the text under review.

The other questions presenting themselves, are—1. Whether indications have appeared of a design to expound certain general phrases copied from the "articles of confederation," so as to destroy the effect of the particular enumeration explaining and limiting their meaning. 2. Whether this exposition would by degrees consolidate the states into one sovereignty. 3. Whether the tendency and result of this consolidation would be to transform the Republican system of the United States into a monarchy.

1. The general phrases here meant must be those "of providing for the common defence and general welfare."

In the "articles of confederation" the phrases are used as follows, in article VIII. "All charges of war, and all other expences that shall be incurred *for the common defence and general welfare*, and allowed by the United States in Congress assembled, shall be defrayed out of a common treasury, which shall be supplied by the several states, in proportion to the value of all land within each state, granted to or surveyed for any person, as such land and the buildings and improvements thereon shall be estimated, according to such mode as the United States in Congress assembled, shall from time to time direct and appoint."

In the existing constitution, they make the following part of section 8. "The Congress shall have power, to lay and collect taxes, duties, imposts and excises to pay the debts, and provide for the common defence and general welfare of the United States."

This similarity in the use of these phrases in the two great federal charters, might well be considered, as rendering their meaning less liable to be misconstrued in the latter; because it will scarcely be said that in the former they were ever understood to be either a general grant of power, or to authorize the requisition or application of money by the old Congress to the common defence and general welfare, except in the cases afterwards enumerated which explained and limited their meaning; and if such was the limited meaning attached to these phrases in the very instrument revised and remodelled by the present constitution, it can never be supposed that when copied into this constitution, a different meaning ought to be attached to them.

That notwithstanding this remarkable security against misconstruction, a design has been indicated to expound these phrases in the Constitution so as to destroy the effect of the particular enumeration of powers by which it explains and limits them, must have fallen under the observation of those who have attended to the course of public transactions. Not to multiply proofs on this subject, it will suffice to refer to the debates of the Federal Legislature in which arguments have on different occasions been drawn, with apparent effect from these phrases in their indefinite meaning.

To these indications might be added without looking farther, the official report on manufactures by the late Secretary of the Treasury, made on the 5th of December, 1791; and the report of a committee of Congress in January 1797, on the promotion of agriculture. In the first of these it is expressly contended to belong "to the discretion of the National legislature to pronounce upon the objects which concern the *general welfare*, and for which under that description, an appropriation of money is requisite and proper. And there seems to be no room for a doubt that whatever concerns the general interests of LEARNING, of AGRICULTURE, of MANUFACTURES, and of COMMERCE, are within the sphere of the national councils, *as far as regards an application of money.*" The latter report assumes the same latitude of power in the national councils and applies it to the encouragement of agriculture, by means of a society to be established at the seat of government. Although neither of these reports may have received the sanction of a law carrying it into effect; yet, on the other hand, the extraordinary doctrine contained in both, has passed without the slightest positive mark of disapprobation from the authority to which it was addressed.

Now whether the phrases in question be construed to authorise every measure relating to the common defence and general welfare, as contended by some; or every measure only in which there might be an application of money, as suggested by the caution of others, the effect must substantially be the same, in destroying the import and force of the particular enumeration of powers, which follow these general phrases in the Constitution. For it is evident that there is not a single power whatever, which may not have some reference to the common defence, or the general welfare; nor a power of any magnitude which in its exercise does not involve or admit an application of money. The government therefore which possesses power in either one or other of these extents, is a government without the limitations formed by a particular enumeration of powers; and consequently the meaning and effect of this particular enumeration, is destroyed by the exposition given to these general phrases.

This conclusion will not be affected by an attempt to qualify the power over the "general welfare," by referring it to cases where the *general welfare* is beyond the reach of *separate* provisions by the *individual states*; and leaving to these their jurisdictions in cases, to which their separate provisions may be competent. For as the authority of the individual states must in all cases be incompetent to general regulations operating through the whole, the authority of the United States would be extended to every object relating to the general welfare, which might by any possibility be provided for by the general authority. This qualifying construction therefore would have little, if any tendency, to circumscribe the power claimed under the latitude of the terms "general welfare."

The true and fair construction of this expression, both in the original and existing federal compacts appears to the committee too obvious to be mistaken. In both, the Congress is authorized to provide money for the common defence and *general welfare*. In both, is subjoined to this authority, an enumeration of the cases, to which their powers shall extend. Money cannot be applied to the *general welfare*, otherwise than by an application of it to some *particular* measure conducive to the general welfare. Whenever therefore, money has been raised by the general authority, and is to be applied to a particular measure, a question arises, whether the particular measure be within the enumerated authorities vested in Congress. If it be, the money requisite for it may be applied to it; if it be not, no such application can be made. This fair and obvious interpretation coincides with, and is enforced by, the clause in the Constitution which declares that "no money shall be drawn from the treasury, but in consequence of appropriations by law." An appropriation of money to the general welfare, would be deemed rather a mockery than an observance of this constitutional injunction.

2. Whether the exposition of the general phrases here combated, would not, by degrees consolidate the states into one sovereignty, is a question concerning which, the committee can perceive little room for difference of opinion. To consolidate the States into one sovereignty, nothing more can be

wanted, than to supercede their respective sovereignties in the cases reserved to them, by extending the sovereignty of the United States to all cases of the "general welfare," that is to say, to *all cases whatever*.

3. That the obvious tendency and inevitable result of a consolidation of the states into one sovereignty, would be, to transform the republican system of the United States into a monarchy, is a point which seems to have been sufficiently decided by the general sentiment of America. In almost every instance of discussion, relating to the consolidation in question, its certain tendency to pave the way to monarchy, seems not to have been contested. The prospect of such a consolidation has formed the only topic of controversy. It would be unnecessary therefore, for the committee to dwell long on the reasons which support the position of the General Assembly. It may not be improper however to remark two consequences evidently flowing from an extension of the federal powers to every subject falling within the idea of the "general welfare."

One consequence must be, to enlarge the sphere of discretion allotted to the executive magistrate. Even within the legislative limits properly defined by the constitution, the difficulty of accomodating legal regulations to a country so great in extent, and so various in its circumstances, has been much felt; and has led to occasional investments of power in the executive, which involve perhaps as large a portion of discretion, as can be deemed consistent with the nature of the executive trust. In proportion as the objects of legislative care might be multiplied, would the time allowed for each be diminished, and the difficulty of providing uniform and particular regulations for all, be increased. From these sources would necessarily ensue, a greater latitude to the agency of that department which is always in existence, and which could best mould regulations of a general nature, so as to suit them to the diversity of particular situations. And it is in this latitude, as a supplement to the deficiency of the laws, that the degree of executive prerogative materially consists.

The other consequence would be, that of an excessive augmentation of the offices, honors, and emoluments depending on the executive will. Add to the present legitimate stock, all those of every description which a consolidation of the states would take from them, and turn over to the federal government, and the patronage of the executive would necessarily be as much swelled in this case, as its prerogative would be in the other.

This disproportionate increase of prerogative and patronage must, evidently, either enable the chief magistrate of the union, by quiet means, to secure his re-election from time to time, and finally, to regulate the succession as he might please; or, by giving so transcendent an importance to the office, would render the elections to it so violent and corrupt, that the public voice itself might call for an hereditary, in place of an elective succession. Which ever of these events might follow, the transformation of the Republican system of the United States into a monarchy, anticipated by the General Assembly from a consolidation of the states into one sovereignty, would be equally accomplished; and whether it would be into a mixt or an absolute monarchy, might depend on too many contingencies to admit of any certain foresight.

The resolution next in order, is contained in the following terms:

That the General Assembly doth particularly protest against the palpable, and alarming infractions of the constitution, in the two late cases of the "Alien and Sedition acts," passed at the last session of Congress; the first of which, exercises a power no where delegated to the federal government; and which by uniting legislative and judicial powers to those of executive, subverts the general principles of a free government, as well as the particular organization, and positive provisions of the federal constitution; and the other of which acts, exercises in like manner, a power not delegated by the constitution, but on the contrary, expressly and positively forbidden by one of the amendments thereto; a power, which more than any other, ought to produce universal alarm; because it is levelled against that right of freely examining public characters and measures, and of free communication among the people thereon, which has ever been justly deemed the only effectual guardian of every other right.

The subject of this resolution having, it is presumed, more particularly led the General Assembly into the proceedings which they communicated to the other states, and being in itself of peculiar importance; it deserves the most critical and faithful investigation; for the length of which no other apology will be necessary.

The subject divides itself into *first*, "The Alien Act," *secondly*, "The Sedition Act."

Of the "Alien act," it is affirmed by the resolution, 1st. That it exercises a power no where delegated to the federal government. 2d. That it unites legislative and judicial powers to those of the executive. 3d. That this union of power, subverts the general principles of free government. 4th. That it subverts the particular organization and positive provisions of the federal constitution.

In order to clear the way for a correct view of the first position, several observations will be premised.

In the first place; it is to be borne in mind, that it being a characteristic feature of the Federal constitution, as it was originally ratified, and an amendent thereto having precisely declared, "That the powers not delegated to the United States by the constitution, nor prohibited by it to the states, are reserved to the states respectively, or to the people"; it is incumbent in this, as in every other exercise of power by the federal government, to prove from the constitution, that it grants the particular power exercised.

The next observation to be made, is, that much confusion and fallacy, have been thrown into the question, by blending the two cases of *aliens, members of a hostile nation*; and *aliens, members of friendly nations*. These two cases are so obviously, and so essentially distinct, that it occasions no little surprise that the distinction should have been disregarded: and the surprise is so much the greater, as it appears that the two cases are actually distinguished by two separate acts of Congress, passed at the same session, and comprised in the same publication; the one providing for the case of "alien enemies"; the other "concerning aliens" indiscriminately; and consequently extending to aliens of every nation in peace and amity with the United States. With respect to alien enemies, no doubt has been intimated as to the federal authority over them; the constitution having expressly delegated to Congress the power to declare war against any nation, and of course to treat it and all its members as enemies. With respect to aliens, who are not enemies, but members of nations in peace and amity with the United States, the power assumed by the act of Congress, is denied to be constitutional; and it is accordingly against this act, that the protest of the General Assembly is expressly and exclusively directed.

A third observation is, that were it admitted as is contended, that the "act concerning aliens," has for its object, not a *penal*, but a *preventive* justice; it would still remain to be proved that it comes within the constitutional power of the federal legislature, and if within its power, that the legislature has exercised it in a constitutional manner.

In the administration of preventive justice, the following principles have been held sacred; that some probable ground of suspicion be exhibited before some judicial authority; that it be supported by oath or affirmation; that the party may avoid being thrown into confinement, by finding pledges or sureties for his legal conduct sufficient in the judgment of some judicial authority; that he may have the benefit of a writ of habeas corpus, and thus obtain his release, if wrongfully confined; and that he may at any time be discharged from his recognizance, or his confinement, and restored to his former liberty and rights, on the order of the proper judicial authority; if it shall see sufficient cause.

All these principles of the only preventive justice known to American jurisprudence, are violated by the alien act. The ground of suspicion is to be judged of, not by any judicial authority, but by the executive magistrate alone; no oath or affirmation is required; if the suspicion be held reasonable by the President, he may order the suspected alien to depart the territory of the United States, without the opportunity of avoiding the sentence, by finding pledges for his future good conduct; as the President may limit the time of departure as he pleases, the benefit of the writ of habeas corpus, may be suspended with respect to the party, although the constitution ordains, that it shall not be suspended, unless when the public safety may require it in case of rebellion or invasion, neither of which existed at the passage of the act: And the party being, under the sentence of the President, either removed from the United States, or being punished by imprisonment, or disqualification ever to become a citizen on conviction of not obeying the order of removal, he cannot be discharged from the proceedings against him, and restored to the benefits of his former situation, although the *highest judicial authority* should see the most sufficient cause for it.

But, in the last place, it can never be admitted, that the removal of aliens, authorised by the act, is to be considered, not as punishment for an offence; but as a measure of precaution and prevention. If the banishment of an alien from a country into which he has been invited, as the asylum most auspicious to his happiness; a country, where he may have formed the most tender of connections, where he may have vested his entire property, and acquired property of the real and permanent, as well as the moveable and temporary kind; where he enjoys under the laws, a greater share of the blessings of personal security and personal liberty, than he can elsewhere hope for, and where he may have nearly compleated his probationary title to citizenship; if moreover, in the execution of the sentence against him, he is to be exposed, not only to the ordinary dangers of the sea, but to the peculiar casualties incident to a crisis of war, and of unusual licentiousness on that element, and possibly to vindictive purposes which his emigration itself may have provoked; if a banishment of this sort be not a punishment, and among the severest of punishments, it will be difficult to imagine a doom to which the name can be applied. And if it be a punishment, it will remain to be enquired, whether it can be constitutionally inflicted, on mere suspicion, by the single will of the executive magistrate, on persons convicted of no personal offence against the laws of the land, nor involved in any offence against the law of nations, charged on the foreign state of which they are members.

One argument offered in justification of this power exercised over aliens, is, that the admission of them into the country being of favor not of right, the favor is at all times revokable.

To this argument it might be answered, that allowing the truth of the inference, it would be no proof of what is required. A question would still occur, whether the constitution had vested the discretionary power of admitting aliens in the federal government or in the state governments.

But it can not be a true inference, that because the admission of an alien is a favor, the favor may be revoked at pleasure. A grant of land to an individual, may be of favor not of right; but the moment the grant is made, the favor becomes a right, and must be forfeited before it can be taken away. To pardon a malefactor may be a favor, but the pardon is not, on that account, the less irrevocable. To admit an alien to naturalization, is as much a favor, as to admit him to reside in the country; yet it cannot be pretended, that a person naturalized can be deprived of the benefit, any more than a native citizen can be disfranchised.

Again it is said, that aliens not being parties to the constitution, the rights and privileges which it secures, cannot be at all claimed by them.

To this reasoning also, it might be answered, that although aliens are not parties to the constitution, it does not follow that the constitution has vested in Congress an absolute power over them. The parties to the constitution may have granted, or retained, or modified the power over aliens, without regard to that particular consideration.

But a more direct reply is, that it does not follow, because aliens are not parties to the constitution, as citizens are parties to it, that whilst they actually conform to it, they have no right to its protection. Aliens are not more parties to the laws, than they are parties to the constitution; yet it will not be disputed, that as they owe on one hand, a temporary obedience, they are entitled in return, to their protection and advantage.

If aliens had no rights under the constitution, they might not only be banished, but even capitally punished, without a jury or the other incidents to a fair trial. But so far has a contrary principle been carried, in every part of the United States, that except on charges of treason, an alien has, besides all the common privileges, the special one of being tried by a jury, of which one half may be also aliens.

It is said, further, that by the law and practice of nations, aliens may be removed at discretion, for offences against the law of nations; that Congress are authorised to define and punish such offences; and that to be dangerous to the peace of society is, in aliens, one of those offences.

The distinction between alien enemies and alien friends, is a clear and conclusive answer to this argument. Alien enemies are under the law of nations, and liable to be punished for offences against it. Alien friends, except in the single case of public ministers, are under the municipal law, and must be tried and punished according to that law only.

This argument also, by referring the alien act, to the power of Congress to define and *punish* offences against the law of nations, yields the point that the act is of a *penal*, not merely of a preventive operation. It must, in truth be so considered. And if it be a penal act, the punishment it inflicts, must be justified by some offence that deserves it.

Offences for which aliens within the jurisdiction of a country, are punishable, are first, offences committed by the nation of which they make a part, and in whose offences they are involved: Secondly, offences committed by themselves alone, without any charge against the nation to which they belong. The first is the case of alien enemies; the second the case of alien friends. In the first case, the offending nation can no otherwise be punished than by war, one of the laws of which authorizes the expulsion of such of its members, as may be found within the country, against which the offence has been committed. In the second case, the offence being committed by the individual, not by his nation, and against the municipal law, not against the law of nations; the individual only, and not the nation is punishable; and the punishment must be conducted according to the municipal law, not according to the law of nations. Under this view of the subject, the act of Congress, for the removal of alien enemies, being conformable to the law of nations, is justified by the constitution: and the "act," for the removal of alien friends, being repugnant to the constitutional principles of municipal law, is unjustifiable.

Nor is the act of Congress, for the removal of alien friends, more agreeable to the general practice of nations, than it is within the purview of the law of nations. The general practice of nations, distinguishes between alien friends and alien enemies. The latter it has proceeded against, according to the law of nations, by expelling them as enemies. The former it has considered as under a local and temporary allegiance, and entitled to a correspondent protection. If contrary instances are to be found in barbarous countries, under undefined prerogatives, or amid revolutionary dangers; they will not be deemed fit precedents for the government of the United States, even if not beyond its constitutional authority.

It is said, that Congress may grant letters of marque and reprisal; that reprisals may be made on persons, as well as property; and that the removal of aliens may be considered as the exercise in an inferior degree, of the general power of reprisal on persons.

Without entering minutely into a question that does not seem to require it; it may be remarked, that reprisal is a seizure of foreign persons or property, with a view to obtain that justice for injuries done by one state or its members, to another state or its members; for which a refusal of the aggressor requires such a resort to force under the law of nations. It must be considered as an abuse of words to call the removal of persons from a country, a seizure or reprisal on them; nor is the distinction to be overlooked between reprisals on persons within the country and under the faith of its laws, and on persons out of the country. But, laying aside these considerations; it is evidently impossible to bring the alien act within the power of granting reprisals; since it does not alledge or imply any injury received from any particular nation, for which this proceeding against its members was intended as a reparation. The proceeding is authorized against aliens *of every nation*; of nations charged neither with any similar proceeding against American citizens, nor with any injuries for which justice might be sought, in the mode prescribed by the act. Were it true therefore, that good causes existed for reprisals against one or more foreign nations, and that neither the persons nor property of its members under the faith of our laws, could plead an exemption; the operation of the act ought to have been limited to the aliens among us, belonging to such nations. To license reprisals against all nations, for aggressions charged on one only, would be a measure as contrary to every principle of justice and public law, as to a wise policy, and the universal practice of nations.

It is said, that the right of removing aliens is an incident to the power of war, vested in Congress by the constitution.

This is a former argument in a new shape only; and is answered by repeating, that the removal of alien enemies is an incident to the power of war; that the removal of alien friends, is not an incident to the power of war.

It is said, that Congress, are, by the constitution, to protect each state against invasion; and that the means of *preventing* invasion, are included in the power of protection against it.

The power of war in general, having been before granted by the constitution; this clause must either be a mere specification for greater caution and certainty, of which there are other examples in the instrument; or be the injunction of a duty, superadded to a grant of the power. Under either explanation, it cannot enlarge the powers of Congress on the subject. The power and the duty to protect each state against an invading enemy, would be the same under the general power, if this regard to greater caution had been omitted.

Invasion is an operation of war. To protect against invasion is an exercise of the power of war. A power therefore not incident to war, cannot be incident to a particular modification of war. And as the removal of alien friends has appeared to be no incident to a general state of war, it cannot be incident to a partial state, or a particular modification of war.

Nor can it ever be granted, that a power to act on a case when it actually occurs, includes a power over all the means that may *tend to prevent* the occurrence of the case. Such a latitude of construction would render unavailing, every practicable definition of particular and limited powers. Under the idea of preventing war in general, as well as invasion in particular, not only an indiscriminate removal of all aliens, might be enforced; but a thousand other things still more remote from the operations and precautions appurtenant to war, might take place. A bigoted or tyrannical nation might threaten us with war, unless certain religious or political regulations were adopted by us; yet it never could be inferred, if the regulations which would prevent war, were such as Congress had otherwise no power to make, that the power to make them would grow out of the purpose they were to answer. Congress have power to suppress insurrections, yet it would not be allowed to follow, that they might employ all the means tending to prevent them; of which a system of moral instruction for the ignorant, and of provident support for the poor, might be regarded as among the most efficacious.

One argument for the power of the General Government to remove aliens would have been passed in silence, if it had appeared under any authority inferior to that of a report, made during the last session of Congress, to the House of Representatives by a committee, and approved by the house. The doctrine on which this argument is founded, is of so new and so extraordinary a character, and strikes so radically at the political system of America, that it is proper to state it in the very words of the report.

"The act (concerning aliens) is said to be unconstitutional, because to remove aliens, is a direct breach of the Constitution which provides, by the 9th section of the 1st article: that the migration or importation of such persons as any of the states shall think proper to admit, shall not be prohibited by the Congress, prior to the year 1808."

Among the answers given to this objection to the constitutionality of the act, the following very remarkable one is extracted.

"Thirdly, that as the Constitution has *given to the states*, no power to remove aliens, during the period of the limitation under consideration, in the mean time, on the construction assumed, there would be no authority in the country, empowered to send away dangerous aliens which cannot be admitted."

The reasoning here used, would not in any view, be conclusive; because there are powers exercised by most other governments, which, in the United States are withheld by the people, both from the general government and from the state governments. Of this sort are many of the powers prohibited by the Declarations of right prefixed to the Constitutions, or by the clauses in the Constitutions, in the nature of such Declarations. Nay, so far is the political system of the United States distinguishable from that of other countries, by the caution with which powers are delegated and defined; that in one very important case, even of commercial regulation and revenue, the power is absolutely locked up against the hands of both governments. A tax on exports can be laid by no Constitutional authority whatever. Under a system thus pecu-

liarly guarded, there could surely be no absurdity in supposing, that alien friends, who if guilty of treasonable machinations may be punished, or if suspected on probable grounds,
may be secured by pledges or imprisonment, in like manner
with permanent citizens, were never meant to be subjected to
banishment by any arbitrary and unusual process, either under the one government or the other.

But it is not the inconclusiveness of the general reasoning
in this passage, which chiefly calls the attention to it. It is the
principle assumed by it, that the powers held by the states, are
given to them by the constitution of the United States; and
the inference from this principle, that the powers supposed to
be necessary which are not so given to the state governments,
must reside in the government of the United States.

The respect which is felt for every portion of the constituted authorities, forbids some of the reflections which this
singular paragraph might excite; and they are the more readily suppressed, as it may be presumed, with justice perhaps, as
well as candour, that inadvertence may have had its share in
the error. It would be an unjustifiable delicacy nevertheless, to
pass by so portentous a claim, proceeding from so high an authority, without a monitory notice of the fatal tendencies with
which it would be pregnant.

Lastly, it is said, that a law on the same subject with the
alien act, passed by this state originally in 1785, and re-enacted
in 1792, is a proof that a summary removal of suspected aliens,
was not heretofore regarded by the Virginia Legislature as liable to the objections now urged against such a measure.

This charge against Virginia, vanishes before the simple remark, that the law of Virginia relates to "suspicious persons,
being the subjects of any foreign power or state, who shall
have *made a declaration of war*, or actually *commenced hostilities*, or from whom the President shall apprehend *hostile designs*"; whereas the act of Congress relates to aliens, being the
subjects of foreign powers and states, who have *neither declared war, nor commenced hostilities, nor from whom hostile
designs are apprehended.*

II. It is next affirmed of the alien act, that it unites legislative, judicial and executive powers in the hands of the
President.

However difficult it may be to mark, in every case, with clearness and certainty, the line which divides legislative power, from the other departments of power; all will agree, that the powers referred to these departments may be so general and undefined, as to be of a legislative, not of an executive or judicial nature; and may for that reason be unconstitutional. Details, to a certain degree, are essential to the nature and character of a law; and, on criminal subjects, it is proper, that details should leave as little as possible to the discretion of those who are to apply and to execute the law. If nothing more were required, in exercising a legislative trust, than a general conveyance of authority, without laying down any precise rules, by which the authority conveyed, should be carried into effect; it would follow, that the whole power of legislation might be transferred by the legislature from itself, and proclamations might become substitutes for laws. A delegation of power in this latitude, would not be denied to be a union of the different powers.

To determine then, whether the appropriate powers of the distinct departments are united by the act authorising the executive to remove aliens, it must be enquired whether it contains such details, definitions, and rules, as appertain to the true character of a law; especially, a law by which personal liberty is invaded, property deprived of its value to the owner, and life itself indirectly exposed to danger.

The alien act, declares, "that it shall be lawful for the president to order all such aliens as he shall judge *dangerous* to the peace and safety of the United States, or shall have reasonable grounds to *suspect*, are concerned in any treasonable, *or secret machinations*, against the government thereof, to depart," &c.

Could a power be well given in terms less definite, less particular, and less precise. To be *dangerous to the public safety*; to be *suspected of secret machinations* against the government: these can never be mistaken for legal rules or certain definitions. They leave every thing to the President. His will is the law.

But it is not a legislative power only that is given to the President. He is to stand in the place of the judiciary also. His suspicion is the only evidence which is to convict: his order the only judgment which is to be executed.

Thus it is the President whose will is to designate the offensive conduct; it is his will that is to ascertain the individuals on whom it is charged; and it is his will, that is to cause the sentence to be executed. It is rightly affirmed therefore, that the act unites legislative and judicial powers to those of the executive.

III. It is affirmed that this union of powers subverts the general principles of free government.

It has become an axiom in the science of government, that a separation of the legislative, executive and judicial departments, is necessary to the preservation of public liberty. No where has this axiom been better understood in theory, or more carefully pursued in practice, than in the United States.

IV. It is affirmed that such a union of power subverts the particular organization and positive provisions of the federal constitution.

According to the particular organization of the constitution, its legislative powers are vested in the Congress; its executive powers in the President, and its judicial powers, in a supreme and inferior tribunals. The union of any two of these powers, and still more of all three, in any one of these departments, as has been shewn to be done by the alien act, must consequently subvert the constitutional organization of them.

That positive provisions in the constitution, securing to individuals the benefits of fair trial, are also violated by the union of powers in the alien act, necessarily results from the two facts, that the act relates to alien friends, and that alien friends being under the municipal law only, are entitled to its protection.

The *second* object against which the resolution protests is the sedition act.

Of this act it is affirmed 1. That it exercises in like manner a power not delegated by the constitution. 2d. That the power, on the contrary, is expressly and positively forbidden by one of the amendments to the constitution. 3d. That this is a power, which more than any other ought to produce universal alarm; because it is levelled against that right of freely examining public characters and measures, and of free communication thereon; which has ever been justly deemed the only effectual guardian of every other right.

I. That it exercises a power not delegated by the constitution.

Here, again it will be proper to recollect, that the Federal Government being composed of powers specifically granted, with a reservation of all others to the states or to the people, the positive authority under which the sedition act could be passed must be produced by those who assert its constitutionality. In what part of the constitution then is this authority to be found?

Several attempts have been made to answer this question, which will be examined in their order. The committee will begin with one, which has filled them with equal astonishment and apprehension; and which, they cannot but persuade themselves, must have the same effect on all, who will consider it with coolness and impartiality, and with a reverence for our constitution, in the true character in which it issued from the sovereign authority of the people. The committee refer to the doctrine lately advanced as a sanction to the sedition act: "that the common or unwritten law," a law of vast extent and complexity, and embracing almost every possible subject of legislation, both civil and criminal, "makes a part of the law of these states; in their united and national capacity."

The novelty, and in the judgment of the committee, the extravagance of this pretension, would have consigned it to the silence, in which they have passed by other arguments, which an extraordinary zeal for the act has drawn into the discussion. But the auspices, under which this innovation presents itself, have constrained the committee to bestow on it an attention, which other considerations might have forbidden.

In executing the task, it may be of use, to look back to the colonial state of this country, prior to the revolution; to trace the effect of the revolution which converted the colonies into independent states; to enquire into the import of the articles of confederation, the first instrument by which the union of the states was regularly established; and finally to consult the Constitution of 1788, which is the oracle that must decide the important question.

In the state prior to the revolution, it is certain that the common law under different limitations, made a part of the colonial codes. But whether it be understood that the original colonists brought the law with them, or made it their law by adoption; it is equally certain that it was the separate law of each colony within its respective limits, and was unknown to them, as a law pervading and operating through the whole, as one society.

It could not possibly be otherwise. The common law was not the same in any two of the colonies; in some, the modifications were materially and extensively different. There was no common legislature, by which a common will, could be expressed in the form of a law; nor any common magistracy, by which such a law could be carried into practice. The will of each colony alone and separately, had its organs for these purposes.

This stage of our political history, furnishes no foothold for the patrons of this new doctrine.

Did then, the principle or operation of the great event which made the colonies, independent states, imply or introduce the common law, as a law of the union?

The fundamental principle of the revolution was, that the colonies were co-ordinate members with each other, and with Great-Britain; of an Empire, united by a common Executive Sovereign, but not united by any common Legislative Sovereign. The Legislative power was maintained to be as complete in each American Parliament, as in the British Parliament. And the royal prerogative was in force in each colony, by virtue of its acknowledging the King for its Executive Magistrate, as it was in Great-Britain, by virtue of a like acknowledgment there. A denial of these principles by Great-Britain, and the assertion of them by America, produced the revolution.

There was a time indeed, when an exception to the Legislative separation of the several component and co-equal parts of the Empire, obtained a degree of acquiescence. The British Parliament was allowed to regulate the trade with foreign nations, and between the different parts of the Empire. This was however mere practice without right, and contrary to the true theory of the constitution. The conveniency of some regulations in both those cases, was apparent; and as there was no Legislature with power over the whole, nor any constitutional pre-eminence among the Legislatures of the several parts; it was natural for the Legislature of that particular part which was the eldest and the largest, to assume this function, and for the others to acquiesce in it. This tacit arrangement was the less criticised, as the regulations established by the British Parliament, operated in favor of that part of the Empire, which seemed to bear the principal share of the public burdens, and were regarded as an indemnification of its advances for the other parts. As long as this regulating power was confined to the two objects of conveniency and equity, it was not complained of, nor much enquired into. But no sooner was it perverted to the selfish views of the party assuming it, than the injured parties began to feel and to reflect; and the moment the claim to a direct and indefinite power was ingrafted on the precedent of the regulating power, the whole charm was dissolved, and every eye opened to the usurpation. The assertion by G.B. of a power to make laws for the other members of the Empire *in all cases whatsoever*, ended in the discovery, that she had a right to make laws for them, *in no cases whatsoever*.

Such being the ground of our revolution, no support nor colour can be drawn from it, for the doctrine that the common law is binding on these states as one society. The doctrine on the contrary, is evidently repugnant to the fundamental principle of the revolution.

The articles of confederation, are the next source of information on this subject.

In the interval between the commencement of the revolution, and the final ratification of these articles, the nature and extent of the union was determined by the circumstances of the crisis, rather than by any accurate delineation of the general authority. It will not be alledged that the "common law," could have had any legitimate birth as a law of the United States, during that state of things. If it came as such, into existence at all, the charter of confederation must have been its parent.

Here again, however, its pretensions are absolutely destitute of foundation. This instrument does not contain a sentence or syllable, that can be tortured into a countenance of the idea, that the parties to it were with respect to the objects of the common law, to form one community. No such law is named or implied, or alluded to, as being in force, or as brought into force by that compact. No provision is made by which such a law could be carried into operation; whilst on the other hand, every such inference or pretext is absolutely precluded, by article 2d, which declares, "that each state retains its sovereignty, freedom and independence, and every power, jurisdiction and right, which is not by this confederation expressly delegated to the United States, in Congress assembled."

Thus far it appears, that not a vestige of this extraordinary doctrine can be found, in the origin or progress of American institutions. The evidence against it, has, on the contrary, grown stronger at every step; till it has amounted to a formal and positive exclusion, by written articles of compact among the parties concerned.

Is this exclusion revoked, and the common law introduced as a national law, by the present constitution of the United States? This is the final question to be examined.

It is readily admitted, that particular parts of the common law, may have a sanction from the constitution, so far as they are necessarily comprehended in the technical phrases which express the powers delegated to the government; and so far also, as such other parts may be adopted as necessary and proper, for carrying into execution the powers expressly delegated. But the question does not relate to either of these portions of the common law. It relates to the common law, beyond these limitations.

The only part of the constitution which seems to have been relied on in this case, is the 2d sect. of art. III. "The judicial power shall extend to all cases, *in law and equity*, arising *under this constitution*, the laws of the United States, and treaties made or which shall be made under their authority."

It has been asked what cases distinct from those arising under the laws and treaties of the United States, can arise under the constitution, other than those arising under the common law; and it is inferred, that the common law is accordingly adopted or recognized by the constitution.

Never perhaps was so broad a construction applied to a text so clearly unsusceptible of it. If any colour for the inference could be found, it must be in the impossibility of finding any other cases in law and equity, within the provisions of the constitution, to satisfy the expression; and rather than resort to a construction affecting so essentially the whole character of the government, it would perhaps be more rational to consider the expression as a mere pleonasm or inadvertence. But it is not necessary to decide on such a dilemma. The expression is fully satisfied, and its accuracy justified, by two descriptions of cases, to which the judicial authority is extended, and neither of which implies that the common law is the law of the United States. One of these descriptions comprehends the cases growing out of the restrictions on the legislative power of the states. For example, it is provided that "no state shall emit bills of credit," or "make any thing but gold and silver coin a tender in payment of debts." Should this prohibition be violated, and a suit *between citizens of the same state* be the consequence, this would be a case arising under the constitution before the judicial power of the United States. A second description comprehends suits between citizens and foreigners, or citizens of different states, to be decided according to the state or foreign laws; but submitted by the constitution to the judicial power of the United States; the judicial power being, in several instances, extended beyond the legislative power of the United States.

To this explanation of the text, the following observations may be added.

The expression, cases in law and equity, is manifestly confined to cases of a civil nature; and would exclude cases of criminal jurisdiction. Criminal cases in law and equity, would be a language unknown to the law.

The succeeding paragraph of the same section, is in harmony with this construction. It is in these words—"In all cases affecting ambassadors, other public ministers and consuls, and those in which a state shall be a party, the Supreme Court shall have original jurisdiction. *In all* the other cases (including cases in law and equity arising under the constitution) the Supreme Court shall have *appellate* jurisdiction both as to law and *fact*; with such exceptions, and under such regulations as Congress shall make."

This paragraph, by expressly giving an *appellate* jurisdiction, in cases of law and equity arising under the constitution, to *fact*, as well as to law, clearly excludes criminal cases, where the trial by jury is secured; because the fact, in such cases, is not a subject of appeal. And although the appeal is liable to such *exceptions* and regulations as Congress may adopt; yet it is not to be supposed that an exception of all criminal cases could be contemplated; as well because a discretion in Congress to make or omit the exception would be improper; as because it would have been unnecessary. The exception could as easily have been made by the constitution itself, as referred to the Congress.

Once more, the amendment last added to the constitution, deserves attention, as throwing light on this subject. "The judicial power of the United States shall not be construed to extend to any suit in *law* or *equity*, commenced or prosecuted against one of the United States, by citizens of another state, or by citizens or subjects of any foreign power." As it will not be pretended that any criminal proceeding could take place against a state; the terms *law* or *equity*, must be understood as appropriate to *civil* in exclusion of *criminal* cases.

From these considerations, it is evident, that this part of the constitution, even if it could be applied at all, to the purpose for which it has been cited, would not include any cases whatever of a criminal nature; and consequently, would not authorise the inference from it, that the judicial authority extends to offences against the common law, as offences arising under the constitution.

It is further to be considered, that even if this part of the constitution could be strained into an application to every common law case, criminal as well as civil, it could have no effect in justifying the sedition act; which is an exercise of legislative, and not of judicial power: and it is the judicial power only of which the extent is defined in this part of the constitution.

There are two passages in the constitution, in which a description of the law of the United States, is found—The first is contained in article III. sect. 2, in the words following: "This constitution, the laws of the United States, and treaties made, or which shall be made under their authority." The second is contained in the 2d paragraph of art. VI. as follows: "This constitution and the laws of the United States which shall be made in pursuance thereof, and all treaties made, or which shall be made under the authority of the United States, shall be the supreme law of the land." The first of these descriptions was meant as a guide to the judges of the United States; the second as a guide to the judges in the several states. Both of them consist of an enumeration, which was evidently meant to be precise and compleat. If the common law had been understood to be a law of the United states, it is not possible to assign a satisfactory reason why it was not expressed in the enumeration.

In aid of these objections, the difficulties and confusion inseparable from a constructive introduction of the common law, would afford powerful reasons against it.

Is it to be the common law with, or without the British statutes?

If without the statutory amendments, the vices of the code would be insupportable.

If with these amendments, what period is to be fixed for limiting the British authority over our laws?

Is it to be the date of the eldest or the youngest of the colonies?

Or are the dates to be thrown together, and a medium deduced?

Or is our independence to be taken for the date?

Is, again, regard to be had to the various changes in the common law made by the local codes of America?

Is regard to be had to such changes, subsequent, as well as prior, to the establishment of the constitution?

Is regard to be had to future, as well as past changes?

Is the law to be different in every state, as differently modified by its code; or are the modifications of any particular state, to be applied to all?

And on the latter supposition, which among the state codes would form the standard?

Questions of this sort might be multiplied with as much ease, as there would be difficulty in answering them.

The consequences flowing from the proposed construction, furnish other objections equally conclusive; unless the text were peremptory in its meaning, and consistent with other parts of the instrument.

These consequences may be in relation; to the legislative authority of the United States; to the executive authority; to the judicial authority, and to the governments of the several states.

If it be understood that the common law is established by the constitution, it follows that no part of the law can be altered by the legislature; such of the statutes already passed as may be repugnant thereto, would be nullified, particularly the "sedition act" itself which boasts of being a melioration of the common law; and the whole code with all its incongruities, barbarisms, and bloody maxims would be inviolably saddled on the good people of the United States.

Should this consequence be rejected, and the common law be held, like other laws, liable to revision and alteration, by the authority of Congress; it then follows, that the authority of Congress is co-extensive with the objects of common law; that is to say, with every object of legislation: For to every such object, does some branch or other of the common law extend. The authority of Congress would therefore be no longer under the limitations, marked out in the constitution. They would be authorized to legislate in all cases whatsoever.

In the next place, as the President possesses the executive powers of the constitution, and is to see that the laws be faithfully executed, his authority also must be co-extensive with every branch of the common law. The additions which this would make to his power, though not readily to be estimated, claim the most serious attention.

This is not all; it will merit the most profound consideration, how far an indefinite admission of the common law, with a latitude in construing it, equal to the construction by which it is deduced from the constitution, might draw after it the various prerogatives making part of the unwritten law of England. The English constitution itself is nothing more than a composition of unwritten laws and maxims.

In the third place, whether the common law be admitted as of legal or of constitutional obligation, it would confer on the judicial department a discretion little short of a legislative power.

On the supposition of its having a constitutional obligation, this power in the judges would be permanent and irremediable by the legislature. On the other supposition, the power would not expire, until the legislature should have introduced a full system of statutory provisions. Let it be observed too, that besides all the uncertainties above enumerated, and which present an immense field for judicial discretion, it would remain with the same department to decide what parts of the common law would, and what would not, be properly applicable to the circumstances of the United States.

A discretion of this sort, has always been lamented as incongruous and dangerous, even in the colonial and state courts; although so much narrowed by positive provisions in the local codes on all the principal subjects embraced by the common law. Under the United States, where so few laws exist on those subjects, and where so great a lapse of time must happen before the vast chasm could be supplied, it is manifest that the power of the judges over the law would, in fact, erect them into legislators; and that for a long time, it would be impossible for the citizens to conjecture, either what was, or would be law.

In the last place, the consequence of admitting the common law as the law of the United States, on the authority of the individual states, is as obvious as it would be fatal. As this law relates to every subject of legislation, and would be paramount to the constitutions and laws of the states; the admission of it would overwhelm the residuary sovereignty of the states, and by one constructive operation new model the whole political fabric of the country.

From the review thus taken of the situation of the American colonies prior to their independence; of the effect of this event on their situation; of the nature and import of the articles of confederation; of the true meaning of the passage in the existing constitution from which the common law has been deduced; of the difficulties and uncertainties incident to the doctrine; and of its vast consequences in extending the powers of the federal government, and in superceding the authorities of the state governments; the committee feel the utmost confidence in concluding that the common law never was, nor by any fair construction, ever can be, deemed a law for the American people as one community; and they indulge the strongest expectation that the same conclusion will finally be drawn, by all candid and accurate enquirers into the subject. It is indeed distressing to reflect, that it ever should have been made a question, whether the constitution, on the whole face of which is seen so much labour to enumerate and define the several objects of federal power, could intend to introduce in the lump, in an indirect manner, and by a forced construction of a few phrases, the vast and multifarious jurisdiction involved in the common law; a law filling so many ample volumes; a law overspreading the entire field of legislation; and a law that would sap the foundation of the constitution as a system of limited and specified powers. A severer reproach could not in the opinion of the committee be thrown on the constitution, on those who framed, or on those who established it, than such a supposition would throw on them.

The argument then drawn from the common law, on the ground of its being adopted or recognized by the constitution, being inapplicable to the Sedition act, the committee will proceed to examine the other arguments which have been founded on the constitution.

They will waste but little time on the attempt to cover the act by the preamble to the constitution; it being contrary to every acknowledged rule of construction, to set up this part of an instrument, in opposition to the plain meaning, expressed in the body of the instrument. A preamble usually contains the general motives or reasons, for the particular regulations or measures which follow it; and is always understood to be explained and limited by them. In the present instance, a contrary interpretation would have the inadmissable effect, of rendering nugatory or improper, every part of the constitution which succeeds the preamble.

The paragraph in art. I, sect. 8, which contains the power to lay and collect taxes, duties, imposts, and excises, to pay the debts, and provide for the common defence and general welfare, having been already examined, will also require no particular attention in this place. It will have been seen that in its fair and consistent meaning, it cannot enlarge the enumerated powers vested in Congress.

The part of the constitution which seems most to be recurred to, in defence of the "Sedition Act," is the last clause of the above section, empowering Congress "to make all laws which shall be necessary and proper for carrying into execution the foregoing powers, and all other powers vested by this constitution in the government of the United States, or in any department or officer thereof."

The plain import of this clause is, that Congress shall have all the incidental or instrumental powers, necessary and proper for carrying into execution all the express powers; whether they be vested in the government of the United States, more collectively, or in the several departments, or officers thereof. It is not a grant of new powers to Congress, but merely a declaration, for the removal of all uncertainty, that the means of carrying into execution, those otherwise granted, are included in the grant.

Whenever, therefore a question arises concerning the constitutionality of a particular power; the first question is, whether the power be expressed in the constitution. If it be, the question is decided. If it be not expressed; the next enquiry must be, whether it is properly an incident to an express power, and necessary to its execution. If it be, it may be exercised by Congress. If it be not; Congress cannot exercise it.

Let the question be asked, then, whether the power over the press exercised in the "sedition act," be found among the powers expressly vested in the Congress? This is not pretended.

Is there any express power, for executing which, it is a necessary and proper power?

The power which has been selected, as least remote, in answer to this question, is that of "suppressing insurrections"; which is said to imply a power to *prevent* insurrections, by punishing whatever may *lead* or *tend* to them. But it surely cannot, with the least plausibility, be said, that a regulation of the press, and a punishment of libels, are exercises of a power to suppress insurrections. The most that could be said, would be, that the punishment of libels, if it had the tendency ascribed to it, might prevent the occasion, of passing or executing laws, necessary and proper for the suppression of in-surrections.

Has the federal government no power, then, to prevent as well as to punish resistance to the laws?

They have the power which the constitution deemed most proper in their hands for the purpose. The Congress has power, before it happens, to pass laws for punishing it; and the Executive and Judiciary have power to enforce those laws when it does happen.

It must be recollected by many, and could be shewn to the satisfaction of all, that the construction here put on the terms 'necessary and proper' is precisely the construction which pre-vailed during the discussions and ratifications of the constitu-tion. It may be added, and cannot too often be repeated, that it is a construction absolutely necessary to maintain their con-sistency with the peculiar character of the government, as pos-sessed of particular and defined powers only; not of the general and indefinite powers vested in ordinary govern-ments. For if the power to *suppress insurrections*, includes a power to *punish libels*; or if the power to *punish*, includes a power to *prevent*, by all the means that may have that *ten-dency*; such is the relation and influence among the most re-mote subjects of legislation, that a power over a very few, would carry with it a power over all. And it must be wholly immaterial, whether unlimited powers be exercised under the name of unlimited powers, or be exercised under the name of unlimited means of carrying into execution, limited powers.

This branch of the subject will be closed with a reflection which must have weight with all; but more especially with those who place peculiar reliance on the Judicial exposition of the constitution, as the bulwark provided against undue ex-tensions of the Legislative power. If it be understood that the powers implied in the specified powers, have an immediate and appropriate relation to them, as means, necessary and proper for carrying them into execution, questions on the constitutionality of laws passed for this purpose, will be of a nature sufficiently precise and determinate for Judicial cog-nizance and controul. If, on the other hand, Congress are not limited in the choice of means by any such appropriate rela-tion of them to the specified powers; but may employ all such means as they may deem fitted to *prevent* as well as to *punish*, crimes subjected to their authority; such as may have a *tendency* only to *promote* an object for which they are authorized to provide; every one must perceive that questions relating to means of this sort, must be questions of mere policy and expediency; on which legislative discretion alone can decide, and from which the judicial interposition and controul are completely excluded.

II. The next point which the resolution requires to be proved, is, that the power over the press exercised by the sedition act, is positively forbidden by one of the amendments to the constitution.

The amendment stands in these words—"Congress shall make no law respecting an establishment of religion, or prohibiting the free exercise thereof, *or abridging the freedom of speech or of the press*, or the right of the people peaceably to assemble, and to petition the government for a redress of grievances."

In the attempts to vindicate the "Sedition act," it has been contended, 1. That the "freedom of the press" is to be determined by the meaning of these terms in the common law. 2. That the article supposes the power over the press to be in Congress, and prohibits them only from *abridging* the freedom allowed to it by the common law.

Although it will be shewn, in examining the second of these positions, that the amendment is a denial to Congress of all power over the press; it may not be useless to make the following observations on the first of them.

It is deemed to be a sound opinion, that the sedition act, in its definition of some of the crimes created, is an abridgment of the freedom of publication, recognized by principles of the common law in England.

The freedom of the press under the common law, is, in the defences of the sedition act, made to consist in an exemption from all *previous* restraint on printed publications, by persons authorized to inspect and prohibit them. It appears to the committee, that this idea of the freedom of the press, can never be admitted to be the American idea of it: since a law inflicting penalties on printed publications, would have a similar effect with a law authorizing a previous restraint on them.

It would seem a mockery to say, that no law should be passed, preventing publications from being made, but that laws might be passed for punishing them in case they should be made.

The essential difference between the British government, and the American constitutions, will place this subject in the clearest light.

In the British government, the danger of encroachments on the rights of the people, is understood to be confined to the executive magistrate. The representatives of the people in the legislature, are not only exempt themselves, from distrust, but are considered as sufficient guardians of the rights of their constituents against the danger from the executive. Hence it is a principle, that the parliament is unlimited in its power; or in their own language, is omnipotent. Hence too, all the ramparts for protecting the rights of the people, such as their magna charta, their bill of rights, &c. are not reared against the parliament, but against the royal prerogative. They are merely legislative precautions, against executive usurpations. Under such a government as this, an exemption of the press from previous restraint by licensers appointed by the king, is all the freedom that can be secured to it.

In the United States, the case is altogether different. The people, not the government, possess the absolute sovereignty. The legislature, no less than the executive, is under limitations of power. Encroachments are regarded as possible from the one, as well as from the other. Hence in the United States, the great and essential rights of the people are secured against legislative, as well as against executive ambition. They are secured, not by laws paramount to prerogative; but by constitutions paramount to laws. This security of the freedom of the press, requires that it should be exempt, not only from previous restraint by the executive, as in Great Britain; but from legislative restraint also; and this exemption, to be effectual, must be an exemption, not only from the previous inspection of licensers, but from the subsequent penalty of laws.

The state of the press, therefore, under the common law, can not in this point of view, be the standard of its freedom, in the United States.

But there is another view, under which it may be necessary to consider this subject. It may be alledged, that although the security for the freedom of the press, be different in Great Britain and in this country; being a legal security only in the former, and a constitutional security in the latter; and although there may be a further difference, in an extension of the freedom of the press, here, beyond an exemption from previous restraint, to an exemption from subsequent penalties also; yet that the actual legal freedom of the press, under the common law, must determine the degree of freedom, which is meant by the terms and which is constitutionally secured against both previous and subsequent restraints.

The committee are not unaware of the difficulty of all general questions which, may turn on the proper boundary between the liberty and licentiousness of the press. They will leave it therefore for consideration only, how far the difference between the nature of the British government, and the nature of the American governments, and the practice under the latter, may shew the degree of rigor in the former, to be inapplicable to, and not obligatory in, the latter.

The nature of governments elective, limited and responsible, in all their branches, may well be supposed to require a greater freedom of animadversion, than might be tolerated by the genius of such a government as that of Great Britain. In the latter, it is a maxim, that the king, an hereditary, not a responsible magistrate, can do no wrong; and that the legislature, which in two thirds of its composition, is also hereditary, not responsible, can do what it pleases. In the United States, the executive magistrates are not held to be infallible, nor the legislatures to be omnipotent; and both being elective, are both responsible. Is it not natural and necessary, under such different circumstances, that a different degree of freedom, in the use of the press, should be contemplated?

Is not such an inference favored by what is observable in Great Britain itself? Notwithstanding the general doctrine of the common law, on the subject of the press, and the occasional punishment of those, who use it with a freedom offensive to the government; it is well known, that with respect to the responsible members of the government, where the reasons operating here, become applicable there; the freedom exercised by the press, and protected by the public opinion, far exceeds the limits prescribed by the ordinary rules of law.

The ministry, who are responsible to impeachment, are at all times, animadverted on, by the press, with peculiar freedom; and during the elections for the House of Commons, the other responsible part of the government, the press is employed with as little reserve towards the candidates.

The practice in America must be entitled to much more respect. In every state, probably, in the union, the press has exerted a freedom in canvassing the merits and measures of public men, of every description, which has not been confined to the strict limits of the common law. On this footing, the freedom of the press has stood; on this footing it yet stands. And it will not be a breach, either of truth or of candour, to say, that no persons or presses are in the habit of more unrestrained animadversions on the proceedings and functionaries of the state governments, than the persons and presses most zealous, in vindicating the act of Congress for punishing similar animadversions on the government of the United States.

The last remark will not be understood, as claiming for the state governments, an immunity greater than they have heretofore enjoyed. Some degree of abuse is inseparable from the proper use of every thing; and in no instance is this more true, than in that of the press. It has accordingly been decided by the practice of the states, that it is better to leave a few of its noxious branches, to their luxuriant growth, than by pruning them away, to injure the vigor of those yielding the proper fruits. And can the wisdom of this policy be doubted by any who reflect, that to the press alone, chequered as it is with abuses, the world is indebted for all the triumphs which have been gained by reason and humanity, over error and oppression; who reflect that to the same beneficent source, the United States owe much of the lights which conducted them to the rank of a free and independent nation; and which have improved their political system, into a shape so auspicious to their happiness. Had "Sedition acts," forbidding every publication that might bring the constituted agents into contempt or disrepute, or that might excite the hatred of the people against the authors of unjust or pernicious measures, been uniformly enforced against the press; might not the United States have been languishing at this day, under the infirmities of a sickly confederation? Might they not possibly be miserable colonies, groaning under a foreign yoke?

To these observations one fact will be added, which demonstrates that the common law cannot be admitted as the *universal* expositor of American terms, which may be the same with those contained in that law. The freedom of conscience, and of religion, are found in the same instruments, which assert the freedom of the press. It will never be admitted, that the meaning of the former, in the common law of England, is to limit their meaning in the United States.

Whatever weight may be allowed to these considerations, the committee do not, however, by any means, intend to rest the question on them. They contend that the article of amendment, instead of supposing in Congress, a power that might be exercised over the press, provided its freedom be not abridged, was meant as a positive denial to Congress, of any power whatever on the subject.

To demonstrate that this was the true object of the article, it will be sufficient to recall the circumstances which led to it, and to refer to the explanation accompanying the article.

When the constitution was under the discussions which preceded its ratification, it is well known, that great apprehensions were expressed by many, lest the omission of some positive exception from the powers delegated, of certain rights, and of the freedom of the press particularly, might expose them to the danger of being drawn by construction within some of the powers vested in Congress; more especially of the power to make all laws necessary and proper, for carrying their other powers into execution. In reply to this objection, it was invariably urged to be a fundamental and characteristic principle of the constitution; that all powers not given by it, were reserved; that no powers were given beyond those enumerated in the constitution, and such as were fairly incident to them; that the power over the rights in question, and particularly over the press, was neither among the enumerated powers, nor incident to any of them; and consequently that an exercise of any such power, would be a manifest usurpation. It is painful to remark, how much the arguments now employed in behalf of the sedition act, are at variance with the reasoning which then justified the constitution, and invited its ratification.

From this posture of the subject, resulted the interesting question in so many of the conventions, whether the doubts and dangers ascribed to the constitution, should be removed by any amendments previous to the ratification, or be postponed, in confidence that as far as they might be proper, they would be introduced in the form provided by the constitution. The latter course was adopted; and in most of the states, the ratifications were followed by propositions and instructions for rendering the constitution more explicit, and more safe to the rights, not meant to be delegated by it. Among those rights, the freedom of the press, in most instances, is particularly and emphatically mentioned. The firm and very pointed manner, in which it is asserted in the proceedings of the convention of this state will be hereafter seen.

In pursuance of the wishes thus expressed, the first Congress that assembled under the constitution, proposed certain amendments which have since, by the necessary ratifications, been made a part of it; among which amendments is the article containing, among other prohibitions on the Congress, an express declaration that they should make no law abridging the freedom of the press.

Without tracing farther the evidence on this subject, it would seem scarcely possible to doubt, that no power whatever over the press, was supposed to be delegated by the constitution, as it originally stood; and that the amendment was intended as a positive and absolute reservation of it.

But the evidence is still stronger. The proposition of amendments made by Congress, is introduced in the following terms: *"The Conventions of a number of the states having at the time of their adopting the Constitution, expressed a desire, in order to prevent misconstructions or abuse of its powers, that further declaratory and restrictive clauses should be added; and as extending the ground of public confidence in the government, will best ensure the beneficent ends of its institution."*

Here is the most satisfactory and authentic proof, that the several amendments proposed, were to be considered as either declaratory or restrictive; and whether the one or the other, as corresponding with the desire expressed by a number of the states, and as extending the ground of public confidence in the government.

Under any other construction of the amendment relating to the press, than that it declared the press to be wholly exempt from the power of Congress, the amendment could neither be said to correspond with the desire expressed by a number of the states, nor be calculated to extend the ground of public confidence in the government.

Nay more; the construction employed to justify the "sedition act," would exhibit a phenomenon, without a parallel in the political world. It would exhibit a number of respectable states, as denying first that any power over the press was delegated by the constitution; as proposing next, that an amendment to it, should explicitly declare that no such power was delegated; and finally, as concurring in an amendment actually recognizing or delegating such a power.

Is then the federal government, it will be asked, destitute of every authority for restraining the licentiousness of the press, and for shielding itself against the libellous attacks which may be made on those who administer it?

The constitution alone can answer this question. If no such power be expressly delegated, and it be not both necessary and proper to carry into execution an express power; above all, if it be expressly forbidden by a declaratory amendment to the constitution, the answer must be, that the federal government is destitute of all such authority.

And might it not be asked in turn, whether it is not more probable, under all the circumstances which have been reviewed, that the authority should be withheld by the constitution, than that it should be left to a vague and violent construction: whilst so much pains were bestowed in enumerating other powers, and so many less important powers are included in the enumeration.

Might it not be likewise asked, whether the anxious circumspection which dictated so many *peculiar* limitations on the general authority, would be unlikely to exempt the press altogether from that authority? The peculiar magnitude of some of the powers necessarily committed to the federal government; the peculiar duration required for the functions of some of its departments; the peculiar distance of the seat of its proceedings from the great body of its constituents; and the peculiar difficulty of circulating an adequate knowledge of them through any other channel; will not these considerations, some or other of which produced other exceptions from the powers of ordinary governments, all together, account for the policy of binding the hand of the federal government, from touching the channel which alone can give efficacy to its responsibility to its constituents; and of leaving those who administer it, to a remedy for injured reputations, under the same laws, and in the same tribunals, which protect their lives, their liberties, and their properties.

But the question does not turn either on the wisdom of the constitution, or on the policy which gave rise to its particular organization. It turns on the actual meaning of the instrument; by which it has appeared, that a power over the press is clearly excluded, from the number of powers delegated to the federal government.

III. And in the opinion of the committee well may it be said, as the resolution concludes with saying, that the unconstitutional power exercised over the press by the "sedition act," ought "more than any other, to produce universal alarm; because it is leveled against that right of freely examining public characters and measures, and of free communication among the people thereon, which has ever been justly deemed the only effectual guardian of every other right."

Without scrutinising minutely into all the provisions of the "sedition act," it will be sufficient to cite so much of section 2. as follows: "And be it further enacted, that if any person shall write, print, utter or publish, or shall cause or procure to be written, printed, uttered or published, or shall knowingly and willingly assist or aid in writing, printing, uttering or publishing any false, scandalous, and malicious writing or writings against the government of the United States, or either house of the Congress of the United States, or the President of the United States, *with an intent to defame the said government, or either house of the said Congress, or the President, or to bring them, or either of them, into contempt or disrepute; or to excite against them, or either, or any of them, the hatred of the good people of the United States, &c. then such person being thereof convicted before any court of the United States, having jurisdiction thereof, shall be punished by a fine not exceeding two thousand dollars, and by imprisonment not exceeding two years."*

On this part of the act the following observations present themselves.

1. The constitution supposes that the President, the Congress, and each of its houses, may not discharge their trusts, either from defect of judgment, or other causes. Hence, they are all made responsible to their constituents, at the returning periods of election; and the President, who is singly entrusted with very great powers, is, as a further guard, subjected to an intermediate impeachment.

2. Should it happen, as the constitution supposes it may happen, that either of these branches of the government, may not have duly discharged its trust; it is natural and proper, that according to the cause and degree of their faults, they should be brought into contempt or disrepute, and incur the hatred of the people.

3. Whether it has, in any case, happened that the proceedings of either, or all of those branches, evinces such a violation of duty as to justify a contempt, a disrepute or hatred among the people, can only be determined by a free examination thereof, and a free communication among the people thereon.

4. Whenever it may have actually happened, that proceedings of this sort are chargeable on all or either of the branches of the government, it is the duty as well as right of intelligent and faithful citizens, to discuss and promulge them freely, as well to controul them by the censorship of the public opinion, as to promote a remedy according to the rules of the constitution. And it cannot be avoided, that those who are to apply the remedy must feel, in some degree, a contempt or hatred against the transgressing party.

5. As the act was passed on July 14, 1798, and is to be in force until March 3, 1801, it was of course, that during its continuance, two elections of the entire House of Representatives, an election of a part of the Senate, and an election of a President, were to take place.

6. That consequently, during all these elections, intended by the constitution to preserve the purity, or to purge the

faults of the administration, the great remedial rights of the people were to be exercised, and the responsibility of their public agents to be skreened, under the penalties of this act.

May it not be asked of every intelligent friend to the liberties of his country whether, the power exercised in such an act as this, ought not to produce great and universal alarm? Whether a rigid execution of such an act, in time past, would not have repressed that information and communication among the people, which is indispensible to the just exercise of their electoral rights? And whether such an act, if made perpetual, and enforced with rigor, would not, in time to come, either destroy our free system of government, or prepare a convulsion that might prove equally fatal to it.

In answer to such questions, it has been pleaded that the writings and publications forbidden by the act, are those only which are false and malicious, and intended to defame; and merit is claimed for the privilege allowed to authors to justify, by proving the truth of their publications, and for the limitations to which the sentence of fine and imprisonment is subjected.

To those who concurred in the act, under the extraordinary belief, that the option lay between the passing of such an act, and leaving in force the common law of libels, which punishes truth equally with falsehood, and submits the fine and imprisonment to the indefinite discretion of the court, the merit of good intentions ought surely not to be refused. A like merit may perhaps be due for the discontinuance of the *corporal punishment* which the common law also leaves to the discretion of the court. This merit of *intention*, however, would have been greater, if the several mitigations had not been limited to so short a period; and the apparent inconsistency would have been avoided, between justifying the act at one time, by contrasting it with the rigors of the common law, otherwise in force; and at another time by appealing to the nature of the crisis, as requiring the temporary rigor exerted by the act.

But whatever may have been the meritorious intentions of all or any who contributed to the sedition act; a very few reflections will prove, that its baneful tendency is little diminished by the privilege of giving in evidence the truth of the matter contained in political writings.

In the first place, where simple and naked facts alone are in question, there is sufficient difficulty in some cases, and sufficient trouble and vexation in all, of meeting a prosecution from the government, with the full and formal proof, necessary in a court of law.

But in the next place, it must be obvious to the plainest minds, that opinions, and inferences, and conjectural observations, are not only in many cases inseparable from the facts, but may often be more the objects of the prosecution than the facts themselves; or may even be altogether abstracted from particular facts; and that opinions and inferences, and conjectural observations, cannot be subjects of that kind of proof which appertains to facts, before a court of law.

Again, it is no less obvious, that the *intent* to defame or bring into contempt or disrepute, or hatred, which is made a condition of the offence created by the act; cannot prevent its pernicious influence, on the freedom of the press. For omitting the enquiry, how far the malice of the intent is an inference of the law from the mere publication; it is manifestly impossible to punish the intent to bring those who administer the government into disrepute or contempt, without striking at the right of freely discussing public characters and measures: because those who engage in such discussions, must expect and *intend* to excite these unfavorable sentiments, so far as they may be thought to be deserved. To prohibit therefore the intent to excite those unfavorable sentiments against those who administer the government, is equivalent to a prohibition of the actual excitement of them; and to prohibit the actual excitement of them, is equivalent to a prohibition of discussions having that tendency and effect; which, again, is equivalent to a protection of those who administer the government, if they should at any time deserve the contempt or hatred of the people, against being exposed to it, by free animadversions on their characters and conduct. Nor can there be a doubt, if those in public trust be shielded by penal laws from such strictures of the press, as may expose them to contempt or disrepute, or hatred, where they may deserve it, that in exact proportion as they may deserve to be exposed, will be the certainty and criminality of the intent to expose them, and the vigilance of prosecuting and punishing it; nor a doubt, that a government thus intrenched in penal statutes, against the just and natural effects of a culpable administration, will easily evade the responsibility, which is essential to a faithful discharge of its duty.

Let it be recollected, lastly, that the right of electing the members of the government, constitutes more particularly the essence of a free and responsible government. The value and efficacy of this right, depends on the knowledge of the comparative merits and demerits of the candidates for public trust; and on the equal freedom, consequently, of examining and discussing these merits and demerits of the candidates respectively. It has been seen that a number of important elections will take place whilst the act is in force; although it should not be continued beyond the term to which it is limited. Should there happen, then, as is extremely probable in relation to some or other of the branches of the government, to be competitions between those who are, and those who are not, members of the government; what will be the situations of the competitors? Not equal; because the characters of the former will be covered by the "sedition act" from animadversions exposing them to disrepute among the people; whilst the latter may be exposed to the contempt and hatred of the people, without a violation of the act. What will be the situation of the people? Not free; because they will be compelled to make their election between competitors, whose pretensions they are not permitted by the act, equally to examine, to discuss, and to ascertain. And from both these situations, will not those in power derive an undue advantage for continuing themselves in it; which by impairing the right of election, endangers the blessings of the government founded on it.

It is with justice, therefore, that the General Assembly hath affirmed in the resolution, as well that the right of freely examining public characters and measures, and of free communication thereon, is the only effectual guardian of every other right; as that this particular right is leveled at, by the power exercised in the "sedition act."

The resolution next in order is as follows:

That this state having by its Convention, which ratified the Federal Constitution expressly declared, that among other essential rights, "the liberty of conscience and of the press cannot be cancelled, abridged, restrained or modified by any authority of the United States," and from its extreme anxiety to guard these rights from every possible attack of sophistry and ambition, having with other states, recommended an amendment for that purpose, which amendment was, in due time, annexed to the constitution; it would mark a reproachful inconsistency, and criminal degeneracy, if an indifference were not shewn, to the most palpable violation of one of the rights, thus declared and secured; and to the establishment of a precedent, which may be fatal to the other.

To place this resolution in its just light, it will be necessary to recur to the act of ratification by Virginia which stands in the ensuing form.

We, the Delegates of the people of Virginia, duly elected in pursuance of a recommendation from the General Assembly, and now met in Convention, having fully and freely investigated and discussed the proceedings of the federal convention, and being prepared as well as the most mature deliberation hath enabled us, to decide thereon; DO, in the name and in behalf of the people of Virginia, declare and make known, that the powers granted under the constitution, being derived from the people of the United States, may be resumed by them, whensoever the same shall be perverted to their injury or oppression; and that every power not granted thereby, remains with them, and at their will. That therefore, no right of any denomination can be cancelled, abridged, restrained or modified, by the Congress, by the Senate or House of Representatives acting in any capacity, by the President, or any department or officer of the United States, except in those instances in which power is given by the constitution for those purposes; and, that among other essential rights, the liberty of conscience and of the press, cannot be cancelled, abridged, restrained or modified by any authority of the United States.

Here is an express and solemn declaration by the convention of the state, that they ratified the constitution in the sense, that no right of any denomination can be cancelled, abridged, restrained or modified by the government of the United States or any part of it; except in those instances in which power is given by the constitution; and in the sense particularly, "that among other essential rights, the liberty of conscience and freedom of the press cannot be cancelled, abridged, restrained or modified, by any authority of the United States."

Words could not well express, in a fuller or more forcible manner, the understanding of the convention, that the liberty of conscience and the freedom of the press, were *equally* and *completely* exempted from all authority whatever of the United States.

Under an anxiety to guard more effectually these rights against every possible danger, the convention, after ratifying the constitution, proceeded to prefix to certain amendments proposed by them, a declaration of rights, in which are two articles providing, the one for the liberty of conscience, the other for the freedom of speech and of the press.

Similar recommendations having proceeded from a number of other states; and Congress, as has been seen, having in consequence thereof, and with a view to extend the ground of public confidence, proposed among other declaratory and restrictive clauses, a clause expressly securing the liberty of conscience and of the press; and Virginia having concurred in the ratifications which made them a part of the constitution; it will remain with a candid public to decide, whether it would not mark an inconsistency and degeneracy, if an indifference were now shewn to a palpable violation of one of those rights, the freedom of the press; and to a precedent therein, which may be fatal to the other, the free exercise of religion.

That the precedent established by the violation of the former of these rights, may, as is affirmed by the resolution, be fatal to the latter, appears to be demonstrable, by a comparison of the grounds on which they respectively rest; and from the scope of reasoning, by which the power over the former has been vindicated.

First. Both of these rights, the liberty of conscience and of the press, rest equally on the original ground of not being delegated by the constitution, and consequently withheld from the government. Any construction therefore, that would attack this original security for the one must have the like effect on the other.

Secondly. They are both equally secured by the supplement to the constitution; being both included in the same amendment, made at the same time, and by the same authority. Any construction or argument then which would turn the amendment into a grant or acknowledgment of power with respect to the press, might be equally applied to the freedom of religion.

Thirdly. If it be admitted that the extent of the freedom of the press secured by the amendment, is to be measured by the common law on this subject; the same authority may be resorted to, for the standard which is to fix the extent of the "free exercise of religion." It cannot be necessary to say what this standard would be; whether the common law be taken solely as the unwritten, or as varied by the written, law of England.

Fourthly. If the words and phrases in the amendment, are to be considered as chosen with a studied discrimination, which yields an argument for a power over the press, under the limitation that its freedom be not abridged; the same argument results from the same consideration, for a power over the exercise of religion, under the limitation that its freedom be not prohibited.

For if Congress may regulate the freedom of the press, provided they do not abridge it: because it is said only, "they shall not abridge it"; and is not said, "they shall make no law respecting it": the analogy of reasoning is conclusive, that Congress may *regulate* and even *abridge* the free exercise of religion; provided they do not *prohibit* it; because it is said only "they shall not prohibit it"; and is *not* said "they shall make no law *respecting* or no law *abridging* it."

The General Assembly were governed by the clearest reason, then, in considering the "Sedition act," which legislates on the freedom of the press, as establishing a precedent that may be fatal to the liberty of conscience and it will be the duty of all, in proportion as they value the security of the latter, to take the alarm at every encroachment on the former.

The two concluding resolutions only remain to be examined. They are in the words following.

"That the good people of this commonwealth, having ever felt, and continuing to feel the most sincere affection for their brethren of the other states; the truest anxiety for establishing and perpetuating the union of all; and the most scrupulous fidelity to that constitution, which is the pledge of mutual friendship, and the instrument of mutual happiness; the General Assembly doth solemnly appeal to the like dispositions in the other states, in confidence that they will concur with this commonwealth in declaring, as it does hereby declare, that the acts aforesaid, are unconstitutional; and, that the necessary and proper measures will be taken by each, for co-operating with this state, in maintaining unimpaired, the authorities, rights, and liberties, reserved to the states respectively, or to the People."

"That the Governor be desired, to transmit a copy of the foregoing resolutions to the executive authority of each of the other states, with a request that the same may be communicated to the Legislature thereof; and that a copy be furnished to each of the Senators and Representatives representing this state in the Congress of the United States."

The fairness and regularity of the course of proceeding, here pursued, have not protected it, against objections even from sources too respectable to be disregarded.

It has been said that it belongs to the judiciary of the United States, and not to the state legislatures, to declare the meaning of the Federal Constitution.

But a declaration that proceedings of the Federal Government are not warranted by the constitution, is a novelty neither among the citizens nor among the legislatures of the states; nor are the citizens or the legislature of Virginia, singular in the example of it.

Nor can the declarations of either, whether affirming or denying the constitutionality of measures of the Federal Government; or whether made before or after judicial decisions thereon, be deemed, in any point of view, an assumption of the office of the judge. The declarations in such cases, are expressions of opinion, unaccompanied with any other effect, than what they may produce on opinion, by exciting reflection. The expositions of the judiciary, on the other hand, are carried into immediate effect by force. The former may lead to a change in the legislative expression of the general will; possibly to a change in the opinion of the judiciary: the latter enforces the general will, whilst that will and that opinion continue unchanged.

And if there be no impropriety in declaring the unconstitu

tionality of proceedings in the Federal Government; where can be the impropriety of communicating the declaration to other states, and inviting their concurrence in a like declaration? What is allowable for one, must be allowable for all; and a free communication among the states, where the constitution imposes no restraint, is as allowable among the state governments, as among other public bodies, or private citizens. This consideration derives a weight, that cannot be denied to it, from the relation of the state legislatures, to the federal legislature, as the immediate constituents of one of its branches.

The legislatures of the states have a right also, to originate amendments to the constitution, by a concurrence of two thirds of the whole number, in applications to Congress for the purpose. When new states are to be formed by a junction of two or more states, or parts of states, the legislatures of the states concerned, are, as well as Congress, to concur in the measure. The states have a right also, to enter into agreements, or compacts, with the consent of Congress. In all such cases, a communication among them, results from the object which is common to them.

It is lastly to be seen, whether the confidence expressed by the resolution, that the *necessary and proper measures*, would be taken by the other states, for co-operating with Virginia, in maintaining the rights reserved to the states, or to the people, be in any degree liable to the objections which have been raised against it.

If it be liable to objection, it must be, because either the object, or the means, are objectionable.

The object being to maintain what the constitution has ordained, is in itself a laudable object.

The means are expressed in the terms "the necessary and proper measures." A proper object was to be pursued, by means both necessary and proper.

To find an objection then, it must be shewn, that some meaning was annexed to these general terms, which was not proper; and for this purpose, either that the means used by the General Assembly, were an example of improper means, or that there were no proper means to which the terms could refer.

In the example given by the state, of declaring the alien and sedition acts to be unconstitutional, and of communicating the declaration to the other states, no trace of improper means has appeared. And if the other states had concurred in making a like declaration, supported too by the numerous applications flowing immediately from the people, it can scarcely be doubted, that these simple means would have been as sufficient, as they are unexceptionable.

It is no less certain, that other means might have been employed, which are strictly within the limits of the constitution. The legislatures of the states might have made a direct representation to Congress, with a view to obtain a rescinding of the two offensive acts; or they might have represented to their respective senators in Congress, their wish, that two thirds thereof would propose an explanatory amendment to the constitution; or two thirds of themselves, if such had been their option, might, by an application to Congress, have obtained a convention for the same object.

These several means, though not equally eligible in themselves, nor probably, to the states, were all constitutionally open for consideration. And if the General Assembly, after declaring the two acts to be unconstitutional, the first and most obvious proceeding on the subject, did not undertake to point out to the other states, a choice among the farther measures that might become necessary and proper, the reserve will not be misconstrued by liberal minds, into any culpable imputation.

These observations appear to form a satisfactory reply, to every objection which is not founded on a misconception of the terms, employed in the resolutions. There is one other however, which may be of too much importance not to be added. It cannot be forgotten, that among the arguments addressed to those, who apprehended danger to liberty, from the establishment of the general government over so great a country; the appeal was emphatically made to the intermediate existence of the state governments, between the people and that government, to the vigilance with which they would descry the first symptoms of usurpation, and to the promptitude with which they would sound the alarm to the public. This argument was probably not without its effect; and if it was a proper one, then, to recommend the establishment of the constitution; it must be a proper one now, to assist in its interpretation.

The only part of the two concluding resolutions, that remains to be noticed, is the repetition in the first, of that warm
affection to the union and its members, and of that scrupulous fidelity to the constitution which have been invariably felt
by the people of this state. As the proceedings were introduced with these sentiments, they could not be more properly
closed, than in the same manner. Should there be any so far
misled, as to call in question the sincerity of these professions,
whatever regret may be excited by the error, the General
Assembly cannot descend into a discussion of it. Those who
have listened to the suggestion, can only be left to their own
recollection, of the part which this state has borne in the establishment of our national independence; in the establishment of our national constitution; and in maintaining under
it, the authority and laws of the union, without a single exception of internal resistance or commotion. By recurring to
these facts, they will be able to convince themselves, that the
representatives of the people of Virginia must be above the
necessity of opposing any other shield to attacks on their national patriotism, than their own consciousness and the justice
of an enlightened public; who will perceive in the resolutions
themselves, the strongest evidence of attachment both to the
constitution and to the union, since it is only by maintaining
the different governments and departments within their respective limits, that the blessings of either can be perpetuated.
The extensive view of the subject thus taken by the committee, has led them to report to the house, as the result of the
whole, the following resolution.

Resolved, That the General Assembly, having carefully and
respectfully attended to the proceedings of a number of the
states, in answer to their resolutions of December 21, 1798,
and having accurately and fully re-examined and re-consid-
ered the latter, find it to be their indispensable duty to adhere
to the same, as founded in truth, as consonant with the constitution, and as conducive to its preservation; and more especially to be their duty, to renew, as they do hereby renew,
their protest against "the alien and sedition acts," as palpable
and alarming infractions of the constitution.

January 7, 1800

To Thomas Jefferson

Dear Sir   Jany. 10. 1801.

Mrs. Browne having been detained at Fredg for some time, I did not receive your favor of the 19th. in time to be conveniently acknowledged by the last mail. The succeeding one of the 26th. came to hand on the 7th. instant only, a delay that fixes blame on the post office either in Washington or Fredg. In all the letters & most of the Newspapers which I have lately recd. thro' the post office, there is equal ground for complaint.

I find that the vote of Kentucky establishes the tie between the Repub: characters, and consequently throws the result into the hands of the H. of R. Desperate as some of the adverse party there may be, I can scarcely allow myself to believe that enough will not be found to frustrate the attempt to strangle the election of the people, and smuggle into the cheif Magistracy the creature of a faction. It would seem that every individual member, who has any standing or stake in society, or any portion of virtue or sober understandg must revolt at the tendency of such a manouvre. Is it possible that Mr. A. shd. give his sanction to it if that should be made a necessary ingredient? or that he would not hold it his duty or his policy, in case the present House should obstinately refuse to give effect to the Constn. to appoint, which he certainly may do before his office expires as early a day as possible, after that event, for the succeeding House to meet, and supply the omission. Should he disappt. a just expectation in either instance, it will be an omen, I think, forbidding the steps towards him which you seem to be meditating. I would not wish to discourage any attentions which friendship, prudence, or benevolence may suggest in his behalf, but I think it not improper to remark, that I find him infinitely sunk in the estimation of all parties. The follies of his administration, the oblique stroke at his Predecessor in the letter to Coxe, and the crooked character of that to T. Pinkney, are working powerfully agst. him. Added to these causes is the pamphlet of H which, tho' its recoil has perhaps more deeply wounded the author, than the Object it was discharged at, has contributed not a little to overthrow the latter staggering as he before was in the public esteem.

On the supposition of either event, whether of an interregnum in the Executive, or of a surreptitious intrusion into it, it becomes a question of the first order, what is the course demanded by the crisis. Will it be best to acquiesce in a suspension or usurpation of the Executive authority till the meeting of Congs. in Der. next, or for Congs. to be summoned by a joint proclamation or recommendation of the two characters havg a majority of votes for President. My present judgment favors the latter expedient. The prerogative of convening the Legislature must reside in one or other of them, and if both concur, must substantially include the requisite will. The intentions of the people would undoubtedly be pursued. And if, in reference to the Constn: the proceeding be not strictly regular, the irregularity will be less in form than any other adequate to the emergency; and will lie in form only rather than substance; whereas the other remedies proposed are substantial violations of the will of the people, of the scope of the Constitution, and of the public order & interest. It is to be hoped however that all such questions will be precluded by a proper decision of nine States in the H. of R.

I observe that the French Convention is represented as highly obnoxious to the Senate. I should not have supposed that the opposition would be hinged on the article surrendering public vessels. As the stipulation is mutual it certainly spares our pride, sufficiently to leave us free to calculate our interest, and on this point there cannot be a difference of opinion. I was less surprized at the obstacle discovered in the British Treaty, the latter of which combined with the repeal of the French Treaty, beget a suspicion that in some quarters at least the present posture of things has been long anticipated. It is certain however that the Convention leaves G. B. on a better footing than the B. Treaty placed her, and it is remarkable that E. D. & Murray, should have concurred in the arrangement, if it have any real interference with bona fide engagements to G. B. It may be recollected that the privilege given to British prizes was not purchased like that to French prizes, by any peculiar services to us; and never had any other pretext, than the alledged policy of putting the two great

rival nations of Europe as nearly as possible on an equal footing. Notwithstanding this pretext for the measure, H. in his
late pamphlet acknowledges the error of it. It would be truly
extraordinary if a measure intended for this equalizing purpose, should be construable into an insuperable barrier to the
equality proposed. It is of vast moment both in a domestic &
foreign view, that the Senate should come to a right decision.
The public mind is already sore & jealous of that body, and
particularly so of the insidious & mischeivous policy of the
British Treaty. It is strongly averse also to war, and would feel
abhorrence of an unjust or unnecessary war with any nation.
It is much to be wished that these facts may not be disregarded in the question before the Senate. If there be any
thing fairly inadmissible in the Convn. it would be better to
follow the example of a qualified ratification, than rush into a
provoking rejection. If there be any thing likely, however unjustly, to beget complaints or discontents on the part of G. B.
early & conciliatory explanations ought not to be omitted.
However difficult our situation has been made, justice & prudence will it is hoped, steer us through it peacefully. In some
respects the task is facilitated at the present moment. France
has sufficiently manifested her friendly disposition, and what
is more, seems to be duly impressed with the interest she has
in being at peace with us. G. B. however intoxicated with her
maritime ascendancy, is more dependent every day on our
commerce for her resources, must for a considerable length
of time look in a great degree to this Country, for bread for
herself, and absolutely for all the necessaries for her islands.
The prospect of a Northern confederacy of Neutrals cannot
fail, in several views, to inspire caution & management towards the U. S., especially as in the event of war or interruption of Commerce with the Baltic, the essential article of
naval Stores can be sought here only. Beside these cogent
motives to peace and moderation, her subjects will not fail to
remind her of the great pecuniary pledge they have in this
Country, and which under any interruption of peace or commerce with it, must fall under great embarrassments, if nothing worse. As I have not restrained my pen from this hasty
effusion, I will add for your consideration one other remark
on the subject. Should it be found that G. B. means to op-

pose pretensions drawn from her Treaty, to any part of the late one with F. may she not be diverted from it, by the idea of driving us into the necessity of soothing France, by stipulations to take effect at the expiration of the Treaty with G. B. and that wd. be a bar to the renewal of the latter; or in case the pretensions of G. B. should defeat the Treaty now before the Senate, might not such an expedient be made a plaister for the wound given to F?

My health still suffers from several complaints, and I am much afraid that any changes that may take place are not likely to be for the better. The age and very declining state of my father are making also daily claims on my attention; and, from appearances it may not be long before these claims may acquire their full force. All these considerations mingle themselves very seriously with one of the eventual arrangements contemplated. It is not my purpose however to retract what has passed in conversation between us on that head. But I can not see the necessity, and I extremely doubt the propriety, should the contest in hand issue as is most probable, of my anticipating a relinquishment of my home. I cannot but think, & feel that there will be an awkwardness to use the softest term, in appearing on the political Theatre before I could be considered as regularly called to it, and even before the commencement of the authority from which the call would proceed. Were any solid advantage at stake, this scruple might be the less applicable, but it does not occur that the difference of not very many days, can be at all material. As little can I admit that the circumstance of my participation in the Ex. business, cou'd have any such effect on either the majority or minority as has occured; or if a partiality in any particular friends would be gratified by a knowledge of such an arrangement, that the end would not be as well attained by its being otherwise made known to them that it was to take place, as by its being announced by my appearance on the spot. I only add that I am sensible of the obligation of respecting your conclusion whatever it may finally be; but I can not but hope that it may be influenced by the considerations which I have taken the liberty to hint. Very affecly. & respectfully I am Dr. Sir Yrs.

You may recollect a difficulty suggested in makg. appts. witht. a Senate, in case of resignations *prior to March 4*. How have you solved it?

SECRETARY OF STATE
AND PRESIDENT
1801–1817

To Robert R. Livingston and James Monroe

Gentlemen,   Department of State July 29th—1803.

Your dispatches, including the Treaty and two conventions signed with a French Plenipotentiary on the 30th of April, were safely delivered on the 14th by Mr. Hughes, to whose care you had committed them.

In concurring with the disposition of the French Government to treat for the whole of Louisiana, altho' the western part of it was not embraced by your powers, you were justified by the solid reasons which you give for it, and I am charged by the President to express to you his entire approbation of your so doing.

This approbation is in no respect precluded by the silence of your Commission and instructions. When these were made out, the object of the most sanguine was limited to the establishment of the Mississippi as our boundary. It was not presumed that more could be sought by the United States either with a chance of success, or perhaps without being suspected of a greedy ambition, than the Island of New Orleans and the two Floridas, it being little doubted that the latter was or would be comprehended in the Cession from Spain to France. To the acquisition of New Orleans and the Floridas, the provision was therefore accommodated. Nor was it to be supposed that in case the French Government should be willing to part with more than the Territory on our side of the Mississippi, an arrangement with Spain for restoring to her the territory on the other side would not be preferred to a sale of it to the United States. It might be added, that the ample views of the subject carried with him by Mr. Monroe and the confidence felt that your judicious management would make the most of favorable occurrences, lessened the necessity of multiplying provisions for every turn which your negotiations might possibly take.

The effect of such considerations was diminished by no information or just presumptions whatever. The note of Mr. Livingston in particular stating to the French Government the idea of ceding the Western Country above the Arkansa and communicated to this Department in his letter of the

29th January, was not received here till April 5 more than a
month after the Commission and instructions had been forwarded. And besides that this project not only left with
France the possession and jurisdiction of one bank of the
Mississippi from its mouth to the Arkansa, but a part of West
Florida, the whole of East Florida, and the harbours for ships
of war in the Gulph of Mexico, the letter inclosing the note
intimated that it had been treated by the French Government
with a decided neglect. In truth the communications in general between Mr. Livingston and the French Government,
both of prior and subsequent date, manifested a repugnance
to our views of purchase which left no expectation of any
arrangement with France by which an extensive acquisition
was to be made, unless in a favorable crisis of which advantage
should be taken. Such was thought to be the crisis which gave
birth to the extraordinary commission in which you are
joined. It consisted of the state of things produced by the
breach of our deposit at New Orleans, the situation of the
French Islands, particularly the important Island of St.
Domingo; the distress of the French finances, the unsettled
posture of Europe, the increasing jealousy between G Britain
and France, and the known aversion of the former to see the
mouth of the Mississippi in the hands of the latter. These considerations it was hoped, might so far open the eyes of France
to her real interest and her ears to the monitory truths which
were conveyed to her thro' different channels, as to reconcile
her to the establishment of the Mississippi as a natural boundary to the United States; or at least to some concessions
which would justify our patiently waiting for a fuller accomplishment of our wishes under auspicious events. The crisis relied on has derived peculiar force from the rapidity with which
the complaints and questions between France and Great
Britain ripened towards a rupture, and it is just ground for
mutual and general felicitation, that it has issued under your
zealous exertions, in the extensive acquisition beyond the
Mississippi.

With respect to the terms on which the acquisition is made,
there can be no doubt that the bargain will be regarded as on
the whole highly advantageous. The pecuniary stipulations
would have been more satisfactory, if they had departed less

from the plan prescribed; and particularly if the two millions of dollars in cash, intended to reduce the price or hasten the delivery of possession had been so applied, and the assumed payments to American claimants on the footing specified in the instructions. The unexpected weight of the draught now to be made on the Treasury will be sensibly felt by it, and may possibly be inconvenient in relation to other important objects.

The President has issued his proclamation convening Congress on the 17th of October, in order that the exchange of the ratifications may be made within the time limitted. It is obvious that the exchange, to be within the time, must be made here and not at Paris; and we infer from your letter of   that the ratifications of the Chief Consul are to be transmitted hither with that view.

I only add the wish of the President to know from you the understanding which prevailed in the negotiation with respect to the Boundaries of Louisiana, and particularly the pretensions and proofs for carrying it to the River Perdigo, or for including any lesser portion of West Florida.

With high respect, &c.

To James Monroe

Sir,   Department of State, July 6th, 1807.
The documents herewith inclosed from No. 1 to No. 9 inclusive, explain the hostile attack, with the insulting pretext for it, lately committed near the Capes of Virginia, by the British ship of War the Leopard, on the American frigate the Chesapeake. No. 10 is a copy of the Proclamation issued by the President, interdicting, in consequence of that outrage, the use of our waters and every other accommodation, to all British Armed ships.

1st. *This enormity is not a subject for discussion.* The immunity of a national ship of War from every species and purpose of search on the high seas, has never been contested by any nation. Great Britain would be second to none, in resenting such a violation of her rights, and such an insult to her flag.

She may bring the case to the test of her own feelings, by supposing that, instead of the customary demand of our marines serving compulsively even, on board her ships of war, opportunities had been seized for rescuing them, in like manner, whenever the superiority of force, or the chance of surprize, might be possessed by our ships of War.

But the present case is marked by circumstances which give it a peculiar die. The seamen taken from the Chesapeake had been ascertained to be native Citizens of the United States; and this fact was made known to the bearer of the demand, and doubtless communicated by him to his commander, previous to the commencement of the attack. It is a fact also, affirmed by two of the men, with every appearance of truth, that they had been impressed from American vessels into the British frigate from which they escaped, and by the third, that having been impressed from a British merchant ship, he had accepted the recruiting bounty under that duress, and with a view to alleviate his situation, till he could escape to his own country: and that the attack was made during a period of negotiation, and in the midst of friendly assurances from the British Government.

The printed papers, herewith sent, will enable you to judge of the spirit which has been roused by the occasion. It pervades the whole community, is abolishing the distinctions of party; and, regarding only the indignity offered to the Sovereignty and flag of the Nation, and the blood of Citizens so wantonly and wickedly shed, demands, in the loudest tone, an honorable reparation.

With this demand you are charged by the President. The tenor of his proclamation will be your guide, in reminding the British Government of the uniform proofs given by the United States of their disposition to maintain, faithfully, every friendly relation; of the multiplied infractions of their rights by British Naval Commanders on our coasts and in our harbours; of the inefficacy of reiterated appeals to the justice and friendship of that Government; and of the moderation on the part of the United States, which reiterated disappointments had not extinguished; till at length no alternative is left, but a voluntary satisfaction on the part of Great Britain, or a resort to means depending on the United States alone.

The nature and extent of the satisfaction ought to be suggested to the British Government, not less by a sense of its own honor, than by justice to that of the United States.

A formal disavowal of the deed, and restoration of the four seamen to the ship from which they were taken, are things of course *and indispensable. As a security for the future, an entire abolition of impressments from vessels under the flag of the United States*, if not already arranged, *is also to make an indispensable part of the satisfaction. The abolition* must be on terms compatible with the instructions to yourself and Mr. Pinkney on this subject; and if possible *without the authorized rejection from the service of the United States of British seamen who have not been two years in it.* Should it be impossible to *avoid this concession on the part of the United States*, it ought of itself, as being more than a reasonable *price for future security*, to extend the reparation due for the past.

But, beyond *these indispensable conditions the United States have a right to expect* every solemnity *of form* and every other ingredient of retribution and respect, which, according to usage and the sentiments of mankind, are proper in the strongest cases of insult, to the rights and sovereignty of a nation. And the British Government is to be apprized of the importance of a full compliance with this expectation, to the thorough healing of the wound which has been made in the feelings of the American Nation.

Should it be alleged as a ground for declining or diminishing the satisfaction in this case, that the United States have themselves taken it, by the interdict contained in the proclamation, the answer will be obvious. The interdict is a measure not of reparation, but of precaution; and would besides be amply justified by occurrences prior to the extraordinary outrage in question.

The exclusion of all armed ships whatever from our waters is, in fact, so much required by the vexations and dangers to our peace experienced from their visits, that the President makes it a special part of the charge to you, to avoid laying the United States under any species of restraint from adopting that remedy. Being extended to all belligerent nations, none of them could of right complain; and with the less reason, as the policy of most nations has limited the admission of foreign ships of war, into their ports, to such number as, being inferior to the naval force of the Country, could be readily made to respect its authority and laws.

As it may be useful in enforcing the justice of the present demands, to bring into view applicable cases, especially where Great Britain has been the complaining party, I refer you to the ground taken, and the language held by her, in those of the Faulkland Islands, and Nootka Sound; notwithstanding the assertion by Spain, in both cases, that the real right was in her, and the possession only in Great Britain. These cases will be found in the Annual Registers for 1771 and 79, and in the parliamentary debates for those years. In the latter you will find also two cases referred to, in one of which the French King sent an Ambassador Extraordinary to the King of Sardinia, in the most public and solemn manner, with an apology for an infringement of his territorial rights in the pursuit of a smuggler and murderer. In the other case, an Ambassador Exty was sent by the British Government to the Court of Portugal, with an apology for the pursuit and destruction by Admiral Boscawen, of certain French ships on the coasts of this last Kingdom. Many other cases more or less analogous may doubtless be found, see particularly the reparation by France to Great Britain for the attack on Turks Island in 1764, as related in the Annual Register and in Smollets continuation of Hume vol. 10; the proceedings in the case of an English merchantman, which suffered much in her crew and otherwise from the fire of certain Spanish Zebecs cruizing in the Mediterranean, and the execution of the Lieutenant of a privateer for firing a gun into a venetian Merchantman, which killed the Capt. as stated in the Annual Register for 1781 page 94. The case of an affront to a Russian Ambassador in the Reign of Queen Ann, tho' less analogous shews, in a general view, the solemnity with which reparation is made for insults having immediate relation to the Sovereignty of a nation.

Altho' the principle which was outraged in the proceedings against the American Frigate, is independent of the question concerning the allegiance of the seamen taken from her, the fact that they were citizens of the United States, and not British subjects may have such an influence on the feelings of all, and perhaps on the feelings of some unacquainted with the laws and usages of nations, that it has been thought proper to seek more regular proofs of their National character than were deemed sufficient in the first instance. These proofs will be added by this conveyance, if obtained in time for it; if not, by the first that succeeds.

The President has an evident right to expect from the British Government, not only an ample reparation to the United States in this case, but that it will be decided without difficulty or delay. *Should this expectation fail*, and above *all, should reparation be refused, it will be incumbent on you to take the proper measures for hastening home, according to the degree of urgency, all American vessels remaining in British ports; using for the purpose the mode least likely to awaken the attention of the British Government. Where there may be no ground to distrust the prudence or fidelity of Consuls, they will probably be found the fittest vehicles for your intimations.* It will be particularly *requisite to communicate to our public ships in the Mediterranean the state of appearances, if it be such as ought to influence their movements.*

All negotiation with the British Government on other subjects will of course be suspended until satisfaction on this be so pledged and arranged as to render negotiation honorable.

Whatever may be the *result or the prospect*, you will please to *forward to us the earliest information.*

The scope of the proclamation will signify to you, that the President has yielded to the presumption, that the hostile act of the British Commander did not pursue the intentions of his Government. It is not indeed easy to suppose, that so rash and critical a step, should have originated with the admiral; but it is still more difficult to believe, that such orders were prescribed by any Government, under circumstances, such as existed between Great Britain and the United States.

Calculations founded on dates, are also strongly opposed to the supposition, that the orders in question could have been transmitted from England. In the same scale are to be put the apparent and declared persuasion of the British representative Mr. Erskine, that no orders of a hostile spirit could have been issued or authorized by his Government, and the coincidence of this assurance with the amicable professions of Mr. Canning,

the organ of the new administration, as stated in the dispatch
of the 22d April from yourself and Mr. Pinkney.

Proceeding on these considerations, the President has inferred, that the justice and honor of the British Government
will readily make the atonement required; and in that expectation, he has forborne an immediate call of Congress,
notwithstanding the strong wish which has been manifested
by many, that measures depending on their authority, should
without delay be adopted. *The motives to this forbearance have,
at the same time, been strengthened by the policy of avoiding a
course, which might stimulate the British cruizers in this quarter to arrest our ships and seamen now arriving* and shortly expected *in great numbers, from all quarters.* It is probable,
however, that *the Legislature will be convened in time to receive
the answer of the British Government on the subject of this dispatch; or even* sooner *if the conduct of the British squadron here,
or other occurrences, should require immediate measures beyond
the authority of the Executive.*

You are not unaware of the good will and respect for the
United States, and personally even for the President, which
have been manifested *by the Emperor of Russia,* nor of the inducements to cultivate *the friendship of so great a power,* en-
tertaining principles *and having interests, according* in some
important views, *with those of the United States.* This consideration combined with the *subsisting relations between Russia
and Great Britain,* make it proper in the opinion of the
President, that *in case of an express or probable refusal of the
satisfaction demanded of the British Government, you should
take an early occasion,* if there be no special objections unknown here, *of communicating to the Russian Minister at
London, the hostile insult* which has been offered, as well as the
resort which may become necessary on our part, to measures constituting *or leading to war,* and of making *him sensible of the
regret which will be felt, at a rupture with a power, to which the
Emperor is allied by so many close and important interests.*

In order to give you the more expedition and security to
the present dispatch, a public armed vessel, the Revenge, is
especially employed, and Dr. Bullus is made the bearer, who
was on board the Chesapeake on his way to a Consulate in
the Mediterranean, and will be able to detail and explain

circumstances, which may possibly become interesting *in the course of your communications with the British Government.*

The vessel after depositing Dr. Bullus at a British port will proceed *with dispatches to a French port,* but will return to England with a view to bring the result of your transactions with the British Government. *The trip to France will afford you* and *Mr. Pinkney a favorable opportunity for communicating with our ministers at Paris, who* being *instructed to regulate their conduct on the present occasion, by the advices they may receive from you will need every explanation that can throw light on the probable turn and issue of things with Great Britain.*

I have, &c.

First Inaugural Address

Unwilling to depart from examples, of the most revered authority, I avail myself of the occasion now presented, to express the profound impression made on me, by the call of my Country to the station, to the duties of which I am about to pledge myself, by the most solemn of sanctions. So distinguished a mark of confidence, proceeding from the deliberate and tranquil suffrage of a free and virtuous nation, would, under any circumstances, have commanded my gratitude and devotion; as well as filled me with an awful sense of the trust to be assumed. Under the various circumstances which give peculiar solemnity to the existing period, I feel that both the honor and the responsibility allotted to me, are inexpressibly enhanced.

The present situation of the world is indeed without a parallel; and that of our own Country full of difficulties. The pressure of these too is the more severely felt, because they have fallen upon us at a moment, when the national prosperity being at a height not before attained, the contrast resulting from the change, has been rendered the more striking. Under the benign influence of our Republican institutions, and the maintainance of peace with all nations, whilst so many of them were engaged in bloody and wasteful wars, the fruits of a just policy were enjoyed in an unrivalled growth of our faculties and resources. Proofs of this were seen in the improvements of agriculture; in the successful enterprizes of commerce; in the progress of manufactures, and useful arts; in the increase of the public revenue, and the use made of it in reducing the public debt; and in the valuable works and establishments every where multiplying over the face of our land.

It is a precious reflection that the transition from this prosperous condition of our Country, to the scene which has for some time been distressing us, is not chargeable on any unwarrantable views, nor, as I trust, on any involuntary errors, in the public Councils. Indulging no passions which trespass on the rights or the repose of other nations, it has been the true glory of the United States to cultivate peace by observing justice, and to entitle themselves to the respect of the nations at war, by fulfilling their neutral obligations, with the most scrupulous impartiality. If there be candor in the world, the truth of these assertions, will not be questioned. Posterity at least will do justice to them.

This unexceptionable course could not avail against the injustice and violence of the Belligerent powers. In their rage against each other, or impelled by more direct motives, principles of retaliation have been introduced, equally contrary to universal reason, and acknowledged law. How long their arbitrary edicts will be continued, in spite of the demonstrations that not even a pretext for them has been given by the United States, and of the fair and liberal attempts to induce a revocation of them, cannot be anticipated. Assuring myself, that under every vicisitude, the determined spirit and united Councils of the nation, will be safeguards to its honor and its essential interests, I repair to the post assigned me, with no other discouragement, than what springs from my own inadequacy to its high duties. If I do not sink under the weight of this deep conviction, it is because I find some support in a consciousness of the purposes, and a confidence in the principles which I bring with me into this arduous service.

To cherish peace and friendly intercourse with all nations having correspondent dispositions; to maintain sincere neutrality towards belligerent nations; to prefer in all cases, amicable discussion and reasonable accommodation of differences, to a decision of them by an appeal to Arms; to exclude foreign intrigues and foreign partialities, so degrading to all Countries, and so baneful to free ones; to foster a spirit of independence too just to invade the rights of others, too proud to surrender our own, too liberal to indulge unworthy prejudices ourselves, and too elevated not to look down upon them in others; to hold the Union of the States as the basis of their peace and happiness; to support the Constitution, which is the cement of the Union, as well in its limitations as in its authorities; to respect the rights and authorities reserved to the States and to the people, as equally incorporated with, and essential to the success of, the general system; to avoid the slightest interference with the rights of conscience, or the functions of religion so wisely exempted from civil jurisdiction; to preserve in their full energy, the other salutary provisions in behalf of private and personal rights, and of the freedom of the press; to observe œconomy in public expenditures; to liberate the public resources by an honorable discharge of the public debts; to keep within the requisite limits a standing military force, always remembering, that an Armed and trained militia is the firmest bulwark of Republics; that without standing Armies their liberty can never be in danger; nor with large ones, safe; to promote by authorized means, improvements friendly to agriculture, to manufactures and to external as well as internal commerce; to favor, in like manner, the advancement of science and the diffusion of information as the best aliment to true liberty; to carry on the benevolent plans which have been so meritoriously applied to the conversion of our aboriginal neighbours from the degradation and wretchedness of savage life, to a participation of the improvements of which the human mind and manners are susceptible in a civilized state: As far as sentiments and intentions such as these can aid the fulfilment of my duty, they will be a resource which cannot fail me.

It is my good fortune, moreover, to have the path in which I am to tread, lighted by examples of illustrious services, successfully rendered in the most trying difficulties, by those who have marched before me. Of those of my immediate predecessor, it might least become me here to speak. I may however, be pardoned for not suppressing the sympathy with which my heart is full, in the rich reward he enjoys in the benedictions of a beloved Country, gratefully bestowed for exalted talents, zealously devoted, thro' a long career, to the advancement of its highest interest and happiness.

But the source to which I look for the aids which alone can supply my deficiences, is in the well tried intelligence and virtue of my fellow Citizens, and in the Councils of those representing them, in the other Departments associated in the care of the national interests. In these my confidence will, under every difficulty be best placed; next to that which we have all been encouraged to feel in the guardianship and guidance of that Almighty Being whose power regulates the destiny of nations, whose blessings have been so conspicuously dispensed to this rising Republic, and to whom we are bound to address our devout gratitude for the past, as well as our fervent supplications and best hopes for the future.

March 4, 1809

Veto Message to Congress

February 21st 1811

Having examined and considered the Bill, entitled "An Act incorporating the protestant Episcopal Church in the Town of Alexandria in the District of Columbia," I now return the Bill to the House of Representatives, in which it originated, with the following objections:

Because the Bill exceeds the rightful authority, to which Governments are limited by the essential distinction between Civil and Religious functions, and violates, in particular, the Article of the Constitution of the United States which declares, that "Congress shall make no law respecting a Religious establishment." The Bill enacts into, and establishes by law, sundry rules and proceedings relative purely to the organization and polity of the Church incorporated, and comprehending even the election and removal of the Minister of the same; so that no change could be made therein, by the particular Society, or by the General Church of which it is a member, and whose authority it recognizes. This particular Church, therefore, would so far be a religious establishment by law; a legal force and sanction being given to certain articles in its constitution and administration. Nor can it be considered that the articles thus established, are to be taken as the descriptive criteria only, of the corporate identity of the Society; in as much as this identity, must depend on other characteristics; as the regulations established are generally unessential and alterable, according to the principles and cannons, by which Churches of that denomination govern themselves; and as the injunctions & prohibitions contained in the regulations would be enforced by the penal consequences applicable to a violation of them according to the local law.

Because the Bill vests in the said incorporated Church, an authority to provide for the support of the poor, and the education of poor children of the same; an authority, which being altogether superfluous if the provision is to be the result of pious charity, would be a precident for giving to religious Societies as such, a legal agency in carrying into effect a public and civil duty.

To Thomas Jefferson

Dear Sir,   Washington May 25, 1812

The inclosed letters came under cover to me, by the Hornet. France has done nothing towards adjusting our differences with her. It is understood that the B. & M. Decrees are not in force agst. the U. S. and no contravention of them can be established agst. her. On the contrary positive cases rebut the allegation. Still the manner of the F. Govt. betrays the design of leaving G. B. a pretext for enforcing her O. in C. And in all other respects, the grounds of our complaints remain the same. The utmost address has been played off on Mr. Barlow's wishes & hopes; in much that at the Departure of the Hornet which had been so long detained for a final answer without its being obtained, he looked to the return of the Wasp which had just arrived, without despair of making her the Bearer of some satisfactory arrangement. Our calculations differ widely. In the mean time, the business is become more than ever puzzling. To go to war with Engd and not with France arms the federalists with new matter, and divides the Republicans some of whom with the Quids make a display of impartiality. To go to war agst both, presents a thousand difficulties, above all, that of shutting all the ports of the Continent of Europe agst our Cruisers who can do little without the use of them. It is pretty certain also, that it would not gain over the Federalists, who wd. turn all those difficulties agst the Administration. The only consideration of weight in favor of this triangular war as it is called, is that it might hasten thro' a peace with G. B. or F. a termination, for a while at least, of the obstinate questions now depending with both.

But even this advantage is not certain. For a prolongation of such a war might be viewed by both Belligts. as desirable, with as little reason for the opinion, as has prevailed in the past conduct of both.

Affectionate respects

War Message to Congress

Washington, June 1, 1812.

To the Senate and House of Representatives of the United States:

I communicate to Congress certain documents, being a continuation of those heretofore laid before them on the subject of our affairs with Great Britain.

Without going back beyond the renewal in 1803 of the war in which Great Britain is engaged, and omitting unrepaired wrongs of inferior magnitude, the conduct of her Government presents a series of acts hostile to the United States as an independent and neutral nation.

British cruisers have been in the continued practice of violating the American flag on the great highway of nations, and of seizing and carrying off persons sailing under it, not in the exercise of a belligerent right founded on the law of nations against an enemy, but of a municipal prerogative over British subjects. British jurisdiction is thus extended to neutral vessels in a situation where no laws can operate but the law of nations and the laws of the country to which the vessels belong, and a self-redress is assumed which, if British subjects were wrongfully detained and alone concerned, is that substitution of force for a resort to the responsible sovereign which falls within the definition of war. Could the seizure of British subjects in such cases be regarded as within the exercise of a belligerent right, the acknowledged laws of war, which forbid an article of captured property to be adjudged without a regular investigation before a competent tribunal, would imperiously demand the fairest trial where the sacred rights of persons were at issue. In place of such a trial these rights are subjected to the will of every petty commander.

The practice, hence, is so far from affecting British subjects alone that, under the pretext of searching for these, thousands of American citizens, under the safeguard of public law and of their national flag, have been torn from their country and from everything dear to them; have been dragged on board ships of war of a foreign nation and exposed, under the severities of their discipline, to be exiled to the most distant and deadly climes, to risk their lives in the battles of their oppressors, and to be the melancholy instruments of taking away those of their own brethren.

Against this crying enormity, which Great Britain would be so prompt to avenge if committed against herself, the United States have in vain exhausted remonstrances and expostulations, and that no proof might be wanting of their conciliatory dispositions, and no pretext left for a continuance of the practice, the British Government was formally assured of the readiness of the United States to enter into arrangements such as could not be rejected if the recovery of British subjects were the real and the sole object. The communication passed without effect.

British cruisers have been in the practice also of violating the rights and the peace of our coasts. They hover over and harass our entering and departing commerce. To the most insulting pretensions they have added the most lawless proceedings in our very harbors, and have wantonly spilt American blood within the sanctuary of our territorial jurisdiction. The principles and rules enforced by that nation, when a neutral nation, against armed vessels of belligerents hovering near her coasts and disturbing her commerce are well known. When called on, nevertheless, by the United States to punish the greater offenses committed by her own vessels, her Government has bestowed on their commanders additional marks of honor and confidence.

Under pretended blockades, without the presence of an adequate force and sometimes without the practicability of applying one, our commerce has been plundered in every sea, the great staples of our country have been cut off from their legitimate markets, and a destructive blow aimed at our agricultural and maritime interests. In aggravation of these predatory measures they have been considered as in force from the dates of their notification, a retrospective effect being thus added, as has been done in other important cases, to the unlawfulness of the course pursued. And to render the outrage the more signal these mock blockades have been reiterated and enforced in the face of official communications from the British Government declaring as the true definition of a legal blockade "that particular ports must be actually invested and previous warning given to vessels bound to them not to enter."

Not content with these occasional expedients for laying waste our neutral trade, the cabinet of Britain resorted at length to the sweeping system of blockades, under the name of orders in council, which has been molded and managed as might best suit its political views, its commercial jealousies, or the avidity of British cruisers.

To our remonstrances against the complicated and transcendent injustice of this innovation the first reply was that the orders were reluctantly adopted by Great Britain as a necessary retaliation on decrees of her enemy proclaiming a general blockade of the British Isles at a time when the naval force of that enemy dared not issue from his own ports. She was reminded without effect that her own prior blockades, unsupported by an adequate naval force actually applied and continued, were a bar to this plea; that executed edicts against millions of our property could not be retaliation on edicts confessedly impossible to be executed; that retaliation, to be just, should fall on the party setting the guilty example, not on an innocent party which was not even chargeable with an acquiescence in it.

When deprived of this flimsy veil for a prohibition of our trade with her enemy by the repeal of his prohibition of our trade with Great Britain, her cabinet, instead of a corresponding repeal or a practical discontinuance of its orders, formally avowed a determination to persist in them against the United States until the markets of her enemy should be laid open to British products, thus asserting an obligation on a neutral power to require one belligerent to encourage by its internal regulations the trade of another belligerent, contradicting her own practice toward all nations, in peace as well as in war, and betraying the insincerity of those professions which inculcated a belief that, having resorted to her orders with regret, she was anxious to find an occasion for putting an end to them.

Abandoning still more all respect for the neutral rights of the United States and for its own consistency, the British Government now demands as prerequisites to a repeal of its orders as they relate to the United States that a formality should be observed in the repeal of the French decrees nowise necessary to their termination nor exemplified by British usage, and that the French repeal, besides including that portion of the decrees which operates within a territorial jurisdiction, as well as that which operates on the high seas, against the commerce of the United States should not be a single and special repeal in relation to the United States, but should be extended to whatever other neutral nations unconnected with them may be affected by those decrees. And as an additional insult, they are called on for a formal disavowal of conditions and pretensions advanced by the French Government for which the United States are so far from having made themselves responsible that, in official explanations which have been published to the world, and in a correspondence of the American minister at London with the British minister for foreign affairs such a responsibility was explicitly and emphatically disclaimed.

It has become, indeed, sufficiently certain that the commerce of the United States is to be sacrificed, not as interfering with the belligerent rights of Great Britain; not as supplying the wants of her enemies, which she herself supplies; but as interfering with the monopoly which she covets for her own commerce and navigation. She carries on a war against the lawful commerce of a friend that she may the better carry on a commerce with an enemy—a commerce polluted by the forgeries and perjuries which are for the most part the only passports by which it can succeed.

Anxious to make every experiment short of the last resort of injured nations, the United States have withheld from Great Britain, under successive modifications, the benefits of a free intercourse with their market, the loss of which could not but outweigh the profits accruing from her restrictions of our commerce with other nations. And to entitle these experiments to the more favorable consideration they were so framed as to enable her to place her adversary under the exclusive operation of them. To these appeals her Government has been equally inflexible, as if willing to make sacrifices of every sort rather than yield to the claims of justice or renounce the errors of a false pride. Nay, so far were the attempts carried to overcome the attachment of the British cabinet to its unjust edicts that it received every encouragement within the competency of the executive branch of our Government to expect that a repeal of them would be followed by a war between the United States and France, unless the French edicts should also be repealed. Even this communication, although silencing forever the plea of a disposition in the United States to acquiesce in those edicts originally the sole plea for them, received no attention.

If no other proof existed of a predetermination of the British Government against a repeal of its orders, it might be found in the correspondence of the minister plenipotentiary of the United States at London and the British secretary for foreign affairs in 1810, on the question whether the blockade of May, 1806, was considered as in force or as not in force. It had been ascertained that the French Government, which urged this blockade as the ground of its Berlin decree, was willing in the event of its removal, to repeal that decree, which, being followed by alternate repeals of the other offensive edicts, might abolish the whole system on both sides. This inviting opportunity for accomplishing an object so important to the United States, and professed so often to be the desire of both the belligerents, was made known to the British Government. As that Government admits that an actual application of an adequate force is necessary to the existence of a legal blockade, and it was notorious that if such a force had ever been applied its long discontinuance had annulled the blockade in question, there could be no sufficient objection on the part of Great Britain to a formal revocation of it, and no imaginable objection to a declaration of the fact that the blockade did not exist. The declaration would have been consistent with her avowed principles of blockade, and would have enabled the United States to demand from France the pledged repeal of her decrees, either with success, in which case the way would have been opened for a general repeal of the belligerent edicts, or without success, in which case the United States would have been justified in turning their measures exclusively against France. The British Government would, however, neither rescind the blockade nor declare its nonexistence, nor permit its non-existence to be inferred and affirmed by the American plenipotentiary. On the contrary, by representing the blockade to be comprehended in the orders in council, the United States were compelled so to regard it in their subsequent proceedings.

There was a period when a favorable change in the policy of the British cabinet was justly considered as established. The minister plenipotentiary of His Britannic Majesty here proposed an adjustment of the differences more immediately endangering the harmony of the two countries. The proposition was accepted with the promptitude and cordiality corresponding with the invariable professions of this Government. A foundation appeared to be laid for a sincere and lasting reconciliation. The prospect, however, quickly vanished. The whole proceeding was disavowed by the British Government without any explanations which could at that time repress the belief that the disavowal proceeded from a spirit of hostility to the commercial rights and prosperity of the United States; and it has since come into proof that at the very moment when the public minister was holding the language of friendship and inspiring confidence in the sincerity of the negotiation with which he was charged a secret agent of his Government was employed in intrigues having for their object a subversion of our Government and a dismemberment of our happy union.

In reviewing the conduct of Great Britain toward the United States our attention is necessarily drawn to the warfare just renewed by the savages on one of our extensive frontiers—a warfare which is known to spare neither age nor sex and to be distinguished by features peculiarly shocking to humanity. It is difficult to account for the activity and combinations which have for some time been developing themselves among tribes in constant intercourse with British traders and garrisons without connecting their hostility with that influence and without recollecting the authenticated examples of such interpositions heretofore furnished by the officers and agents of that Government.

Such is the spectacle of injuries and indignities which have been heaped on our country, and such the crisis which its unexampled forbearance and conciliatory efforts have not been able to avert. It might at least have been expected that an enlightened nation, if less urged by moral obligations or invited by friendly dispositions on the part of the United States, would have found its true interest alone a sufficient motive to respect their rights and their tranquillity on the high seas; that an enlarged policy would have favored that free and general circulation of commerce in which the British nation is at all times interested, and which in times of war is the best alleviation of its calamities to herself as well as to other belligerents; and more especially that the British cabinet would not, for the sake of a precarious and surreptitious intercourse with hostile markets, have persevered in a course of measures which necessarily put at hazard the invaluable market of a great and growing country, disposed to cultivate the mutual advantages of an active commerce.

Other counsels have prevailed. Our moderation and conciliation have had no other effect than to encourage perseverance and to enlarge pretensions. We behold our seafaring citizens still the daily victims of lawless violence, committed on the great common and highway of nations, even within sight of the country which owes them protection. We behold our vessels, freighted with the products of our soil and industry, or returning with the honest proceeds of them, wrested from their lawful destinations, confiscated by prize courts no longer the organs of public law but the instruments of arbitrary edicts, and their unfortunate crews dispersed and lost, or forced or inveigled in British ports into British fleets, whilst arguments are employed in support of these aggressions which have no foundation but in a principle equally supporting a claim to regulate our external commerce in all cases whatsoever.

We behold, in fine, on the side of Great Britain, a state of war against the United States, and on the side of the United States a state of peace toward Great Britain.

Whether the United States shall continue passive under these progressive usurpations and these accumulating wrongs, or, opposing force to force in defense of their national rights, shall commit a just cause into the hands of the Almighty Disposer of Events, avoiding all connections which might entangle it in the contest or views of other powers, and preserving a constant readiness to concur in an honorable re-establishment of peace and friendship, is a solemn question which the Constitution wisely confides to the legislative department of the Government. In recommending it to their early deliberations I am happy in the assurance that the decision will be worthy the enlightened and patriotic councils of a virtuous, a free, and a powerful nation.

Having presented this view of the relations of the United States with Great Britain and of the solemn alternative growing out of them, I proceed to remark that the communications last made to Congress on the subject of our relations with France will have shewn that since the revocation of her decrees, as they violated the neutral rights of the United States, her Government has authorized illegal captures by its privateers and public ships, and that other outrages have been practised on our vessels and our citizens. It will have been seen also that no indemnity had been provided or satisfactorily pledged for the extensive spoliations committed under the violent and retrospective orders of the French Government against the property of our citizens seized within the jurisdiction of France. I abstain at this time from recommending to the consideration of Congress definitive measures with respect to that nation, in the expectation that the result of unclosed discussions between our minister plenipotentiary at Paris and the French Government will speedily enable Congress to decide with greater advantage on the course due to the rights, the interests, and the honor of our country.

Second Inaugural Address

About to add the solemnity of an oath to the obligations imposed by a second call to the station in which my country heretofore placed me, I find in the presence of this respectable assembly an opportunity of publicly repeating my profound sense of so distinguished a confidence and of the responsibility united with it. The impressions on me are strengthened by such an evidence that my faithful endeavors to discharge my arduous duties have been favorably estimated, and by a consideration of the momentous period at which the trust has been renewed. From the weight and magnitude now belonging to it I should be compelled to shrink if I had less reliance on the support of an enlightened and generous people, and felt less deeply a conviction that the war with a powerful nation, which forms so prominent a feature in our situation, is stamped with that justice which invites the smiles of Heaven on the means of conducting it to a successful termination.

May we not cherish this sentiment without presumption when we reflect on the characters by which this war is distinguished?

It was not declared on the part of the United States until it had been long made on them, in reality though not in name; until arguments and expostulations had been exhausted; until a positive declaration had been received that the wrongs provoking it would not be discontinued; nor until this last appeal could no longer be delayed without breaking down the spirit of the nation, destroying all confidence in itself and in its political institutions, and either perpetuating a state of disgraceful suffering or regaining by more costly sacrifices and more severe struggles our lost rank and respect among independent powers.

On the issue of the war are staked our national sovereignty on the high seas and the security of an important class of citizens, whose occupations give the proper value to those of every other class. Not to contend for such a stake is to surrender our equality with other powers on the element common to all and to violate the sacred title which every member of the society has to its protection. I need not call into view the unlawfulness of the practice by which our mariners are forced at the will of every cruising officer from their own vessels into foreign ones, nor paint the outrages inseparable from it. The proofs are in the records of each successive Administration of our Government, and the cruel sufferings of that portion of the American people have found their way to every bosom not dead to the sympathies of human nature.

As the war was just in its origin and necessary and noble in its objects, we can reflect with a proud satisfaction that in carrying it on no principle of justice or honor, no usage of civilized nations, no precept of courtesy or humanity, have been infringed. The war has been waged on our part with scrupulous regard to all these obligations, and in a spirit of liberality which was never surpassed.

How little has been the effect of this example on the conduct of the enemy!

They have retained as prisoners of war citizens of the United States not liable to be so considered under the usages of war.

They have refused to consider as prisoners of war, and threatened to punish as traitors and deserters, persons emigrating without restraint to the United States, incorporated by naturalization into our political family, and fighting under the authority of their adopted country in open and honorable war for the maintenance of its rights and safety. Such is the avowed purpose of a Government which is in the practice of naturalizing by thousands citizens of other countries, and not only of permitting but compelling them to fight its battles against their native country.

They have not, it is true, taken into their own hands the hatchet and the knife, devoted to indiscriminate massacre, but they have let loose the savages armed with these cruel instruments; have allured them into their service, and carried them to battle by their sides, eager to glut their savage thirst with the blood of the vanquished and to finish the work of torture and death on maimed and defenseless captives. And, what was never before seen, British commanders have extorted victory over the unconquerable valor of our troops by presenting to the sympathy of their chief captives awaiting massacre from their savage associates.

And now we find them, in further contempt of the modes of honorable warfare, supplying the place of a conquering force, by attempts to disorganize our political society, to dismember our confederated Republic. Happily, like others, these will recoil on the authors; but they mark the degenerate counsels from which they emanate: and if they did not belong to a series of unexampled inconsistencies, might excite the greater wonder, as proceeding from a Government which founded the very war in which it has been so long engaged, on a charge against the disorganizing and insurrectional policy of its adversary.

To render the justice of the war on our part the more conspicuous, the reluctance to commence it was followed by the earliest and strongest manifestations of a disposition to arrest its progress. The sword was scarcely out of the scabbard, before the enemy was apprized of the reasonable terms on which it would be resheathed. Still more precise advances were repeated, and have been received in a spirit forbidding every reliance not placed on the military resources of the nation.

These resources are amply sufficient to bring the war to an honorable issue. Our nation is, in number, more than half that of the British isles. It is composed of a brave, a free, a virtuous, and an intelligent people. Our country abounds in the necessaries, the arts, and the comforts of life. A general prosperity is visible in the public countenance. The means employed by the British Cabinet to undermine it, have recoiled on themselves; have given to our national faculties a more rapid development; and draining or diverting the precious metals from British circulation and British vaults, have poured them into those of the United States. It is a propitious consideration, that an unavoidable war should have found this seasonable facility for the contributions required to support it. When the public voice called for war, all knew and still know, that without them it could not be carried on through the period which it might last; and the patriotism, the good sense, and the manly spirit of our fellow-citizens, are pledges for the cheerfulness with which they will bear each his share of the common burden. To render the war short, and its success sure, animated, and systematic exertions alone are necessary; and the success of our arms now may long preserve our country from the necessity of another resort to them. Already have the gallant exploits of our naval heroes proved to the world our inherent capacity to maintain our rights on one element. If the reputation of our arms has been thrown under clouds on the other, presaging flashes of heroic enterprise assure us that nothing is wanting to correspondent triumphs there also, but the discipline and habits which are in daily progress.

March 4, 1813

To John Nicholas

Dear Sir   Washington April 2d, 1813.

Your favor of the 11th March came duly to hand and I feel myself obliged by the friendly spirit of the observations it contains. The circumstances under which the war commenced on our part require that it should be reviewed with a liberality above the ordinary rules and dispositions indulged in such cases. It had become impossible to avoid or even delay war, at a moment when we were not prepared for it, and when it was certain that effective preparations would not take place, whilst the question of war was undecided. Another feature was, the discord and variety of opinions and views in the public councils, of which sufficient evidence has been seen, in the public debates and proceedings; and of which much more is known than ever has been published. The Calculations of the Ex. were that it would be best to open the war with a force of a kind and amount that would be soon procured, & that might strike an important blow, before the Enemy, who was known to disbelieve the approach of such an event, could be reinforced. These calculations were defeated, as you observe by mixing, and substituting preparations necessarily producing fatal delays; and in some respects thwarting each other. At this moment, notwithstanding the additional stimuli, it is not certain that the regular force exceeds that which was in the first instance recommended, which would have been more an overmatch for the then strength of the enemy, than the force voted, if realized, would be for his present strength; and which could have been easily augmented as fast as might be necessary to maintain conquered ground, or meet reinforcements from Europe or elsewhere. The failure of our calculations, with respect to the expedition under Hull, needs no comment. The worst of it was that we were misled by a reliance authorized by himself, on its securing to us the command of the Lakes. The decisive importance of this advantage has always been well understood; but until the first prospect ceased, other means of attaining it were repressed by certain difficulties in carrying them into effect. These means have since been pushed with alacrity; and we hope will enable us to open the campaign in relation to Canada, with a retort of the success which the last turned against us. With the command of L. Ontario, the treasonable commerce at which you point, will probably be found too hazardous to be prosecuted. I have furnished you hints however, for the consideration of the proper Departments.

We are at present occupied with the Mediation of Russia. That is the only power in Europe which can command respect from both France and England; and at this moment it is in its zenith. We shall endeavour to turn this mediation to the best account, in promoting a just peace. We are encouraged in this policy by the known friendship of the Emperor Alexander to this country; and by the probability that the greater affinity between the Baltic and American ideas of maritime law, than between those of the former and of G. B. will render his interposition as favorable as will be consistent with the character assumed by him.

Accept &c.

To John Armstrong

For the Department of War.

On viewing the course which the proceedings of the War Department have not unfrequently taken, I find that I owe it to my own responsibility as well as to other considerations, to make some remarks on the relations in which the Head of the Department stands to the President, and to lay down some rules for conducting the business of the Department, which are dictated by the nature of those relations.

In general the Secretary of War, like the Heads of the other Depts. as well by express statute as by the structure of the constitution, acts under the authority & subject to the decisions & instructions of the President; with the exception of cases where the law may vest special & independent powers in the head of the Department.

From the great number & variety of subjects, however, embraced by that Department and the subordinate & routine character of a great portion of them, it cannot be either necessary or convenient that proceedings relative to every subject should receive a previous & positive sanction of the Executive. In cases of that minor sort it is requisite only that they be subsequently communicated as far and as soon as a knowledge of them can be useful or satisfactory.

In cases of a higher character & importance, involving necessarily, and in the public understanding, a just responsibility of the President, the acts of the Department ought to be either prescribed by him, or preceded by his sanction.

It is not easy to define in theory the cases falling within these different classes, or in practice to discriminate them with uniform exactness. But substantial observance of the distinction is not difficult, and will be facilitated by the confidence between the Executive & the Head of the Department.

This distinction has not been sufficiently kept in view.

I need not repeat the notice heretofore taken of the measure consolidating certain regiments; a measure highly important under more than one aspect; and which was adopted & executed without the knowledge or sanction of the President; nor was it subsequently made known to him otherwise than through the publication of the act in the newspapers.

The like may be said of certain rules & regulations, particularly a Body of them for the Hospital & Medical Depts. of which the law expressly required the approbation of the President, and which comprise a rule to be observed by the P. himself in future appointments. The first knowledge of these latter regulations was derived from the newspapers.

A very remarkable instance is a late general order prohibiting Duels and challenges, on pain of dismission from the army. However proper such an order may be in itself, it would never be supposed to have been issued without the deliberate sanction of the President, the more particularly as it pledged an exercise of one of the most responsible of the Executive functions, that of summarily dismissing from military offices without the intervention of the Military Tribunal provided by law. This order was adopted & promulgated without the previous knowledge of the P. nor was it ever made known to him otherwise than by its promulgation. Instructions to military Comanders relating to important plans & operations have been issued without any previous or even any subsequent communication thereof to the Executive; and letters expressly intended & proper for the knowledge & decision of the Ex. have been recd. & acted on without being previously communicated or the measures taken being made known to him.

Other illustrations might be drawn from instances of other sorts, leading to the result of these remarks. The above may suffice, with the addition of one which with the circumstances attending it will be explained by a reference to the letter of resignation from Genl. Harrison, to the letter of the P. to the Secretary of War of May 24, to the issuing of the commission of Major General to General Jackson, and the letter of the Secretary of War accompanying it.

The following course will be observed in future:

To be previously communicated to the President:

1. Orders from the Dept. of War establishing general or permanent regulations.

2. Orders for Courts of Enquiry or Courts Martial, on general officers; or designating the numbers or members of the Courts.

3. Commissions or notifications of appointment to officers other than regular promotions, in uncontested cases.

4. Dismissions of officers from the service.

5. Consolidations of Corps or parts of Corps & translations of Fd. officers from one Regiment to another.

6. Acceptances & refusals of resignations from officers above the rank of Captains.

7. Requisitions & receptions of militia into the service & pay of the U. S.

8. Instructions relating to Treaties with Indians.

9. Instructions to officers commanding military Districts, or Corps or Stations, relative to military movements or operations.

10. Changes in the boundaries of military Districts, or the establishmt. of separate commands therein; or the transfer of General officers from one District or command to another District or command.

In the absence of the P. from the seat of Govt. previous communications to him may be waived in urgent cases, but to be subsequently made without delay.

All letters giving military intelligence or containing other matters intended or proper for the knowledge of the P. will of course be immediately communicated to him.

These rules may omit cases falling within, and embrace cases not entirely within, the reason of them. Experience therefore may improve the rules. In the meantime, they will give a more suitable order & course to the business of the Dept. will conduce to a more certain harmony & cooperation in the proceedings of the several Departments, and will furnish the proper opportunity for the advantage of cabinet consultations on cases of a nature to render them expedient.

August 13, 1814

Memorandum on the Battle of Bladensburg

In the morning, a note, by an express from General Winder was handed me. It was addressed to the Secretary of War. Not doubting the urgency of the occasion, I opened and read it, and it went on immediately by the Express to Genl. Armstrong who lodged in the Seven Buildings. Finding by the note that the General requested the speediest counsel, I proceeded to his Head Quarters on the Eastern Branch, trusting for notice to the Secretary of War to follow, to the note from Winder. On my reaching his quarters, we were successively joined by the Secretary of State the Secretary of the Navy, and Mr. Rush, the Attorney General. After an hour or so, the Secretary of the Treasury arrived, and quickly after the Secretary of War. The latter had been impatiently expected, and surprize at his delay manifested. Gen. Winder was, at the moment setting off to hurry on the troops to Bladensburg in consequence of certain intelligence that the Enemy had taken that direction. Barney's corps was also ordered thither, leaving the Bridge to be blown up if necessary. On Gen. Armstrong's coming into the room, he was informed of the certain march of the enemy for Bladensburg, and of what had passed before his arrival; and he was asked whether he had any arrangement or advice to offer in the emergency. He said he had not; adding, that as the battle would be between Militia and regular troops, the former would be beaten.

On coming out of the house and mounting our horses, the Secretary of the Treasury, who though in a very languid state of health had turned out to join us, observed to me privately that he was grieved to see the great reserve of the Secretary of War, who was taking no part on so critical an occasion; that he found him under the impression, that as the means of defending the District had been committed to Genl. Winder, it might not be delicate to intrude his opinions without the approbation of the President; tho' with that approbation he was ready to give any aid he could. Mr. Campbell said that notwithstanding his just confidence in Genl. Winder, he thought, in the present state of things which called for all the military skill possible, the Military knowledge and experience of the Secretary of War ought to be availed of, and that no considerations of delicacy ought to jeopard the public safety. With these impressions he said, he had thought it his duty to make this communication, and was very anxious, that I should take some proper steps in the case. I told him I could scarcely conceive it possible that Genl. Armstrong could have so misconstrued his functions and duty as Secretary of war; that he could not but know that any proper directions from him would receive any sanction that might be necessary from the Executive; nor doubt that any suggestions or advice from him to Genl. Winder would be duly attended to I told Mr. C. that I would speak to the Secretary of War explicitly on the subject; and accordingly turning my horse to him, expressed to him my concern and surprise at the reserve he shewed at the present crisis, and at the scruples I understood he had at offering his advice or opinions; that I hoped he had not construed the paper of instructions given him some time before, so as to restrain him in any respect from the exercise of functions belonging to his office; that at such a juncture it was to be expected that he should omit nothing within the proper agency of Secretary of War, towards the public defence; and that I thought it proper particularly that he should proceed to Bladensburg and give any aid to Genl. Winder that he could; observing that if any difficulty on the score of authority should arise, which was not likely, I should be near at hand to remove it. He said in reply that he had put no such construction on the paper of instructions as was alluded to; and that as I thought it proper, he would proceed to Bladensburg, and be of any service to Genl. Winder he could. The purport of this conversation I communicated to Mr. Campbell who remained near us. The Secretary of War set off without delay to Bladensburg.

After a short turn to the Marine barracks whither the Secretary of the Navy had gone, I mentioned to Mr. Rush who was with me my purpose of going to Bladensburg and my object in so doing. He readily accompanied me. On approaching the Town, we learned from William Simmons, that Winder was not there, and that the enemy were entering it. We rode up to him instantly. The Secretaries of State and War were with him. I asked the latter whether he had spoken with Genl. Winder on the subject of his arrangements and views. He said he had not. I remarked that tho' there was so little time for it, it was possible he might offer some advice or suggestion that might not be too late, to be turned to account; on which he rode up to the General as I did myself. The unruliness of my horse prevented me from joining in the short conversation that took place. When it was over, I asked Genl. Armstrong whether he had seen occasion to suggest any improvement in any part of the arrangements. He said that he had not; that from his view of them they appeared to be as good as circumstances admitted.

When the Battle had decidedly commenced, I observed to the Secretary of War and Secretary of State that it would be proper to withdraw to a position in the rear, where we could act according to circumstances; leaving military movements now to the military functionaries who were responsible for them. This we did, Mr. Rush soon joining us. When it became manifest that the battle was lost; Mr. Rush accompanying me, I fell down into the road leading to the city and returned to it.

It had been previously settled that in the event of the enemy's taking possession of the city, and the necessity of Executive consultations elsewhere, Fredericktown would be the proper place for the assembling of the Cabinet.

c. August 24, 1814

Memorandum on Armstrong's Resignation

In the evening of the 29th of August, 1814, Being on horseback, I stopped at General Armstrong's lodgings for the purpose of communicating with him on the state of things in the District, then under apprehensions of an immediate visit from the force of the enemy at Alexandria.

I observed to him that he could not be unaware of the great excitement in the District produced by the unfortunate event which had taken place in the city; that violent prejudices were known to exist against the administration, as having failed in its duty to protect it, particularly against me and himself as head of the War Department; that threats of personal violence had, it was said, been thrown out against us both, but more especially against him; that it had been sufficiently known for several days, and before his return* to the city (which was about one o'clock P.M. of the 29th) that the temper of the troops was such as made it expedient, if possible, that he should have nothing to do with them; that I had within a few hours received a message from the commanding General of the Militia informing me that every officer would tear off his epauletts if Genl Armstrong was to have anything to do with them; that before his arrival there was less difficulty, as Mr. Monroe who was very acceptable to them, had,

*He had repaired to Fredericktown, the place appointed for the rendezvous of the Executive in the event of their being driven from the city. The turn which things took after his departure prevented the other members from joining him.

as on preceding occasions of his absence, though very reluctantly on this, been the medium for the functions of Secretary
of War, but that since his return and presence, the expedient
could not be continued, and the question was, what was best
to be done. Any convulsion at so critical a moment could not
but have the worst consequences.

He said he had been aware of the excitement against him;
that it was altogether artificial, and that he knew the sources
of it, and the intrigues by which it had been effected, which
this was not the proper time for examining; that the excitement was founded on the most palpable falsehoods, and was
limited to this spot; that it was evident he could not remain
here, and the functions belonging to him divided or exercised
by any one else, without forgetting what he owed to his station, and to himself; that he had come into his office with the
sole view of serving the public, and was willing to resign it
when he could no longer do so with honor and effect; that
if it was thought best therefore that he should adopt this
course, he was ready to give up his appointment; or he could,
with my permission, retire from the scene, by setting out immediately on a visit to his family in the State of New York.

I observed that a resignation was an extent which had not
been contemplated; that if made under such circumstances, it
might receive constructions which could not be desirable,
either in a public or a personal view; that a temporary retirement, as he suggested, tho' also subject to be viewed in some
lights not agreeable, was on the whole less objectionable, and
would avoid the existing embarrassment, without precluding
any future course which might be deemed most fit.

He dwelt on the groundless nature of the charges which
had produced the excitement, and on the limits within which
they had and would operate; affirming that his conduct in relation to the defence of the city &c. had proved that there
had been no deficiency on his part.

I told him that I well knew that some of the particular
charges brought against him were destitute of foundation,
and that as far as they produced the discontents, these would
be limited both as to time and space; but that I suspected the
discontents to be in a great measure rooted in the belief that
he had not taken a sufficient interest in the defence of the

city, nor promoted the measures for it; and considering the heavy calamity which had fallen on the place and on its inhabitants, it was natural that strong feelings would be excited on the spot; and as the place was the Capital of the nation every where else also. I added that it would not be easy to satisfy the nation that the event was without blame somewhere, and I could not in candour say that all that ought to have been done had been done & in proper time.

He returned to an exculpation of himself, and remarked that he had omitted no preparations or steps whatever for the safety of the place which had been enjoined on him.

I replied that as the conversation was a frank one, I could not admit this justification; that it was the duty of the Secretary of War not only to execute plans, or orders committed to him, but to devise and propose such as would in his opinion be necessary and proper; that it was an obvious and essential part of his charge, and that in what related to military plans and proceedings elsewhere, he had never been scrupulous or backward in taking this course; that on the contrary he well knew from what on another occasion* had passed between us, he had taken a latitude in this respect which I was not satisfied with; that it was due to truth and to myself to say, that he had never appeared to enter into a just view either of the danger to the city which was to be apprehended, or of the consequences of its falling into the hands of the Enemy; that he had never himself proposed or suggested a single precaution or arrangement for its safety, everything done on that subject having been brought forward by myself, and that the apparent difference of his views on that subject from mine had naturally induced a reduction of my arrangements to the minimum, in order to obtrude the less on a reluctant execution. I reminded him also that he had fallen short of the preparations even decided on in the Cabinet, in some respects; particularly in not having arms and equipments brought to convenient depôts from distant ones, some of the militia, when called on for the defence of the City, being obliged to get arms first at Harper's ferry.

I remarked that it was not agreeable thus to speak, nor on

*See the instructions to him on the 13th day of August 1814.

an occasion less urgent would it be done; that I had selected him for the office he filled from a respect to his talents, and a confidence that he would exert them for the public good; that I had always treated him with friendliness and confidence and that as there was but a short distance before me to the end of my public career, my great wish, next to leaving my country in a state of peace and prosperity, was to have preserved harmony and avoid changes, and that I had accordingly as he well knew acquiesced in many things, to which no other consideration would have reconciled me.

He said he was very sensible of my friendly conduct towards him, and always had, and always should respect me for it.

The conversation was closed by my referring to the idea of his setting out in the Morning on a visit to his family; and observing that he would of course revolve it further, and if he continued to think of it as he then did, he would consider me as opposing no restraint. We parted as usual in a friendly manner. On the next morning he sent me word by Mr. Parker that he should proceed immediately to visit his family; and on his arrival at Baltimore, transmitted his resignation.

August 29, 1814

To Wilson Cary Nicholas

Dear Sir,   Washington, Novr 26, 1814.

I did not receive your favor of the 11th instant till a few days ago, and I have till now been too much indisposed to acknowledge it.

You are not mistaken in viewing the conduct of the Eastern States as the source of our greatest difficulties in carrying on the war, as it certainly is the greatest, if not the sole, inducement with the enemy to persevere in it. The greater part of the people in that quarter have been brought by their leaders, aided by their priests, under a delusion scarcely exceeded by that recorded in the period of witchcraft; and the leaders are becoming daily more desperate in the use they make of it. Their object is power. If they could obtain it by menaces, their efforts would stop there. These failing, they are ready to go every length for which they can train their followers. Without foreign co-operation, revolts & separation will be hardly risked; and what the effect of so profligate an experiment may be, first on deluded partizans, and next on those remaining faithful to the nation who are respectable for their consistency, and even for their numbers, is for conjecture only. The best may be hoped, but the worst ought to be kept in view. In the mean time the course to be taken by the Govt is full of delicacy & perplexity; and the more so under the pinch which exists in our fiscal affairs, & the lamentable tardiness of the Legislature in applying some relief.

At such a moment the vigorous support of the well disposed States is peculiarly important to the General Govt; and it would be impossible for me to doubt that Virga, under your administration of its Executive Govt, will continue to be among the foremost in zealous exertions for the national rights and success.

Be pleased to accept assurances of my esteem & respect

Message to Congress on Peace Treaty

Washington, February 18, 1815.
To the Senate and House of Representatives of the United States:
I lay before Congress copies of the treaty of peace and amity between the United States and His Britannic Majesty, which was signed by the commissioners of both parties at Ghent on the 24th of December, 1814, and the ratifications of which have been duly exchanged.

While performing this act I congratulate you and our constituents upon an event which is highly honorable to the nation, and terminates with peculiar felicity a campaign signalized by the most brilliant successes.

The late war, although reluctantly declared by Congress, had become a necessary resort to assert the rights and independence of the nation. It has been waged with a success which is the natural result of the wisdom of the legislative councils, of the patriotism of the people, of the public spirit of the militia, and of the valor of the military and naval forces of the country. Peace, at all times a blessing, is peculiarly welcome, therefore, at a period when the causes for the war have ceased to operate, when the Government has demonstrated the efficiency of its powers of defense, and when the nation can review its conduct without regret and without reproach.

I recommend to your care and beneficence the gallant men whose achievements in every department of the military service, on the land and on the water, have so essentially contributed to the honor of the American name and to the restoration of peace. The feelings of conscious patriotism and worth will animate such men under every change of fortune and pursuit, but their country performs a duty to itself when it bestows those testimonials of approbation and applause which are at once the reward and the incentive to great actions.

The reduction of the public expenditures to the demands of a peace establishment will doubtless engage the immediate attention of Congress. There are, however, important considerations which forbid a sudden and general revocation of the measures that have been produced by the war. Experience has taught us that neither the pacific dispositions of the American people nor the pacific character of their political institutions can altogether exempt them from that strife which appears beyond the ordinary lot of nations to be incident to the actual period of the world, and the same faithful monitor demonstrates that a certain degree of preparation for war is not only indispensable to avert disasters in the onset, but affords also the best security for the continuance of peace. The wisdom of Congress will therefore, I am confident, provide for the maintenance of an adequate regular force; for the gradual advancement of the naval establishment; for improving all the means of harbor defense; for adding discipline to the distinguished bravery of the militia, and for cultivating the military art in its essential branches, under the liberal patronage of Government.

The resources of our country were at all times competent to the attainment of every national object, but they will now be enriched and invigorated by the activity which peace will introduce into all the scenes of domestic enterprise and labor.

The provision that has been made for the public creditors during the present session of Congress must have a decisive effect in the establishment of the public credit both at home and abroad. The reviving interests of commerce will claim the legislative attention at the earliest opportunity, and such regulations will, I trust, be seasonably devised as shall secure to the United States their just proportion of the navigation of the world. The most liberal policy toward other nations, if met by corresponding dispositions, will in this respect be found the most beneficial policy toward ourselves. But there is no subject that can enter with greater force and merit into the deliberations of Congress than a consideration of the means to preserve and promote the manufactures which have sprung into existence and attained an unparalleled maturity throughout the United States during the period of the European wars. This source of national independence and wealth I anxiously recommend, therefore, to the prompt and constant guardianship of Congress.

The termination of the legislative sessions will soon separate you, fellow-citizens, from each other, and restore you to your constituents. I pray you to bear with you the expressions of my sanguine hope that the peace which has been just declared, will not only be the foundation of the most friendly intercourse between the United States and Great Britain, but that it will also be productive of happiness and harmony in every section of our beloved country. The influence of your precepts and example must be every where powerful; and while we accord in grateful acknowledgments for the protection which Providence has bestowed upon us, let us never cease to inculcate obedience to the laws, and fidelity to the union, as constituting the palladium of the national independence and prosperity.

Seventh Annual Message to Congress

Washington, December 5, 1815.

Fellow-Citizens of the Senate and of the House of
Representatives:

I have the satisfaction on our present meeting of being able to communicate to you the successful termination of the war which had been commenced against the United States by the Regency of Algiers. The squadron in advance on that service, under Commodore Decatur, lost not a moment after its arrival in the Mediterranean in seeking the naval force of the enemy then cruising in that sea, and succeeded in capturing two of his ships, one of them the principal ship, commanded by the Algerine admiral. The high character of the American commander was brilliantly sustained on that occasion which brought his own ship into close action with that of his adversary, as was the accustomed gallantry of all the officers and men actually engaged. Having prepared the way by this demonstration of American skill and prowess, he hastened to the port of Algiers, where peace was promptly yielded to his victorious force. In the terms stipulated the rights and honor of the United States were particularly consulted by a perpetual relinquishment on the part of the Dey of all pretensions to tribute from them. The impressions which have thus been made, strengthened as they will have been by subsequent transactions with the Regencies of Tunis and of Tripoli by the appearance of the larger force which followed under Commodore Bainbridge, the chief in command of the expedition, and by the judicious precautionary arrangements left by him in that quarter, afford a reasonable prospect of future security for the valuable portion of our commerce which passes within reach of the Barbary cruisers.

It is another source of satisfaction that the treaty of peace with Great Britain has been succeeded by a convention on the subject of commerce concluded by the plenipotentiaries of the two countries. In this result a disposition is manifested on the part of that nation corresponding with the disposition of the United States, which it may be hoped will be improved into liberal arrangements on other subjects on which the parties have mutual interests, or which might endanger their future harmony. Congress will decide on the expediency of promoting such a sequel by giving effect to the measure of confining the American navigation to American seamen— a measure which, at the same time that it might have that conciliatory tendency, would have the further advantage of increasing the independence of our navigation and the resources for our maritime defence.

In conformity with the articles in the treaty of Ghent relating to the Indians, as well as with a view to the tranquillity of our western and northwestern frontiers, measures were taken to establish an immediate peace with the several tribes who had been engaged in hostilities against the United States. Such of them as were invited to Detroit acceded readily to a renewal of the former treaties of friendship. Of the other tribes who were invited to a station on the Mississippi the greater number have also accepted the peace offered to them. The residue, consisting of the more distant tribes or parts of tribes, remain to be brought over by further explanations, or by such other means as may be adapted to the dispositions they may finally disclose.

The Indian tribes within and bordering on the southern frontier, whom a cruel war on their part had compelled us to chastise into peace, have latterly shown a restlessness which has called for preparatory measures for repressing it, and for protecting the commissioners engaged in carrying the terms of the peace into execution.

The execution of the act fixing the military peace establishment has been attended with difficulties which even now can only be overcome by legislative aid. The selection of officers, the payment and discharge of the troops enlisted for the war, the payment of the retained troops and their reunion from detached and distant stations, the collection and security of the public property in the Quartermaster, Commissary, and Ordnance departments, and the constant medical assistance required in hospitals and garrisons rendered a complete execution of the act impracticable on the 1st of May, the period more immediately contemplated. As soon, however, as circumstances would permit, and as far as it has been practicable consistently with the public interests, the reduction of the

Army has been accomplished; but the appropriations for its pay and for other branches of the military service having proved inadequate, the earliest attention to that subject will be necessary; and the expediency of continuing upon the peace establishment the staff officers who have hitherto been provisionally retained is also recommended to the consideration of Congress.

In the performance of the Executive duty upon this occasion there has not been wanting a just sensibility to the merits of the American Army during the late war; but the obvious policy and design in fixing an efficient military peace establishment did not afford an opportunity to distinguish the aged and infirm on account of their past services nor the wounded and disabled on account of their present sufferings. The extent of the reduction, indeed, unavoidably involved the exclusion of many meritorious officers of every rank from the service of their country; and so equal as well as so numerous were the claims to attention that a decision by the standard of comparative merit could seldom be attained. Judged, however, in candor by a general standard of positive merit, the Army register will, it is believed, do honor to the establishment, while the case of those officers whose names are not included in it devolves with the strongest interest upon the legislative authority for such provision as shall be deemed the best calculated to give support and solace to the veteran and the invalid, to display the beneficence as well as the justice of the Government, and to inspire a martial zeal for the public service upon every future emergency.

Although the embarrassments arising from the want of an uniform national currency have not been diminished since the adjournment of Congress, great satisfaction has been derived in contemplating the revival of the public credit and the efficiency of the public resources. The receipts into the Treasury from the various branches of revenue during the nine months ending on the 30th of September last have been estimated at $12,500,000; the issues of Treasury notes of every denomination during the same period amounted to the sum of $14,000,000, and there was also obtained upon loan during the same period a sum of $9,000,000, of which the sum of $6,000,000 was subscribed in cash and the sum of

$3,000,000 in Treasury notes. With these means, added to the sum of $1,500,000, being the balance of money in the Treasury on the 1st day of January, there has been paid between the 1st of January and the 1st of October on account of the appropriations of the preceding and of the present year (exclusively of the amount of the Treasury notes subscribed to the loan and of the amount redeemed in the payment of duties and taxes) the aggregate sum of $33,500,000, leaving a balance then in the Treasury estimated at the sum of $3,000,000. Independent, however, of the arrearages due for military services and supplies, it is presumed that a further sum of $5,000,000, including the interest on the public debt payable on the 1st of January next, will be demanded at the Treasury to compete the expenditures of the present year, and for which the existing ways and means will sufficiently provide.

The national debt, as it was ascertained on the 1st of October last, amounted in the whole to the sum of $120,000,000, consisting of the unredeemed balance of the debt contracted before the late war ($39,000,000), the amount of the funded debt contracted in consequence of the war ($64,000,000), and the amount of the unfunded and floating debt, including the various issues of Treasury notes, $17,000,000, which is in a gradual course of payment. There will probably be some addition to the public debt upon the liquidation of various claims which are depending, and a conciliatory disposition on the part of Congress may lead honorably and advantageously to an equitable arrangement of the militia expenses incurred by the several States without the previous sanction or authority of the Government of the United States; but when it is considered that the new as well as the old portion of the debt has been contracted in the assertion of the national rights and independence, and when it is recollected that the public expenditures, not being exclusively bestowed upon subjects of a transient nature, will long be visible in the number and equipments of the American Navy, in the military works for the defense of our harbors and our frontiers, and in the supplies of our arsenals and magazines the amount will bear a gratifying comparison with the objects which have been attained, as well as with the resources of the country.

The arrangements of the finances with a view to the

receipts and expenditures of a permanent peace establishment will necessarily enter into the deliberations of Congress during the present session. It is true that the improved condition of the public revenue will not only afford the means of maintaining the faith of the Government with its creditors inviolate, and of prosecuting successfully the measures of the most liberal policy, but will also justify an immediate alleviation of the burdens imposed by the necessities of the war. It is, however, essential to every modification of the finances that the benefits of an uniform national currency should be restored to the community. The absence of the precious metals will, it is believed, be a temporary evil, but until they can again be rendered the general medium of exchange it devolves on the wisdom of Congress to provide a substitute which shall equally engage the confidence and accommodate the wants of the citizens throughout the Union. If the operation of the State banks can not produce this result, the probable operation of a national bank will merit consideration; and if neither of these expedients be deemed effectual it may become necessary to ascertain the terms upon which the notes of the Government (no longer required as an instrument of credit) shall be issued upon motives of general policy as a common medium of circulation.

Notwithstanding the security for future repose which the United States ought to find in their love of peace and their constant respect for the rights of other nations, the character of the times particularly inculcates the lesson that, whether to prevent or repel danger, we ought not to be unprepared for it. This consideration will sufficiently recommend to Congress a liberal provision for the immediate extension and gradual completion of the works of defense, both fixed and floating, on our maritime frontier, and an adequate provision for guarding our inland frontier against dangers to which certain portions of it may continue to be exposed.

As an improvement in our military establishment, it will deserve the consideration of Congress whether a corps of invalids might not be so organized and employed as at once to aid in the support of meritorious individuals excluded by age or infirmities from the existing establishment, and to procure to the public the benefit of their stationary services and of their exemplary discipline. I recommend also an enlargement of the Military Academy already established, and the establishment of others in other sections of the Union; and I can not press too much on the attention of Congress such a classification and organization of the militia as will most effectually render it the safeguard of a free state. If experience has shewn in the recent splendid achievements of militia the value of this resource for the public defense, it has shewn also the importance of that skill in the use of arms and that familiarity with the essential rules of discipline which can not be expected from the regulations now in force. With this subject is intimately connected the necessity of accommodating the laws in every respect to the great object of enabling the political authority of the Union to employ promptly and effectually the physical power of the Union in the cases designated by the Constitution.

The signal services which have been rendered by our Navy and the capacities it has developed for successful co-operation in the national defense will give to that portion of the public force its full value in the eyes of Congress, at an epoch which calls for the constant vigilance of all governments. To preserve the ships now in a sound state, to complete those already contemplated, to provide amply the imperishable materials for prompt augmentations, and to improve the existing arrangements into more advantageous establishments for the construction, the repairs, and the security of vessels of war is dictated by the soundest policy.

In adjusting the duties on imports to the object of revenue the influence of the tariff on manufactures will necessarily present itself for consideration. However wise the theory may be which leaves to the sagacity and interest of individuals the application of their industry and resources, there are in this as in other cases exceptions to the general rule. Besides the condition which the theory itself implies of a reciprocal adoption by other nations, experience teaches that so many circumstances must concur in introducing and maturing manufacturing establishments, especially of the more complicated kinds, that a country may remain long without them, although sufficiently advanced and in some respects even peculiarly fitted for carrying them on with success. Under circumstances giving a powerful impulse to manufacturing industry it has made among us a progress and exhibited an efficiency which justify the belief that with a protection not more than is due to the enterprising citizens whose interests are now at stake it will become at an early day not only safe against occasional competitions from abroad, but a source of domestic wealth and even of external commerce. In selecting the branches more especially entitled to the public patronage a preference is obviously claimed by such as will relieve the United States from a dependence on foreign supplies ever subject to casual failures, for articles necessary for the public defense or connected with the primary wants of individuals. It will be an additional recommendation of particular manufactures where the materials for them are extensively drawn from our agriculture, and consequently impart and insure to that great fund of national prosperity and independence an encouragement which can not fail to be rewarded.

Among the means of advancing the public interest the occasion is a proper one for recalling the attention of Congress to the great importance of establishing throughout our country the roads and canals which can best be executed under the national authority. No objects within the circle of political economy so richly repay the expense bestowed on them; there are none the utility of which is more universally ascertained and acknowledged; none that do more honor to the governments whose wise and enlarged patriotism duly appreciates them. Nor is there any country which presents a field where nature invites more the art of man to complete her own work for his accommodation and benefit. These considerations are strengthened, moreover, by the political effect of these facilities for intercommunication in bringing and binding more closely together the various parts of our extended confederacy. Whilst the States individually, with a laudable enterprise and emulation, avail themselves of their local advantages by new roads, by navigable canals, and by improving the streams susceptible of navigation, the General Government is the more urged to similar undertakings, requiring a national jurisdiction and national means, by the prospect of thus systematically completing so inestimable a work; and it is a happy reflection that any defect of constitutional authority which may be encountered can be supplied in a mode which the Constitution itself has providently pointed out.

The present is a favorable season also for bringing again into view the establishment of a national seminary of learning within the District of Columbia, and with means drawn from the property therein, subject to the authority of the General Government. Such an institution claims the patronage of Congress as a monument of their solicitude for the advancement of knowledge, without which the blessings of liberty can not be fully enjoyed or long preserved; as a model instructive in the formation of other seminaries; as a nursery of enlightened preceptors, and as a central resort of youth and genius from every part of their country, diffusing on their return examples of those national feelings, those liberal sentiments, and those congenial manners which contribute cement to our Union and strength to the great political fabric of which that is the foundation.

In closing this communication I ought not to repress a sensibility, in which you will unite, to the happy lot of our country and to the goodness of a superintending Providence, to which we are indebted for it. Whilst other portions of mankind are laboring under the distresses of war or struggling with adversity in other forms, the United States are in the tranquil enjoyment of prosperous and honorable peace. In reviewing the scenes through which it has been attained we can rejoice in the proofs given that our political institutions, founded in human rights and framed for their preservation, are equal to the severest trials of war as well as adapted to the ordinary periods of repose. As fruits of this experience and of the reputation acquired by the American arms on the land and on the water, the nation finds itself possessed of a growing respect abroad and of a just confidence in itself, which are among the best pledges for its peaceful career. Under other aspects of our country the strongest features of its flourishing condition are seen in a population rapidly increasing on a territory as productive as it is extensive; in a general industry and fertile ingenuity which find their ample rewards, and in an affluent revenue which admits a reduction of the public burdens without withdrawing the means of sustaining the public credit, of gradually discharging the public debt, of providing for the necessary defensive and precautionary establishments, and of patronizing in every authorized mode undertakings conducive to the aggregate wealth and individual comfort of our citizens.

It remains for the guardians of the public welfare to persevere in that justice and good will toward other nations which invite a return of these sentiments toward the United States; to cherish institutions which guarantee their safety and their liberties, civil and religious; and to combine with a liberal system of foreign commerce an improvement of the national advantages and a protection and extension of the independent resources of our highly favored and happy country.

In all measures having such objects my faithful co-operation will be afforded.

Veto Message to Congress

March 3, 1817.

To the House of Representatives of the United States:

Having considered the bill this day presented to me entitled "An act to set apart and pledge certain funds for internal improvements," and which sets apart and pledges funds "for constructing roads and canals, and improving the navigation of water courses, in order to facilitate, promote, and give security to internal commerce among the several States, and to render more easy and less expensive the means and provisions for the common defense," I am constrained by the insuperable difficulty I feel in reconciling the bill with the Constitution of the United States to return it with that objection to the House of Representatives, in which it originated.

The legislative powers vested in Congress are specified and enumerated in the eighth section of the first article of the Constitution, and it does not appear that the power proposed to be exercised by the bill is among the enumerated powers, or that it falls by any just interpretation within the power to make laws necessary and proper for carrying into execution those or other powers vested by the Constitution in the Government of the United States.

"The power to regulate commerce among the several States" can not include a power to construct roads and canals, and to improve the navigation of water courses in order to facilitate, promote, and secure such a commerce without a latitude of construction departing from the ordinary import of the terms strengthened by the known inconveniences which doubtless led to the grant of this remedial power to Congress.

To refer the power in question to the clause "to provide for the common defense and general welfare" would be contrary to the established and consistent rules of interpretation, as rendering the special and careful enumeration of powers which follow the clause nugatory and improper. Such a view of the Constitution would have the effect of giving to Congress a general power of legislation instead of the defined and limited one hitherto understood to belong to them, the terms "common defense and general welfare" embracing every object and act within the purview of a legislative trust. It would have the effect of subjecting both the Constitution and laws of the several States in all cases not specifically exempted to be superseded by laws of Congress, it being expressly declared "that the Constitution of the United States and laws made in pursuance thereof shall be the supreme law of the land, and the judges of every State shall be bound thereby, anything in the constitution or laws of any State to the contrary notwithstanding." Such a view of the Constitution, finally, would have the effect of excluding the judicial authority of the United States from its participation in guarding the boundary between the legislative powers of the General and the State Governments, inasmuch as questions relating to the general welfare, being questions of policy and expediency, are unsusceptible of judicial cognizance and decision.

A restriction of the power "to provide for the common defense and general welfare" to cases which are to be provided for by the expenditure of money would still leave within the legislative power of Congress all the great and most important measures of Government, money being the ordinary and necessary means of carrying them into execution.

If a general power to construct roads and canals, and to improve the navigation of water courses, with the train of powers incident thereto, be not possessed by Congress, the assent of the States in the mode provided in the bill cannot confer the power. The only cases in which the consent and cession of particular States can extend the power of Congress are those specified and provided for in the Constitution.

I am not unaware of the great importance of roads and canals and the improved navigation of water courses, and that a power in the National Legislature to provide for them might be exercised with signal advantage to the general prosperity. But seeing that such a power is not expressly given by the Constitution, and believing that it can not be deduced from any part of it without an inadmissible latitude of construction and a reliance on insufficient precedents; believing also that the permanent success of the Constitution depends on a definite partition of powers between the General and the State Governments, and that no adequate landmarks would be left by the constructive extension of the powers of Congress as proposed in the bill, I have no option but to withhold my signature from it, and to cherishing the hope that its beneficial objects may be attained by a resort for the necessary powers to the same wisdom and virtue in the nation which established the Constitution in its actual form and providently marked out in the instrument itself a safe and practicable mode of improving it as experience might suggest.

RETIREMENT
1817–1836

To Robert Walsh

Dr. Sir   Montpellier, Mar. 2, 1819
I recd. some days ago your letter of Feby 15, in which you intimate your intention to vindicate our Country against misrepresentations propagated abroad, and your desire of information on the subject of Negro slavery, of moral character, of religion, and of education in Virginia, as affected by the Revolution, and our public Institutions.

The general condition of slaves must be influenced by various causes. Among these are 1. the ordinary price of food, on which the quality and quantity allowed them will more or less depend. This cause has operated much more unfavorably against them in some quarters than in Virga. 2. the kinds of labour to be performed, of wch the Sugar & Rice plantations afford elsewhere & not here unfavorable examples. 3. the national spirit of their Masters, which has been graduated by Philosophical writers among the slaveholding Colonies of Europe. 4. the circumstance of conformity or difference in the physical characters of the two classes; such a difference cannot but have a material influence, and is common to all the slave-holding Countries within the American Hemisphere. Even in those where there are other than black slaves, as Indians & mixed breeds, there is a difference of Colour not without its influence. 5. the proportion which the slaves bear to the free part of the community, and especially the greater or smaller numbers in which they belong to individuals.

This last is, perhaps, the most powerful of all the causes deteriorating the condition of the slave, and furnishes the best scale for determining the degree of its hardship.

In reference to the actual condition of slaves in Virga. it may be confidently stated, as better beyond comparison, than it was before the Revolution. The improvement strikes every one who witnessed their former condition, and attends to their present. They are better fed, better clad, better lodged, and better treated in every respect: insomuch that what was formerly deemed a moderate treatment, wd. now be a rigid one, and what formerly a rigid one, would now be denounced by the Public feeling. With respect to the great article of food particularly it is a common remark among those who have visited Europe, that it includes a much greater proportion of the animal ingredient, than is attainable by the free labourers even in that quarter of the Globe. As the two great causes of the general melioration in the lot of the slaves since the establishment of our Independence, I should set down 1. the sensibility to human rights, and sympathy with human sufferings excited and cherished by the discussions preceding, & the spirit of the Institutions growing out of, that event. 2. the decreasing proportion which the slaves bear to the individual holders of them; a consequence of the abolition of entails, & the rule of primogeniture, and of the equalizing tendency of parental affection unfettered from all prejudices, as well as from the restrictions of law.

With respect to the moral features of Virga. it may be observed, that pictures which have been given of them are, to say the least, outrageous caricatures even when taken from the state of Society previous to the Revolution; and that so far as there was any ground or colour for them, then, the same cannot be found for them now.

Omitting more minute or less obvious causes tainting the habits and manners of the people under the Colonial Govt., the following offer themselves. 1. the negro slavery chargeable in so great a degree on the very quarter which has furnished most of the libellers. It is well known that during the Colonial dependence of Virga. repeated attempts were made to stop the importation of slaves each of which attempts was successively defeated by the foreign negative on the laws, and that one of the first offsprings of independent & Republican legislation was an Act of perpetual prohibition. 2. the too unequal distribution of property favored by laws derived from the British code, which generated examples in the opulent class inauspicious to the habits of the other classes. 3. the indolence of most & the irregular lives of many of the established Clergy, consisting, in a very large proportion, of foreigners, and these in no inconsiderable proportion, of men willing to leave their homes in the parent Country where their demerit was an obstacle to a provision for them, and whose degeneracy here was promoted by their distance from the controuling eyes of their kindred & friends, by the want of Ecclesiastical superiors in the Colony, or efficient ones in G. B. who might maintain a salutary discipline among them, and finally by their independence both of their congregations and of the Civil authority for their stipends. 4. A source of contagious dissipation might be traced in the British Factors chiefly from Scotland, who carried on the general trade external & internal of the Colony. These being interdicted by their principals from marrying in the Country, being little prone to apply their leisure to intellectual pursuits, and living in knots scattered in small towns or detached spots affording few substitutes of social amusement easily fell into irregularities of different sorts, and of evil example. I ought not however to make this remark, without adding not only that there were exceptions to it, but that those to whom the remark is applicable, often combined with those traits of character others of a laudable & amiable kind. Such of them as eventually married & settled in the Country were in most cases remarked for being good husbands, parents & masters, as well as good neighbours as far as was consistent with habits of intemperance, to which not a few became victims. The weight of this mercantile class, in the community may be inferred from the fact that they had their periodical meetings at the seat of Govt. at which they fixed the rate of foreign exchange, the advance on their imported merchandise universally sold on credit, and the price of Tobo. the great & indeed the only staple commodity for exportation; regulations affecting more deeply the interests of the people at large, than the ordinary proceedings of the Legislative Body. As a further mark of their importance, their influence as creditors was felt in elections of the popular branch of that Body. It had the common name of the Ledger interest. 5. Without laying undue stress on it, I may refer to the rule of septennial elections for the Legislature, which led of course to the vitiating means to which candidates are more tempted to resort by so durable, than by a shorter, period of power.

With the exception of slavery these demoralizing causes have ceased or are wearing out; and even that as already noticed, has lost no small share of its former character. On the whole the moral aspect of the State may at present be fairly said to bear no unfavorable comparison with the average standard of the other States. It certainly gives the lie to the foreign Calumniators whom you propose to arraign.

That there has been an increase of religious instruction since the revolution can admit of no question. The English church was originally the established religion; the character of the clergy that above described. Of other sects there were but few adherents, except the Presbyterians who predominated on the W. side of the Blue Mountains. A little time previous to the Revolutionary struggle the Baptists sprang up, and made a very rapid progress. Among the early acts of the Republican Legislature, were those abolishing the Religious establishment, and putting all Sects at full liberty and on a perfect level. At present the population is divided, with small exceptions, among the Protestant Episcopalians, the Presbyterians, the Baptists & the Methodists. Of their comparative numbers I can command no sources of information. I conjecture the Presbyterians & Baptists to form each abt. a third, & the two other sects together of which the Methodists are much the smallest, to make up the remaining third. The Old churches, built under the establisht. at the public expence, have in many instances gone to ruin, or are in a very dilapidated state, owing chiefly to a transition desertion of the flocks to other worships. A few new ones have latterly been built particularly in the towns. Among the other sects, Meeting Houses, have multiplied & continue to multiply; tho' in general they are of the plainest and cheapest sort. But neither the number nor the style of the Religious edifices is a true measure of the state of religion. Religious instruction is now diffused throughout the Community by preachers of every sect with almost equal zeal, tho' with very unequal acquirements; and at private houses & open stations and occasionally in such as are appropriated to Civil use, as well as buildings appropriated to that use. The qualifications of the Preachers, too among the new sects where there was the greatest deficiency, are understood to be improving. On a general comparison of the present & former times, the balance is certainly & vastly on the side of the present, as to the number of religious teachers the zeal which actuates them, the purity of their lives, and the attendance of the people on their instructions. It was the Universal opinion of the Century preceding the last, that Civil Govt.

could not stand without the prop of a Religious establishment, & that the Xn. religion itself, would perish if not supported by a legal provision for its Clergy. The experience of Virginia conspicuously corroborates the disproof of both opinions. The Civil Govt. tho' bereft of everything like an associated hierarchy possesses the requisite stability and performs its functions with complete success; Whilst the number, the industry, and the morality of the Priesthood, & the devotion of the people have been manifestly increased by the total separation of the Church from the State.

On the subject of education I am not eno' informed to give a view of its increase. The system contemplated by the literary fund cannot yet be taken into the estimate, farther than as it may be an index of the progress of knowledge prerequisite to its adoption. Those who are best able to compare the present intelligence of the Mass of the people, with that antecedent to the revolution, will all agree I believe, in the great superiority of the present.

I know not how far these notices may fall within the precise scope of your meditated Exposition. Should any of them do so, I communicate them with pleasure; well assured that they will be in good hands for a good purpose. The only restriction I wish in the use of them is that my name may not be referred to.

In compliance with your request I send a copy of the observations addressed to the Agricult: Socy. of Albemarle. I regret that they are not more worthy of the place to which you destine them. I am not unaware that some of the topics introduced may be interesting ones; but they required a development very different from that which I gave them.

As you intend to notice the variance between my statement and that of Mr. Hamilton relating to certain nos. in the Federalist, I take the liberty of remarking, that independent of any internal evidences that may be discernible, the inaccuracy of Mr. H's memory is illustrated by the circumstance, that his memorandum ascribes, not only to Mr. Jay, a paper No. 54, not written by him, but to himself a paper No. 64 written by Mr. Jay. This appears by the statement (presumed to be authentic) in the life of Mr. Jay by Delaplaine. If I have any interest in proving the fallibility of Mr. H's memory, or the error of his statement however occasioned, it is not that the authorship in question is of itself a point deserving the solicitude of either of the parties; but because I had, at the request of a confidential friend or two, communicated a list of the nos. in that publication with the names of the writers annexed, at a time & under circumstances depriving me of a plea for so great a mistake in a slip of the memory or attention. Be pleased to accept my esteem & friendly respects.

To Robert J. Evans

Sir,   Montpellier, June 15, 1819

I have recd. your letter of the 3d instant, requesting such hints as may have occurred to me on the subject of an eventual extinguishment of slavery in the U. S.

Not doubting the purity of your views, and relying on the discretion by which they will be regulated, I cannot refuse such a compliance as will at least manifest my respect for the object of your undertaking.

A general emancipation of slaves ought to be 1. gradual. 2. equitable & satisfactory to the individuals immediately concerned. 3. consistent with the existing & durable prejudices of the nation.

That it ought, like remedies for other deeprooted and wide-spread evils, to be gradual, is so obvious that there seems to be no difference of opinion on that point.

To be equitable & satisfactory, the consent of both the Master & the slave should be obtained. That of the Master will require a provision in the plan for compensating a loss of what he held as property guarantied by the laws, and recognised by the Constitution. That of the slave, requires that his condition in a state of freedom, be preferable in his own estimation, to his actual one in a state of bondage.

To be consistent with existing and probably unalterable prejudices in the U. S. the freed blacks ought to be permanently removed beyond the region occupied by or allotted to a White population. The objections to a thorough incorporation of the two people are, with most of the Whites insuperable; and are admitted by all of them to be very powerful. If the blacks, strongly marked as they are by Physical & lasting peculiarities, be retained amid the Whites, under the degrading privation of equal rights political or social, they must be always dissatisfied with their condition as a change only from one to another species of oppression; always secretly confederated agst. the ruling & privileged class; and always uncontroulled by some of the most cogent motives to moral and respectable conduct. The character of the free blacks, even where their legal condition is least affected by their colour, seems to put these truths beyond question. It is material also that the removal of the blacks be to a distance precluding the jealousies & hostilities to be apprehended from a neighboring people stimulated by the contempt known to be entertained for their peculiar features; to say nothing of their vindictive recollections, or the predatory propensities which their State of Society might foster. Nor is it fair, in estimating the danger of Collisions with the Whites, to charge it wholly on the side of the Blacks. There would be reciprocal antipathies doubling the danger.

The colonizing plan on foot, has as far as it extends, a due regard to these requisites; with the additional object of bestowing new blessings civil & religious on the quarter of the Globe most in need of them. The Society proposes to transport to the African Coast all free & freed blacks who may be willing to remove thither; to provide by fair means, &, it is understood with a prospect of success, a suitable territory for their reception; and to initiate them into such an establishment as may gradually and indefinitely expand itself.

The experiment, under this view of it, merits encouragement from all who regard slavery as an evil, who wish to see it diminished and abolished by peaceable & just means; and who have themselves no better mode to propose. Those who have most doubted the success of the experiment must at least have wished to find themselves in an error.

But the views of the Society are limited to the case of blacks already free, or who may be *gratuitously* emancipated. To provide a commensurate remedy for the evil, the plan must be extended to the great Mass of blacks, and must embrace a fund sufficient to induce the Master as well as the slave to concur in it. Without the concurrence of the Master, the benefit will be very limited as it relates to the Negroes; and essentially defective, as it relates to the U. States; and the concurrence of Masters, must, for the most part, be obtained by purchase.

Can it be hoped that voluntary contributions, however adequate to an auspicious commencement, will supply the sums necessary to such an enlargement of the remedy? May not another question be asked? Would it be reasonable to throw so great a burden on the individuals distinguished by their philanthropy and patriotism?

The object to be obtained, as an object of humanity, appeals alike to all; as a National object, it claims the interposition of the nation. It is the nation which is to reap the benefit. The nation therefore ought to bear the burden.

Must then the enormous sums required to pay for, to transport, and to establish in a foreign land all the slaves in the U. S. as their Masters may be willg. to part with them, be taxed on the good people of the U. S. or be obtained by loans swelling the public debt to a size pregnant with evils next in degree to those of slavery itself?

Happily it is not necessary to answer this question by remarking that if slavery as a national evil is to be abolished, and it be just that it be done at the national expence, the amount of the expence is not a paramount consideration. It is the peculiar fortune, or, rather a providential blessing of the U. S. to possess a resource commensurate to this great object, without taxes on the people, or even an increase of the public debt.

I allude to the vacant territory the extent of which is so vast, and the vendible value of which is so well ascertained.

Supposing the number of slaves to be 1,500,000, and their price to average 400 drs, the cost of the whole would be 600 millions of dollrs. These estimates are probably beyond the fact; and from the no. of slaves should be deducted 1. those whom their Masters would not part with. 2. those who may be gratuitously set free by their Masters. 3. those acquiring freedom under emancipating regulations of the States. 4. those preferring slavery where they are, to freedom in an African settlement. On the other hand, it is to be noted that the expence of removal & settlement is not included in the estimated sum; and that an increase of the slaves will be going on during the period required for the execution of the plan.

On the whole the aggregate sum needed may be stated at about 600 Mils. of dollars.

This will require 200 mils. of Acres at 3 dolrs. per Acre; or 300 mils. at 2 dollrs. per Acre a quantity which tho' great in itself, is perhaps not a third part of the disposable territory belonging to the U. S. And to what object so good so great & so glorious, could that peculiar fund of wealth be appropriated? Whilst the sale of territory would, on one hand be planting one desert with a free & civilized people, it would on the other, be giving freedom to another people, and filling with them another desert. And if in any instances, wrong has been done by our forefathers to people of one colour, by dispossessing them of their soil, what better atonement is now in our power than that of making what is rightfully acquired a source of justice & of blessings to a people of another colour?

As the revolution to be produced in the condition of the negroes must be gradual, it will suffice if the sale of territory keep pace with its progress. For a time at least the proceeds wd. be in advance. In this case it might be best, after deducting the expence incident to the surveys & sales, to place the surplus in a situation where its increase might correspond with the natural increase of the unpurchased slaves. Should the proceeds at any time fall short of the calls for their application, anticipations might be made by temporary loans to be discharged as the land should find a Market.

But it is probable that for a considerable period, the sales would exceed the calls. Masters would not be willing to strip their plantations & farms of their laborers too rapidly. The slaves themselves, connected as they generally are by tender ties with others under other Masters, would be kept from the list of emigrants by the want of the multiplied consents to be obtained. It is probable indeed that for a long time a certain portion of the proceeds might safely continue applicable to the discharge of the debts or to other purposes of the Nation. Or it might be most convenient, in the outset, to appropriate a certain proportion only of the income from sales, to the object in view, leaving the residue otherwise applicable.

Should any plan similar to that I have sketched, be deemed eligible in itself no particular difficulty is foreseen from that portion of the nation which with a common interest in the vacant territory has no interest in slave property. They are too just to wish that a partial sacrifice shd. be made for the general good; and too well aware that whatever may be the intrinsic character of that description of property, it is one known to the constitution, and, as such could not be constitutionally taken away without just compensation. That part of the Nation has indeed shewn a meritorious alacrity in promoting, by pecuniary contributions, the limited scheme for colonizing the Blacks, & freeing the nation from the unfortunate stain on it, which justifies the belief that any enlargement of the scheme, if founded on just principles would find among them its earliest & warmest patrons. It ought to have great weight that the vacant lands in question have for the most part been derived from grants of the States holding the slaves to be redeemed & removed by the sale of them.

It is evident however that in effectuating a general emancipation of slaves, in the mode which has been hinted, difficulties of other sorts would be encountered. The provision for ascertaining the joint consent of the masters & slaves; for guarding agst. unreasonable valuations of the latter; and for the discrimination of those not proper to be conveyed to a foreign residence, or who ought to remain a charge on Masters in whose service they had been disabled or worn out and for the annual transportation of such numbers, would Require the mature deliberations of the National Councils. The measure implies also the practicability of procuring in Africa, an enlargement of the district or districts, for receiving the exiles, sufficient for so great an augmentation of their numbers.

Perhaps the Legislative provision best adapted to the case would be an incorporation of the Colonizing Society or the establishment of a similar one, with proper powers, under the appointment & superintendence of the National Executive.

In estimating the difficulties however incident to any plan of general emancipation, they ought to be brought into comparison with those inseparable from other plans, and be yielded to or not according to the result of the comparison.

One difficulty presents itself which will probably attend every plan which is to go into effect under the Legislative provisions of the National Govt. But whatever may be the defect of existing powers of Congress, the Constitution has pointed out the way in which it can be supplied. And it can hardly be doubted that the requisite powers might readily be procured for attaining the great object in question, in any mode whatever approved by the Nation.

If these thoughts can be of any aid in your search of a remedy for the great evil under which the nation labors, you are very welcome to them. You will allow me however to add that it will be most agreeable to me, not to be publickly referred to in any use you may make of them.

To Spencer Roane

Dear Sir   Septr. 2; 1819.

I have recd. your favor of the 22d Ult inclosing a copy of your observations on the Judgment of the Supreme Court of the U. S. in the case of M'Culloch agst. the State of Maryland; and I have found their latitudinary mode of expounding the Constitution, combated in them with the ability and the force which were to be expected.

It appears to me as it does to you that the occasion did not call for the general and abstract doctrine interwoven with the decision of the particular case. I have always supposed that the meaning of a law, and for a like reason, of a Constitution, so far as it depends on Judicial interpretation, was to result from a course of particular decisions, and not these from a previous and abstract comment on the subject. The example in this instance tends to reverse the rule and to forego the illustration to be derived from a series of cases actually occurring for adjudication.

I could have wished also that the Judges had delivered their opinions seriatim. The case was of such magnitude, in the scope given to it, as to call, if any case could do so, for the

views of the subject separately taken by them. This might either by the harmony of their reasoning have produced a
greater conviction in the Public mind; or by its discordance
have impaired the force of the precedent now ostensibly supported by a unanimous & perfect concurrence in every argument & dictum in the judgment pronounced.

But what is of most importance is the high sanction given
to a latitude in expounding the Constitution which seems to
break down the landmarks intended by a specification of the
Powers of Congress, and to substitute for a definite connection between means and ends, a Legislative discretion as to
the former to which no practical limit can be assigned. In the
great system of Political Economy having for its general object the national welfare, everything is related immediately or
remotely to every other thing; and consequently a Power over
any one thing, if not limited by some obvious and precise
affinity, may amount to a Power over every other. Ends &
means may shift their character at the will & according to the
ingenuity of the Legislative Body. What is an end in one case
may be a means in another; nay in the same case, may be either an end or a means at the Legislative option. The British
Parliament in collecting a revenue from the commerce of
America found no difficulty in calling it either a tax for the
regulation of trade, or a regulation of trade with a view to the
tax, as it suited the argument or the policy of the moment.

Is there a Legislative power in fact, not expressly prohibited
by the Constitution, which might not, according to the doctrine of the Court, be exercised as a means of carrying into effect some specified Power?

Does not the Court also relinquish by their doctrine, all
controul on the Legislative exercise of unconstitutional powers? According to that doctrine, the expediency & constitutionality of means for carrying into effect a specified Power
are convertible terms; and Congress are admitted to be
Judges of the expediency. The Court certainly cannot be so; a
question, the moment it assumes the character of mere expediency or policy, being evidently beyond the reach of Judicial
cognizance.

It is true, the Court are disposed to retain a guardianship of
the Constitution against legislative encroachments. "Should

Congress," say they, "under the pretext of executing its Powers, pass laws for the accomplishment of objects not entrusted to the Government, it would become the painful duty of this Tribunal to say that such an act was not the law of the land." But suppose Congress should, as would doubtless happen, pass unconstitutional laws not to accomplish objects not specified in the Constitution, but the same laws as means expedient, convenient or conducive to the accomplishment of objects entrusted to the Government; by what handle could the Court take hold of the case? We are told that it was the policy of the old Government of France to grant monopolies, such as that of Tobacco, in order to create funds in particular hands from which loans could be made to the Public, adequate capitalists not being formed in that Country in the ordinary course of commerce. Were Congress to grant a like monopoly merely to aggrandize those enjoying it, the Court might consistently say, that this not being an object entrusted to the Governt. the grant was unconstitutional and void. Should Congress however grant the monopoly according to the French policy as a means judged by them to be necessary, expedient or conducive to the borrowing of money, which is an object entrusted to them by the Constitution, it seems clear that the Court, adhering to its doctrine, could not interfere without stepping on Legislative ground, to do which they justly disclaim all pretension.

It could not but happen, and was foreseen at the birth of the Constitution, that difficulties and differences of opinion might occasionally arise in expounding terms & phrases necessarily used in such a charter; more especially those which divide legislation between the General & local Governments; and that it might require a regular course of practice to liquidate & settle the meaning of some of them. But it was anticipated I believe by few if any of the friends of the Constitution, that a rule of construction would be introduced as broad & as pliant as what has occurred. And those who recollect, and still more those who shared in what passed in the State Conventions, thro' which the people ratified the Constitution, with respect to the extent of the powers vested in Congress, cannot easily be persuaded that the avowal of such a rule would not have prevented its ratification. It has been the misfortune, if not the reproach, of other nations, that their Govts. have not been freely and deliberately established by themselves. It is the boast of ours that such has been its source and that it can be altered by the same authority only which established it. It is a further boast that a regular mode of making proper alterations has been providently inserted in the Constitution itself. It is anxiously to be wished therefore, that no innovations may take place in other modes, one of which would be a constructive assumption of powers never meant to be granted. If the powers be deficient, the legitimate source of additional ones is always open, and ought to be resorted to.

Much of the error in expounding the Constitution has its origin in the use made of the species of sovereignty implied in the nature of Govt. The specified powers vested in Congress, it is said, are sovereign powers, and that as such they carry with them an unlimited discretion as to the means of executing them. It may surely be remarked that a limited Govt. may be limited in its sovereignty as well with respect to the means as to the objects of his powers; and that to give an extent to the former, superseding the limits to the latter, is in effect to convert a limited into an unlimited Govt. There is certainly a reasonable medium between expounding the Constitution with the strictness of a penal law, or other ordinary statute, and expounding it with a laxity which may vary its essential character, and encroach on the local sovereignties with wch. it was meant to be reconcilable.

The very existence of these local sovereignties is a controul on the pleas for a constructive amplification of the powers of the General Govt. Within a single State possessing the entire sovereignty, the powers given to the Govt. by the People are understood to extend to all the Acts whether as means or ends required for the welfare of the Community, and falling within the range of just Govt. To withhold from such a Govt. any particular power necessary or useful in itself, would be to deprive the people of the good dependent on its exercise; since the power must be there or not exist at all. In the Govt. of the U. S. the case is obviously different. In establishing that Govt. the people retained other Govts. capable of exercising such necessary and useful powers as were not to be exercised by the General Govt. No necessary presumption therefore arises from the importance of any particular power in itself, that it has been vested in that Govt. because tho' not vested there, it may exist elsewhere, and the exercise of it elsewhere might be preferred by those who alone had a right to make the distribution. The presumption which ought to be indulged is that any improvement of this distribution sufficiently pointed out by experience would not be withheld.

Altho' I have confined myself to the single question concerning the rule of interpreting the Constitution, I find that my pen has carried me to a length which would not have been permitted by a recollection that my remarks are merely for an eye to which no aspect of the subject is likely to be new. I hasten therefore to conclude with assurances &c &c.

To Robert Walsh

Dear Sir,   Montpellier, Novr. 27 1819.
Your letter of the 11th was duly recd. and I should have given it a less tardy answer, but for a succession of particular demands on my attention, and a wish to assist my recollections, by consulting both Manuscript & printed sources of information on the subjects of your enquiry. Of these, however, I have not been able to avail myself but very partially.

As to the intention of the framers of the Constitution in the clause relating to "the migration and importation of persons, &c" the best key may perhaps be found in the case which produced it. The African trade in slaves had long been odious to most of the States, and the importation of slaves into them had been prohibited. Particular States however continued the importation, and were extremely averse to any restriction on their power to do so. In the convention the former States were anxious, in framing a new constitution, to insert a provision for an immediate and absolute stop to the trade. The latter were not only averse to any interference on the subject; but solemnly declared that their constituents would never accede to a Constitution containing such an article. Out of this conflict grew the middle measure providing that Congress should not interfere until the year 1808; with an implication, that after that date, they might prohibit the importation of slaves into the States then existing, & previous thereto, into the States not then existing. Such was the tone of opposition in the States of S. Carolina & Georgia, & such the desire to gain their acquiescence in a prohibitory power, that on a question between the epochs of 1800 & 1808, the States of N. Hampshire, Masstts. & Connecticut, (all the eastern States in the Convention,) joined in the vote for the latter, influenced however by the collateral motive of reconciling those particular States to the power over commerce & navigation; against which they felt, as did some other States, a very strong repugnance. The earnestness of S. Carolina & Georgia was farther manifested by their insisting on the security in the V article, against any amendment to the Constitution affecting the right reserved to them, & their uniting with the small states, who insisted on a like security for their equality in the Senate.

But some of the States were not only anxious for a Constitutional provision against the introduction of slaves. They had scruples against admitting the term "slaves" into the Instrument. Hence the descriptive phrase, "migration or importation of persons;" the term migration allowing those who were scrupulous of acknowledging expressly a property in human beings, to view *imported* persons as a species of emigrants, while others might apply the term to foreign malefactors sent or coming into the country. It is possible tho' not recollected, that some might have had an eye to the case of freed blacks, as well as malefactors.

But whatever may have been intended by the term "migration" or the term "persons," it is most certain, that they referred exclusively to a migration or importation from other countries into the U. States; and not to a removal, voluntary or involuntary, of slaves or freemen, from one to another part of the U. States. Nothing appears or is recollected that warrants this latter intention. Nothing in the proceedings of the State conventions indicates such a construction there.* Had

*The debates of the Pennsylvania Convention contain a speech of Mr. Willson, (Decr. 3, 1787) who had been a member of the general convention, in which, alluding to the clause tolerating for a time, the farther importation

such been the construction it is easy to imagine the figure it would have made in many of the states, among the objections to the constitution, and among the numerous amendments to it proposed by the State conventions* not one of which amendments refers to the clause in question. Neither is there any indication that Congress have heretofore considered themselves as deriving from this Clause a power over the migration or removal of individuals, whether freemen or slaves, from one State to another, whether new or old: For it must be kept in view that if the power was given at all, it has been in force eleven years over all the States existing in 1808, and at all times over the States not then existing. Every indication is against such a construction by Congress of their constitutional powers. Their alacrity in exercising their powers

---

of slaves, he consoles himself with the hope that, in a few years it would be prohibited altogether; observing that in the mean time, the new States which were to be formed would be under the controul of Congress *in this particular*, and slaves would never be introduced among them. In another speech on the day following and alluding to the same clause, his words are "yet the lapse of a few years & Congress will have power to *exterminate* slavery within our borders." How far the language of Mr. W. may have been accurately reported is not known. The expressions used, are more vague & less consistent than would be readily ascribed to him. But as they stand, the fairest construction would be, that he considered the power given to Congress, to arrest the importation of slaves as "laying a foundation for banishing slavery out of the country; & tho' at a period more distant than might be wished, producing the same kind of gradual change which was pursued in Pennsylvania." (See his speech, page 90 of the Debates.) By this "change," after the example of Pennsylvania, he must have meant a change by the other States influenced by that example, & yielding to the general way of thinking & feeling, produced by the policy of putting an end to the importation of slaves. He could not mean by "banishing slavery," more than by a power "to exterminate it," that Congress were authorized to do what is literally expressed.

*In the convention of Virga. the opposition to the Constitution comprised a number of the ablest men in the State. Among them were Mr. Henry & Col. Mason, both of them distinguished by their acuteness, and anxious to display unpopular constructions. One of them Col. Mason, had been a member of the general convention and entered freely into accounts of what passed within it. Yet neither of them, nor indeed any of the other opponents, among the multitude of their objections, and farfetched interpretations, ever hinted, in the debates on the 9th Sect. of Ar. 1, at a power given by it to prohibit an interior migration of any sort. The meaning of the Secn. as levelled against migrations or importations from abroad, was not contested.

relating to slaves, is a proof that they did not claim what they did not exercise. They punctually and unanimously put in force the power accruing in 1808 against the further importation of slaves from abroad. They had previously directed their power over American vessels on the high seas, against the African trade. They lost no time in applying the prohibitory power to Louisiana, which having maritime ports, might be an inlet for slaves from abroad. But they forebore to extend the prohibition to the introduction of slaves from other parts of the Union. They had even prohibited the importation of slaves into the Mississippi Territory from *without the limits of the U. S.* in the year 1798, without extending the prohibition to the introduction of slaves from *within those limits*; altho' at the time the ports of Georgia and S. Carolina were open for the importation of slaves from abroad, and increasing the mass of slavery within the U. States.

If these views of the subject be just, a power in Congress to controul the interior migration or removals of persons, must be derived from some other source than Sect 9, Art. 1; either from the clause giving power "to make all needful rules and regulations respecting the Territory or other property belonging to the U. S. or from that providing for the admission of New States into the Union."

The terms in which the 1st. of these powers is expressed, tho' of a ductile character, cannot well be extended beyond a power over the Territory as property, & a power to make the provisions really needful or necessary for the Govt. of settlers until ripe for admission as States into the Union. It may be inferred that Congress did not regard the interdict of slavery among the needful regulations contemplated by the constitution; since in none of the Territorial Governments created by them, is such an interdict found. The power, however be its import what it may, is obviously limited to a Territory whilst remaining in that character as distinct from that of a State.

As to the power of admitting new States into the federal compact, the questions offering themselves are; whether congress can attach conditions, or the new States concur in conditions, which after admission, would abridge or *enlarge* the constitutional rights of legislation common to the other

States; whether Congress can by a compact with a new member take power either to or from itself, or place the new member above or below the equal rank & rights possessed by the others; whether all such stipulations, expressed or implied would not be nullities, and so pronounced when brought to a practical test. It falls within the Scope of your enquiry, to state the fact, that there was a proposition in the convention to discriminate between the old and new States, by an Article in the Constitution declaring that the aggregate number of representatives from the States thereafter to be admitted should never exceed that of the States originally adopting the Constitution. The proposition happily was rejected. The effect of such a discrimination, is sufficiently evident.

In the case of Louisiana, there is a circumstance which may deserve notice. In the Treaty ceding it, a privilege was retained by the ceding party, which distinguishes between its ports & others of the U. S. for a special purpose & a short period. This privilege however was the result not of an ordinary legislative power in Congress; nor was it the result of an arrangement between Congress & the people of Louisiana. It rests on the ground that the same entire power, even in the nation, over that territory, as over the original territory of the U. S. never existed; the privilege alluded to being in the deed of cession carved by the foreign owner, out of the title conveyed to the purchaser. A sort of necessity therefore was thought to belong to so peculiar & extraordinary a case. Notwithstanding this plea it is presumable that if the privilege had materially affected the rights of other ports, or had been of a permanent or durable character, the occurrence would not have been so little regarded. Congress would not be allowed to effect through the medium of a Treaty, obnoxious discriminations between new and old States, more than among the latter.

With respect to what has taken place in the N. W. Territory, it may be observed, that the ordinance giving its distinctive character on the Subject of Slaveholding proceeded from the old Congress, acting, with the best intentions, but under a charter which contains no shadow of the authority exercised. And it remains to be decided how far the States formed within that Territory & admitted into the Union, are on a different footing from its other members, as to their legislative sovereignty.

For the grounds on which ⅗ of the slaves were admitted into the ratio of representation, I will with your permission, save trouble by referring to No. 54 of the Federalist. In addition, it may be stated that this feature in the Constitution was combined with that relating to the power over Commerce & navigation. In truth these two powers, with those relating to the importation of slaves, & the Articles establishing the equality of representation in the Senate & the rule of taxation, had a complicated influence on each other which alone would have justified the remark, that the Constitution was "the result of mutual deference & Concession."

It was evident that the large States holding slaves, and those not large which felt themselves so by anticipation, would not have concurred in a constitution, allowing them no more Representation in one legislative branch than the smallest States, and in the other less than their proportional contributions to the Common Treasury.

The considerations which led to this mixed ratio which had been very deliberately agreed on in Apl., 1783, by the old Congress, make it probable that the Convention could not have looked to a departure from it, in any instance where slaves made a part of the local population.

Whether the Convention could have looked to the existence of slavery at all in the new States is a point on which I can add little to what has been already stated. The great object of the Convention seemed to be to prohibit the increase by the *importation* of slaves. A power to emancipate slaves was disclaimed; Nor is anything recollected that denoted a view to controul the distribution of those within the Country. The case of the N. Western Territory was probably superseded by the provision agst. the importation of slaves by S. Carolina & Georgia, which had not then passed laws prohibiting it. When the existence of slavery in that territory was precluded, the importation of slaves was rapidly going on, and the only mode of checking it was by narrowing the space open to them. It is not an unfair inference that the expedient would not have been undertaken, if the power afterward given to terminate the importation everywhere, had existed or been even anticipated. It has appeared that the present Congress never followed the example during the twenty years preceding the prohibitory epoch.

The *expediency* of exercising a supposed power in Congress, to prevent a diffusion of the slaves actually in the Country, as far as the local authorities may admit them, resolves itself into the probable effects of such a diffusion on the interests of the slaves and of the Nation.

Will it or will it not better the condition of the slaves, by lessening the number belonging to individual masters, and intermixing both with greater masses of free people? Will partial manumissions be more or less likely to take place, and a general emancipation be accelerated or retarded? Will the moral & physical condition of slaves, in the mean time, be improved or deteriorated? What do experiences and appearances decide as to the comparative rates of generative increase, in their present, and, in a dispersed situation?

Will the aggregate strength security tranquillity and harmony of the whole nation be advanced or impaired by lessening the proportion of slaves to the free people in particular sections of it?

How far an occlusion of the space now vacant, agst. the introduction of slaves may be essential to prevent compleatly a smuggled importation of them from abroad, ought to influence the question of expediency, must be decided by a reasonable estimate of the degree in which the importation would take place in spight of the spirit of the times, the increasing co-operation of foreign powers agst the slave trade, the increasing rigor of the Acts of Congress and the vigilant enforcement of them by the Executive; and by a fair comparison of this estimate with the considerations opposed to such an occlusion.

Will a multiplication of States holding slaves, multiply advocates of the importation of foreign slaves, so as to endanger the continuance of the prohibitory Acts of Congress? To such an apprehension seem to be opposed the facts, that the States holding fewest slaves are those which most readily abolished slavery altogether; that of the 13 primitive States, Eleven had prohibited the importation before the power was given to Congs., that all of them, with the newly added

States, unanimously concurred in exerting that power; that most of the present slaveholding States cannot be tempted by motives of interest to favor the reopening of the ports to foreign slaves; and that these, with the States which have even abolished slavery within themselves, could never be outnumbered in the National Councils by new States wishing for slaves, and not satisfied with the supply attainable within the U. S.

On the whole, the Missouri question, as a constitutional one, amounts to the question whether the condition proposed to be annexed to the admission of Missouri would or would not be void in itself, or become void the moment the territory should enter as a State within the pale of the Constitution. And as a question of expediency & humanity, it depends essentially on the probable influence of such restrictions on the quantity & duration of slavery, and on the general condition of slaves in the U. S.

The question raised with regard to the tenor of the stipulation in the Louisiana Treaty, on the subject of its admission, is one which I have not examined, and on which I could probably throw no light if I had.

Under one aspect of the general subject, I cannot avoid saying, that apart from its merits under others, the tendency of what has passed and is passing, fills me with no slight anxiety. Parties under some denominations or other must always be expected in a Govt. as free as ours. When the individuals belonging to them are intermingled in every part of the whole Country, they strengthen the Union of the Whole, while they divide every part. Should a State of parties arise, founded on geographical boundaries and other Physical & permanent distinctions which happen to coincide with them, what is to controul those great repulsive Masses from awful shocks agst. each other?

The delay in answering your letter made me fear you might doubt my readiness to comply with its requests. I now fear you will think I have done more than these justified. I have been the less reserved because you are so ready to conform to my inclination formerly expressed, not to be drawn from my sequestered position into public view.

Since I thanked you for the copy of your late volume I have

had the pleasure of going thro' it; and I should have been much disappointed, if it had been recd. by the public with less favor than is everywhere manifested. According to all accounts from the Continent of Europe, the American character has suffered much there by libels conveyed by British Prints, or circulated by itinerant Calumniators. It is to be hoped the truths in your book may find their way thither. Good translations of the Preface alone could not but open many eyes which have been blinded by prejudices against this Country.

Detached Memoranda

Doctor Franklin

I did not become acquainted with Dr. Franklin till after his return from France and election to the Chief Magistracy of Pennsylvania. During the Session of the Grand Convention, of which he was a member and as long after as he lived, I had opportunities of enjoying much of his conversation, which was always a feast to me. I never passed half an hour in his company without hearing some observation or anicdote worth remembering.

Among those which I have often repeated, and can therefore be sure that my memory accurately retains, are the following.

Previous to the Convention, and whilst the States were seeking by their respective regulations, to enlarge as much as possible their share of the general commerce, the Dr. alluding to their jealousies and competitions remarked that it would be best for all of them to let the trade be free, in which case it would level itself, and leave to each its proper share. These contests he said, put him in mind of what had once passed between a little boy & little girl eating milk & bread out of the same bowl, "Brother," cried the little girl, "eat on your side, you get more than your share."

In the Convention, the difference of opinions was often very great, and it occasionally happened that the votes of the States were equally divided, and the questions undecided. On a particular day, when several subjects of great importance were successively discussed, and great diversity of opinions expressed, it happened that on each of them this was the case; so that nothing was done through the whole day and appearances were not a little discouraging, as to a successful issue to the undertaking. After the adjournment, the Docr. observed to several of us who were near him in allusion to the poor sample wch had been given, of human reason that there was on board a ship in which he once crossed the Atlantic, a man who had from his birth been without the sense of smelling. On sitting down to dinner one day one of the men, cut off a piece of beef, and putting it to his nose cried out, this beef stinks. The one next to him, cutting and smelling a piece, said not at all, it is as sweet as any meat I ever smelt. A third passing a piece across his nose several times; stinks, says he, no, I believe not: yes, I believe it does, repeating the opposite opinions as often as he made the trial. The same doubts and contrarieties went round as the company, one after the other, expressed their opinions. Now, gentlemen, exclaimed the man, without the sense of smelling, I am satisfied of what I have long suspected, that what you call smelling has no existence, and that it is nothing but mere fancy & prejudice.

For the anicdote at the close of the Convention relating to the rising sun painted on the wall behind the Presidts chair see note att the end of the Debates.

In a conversation with him one day whilst he was confined to his bed, the subject of religion with its various dotrines & modes happening to turn up, the Dr. remarked that he should be glad to see an experiment made of a religion that admitted of no pardon for trangressions; the hope of impunity being the great encouragement to them. In illustration of this tendency, he said that when he was a young man he was much subject to fits of indigestion brought on by indulgence at the table. On complaining of it to a friend, he recommended as a remedy a few drops of oil of wormwood, whenever that happened; and that he should carry a little viol of it about him. On trial he said he found the remedy to answer, and then said he, having my absolution in my pocket, I went on sinning more freely than ever.

On entering his chamber in his extreme age when he had

been much exhausted by pain and was particularly sensible of his weakness, Mr. M. said he, these machines of ours however admirably formed will not last always. Mine I find is just worn out. It must have been an uncommonly good one I observed to last so long, especially under the painful malady which had co-operated with age in preying on it; adding that I could not but hope that he was yet to remain some time with us, and that the cause of his suffering might wear out faster than his Constitution. The only alleviation he said to his pain was opium, and that he found as yet to be a pretty sure one. I told him I took for granted he used it as sparingly as possible as frequent doses must otherwise impair his constitutional strength. He was well aware he said that every Dose he took had that effect; but he had no other remedy; and thought the best terms he cd make with his complaint was to give up a part of his remaining life, for the greater ease of the rest.

The following anecdotes are from the report of others.

Among the measures of the first Revolutionary Congress, it was proposed that a Committee should be appointed to provide a Medical Chest for the army. The Docr voted agst it. Much surprize being manifested by some members, the Docr in his justification, related an anecdote of the Celebrated Dr. Fothergill, who being desired by a philosophical friend to say candidly whether he thought Physicians of real service to mankind, replied by observing that he must first know whether his friend included old women among Physicians; If he did he thought they were of great service.

Whilst the plan of the original "Articles of Confederation" were depending, great difficulty was found in agreeing on the powers proper to be granted by the States to the general Congress, much jealousy being entertained by the former lest the latter being possessed of too many powers, should by degrees swallow up those of the States. The Docr was more apprehensive of encroachments by the States, and in support of his opinion related what had occurred when the Union in 1706 between England & Scotland was on foot. The Scotch orators & patriots opposed the measure as pregnant with ruin to their Country. In a Sermon one of their Preachers vehemently declaimed agst it. Not only would the dignity the independence & commerce of Scotland be lost. Her religious as well as Civil interests would be sacrificed in favor of England. In a word the whale would swallow Jonas. But how said the Docr has it turned out, Why that Jonas had in fact swallowed the whale (Bute & other Scotsmen having then the sway in the Br. Cabinet)

> case of the story concerning Abraham and the
> angels against persecution—Dialogue with
> —see F's (Franklin's) Gazette See the sundry
> accts of it in   & his improvemt by adding to
> the alleged original in the appeal to Abraham—
> the words "who art thyself a sinner."

General Washington

(See the papers referred to in this, annexed to the letters to Genl Washington.)

See correspondence with him and memoranda of conversations.

The strength of his character lay in his integrity, his love of justice, his fortitude, the soundness of his judgment, and his remarkable prudence to which he joined an elevated sense of patriotic duty, and a reliance on the enlightened & impartial world as the tribunal by which a lasting sentence on his career would be pronounced. Nor was he without the advantage of a Stature & figure, which however insignificant when separated from greatness of character do not fail when combined with it to aid the attraction. But what particularly distinguished him, was a modest dignity which at once commanded the highest respect, and inspired the purest attachment. Although not idolizing public opinion, no man could be more attentive to the means of ascertaining it. In comparing the candidates for office, he was particularly inquisitive as to their standing with the public and the opinion entertained of them by men of public weight. On important questions to be decided by him, he spared no pains to gain information from all quarters; freely asking from all whom he held in esteem, and who were intimate with him, a free communication of their sentiments, receiving with great attention the different arguments and opinions offered to him, and making up his own judgment with all the leisure that was permitted. If any erroneous changes took place in his views of persons and public affairs near the close of his life as has been insinuated, they may probably be accounted for by circumstances which threw him into an exclusive communication with men of one party, who took advantage of his retired situation to make impressions unfavorable to their opponents.

> Note the circumstances relating to his first inaugural address to Congress.
> Explain what passed in relation to the title & place proper in answering him.

When the navigation bill (at the 1st Congress under the new Constitution) in which the proposed discrimination between foreign nations & against G. Britain had been defeated by the Senate, he (Gen W) was so much disappointed, that he told Mr Dalton, one of the Senators from Massachussetts, that he would not have signed the Bill, but for the expectation given him that the Senate would provide for the object in some other mode deemed more eligible.

The constitutionality of the National Bank, was a question on which his mind was greatly perplexed. His belief in the utility of the establishment & his disposition to favor a liberal construction of the national powers, formed a bias on one side. On the other, he had witnessed what passed in the Convention which framed the Constitution, and he knew the tenor of the reasonings & explanations under which it had been ratified by the State Conventions. His perplexity was increased by the opposite arguments and opinions of his official advisers Mr Jefferson & Mr Hamilton. He held several free conversations with me on the Subject, in which he listened favorably as I thought to my views of it, but certainly without committing himself in any manner whatever. Not long before the expiration of the ten days allowed for his decision, he desired me to reduce into form, the objections to the Bill, that he might be prepared, in case he should return it without his signature. This I did in a paper of which the following is a copy. (which see & here insert)

From this circumstance, with the manner in which the paper had been requested & received, I had inferred that he

would not sign the Bill: but it was an inference nowise implying that he had precluded himself from consistently signing it.

As it was, he delayed to the last moment, the message communicating his signature. The delay had begotten strong suspicions in the zealous friends of the Bill, that it would be
rejected. One of its ablest Champions, under this impression,
told me he had been making an exact computation of the
time elapsed, and that the Bill would be a law, in spite of its
return with objections, in consequence of the failure to make
the return within the limited term of ten days. I did not
doubt that if such had been the case advantage would have
been taken of it, and that the disappointed party would have
commenced an open opposition to the President; so great was
their confidence in the wealth and strength they possessed,
and such the devotion of the successful speculators in the
funds, and of the anti-republican partizans, to the plans &
principles of the Secretary of the Treasury. The conversation
had scarcely ended, when the message arrived with notice that
the Bill had been approved and signed.

In explaining the grounds on which he refused to comply
with the call of the House of Reps for the papers relating to
Mr Jay's negociations & Treaty with G. B. in 1795, he was led
into a reference to a vote in the Grand Convention negativing a proposition to allow the H. of Reps. a participation in
concluding Treaties as an argument agst their right to the papers called for. The reference and inference were misjudged.
1.—The question on wch the vote in the Convention was
taken, was not the same with that on wch the call for papers
turned; since the House tho' not a party to a Treaty might, as
in the case of the British Parlt have a legislative right to deliberate on the provisions depending on them for its execution. 2. The vote in the Convention, as nakedly stated, did
not necessarily imply a negative on the powers of the House,
as it might have proceeded from collateral motives distinct
from the merits of the question, such as its being out of time
or place, or a belief that without an affirmative vote, an
agency of the House of Reps in the case of Treaties, sufficiently resulted from the text of the Constitutional plan then
before the Convention. 3. If the meaning of the Constitution

was to be looked for elsewhere than in the instrument, it was not in the General Convention, but the State Conventions. The former proposed it only; it was from the latter that it derived its validity and authority. The former were the Committee that prepared the Bill, the latter the authoritative Bodies which made it a law, or rather through which the Nation made it its own Act. It is the sense of the nation therefore not the sense of the General Convention, that is to be consulted; and that sense, if not taken from the act itself, is to be taken from the proceedings of the State Conventions & other public indications as the true keys to the sense of the Nation. 4. But what rendered the argument from the case cited particularly unfortunate was the circumstance, that the Bank-Bill had been signed, notwithstanding the vote in the General Convention negativing expressly a proposition to give to Congress a power to establish a Bank. On the other hand the call of the H. of Reps for papers which might be of a confidential nature, was in terms too peremptory and unqualified; and the President might therefore justifiably decline, on his responsibility to the Nation, to comply with it. Having myself at the time, taken this view of the subject I proposed that the call should be so varied, as to limit it to such papers as in the judgment of the President might with propriety be communicated. The proposition was very disagreeable to the warmest advocates for the Call, and brought on me some displeasure from a few with whom I was most intimate. The proposition being rejected, I voted for the call, in its unqualified terms, taking for granted that the President would exercise his responsible discretion on the subject. The practice of the House has since expressly limited the calls for paper Executive Communications to such as in the judgment of the President the public interest might not forbid.

In the original plan of the Bank contained in the Bill of 179   was a clause making the Bank co-durable with the public debt. It was not without some difficulty limited to the period of years fixed in the law. A more impolitic mode of regulating its duration than the original one could not have been devised. Instead of motives with the B. to aid the Govt in making the most of its resources, it gave the B. a direct &

powerful interest in prolonging the Pub. debt, by embarrassing them, & even promoting wars & wasteful & expensive establishments military as well as civil.

See sheet headed "Bank."

On the 28th of Feby 1793. Mr Giles moved in the House of Reps certain Resolutions charging the Secy of the Treasury with drawing a sum of money borrowed in Europe, into the U. S. and applying it, contrary to the legal appropriation, and also contrary to the instruction of the President (accompanying his commission to the Secy as the agent for borrowing.) It was suspected that the object of the Secy had been to divert money from an intended payment to France, which he disliked, and to aid the Bank to which he was partial.

As the instruction of the President to the Secy which was before the House was violated by the act of the latter, his friends contended that he might, as was to be presumed, have recd subsequent instructions authorizing it, which had not been communicated, and that in any view, if there had been a violation of the appropriating law the President was the responsible functionary, and that the charge was an imputation on him rather than on the Secretary.

On the other side it was insisted that if subsequent & different instructions had been given by the Presidt the Secy would not have failed to make them known in his own defence, which had not been done.

The perfect confidence felt in the integrity of the President, and the delicacy & respect for his feelings, had their natural effect on the occasion. Still it was considered as not a little remarkable that if he had given a sanction to the conduct of the Secy he should not have protected him agst the Charge, by authorizing the Secy to disclose the fact: and if the Secy had proceeded contrary to his instructions as well as to the law, that he shd have exposed himself to the inferences from his reserve under such circumstances.

The mystery is explained by the following extract from letters from Ed: Randolph at that time Attorney Genl of the U. S.

July 9. 1811. E. R. to J. Madison

"Without one feeling left of the character of a partizan, but still living to friendship, a man whose hand is known to Mr Madison asks him whether he recollects or ever heard that after Col: Hamilton had been severely pressed for a supposed misappropriation of the money devoted by law to special purposes, he Col: H produced a letter, authorizing it, signed by President Washington, while on his tour to South Carolina; that the President at first denied its existence in positive & vehement terms, *not having preserved a copy of it*; but that it was afterwards acknowledged by him, and registered in the Treasury Department, ut valeret quantum valere potuit"

From the same to the same. Aug. 8, 1811
"The following clue (to) a second search at the Treasury may perhaps succeed. Giles' Resolutions had been defeated before Col: H. suggested thro' one of his indirect conduits to the ear of the President, that during his tour in the south, he had sanctioned by two letters, the measure which was so severely criminated. He (the P.) mentioned the circumstances to me, with surprize & passion declaring in the most excluding terms, that he never did write or cause to be written letters to that purport. Some days afterwards Col: H put them into the President's hands, and by him they were communicated to me with an instruction to write to Col: H. avowing them. This I did, and it would seem impossible that upon a subject on which his sensibility was so much kindled, that a document of justification should have been laid aside as a private paper. These facts are most distinctly recollected."

The communication in these letters is to be ascribed to the friendly feeling in the writer to J. M. who had taken an active part in the discussions produced by Mr Giles' Resolutions. The second letter was written in consequence of an intimation, that from an enquiry at the Treasury Department it did not appear that any such paper as that described had been deposited there.
The inference from the whole seems to be that the Secretary of the Treasury, must have prepared as was not unusual with Heads of Depts in the ordinary course of business, & forwarded to the P. letters to be signed by him, that the Presidt in the hurry of a journey, & regarding them as fiscal

operations merely requiring his formal sanction, signed & returned them without particularly attending to or charging his memory with them & that the Secy of the Treasury aware that this might be the case, forbore to avail himself of the document he possessed, or to involve the President in the responsibility he was willing to take on himself.

It is proper to remark that Mr Randolph's statement came from a dismissed officer, and that it was subsequent to a paralytic stroke which ended in greatly enfeebling his mind. But there is reason to confide in his declaration that he retained no feeling of a partizan; and the tenor of his letters indicates no incompetency to the task assumed in them. The explanatory facts stated, carry indeed the greatest probability on the face of them. If the acknowledgt by President Washington referred to, shd not have escaped the search made in the Treasury Dept it must be among the papers of Col: Hamilton unless indeed involved in some destruction of that Department: for it can not be presumed that the preservation of such a paper could have been wholly neglected.

Bank

(These essays belong with the printed ones in
Freneau to the class of political economy.)

Banks, in their accommodations to prudent borrowers & in furnishing a currency more easy to be counted and transmitted than the metals have acquired so many friends, that if it were desirable to abolish them entirely & everywhere, the attempt would be hopeless. But the more impossible or unadvisable it may be to abolish them, the more necessary it is to guard agst the evils resulting from their number, and agst the abuses incident to the ordinary constitution of them. These abuses may be diminished by a variety of particular regulations. Might not a more radical remedy be found in a different Construction and organization of the administrative Body?

The greatest, certainly the most offensive abuses of Banks proceed from the opportunities and interests of the Directors. They can obtain discounts for themselves, even it is said to *privileged amounts*. They, can suspend limit and resume the discounts to others as they please. Their stations inform them of the wants and business of all who deal with and depend on the Bank under their management. With these advantages alone, they may by first lending money to themselves, and then immediately shutting the Bank to others, with a knowledge of the effect on others carry on speculations as gainful as reproachful. Whether the following case happened or not, it will illustrate this source of abuse. A combination of a few influencial Bank Directors, who were shippers of flour, after drawing under the rules of the B. the amount permitted to Directors, procured a curtailment of discounts, which compelled the Holders of flour, as was foreseen, to sell at reduced prices. As soon as the Mercantile Directors had loaded their ships, and appearances would allow, the ordinary course of discounts was restored. A candid or an incautious Bank Director many years ago was heard to say, that altho' there was no salary annexed to the place, it was *fairly* worth five thousand dollars a year.

As a remedial plan of a Bank the Directors might be converted into impartial Judges, in the discharge of their trust, by receiving a liberal salary paid out of the Bank dividends, might be disabled from holding Bank Stock & from borrowing directly or indirectly from the Institution, and might take a customary oath of office. Under these regulations, they might without bias, at least without the temptations now before them, exercise the functions required from them & fulfill the ends of the Institution. If it be objected that by holding an interest in the Institution they will be more solicitous to increase its profits, the answer is that at present they may promote their particular interest, in ways impairing those profits. If objected that the men engaged in the business connecting people with the Banks make the best directors, because best acquainted with the affairs of the Customers of the Bank; the answer is that the Directors soon acquire in their places, more of that sort of information than they carry into them. And it is a general answer to objections, that the question is whether all the advantages claimed for the present constitution of Boards of Directors, are not overbalanced by its disadvantages, and by the advantages of a Board such as that suggested.

Force of precedents in case of the Bank—& in
expounding the Constn. equal division of Senate,
when the Bill negatived by V. P. not occasioned by
unconstitutionality but inexpediency of the Bill.
reasoning of Supreme Ct—founded on erroneous
views &—1. as to the ratification of Const: by people if meant people collectively & not by States.
2. imputing concurrence of those formerly opposed to change of opinion, instead of precedents
superseding opinion. 3. endeavoring to retain right
of Court to pronounce on the consty of law after
making Legisl omnipotent as to the expediency of
means. 4. expounding power of Congs—as if no
other Sovereignty existed in the States supplemental to the enumerated powers of Congs—
5. making the Judy-exclusive expositor of the
Constitutionality of laws: the co-ordinate authorities Legisl—& Execut—being equally expositors
within the scope of their functions.

Monopolies. Perpetuities. Corporations. Ecclesiastical Endowments.

Monoplies tho' in certain cases useful ought to be granted
with caution, and guarded with strictness agst abuse. The
Constitution of the U. S. has limited them to two cases, the
authors of Books, and of useful inventions, in both which
they are considered as a compensation for a benefit actually
gained to the community as a purchase of property which the
owner might otherwise withold from public use. There can be
no just objection to a temporary monopoly in these cases: but
it ought to be temporary, because under that limitation a sufficient recompence and encouragement may be given. The
limitation is particularly proper in the case of inventions, because they grow so much out of preceding ones that there is
the less merit in the authors: and because for the same reason,
the discovery might be expected in a short time from other
hands.

Monopolies have been granted in other Countries, and by
some of the States in this, on another principle, that of sup-

porting some useful undertaking untill experience and success should render the monopoly unnecessary, & lead to a salutary competition. This was the policy of the monopoly granted in Virga to Col: Jno Hoomes to establish a passenger-stage from   to   . But grants of this sort can be justified in very peculiar cases only, if at all; the danger being very great that the good resulting from the operation of the monopoly, will be overbalanced by the evil effect of the precedent; and it being not impossible that the monopoly itself, in its original operation, may produce more evil than good.

In all cases of monopoly, not excepting those specified in favor of authors & inventors, it would be well to reserve to the State, a right to terminate the monopoly by paying a specified and reasonable sum. This would guard against the public discontents resulting from the exorbitant gains of individuals, and from the inconvenient restrictions combined with them. This view of the subject suggested, the clause in the bill relating to J. Rumsey in the Virga Legislature in the year 178 providing that the State might cancel his privilege by paying him ten thousand dollars. and to secure him agst the possibility of a payment in depreciated medium, then a prevalent apprehension, it was proposed that the sum should be paid in metal & that of a specified weight & fineness.

One objection to a Bank is that it involves a qualified monopoly; and the objection certainly has weight in proportion to the degree & duration of the monopoly.

Perpetual monopolies of every sort, are forbidden not only by the genius of free Govts, but by the imperfection of human foresight. (Among such monopolies, cannot be included the grants in perpetuity of public lands to individuals, the grants being made according to rules of impartiality, for a valuable consideration; and all lands being held equally by that tenure from the public, the vital principle of monopoly is lost. The benefit is not confined to one or a few, but is enjoyed by the whole or a majority of the Community. The evil of an excessive & dangerous cumulation of landed property in the hands of individuals is best precluded by the prohibition of entails, by the suppression of the right of primogeniture, and by the liability of landed property to the payment of debts. In Countries where there is a rapid increase of

population as the U. S. these provisions are evidently sufficient; and in all countries wd probably be found so) Where
charters of incorporation, even the common ones to towns
for the sake of local police, contain clauses implying contracts,
and irrevocably, they are liable to objections of equal force.
The ordinary limitation on incorporated Societies is a proviso
that their laws shall not violate the laws of the land. But how
easily may it happen that redress for such violations may not
be pursued into effect? How much injury may accrue during
the pursuit of redress. And above all how much local injustice
and oppression may be committed by laws & regulations, not
in strict construction violating any law of the land. Within the
local limits, parties generally exist, founded on different sorts
of property, sometimes on divisions by streets or little
streams; frequently on political and religious differences. Attachments to rival individuals, are not seldom a source of the
same divisions. In all these cases the party animosities are the
more violent as the compass of the Society may more easily
admit of the contagion & collision of the passions; and according to that violence is the danger of oppression by one
party on the other; by the majority on the minority. The ways
in which this can be effected, even beyond the cognizance of
the paramount law of the land have scarce any other limits
than the ingenuity and interest of those who possess the
power. Is a tax to be collected? What inequality may attend
the rule or modes of assessment? Is a public building to be
erected, what is to guard agst partiality or favoritism in fixing
its site? Is there a single regulation of police which will not
differently affect the component parts of the society, and afford an opportunity to the majority to sacrifice to their prejudices or their conveniency the conveniency or the interests of
the minor party.

When the town incorporated is not only a Market town for
the neighbourhood, but a port for an external commerce the
effect of its police has a wider range, and its corporate powers
the greater need of some other controul than the vague & inefficient one, of the law of the land.

The best illustration of these remarks is to be found in the
recorded proceedings of the various local Corporations. What
is generally known sufficiently justifies them. Without even a

recurrence to facts a common knowledge of human nature, would suggest the probability of the abuses on which they are founded.

The most effectual & perhaps the least exceptionable provision agst them, seems to be that of superadding to the general restraint of the law of the land, a previous veto in some impartial & convenient quarter on each particular by law. The Executive authority of the State or that authority in consultation with a judge or judges of the highest grade might perhaps be relied on for the controul on these local legislatures, most likely to preserve a just, a uniform, and an impartial exercise of their subordinate powers.

The danger of silent accumulations & encroachments by Ecclesiastical Bodies have not sufficiently engaged attention in the U. S. They have the noble merit of first unshackling the conscience from persecuting laws, and of establishing among religious Sects a legal equality. If some of the States have not embraced this just and this truly Xn principle in its proper latitude, all of them present examples by which the most enlightened States of the old world may be instructed; and there is one State at least, Virginia, where religious liberty is placed on its true foundation and is defined in its full latitude. The general principle is contained in her declaration of rights, prefixed to her Constitution: but it is unfolded and defined, in its precise extent, in the act of the Legislature, usually named the Religious Bill, which passed into a law in the year 1786. Here the separation between the authority of human laws, and the natural rights of Man excepted from the grant on which all political authority is founded, is traced as distinctly as words can admit, and the limits to this authority established with as much solemnity as the forms of legislation can express. The law has the further advantage of having been the result of a formal appeal to the sense of the Community and a deliberate sanction of a vast majority, comprizing every sect of Christians in the State. This act is a true standard of Religious liberty: its principle the great barrier agst usurpations on the rights of conscience. As long as it is respected & no longer, these will be safe. Every provision for them short of this principle, will be found to leave crevices at least thro' which bigotry may introduce persecution; a monster, that feeding & thriving on its own venom, gradually swells to a size and strength over-whelming all laws divine & human.

Ye States of America, which retain in your Constitutions or Codes, any aberration from the sacred principle of religious liberty, by giving to Caesar what belongs to God, or joining together what God has put asunder, hasten to revise & purify your systems, and make the example of your Country as pure & compleat, in what relates to the freedom of the mind and its allegiance to its maker, as in what belongs to the legitimate objects of political & civil institutions.

Strongly guarded as is the separation between Religion & Govt in the Constitution of the United States the danger of encroachment by Ecclesiastical Bodies, may be illustrated by precedents already furnished in their short history. (See the cases in which negatives were put by J. M. on two bills passd by Congs and his signature withheld from another. See also attempt in Kentucky for example, where it was proposed to exempt Houses of Worship from taxes.

The most notable attempt was that in Virga to establish a Genl assessment for the support of all Xn sects. This was pro-posed in the year   by P. H. and supported by all his elo-quence, aided by the remaining prejudices of the Sect which before the Revolution had been established by law. The progress of the measure was arrested by urging that the re-spect due to the people required in so extraordinary a case an appeal to their deliberate will. The bill was accordingly printed & published with that view. At the instance of Col: George Nicholas, Col: George Mason & others, the memor-ial & remonstrance agst it was drawn up, (which see) and printed Copies of it circulated thro' the State, to be signed by the people at large. It met with the approbation of the Baptists, the Presbyterians, the Quakers, and the few Roman Catholics, universally; of the Methodists in part; and even of not a few of the Sect formerly established by law. When the Legislature assembled, the number of Copies & signatures prescribed displayed such an overwhelming opposition of the people, that the proposed plan of a genl assessmt was crushed under it; and advantage taken of the crisis to carry thro' the Legisl: the Bill above referred to, establishing religious liberty. In the course of the opposition to the bill in the House of

Delegates, which was warm & strenuous from some of the
minority, an experiment was made on the reverence entertained for the name & sanctity of the Saviour, by proposing
to insert the words "Jesus Christ" after the words "our lord"
in the preamble, the object of which, would have been, to imply a restriction of the liberty defined in the Bill, to those pro-
fessing his religion only. The amendment was discussed, and
rejected by a vote of   agst (See letter of J. M. to Mr
Jefferson dated   ) The opponents of the amendment
having turned the feeling as well as judgment of the House
agst it, by successfully contending that the better proof of reverence for that holy name wd be not to profane it by making
it a topic of legisl. discussion, & particularly by making his religion the means of abridging the natural and equal rights of
all men, in defiance of his own declaration that his Kingdom
was not of this world. This view of the subject was much enforced by the circumstance that it was espoused by some
members who were particularly distinguished by their reputed
piety and Christian zeal.

But besides the danger of a direct mixture of Religion &
civil Government, there is an evil which ought to be guarded
agst in the indefinite accumulation of property from the capacity of holding it in perpetuity by ecclesiastical corporations. The power of all corporations, ought to be limited in
this respect. The growing wealth acquired by them never fails
to be a source of abuses. A warning on this subject is emphatically given in the example of the various Charitable establishments in G. B. the management of which has been
lately scrutinized. The excessive wealth of ecclesiastical Corporations and the misuse of it in many Countries of Europe
has long been a topic of complaint. In some of them the
Church has amassed half perhaps the property of the nation.
When the reformation took place, an event promoted if not
caused, by that disordered state of things, how enormous
were the treasures of religious societies, and how gross the
corruptions engendered by them; so enormous & so gross as
to produce in the Cabinets & Councils of the Protestant
states a disregard, of all the pleas of the interested party drawn
from the sanctions of the law, and the sacredness of property
held in religious trust. The history of England during the

period of the reformation offers a sufficient illustration for the present purpose.

Are the U. S. duly awake to the tendency of the precedents they are establishing, in the multiplied incorporations of Religious Congregations with the faculty of acquiring & holding property real as well as personal? Do not many of these acts give this faculty, without limit either as to time or as to amount? And must not bodies, perpetual in their existence, and which may be always gaining without ever losing, speedily gain more than is useful, and in time more than is safe? Are there not already examples in the U. S. of ecclesiastical wealth equally beyond its object and the foresight of those who laid the foundation of it? In the U. S. there is a double motive for fixing limits in this case, because wealth may increase not only from additional gifts, but from exorbitant advances in the value of the primitive one. In grants of vacant lands, and of lands in the vicinity of growing towns & Cities the increase of value is often such as if foreseen, would essentially controul the liberality confirming them. The people of the U. S. owe their Independence & their liberty, to the wisdom of descrying in the minute tax of 3 pence on tea, the magnitude of the evil comprized in the precedent. Let them exert the same wisdom, in watching agst every evil lurking under plausible disguises, and growing up from small beginnings. Obsta principiis.

see the Treatise of Father Paul on beneficiary matters.

Is the appointment of Chaplains to the two Houses of Congress consistent with the Constitution, and with the pure principle of religious freedom?

In strictness the answer on both points must be in the negative. The Constitution of the U. S. forbids everything like an establishment of a national religion. The law appointing Chaplains establishes a religious worship for the national representatives, to be performed by Ministers of religion, elected by a majority of them; and these are to be paid out of the national taxes. Does not this involve the principle of a national establishment, applicable to a provision for a religious worship for the Constituent as well as of the representative Body, approved by the majority, and conducted by Ministers of religion paid by the entire nation.

The establishment of the chaplainship to Congs is a palpable violation of equal rights, as well as of Constitutional principles: The tenets of the chaplains elected shut the door of worship agst the members whose creeds & consciences forbid a participation in that of the majority. To say nothing of other sects, this is the case with that of Roman Catholics & Quakers who have always had members in one or both of the Legislative branches. Could a Catholic clergyman ever hope to be appointed a Chaplain? To say that his religious principles are obnoxious or that his sect is small, is to lift the evil at once and exhibit in its naked deformity the doctrine that religious truth is to be tested by numbers, or that the major sects have a right to govern the minor.

If Religion consist in voluntary acts of individuals, singly, or voluntarily associated, and it be proper that public functionaries, as well as their Constituents shd discharge their religious duties, let them like their Constituents, do so at their own expence. How small a contribution from each member of Congs wd suffice for the purpose? How just wd it be in its principle? How noble in its exemplary sacrifice to the genius of the Constitution; and the divine right of conscience? Why should the expence of a religious worship be allowed for the Legislature, be paid by the public, more than that for the Ex. or Judiciary branch of the Govt

Were the establishment to be tried by its fruits, are not the daily devotions conducted by these legal Ecclesiastics, already degenerating into a scanty attendance, and a tiresome formality?

Rather than let this step beyond the landmarks of power have the effect of a legitimate precedent, it will be better to apply to it the legal aphorism de minimis non curat lex: or to class it cum "maculis quas aut incuria fudit, aut humana parum cavit natura."

Better also to disarm in the same way, the precedent of Chaplainships for the army and navy, than erect them into a political authority in matters of religion. The object of this establishment is seducing; the motive to it is laudable. But is it not safer to adhere to a right principle, and trust to its

consequences, than confide in the reasoning however specious in favor of a wrong one. Look thro' the armies & navies
of the world, and say whether in the appointment of their
ministers of religion, the spiritual interest of the flocks or the
temporal interest of the Shepherds, be most in view: whether
here, as elsewhere the political care of religion is not a nominal more than a real aid. If the spirit of armies be devout, the
spirit out of the armies will never be less so; and a failure of
religious instruction & exhortation from a voluntary source
within or without, will rarely happen: and if such be not the
spirit of armies, the official services of their Teachers are not
likely to produce it. It is more likely to flow from the labours
of a spontaneous zeal. The armies of the Puritans had their
appointed Chaplains; but without these there would have
been no lack of public devotion in that devout age.

The case of navies with insulated crews may be less within
the scope of these reflections. But it is not entirely so. The
chance of a devout officer, might be of as much worth to religion, as the service of an ordinary chaplain. But we are always to keep in mind that it is safer to trust the consequences
of a right principle, than reasonings in support of a bad one.

Religious proclamations by the Executive recommending
thanksgivings & fasts are shoots from the same root with the
legislative acts reviewed.

Altho' recommendations only, they imply a religious
agency, making no part of the trust delegated to political
rulers.

The objections to them are 1. that Govts ought not to interpose in relation to those subject to their authority but in
cases where they can do it with effect. An *advisory* Govt is a
contradiction in terms. 2. The members of a Govt as such can
in no sense, be regarded as possessing an advisory trust from
their Constituents in their religious capacities. They cannot
form an ecclesiastical Assembly, Convocation, Council, or
Synod, and as such issue decrees or injunctions addressed to
the faith or the Consciences of the people. In their individual
capacities, as distinct from their official station, they might
unite in recommendations of any sort whatever, in the same
manner as any other individuals might do. But then their
recommendations ought to express the true character from

which they emanate. 3. They seem to imply and certainly nourish the erronious idea of a *national* religion. The idea just as it related to the Jewish nation under a theocracy, having been improperly adopted by so many nations which have embraced Xnity, is too apt to lurk in the bosoms even of Americans, who in general are aware of the distinction between religious & political societies. The idea also of a union of all to form one nation under one Govt in acts of devotion to the God of all is an imposing idea. But reason and the principles of the Xn religion require that all the individuals composing a nation even of the same precise creed & wished to unite in a universal act of religion at the same time, the union ought to be effected thro' the intervention of their religious not of their political representatives. In a nation composed of various sects, some alienated widely from others, and where no agreement could take place thro' the former, the interposition of the latter is doubly wrong: 4. The tendency of the practice, to narrow the recommendation to the standard of the predominant sect. The 1st proclamation of Genl Washington dated Jany 1. 1795 (see if this was the 1st) recommending a day of thanksgiving, embraced all who believed in a supreme ruler of the Universe. That of Mr Adams called for a *Xn* worship. Many private letters reproached the Proclamations issued by J. M. for using general terms, used in that of Presidt W—n; and some of them for not inserting particulars according with the faith of certain Xn sects. The practice if not strictly guarded naturally terminates in a conformity to the creed of the majority and a single sect, if amounting to a majority. 5. The last & not the least objection is the liability of the practice to a subserviency to political views; to the scandal of religion, as well as the increase of party animosities. Candid or incautious politicians will not always disown such views. In truth it is difficult to frame such a religious Proclamation generally suggested by a political State of things, without referring to them in terms having some bearing on party questions. The Proclamation of Pres: W. which was issued just after the suppression of the Insurrection in Penna and at a time when the public mind was divided on several topics, was so construed by many. Of this the Secretary of State himself, E. Randolph seems to have had an anticipation.

The original draught of that Instrument filed in the Dept. of State (see copies of these papers on the files of J. M.) in the hand writing of Mr Hamilton the Secretary of the Treasury. It appears that several slight alterations only had been made at the suggestion of the Secretary of State; and in a marginal note in his hand, it is remarked that "In short this proclamation ought to savour as much as possible of religion, & not too much of having a political object." In a subjoined note in the hand of Mr. Hamilton, this remark is answered by the counter-remark that "A proclamation of a Government which is a national act, naturally embraces objects which are political" so *naturally*, is the idea of policy associated with religion, whatever be the mode or the occasion, when a function of the latter is assumed by those in power.

During the administration of Mr Jefferson no religious proclamation was issued. It being understood that his successor was disinclined to such interpositions of the Executive and by some supposed moreover that they might originate with more propriety with the Legislative Body, a resolution was passed requesting him to issue a proclamation. (see the resolution in the Journals of Congress.

It was thought not proper to refuse a compliance altogether; but a form & language were employed, which were meant to deaden as much as possible any claim of political right to enjoin religious observances by resting these expressly on the voluntary compliance of individuals, and even by limiting the recommendation to such as wished simultaneous as well as voluntary performance of a religious act on the occasion. The following is a copy of the proclamation: (see it in

Popular elections

On the purity of these depend the reputation & success of Representative Govts. In some of the States whilst they were Colonies, the original maners & usage of the people maintained this purity. It was much favored also by the frequency of elections, which were annual; nor were half yearly elections without example. The rule of voting by ballot was another precaution and guard agst the use of undue means by Candidates for the popular suffrage. In a number of the Colonies Candidates were in the practice not only of publicly offering their services, but of soliciting the votes of the people and of giving them treats, particularly of intoxicating drinks. In Virga when the elections for the Colonial Legislature were septennial, & the original Settlers of the prevailing sentiments & religious manners of the parent nation, the modes of canvassing for popular votes in that Country were generally practiced. The people not only tolerated, but expected and even required to be courted and treated. No Candidate who neglected these attentions could be elected. His forbearance wd have been ascribed to a mean parsimony, or to a proud disrespect for the voters.

The spirit of the revolution and adoption of anual Elections seeming to favor a more chaste mode of conducting elections in Virga my way of thinking on the subject determined me to attempt by an example to introduce one. It was found that the old habits were too deeply rooted to be suddenly reformed. Particular circumstances obtained for me success in the first election at which I was a Candidate. At the next I was outvoted by two Candidates, neither of them having superior pretensions and one peculiarly deficient in them; but both of them availing themselves fully of all the means of influence familiar to the people. My reserve was imputed to want of respect for them, if to no other unpopular motive.

Time, the genius of her Govn and the shortness of the term, have considerably diminished the undue means of canvassing; but the practice still prevails too much of treating the people, and the Candidates failing to do so would be charged with or suspected of unworthy motives.—As a remedy—Let one or more of the Candidates, propose in the outset, that all should, instead of spending money on ardent spirits and other treats contribute the estimated amount, as a fund for supporting & educating the poor; and if not agreed to by others let him take that course as an example. So beneficent a substitute, for a corrupting practice wd be espoused by all the most virtuous & respectable voters—& might soon triumph over the remaining prejudices.

The "Federalist"

The papers, so entitled, were written in the latter part of 1787, & the early part of 1788 by Alexander Hamilton, John Jay and James Madison. The original and immediate object of them was to promote the ratification of the new Constitution by the State of N. York where it was powerfully opposed, and where its success was deemed of critical importance. According to the original plan & in the early numbers, the papers went out as from a Citizen of N. Y. It being found however that they were republished in other States and were making a diffusive impression in favor of the Constitution, that limited character was laid aside.

The undertaking was proposed by A. Hamilton to J. M. with a request to join him & Mr. Jay in carrying it into effect. William Duer was also included in the original plan & wrote two or perhaps more papers, which tho' intelligent & sprightly, were not continued; nor did they make a part of the printed Collection.

The papers were first published in the Newspapers of the City. They were written most of them in great haste, and without any special allotment of the different parts of the subject to the several writers, J. M. being at the time a member of the then Congress, and A. H. being also a member, and occupied moreover in his profession at the bar, it was understood that each was to write as their respective situations permitted, preserving as much as possible an order & connection in the papers successively published. This will account for deficiency in that respect, and also for an occasional repetition of the views taken of particular branches of the subject. The haste with which many of the papers were penned, in order to get thro the subject whilst the Constitution was before the public, and to comply with the arrangement by which the printer was to keep his newspaper open for four numbers every week, was such that the performance must have borne a very different aspect without the aid of historical and other notes which had been used in the Convention and without the familiarity with the whole subject produced by the discussions there. It frequently happened that whilst the printer was putting into type the parts of a number, the following parts were under the pen, & to be furnished in time for the press.

In the beginning it was the practice of the writers, of A. H. & J. M. particularly to communicate each to the other, their respective papers before they were sent to the press. This was rendered so inconvenient, by the shortness of the time allowed, that it was dispensed with. Another reason was, that it was found most agreeable to each, not to give a positive sanction to all the doctrines and sentiments of the other; there being a known difference in the general complexion of their political theories.

The particular papers assigned to each of the writers have been differently presented to the public. The statement from a memorandum left by Mr H. with Mr Benson just before his death, is very erroneous, owing doubtless to the hurry in which the memorandum was made out. Besides the considerable number of papers written by J. M. and in the lump classed with those written by himself, he ascribes to himself No 64 written by Mr. Jay; and to Mr. Jay No   written not by him, but by J. M. (see life of Mr Jay by Delaplaine) The paper No 49 also in which Mr Jefferson is painted in such strong colours was not likely to be even approved by Mr H: and the paper No 54, on the subject of the negroes as comprized in the ratio of representation, was most likely to be within the share executed by the Southern member of the Club. There can be little difficulty in admitting this instance of the fallibility of Mr H's memory; on comparing it with a far more extraordinary one furnished in his letter to Mr Pickering written at full leisure, in which, among other things which ought not to have been written, he says that in his plan of a Constitution deposited with J. M. he proposed that the President shd be chosen for *three years* (see Nile's Register   ) when in fact, as the original in his own hand must show, that there as elsewhere he desired a President *"during good behaviour."*

(This original stated by Mr Mason to Mr Eustis (see the letter of E. to J. M.) to be among the papers left by Mr Hamilton: A copy is among the papers of J. M. with whom the document was placed for preservation by Mr H. who regarded it as a permanent evidence of his opinion, on the subject.)

A true distribution of the numbers of the Federalist among the three writers is contained in the Edition of that work by Jacob Gideon. It was furnished to him by me with a perfect knowledge of its accuracy as it relates to myself, and a full confidence in its equal accuracy as it relates to the two others.

In the same volume, edited by J. G. he has published along with Mr H's pamphlet under the name of "Pacificus" a pamphlet in answer to it by me under the name of "Helvidius" whose distinguished character was drawn by the pencil of Tacitus. The Pamphlet "Pacificus" had been improperly included in a former Edition of the "Federalist," of which it could not make a part, being not written as that was, conjointly with others, to recommend the adoption of the Constitution, but in opposition to one at least of the others, and as a comment on the Constitution long after its adoption. I suggested to Mr Gideon the impropriety of what had been done, with a view to a publication of the Federalist without combining with it, what was entirely foreign to it. The Editor having determined to publish both of the pamphlets, rather than omit what had been included in a former Edition, I sent him the copy of Helvidius which he published.

I ought not perhaps to acknowlege my having written this polemic tract, without acknowleging at the same time my consciousness & regret, that it breathes a spirit which was of no advantage either to the subject, or to the Author. If an apology for this, & for other faults can be made it must be furnished by the circumstances, of the pamphlet being written in much haste, during an intense heat of the weather, and under an excitement stimulated by friends, agst a publication breathing not only the intemperance of party, but giving as was believed a perverted view of Presidt Washington's proclamation of neutrality, and calculated to put a dangerous gloss on the Constitution of the U. S.

1819?

To James Monroe

Dear Sir,   Montplr., Feby 10, 1820.

I have duly recd. your favr. of the 5th, followed by a copy of the public documents, for which I give you many thanks. I shd. like to get a copy of the Journals of the Convention. Are they to be purchased & where?

It appears to me as it does to you, that a coupling of Missouri with Maine, in order to force the entrance of the former thro' the door voluntarily opened to the latter is, to say the least, a very doubtful policy. Those who regard the claims of both as similar & equal, and distrust the views of such as wish to disjoin them may be strongly tempted to resort to the expedient; and it wd. perhaps, be too much to say that in no possible case such a resort cd. be justified. But it may at least be said that a very peculiar case only could supersede the general policy of a direct & magnanimous course, appealing to the justice & liberality of others, and trusting to the influence of conciliatory example.

I find the idea is fast spreading that the zeal wth. which the extension, so called, of slavery is opposed, has, with the coalesced *leaders*, an object very different from the welfare of the slaves, or the check to their increase; and that their real object is, as you intimate, to form a new state of parties founded on local instead of political distinctions; thereby dividing the Republicans of the North from those of the South, and making the former instrumental in giving to the opponents of both an ascendancy over the whole. If this be the view of the subject at Washington it furnishes an additional reason for a conciliatory proceeding in relation to Maine.

I have been truly astonished at some of the doctrines and deliberations to which the Missouri question has led; and particularly so at the interpretations put on the terms "migration or importation &c." Judging from my own impressions I shd. deem it impossible that the memory of any one who was a member of the Genl. Convention, could favor an opinion that the terms did not *exclusively* refer to Migration & importation *into the U. S.* Had they been understood in that Body in the sense now put on them, it is easy to conceive the alienation they would have there created in certain States; And no one can decide better than yourself the effect they would have had in the State Conventions, if such a meaning had been avowed by the Advocates of the Constitution. If a suspicion had existed of such a construction, it wd. at least have made a conspicuous figure among the amendments proposed to the Instrument.

I have observed *as yet*, in none of the views taken of the Ordinance of 1787, interdicting slavery N. W. of the Ohio, an allusion to the circumstance, that when it passed, the Congs. had no authority to prohibit the importaton of slaves from abroad; that all the States had, & some were in the full exercise of the right to import them; and, consequently, that there was no mode in which Congs. could check the evil, but the indirect one of narrowing the space open for the reception of slaves. Had a federal authority then existed to prohibit directly & totally the importation from abroad, can it be doubted that it wd. have been exerted? and that a regulation having merely the effect of preventing an interior dispersion of the slaves actually in the U. S. & creating a distinction among the States in the degrees of their sovereignty, would not have been adopted, or perhaps, thought of?

No folly in the Spanish Govt. can now create surprise. I wish you happily thro' the thorny circumstances it throws in your way. Adieu &c.

To Spencer Roane

Dear Sir,   Montpr., May 6, 1821

I recd. more than two weeks ago, your letter of Apl. 17. A visit to a sick friend at a distance, with a series of unavoidable attentions have prevented an earlier acknowledgment of it.

Under any circumstances I should be disposed rather to put such a subject as that to which it relates into your hands than to take it out of them. Apart from this consideration, a variety of demands on my time would restrain me from the task of unravelling the arguments applied by the Supreme Court of the U. S. to their late decision. I am particularly aware moreover that they are made to rest not a little on technical points of law, which are as foreign to my studies as they are familiar to yours.

It is to be regretted that the Court is so much in the practice of mingling with their judgments pronounced, comments & reasonings of a scope beyond them; and that there is often an apparent disposition to amplify the authorities of the Union at the expence of those of the States. It is of great importance as well as of indispensable obligation, that the constitutional boundary between them should be impartially maintained. Every deviation from it in practice detracts from the superiority of a Chartered over a traditional Govt. and mars the experiment which is to determine the interesting Problem whether the organization of the Political system of the U. S. establishes a just equilibrium; or tends to a preponderance of the National or the local powers, and in the latter case, whether of the national or of the local.

A candid review of the vicissitudes which have marked the progress of the General Govt. does not preclude doubts as to the ultimate & fixed character of a Political Establishment distinguished by so novel & complex a mechanism. On some occasions the advantage taken of favorable circumstances gave an impetus & direction to it which seemed to threaten subversive encroachments on the rights & authorities of the States. At a certain period we witnessed a spirit of usurpation by some of these on the necessary & legitimate functions of the former. At the present date, theoretic innovations at least are putting new weights into the scale of federal sovereignty which make it highly proper to bring them to the Bar of the Constitution.

In looking to the probable course and eventual bearing of the compound Govt. of our Country, I cannot but think that much will depend not only on the moral changes incident to the progress of society; but on the increasing number of the members of the Union. Were the members very few, and each very powerful, a feeling of self-sufficiency would have a relaxing effect on the bands holding them together. Were they numerous & weak, the Gov. over the whole would find less difficulty in maintaining & increasing subordination. It happens that whilst the power of some is swelling to a great size, the entire number is swelling also. In this respect a corresponding increase of centripetal & centrifugal forces, may be equivalent to no increase of either.

In the existing posture of things, my reflections lead me to infer that whatever may be the latitude of Jurisdiction assumed by the Judicial Power of the U. S. it is less formidable to the reserved sovereignty of the States than the latitude of power which it has assigned to the National Legislature; & that encroachments of the latter are more to be apprehended from impulses given to it by a majority of the States seduced by expected advantages, than from the love of Power in the Body itself, controuled as it *now* is by its responsibility to the Constituent Body.

Such is the plastic faculty of Legislation, that notwithstanding the firm tenure which judges have on their offices, they can by various regulations be kept or reduced within the paths of duty; more especially with the aid of their amenability to the Legislative tribunal in the form of impeachment. It is not probable that the Supreme Court would long be indulged in a career of usurpation opposed to the decided opinions & policy of the Legislature.

Nor do I think that Congress, even seconded by the Judicial Power, can, without some change in the character of the nation, succeed in *durable* violations of the rights & authorities of the States. The responsibility of one branch to the people, and of the other branch to the Legislatures, of the States, seem to be, in the present stage at least of our political history, an adequate barrier. In the case of the alien & sedition laws, which violated the general *sense* as well as the *rights* of the States, the usurping experiment was crushed at once, notwithstanding the co-operation of the federal Judges with the federal laws.

But what is to controul Congress when backed & even pushed on by a majority of their Constituents, as was the case in the late contest relative to Missouri, and as may again happen in the constructive power relating to Roads & Canals? Nothing within the pale of the Constitution but sound arguments & conciliatory expostulations addressed both to Congress & to their Constituents.

On the questions brought before the Public by the late doctrines of the Supreme Court of the U. S. concerning the extent of their own powers, and that of the exclusive jurisdiction of Congress over the ten miles square and other specified places, there is as yet no evidence that they express either the opinions of Congress or those of their Constituents. There is nothing therefore to discourage a development of whatever flaws the doctrines may contain, or tendencies they may threaten. Congress if convinced of these may not only abstain from the exercise of Powers claimed for them by the Court, but find the means of controuling those claimed by the Court for itself. And should Congress not be convinced, their Constituents, if so, can certainly under the forms of the Constitution effectuate a compliance with their deliberate judgment and settled determination.

In expounding the Constitution the Court seems not insensible that the intention of the parties to it ought to be kept in view; and that as far as the language of the instrument will permit, this intention ought to be traced in the contemporaneous expositions. But is the Court as prompt and as careful in citing and following this evidence, when agst. the federal Authority as when agst. that of the States? (See the partial reference of the Court to "The Federalist.")

The exclusive jurisdiction over the ten miles square is itself an anomaly in our Representative System. And its object being manifest, and attested by the views taken of it, at its date, there seems a peculiar impropriety in making it the fulcrum for a lever stretching into the most distant parts of the Union, and overruling the municipal policy of the States. The remark is still more striking when applied to the smaller places over which an exclusive jurisdiction was suggested by a regard to the defence & the property of the Nation.

Some difficulty, it must be admitted may result in particular cases from the impossibility of executing some of these powers within the defined spaces, according to the principles and rules enjoined by the Constitution; and from the want of a constitutional provision for the surrender of malefactors whose escape must be so easy, on the demand of the U. States as well as of the Individual States. It is true also that these exclusive jurisdictions are in the class of enumerated powers, to wch. is subjoined the "power in Congress to pass all laws necessary & proper for their execution." All however that could be exacted by these considerations would be that the means of execution should be of the most obvious & essential kind; & exerted in the ways as little intrusive as possible on the powers and police of the States. And, after all, the question would remain whether the better course would not be to regard the case as an omitted one, to be provided for by an amendment of the Constitution. In resorting to legal precedents as sanctions to power, the distinctions should ever be strictly attended to, between such as take place under transitory impressions, or without full examination & deliberation, and such as pass with solemnities and repetitions sufficient to imply a concurrence of the judgment & the will of those, who having granted the power, have the ultimate right to explain the grant. Altho' I cannot join in the protest of some against the validity of all precedents, however uniform & multiplied, in expounding the Constitution, yet I am persuaded that Legislative precedents are frequently of a character entitled to little respect, and that those of Congress are sometimes liable to peculiar distrust. They not only follow the example of other Legislative assemblies in first procrastinating and then precipitating their acts; but, owing to the termination of their session every other year at a fixed day & hour, a mass of business is struck off, as it were at shorthand, and in a moment. These midnight precedents of every sort ought to have little weight in any case.

On the question relating to involuntary submissions of the States to the Tribunal of the Supreme Court, the Court seems not to have adverted at all to the expository language when the Constitution was adopted; nor to that of the Eleventh Amendment, which may as well import that it was declaratory, as that it was restrictive of the meaning of the original text. It seems to be a strange reasoning also that would imply that a State in controversies with its own Citizens might have less of sovereignty, than in controversies with foreign individuals, by which the national relations might be affected. Nor is it less to be wondered that it should have appeared to the Court that the dignity of a State was not more compromitted by being made a party agst. a private person than agst a coordinate Party.

The Judicial power of the U. S. over cases arising under the

Constitution, must be admitted to be a vital part of the System. But that there are limitations and exceptions to its efficient character, is among the admissions of the Court itself. The Eleventh Amendment introduces exceptions if there were none before. A liberal & steady course of practice can alone reconcile the several provisions of the Constitution literally at variance with each other; of which there is an example in the Treaty Power & the Legislative Power on subjects to which both are extended by the words of the Constitution. It is particularly incumbent, in taking cognizance of cases arising under the Constitution, and in which the laws and rights of the States may be involved, to let the proceedings touch individuals only. Prudence enjoins this if there were no other motive, in consideration of the impracticability of applying coercion to States

I am sensible Sir, that these ideas are too vague to be of value, and that they may not even hint for consideration anything not occurring to yourself. Be so good as to see in them at least an unwillingness to disregard altogether your request. Should any of the ideas be erroneous as well as vague, I have the satisfaction to know that they will be viewed by a friendly as well as a candid eye.

To Spencer Roane

Dear Sir,   Montpellier, June 29, 1821
I have recd., and return my thanks for your obliging communication of the 20th instant. The papers of "Algernon Sidney" have given their full lustre to the arguments agst the suability of States by individuals, and agst the projectile capacity of the power of Congress within the "ten miles square." The publication is well worthy of a Pamphlet form, but must attract Public attention in any form.

The Gordian Knot of the Constitution seems to lie in the problem of collision between the federal & State powers, especially as eventually exercised by their respective Tribunals. If the knot cannot be untied by the text of the Constitution it ought not, certainly, to be cut by any Political Alexander.

I have always thought that a construction of the instrument ought to be favoured, as far as the text would warrant, which would obviate the dilemma of a Judicial rencounter or a mutual paralysis; and that on the abstract question whether the federal or the State decisions ought to prevail, the sounder policy would yield to the claims of the former.

Our Governmental System is established by a compact, not between the Government of the U. States, and the State Governments; but between the States, as sovereign communities, stipulating each with the others, a surrender of certain portions, of their respective authorities, to be exercised by a Common Govt. and a reservation, for their own exercise, of all their other Authorities. The possibility of disagreements concerning the line of division between these portions could not escape attention; and the existence of some Provision for terminating regularly & authoritatively such disagreements, not but be regarded as a material desideratum.

Were this trust to be vested in the States in their individual characters, the Constitution of the U. S. might become different in every State, and would be pretty sure to do so in some; the State Govts. would not stand all in the same relation to the General Govt., some retaining more, others less of sovereignty; and the vital principle of equality, which cements their Union thus gradually be deprived of its virtue. Such a trust vested in the Govt. representing the whole and exercised by its tribunals, would not be exposed to these consequences; whilst the trust itself would be controulable by the States who directly or indirectly appoint the Trustees: whereas in the hands of the States no federal controul direct or indirect would exist the functionaries holding their appointments by tenures altogether independent of the General Govt.

Is it not a reasonable calculation also that the room for jarring opinions between the National & State tribunals will be narrowed by successive decisions sanctioned by the Public concurrence; and that the weight of the State tribunals will be increased by improved organizations, by selections of abler Judges, and consequently by more enlightened proceedings? Much of the distrust of these departments in the States, which prevailed when the National Constitution was formed has already been removed. Were they filled everywhere, as they are in some of the States, one of which I need not name, their decisions at once indicating & influencing the sense of their Constituents, and founded on united interpretations of constitutional points, could scarcely fail to frustrate an assumption of unconstitutional powers by the federal tribunals.

Is it too much to anticipate even that the federal & State Judges, as they become more & more co-ordinate in talents, with equal integrity, and feeling alike the impartiality enjoined by their oaths, will vary less & less also in their reasonings & opinions on all Judicial subjects; and thereby mutually contribute to the clearer & firmer establishment of the true boundaries of power, on which must depend the success & permanency of the federal republic, the best Guardian, as we believe, of the liberty, the safety, and the happiness of men. In these hypothetical views I may permit my wishes to sway too much my hopes. I submit the whole nevertheless to your perusal, well assured that you will approve the former, if you cannot join fully in the latter.

Under all circumstances I beg you to be assured of my distinguished esteem & sincere regard.

Jonathan Bull and Mary Bull

(*Written but not published at the period of the Missouri question.*)

Jonathan Bull & Mary Bull, who were descendants of old Jno. Bull, the head of the family, had inherited contiguous estates in large tracts of land. As they grew up & became well acquainted, a partiality was mutually felt, and advances on several occasions made towards a matrimonial connection. This was particularly recommended by the advantage of putting their two estates under a common superintendence. Old B. however as guardian of both and having long been allowed certain valuable privileges within the Estates with which he was not long content had always found the means of breaking off the match which he regarded as a fatal obstacle to his secret design of getting the whole property into his own hands.

At a moment favorable as he thought for the attempt, he

brought suit agst. both, but with a view of carrying it on in a way that would make the process bear on the parties in such different modes times and degrees as might create a jealousy & discord between them. J. & M. had too much sagacity to be duped. They understood well old Bull's character and situation. They knew that he was deeply versed in all the subtleties of the law, that he was of a stubborn & persevering temper, and that he had moreover a very long purse. They were sensible therefore that the more he endeavoured to divide their interests & their defence of the suit the more they ought to make a common cause, and proceed in a concert of measures. As this could best be done by giving effect to the feelings long entertained for each other, an intermarriage was determined on, & solemnized with a deed of settlement as usual in such opulent matches, duly executed, and no event certainly of the sort was ever celebrated by a greater fervor or variety of rejoicings among the respective tenants of the parties. They had a great horror of falling into the hands of old B. and regarded the marriage of their proprietors under whom they held their freeholds as the surest mode of warding off the danger. They were not disappointed. United purses and good advocates compelled old B. after a hard struggle to withdraw the suit, and relinquish forever not only the new pretensions he had set up but the old privileges he had been allowed.

The marriage of J. and M. was not a barren one. On the contrary every year or two added a new member to the family and on such occasions the practice was to set off a portion of land sufficient for a good farm to be put under the authority of the child on its attaining the age of manhood, and these lands were settled very rapidly by tenants going as the case might be from the estates, sometimes of J. sometimes of M. and sometimes partly from one & partly from the other.

It happened that at the expiration of the non-age of the 10th. or 11th. fruit of the marriage some difficulties were started concerning the rules & conditions of declaring the young party of age, and of giving him as a member of the family, the management of his patrimony. Jonathan became possessed with a notion that an arrangement ought to be made that would prevent the new farm from being settled and cultivated, as in all the latter instances, indiscriminately by persons removing from his and M's estate and confine this privilege to those going from his own; and in the perverse humour which had seized him, he listened moreover to suggestions that M. had some undue advantage from the selections of the Head Stewards which happened to have been made much oftener out of her tenants than his.

Now the prejudice suddenly taken up by J. agst. the equal right of M's tenants to remove with their property to new farms, was connected with a peculiarity in Mary's person not as yet noticed. Strange as it may appear, the circumstance is not the less true, that M. when a Child had unfortunately recd. from a certain African dye, a stain on her left arm which had made it perfectly black, and withal somewhat weaker than the other arm. The misfortune arose from a Ship from Africa loaded with the article which had been permitted to enter a river running thro' her estate, and dispose of a part of the noxious cargo. The fact was well known to J. at the time of their marriage, and if felt as an objection, it was in a manner reduced to nothing by the comely form and pleasing features of M. in every other respect; by her good sense and amiable manners; and in part perhaps by the large and valuable estate she brought with her.

In the unlucky fit however which was upon him, he looked at the black arm, and forgot all the rest. To such a pitch of feeling was he wrought up that he broke out into the grossest taunts on M. for her misfortune; not omitting at the same time to remind her of his long forbearance to exert his superior voice in the appointment of the Head Steward. He had now he said got his eyes fully opened, he saw everything in a new light, and was resolved to act accordingly. As to the Head Steward he wd. let her see that the appointment was virtually in his power; and she might take her leave of all chance of ever having another of her tenants advanced to that station, and as to the black arm, she should, if the colour could not be taken out, either tear off the skin from the flesh or cut off the limb; For it was his fixed determination, that one or other should be done, or he wd. sue out a divorce, & there should be an end of all connection between them and their Estates. I have examined he said well the marriage settlement, and flaws have been pointed out to me, that never occurred before, by which I shall be able to set the whole aside. White as I am all over, I can no longer consort with one marked with such a deformity as the blot on your person.

Mary was so stunned with the language she heard that it was some time before she could speak at all; and as the surprise abated, she was almost choked with the anger & indignation swelling in her bosom. Generous and placable as her temper was, she had a proud sensibility to what she thought an unjust & degrading treatment, which did not permit her to suppress the violence of her first emotions. Her language accordingly for a moment was such as these emotions prompted. But her good sense, and her regard for J. whose qualities as a good husband she had long experienced, soon gained an ascendency, and changed her tone to that of sober reasoning & affectionate expostulation. Well my dear husband you see what a passion you had put me into. But it is now over, and I will endeavor to express my thoughts with the calmness and good feelings which become the relation of wife & husband.

As to the case of providing for our child just coming of age, I shall say but little. We both have such a tender regard for him and such a desire to see him on a level with his brethren as to the chance of making his fortune in the world, that I am sure the difficulties which have occurred will in some way or other be got over.

But I cannot pass so lightly over the reproaches you cast on the colour of my left arm, and on the more frequent appointment of my tenants than of yours to the head-stewardship of our joint estates.

Now as to the first point, you seem to have forgotten, my worthy partner, that this infirmity was fully known to you before our marriage, and is proved to be so by the deed of settlement itself. At that time you made it no objection whatever to our Union; and indeed how could you urge such an objection, when you were conscious that you yourself was not entirely free from a like stain on your own person. The fatal African dye, as you well know, had found its way into your abode as well as mine; and at the time of our marriage had spots & specks scattered over your body as black as the skin on my arm. And altho' you have by certain abrasions and other applications, taken them in some measure out, there are visible remains which ought to soften at least your language when reflecting on my situation. You ought surely when you have so slowly and imperfectly relieved yourself from the mortifying stain altho' the task was comparatively so easy, to have some forbearance and sympathy with me who have a task so much more difficult to perform. Instead of that you abuse me as if I had brought the misfortune on myself, and could remove it at will; or as if you had pointed out a ready way to do it, and I had slighted your advice. Yet so far is this from being the case that you know as well as I do that I am not to be blamed for the origin of the sad mishap, that I am as anxious as you can be to get rid of it; that you are as unable as I am to find out a safe & feasible plan for the purpose; and moreover that I have done everything I could, in the meantime, to mitigate an evil that cannot as yet be removed. When you talk of tearing off the skin or cutting off the unfortunate limb, must I remind you of what you cannot be ignorant that the most skilful surgeons have given their opinions that if so cruel an operation were to be tried, it could hardly fail to be followed by a mortification or a bleeding to death. Let me ask too whether, should neither of the fatal effects ensue, you would like me better in my mangled or mutilated condition than you do now? And when you threaten a divorce and an annulment of the marriage settlement, may I not ask whether your estate wd. not suffer as much as mine by dissolving the partnership between them? I am far from denying that I feel the advantage of having the pledge of your arm, your stronger arm if you please, for the protection of me & mine; and that my interests in general have been and must continue to be the better for your aid & counsel in the management of them. But on the other hand you must be equally sensible that the aid of my purse will have its value, in case old B. or any other rich litigious fellow should put us to the expense of another tedious lawsuit. And now that we are on the subject of loss & gain, you will not be offended if I take notice of a report that you sometimes insinuate that my estate according to the rates of assessment, does not pay its due share into the common purse. I think my dear J. that if you ever entertained this opinion you must have been led into it by a very wrong

view of the subject as to the direct income from rents, there
can be no deficiency on my part there; the rule of apportionment being clear & founded on a calculation by numbers.
And as to what is raised from the articles bought & used by
my tenants, it is difficult to conceive that my tenants buy or
use less than yours, considering that they carry a greater
amount of crops to market the whole of which it is well
known they lay out in articles from the use of which the bailiff
regularly collects the sum due. It wd. seem then that my tenants selling more, buy more; buying more use more, and
using more pay more. Meaning however not to put you in the
wrong, but myself in the right, I do not push the argument
to that length, because I readily agree that in paying for articles bought & used you have beyond the fruits of the soil on
which I depend ways & means which I have not. You draw
chiefly the interest we jointly pay for the funds we were
obliged to borrow for the fees & costs the suit of Old Bull
put us to. Your tenants also turn their hands so ingeniously to
a variety of handicrafts & other mechanical productions, that
they make not a little money from that source. Besides all
this, you gain much by the fish you catch & carry to market;
by the use of your teams and boats in transporting and trading on the crops of my tenants; and indeed in doing that sort
of business for strangers also. This is a fair statement on your
side of the account, with the drawback however, that as your
tenants are supplied with a greater proportion of articles
made by themselves, than is the case with mine, the use of
which articles does not contribute to the common purse, they
avoid in the same proportion, the payments collected from
my tenants. If I were to look still farther into this matter and
refer you to every advantage you draw from the union of our
persons & property, I might remark that the profits you make
from your teams & boats & which enable you to pay your
quota in great part, are drawn from the preference they have
in conveying & disposing of the products of my soil; a business that might fall into other hands in the event of our separation. I mention this as I have already sd. not by way of
complaint for I am well satisfied that your gain is not altogether my loss in this more than in many other instances; and
that what profits you immediately may profit me also in the

long run. But I will not dwell on these calculations & comparisons of interest which you ought to weigh as well as myself as reasons agst. the measure to which you threaten a resort. For when I consult my own heart & call to mind all the endearing proofs you have given of yours being in sympathy with it, I must needs hope that there are other ties than mere interest to prevent us from ever suffering a transient resentment on either side, with or without cause, to bring on both all the consequences of a divorce; consequences too which wd. be a sad inheritance indeed for our numerous and beloved offspring.

As to the other point relative to the Head Stewards I must own, my worthy husband, that I am altogether at a loss for any cause of dissatisfaction on your part or blame on mine. It is true as you say that they have been oftener taken from among my tenants than yours, but under other circumstances the reverse might as well have happened. If the individls. appointed had made their way to the important trust by corrupt or fallacious means; if they had been preferred merely because they dwelt on my estate, or had succeeded by any interposition of mine contrary to your inclination; or finally if they had administered the trust unfaithfully, sacrificing your interests to mine, or the interests of both to selfish or unworthy purposes in either of these cases you wd have ground for your complaints. But I know J. that you are too just and too candid not to admit that no such ground exists. The head Stewards in question cd. not have been appointed without your own participation as well as mine. They were recommended to our joint choice by the reputed fairness of their characters, by their tried fidelity & competency in previous trusts, and by their exemption from all charges of impure & grasping designs, and so far were they from being partial to my interest at the expense of yours, that they were rather considered by my tenants as leaning to a management more favorable to yours than to mine. I need not say that I allude to the bounties direct or indirect to your teams & boats, to the hands employed in your fisheries, and to the looms and other machineries which witht. such encouragement wd. not be able to meet the threatened rivalships of interfering neighbors. I say only that these ideas were in the heads of some of my tenants.

For myself I shd. not have mentioned them but as a defence agst. what I must regard as so unfounded that it ought not to be permitted to make a lasting impression.

But laying aside all these considerations, I repeat my dear J. that the appt of the Head Steward lies as much if not more with you than with me. Let the choice fall where it may, you will find me faithfully abiding by it, whether it be thought the best possible one or not, and sincerely wishing that he may equally improve better opportunities of serving us both than was the lot of any of those who have gone before him.

J. who had a good heart as well as sound head & steady temper was touched with this tender & considerate language of M. and the bickering wch had sprung up ended as the quarrels of lovers *always*, & of married folks *sometimes* do, in increased affection & confidence between the parties.

c. 1821

To Edward Livingston

Dr Sir,   Montpr., July 10, 1822

I was favored some days ago with your letter of May 19, accompanied by a copy of your Report to the Legislature of the State on the subject of a penal Code.

I should commit a tacit injustice if I did not say that the Report does great honor to the talents and sentiments of the Author. It abounds with ideas of conspicuous value and presents them in a manner not less elegant than persuasive.

The reduction of an entire code of criminal jurisprudence, into statutory provisions, excluding a recurrence to foreign or traditional codes, and substituting for technical terms, more familiar ones with or without explanatory notes, cannot but be viewed as a very arduous task. I sincerely wish your execution of it may fulfil every expectation.

I cannot deny, at the same time, that I have been accustomed to doubt the practicability of giving all the desired simplicity to so complex a subject, without involving a discretion, inadmissible in free Govt. to those who are to expound and apply the law. The rules and usages which make a part of the law, tho' to be found only in elementary treatises, in respectable commentaries, and in adjudged cases, seem to be too numerous & too various to be brought within the requisite compass; even if there were less risk of creating uncertainties by defective abridgments, or by the change of phraseology.

This risk wd. seem to be particularly incident to a substitution of new words & definitions for a technical language, the meaning of which had been settled by long use and authoritative expositions. When a technical term may express a very simple idea, there might be no inconveniency or rather an advantage in exchanging it for a more familiar synonyme, if a precise one could be found. But where the technical terms & phrases have a complex import, not otherwise to be reduced to clearness & certainty, than by practical applications of them, it might be unsafe to introduce new terms & phrases, tho' aided by brief explanations. The whole law expressed by single terms, such as "trial by jury, evidence, &c, &c." fill volumes, when unfolded into the details which enter into their meaning.

I hope it will not be thought by this intimation of my doubts I wish to damp the enterprize from which you have not shrunk. On the contrary I not only wish that you may overcome all the difficulties which occur to me; but am persuaded that if compleat success shd. not reward your labors, there is ample room for improvements in the criminal jurisprudence of Louisiana as elsewhere which are well worthy the exertion of your best powers, and wh will furnish useful examples to other members of the Union. Among the advantages distinguishing our compound Govt. it is not the least that it affords so many opportunities and chances in the local Legislatures, for salutary innovations by some, which may be adopted by others; or for important experiments, which, if unsuccessful, will be of limited injury, and may even prove salutary as beacons to others. Our political system is found also to have the happy merit of exciting a laudable emulation among the States composing it, instead of the enmity marking competitions among powers wholly alien to each other.

I observe with particular pleasure the view you have taken of the immunity of Religion from civil jurisdiction, in every case where it does not trespass on private rights or the public peace. This has always been a favorite principle with me; and it was not with my approbation, that the deviation from it took place in Congs., when they appointed Chaplains, to be paid from the Natl. Treasury. It would have been a much better proof to their Constituents of their pious feeling if the members had contributed for the purpose, a pittance from their own pockets. As the precedent is not likely to be rescinded, the best that can now be done, may be to apply to the Constn. the maxim of the law, de minimis non curat.

There has been another deviation from the strict principle in the Executive Proclamations of fasts & festivals, so far, at least, as they have spoken the language of *injunction*, or have lost sight of the equality of *all* religious sects in the eye of the Constitution. Whilst I was honored with the Executive Trust I found it necessary on more than one occasion to follow the example of predecessors. But I was always careful to make the Proclamations absolutely indiscriminate, and merely recommendatory; or rather mere *designations* of a day, on which all who thought proper might *unite* in consecrating it to religious purposes, according to their own faith & forms. In this sense, I presume you reserve to the Govt. a right to *appoint* particular days for religious worship throughout the State, without any penal sanction *enforcing* the worship. I know not what may be the way of thinking on this subject in Louisiana. I should suppose the Catholic portion of the people, at least, as a small & even unpopular sect in the U. S., would rally, as they did in Virga. when religious liberty was a Legislative topic, to its broadest principle. Notwithstanding the general progress made within the two last centuries in favour of this branch of liberty, & the full establishment of it, in some parts of our Country, there remains in others a strong bias towards the old error, that without some sort of alliance or coalition between Govt. & Religion neither can be duly supported. Such indeed is the tendency to such a coalition, and such its corrupting influence on both the parties, that the danger cannot be too carefully guarded agst. And in a Govt. of opinion, like ours, the only effectual guard must be found in the soundness and stability of the general opinion on the subject. Every new & successful example therefore of a perfect separation between ecclesiastical and civil matters, is of importance. And I have no doubt that every new example, will succeed, as every past one has done, in shewing that religion & Govt. will both exist in greater purity, the less they are mixed together. It was the belief of all sects at one time that the establishment of Religion by law, was right & necessary; that the true religion ought to be established in exclusion of every other; And that the only question to be decided was which was the true religion. The example of Holland proved that a toleration of sects, dissenting from the established sect, was safe & even useful. The example of the Colonies, now States, which rejected religious establishments altogether, proved that all Sects might be safely & advantageously put on a footing of equal & entire freedom; and a continuance of their example since the declaration of Independence, has shewn that its success in Colonies was not to be ascribed to their connection with the parent Country. If a further confirmation of the truth could be wanted, it is to be found in the examples furnished by the States, which have abolished their religious establishments. I cannot speak particularly of any of the cases excepting that of Virga. where it is impossible to deny that Religion prevails with more zeal, and a more exemplary priesthood than it ever did when established and patronised by Public authority. We are teaching the world the great truth that Govts. do better without Kings & Nobles than with them. The merit will be doubled by the other lesson that Religion flourishes in greater purity, without than with the aid of Govt.

My pen I perceive has rambled into reflections for which it was not taken up. I recall it to the proper object of thanking you for your very interesting pamphlet, and of tendering you my respects and good wishes.

J. M. presents his respects to Mr. Livingston and requests the favor of him to forward the above inclosed letter to N. Orleans or to retain it as his brother may or may not be expected at N. York.

To William T. Barry

Dr Sir,   Aug 4, 1822

I recd. some days ago your letter of June 30, and the printed Circular to which it refers.

The liberal appropriations made by the Legislature of Kentucky for a general system of Education cannot be too much applauded. A popular Government, without popular information, or the means of acquiring it, is but a Prologue to a Farce or a Tragedy; or, perhaps both. Knowledge will forever govern ignorance: And a people who mean to be their own Governors, must arm themselves with the power which knowledge gives.

I have always felt a more than ordinary interest in the destinies of Kentucky. Among her earliest settlers were some of my particular friends and Neighbors. And I was myself among the foremost advocates for submitting to the Will of the "District" the question and the time of its becoming a separate member of the American family. Its rapid growth & signal prosperity in this character have afforded me much pleasure; which is not a little enhanced by the enlightened patriotism which is now providing for the State a Plan of Education embracing every class of Citizens, and every grade & department of Knowledge. No error is more certain than the one proceeding from a hasty & superficial view of the subject: that the people at large have no interest in the establishment of Academies, Colleges, and Universities, where a few only, and those not of the poorer classes can obtain for their sons the advantages of superior education. It is thought to be unjust that all should be taxed for the benefit of a part, and that too the part least needing it.

If provision were not made at the same time for every part, the objection would be a natural one. But, besides the consideration when the higher Seminaries belong to a plan of general education, that it is better for the poorer classes to have the aid of the richer by a general tax on property, than that every parent should provide at his own expence for the education of his children, it is certain that every Class is interested in establishments which give to the human mind its highest improvements, and to every Country its truest and most durable celebrity.

Learned Institutions ought to be favorite objects with every free people. They throw that light over the public mind which is the best security against crafty & dangerous encroachments on the public liberty. They are the nurseries of skilful Teachers for the schools distributed throughout the Community. They are themselves schools for the particular talents required for some of the Public Trusts, on the able execution of which the welfare of the people depends. They multiply the educated individuals from among whom the people may elect a due portion of their public Agents of every description; more especially of those who are to frame the laws; by the perspicuity, the consistency, and the stability, as well as by the just & equal spirit of which the great social purposes are to be answered.

Without such Institutions, the more costly of which can scarcely be provided by individual means, none but the few whose wealth enables them to support their sons abroad can give them the fullest education; and in proportion as this is done, the influence is monopolized which superior information every where possesses. At cheaper & nearer seats of Learning parents with slender incomes may place their sons in a course of education putting them on a level with the sons of the Richest. Whilst those who are without property, or with but little, must be peculiarly interested in a System which unites with the more Learned Institutions, a provision for diffusing through the entire Society the education needed for the common purposes of life. A system comprizing the Learned Institutions may be still further recommended to the more indigent class of Citizens by such an arrangement as was reported to the General Assembly of Virginia, in the year 1779, by a Committee* appointed to revise laws in order to adapt them to the genius of Republican Government. It made part of a "Bill for the more general diffusion of knowledge" that wherever a youth was ascertained to possess talents meriting an education which his parents could not afford, he should be carried forward at the public expence, from

*The report was made by Mr. Jefferson, Mr. Pendleton, and Mr. Wythe.

seminary to seminary, to the completion of his studies at the highest.

But why should it be necessary in this case, to distinguish the Society into classes according to their property? When it is considered that the establishment and endowment of Academies, Colleges, and Universities are a provision, not merely for the existing generation, but for succeeding ones also; that in Governments like ours a constant rotation of property results from the free scope to industry, and from the laws of inheritance, and when it is considered moreover, how much of the exertions and privations of all are meant not for themselves, but for their posterity, there can be little ground for objections from any class, to plans of which every class must have its turn of benefits. The rich man, when contributing to a permanent plan for the education of the poor, ought to reflect that he is providing for that of his own descendants; and the poor man who concurs in a provision for those who are not poor that at no distant day it may be enjoyed by descendants from himself. It does not require a long life to witness these vicissitudes of fortune.

It is among the happy peculiarities of our Union, that the States composing it derive from their relation to each other and to the whole, a salutary emulation, without the enmity involved in competitions among States alien to each other. This emulation, we may perceive, is not without its influence in several important respects; and in none ought it to be more felt than in the merit of diffusing the light and the advantages of Public Instruction. In the example therefore which Kentucky is presenting, she not only consults her own welfare, but is giving an impulse to any of her sisters who may be behind her in the noble career.

Throughout the Civilized World, nations are courting the praise of fostering Science and the useful Arts, and are opening their eyes to the principles and the blessings of Representative Government. The American people owe it to themselves, and to the cause of free Government, to prove by their establishments for the advancement and diffusion of Knowledge, that their political Institutions, which are attracting observation from every quarter, and are respected as Models, by the new-born States in our own Hemisphere, are as favorable to the intellectual and moral improvement of Man as they are conformable to his individual & social Rights. What spectacle can be more edifying or more seasonable, than that of Liberty & Learning, each leaning on the other for their mutual & surest support?

The Committee, of which your name is the first, have taken a very judicious course in endeavouring to avail Kentucky of the experience of elder States, in modifying her Schools. I enclose extracts from the laws of Virginia on that subject; though I presume they will give little aid; the less as they have as yet been imperfectly carried into execution. The States where such systems have been long in operation will furnish much better answers to many of the enquiries stated in your Circular. But after all, such is the diversity of local circumstances, more particularly as the population varies in density & sparseness, that the details suited to some may be little so to others. As the population however, is becoming less & less sparse, and it will be well in laying the foundation of a Good System, to have a view to this progressive change, much attention seems due to examples in the Eastern States, where the people are most compact, & where there has been the longest experience in plans of popular education.

I know not that I can offer on the occasion any suggestions not likely to occur to the Committee. Were I to hazard one, it would be in favour of adding to Reading, Writing, & Arithmetic, to which the instruction of the poor, is commonly limited, some knowledge of Geography; such as can easily be conveyed by a Globe & Maps, and a concise Geographical Grammar. And how easily & quickly might a general idea even, be conveyed of the Solar System, by the aid of a Planatarium of the Cheapest construction. No information seems better calculated to expand the mind and gratify curiosity than what would thus be imparted. This is especially the case, with what relates to the Globe we inhabit, the Nations among which it is divided, and the characters and customs which distinguish them. An acquaintance with foreign Countries in this mode, has a kindred effect with that of seeing them as travellers, which never fails, in uncorrupted minds, to weaken local prejudices, and enlarge the sphere of benevolent feelings. A knowledge of the Globe & its various inhabitants, however slight, might moreover, create a taste for Books of Travels and Voyages; out of which might grow a general taste for History, an inexhaustible fund of entertainment & instruction. Any reading not of a vicious species must be a good substitute for the amusements too apt to fill up the leisure of the labouring classes.

I feel myself much obliged Sir by your expressions of personal kindness, and pray you to accept a return of my good wishes, with assurances of my great esteem & respect.

P. S. On reflection I omit the extracts from the laws of Virga., which it is probable may be within your reach at home. Should it be otherwise, and you think them worth the transmission by the mail, the omission shall be supplied.

To Edward Everett

Dear Sir   Montpellier, March 19, 1823

I received, on the 15th, your favour of the 2d inst:, with the little pamphlet of remarks on your brother's "Europe."

The pamphlet wd. have been much improved by softer words and harder arguments. To support its construction of Art. 18, of the Treaty of 1794, the writer ought to have shewn that there are cases in which provisions become contraband according to the Law of Nations; and that the cases are of such recurrence and importance as to make them a probable object of such an article. He does not point at a single one.

If he be not right in contending that the U. S. always resisted the Rule of 1756 he is still more astray in saying that G. B. relinquished it. The indemnities for violations of the Rule allowed by the Joint Commissioners can be no evidence of the fact. This award might be the result of the casting vote on the American side; or the concurrence of the British side, the result of the individual opinions of honest Umpires. That the British Govt. made no such relinquishment is demonstrated by the reasonings & adjudications of Sir Wm Scott, whether he be regarded as the Organ, or as the Oracle of his Govt. There is no question of public law, on which he exerts his talents with more pertinacity than he does in giving effect to the rule of '56, in all its ductile applications to emerging cases. His testimony on this point admits no reply. The payment of the awards of the Board of Com. by the British Govt. is an evidence merely of its good faith; the more to its credit, the more they disappointed its calculations & wishes.

Our University has lately recd. a further loan from the Legislature which will prepare the Buildings for ten Professors and about 200 Students. Should all the loans be converted into donations, at the next Session, as is generally expected, but for which no pledge has been given, the Visitors, with an annuity of $15,000 settled on the Institution, will turn their thoughts towards opening it, and to the preliminary engagement of Professors.

I am not surprised at the dilemma produced at your University by making theological professorships an integral part of the System. The anticipation of such an one led to the omission in ours; the Visitors being merely authorized to open a public Hall for religious occasions, under *impartial* regulations; with the opportunity to the different sects to establish Theological schools so near that the Students of the University may respectively attend the religious exercises in them. The village of Charlottesville also, where different religious worships will be held, is also so near, that resort may conveniently be had to them.

A University with sectarian professorships, becomes, of course, a Sectarian Monopoly: with professorships of rival sects, it would be an Arena of Theological Gladiators. Without any such professorships, it may incur for a time at least, the imputation of irreligious tendencies, if not designs. The last difficulty was thought more manageable than either of the others.

On this view of the subject, there seems to be no alternative but between a public University without a theological professorship, and sectarian Seminaries without a University.

I recollect to have seen, many years ago, a project of a prayer, by Govr. Livingston father of the present Judge, intended to comprehend & conciliate College Students of every Xn denomination, by a Form composed wholly of texts & phrases of scripture. If a trial of the expedient was ever made, it must have failed, notwithstanding its winning aspect from the single cause that many sects reject all set forms of Worship.

The difficulty of reconciling the Xn mind to the absence of a religious tuition from a University established by law and at the common expence, is probably less with us than with you. The settled opinion here is that religion is essentially distinct from Civil Govt. and exempt from its cognizance; that a connexion between them is injurious to both; that there are causes in the human breast, which ensure the perpetuity of religion without the aid of the law; that rival sects, with equal rights, exercise mutual censorships in favor of good morals; that if new sects arise with absurd opinions or overheated maginations, the proper remedies lie in time, forbearance and example; that a legal establishment of religion without a toleration could not be thought of, and with a toleration, is no security for public quiet & harmony, but rather a source itself of discord & animosity; and finally that these opinions are supported by experience, which has shewn that every relaxation of the alliance between Law & religion, from the partial example of Holland, to its consummation in Pennsylvania Delaware N. J., &c, has been found as safe in practice as it is sound in theory. Prior to the Revolution, the Episcopal Church was established by law in this State. On the Declaration of independence it was left with all other sects, to a self-support. And no doubt exists that there is much more of religion among us now than there ever was before the change; and particularly in the Sect which enjoyed the legal patronage. This proves rather more than, that the law is not necessary to the support of religion.

With such a public opinion, it may be expected that a University with the feature peculiar to ours will succeed here if anywhere. Some of the Clergy did not fail to arraign the peculiarity; but it is not improbable that they had an eye to the chance of introducing their own creed into the professor's chair. A late resolution for establishing an Episcopal school within the College of William & Mary, tho' in a very guarded manner, drew immediate animadversions from the press, which if they have not put an end to the project, are a proof of what would follow such an experiment in the University of the State, endowed and supported as this will be, altogether by the Public authority and at the common expence.

I know not whence the rumour sprang of my being engaged in a Poll. History of our Country. Such a task, cd. I presume on a capacity for it, belongs to those who have more time before them than the remnant to wch. mine is limited.

On reviewing my political papers & correspondence, I find much that may deserve to be put into a proper state for preservation; and some things that may not in equal amplitude be found elsewhere. The case is doubtless the same with other individuals whose public lives have extended thro' the same long & pregnant period. It has been the misfortune of history, that a personal knowledge and an impartial judgment of things rarely meet in the historian. The best history of our Country therefore must be the fruit of contributions bequeathed by contemporary actors & witnesses, to successors who will make an unbiassed use of them. And if the abundance & authenticity of the materials which still exist in the private as well as public repositories among us shd. descend to hands capable of doing justice to them, the American History may be expected to contain more truth, and lessons, certainly not less valuable, than those of any Country or age.

I have been so unlucky as not yet to have received the Nos. of the N. Amn. Review written for the   . I expect them every moment, but the delay has deprived me as yet of the criticism in that work on Your Brother's Book.

The difference to wch. you allude between the profits of authorship in England & in the U. S. is very striking. It proceeds, mainly, no doubt from the difference of the area over wch. the population is spread, and of the manner in wch. the aggregate wealth is distributed in the 2 Countries. The number of people in this is perhaps equal to that in England, and the number of readers of popular works at least, probably not less, if not greater. But in their scattered situation here, they are with more difficulty supplied with new publications than when they are condensed within an easy reach of them, and where indeed a vast proportion, being in the Metropolis, are on the same spot with the printing offices. But the unequal division of wealth in Engd. enters much into the advantage given there to Authors & Editors. With us there are more readers than buyers of books. In England there are more buyers than readers. Hence those Gorgeous Editions, which are destined to sleep in the private libraries of the Rich whose vanity aspires to that species of furniture, or who give that turn to their public spirit & patronage of letters.

Whatever may be the present obstacles to the diffusion of literature in our Country, it is a consolation that its growing improvements are daily diminishing them, and that in the meantime individuals are seen making generous efforts to overcome them. With my wishes for the success of yours, I repeat assurances of my esteem & cordial respect.

To Thomas Jefferson

Dear Sir   Montpellier, June 27, 1823

I return the copy of your letter to Judge Johnson inclosed in your favor of the —— instant. Your statement relating to the farewell Address of Genl. Washington is substantially correct. If there be any circumstantial inaccuracy, it is in imputing to him more agency in composing the document than he probably had. Taking for granted that it was drawn up by Hamilton, the best conjecture is that the General put into his hands his own letter to me suggesting his general ideas, with the paper prepared by me in conformity with them; and if he varied the draught of Hamilton at all, it was by a few verbal or qualifying amendments only. It is very inconsiderate in the friends of Genl. Washington to make the merit of the Address a question between him & Col: Hamilton, & somewhat extraordinary, if countenanced by those who possess the files of the General where it is presumed the truth might be traced. They ought to claim for him the merit only of cherishing the principles & views addressed to his Country, & for the Address itself the weight given to it by his sanction; leaving the literary merit whatever it be to the friendly pen employed on the occasion, the rather as it was never understood that Washington valued himself on his writing talent, and no secret to some that he occasionally availed himself of the friendship of others whom he supposed more practised than himself in studied composition. In a general view it is to be regretted that the Address is likely to be presented to the public not as the pure legacy of the Father of his Country, as has been all along believed, but as the performance of another held in different estimation. It will not only lose the charm of the name subscribed to it; but it will not be surprizing if particular passages be understood in new senses, & with applications derived from the political doctrines and party feelings of the discovered Author.

At some future day it may be an object with the curious to compare the two draughts made at different epochs with each other, and the letter of Genl. W. with both. The comparison will shew a greater conformity in the first with the tenor & tone of the letter, than in the other; and the difference will be more remarkable perhaps in what is omitted, than in what is added in the Address as it stands.

If the solicitude of Genl. Washington's connexions be such as is represented, I foresee that I shall share their displeasure, if public use be made of what passed between him & me at the approaching expiration of his first term. Altho' it be impossible to question the facts, I may be charged with indelicacy, if not breach of confidence, in making them known; and the irritation will be the greater, if the Authorship of the Address continue to be claimed for the signer of it; since the call on me on one occasion, will favor the allegation of a call on another occasion. I hope therefore that the Judge will not understand your communication as intended for the new work he has in hand. I do not know that your statement would justify all the complaint its public appearance might bring on me; but there certainly was a species of confidence at the time in what passed, forbidding publicity, at least till the lapse of time should wear out the seal on it, & the truth of history should put in a fair claim to such disclosures.

I wish the rather that the Judge may be put on his guard, because with all his good qualities, he has been betrayed into errors which shew that his discretion is not always awake. A remarkable instance is his ascribing to Gouverneur Morris the Newburg letters written by Armstrong, which has drawn from the latter a corrosive attack which must pain his feelings, if it should not affect his standing with the Public. Another appears in a stroke at Judge Cooper in a letter to the Education Committee in Kentucky, which has plunged him into an envenomed dispute with an antagonist, the force of whose mind & pen you well know. And what is worse than all, I perceive from one of Cooper's publications casually falling within my notice, that, among the effects of Judge Johnson's excitement, he has stooped to invoke the religious prejudices circulated agst. Cooper.

Johnson is much indebted to you for your remarks on the definition of parties. The radical distinction between them has always been a confidence of one, and distrust of the other, as to the capacity of Mankind for self Government. He expected far too much, in requesting a precise demarkation of the boundary between the Federal & the State Authorities. The answer would have required a critical commentary on the whole text of the Constitution. The two general Canons you lay down would be of much use in such a task; particularly that which refers to the sense of the State Conventions, whose ratifications alone made the Constitution what it is. In exemplifying the other Canon, there are more exceptions than occurred to you, of cases in which the federal jurisdiction is extended to controversies between Citizens of the same State. To mention one only: In cases arising under a Bankrupt law, there is no distinction between those to which Citizens of the same & of different States are parties.

But after surmounting the difficulty in tracing the boundary between the General & State Govts. the problem remains for maintaining it in practice; particularly in cases of Judicial cognizance. To refer every point of disagreement to the people in Conventions would be a process too tardy, too troublesome, & too expensive; besides its tendency to lessen a salutary veneration for an instrument so often calling for such explanatory interpositions. A paramount or even a definitive Authority in the individual States, would soon make the Constitution & laws different in different States, and thus destroy that equality & uniformity of rights & duties which form the essence of the Compact; to say nothing of the opportunity given to the States individually of involving by their decisions the whole Union in foreign Contests. To leave conflicting decisions to be settled between the Judicial parties could not promise a happy result. The end must be a trial of strength between the Posse headed by the Marshal and the Posse headed by the Sheriff. Nor would the issue be safe if left to a compromise between the two Govts. the case of a disagreement between different Govts. being essentially different from a disagreement between branches of the same Govt. In the latter case neither party being able to consummate its will without the concurrence of the other, there is a necessity on both to consult and to accommodate. Not so, with different Govts. each possessing every branch of power necessary to carry its purpose into compleat effect. It here becomes a question between Independent Nations, with no other *dernier* resort than physical force. Negotiation might indeed in some instances avoid this extremity; but how often would it happen, among so many States, that an unaccommodating spirit in some would render that resource unavailing.

We arrive at the agitated question whether the Judicial Authority of the U. S. be the constitutional resort for determining the line between the federal & State jurisdictions. Believing as I do that the General Convention regarded a provision within the Constitution for deciding in a peaceable & regular mode all cases arising in the course of its operation, as essential to an adequate System of Govt. that it intended the Authority vested in the Judicial Department as a final resort in relation to the States, for cases resulting to it in the exercise of its functions, (the concurrence of the Senate chosen by the State Legislatures, in appointing the Judges, and the oaths & official tenures of these, with the surveillance of public Opinion, being relied on as guarantying their impartiality); and that this intention is expressed by the articles declaring that the federal Constitution & laws shall be the supreme law of the land, and that the Judicial Power of the U. S. shall extend to all cases arising under them: Believing moreover that this was the prevailing view of the subject when the Constitution was adopted & put into execution; that it has so continued thro' the long period which has elapsed; and that even at this time an appeal to a national decision would prove that no general change has taken place: thus believing I have never yielded my original opinion indicated in the "Federalist"

No. 39 to the ingenious reasonings of Col: Taylor agst. this construction of the Constitution.

I am not unaware that the Judiciary career has not corresponded with what was anticipated. At one period the Judges perverted the Bench of Justice into a rostrum for partizan harangues. And latterly the Court, by some of its decisions, still more by extrajudicial reasonings & dicta, has manifested a propensity to enlarge the general authority in derogation of the local, and to amplify its own jurisdiction, which has justly incurred the public censure. But the abuse of a trust does not disprove its existence. And if no remedy of the abuse be practicable under the forms of the Constitution, I should prefer a resort to the Nation for an amendment of the Tribunal itself, to continual appeals from its controverted decisions to that Ultimate Arbiter.

In the year 1821, I was engaged in a correspondence with Judge Roane, which grew out of the proceedings of the Supreme Court of the U. S. Having said so much here I will send you a copy of my letters to him as soon as I can have a legible one made, that a fuller view of my ideas with respect to them may be before you.

I agree entirely with you on the subject of seriatim opinions by the Judges, which you have placed in so strong a light in your letter to Judge Johnson, whose example it seems is in favor of the practice. An argument addressed to others, all of whose dislikes to it are not known, may be a delicate experiment. My particular connexion with Judge Todd, whom I expect to see, may tempt me to touch on the subject; and, if encouraged, to present views of it wch. thro' him may find the way to his intimates.

In turning over some bundles of Pamphlets, I met with several Copies of a very small one which at the desire of my political associates I threw out in 1795. As it relates to the state of parties I inclose a Copy. It had the advantage of being written with the subject full & fresh in my mind, and the disadvantage of being hurried, at the close of a fatiguing session of Congs. by an impatience to return home, from which I was detained by that Job only. The temper of the pamphlet is explained if not excused by the excitements of the period.

Always & Affectionately yours.

To Henry Lee

Montpellier, June 25, 1824.

I have received, Sir, your letter of the 18th, inclosing the proposal of a new publication, under the title of "American Gazette & Literary Journal." Of the prospectus I cannot say less than that it is an interesting specimen of cultivated talents.

I must say at the same time that I think it concedes too much to a remedial power in the press over the spirit of party.

Besides the occasional and transient subjects on which parties are formed, they seem to have a permanent foundation in the variance of political opinions in free States, and of occupations and interests in all civilized States. The Constitution itself, whether written or prescriptive, influenced as its exposition and administration will be, by those causes, must be an unfailing source of party distinctions. And the very peculiarity which gives pre-eminent value to that of the United States, the partition of power between different governments, opens a new door for controversies and parties. There is nevertheless sufficient scope for combating the spirit of party, as far as it may not be necessary to fan the flame of liberty, in efforts to divert it from the more noxious channels; to moderate its violence, especially in the ascendant party; to elucidate the policy which harmonizes jealous interests; and particularly to give to the Constitution that just construction, which, with the aid of time and habit, may put an end to the more dangerous schisms otherwise growing out of it.

With a view to this last object, I entirely concur in the propriety of resorting to the sense in which the Constitution was accepted and ratified by the nation. In that sense alone it is the legitimate Constitution. And if that be not the guide in expounding it, there can be no security for a consistent and stable, more than for a faithful exercise of its powers. If the meaning of the text be sought in the changeable meaning of the words composing it, it is evident that the shape and attributes of the Government must partake of the changes to which the words and phrases of all living languages are constantly subject. What a metamorphosis would be produced in the code of law if all its ancient phraseology were to be taken

in its modern sense. And that the language of our Constitution is already undergoing interpretations unknown to its
founders, will I believe appear to all unbiased Enquirers into
the history of its origin and adoption. Not to look farther for
an example, take the word "consolidate" in the Address of the
Convention prefixed to the Constitution. It there and then
meant to give strength and solidity to the Union of the
States. In its current & controversial application it means a
destruction of the States, by transfusing their powers into the
government of the Union.

   On the other point touched in your letter, I fear I shall not
very soon be able to say anything. Notwithstanding the importance of such a work as that of Judge Johnson, and the
public standing of the author, I have never given it a reading.
I have put it off, as in several other voluminous cases, till I
could go through the task with a less broken attention. While
I find that the span of life is contracting much faster than the
demands on it can be discharged, I do not however abandon
the proposed perusal of both the "Life of Greene," and "the
Campaign of 1781."

To Peter S. DuPonceau

Dr. Sir   Montpellier Aug 1824.
   I recd. the copy of your discourse on the Jurisdiction of the
courts of the U. S. with which you favoured me, at a time
when I could not conveniently read it; and I have since been
obliged to do it with such interruptions that I am not sure of
having done entire justice to your investigations. I have certainly found in the volume ample evidence of the distinguished ability of which the public had been made sensible by
other fruits of your pen.
   I must say at the same time that I have not been made a
convert to the doctrine that the "Common Law" as such is a
part of the law of the U. S. in their federo-national capacity. I
can perceive no legitimate avenue for its admission beyond
the portions fairly embraced by the Common law terms used

in the Constitution, and by acts* of Congress authorized by the Constitution as necessary & proper for executing the powers which it vests in the Government.

A characteristic peculiarity of the Govt. of the U. States is, that its powers consist of special grants taken from the general mass of power, whereas other Govts. possess the general mass with special exceptions only. Such being the plan of the Constitution, it cannot well be supposed that the Body which framed it with so much deliberation, and with so manifest a purpose of specifying its objects, and defining its boundaries, would, if intending that the Common Law shd. be a part of the national code, have omitted to express or distinctly indicate the intention; when so many far inferior provisions are so carefully inserted, and such appears to have been the public view taken of the Instrument, whether we recur to the period of its ratification by the States, or to the federal practice under it.

That the Constitution is predicated on the existence of the Common Law cannot be questioned; because it borrows therefrom terms which must be explained by Com: Law authorities: but this no more implies a general adoption or recognition of it, than the use of terms embracing articles of the Civil Law would carry such an implication.

Nor can the Common Law be let in through the authority of the Courts. That the whole of it is within their jurisdiction, is never alledged, and a separation of the parts *suited* from those *not suited* to the peculiar structure & circumstances of the U. States involves questions of *expediency* & *discretion*, of a Legislative not Judicial character. On questions of criminal law & jurisdiction the strict rule of construction prescribed by the Com: Law itself would seem to bar at once an assumption of such a power by the Courts.

If the Common Law has been called our birthright, it has been done with little regard to any precise meaning. It could have been no more our birthright than the Statute law of

*By these the common Law or any other laws may be sanctioned or introduced within the territories or other places subject to the conclusive power of Legislation vested in Congress.

England, or than the English Constitution itself. If the one was brought by our ancestors with them, so must the others; and the whole consequently as it stood during the Dynasty of the Stuarts, the period of their emigration, with no other exceptions than such as necessarily resulted from inapplicability to the colonial state of things. As men our birthright was from a much higher source than the common or any other human law and of much greater extent than is imparted or admitted by the common law. And as far as it might belong to us as British subjects it must with its correlative obligations have expired when we ceased to be such. It would seem more correct therefore & preferable in every respect that the common law, even during the Colonial State, was in force not by virtue of its adhesion to the emigrants & their descendants in their individual capacity but by virtue of its adoption in their social & political capacity.

How far this adoption may have taken place through the mere agency of the courts cannot perhaps be readily traced. But such a mode of introducing laws not otherwise in force ought rather to be classed among the irregularities incident to the times & the occasion, than referred to any in G. Britain, where the courts though sometimes making legal innovations per saltus profess that these should grow out of a series of adjudications, gradually accommodating the law to the gradual change of circumstances in the ordinary progress of society. On sound principles, no change whatever in the state of the Law can be made but by the Legislative authority; Judicial decisions being not more competent to it than Executive proclamations.

But whatever may have been the mode or the process by which the Common law found its way into the colonial codes, no regular passage appears to have been opened for it into that of the U. S. other than through the two channels above mentioned; whilst every plea for an irregular one is taken away, by the provident article in the constitution for correcting its errors & supplying its defects. And although a frequent resort to this remedy be very undesirable, it may be a happy relief from the alternative of enduring an evil or getting rid of it by an open or surreptitious usurpation.

I must not forget however that it is not my intention to

enter into a critical, much less a controversial examination of the subject; and I turn with pleasure from points on which we may differ, to an important one on which I entirely agree with you. It has always appeared to me impossible to digest the unwritten law or even the penal part of it, into a text that would be a compleat substitute. A Justinian or Napoleon Code may ascertain, may elucidate, and even improve the existing law, but the meaning of its complex technical terms, in their application to particular cases, must be sought in like sources as before; and the smaller the compass of the text the more general must be its terms & the more necessary the resort to the usual guides in its particular applications.

With assurances of my high esteem I pray you Sir, to accept my unfeigned good wishes

To Thomas Jefferson

Dear Sir   Montpellier, Feby 8, 1825.
The letters from Mr Cabell are herein returned. I just see that he has succeeded in defeating the project for removing the College from Williamsburg.

I hope your concurrence in what I said of Mr Barbour will not divert your thoughts from others. It is possible that the drudgery of his profession, the uncertainty of Judicial appointment acceptable to him, and some other attractions at the University for his young family, might reconcile him to a removal thither; but I think the chance slender.

I have looked with attention over your intended proposal of a text book for the Law School. It is certainly very material that the true doctrines of liberty, as exemplified in our Political System, should be inculcated on those who are to sustain and may administer it. It is, at the same time, not easy to find standard books that will be both guides & guards for the purpose. Sidney & Locke are admirably calculated to impress on young minds the right of Nations to establish their own Governments, and to inspire a love of free ones; but afford no aid in guarding our Republican Charters against constructive violations. The Declaration of Independence, tho' rich in fundamental principles, and saying every thing that could be said in the same number of words, falls nearly under a like observation. The "Federalist" may fairly enough be regarded as the most authentic exposition of the text of the federal Constitution, as understood by the Body which prepared & the Authority which accepted it. Yet it did not foresee all the misconstructions which have occurred; nor prevent some that it did foresee. And what equally deserves remark, neither of the great rival Parties have acquiesced in all its comments. It may nevertheless be admissible as a School book, if any will be that goes so much into detail. It has been actually admitted into two Universities, if not more—those of Harvard and Rh: Island; but probably at the choice of the Professors, without any injunction from the superior authority. With respect to the Virginia Document of 1799, there may be more room for hesitation. Tho' corresponding with the predominant sense of the Nation; being of local origin & having reference to a state of Parties not yet extinct, an absolute prescription of it, might excite prejudices against the University as under Party Banners, and induce the more bigoted to withhold from it their sons, even when destined for other than the studies of the Law School. It may be added that the Document is not on every point satisfactory to all who belong to the same Party. Are we sure that to our brethren of the Board it is so? In framing a political creed, a like difficulty occurs as in the case of religion tho' the public right be very different in the two cases. If the Articles be in very general terms, they do not answer the purpose; if in very particular terms, they divide & exclude where meant to unite & fortify. The best that can be done in our case seems to be, to avoid the two extremes, by referring to selected Standards without requiring an unqualified conformity to them, which indeed might not in every instance be possible. The selection would give them authority with the Students, and might controul or counteract deviations of the Professor. I have, for your consideration, sketched a modification of the operative passage in your draught, with a view to relax the absoluteness of its injunction, and added to your list of Documents the Inaugural Speech and the Farewell Address of President Washington. They may help down what might be less readily swallowed, and contain nothing which is not good; unless it be the laudatory reference in the Address to the Treaty of 1795 with G. B. which ought not to weigh against the sound sentiments characterizing it.

After all, the most effectual safeguard against heretical intrusions into the School of Politics, will be an Able & Orthodox Professor, whose course of instruction will be an example to his successors, and may carry with it a sanction from the Visitors.

Affectionately yours.

Sketch.

And on the distinctive principles of the Government of our own State, and of that of the U. States, the best guides are to be found in—1. The Declaration of Independence, as the fundamental act of Union of these States. 2. the book known by the title of the "Federalist," being an Authority to which appeal is habitually made by all & rarely declined or denied by any, as evidence of the general opinion of those who framed & those who accepted the Constitution of the U. States on questions as to its genuine meaning. 3. the Resolutions of the General Assembly of Virga. in 1799, on the subject of the Alien & Sedition laws, which appeared to accord with the predominant sense of the people of the U. S. 4. The Inaugural Speech & Farewell Address of President Washington, as conveying political lessons of peculiar value; and that in the branch of the School of law which is to treat on the subject of Govt., these shall be used as the text & documents of the School.

To Thomas Jefferson

Dear Sir,   Montpellier, Feby 24, 1826.
Yours of the 17th was duly recd. The awkward state of the Law Professorship is truly distressing, but seems to be without immediate remedy. Considering the hopeless condition of Mr. Gilmour, a temporary appointment, if an acceptable

successor were at hand, whilst not indelicate towards the worthy moribond incumbent, might be regarded as equivalent to a permanent one. And if the hesitation of our Colleagues at Richmond has no reference to Mr. Terril, but is merely tenderness towards Mr. Gilmour, I see no objection to a communication to Mr. T. that would bring him to Virga. at once, and thus abridge the loss of time. The hardheartedness of the Legislature towards what ought to be the favorite offspring of the State, is as reproachful as deplorable. Let us hope that the reflections of another year, will produce a more parental sensibility.

I had noticed the disclosures at Richmond with feelings which I am sure I need not express; any more than the alleviation of them by the sequel. I had not been without fears, that the causes you enumerate were undermining your estate. But they did not reach the extent of the evil. Some of these causes were indeed forced on my attention by my own experience. Since my return to private life (and the case was worse during my absence in Public) such have been the unkind seasons, & the ravages of insects, that I have made but one tolerable crop of Tobacco, and but one of Wheat; the proceeds of both of which were greatly curtailed by mishaps in the sale of them. And having no resources but in the earth I cultivate, I have been living very much throughout on borrowed means. As a necessary consequence, my debts have swelled to an amount, which if called for at the present conjuncture, would give to my situation a degree of analogy to yours. Fortunately I am not threatened with any rigid pressure, and have the chance of better crops & prices, with the prospect of a more leisurely disposal of the property which must be a final resort.

You do not overrate the interest I feel in the University, as the Temple thro which alone lies the road to that of Liberty. But you entirely do my aptitude to be your successor in watching over its prosperity. It would be the pretension of a mere worshipper "remplacer" the Tutelary Genius of the Sanctuary. The best hope is, in the continuance of your cares, till they can be replaced by the stability and selfgrowth of the Institution. Little reliance can be put even on the fellowship of my services. The past year has given me sufficient intima-

tion of the infirmities in wait for me. In calculating the prob-
abilities of survivorship, the inferiority of my constitution
forms an equation at least with the seniority of yours.

It would seem that some interposition is meditated at
Richmond against the assumed powers of Internal Improvement; and in the mode recommended by Govr. Pleasants, in
which my letter to Mr. Ritchie concurred, of instructions to
the Senators in Congress. No better mode, can perhaps be
taken, if an interposition be likely to do good; a point on
which the opinion of the Virginia members at Washington
ought to have much weight. They can best judge of the tendency of such a measure at the present moment. The public
mind is certainly more divided on the subject than it lately
was. And it is not improbable that the question, whether the
powers exist, will more & more give way to the question, how
far they ought to be granted.

You cannot look back to the long period of our private
friendship & political harmony, with more affecting recollections than I do. If they are a source of pleasure to you, what
ought they not to be to me? We cannot be deprived of the
happy consciousness of the pure devotion to the public good
with which we discharged the trusts committed to us. And I
indulge a confidence that sufficient evidence will find its way
to another generation, to ensure, after we are gone, whatever
of justice may be withheld whilst we are here. The political
horizon is already yielding in your case at least, the surest au-
guries of it. Wishing & hoping that you may yet live to increase the debt which our Country owes you, and to witness
the increasing gratitude, which alone can pay it, I offer you
the fullest return of affectionate assurances.

To Nicholas P. Trist

Dear Sir   Montpellier, July 6, 1826.
I have just recd. yours of the 4th. A few lines from Dr.
Dunglison had prepared me for such a communication; and I
never doubted that the last Scene of our illustrious friend
would be worthy of the life which it closed. Long as this has

been spared to his Country & to those who loved him, a few years more were to have been desired for the sake of both. But we are more than consoled for the loss, by the gain to him; and by the assurance that he lives and will live in the memory and gratitude of the wise & good, as a luminary of Science, as a votary of liberty, as a model of patriotism, and as a benefactor of human kind. In these characters, I have known him, and not less in the virtues & charms of social life, for a period of fifty years, during which there has not been an interruption or diminution of mutual confidence and cordial friendship, for a single moment in a single instance. What I feel therefore now, need not, I should say, cannot, be expressed. If there be any possible way, in which I can *usefully* give evidence of it, do not fail to afford me an opportunity. I indulge a hope that the unforeseen event will not be permitted to impair *any* of the beneficial measures which were in progress or in project. It cannot be unknown that the anxieties of the deceased were for others, not for himself.

Accept my dear Sir, my best wishes for yourself, & for all with whom we sympathize; in which Mrs. M. most sincerely joins.

To Henry Colman

Dr Sir   Montpr, August 25, 1826.

I have read with pleasure the copy of your Oration on the 4th of July, obligingly sent me, and for which I beg you to accept my thanks.

With the merits which I have found in the Oration, may I be permitted to notice a passage, which tho' according with a language often held on the subject, I cannot but regard as at variance with reality.

In doing justice to the virtue and valour of the revolutionary army, you add as a signal proof of the former, their readiness in laying down their arms at the triumphant close of the war, "when they had the liberties of their Country within their grasp."

Is it a fact that they had the liberties of their country within their grasp; that the troops then in command, even if led on by their illustrious chief, and backed by the apostates from the revolutionary cause, could have brought under the Yoke the great body of their fellow Citizens, most of them with arms in their hands, no inconsiderable part fresh from the use of them, all inspired with rage at the patricidal attempt, and not only guided by the federal head, but organized & animated by their local Governments possessing the means of appealing to their interests, as well as other motives, should such an appeal be required?

I have always believed that if General Washington had yielded to a usurping ambition, he would have found an insuperable obstacle in the incorruptibility of a sufficient portion of those under his command, and that the exalted praise due to him & them, was derived not from a forbearance to effect a revolution within their power, but from a love of liberty and of country which there was abundant reason to believe, no facility of success could have seduced. I am not less sure that General Washington would have spurned a sceptre if within his grasp, than I am that it was out of his reach, if he had secretly sighed for it. It must be recollected also that the practicability of a successful usurpation by the army cannot well be admitted, without implying a folly or pusillanimity reproachful to the American character, and without casting some shade on the vital principle of popular Government itself.

If I have taken an undue liberty in these remarks, I have a pledge in the candour of which you have given proofs, that they will be pardoned, and that they will not be deemed, inconsistent with the esteem and cordial respect, which I pray you to accept.

To Joseph Cabell

Dear Sir   Montpr Sepr 18 1828.
    Your late letter reminds me of our Conversation on the constitutionality of the power in Congs. to impose a tariff for the encouragemt. of Manufactures; and of my promise to

sketch the grounds of the confident opinion I had expressed that it was among the powers vested in that Body. I had not forgotten my promise, & had even begun the task of fulfilling it; but frequent interruptions from other causes, being followed by a bilious indisposition, I have not been able sooner to comply with your request. The subjoined view of the subject, might have been advantageously expanded; but I leave that improvement to your own reflections and researches.

The Constitution vests in Congress expressly "the power to lay & collect taxes duties imposts & excises;" and "the power to regulate trade"

That the former Power, if not particularly expressed, would have been included in the latter, as one of the objects of a general power to regulate trade, is not necessarily impugned, as has been alledged, by its being so expressed. Examples of this sort, cannot sometimes be easily avoided, and are to be seen elsewhere in the Constitution. Thus the power "to define & punish offences agst. the law of Nations" includes the power, afterward particularly expressed "to make rules concerning captures &c., from offending Neutrals." So also, a power "to coin money," would doubtless include that of "regulating its value," had not the latter power been expressly inserted. The term taxes, if standing *alone*, would certainly have included, duties, imposts & excises. In another clause it is said, "no tax or duty shall be laid on imports," &c. Here the two terms are used as synonymous. And in another clause where it is said, "no State shall lay any imposts or duties" &c, the terms imposts & duties are synonymous. Pleonasms, tautologies & the promiscuous use of terms & phrases differing in their shades of meaning, (always to be expounded with reference to the context and under the controul of the general character & manifest scope of the Instrument in which they are found) are to be ascribed sometimes to the purpose of greater caution; sometimes to the imperfections of language; & sometimes to the imperfection of man himself. In this view of the subject, it was quite natural, however certainly the general power to regulate trade might include a power to impose duties on it, not to omit it in a clause enumerating the several modes of revenue authorized by the Constitution. In few cases could the "*ex majori cautela*" occur with more claim to respect.

Nor can it be inferred, as has been ingeniously attempted, that a power to regulate trade does not involve a power to tax it, from the distinction made in the original controversy with G. Britain, between a power to regulate trade with the Colonies & a power to tax them. A power to regulate trade between different parts of the Empire was confessedly *necessary*; and was admitted to lie, as far as that was the case in the British Parliament, the taxing part being at the same time denied to the Parliament, & asserted to be necessarily inherent in the Colonial Legislatures, as sufficient & the only safe depositories of the taxing power. So difficult was it nevertheless to maintain the distinction in practice, that the ingredient of revenue was occasionally overlooked or disregarded in the British regulations; as in the duty on sugar & Molasses imported into the Colonies. And it was fortunate that the attempt at an internal and direct tax in the case of the Stamp Act, produced a radical examination of the subject, before a regulation of trade with a view to revenue had grown into an established Authority. One thing at least is certain, that the main & admitted object of the Parliamentary *regulations* of trade with the Colonies, was the encouragement of *manufactures* in G. B.

But the present question is unconnected, with the former relations between G. B. and her Colonies, which were of a peculiar, a complicated, and, in several respects, of an undefined character. It is a simple question under the Constitution of the U. S. whether "the power to regulate trade with foreign nations" as a distinct & substantive item in the enumerated powers, embraces the object of encouraging by duties restrictions and prohibitions the manufactures & products of the Country? And the affirmative must be inferred from the following considerations:

1. The meaning of the Phrase "to regulate trade" must be sought in the general use of it, in other words in the objects to which the power was generally understood to be applicable, when the Phrase was inserted in the Constn.

2. The power has been understood and used by all commercial & manufacturing Nations as embracing the object of encouraging manufactures. It is believed that not a single exception can be named.

3. This has been particularly the case with G. B., whose commercial vocabulary is the parent of ours. A primary object of her commercial regulations is well known to have been the protection and encouragement of her manufactures

4. Such was understood to be a proper use of the power by the States most prepared for manufacturing industry, while retaining the power over their foreign trade. It was the aim of Virginia herself, as will presently appear, tho' at the time among the least prepared for such a use of her power to regulate trade.

5. Such a use of the power by Cong accords with the intention and expectation of the States in transferring the power over trade from themselves to the Govt. of the U. S. This was emphatically the case in the Eastern, the more manufacturing members of the Confederacy. Hear the language held in the Convention of Massts. p. 84, 86, 136.

By Mr. Dawes an advocate for the Constitution, it was observed: "our manufactures are another great subject which has recd. no encouragement by national Duties on foreign manufactures, and they never can by any authority in the Old Confedn" again "If we wish to *encourage our own manufactures*, to preserve our own commerce, to raise the value of our own lands, we must give Congs. the powers in question.

By Mr. Widgery, an opponent, "All we hear is, that the mercht. & farmer will flourish, & that the mechanic & tradesman are to make their fortunes directly, if the Constitution goes down.

The Convention of Massts. was the only one in N. Engd. whose debates have been preserved. But it cannot be doubted that the sentiment there expressed was common to the other States in that quarter, more especially to Connecticut & Rh Isld., the most thickly peopled of all the States, and having of course their thoughts most turned to the subject of manufactures. A like inference may be confidently applied to N. Jersey, whose debates in Convention have not been preserved. In the populous and manufacturing State of Pa., a partial account only of the debates having been published, nothing certain is known of what passed in her Convention on this point. But ample evidence may be found elsewhere, that regulations of trade for the encouragement of manufactures, were considered as within the power to be granted to the new Congress, as well as within the scope of the National Policy. Of the States south of Pena., the only two in whose Conventions the debates have been preserved are Virga & N. Carola., and from these no adverse inferences can be drawn. Nor is there the slightest indication that either of the two States farthest South, whose debates in Convention if preserved have not been made public, viewed the encouragement of manufactures as not within the general power over trade to be transferred to the Govt. of the U. S.

6 If Congress have not the power it is annihilated for the nation; a policy without example in any other nation, and not within the reason of the solitary one in our own. The example alluded to is the prohibition of a tax on exports which resulted from the apparent impossibility of raising in that mode a revenue from the States proportioned to the ability to pay it; the ability of some being derived in a great measure, not from their exports, but from their fisheries, from their freights and from commerce at large, in some of its branches altogether external to the U. S.; the profits from all which being invisible & intangible would escape a tax on exports. A tax on imports, on the other hand, being a tax on consumption which is in proportion to the ability of the consumers whencesoever derived was free from that inequality.

7 If revenue be the sole object of a legitimate impost, and the encouragt. of domestic articles be not within the power of regulating trade it wd. follow that no monopolizing or unequal regulations of foreign Nations could be counteracted; that neither the staple articles of subsistence nor the essential implements for the public safety could under any circumstances be ensured or fostered at home by regulations of commerce, the usual & most convenient mode of providing for both; and that the American navigation, tho the source of naval defence, of a cheapening competition in carrying our valuable & bulky articles to Market, and of an independent carriage of them during foreign wars, when a foreign navigation might be withdrawn, must be at once abandoned or speedily destroyed; it being evident that a tonnage duty merely

in foreign ports agst. our vessels, and an exemption from such a duty in our ports in favor of foreign vessels, must have the inevitable effect of banishing ours from the Ocean.

To assume a power to protect our navigation, & the cultivation & fabrication of all articles requisite for the Public safety as incident to the war power, would be a more latitudinary construction of the text of the Constitution, than to consider it as embraced by the specified power to regulate trade; a power which has been exercised by all Nations for those purposes; and which effects those purposes with less of interference with the authority & conveniency of the States, than might result from internal & direct modes of encouraging the articles, any of which modes would be authorized as far as deemed "necessary & proper," by considering the Power as an incidental Power.

8 That the encouragement of Manufactures, was an object of the power, to regulate trade, is proved by the use made of the power for that object, in the first session of the first Congress under the Constitution; when among the members present were so many who had been members of the federal Convention which framed the Constitution, and of the State Conventions which ratified it; each of these classes consisting also of members who had opposed & who had espoused, the Constitution in its actual form. It does not appear from the printed proceedings of Congress on that occasion that the power was denied by any of them. And it may be remarked that members from Virga. in particular, as well of the antifederal as the federal party, the names then distinguishing those who had opposed and those who had approved the Constitution, did not hesitate to propose duties, & to suggest even prohibitions, in favor of several articles of her production. By one a duty was proposed on mineral Coal in favor of the Virginia Coal-Pits; by another a duty on Hemp was proposed to encourage the growth of that article; and by a third a prohibition even of foreign Beef was suggested as a measure of sound policy. (See *Lloyd's Debates.*)

A further evidence in support of the Cons, power to protect & foster manufactures by regulations of trade, an evidence that ought of itself to settle the question, is the uniform & practical sanction given to the power, by the Genl.

Govt. for nearly 40 years with a concurrence or acquiescence of every State Govt. throughout the same period; and it may be added thro all the vicissitudes of Party, which marked the period. No novel construction however ingeniously devised, or however respectable and patriotic its Patrons, can withstand the weight of such authorities, or the unbroken current of so prolonged & universal a practice. And well it is that this cannot be done without the intervention of the same authority which made the Constitution. If it could be so done, there would be an end to that stability in Govt. and in Laws which is essential to good Govt. & good Laws; a stability, the want of which is the imputation which has at all times been levelled agst. Republicanism with most effect by its most dexterous adversaries. The imputation ought never therefore to be countenanced, by innovating constructions, without any plea of a precipitancy or a paucity of the constructive precedents they oppose; without any appeal to material facts newly brought to light; and without any claim to a better knowledge of the original evils & inconveniences, for which remedies were needed, the very best keys to the true object & meaning of all laws & constitutions.

And may it not be fairly left to the unbiased judgment of all men of experience & of intelligence, to decide which is most to be relied on for a sound and safe test of the meaning of a Constitution, a uniform interpretation by all the successive authorities under it, commencing with its birth, and continued for a long period, thro' the varied state of political contests, or the opinion of every new Legislature heated as it may be by the strife of parties, or warped as often happens by the eager pursuit of some favourite object; or carried away possibly by the powerful eloquence, or captivating address of a few popular Statesmen, themselves influenced, perhaps, by the same misleading causes. If the latter test is to prevail, every new Legislative opinion might make a new Constitution; as the foot of every new Chancellor would make a new standard of measure.

It is seen with no little surprize, that an attempt has been made, in a highly respectable quarter, and at length reduced to a resolution formally proposed in Congress, to substitute for the power of Congs. to regulate trade so as to encourage manufactures, a power in the several States to do so, with the consent of that Body; and this expedient is derived from a clause in the 10 sect. of Art: I. of the Const; which says:

To say nothing of the clear indications in the Journal of the Convention of 1787, that the clause was intended merely to provide for expences incurred by particular States in their inspection laws, and in such improvements as they might chuse to make in their Harbours & rivers with the sanction of Congr., objects to which the reserved power has been applied in several instances, at the request of Virginia & of Georgia, how could it ever be imagined that any State would wish to tax its own trade for the encouragement of manufactures, if possessed of the authority, or could in fact do so, if wishing it?

A tax on imports would be a tax on its own consumption; and the nett proceeds going, according to the clause, not into its own treasury, but into the treasury of the U. S., the State would tax itself separately for the equal gain of all the other States; and as far as the manufactures so encouraged might succeed in ultimately increasing the Stock in Market, and lowering the price by competition, this advantage also, procured at the sole expence of the State, would be common to all the others.

But the very suggestion of such an expedient to any State would have an air of mockery, when its *experienced* impracticability is taken into view. No one who recollects or recurs to the period when the power over Commerce was in the individual States, & separate attempts were made to tax or otherwise regulate it, needs be told that the attempts were not only abortive, but by demonstrating the necessity of general & uniform regulations gave the original impulse to the Constitutional reform which provided for such regulations.

To refer a State therefore to the exercise of a power as reserved to her by the Constitution, the impossibility of exercising which was an inducement to adopt the Constitution, is, of all remedial devices the last that ought to be brought forward. And what renders it the more extraordinary is that, as the tax on commerce as far as it could be separately collected, instead of belonging to the treasury of the State as previous to the Constn. would be a tribute to the U. S.; the State would be in a worse condition, after the adoption of the Constitution, than before, in relation to an important interest, the improvement of which was a particular object in adopting the Constitution.

Were Congress to make the proposed declaration of consent to State tariffs in favour of State manufactures, and the permitted attempts did not defeat themselves, what would be the situation of States deriving their foreign supplies through the ports of other States? It is evident that they might be compelled to pay, in their consumption of particular articles imported, a tax for the common treasury not common to all the States, without having any manufacture or product of their own to partake of the contemplated benefit.

Of the impracticability of separate regulations of trade, & the resulting necessity of general regulations, no State was more sensible than Virga. She was accordingly among the most earnest for granting to Congress a power adequate to the object. On more occasions than one in the proceedings of her Legislative Councils, it was recited, "that the relative situation of the States had been found on *trial* to require *uniformity* in their comercial regulations as the *only* effectual policy for obtaining in the ports of foreign nations a stipulation of privileges reciprocal to those enjoyed by the subjects of such nations in the ports of the U. S., for preventing animosities which cannot fail to arise among the several States from the interference of partial & separate regulations; and for *deriving from comerce* such aids to the public *revenue* as it ought to contribute," &c.

During the delays & discouragts. experienced in the attempts to invest Congs. with the necessary powers, the State of Virga. made various trials of what could be done by her individual laws. She ventured on duties & imposts as a source of Revenue; Resolutions were passed at one time to encourage & protect her own navigation & ship-building; and in consequence of complaints & petitions from Norfolk, Alexa. & other places, agst. the monopolizing navigation laws of G. B., particularly in the trade *between the U. S. & the British W. Indies*, she deliberated with a purpose controuled only by the inefficacy of separate measures, on the experiment of forcing a reciprocity by prohibitory regulations of her own. (See Journal of Hs. of Delegates in 1785.)

The effect of her separate attempts to raise revenue by duties on imports, soon appeared in Representations from her Merchts., that the commerce of the State was banished by them into other channels, especially of Maryd., where imports were less burdened than in Virginia. (See do. 1786.)

Such a tendency of separate regulations was indeed too manifest to escape anticipation. Among the projects prompted by the want of a federal authy. over Comerce, was that of a concert, first proposed on the part of Maryd. for a uniformity of regulations between the 2 States, and comissioners were appointed for that purpose. It was soon perceived however that the concurrence of Pena. was as necessy. to Maryd. as of Maryd. to Virga., and the concurrence of Pennsylvania was accordingly invited. But Pa. could no more concur witht. N. Y. than Md. witht. Pa. nor N. Y. witht. the concurrence of Boston &c.

These projects were superseded for the moment by that of the Convention at Annapolis in 1786, and forever by the Convn at Pha in 1787, and the Consn. which was the fruit of it.

There is a passage in Mr. Necker's work on the finances of France which affords a signal illustration of the difficulty of collecting, in contiguous communities, indirect taxes when not the same in all, by the violent means resorted to against smuggling from one to another of them. Previous to the late revolutionary war in that Country, the taxes were of very different rates in the different Provinces; particularly the tax on salt which was high in the interior Provinces & low in the maritime; and the tax on Tobacco, which was very high in general whilst in some of the Provinces the use of the article was altogether free. The consequence was that the standing army of Patrols agst smuggling, had swollen to the number of twenty three thousand; the annual arrests of men women & children engaged in smuggling, to five thousand five hundred & fifty; and the number annually arrested on account of Salt & Tobacco alone, to seventeen or eighteen hundred, more than three hundred of whom were consigned to the terrible punishment of the Galleys.

May it not be regarded as among the Providential blessings to these States, that their geographical relations multiplied as they will be by artificial channels of intercourse, give such additional force to the many obligations to cherish that Union which alone secures their peace, their safety, and their prosperity. Apart from the more obvious & awful consequences of their entire separation into Independent Sovereignties, it is worthy of special consideration, that divided from each other as they must be by narrow waters & territorial lines merely, the facility of surreptitious introductions of contraband articles, would defeat every attempt at revenue in the easy and indirect modes of impost and excise; so that whilst their expenditures would be necessarily & vastly increased by their new situation, they would, in providing for them, be limited to direct taxes on land or other property, to arbitrary assessments on invisible funds, & to the odious tax on persons.

You will observe that I have confined myself, in what has been said to the constitutionality & expediency of the power in congress to encourage domestic products by regulations of commerce. In the exercise of the power, they are responsible to their Constituents, whose right & duty it is, in that as in all other cases, to bring their measures to the test of justice & of the general good.

Speech in the
Virginia Constitutional Convention

Although the actual posture of the subject before the Committee might admit a full survey of it, it is not my purpose, in rising, to enter into the wide field of discussion, which has called forth a display of intellectual resources and varied powers of eloquence, that any country might be proud of, and which I have witnessed with the highest gratification. Having been, for a very long period, withdrawn from any participation in proceedings of deliberative bodies, and under other disqualifications now of which I am deeply sensible, though perhaps less sensible than others may perceive that I ought to be, I shall not attempt more than a few observations, which may suggest the views I have taken of the subject, and which will consume but little of the time of the Committee, become precious. It is sufficiently obvious, that persons now and property are the two great subjects on which Governments are to act; and that the rights of persons, and the rights of property, are the objects, for the protection of which Government was instituted. These rights cannot well be separated. The personal right to acquire property, which is a natural right, gives to property, when acquired, a right to protection, as a social right. The essence of Government is power; and power, lodged as it must be in human hands, will ever be liable to abuse. In monarchies, the interests and happiness of all may be sacrificed to the caprice and passions of a despot. In aristocracies, the rights and welfare of the many may be sacrificed to the pride and cupidity of the few. In republics, the great danger is, that the majority may not sufficiently respect the rights of the minority. Some gentlemen, consulting the purity and generosity of their own minds, without adverting to the lessons of experience, would find a security against that danger, in our social feelings; in a respect for character; in the dictates of the monitor within; in the interests of individuals; in the aggregate interests of the community. But man is known to be a selfish, as well as a social being. Respect for character, though often a salutary restraint, is but too often overruled by other motives. When numbers of men act in a body, respect for character is often lost, just in proportion as it is necessary to control what is not right. We all know that conscience is not a sufficient safe-guard; and besides, that conscience itself may be deluded; may be misled, by an unconscious bias, into acts which an enlightened conscience would forbid. As to the permanent interest of individuals in the aggregate interests of the community, and in the proverbial maxim, that honesty is the best policy, present temptation is often found to be an overmatch for those considerations. These favourable attributes of the human character are all valuable, as auxiliaries; but they will not serve as a substitute for the coercive provision belonging to Government and Law. They will always, in proportion as they prevail, be favourable to a mild administration of both: but they can never be relied on as a guaranty of the rights of the minority against a majority disposed to take unjust advantage of its power. The only effectual safeguard to the rights of the minority, must be laid in such a basis and structure of the Government itself, as may afford, in a certain degree, directly or indirectly, a defensive authority in behalf of a minority having right on its side.

To come more nearly to the subject before the Committee, viz.: that peculiar feature in our community, which calls for a peculiar division in the basis of our government, I mean the coloured part of our population. It is apprehended, if the power of the Commonwealth shall be in the hands of a majority, who have no interest in this species of property, that, from the facility with which it may be oppressed by excessive taxation, injustice may be done to its owners. It would seem, therefore, if we can incorporate that interest into the basis of our system, it will be the most apposite and effectual security that can be devised. Such an arrangement is recommended to me by many very important considerations. It is due to justice; due to humanity; due to truth; to the sympathies of our nature; in fine, to our character as a people, both abroad and at home, that they should be considered, as much as possible, in the light of human beings, and not as mere property. As such, they are acted upon by our laws, and have an interest in our laws. They may be considered as making a part, though a degraded part, of the families to which they belong.

If they had the complexion of the Serfs in the North of

Europe, or of the Villeins formerly in England; in other terms, if they were of our own complexion, much of the difficulty would be removed. But the mere circumstance of complexion cannot deprive them of the character of men. The Federal number, as it is called, is particularly recommended to attention in forming a basis of Representation, by its simplicity, its certainty, its stability, and its permanency. Other expedients for securing justice in the case of taxation, while they amount in pecuniary effect, to the same thing, have been found liable to great objections: and I do not believe that a majority of this Convention is disposed to adopt them, if they can find a substitute they can approve. Nor is it a small recommendation of the Federal number, in my view, that it is in conformity to the ratio recognized in the Federal Constitution. The cases, it is true, are not precisely the same, but there is more of analogy than might at first be supposed. If the coloured population were equally diffused through the State, the analogy would fail; but existing as it does, in large masses, in particular parts of it, the distinction between the different parts of the State, resembles that between the slave-holding and non-slave-holding States: and, if we reject a doctrine in our own State, whilst we claim the benefit of it in our relations to other States, other disagreeable consequences may be added to the charge of inconsistency, which will be brought against us. If the example of our sister States is to have weight, we find that in Georgia, the Federal number is made the basis of Representation in both branches of their Legislature; and I do not learn, that any dissatisfaction or inconvenience has flowed from its adoption. I wish we could know more of the manner in which particular organizations of Government operate in other parts of the United States. There would be less danger of being misled into error, and we should have the advantage of their experience, as well as our own. In the case I mention, there can, I believe, be no error.

Whether, therefore, we be fixing a basis of Representation, for the one branch or the other of our Legislature, or for both, in a combination with other principles, the Federal ratio is a favourite resource with me. It entered into my earliest views of the subject, before this Convention was assembled: and though I have kept my mind open, have listened to every proposition which has been advanced, and given to them all a candid consideration, I must say, that in my judgment, we shall act wisely in preferring it to others, which have been brought before us. Should the Federal number be made to enter into the basis in one branch of the Legislature, and not into the other, such an arrangement might prove favourable to the slaves themselves. It may be, and I think it has been suggested, that those who have themselves no interest in this species of property, are apt to sympathise with the slaves, more than may be the case with their masters; and would, therefore, be disposed, when they had the ascendancy, to protect them from laws of an oppressive character, whilst the masters, who have a common interest with the slaves, against undue taxation, which must be paid out of their labour, will be their protectors when they have the ascendancy.

The Convention is now arrived at a point, where we must agree on some common ground, all sides relaxing in their opinions, not changing, but mutually surrendering a part of them. In framing a Constitution, great difficulties are necessarily to be overcome; and nothing can ever overcome them, but a spirit of compromise. Other nations are surprised at nothing so much as our having been able to form Constitutions in the manner which has been exemplified in this country. Even the union of so many States, is, in the eyes of the world, a wonder; the harmonious establishment of a common Government over them all, a miracle. I cannot but flatter myself, that without a miracle, we shall be able to arrange all difficulties. I never have despaired, notwithstanding all the threatening appearances we have passed through. I have now more than a hope—a consoling confidence, that we shall at last find, that our labours have not been in vain.

December 2, 1829

A Sketch Never Finished Nor Applied

As the weakness and wants of man naturally lead to an association of individuals, under a common authority, whereby each may have the protection of the whole against danger from without, and enjoy in safety within, the advantages of social intercourse, and an exchange of the necessaries & comforts of life: in like manner feeble communities, independent of each other, have resorted to a Union, less intimate, but with common Councils, for the common safety agst. powerful neighbors, and for the preservation of justice and peace among themselves. Ancient history furnishes examples of these confederal associations, tho' with a very imperfect account, of their structure, and of the attributes and functions of the presiding Authority. There are examples of modern date also, some of them still existing, the modifications and transactions of which are sufficiently known.

It remained for the British Colonies, now United States, of North America, to add to those examples, one of a more interesting character than any of them: which led to a system without a example ancient or modern, a system founded on popular rights, and so combing. a federal form with the forms of individual Republics, as may enable each to supply the defects of the other and obtain the advantages of both.

Whilst the Colonies enjoyed the protection of the parent Country as it was called, against foreign danger; and were secured by its superintending controul, against conflicts among themselves, they continued independent of each other, under a common, tho' limited dependence, on the parental Authority. When however the growth of the offspring in strength and in wealth, awakened the jealousy and tempted the avidity of the parent, into schemes of usurpation & exaction, the obligation was felt by the former of uniting their counsels and efforts to avert the impending calamity.

As early as the year 1754, indications having been given of a design in the British Government to levy contributions on the Colonies, without their consent; a meeting of Colonial deputies took place at Albany, which attempted to introduce a compromising substitute, that might at once satisfy the

British requisitions, and save their own rights from violation. The attempt had no other effect, than by bringing these rights into a more conspicuous view, to invigorate the attachment to them, on one side; and to nourish the haughty & encroaching spirit on the other.

In 1774. The progress made by G. B. in the open assertion of her pretensions, and in the apprehended purpose of otherwise maintaining them than by Legislative enactments and declarations, had been such that the Colonies did not hesitate to assemble, by their deputies, in a formal Congress, authorized to oppose to the British innovations whatever measures might be found best adapted to the occasion; without however losing sight of an eventual reconciliation.

The dissuasive measures of that Congress, being without effect, another Congress was held in 1775, whose pacific efforts to bring about a change in the views of the other party, being equally unavailing, and the commencement of actual hostilities having at length put an end to all hope of reconciliation; the Congress finding moreover that the popular voice began to call for an entire & perpetual dissolution of the political ties which had connected them with G. B., proceeded on the memorable 4th of July, 1776 to declare the 13 Colonies, Independent States.

During the discussions of this solemn Act, a Committee consisting of a member from each colony had been appointed to prepare & digest a form of Confederation, for the future management of the common interests, which had hitherto been left to the discretion of Congress, guided by the exigences of the contest, and by the known intentions or occasional instructions of the Colonial Legislatures.

It appears that as early as the 21st. of July 1775, A plan entitled "Articles of Confederation & *perpetual* Union of the Colonies" had been sketched by Docr. Franklin, the plan being on that day submitted by him to Congress; and tho' not copied into their Journals remaining on their files in his handwriting. But notwithstanding the term "perpetual" observed in the title, the articles provided expressly for the event of a return of the Colonies to a connection with G. Britain.

This sketch became a basis for the plan reported by the Come. on the 12 of July, now also remaining on the files of

Congress, in the handwriting of Mr. Dickinson. The plan, tho' dated after the Declaration of Independence, was probably drawn up before that event; since the name of *Colonies*, not *States* is used throughout the draught. The plan reported, was debated and amended from time to time, till the 17th. of November 1777, when it was agreed to by Congress, and proposed to the Legislatures of the States, with an explanatory and recommendatory letter. The ratifications of these by their Delegates in Congs. duly authorized took place at successive dates; but were not compleated till March 1. 1781. when Maryland who had made it a prerequisite that the vacant lands acquired from the British Crown should be a Common fund, yielded to the persuasion that a final & formal establishment of the federal Union & Govt. would make a favorable impression not only on other foreign Nations, but on G. B. herself.

The great difficulty experienced in so framing the fedl. system as to obtain the unanimity required for its due sanction, may be inferred from the long interval, and recurring discussions, between the commencement and completion of the work; from the changes made during its progress; from the language of Congs. when proposing it to the States, wch. dwelt on the impracticability of devising a system acceptable to all of them; from the reluctant assent given by some; and the various alterations proposed by others; and by a tardiness in others again which produced a special address to them from Congs. enforcing the duty of sacrificing local considerations and favorite opinions to the public safety, and the necessary harmony: Nor was the assent of some of the States finally yielded without strong protests against particular articles, and a reliance on future amendments removing their objections.

It is to be recollected, no doubt, that these delays might be occasioned in some degree, by an occupation of the public Councils both general & local, with the deliberations and measures, essential to a Revolutionary struggle; But there must have been a balance for these causes, in the obvious motives to hasten the establishment of a regular and efficient Govt; and in the tendency of the crisis to repress opinions and pretensions, which might be inflexible in another state of things.

The principal difficulties which embarrassed the progress, and retarded the completion of the plan of Confederation, may be traced to 1. the natural repugnance of the parties to a relinquishment of power: 2 a natural jealousy of its abuse in other hands than their own: 3 the rule of suffrage among parties unequal in size, but equal in sovereignty. 4 the ratio of contributions in money and in troops, among parties, whose inequality in size did not correspond with that of their wealth, or of their military or free population. 5. the selection and definition of the powers, at once necessary to the federal head, and safe to the several members.

To these sources of difficulty, incident to the formation of all such Confederacies, were added two others one of a temporary, the other of a permanent nature. The first was the case of the Crown lands, so called because they had been held by the British Crown, and being ungranted to individuals when its authority ceased, were considered by the States within whose charters or asserted limits they lay, as devolving on them; whilst it was contended by the others, that being wrested from the dethroned authority, by the equal exertion of all, they resulted of right and in equity to the benefit of all. The lands being of vast extent and of growing value, were the occasion of much discussion & heart-burning; & proved the most obstinate of the impediments to an earlier consummation of the plan of federal Govt. The State of Maryland the last that acceded to it held out as already noticed, till March 1, 1781, and then yielded only to the hope that by giving a stable & authoritative character to the Confederation, a successful termination of the Contest might be accelerated. The dispute was happily compromised by successive surrenders of portions of the territory by the States having exclusive claims to it, and acceptances of them by Congress.

The other source of dissatisfaction was the peculiar situation of some of the States, which having no convenient ports for foreign commerce, were subject to be taxed by their neighbors, thro whose ports, their commerce was carryed on. New Jersey, placed between Phila. & N. York, was likened to a cask tapped at both ends; and N. Carolina, between Virga. & S. Carolina to a patient bleeding at both arms. The Articles of Confederation provided no remedy for the complaint:

which produced a strong protest on the part of N. Jersey; and never ceased to be a source of dissatisfaction & discord, until the new Constitution, superseded the old.

But the radical infirmity of the "arts. of Confederation" was the dependence of Congs. on the voluntary and simultaneous compliance with its Requisitions, by so many independent Communities, each consulting more or less its particular interests & convenience and distrusting the compliance of the others. Whilst the paper emissions of Congs. continued to circulate they were employed as a sinew of war, like gold & silver. When that ceased to be the case, the fatal defect of the political System was felt in its alarming force. The war was merely kept alive and brought to a successful conclusion by such foreign aids and temporary expedients as could be applied; a hope prevailing with many, and a wish with all, that a state of peace, and the sources of prosperity opened by it, would give to the Confederacy in practice, the efficiency which had been inferred from its theory.

The close of the war however brought no cure for the public embarrassments. The States relieved from the pressure of foreign danger, and flushed with the enjoyment of independent and sovereign power; [instead of a diminished disposition to part with it,] persevered in omissions and in measures incompatible with their relations to the Federal Govt and with those among themselves;

Having served as a member of Congs. through the period between Mar. 1780 & the arrival of peace in 1783, I had become intimately acquainted with the public distresses and the causes of them. I had observed the successful opposition to every attempt to procure a remedy by new grants of power to Congs. I had found moreover that despair of success hung over the compromising provision of April 1783 for the public necessities which had been so elaborately planned, and so impressively recommended to the States.* Sympathizing, under this aspect of affairs, in the alarm of the friends of free Govt, at the threatened danger of an abortive result to the great & perhaps last experiment in its favour, I could not be insensible to the obligation to co-operate as far as I could in averting the

*See address of Congress.

calamity. With this view I acceded to the desire of my fellow Citizens of the County that I should be one of its representatives in the Legislature, hoping that I might there best contribute to inculcate the critical posture to which the Revolutionary cause was reduced, and the merit of a leading agency of the State in bringing about a rescue of the Union and the blessings of liberty staked on it, from an impending catastrophe.

It required but little time after taking my seat in the House of Delegates in May 1784 to discover that, however favorable the general disposition of the State might be towards the Confederacy the Legislature retained the aversion of its predecessors to transfers of power from the State to the Govt. of the Union; notwithstanding the urgent demands of the Federal Treasury; the glaring inadequacy of the authorized mode of supplying it, the rapid growth of anarchy in the Fedl. System, and the animosity kindled among the States by their conflicting regulations.

The temper of the Legislature & the wayward course of its proceedings may be gathered from the Journals of its Sessions in the years 1784 & 1785.

The failure however of the varied propositions in the Legislature, for enlarging the powers of Congress, the continued failure of the efforts of Congs. to obtain from them the means of providing for the debts of the Revolution; and of countervailing the commercial laws of G. B. a source of much irritation & agst. which the separate efforts of the States were found worse than abortive; these Considerations with the lights thrown on the whole subject, by the free & full discussion it had undergone led to an general acquiescence in the Resoln. passed, on the 21. of Jany 1786. which proposed & invited a meeting of Deputies from all the States to "insert the Resol (See Journal.) 1.

The resolution had been brought forward some weeks before on the failure of a proposed grant of power to Congress to collect a revenue from commerce, which had been abandoned by its friends in consequence of material alterations made in the grant by a Committee of the whole. The Resolution tho introduced by Mr. Tyler an influencial member, who having never served in Congress, had more the ear

of the House than those whose services there exposed them
to an imputable bias, was so little acceptable that it was not
then persisted in. Being now revived by him, on the last day
of the Session, and being the alternative of adjourning without any effort for the crisis in the affairs of the Union, it obtained a general vote; less however with some of its friends
from a confidence in the success of the experiment than from
a hope that it might prove a step to a more comprehensive &
adequate provision for the wants of the Confederacy.

It happened also that Commissioners who had been appointed by Virga. & Maryd. to settle the jurisdiction on waters
dividing the two States had, apart from their official reports,
recommended a uniformity in the regulations of the 2 States
on several subjects & particularly on those having relation to
foreign trade. It apeared at the same time that Maryd. had
deemed a concurrence of her neighbors Pena. & Delaware
indispensable in such a case, who for like reasons would require that of their neighbors. So apt and forceable an illustration of the necessity of a uniformity throughout all the States
could not but favour the passage of a Resolution which proposed a Convention having that for its object.

The commissioners appointed by the Legisl: & who attended the Convention were E. Randolph the Attorney of the
State, St. Geo: Tucker & J. M. The designation of the time &
place for its meeting to be proposed and communicated to
the States having been left to the Comrs. they named for the
time early September and for the place the City of Annapolis
avoiding the residence of Congs. and large Commercial Cities
as liable to suspicions of an extraneous influence.

Altho the invited Meeting appeared to be generally favored,
five States only assembled; some failing to make appointments, and some of the individuals appointed not hastening
their attendance, the result in both cases being ascribed
mainly, to a belief that the time had not arrived for such a political reform, as might be expected from a further experience
of its necessity.

But in the interval between the proposal of the Convention
and the time of its meeting, such had been the advance of
public opinion in the desired direction, stimulated as it had

been by the effect of the contemplated object, of the meeting, in turning the genal attention to the Critical State of things, and in calling forth the sentiments and exertions of the most enlightened & influencial patriots, that the Convention thin as it was did not scruple to decline the limited task assigned to it and to recommend to the States a Convention with powers adequate to the occasion. Nor was it unnoticed that the commission of the N. Jersey Deputation, had extended its object to a general provision for the exigencies of the Union. A recommendation for this enlarged purpose was accordingly reported by a Come. to whom the subject had been referred. It was drafted by Col: H. and finally agreed to unanimously in the following form. Insert it.

The recommendation was well recd. by the Legislature of Virga. which happened to be the *first* that *acted* on it, and the example of her compliance was made as conciliatory and impressive as possible. The Legislature were unanimous or very nearly so on the occasion, and as a proof of the magnitude & solemnity attached to it, they placed Genl. W. at the head of the Deputation from the State; and as a proof of the deep interest he felt in the case he overstepped the obstacles to his acceptance of the appointment.

The law complying with the recommendation from Annapolis was in the terms following:

A resort to a General Convention to remodel the Confederacy, was not a new idea. It had entered at an early date into the conversations and speculations of the most reflecting & foreseeing observers of the inadequacy of the powers allowed to Congress. In a pamphlet published in May 81 at the seat of Congs. Pelatiah Webster an able tho' not conspicuous Citizen, after discussing the fiscal system of the U. States, and suggesting among other remedial provisions including a national Bank remarks that "the Authority of Congs. at present is very inadequate to the performance of their duties; and this indicates the necessity of their calling a *Continental Convention* for the express purpose of ascertaining, defining, enlarging, and limiting, the duties & powers of their Constitution."

On the 1. day of Apl. 1783, Col. Hamilton, in a debate in Congs. observed that

He alluded probably to [see Life of Schuyler in Longacre

It does not appear however that his expectation had been fulfilled.]

In a letter to J. M. from R. H. Lee then President of Congs. dated Novr. 26, 1784 He says

The answer of J. M. remarks

In 1785, Noah Webster whose pol. & other valuable writings had made him known to the public, in one of his publications of American policy brought into view the same resort for supplying the defects of the Fedl. System [see his life in Longacre]

The proposed & expected Convention at Annapolis the first of a general character that appears to have been realized, & the state of the public mind awakened by it had attracted the particular attention of Congs. and favored the idea there of a Convention with fuller powers for amending the Confederacy.

It does not appear that in any of these cases, the reformed system was to be otherwise sanctioned than by the Legislative authy. of the States; nor whether or how far, a change was to be made in the structure of the Depository of Federal powers.

The act of Virga. providing for the Convention at Philada., was succeeded by appointments from other States as their Legislatures were assembled, the appointments being selections from the most experienced & highest standing Citizens. Rh. I. was the only exception to a compliance with the recommendation from Annapolis, well known to have been swayed by an obdurate adherence to an advantage which her position gave her of taxing her neighbors thro' their consumption of imported supplies, an advantage which it was foreseen would be taken from her by a revisal of the "Articles of Confederation.

As the pub. mind had been ripened for a salutary Reform of the pol. System, in the interval between the proposal & the meeting, of Comrs. at Annapolis, the interval between the last event, and the meeting of Deps. at Phila had continued to develop more & more the necessity & the extent of a Systematic provision for the preservation and Govt. of the Union; among the ripening incidents was the Insurrection of Shays, in Massts. against her Govt; which was with difficulty suppressed,

notwithstanding the influence on the insurgents of an apprehended interposition of the Fedl. troops.

At the date of the Convention, the aspect & retrospect of
the pol: condition of the U. S. could not but fill the pub.
mind with a gloom which was relieved only by a hope that so
select a Body would devise an adequate remedy for the existing and prospective evils so impressively demanding it.

It was seen that the public debt rendered so sacred by the
cause in which it had been incurred remained without any
provision for its payment. The reiterated and elaborate efforts
of Cong. to procure from the States a more adequate power
to raise the means of payment had failed. The effect of the ordinary requisitions of Congress had only displayed the inefficiency of the authy. making them; none of the States having
duly complied with them, some having failed altogether or
nearly so; and in one instance, that of N. Jersey a compliance
was expressly refused; nor was more yielded to the expostulations of members of Congs. deputed to her Legislature, than
a mere repeal of the law, without a compliance. [see letter of
Grayson to J. M.

The want of Authy. in Congs. to regulate Commerce had
produced in Foreign nations particularly G. B. a monopolizing policy injurious to the trade of the U. S. and destructive
to their navigation; the imbecilicity and anticipated dissolution of the Confederacy extinguishg. all apprehensions of a
Countervailing policy on the part of the U. States.

The same want of a general power over Commerce, led to
an exercise of the power separately, by the States, wch not
only proved abortive, but engendered rival, conflicting and
angry regulations. Besides the vain attempts to supply their
respective treasuries by imposts, which turned their commerce
into the neighbouring ports, and to co-erce a relaxation of
the British monopoly of the W. Inda. navigation, which was
attempted by Virga. [see the Journal of   ] the States
having ports for foreign commerce, taxed & irritated the adjoining States, trading thro' them, as N. Y. Pena. Virga. & S.
Carolina. Some of the States, as Connecticut, taxed imports
as from Massts. higher than imports even from G. B. of wch
Massts. complained to Virga and doubtless to other States.
[See letter of J. M. In sundry instances as of N. Y. N. J. Pa. &

Maryd. [see   ] the navigation laws treated the Citizens
other States as aliens.

In certain cases the authy. of the Confederacy was disregarded, as in violations not only of the Treaty of peace; but of
Treaties with France & Holland, which were complained of
to Congs.

In other cases the Fedl. Authy. was violated by Treaties &
wars with Indians, as by Geo: by troops raised & kept up
witht. the consent of Congs. as by Massts by compacts witht.
the consent of Congs. as between Pena. and N. Jersey, and between Virga. & Maryd. From the Legisl: Journals of Virga. it
appears, that a vote refusing to apply for a sanction of Congs
was followed by a vote agst. the communication of the
Compact to Congs.

In the internal administration of the States a violation of
Contracts had become familiar in the form of depreciated pa-
per made a legal tender, of property substituted for money, of
Instalment laws, and of the occlusions of the Courts of
Justice; although evident that all such interferences affected
the rights of other States, relatively creditor, as well as
Citizens Creditors within the State.

Among the defects which had been severely felt was that of
a uniformity in cases requiring it, as laws of naturalization,
bankruptcy, a Coercive authority operating on individuals and
a guaranty of the internal tranquility of the States.

As natural consequences of this distracted and dishearten-
ing condition of the union, the Fedl. Authy. had ceased to be
respected abroad, and dispositions shewn there, particularly in
G. B., to take advantage of its imbecility, and to speculate on
its approaching downfall; at home it had lost all confidence &
credit; the unstable and unjust career of the States had also
forfeited the respect & confidence essential to order and good
Govt., involving a general decay of confidence & credit between man & man. It was found moreover, that those least
partial to popular Govt., or most distrustful of its efficacy were
yielding to anticipations, that from an increase of the confusion a Govt. might result more congenial with their taste or
their opinions; whilst those most devoted to the principles
and forms of Republics, were alarmed for the cause of liberty
itself, at stake in the American Experiment, and anxious for a

system that wd. avoid the inefficacy of a mere confederacy without passing into the opposite extreme of a consolidated govt. it was known that there were individuals who had betrayed a bias towards Monarchy [see Knox to G. W. & him to Jay] (Marshall's life) and there had always been some not unfavorable to a partition of the Union into several Confederacies; either from a better chance of figuring on a Sectional Theatre, or that the Sections would require stronger Govts., or by their hostile conflicts lead to a monarchical consolidation. The idea of a dismemberment had recently made its appearance in the Newspapers.

Such were the defects, the deformities, the diseases and the ominous prospects, for which the Convention were to provide a remedy, and which ought never to be overlooked in expounding & appreciating the Constitutional Charter the remedy that was provided.

As a sketch on paper, the earliest perhaps of a Constitutional Govt. for the Union [organized into the regular Departments with physical means operating on individuals] to be sanctioned by *the people of the States*, acting in their original & sovereign character, was contained in a letter of Apl. 8. 1787 from J. M. to Govr. Randolph, a copy of the letter is here inserted.

The feature in the letter which vested in the general Authy. a negative on the laws of the States, was suggested by the negative in the head of the British Empire, which prevented collisions between the parts & the whole, and between the parts themselves. It was supposed that the substitution, of an elective and responsible authority for an hereditary and irresponsible one, would avoid the appearance even of a departure from the principle of Republicanism. But altho' the subject was so viewed in the Convention, and the votes on it were more than once equally divided, it was finally & justly abandoned see note for   for this erasure substitute the amendt. marked * for this page [as, apart from other objections, it was not practicable among so many states, increasing in number, and enacting, each of them, so many laws. Instead of the proposed negative, the objects of it were left as finally provided for in the Constitution.]

On the arrival of the Virginia Deputies at Philada. it

occurred to them that from the early and prominent part taken by that State in bringing about the Convention some initiative step might be expected from them. The Resolutions introduced by Governor Randolph were the result of a Consultation on the subject; with an understanding that they left all the Deputies entirely open to the lights of discussion, and free to concur in any alterations or modifications which their reflections and judgments might approve. The Resolutions as the Journals shew became the basis on which the proceedings of the Convention commenced, and to the developments, variations and modifications of which the plan of Govt. proposed by the Convention may be traced.

The curiosity I had felt during my researches into the History of the most distinguished Confederacies, particularly those of antiquity, and the deficiency I found in the means of satisfying it more especially in what related to the process, the principles, the reasons, & the anticipations, which prevailed in the formation of them, determined me to preserve as far as I could an exact account of what might pass in the Convention whilst executing its trust, with the magnitude of which I was duly impressed, as I was with the gratification promised to future curiosity by an authentic exhibition of the objects, the opinions, & the reasonings from which the new System of Govt. was to receive its peculiar structure & organization. Nor was I unaware of the value of such a contribution to the fund of materials for the History of a Constitution on which would be staked the happiness of a people great even in its infancy, and possibly the cause of Liberty throught the world.

In pursuance of the task I had assumed I chose a seat in front of the presiding member, with the other members on my right & left hands. In this favorable position for hearing all that passed, I noted in terms legible & in abreviations & marks intelligible to myself what was read from the Chair or spoken by the members; and losing not a moment unnecessarily between the adjournment & reassembling of the Convention I was enabled to write out my daily notes [see page 18— during the session or within a few finishing days after its close—see pa. 18 in the extent and form preserved in my own hand on my files.

In the labour & correctness of doing this, I was not a little aided by practice & by a familiarity with the style and the train of observation & reasoning which characterized the principal speakers. It happened, also that I was not absent a single day, nor more than a cassual fraction of an hour in any day, so that I could not have lost a single speech, unless a very short one. Insert the Remark on the — slip of paper marked A.

It may be proper to remark, that, with a very few exceptions, the speeches were neither furnished, nor revised, nor sanctioned, by the speakers, but written out from my notes, aided by the freshness of my recollections. A further remark may be proper, that views of the subject might occasionally be presented in the speeches and proceedings, with a latent reference to a compromise on some middle ground, by mutual concessions. The exceptions alluded to were,—first, the sketch furnished by Mr. Randolph of his speech on the introduction of his propositions, on the twenty-ninth day of May; secondly, the speech of Mr. Hamilton, who happened to call on me when putting the last hand to it, and who acknowledged its fidelity, without suggesting more than a very few verbal alterations which were made; thirdly, the speech of Gouverneur Morris on the second day of May, which was communicated to him on a like occasion, and who acquiesced in it without even a verbal change. The correctness of his language and the distinctness of his enunciation were particularly favorable to a reporter. The speeches of Doctor Franklin, excepting a few brief ones, were copied from the written ones read to the Convention by his colleague, Mr. Wilson, it being inconvenient to the Doctor to remain long on his feet.

Of the ability & intelligence of those who composed the Convention, the debates & proceedings may be a test; as the character of the work which was the offspring of their deliberations must be tested by the experience of the future, added to that of the nearly half century which has passed.

But whatever may be the judgment pronounced on the competency of the architects of the Constitution, or whatever may be the destiny, of the edifice prepared by them, I feel it a duty to express my profound & solemn conviction, derived from my intimate opportunity of observing & appreciating the views of the Convention, collectively & individually, that there never was an assembly of men, charged with a great & arduous trust, who were more pure in their motives, or more exclusively or anxiously devoted to the object committed to them, than were the members of the Federal Convention of 1787, to the object of devising and proposing a constitutional system which would best supply the defects of that which it was to replace, and best secure the permanent liberty and happiness of their country.

1830?

To Edward Everett

Dr. Sir   Augst. 28 1830.
I have duly recd. your letter in wch. you refer to the "nullifying doctrine," advocated as a constitutional right by some of our distinguished fellow citizens; and to the proceedings of the Virga. Legislature in 98 & 99, as appealed to in behalf of that doctrine; and you express a wish for my ideas on those subjects.

I am aware of the delicacy of the task in some respects; and the difficulty in every respect of doing full justice to it. But having in more than one instance complied with a like request from other friendly quarters, I do not decline a sketch of the views which I have been led to take of the doctrine in question, as well as some others connected with them; and of the grounds from which it appears that the proceedings of Virginia have been misconceived by those who have appealed to them. In order to understand the true character of the Constitution of the U. S. the error, not uncommon, must be avoided, of viewing it through the medium either of a consolidated Government or of a confederated Govt. whilst it is neither the one nor the other, but a mixture of both. And having in no model the similitudes & analogies applicable to other systems of Govt it must more than any other be its own interpreter, according to its text & *the facts of the case.*

From these it will be seen that the characteristic peculiarities of the Constitution are 1. The mode of its formation, 2. The division of the supreme powers of Govt between the

States in their united capacity and the States in their individual capacities.

1. It was formed, not by the Governments of the component States, as the Federal Govt. for which it was substituted was formed; nor was it formed by a majority of the people of the U. S. as a single community in the manner of a consolidated Government.

It was formed by the States—that is by the people in each of the States, acting in their highest sovereign capacity; and formed, consequently by the same authority which formed the State Constitutions.

Being thus derived from the same source as the Constitutions of the States, it has within each State, the same authority as the Constitution of the State; and is as much a Constitution, in the strict sense of the term, within its prescribed sphere, as the Constitutions of the States are within their respective spheres; but with this obvious & essential difference, that being a compact among the States in their highest sovereign capacity, and constituting the people thereof one people for certain purposes, it cannot be altered or annulled at the will of the States individually, as the Constitution of a State may be at its individual will.

2. And that it divides the supreme powers of Govt. between the Govt. of the United States, & the Govts. of the individual States, is stamped on the face of the instrument; the powers of war and of taxation, of commerce & of treaties, and other enumerated powers vested in the Govt. of the U. S. being of as high & sovereign a character as any of the powers reserved to the State Govts.

Nor is the Govt. of the U. S. created by the Constitution, less a Govt. in the strict sense of the term, within the sphere of its powers, than the Govts. created by the constitutions of the States are within their several spheres. It is like them organized into Legislative, Executive, & Judiciary Departments. It operates like them, directly on persons & things. And, like them, it has at command a physical force for executing the powers committed to it. The concurrent operation in certain cases is one of the features marking the peculiarity of the system.

Between these different constitutional Govts.—the one

operating in all the States, the others operating separately in each, with the aggregate powers of Govt. divided between them, it could not escape attention that controversies would arise concerning the boundaries of jurisdiction; and that some provision ought to be made for such occurrences. A political system that does not provide for a peaceable & authoritative termination of occurring controversies, would not be more than the shadow of a Govt.; the object & end of a real Govt. being the substitution of law & order for uncertainty confusion, and violence.

That to have left a final decision in such cases to each of the States, then 13 & already 24, could not fail to make the Constn. & laws of the U. S. different in different States was obvious; and not less obvious, that this diversity of independent decisions, must altogether distract the Govt. of the Union & speedily put an end to the Union itself. A uniform authority of the laws, is in itself a vital principle. Some of the most important laws could not be partially executed. They must be executed in all the States or they could be duly executed in none. An impost or an excise, for example, if not in force in some States, would be defeated in others. It is well known that this was among the lessons of experience wch. had a primary influence in bringing about the existing Constitution. A loss of its general authy. would moreover revive the exasperating questions between the States holding ports for foreign commerce and the adjoining States without them, to which are now added all the inland States necessarily carrying on their foreign commerce through other States.

To have made the decisions under the authority of the individual States, co-ordinate in all cases with decisions under the authority of the U. S. would unavoidably produce collisions incompatible with the peace of society, & with that regular & efficient administration which is the essence of free Govts. Scenes could not be avoided in which a ministerial officer of the U. S. and the correspondent officer of an individual State, would have rencounters in executing conflicting decrees, the result of which would depend on the comparative force of the local posse attending them, and that a casualty depending on the political opinions and party feelings in different States.

To have referred every clashing decision under the two authorities for a final decision to the States as parties to the Constitution, would be attended with delays, with inconveniences, and with expenses amounting to a prohibition of the expedient, not to mention its tendency to impair the salutary veneration for a system requiring such frequent interpositions, nor the delicate questions which might present themselves as to the form of stating the appeal, and as to the Quorum for deciding it.

To have trusted to negociation, for adjusting disputes between the Govt. of the U. S. and the State Govts. as between independent & separate sovereignties, would have lost sight altogether of a Constitution & Govt. for the Union; and opened a direct road from a failure of that resort, to the ultima ratio between nations wholly independent of and alien to each other. If the idea had its origin in the process of adjustment between separate branches of the same Govt. the analogy entirely fails. In the case of disputes between independent parts of the same Govt. neither part being able to consummate its will, nor the Gov. to proceed without a concurrence of the parts, necessity brings about an accommodation. In disputes between a State Govt. and the Govt. of the U. States the case is practically as well as theoretically different; each party possessing all the Departments of an organized Govt. Legisl. Ex. & Judiciary; and having each a physical force to support its pretensions. Although the issue of negociation might sometimes avoid this extremity, how often would it happen among so many States, that an unaccommodating spirit in some would render that resource unavailing? A contrary supposition would not accord with a knowledge of human nature or the evidence of our own political history.

The Constitution, not relying on any of the preceding modifications for its safe & successful operation, has expressly declared on the one hand; 1. "That the Constitution, and the laws made in pursuance thereof, and all Treaties made under the authority of the U. S. shall be the supreme law of the land; 2. That the judges of every State shall be bound thereby, anything in the Constn or laws of any State to the contrary notwithstanding; 3. That the judicial power of the U. S. shall extend to all cases in law & equity arising under the

Constitution, the laws of the U. S. and Treaties made under their authority &c."

On the other hand, as a security of the rights & powers of the States in their individual capacities, agst. an undue preponderance of the powers granted to the Government over them in their united capacity, the Constitution has relied on, 1. The responsibility of the Senators and Representatives in the Legislature of the U. S. to the Legislatures & people of the States. 2. The responsibility of the President to the people of the U. States; & 3. The liability of the Ex. and Judiciary functionaries of the U. S. to impeachment by the Representatives of the people of the States, in one branch of the Legislature of the U. S. and trial by the Representatives of the States, in the other branch; the State functionaries, Legislative, Executive, & judiciary, being at the same time in their appointment & responsibility, altogether independent of the agency or authority of the U. States.

How far this structure of the Govt. of the U. S. be adequate & safe for its objects, time alone can absolutely determine. Experience seems to have shown that whatever may grow out of future stages of our national career, there is as yet a sufficient controul in the popular will over the Executive & Legislative Departments of the Govt. When the Alien & Sedition laws were passed in contravention to the opinions and feelings of the community, the first elections that ensued put an end to them. And whatever may have been the character of other acts in the judgment of many of us, it is but true that they have generally accorded with the views of a majority of the States and of the people. At the present day it seems well understood that the laws which have created most dissatisfaction have had a like sanction without doors; and that whether continued varied or repealed, a like proof will be given of the sympathy & responsibility of the Representative Body to the Constituent Body. Indeed, the great complaint now is, not against the want of this sympathy and responsibility, but against the results of them in the legislative policy of the nation.

With respect to the Judicial power of the U. S. and the authority of the Supreme Court in relation to the boundary of jurisdiction between the Federal & the State Govts. I may be permitted to refer to the   number of the "Federalist" for the light in which the subject was regarded by its writer, at the period when the Constitution was depending; and it is believed that the same was the prevailing view then taken of it, that the same view has continued to prevail, and that it does so at this time notwithstanding the eminent exceptions to it.

But it is perfectly consistent with the concession of this power to the Supreme Court, in cases falling within the course of its functions, to maintain that the power has not always been rightly exercised. To say nothing of the period, happily a short one, when judges in their seats did not abstain from intemperate & party harangues, equally at variance with their duty and their dignity, there have been occasional decisions from the Bench which have incurred serious & extensive disapprobation. Still it would seem that, with but few exceptions, the course of the judiciary has been hitherto sustained by the predominant sense of the nation.

Those who have denied or doubted the supremacy of the judicial power of the U. S. & denounce at the same time nullifying power in a State, seem not to have sufficiently adverted to the utter inefficiency of a supremacy in a law of the land, without a supremacy in the exposition & execution of the law; nor to the destruction of all equipoise between the Federal Govt. and the State governments, if, whilst the functionaries of the Fedl. Govt. are directly or indirectly elected by and responsible to the States & the functionaries of the States are in their appointments & responsibility wholly independent of the U. S. no constitutional control of any sort belonged to the U. S. over the States. Under such an organization it is evident that it would be in the power of the States individually, to pass unauthorized laws, and to carry them into complete effect, anything in the Constn. and laws of the U. S. to the contrary notwithstanding. This would be a nullifying power in its plenary character; and whether it had its final effect, thro the Legislative Ex. or Judiciary organ of the State, would be equally fatal to the constitutional relation between the two Govts.

Should the provisions of the Constitution as here reviewed be found not to secure the Govt. & rights of the States agst.

usurpations & abuses on the part of the U. S. the final resort within the purview of the Constn. lies in an amendment of the Constn. according to a process applicable by the States.

And in the event of a failure of every constitutional resort, and an accumulation of usurpations & abuses, rendering passive obedience & non-resistence a greater evil, than resistence & revolution, there can remain but one resort, the last of all, an appeal from the cancelled obligations of the constitutional compact, to original rights & the law of self-preservation. This is the ultima ratio under all Govt. whether consolidated, confederated, or a compound of both; and it cannot be doubted that a single member of the Union, in the extremity supposed, but in that only would have a right, as an extra & ultra constitutional right, to make the appeal.

This brings us to the expedient lately advanced, which claims for a single State a right to appeal agst. an exercise of power by the Govt. of the U. S. decided by the State to be unconstitutional, to the parties of the Const. compact; the decision of the State to have the effect of nullifying the act of the Govt. of the U. S. unless the decision of the State be reversed by three-fourths of the parties.

The distinguished names & high authorities which appear to have asserted and given a practical scope to this doctrine, entitle it to a respect which it might be difficult otherwise to feel for it.

If the doctrine were to be understood as requiring the three-fourths of the States to sustain, instead of that proportion to reverse, the decision of the appealing State, the decision to be without effect during the appeal, it wd. be sufficient to remark, that this extra constl. course might well give way to that marked out by the Const. which authorizes ⅔ of the States to institute and ¾ to effectuate, an amendment of the Constn. establishing a permanent rule of the highest authy in place of an irregular precedent of construction only.

But it is understood that the nullifying doctrine imports that the decision of the State is to be presumed valid, and that it overrules the law of the U. S. unless overuled by ¾ of the States.

Can more be necessary to demonstrate the inadmissibility of such a doctrine than that it puts it in the power of the smallest fraction over ¼ of the U. S.—that is, of 7 States out of 24—to give the law and even the Constn. to 17 States, each of the 17 having as parties to the Constn. an equal right with each of the 7 to expound it & to insist on the exposition. That the 7 might, in particular instances be right and the 17 wrong, is more than possible. But to establish a positive & permanent rule giving such a power to such a minority over such a majority, would overturn the first principle of free Govt. and in practice necessarily overturn the Govt. itself.

It is to be recollected that the Constitution was proposed to the people of the States as a *whole*, and unanimously adopted by the States as a *whole*, it being a part of the Constitution that not less than ¾ of the States should be competent to make any alteration in what had been unanimously agreed to. So great is the caution on this point, that in two cases when peculiar interests were at stake, a proportion even of ¾ is distrusted, and unanimity required to make an alteration.

When the Constitution was adopted as a whole, it is certain that there were many parts which if separately proposed, would have been promptly rejected. It is far from impossible, that every part of the Constitution might be rejected by a majority, and yet, taken together as a whole be unanimously accepted. Free constitutions will rarely if ever be formed without reciprocal concessions; without articles conditioned on & balancing each other. Is there a constitution of a single State out of the 24 that wd. bear the experiment of having its component parts submitted to the people & separately decided on?

What the fate of the Constitution of the U. S. would be if a small proportion of States could expunge parts of it particularly valued by a large majority, can have but one answer.

The difficulty is not removed by limiting the doctrine to cases of construction. How many cases of that sort, involving cardinal provisions of the Constitution, have occurred? How many now exist? How many may hereafter spring up? How many might be ingeniously created, if entitled to the privilege of a decision in the mode proposed?

Is it certain that the principle of that mode wd. not reach farther than is contemplated. If a single State can of right require ¾ of its co-States to overrule its exposition of the Constitution, because that proportion is authorized to amend it, would the plea be less plausible that, as the Constitution was unanimously established, it ought to be unanimously expounded?

The reply to all such suggestions seems to be unavoidable and irresistible, that the Constitution is a compact; that its text is to be expounded according to the provision for expounding it, making a part of the compact; and that none of the parties can rightfully renounce the expounding provision more than any other part. When such a right accrues, as it may accrue, it must grow out of abuses of the compact releasing the sufferers from their fealty to it.

In favour of the nullifying claim for the States individually, it appears, as you observe, that the proceedings of the Legislature of Virga. in 98 & 99 agst. the Alien and Sedition Acts are much dwelt upon.

It may often happen, as experience proves, that erroneous constructions, not anticipated, may not be sufficiently guarded against in the language used; and it is due to the distinguished individuals who have misconceived the intention of those proceedings to suppose that the meaning of the Legislature, though well comprehended at the time, may not now be obvious to those unacquainted with the contemporary indications and impressions.

But it is believed that by keeping in view the distinction between the Govt. of the States & the States in the sense in which they were parties to the Constn.; between the rights of the parties, in their concurrent and in their individual capacities; between the several modes and objects of interposition agst. the abuses of power, and especially between interpositions within the purview of the Constn. & interpositions appealing from the Constn. to the rights of nature paramount to all Constitutions; with these distinctions kept in view, and an attention, always of explanatory use, to the views & arguments which were combated, a confidence is felt, that the Resolutions of Virginia, as vindicated in the Report on them, will be found entitled to an exposition, showing a consistency in their parts and an inconsistency of the whole with the doctrine under consideration.

That the Legislature cd. not have intended to sanction such a doctrine is to be inferred from the debates in the House of Delegates, and from the address of the two Houses to their constitutents on the subject of the resolutions. The tenor of the debates wch. were ably conducted and are understood to have been revised for the press by most, if not all, of the speakers, discloses no reference whatever to a constitutional right in an individual State to arrest by force the operation of a law of the U. S. Concert among the States for redress against the alien & sedition laws, as acts of usurped power, was a leading sentiment, and the attainment of a concert the immediate object of the course adopted by the Legislature, which was that of inviting the other States "to *concur* in declaring the acts to be unconstitutional, and to *co-operate* by the necessary & proper measures in maintaining unimpaired the authorities rights & liberties reserved to the States respectively & to the people." That by the necessary and proper measures to be *concurrently* and co-operatively taken, were meant measures known to the Constitution, particularly the ordinary controul of the people and Legislatures of the States over the Govt. of the U. S. cannot be doubted; and the interposition of this controul as the event showed was equal to the occasion.

It is worthy of remark, and explanatory of the intentions of the Legislature, that the words "not law, but utterly null, void, and of no force or effect," which had followed, in one of the Resolutions, the word "unconstitutional," were struck out by common consent. Tho the words were in fact but synonymous with "unconstitutional," yet to guard against a misunderstanding of this phrase as more than declaratory of opinion, the word unconstitutional alone was retained, as not liable to that danger.

The published address of the Legislature to the people their constituents affords another conclusive evidence of its views. The address warns them against the encroaching spirit of the Genl. Govt., argues the unconstitutionality of the alien & sedition acts, points to other instances in which the constl. limits had been overleaped; dwells upon the dangerous mode of deriving power by implications; and in general presses the necessity of watching over the consolidating tendency of the

Fedl. policy. But nothing is sd. that can be understood to look to means of maintaining the rights of the States beyond the regular ones within the forms of the Constn.

If any farther lights on the subject cd. be needed, a very strong one is reflected in the answers to the Resolutions by the States which protested agst. them. The main objection to these, beyond a few general complaints agst. the inflammatory tendency of the resolutions was directed agst. the assumed authy. of a State Legisle. to declare a law of the U. S. unconstitutional, which they pronounced an unwarrantable interference with the exclusive jurisdiction of the Supreme Ct. of the U. S. Had the resolns. been regarded as avowing & maintaining a right in an indivl. State, to arrest by force the execution of a law of the U. S. it must be presumed that it wd. have been a conspicuous object of their denunciation.

To James Robertson

Dear Sir,   Mar. 27, 1831.

I have recd. your letter of the 8th. but it was not until the 23d. inst.

The veil which was originally over the draft of the resolutions offered in 1798 to the Virga. Assembly having been long since removed, I may say, in answer to your enquiries, that it was penned by me; and that as it went from me, the 3d. Resolution contained the word "alone," which was stricken out by the House of Delegates. Why the alteration was made, I have no particular knowledge, not being a member at the time. I always viewed it as an error. The term was meant to confine the meaning of "*parties* to the constitutional compact," to the States in the capacity in which they formed the compact, in exclusion of the State Govts. which did not form it. And the use of the term "States" throughout in the *plural* number distinguished between the rights belonging to them in their collective, from those belonging to them in their individual capacities.

With respect to the terms following the term "unconstitutional"—viz. "not law, but null void and of no force or effect" which were stricken out of the 7th. Resoln. my memory cannot positively decide whether they were or were not in the original draft, and no copy of it appears to have been retained. On the presumption that they were in the draft as it went from me, I am confident that they must have been regarded only as giving accumulated emphasis to the *declaration*, that the alien & sedition acts had in the opinion of the Assembly violated the Constitution of the U. S. and not that the addition of them could annul the acts or sanction a resistance of them. The Resolution was expressly *declaratory*, and proceeding from the Legislature only which was not even a party to the Constitution, could be declaratory of opinion only.

It may not be out of place here to remark that if the insertion of those terms in the draft could have the effect of showing an inconsistency in its author; the striking them out wd. be a protest agst. the doctrine which has claimed the authority of Virginia in its support.

If the 3d. Resolution be in any degree open to misconstruction on this point, the language and scope of the 7th ought to controul it; and if a more explicit guard against misconstruction was not provided, it is explained in this as in other cases of omission, by the entire absence of apprehension that it could be necessary. Who could, at that day, have foreseen some of the comments on the Constitution advanced at the present?

The task you have in hand is an interesting one, the more so as there is certainly room for a more precise & regular history of the Articles of Confederation & of the Constitution of the U. S. than has yet appeared. I am not acquainted with Pitkin's work, and it was not within the scope of Marshall's Life of Washington to introduce more of Constitutional History than was involved in his main subject. The Journals of the State Legislatures, with the Journal & debates of the State Conventions, and the Journal and other printed accounts of the proceedings of the federal Convention of 1787, are of course the primary sources of information. Some sketches of what passed in that Convention have found their way to the public, particularly those of Judge Yates and of Mr. Luther Martin. But the Judge tho' a highly respectable man, was a zealous partizan, and has committed gross errors in his desultory notes. He left the Convention also before it had reached the stages of its deliberations in which the character of the body and the views of individuals were sufficiently developed. Mr. Martin who was also present but a part of the time betrays, in his communication to the Legislature of Maryland, feelings which had a discolouring effect on his statements. As it has become known that I was at much pains to preserve an account of what passed in the Convention, I ought perhaps to observe, that I have thought it becoming in several views that a publication of it should be at least of a posthumous date.

I know not that I could refer you to any other appropriate sources of information wch. will not have occurred to you, or not fall within your obvious researches. The period which your plan embraces abounds with materials in pamphlets & in newspaper essays not published in that form. You would doubtless find it worth while to turn your attention to the Collections of the Historical Societies now in print in some of the States. The library of Phila. is probably rich in pertinent materials. Its catalogue alone might point to such as are otherwise attainable. Although I might with little risk leave it to your own inference, I take the liberty of noting that this hasty compliance with your request is not for the public eye; adding only my sincere wishes for the success of the undertaking which led to it, and the offer of my friendly respects & salutations.

To Jared Sparks

Dear Sir,   Montpellier, April 8, 1831.
I have duly received your letter of March 30. In answer to your enquiries "respecting the part acted by Gouverneur Morris (whose life, you observe, you are writing) in the Federal Convention of 1787, and the political doctrines maintained by him," it may be justly said that he was an able, an eloquent, and an active member, and shared largely in the discussions succeeding the 1st of July, previous to which, with the exception of a few of the early days, he was absent.

Whether he accorded precisely "with the political doctrines of Hamilton" I cannot say. He certainly did not "incline to the Democratic side," and was very frank in avowing his opinions when most at variance with those prevailing in the Convention. He did not propose any outline of a Constitution, as was done by Hamilton; but he contended for certain articles, (a Senate for life, particularly,) which he held essential to the stability and energy of a Government capable of protecting the rights of property against the spirit of Democracy. He wished to make the weight of wealth to balance that of numbers, which he pronounced to be the only effectual security to each against the encroachments of the other.

The *finish* given to the style and arrangement of the Constitution fairly belongs to the pen of Mr. Morris; the task having been probably handed over to him by the Chairman of the Committee, himself a highly respectable member, with the ready concurrence of the others. A better choice could not have been made, as the performance of the task proved. It is true that the state of the materials, consisting of a reported draught in detail, and subsequent resolutions accurately penned, and falling easily in their proper places, was a good preparation for the symmetry and phraseology of the instrument; but there was sufficient room for the talents and taste stamped by the author on the face of it. The alterations made by the Committee are not recollected. They were not such as to impair the merit of the composition. Those, verbal and others, made in the Convention, may be gathered from the Journal, and will be found also to leave that merit altogether unimpaired.

The anecdote you mention may not be without a foundation, but not in the extent supposed. It is certain that the return of Mr. Morris to the Convention was at a critical stage of its proceedings. The knot felt as the Gordian one was the question between the larger and smaller States on the rule of voting in the Senatorial branch of the Legislature; the latter claiming, the former opposing, the rule of equality. Great zeal and pertinacity had been shewn on both sides; and an equal division of the votes on the question had been reiterated and prolonged till it had become not only distressing but seriously alarming. It was during that period of gloom that

Dr. Franklin made the proposition for a religious service in the Convention, an account of which was so erroneously given, with every semblance of authenticity, through the National Intelligencer, several years ago. The crisis was not over when Mr. Morris is said to have had an interview and conversation with General Washington and Mr. R. Morris, such as may well have occurred; but it appears that on the day of his re-entering the Convention a proposition had been made from another quarter to refer the knotty question to a committee with a view to some compromise; the indications being manifest that sundry members from the larger States were relaxing in their opposition, and that some ground of compromise was contemplated, such as finally took place, and as may be seen in the printed Journal. Mr. Morris was in the deputation from the large State of Pennsylvania, and combated the compromise throughout. The tradition is, however, correct that on the day of his resuming his seat he entered with anxious feelings into the debate, and in one of his speeches painted the consequences of an abortive result to the Convention in all the deep colours suited to the occasion. But it is not believed that any material influence on the turn which things took could be ascribed to his efforts; for, besides the mingling with them some of his most disrelished ideas, the topics of his eloquent appeals to the members had been exhausted during his absence, and their minds were too much made up to be susceptible of new impressions.

It is but due to Mr. Morris to remark, that to the brilliancy and fertility of his genius he added, what is too rare, a candid surrender of his opinions when the lights of discussion satisfied him that they had been too hastily formed, and a readiness to aid in making the best of measures in which he had been overruled.

In making this hastened communication, I have more confidence in the discretion with which it will be used, than in its fulfilment of your anticipations. I hope it will at least be accepted as a proof of my respect for your object, and of the sincerity with which I tender you a reassurance of the cordial esteem and good wishes in which Mrs. Madison always joins me.

I take for granted you have at command all the printed works of Mr. Morris. I recollect that there can be found among my pamphlets a small one by him, intended to prevent the threatened repeal of the law of Pennsylvania which had been passed as necessary to support the Bank of N. America, and when the repeal was viewed as a formidable blow to the establishment. Should a copy be needed, I will hunt it up and forward it.

To Jared Sparks

Dear Sir,   June 1, 1831.
I have duly recd. yours of 24th Ult, and inclose the little pamphlet by Govr. Morris which it refers to. Unless it is to be printed entire in the vols. you are preparing, I shd. wish to re-place it in the collection from which it is taken. Of the other unofficial writings by him, I have but the single recollection that he was a writer for the Newspapers in 1780 (being then a member of Congs.) on our public affairs, chiefly I believe, on the currency & resources of the U. S. It was about the time that the scale of 1 for 40, was applied to the 200,000,000 of dolrs. which had been emitted; and his publications were probably occasioned by the crisis, but of the precise scope of them, I cannot speak. I became a member of Congr. in March of that year, just after the fate of the old Emissions had been decided on; and the subject so far deprived of its interest. In the Phila. newspapers of that period, the writings in question might probably be found, and verified by the style if not the name of the Author. Whether Mr. M. wrote a pamphlet about Deane is a point on wch. I can give no answer.

May I ask of you to let me know the result of your corre-spondence with Charleston on the subject of Mr. Pinckney's draft of a Constn. for the U. S. as soon as it is ascertained.

It is quite certain that since the death of Col. Few I have been the only living signer of the Constn. of the U. S. Of the members who were present & did not sign, & of those who were present part of the time, but had left the Convention, it is equally certain, that not one has remained since the death of Mr. Lansing who disappeared so mysteriously not very long ago. I happen also to be the sole survivor of those who were members of the Revoly. Congs. prior to the close of the war; as I had been for some years, of the members of the Convention in 1776 which formed the first Constn. for Virga. Having outlived so many of my cotemporaries, I ought not to forget that I may be thought to have outlived myself.

With cordl. esteem & all good wishes.

I had not known that the papers of Mr. Hamilton had passed into the hands of Mr. Bayless. Col. Pickering was the last reported selection for the trust.

To Mathew Carey

Dear Sir   Montpellier, July 27, 1831.
I have recd. your favor of the 21st, with your commencing address to the Citizens of S. Carolina. The strange doctrines and misconceptions prevailing in that quarter are much to be deplored; and the tendency of them the more to be dreaded, as they are patronized by Statesmen of shining talents, and patriotic reputations. To trace the great causes of this state of things out of which these unhappy aberrations have sprung, in the effect of markets glutted with the products of the land, and with the land itself; to appeal to the nature of the Constitutional compact, as precluding a right in any one of the parties to renounce it at will, by giving to all an equal right to judge of its obligations; and, as the obligations are mutual, a right to enforce correlative with a right to dissolve them; to make manifest the impossibility as well as injustice, of executing the laws of the Union, particularly the laws of commerce, if even a single State be exempt from their operation; to lay open the effects of a withdrawal of a Single State from the Union on the *practical* conditions & relations of the others; thrown apart by the intervention of a foreign nation; to expose the obvious, inevitable & disastrous consequences of a separation of the States, whether into alien confederacies or

individual nations; these are topics which present a task well worthy the best efforts of the best friends of their country, and I hope you will have all the success, which your extensive information and disinterested views merit. If the States cannot live together in harmony, under the auspices of such a Government as exists, and in the midst of blessings, such as have been the fruits of it, what is the prospect threatened by the abolition of a Common Government, with all the rivalships collisions and animosities, inseparable from such an event. The entanglements & conflicts of commercial regulations, especially as affecting the inland and other non-importing States, & a protection of fugitive slaves, substituted for the present obligatory surrender of them, would of themselves quickly kindle the passions which are the forerunners of war.

My health has not been good for several years, and is at present much crippled by Rheumatism; This with my great age warns me to be as little as possible before the public; and to give way to others who with the same love of their Country, are more able to be useful to it.

To Nicholas P. Trist

Dear Sir   Montpellier, May—, 1832.
I have received your letter of the 8th, with the book referred to and dictate the acknowledgement of it to a pen that is near me. I will read the work as soon as I may be able. When that will be I cannot say. I have been confined to my bed many days by a bilious attack. The fever is now leaving me but in a very enfeebled state, and without any abatement of my Rheumatism; which, besides its general effect on my health, still cripples me in my limbs, and especially in my hands & fingers.

I am glad to find you so readily deciding that the charges against Mr. Jefferson can be duly refuted. I doubt not this will be well done. To be so, it will be expedient to review carefully the correspondences of Mr. Jefferson, to recur to the aspects of things at different epochs of the Government, particularly as presented at its outset, in the unrepublican formalities introduced and attempted, not by President Washington but by the vitiated political taste of others taking the lead on the occasion; and again in the proceedings which marked the Vice Presidency of Mr. Jefferson.

Allowances also ought to be made for a habit in Mr. Jefferson as in others of great genius of expressing in strong and round terms, impressions of the moment.

It may be added that a full exhibition of the correspondences of distinguished public men through the varied scenes of a long period, would without a *single exception* not fail to involve delicate personalities and apparent if not real inconsistencies.

I heartily wish that something may be done with the tariff that will be admissible on both sides and arrest the headlong course in South Carolina. The alternative presented by the dominant party there is so monstrous that it would seem impossible that it should be sustained by any of the most sympathising States; unless there be latent views apart from Constitutional questions, which I hope cannot be of much extent. The wisdom that meets the crisis with the due effect will greatly signalize itself.

The idea that a Constitution which has been so fruitful of blessings, and a Union admitted to be the only guardian of the peace, liberty and happiness of the people of the States comprizing it should be broken up and scattered to the winds without greater than any existing causes is more painful than words can express. It is impossible that this can ever be the deliberate act of the people, if the value of the Union be calculated by the consequences of disunion.

I am much exhausted and can only add an affectionate adieu.

To Andrew Stevenson

My dear Sir   Montpr. Novr 20, 1832
I return you many thanks for the warm cap which came safe to hand a few days ago. It is as comfortable as it may be fashionable, which is more than can be said of all fashions. I recd.

at the same time a duplicate of the excellent pair of gloves as well which Mrs. Stevenson, allow me rather to say, my cousin Sally has favored me. Being the work of her own hands they will impart the more warmth to mine. As they are a gift not a Gauntlet, I may express thro' her husband, the heartfelt acknowledgments with which they are accepted. Mrs. Madison has also provided well for my feet. I am thus equipt cap-a-pie, for the campaign agst. Boreas, & his allies the Frosts & the snows. But there is another article of covering, which I need most of all & which my best friends can not supply. My bones have lost a sad portion of the flesh which clothed & protected them, and the digestive and nutritive organs which alone can replace it, are too slothful in their functions.

I congratulate Richmond & my friends there on the departure of the atmospheric scourge which carried so many deaths and still more of terror with it. I join in the prayer that as it was the first it may also be the last visit.

Mrs. Stevenson in her letter to Mrs. Madison mentions that since you left us, you have had a sharp bilious attack, adding for our gratification that you had quite recovered from it. It is very important that you shd. carry a good share of health into the chair at the capitol, we cannot expect that it will be a seat of Roses, whatever our hopes, that it may be without the thorns that distinguished the last season.

Inclosed is a letter from Mrs. M. to Mrs. S. As she speaks for me as I do for her, Mrs. S. & yourself will have at once joint & several assurances of our constant affection and of all our good wishes.

To Nicholas P. Trist

Dr. Sir   Montpellier, Decr 23, 1832.
I have received yours of the 19th, inclosing some of the South Carolina papers. There are in one of them some interesting views of the doctrine of secession; one that had occurred to me, and which for the first time I have seen in print; namely that if one State can at will withdraw from the others, the others can at will withdraw from her, and turn her,

nolentem, volentem, out of the union. Until of late, there is not a State that would have abhorred such a doctrine more than South Carolina, or more dreaded an application of it to herself. The same may be said of the doctrine of nullification, which she now preaches as the only faith by which the Union can be saved.

I partake of the wonder that the men you name should view secession in the light mentioned. The essential difference between a free Government and Governments not free, is that the former is founded in compact, the parties to which are mutually and equally bound by it. Neither of them therefore can have a greater right to break off from the bargain, than the other or others have to hold them to it. And certainly there is nothing in the Virginia resolutions of —98, adverse to this principle, which is that of common sense and common justice. The fallacy which draws a different conclusion from them lies in confounding a *single* party, with the *parties* to the Constitutional compact of the United States. The latter having made the compact may do what they will with it. The former as one only of the parties, owes fidelity to it, till released by consent, or absolved by an intolerable abuse of the power created. In the Virginia Resolutions and Report the *plural* number, *States*, is in *every* instance used where reference is made to the authority which presided over the Government. As I am now known to have drawn those documents, I may say as I do with a distinct recollection, that the distinction was intentional. It was in fact required by the course of reasoning employed on the occasion. The Kentucky resolutions being less guarded have been more easily perverted. The pretext for the liberty taken with those of Virginia is the word *respective*, prefixed to the "rights" &c to be secured within the States. Could the abuse of the expression have been foreseen or suspected, the form of it would doubtless have been varied. But what can be more consistent with common sense, than that all having the same rights &c, should unite in contending for the security of them to each.

It is remarkable how closely the nullifiers who make the name of Mr. Jefferson the pedestal for their colossal heresy, shut their eyes and lips, whenever his authority is ever so clearly and emphatically against them. You have noticed what he says in his letters to Monroe & Carrington Pages 43 & 203, vol. 2, with respect to the powers of the old Congress to coerce delinquent States, and his reasons for preferring for the purpose a naval to a military force; and moreover that it was not necessary to find a right to coerce in the Federal Articles, that being inherent in the nature of a compact. It is high time that the claim to secede at will should be put down by the public opinion; and I shall be glad to see the task commenced by one who understands the subject.

I know nothing of what is passing at Richmond, more than what is seen in the newspapers. You were right in your foresight of the effect of the passages in the late Proclamation. They have proved a leaven for much fermentation there, and created an alarm against the danger of consolidation, balancing that of disunion. I wish with you the Legislature may not seriously injure itself by assuming the high character of mediator. They will certainly do so if they forget that their real influence will be in the inverse ratio of a boastful interposition of it.

If you can fix, and will name the day of your arrival at Orange Court House, we will have a horse there for you; and if you have more baggage than can be otherwise brought than on wheels, we will send such a vehicle for it. Such is the state of the roads produced by the wagons hurrying flour to market, that it may be impossible to send our carriage which would answer both purposes.

To William Cabell Rives

Dear Sir   Montpr., March 12, 1833.

I have recd. your very kind letter of the 6th, from Washington, and by the same mail a copy of your late Speech in the Senate for which I tender my thanks. I have found as I expected, that it takes a very able and enlightening view of its subject. I wish it may have the effect of reclaiming to the doctrine & language held by all from the birth of the Constitution, & till very lately by themselves, those who now Contend that the States have never parted with an Atom of their sovereignty; and consequently that the Constitutional band which holds them together, is a mere league or partnership, without any of the characteristics of sovereignty or nationality.

It seems strange that it should be necessary to disprove this novel and nullifying doctrine; and stranger still that those who deny it should be denounced as Innovators, heretics & Apostates. Our political system is admitted to be a new Creation—a real nondescript. Its character therefore must be sought within itself; not in precedents, because there are none; not in writers whose comments are guided by precedents. Who can tell at present how Vattel and others of that class, would have qualified (in the Gallic sense of the term) a Compound & peculiar system with such an example of it as ours before them.

What can be more preposterous than to say that the States as united, are in no respect or degree, a Nation, which implies sovereignty; altho' acknowledged to be such by all other Nations & Sovereigns, and maintaining with them, all the international relations, of war & peace, treaties, commerce, &c, and, on the other hand and at the same time, to say that the States separately are compleatly nations & sovereigns; although they can separately neither speak nor harken to any other nation, nor maintain with it any of the international relations whatever and would be disowned as Nations if presenting themselves in that character.

The nullifiers it appears, endeavor to shelter themselves under a distinction between a delegation and a surrender of powers. But if the powers be attributes of sovereignty & nationality & the grant of them be perpetual, as is necessarily implied, where not otherwise expressed, sovereignty & nationality according to the extent of the grant are effectually transferred by it, and a dispute about the name, is but a battle of words. The practical result is not indeed left to argument or inference. The words of the Constitution are explicit that the Constitution & laws of the U. S. shall be supreme over the Constitution & laws of the several States; supreme in their exposition and execution as well as in their authority. Without a supremacy in those respects it would be like a scabbard in the hand of a soldier without a sword in it. The imagination itself is startled at the idea of twenty four independent expounders of a rule that cannot exist, but in a meaning and operation, the same for all.

The conduct of S. Carolina has called forth not only the question of nullification; but the more formidable one of secession. It is asked whether a State by resuming the sovereign form in which it entered the Union, may not of right withdraw from it at will. As this is a simple question whether a State, more than an individual, has a right to violate its engagements, it would seem that it might be safely left to answer itself. But the countenance given to the claim shows that it cannot be so lightly dismissed. The natural feelings which laudably attach the people composing a State, to its authority and importance, are at present too much excited by the unnatural feelings, with which they have been inspired agst. their brethren of other States, not to expose them, to the danger of being misled into erroneous views of the nature of the Union and the interest they have in it. One thing at least seems to be too clear to be questioned; that whilst a State remains within the Union it cannot withdraw its citizens from the operation of the Constitution & laws of the Union. In the event of an actual secession without the Consent of the Co-States, the course to be pursued by these involves questions painful in the discussion of them. God grant that the menacing appearances, which obtruded it may not be followed by positive occurrences requiring the more painful task of deciding them!

In explaining the proceedings of Virga. in 98–99, the state of things at that time was the more properly appealed to, as it has been too much overlooked. The doctrines combated are always a key to the arguments employed. It is but too common to read the expressions of a remote period thro' the modern meaning of them, & to omit guards agst. misconstruction not anticipated. A few words with a prophetic gift, might have prevented much error in the glosses on those proceedings. The remark is equally applicable to the Constitution itself.

Having thrown these thoughts on paper in the midst of interruptions added to other dangers of inaccuracy, I will ask the favor of you to return the letter after perusal. I have latterly taken this liberty with more than one of my corresponding friends. And every lapse of very short periods becomes now a fresh apology for it.

Neither Mrs. M. nor myself have forgotten the promised visit which included Mrs. Rives, and we flatter ourselves the fulfilment of it, will not be very distant. Meanwhile we tender to you both our joint & affecte. salutations.

P. Script. I inclose a little pamphlet rec a few days ago, which so well repaid my perusal, that I submit it to yours, to be returned only at your leisure. It is handsomely written, and its matter well chosen & interesting. A like task as well executed in every State wd. be of historical value; the more so as the examples might both prompt & guide researches, not as yet too late but rapidly becoming so.

Advice to My Country

As this advice, if it ever see the light will not do it till I am no more it may be considered as issuing from the tomb, where truth alone can be respected, and the happiness of man alone consulted. It will be entitled therefore to whatever weight can be derived from good intentions, and from the experience of one who has served his country in various stations through a period of forty years, who espoused in his youth and adhered through his life to the cause of its liberty, and who has borne a part in most of the great transactions which will constitute epochs of its destiny.

The advice nearest to my heart and deepest in my convictions is that the Union of the States be cherished and perpetuated. Let the open enemy to it be regarded as a Pandora with her box opened; and the disguised one, as the Serpent creeping with his deadly wiles into Paradise.

1834

To George Tucker

My dear Sir,   June 27, 1836.

I have received your letter of June 17th, with the paper enclosed in it.

A part from the value put on such a mark of respect from you in a dedication of your "Life of Mr. Jefferson" to me, I could only be governed in accepting it by my confidence in your capacity to do justice to a character so interesting to his country and to the world; and, I may be permitted to add, with whose principles of liberty and political career mine have been so extensively congenial.

It could not escape me that a feeling of personal friendship has mingled itself greatly with the credit you allow to my public services. I am, at the same time, justified by my consciousness in saying, that an ardent zeal was always felt to make up for deficiencies in them by a sincere and steadfast cooperation in promoting such a reconstruction of our political system as would provide for the permanent liberty and happiness of the United States; and that of the many good fruits it has produced which have well rewarded the efforts and anxieties that led to it, no one has been a more rejoicing witness than myself.

With cordial salutations on the near approach to the end of your undertaking, &c.

APPENDIX

The Constitution

We the People of the United States, in Order to form a more perfect Union, establish Justice, insure domestic Tranquility, provide for the common defence, promote the general Welfare, and secure the Blessings of Liberty to ourselves and our Posterity, do ordain and establish this Constitution for the United States of America.

Article. I.

Section. 1.   All legislative Powers herein granted shall be vested in a Congress of the United States, which shall consist of a Senate and House of Representatives.

Section. 2.   The House of Representatives shall be composed of Members chosen every second Year by the People of the several States, and the Electors in each State shall have the Qualifications requisite for Electors of the most numerous Branch of the State Legislature.

No Person shall be a Representative who shall not have attained to the Age of twenty five Years, and been seven Years a Citizen of the United States, and who shall not, when elected, be an Inhabitant of that State in which he shall be chosen.

Representatives and direct Taxes shall be apportioned among the several States which may be included within this Union, according to their respective Numbers, which shall be determined by adding to the whole Number of free Persons, including those bound to Service for a Term of Years, and excluding Indians not taxed, three fifths of all other Persons. The actual Enumeration shall be made within three Years after the first Meeting of the Congress of the United States, and within every subsequent Term of ten Years, in such Manner as they shall by Law direct. The Number of Representatives shall not exceed one for every thirty Thousand, but each State shall have at Least one Representative; and until such enumeration shall be made, the State of New Hampshire shall be entitled to chuse three, Massachusetts eight, Rhode-Island and Providence Plantations one, Connecticut five, New-York six, New Jersey four, Pennsylvania eight, Delaware one, Maryland six, Virginia ten, North Carolina five, South Carolina five, and Georgia three.

When vacancies happen in the Representation from any State, the Executive Authority thereof shall issue Writs of Election to fill such Vacancies.

The House of Representatives shall chuse their Speaker and other Officers; and shall have the sole Power of Impeachment.

Section. 3. The Senate of the United States shall be composed of two Senators from each State, chosen by the Legislature thereof, for six Years; and each Senator shall have one Vote.

Immediately after they shall be assembled in Consequence of the first Election, they shall be divided as equally as may be into three Classes. The Seats of the Senators of the first Class shall be vacated at the Expiration of the second Year, of the second Class at the Expiration of the fourth Year, and of the third Class at the Expiration of the sixth Year, so that one third may be chosen every second Year; and if Vacancies happen by Resignation, or otherwise, during the Recess of the Legislature of any State, the Executive thereof may make temporary Appointments until the next Meeting of the Legislature, which shall then fill such Vacancies.

No Person shall be a Senator who shall not have attained to the Age of thirty Years, and been nine Years a Citizen of the United States, and who shall not, when elected, be an Inhabitant of that State for which he shall be chosen.

The Vice President of the United States shall be President of the Senate, but shall have no Vote, unless they be equally divided.

The Senate shall chuse their other Officers, and also a President pro tempore, in the Absence of the Vice President, or when he shall exercise the Office of President of the United States.

The Senate shall have the sole Power to try all Impeachments. When sitting for that Purpose, they shall be on Oath or Affirmation. When the President of the United States is tried, the Chief Justice shall preside: And no Person shall be convicted without the Concurrence of two thirds of the Members present.

Judgment in Cases of Impeachment shall not extend further than to removal from Office, and disqualification to hold and enjoy any Office of honor, Trust or Profit under the United States: but the Party convicted shall nevertheless be liable and subject to Indictment, Trial, Judgment and Punishment, according to Law.

Section. 4. The Times, Places and Manner of holding Elections for Senators and Representatives, shall be prescribed in each State by the Legislature thereof; but the Congress may at any time by Law make or alter such Regulations, except as to the Places of chusing Senators.

The Congress shall assemble at least once in every Year, and such Meeting shall be on the first Monday in December, unless they shall by Law appoint a different Day.

Section. 5. Each House shall be the Judge of the Elections, Returns and Qualifications of its own Members, and a Majority of each shall constitute a Quorum to do Business; but a smaller Number may adjourn from day to day, and may be authorized to compel the Attendance of absent Members, in such Manner, and under such Penalties as each House may provide.

Each House may determine the Rules of its Proceedings, punish its members for disorderly Behaviour, and, with the Concurrence of two thirds, expel a Member.

Each House shall keep a Journal of its Proceedings, and from time to time publish the same, excepting such Parts as may in their Judgment require Secrecy; and the Yeas and Nays of the Members of either House on any question shall, at the Desire of one fifth of those Present, be entered on the Journal.

Neither House, during the Session of Congress, shall, without the Consent of the other, adjourn for more than three days, nor to any other Place than that in which the two Houses shall be sitting.

Section. 6.   The Senators and Representatives shall receive a Compensation for their Services, to be ascertained by Law, and paid out of the Treasury of the United States. They shall in all Cases, except Treason, Felony and Breach of the Peace, be privileged from Arrest during their Attendance at the Session of their respective Houses, and in going to and returning from the same; and for any Speech or Debate in either House, they shall not be questioned in any other Place.

No Senator or Representative shall, during the Time for which he was elected, be appointed to any civil Office under the Authority of the United States which shall have been created, or the Emoluments whereof shall have been encreased during such time; and no Person holding any Office under the United States, shall be a Member of either House during his Continuance in Office.

Section. 7.   All Bills for raising Revenue shall originate in the House of Representatives; but the Senate may propose or concur with Amendments as on other Bills.

Every Bill which shall have passed the House of Representatives and the Senate shall, before it become a Law, be presented to the President of the United States; If he approve he shall sign it, but if not he shall return it, with his Objections to that House in which it shall have originated, who shall enter the Objections at large on their Journal, and proceed to reconsider it. If after such Reconsideration two thirds of that House shall agree to pass the Bill, it shall be sent, together with the Objections, to the other House, by which it shall likewise be reconsidered, and if approved by two thirds of that House, it shall become a Law. But in all such Cases the Votes of both Houses shall be determined by yeas and Nays, and the Names of the Persons voting for and against the Bill shall be entered on the

Journal of each House respectively. If any Bill shall not be returned by the President within ten Days (Sundays excepted) after it shall have been presented to him, the Same shall be a Law, in like Manner as if he had signed it, unless the Congress by their Adjournment prevent its Return, in which Case it shall not be a Law.

Every Order, Resolution, or Vote to which the Concurrence of the Senate and House of Representatives may be necessary (except on a question of Adjournment) shall be presented to the President of the United States; and before the Same shall take Effect, shall be approved by him, or being disapproved by him, shall be repassed by two thirds of the Senate and House of Representatives, according to the Rules and Limitations prescribed in the Case of a Bill.

Section. 8.   The Congress shall have Power To lay and collect Taxes, Duties, Imposts and Excises, to pay the Debts and provide for the common Defence and general Welfare of the United States; but all Duties, Imposts and Excises shall be uniform throughout the United States;

To borrow Money on the credit of the United States;

To regulate Commerce with foreign Nations, and among the several States, and with the Indian Tribes;

To establish an uniform Rule of Naturalization, and uniform Laws on the subject of Bankruptcies throughout the United States;

To coin Money, regulate the Value thereof, and of foreign Coin, and fix the Standard of Weights and Measures;

To provide for the Punishment of counterfeiting the Securities and current Coin of the United States;

To establish Post Offices and post Roads;

To promote the Progress of Science and useful Arts, by securing for limited Times to Authors and Inventors the exclusive Right to their respective Writings and Discoveries;

To constitute Tribunals inferior to the supreme Court;

To define and punish Piracies and Felonies committed on the high Seas, and Offences against the Law of Nations;

To declare War, grant Letters of Marque and Reprisal, and make Rules concerning Captures on Land and Water;

To raise and support Armies, but no Appropriation of Money to that Use shall be for a longer Term than two Years;

To provide and maintain a Navy;

To make Rules for the Government and Regulation of the land and naval Forces;

To provide for calling forth the Militia to execute the Laws of the Union, suppress Insurrections and repel Invasions;

To provide for organizing, arming, and disciplining, the Militia, and for governing such Part of them as may be employed in the Service of the United States, reserving to the States respectively, the Appointment of the Officers, and the Authority of training the Militia according to the discipline prescribed by Congress;

To exercise exclusive Legislation in all Cases whatsoever, over such District (not exceeding ten Miles square) as may, by Cession of particular States, and the Acceptance of Congress, become the Seat of the Government of the United States, and to exercise like Authority over all Places purchased by the Consent of the Legislature of the State in which the same shall be, for the Erection of Forts, Magazines, Arsenals, dock-Yards, and other needful Buildings;—And

To make all Laws which shall be necessary and proper for carrying into Execution the foregoing Powers, and all other Powers vested by this Constitution in the Government of the United States, or in any Department or Officer thereof.

Section. 9.   The Migration or Importation of such Persons as any of the States now existing shall think proper to admit, shall not be prohibited by the Congress prior to the Year one thousand eight hundred and eight, but a Tax or duty may be imposed on such Importation, not exceeding ten dollars for each Person.

The Privilege of the Writ of Habeas Corpus shall not be suspended, unless when in Cases of Rebellion or Invasion the public Safety may require it.

No Bill of Attainder or ex post facto Law shall be passed.

No Capitation, or other direct, Tax shall be laid, unless in Proportion to the Census or Enumeration herein before directed to be taken.

No Tax or Duty shall be laid on Articles exported from any State.

No Preference shall be given by any Regulation of Commerce or Revenue to the Ports of one State over those of another: nor shall Vessels bound to, or from, one State, be obliged to enter, clear, or pay Duties in another.

No Money shall be drawn from the Treasury, but in Consequence of Appropriations made by Law; and a regular Statement and Account of the Receipts and Expenditures of all public Money shall be published from time to time.

No Title of Nobility shall be granted by the United States: And no Person holding any Office of Profit or Trust under them, shall, without the Consent of the Congress, accept of any present, Emolument, Office, or Title, of any kind whatever, from any King, Prince, or foreign State.

Section. 10.   No State shall enter into any Treaty, Alliance, or Confederation; grant Letters of Marque and Reprisal; coin Money; emit Bills of Credit; make any Thing but gold and silver Coin a

Tender in Payment of Debts; pass any Bill of Attainder, ex post facto
Law, or Law impairing the Obligation of Contracts, or grant any
Title of Nobility.

No State shall, without the Consent of the Congress, lay any Imposts or Duties on Imports or Exports, except what may be absolutely necessary for executing it's inspection Laws: and the net
Produce of all Duties and Imposts, laid by any State on Imports or
Exports, shall be for the Use of the Treasury of the United States;
and all such Laws shall be subject to the Revision and Controul of
the Congress.

No State shall, without the Consent of Congress, lay any Duty of
Tonnage, keep Troops, or Ships of War in time of Peace, enter into
any Agreement or Compact with another State, or with a foreign
Power, or engage in War, unless actually invaded, or in such imminent Danger as will not admit of delay.

Article. II.

Section. 1.   The executive Power shall be vested in a President of
the United States of America. He shall hold his Office during the
Term of four Years, and, together with the Vice President, chosen
for the same Term, be elected, as follows

Each State shall appoint, in such Manner as the Legislature thereof
may direct, a Number of Electors, equal to the whole Number of
Senators and Representatives to which the State may be entitled in
the Congress: but no Senator or Representative, or Person holding
an Office of Trust or Profit under the United States, shall be appointed an Elector.

The Electors shall meet in their respective States and vote by Ballot for two Persons, of whom one at least shall not be an Inhabitant
of the same State with themselves. And they shall make a List of all
the Persons voted for, and of the Number of Votes for each; which
List they shall sign and certify, and transmit sealed to the Seat of the
Government of the United States, directed to the President of the
Senate. The President of the Senate shall, in the Presence of the Senate and House of Representatives, open all the Certificates, and the
Votes shall then be counted. The Person having the greatest Number of Votes shall be the President, if such Number be a Majority of
the whole Number of Electors appointed; and if there be more than
one who have such Majority, and have an equal Number of Votes,
then the House of Representatives shall immediately chuse by Ballot
one of them for President; and if no Person have a Majority, then
from the five highest on the List the said House shall in like Manner

chuse the President. But in chusing the President, the Votes shall be taken by States, the Representation from each State having one Vote; A quorum for this Purpose shall consist of a Member or Members from two thirds of the States, and a Majority of all the States shall be necessary to a Choice. In every Case, after the Choice of the President, the Person having the greatest Number of Votes of the Electors shall be the Vice President. But if there should remain two or more who have equal Votes, the Senate shall chuse from them by Ballot the Vice President.

The Congress may determine the Time of chusing the Electors, and the Day on which they shall give their Votes; which Day shall be the same throughout the United States.

No Persons except a natural born Citizen, or a Citizen of the United States, at the time of the Adoption of this Constitution, shall be eligible to the Office of President; neither shall any Person be eligible to that Office who shall not have attained to the Age of thirty five Years, and been fourteen Years a Resident within the United States.

In Case of the Removal of the President from Office, or of his Death, Resignation, or Inability to discharge the Powers and Duties of the said Office, the Same shall devolve on the Vice President, and the Congress may by Law provide for the Case of Removal, Death, Resignation or Inability, both of the President and Vice President, declaring what Officer shall then act as President, and such Officer shall act accordingly, until the Disability be removed, or a President shall be elected.

The President shall, at stated Times, receive for his Services, a Compensation, which shall neither be encreased nor diminished during the Period for which he shall have been elected, and he shall not receive within that Period any other Emolument from the United States, or any of them.

Before he enter on the Execution of his Office, he shall take the following Oath or Affirmation:—"I do solemnly swear (or affirm) that I will faithfully execute the Office of President of the United States, and will to the best of my Ability, preserve, protect and defend the Constitution of the United States."

Section. 2. The President shall be Commander in Chief of the Army and Navy of the United States, and of the Militia of the several States, when called into the actual Service of the United States; he may require the Opinion, in writing, of the principal Officer in each of the executive Departments, upon any Subject relating to the Duties of their respective Offices, and he shall have Power to grant

Reprieves and Pardons for Offences against the United States, except in Cases of Impeachment.

He shall have Power, by and with the Advice and Consent of the Senate, to make Treaties, provided two thirds of the Senators present concur; and he shall nominate, and by and with the Advice and Consent of the Senate, shall appoint Ambassadors, other public Ministers and Consuls, Judges of the supreme Court, and all other Officers of the United States, whose Appointments are not herein otherwise provided for, and which shall be established by Law: but the Congress may by Law vest the Appointment of such inferior Officers, as they think proper, in the President alone, in the Courts of Law, or in the Heads of Departments.

The President shall have Power to fill up all Vacancies that may happen during the Recess of the Senate, by granting Commissions which shall expire at the End of their next Session.

Section. 3.   He shall from time to time give to the Congress Information of the State of the Union, and recommend to their Consideration such Measures as he shall judge necessary and expedient; he may, on extraordinary Occasions, convene both Houses, or either of them, and in Case of Disagreement between them, with Respect to the Time of Adjournment, he may adjourn them to such Time as he shall think proper; he shall receive Ambassadors and other public Ministers; he shall take Care that the Laws be faithfully executed, and shall Commission all the Officers of the United States.

Section. 4.   The President, Vice President and all civil Officers of the United States, shall be removed from Office on Impeachment for, and Conviction of Treason, Bribery, or other high Crimes and Misdemeanors.

Article. III.

Section. 1.   The judicial Power of the United States, shall be vested in one supreme Court, and in such inferior Courts as the Congress may from time to time ordain and establish. The Judges, both of the supreme and inferior Courts, shall hold their Offices during good Behaviour, and shall, at stated Times, receive for their Services, a Compensation, which shall not be diminished during their Continuance in Office.

Section. 2.   The judicial Power shall extend to all Cases, in Law and Equity, arising under this Constitution, the Laws of the United States, and Treaties made, or which shall be made, under their Authority;—to all Cases affecting Ambassadors, other public Ministers and Consuls;—to all Cases of admiralty and maritime Jurisdiction;—

to Controversies to which the United States shall be a Party;—to Controversies between two or more States;—between a State and Citizens of another State;—between Citizens of different States,— between Citizens of the same State claiming Lands under Grants of different States, and between a State, or the Citizens thereof, and of foreign States, Citizens or Subjects.

In all Cases affecting Ambassadors, other public Ministers and Consuls, and those in which a State shall be Party, the supreme Court shall have original Jurisdiction. In all the other Cases before mentioned, the supreme Court shall have appellate Jurisdiction, both as to Law and Fact, with such Exceptions, and under such Regulations as the Congress shall make.

The Trial of all Crimes, except in Cases of Impeachment, shall be by Jury; and such Trial shall be held in the State where the said Crimes shall have been committed; but when not committed within any State, the Trial shall be at such Place or Places as the Congress may by Law have directed.

Section. 3.   Treason against the United States, shall consist only in levying War against them, or in adhering to their Enemies, giving them Aid and Comfort. No Person shall be convicted of Treason unless on the Testimony of two Witnesses to the same overt Act, or on Confession in open Court.

The Congress shall have Power to declare the Punishment of Treason, but no Attainder of Treason shall work Corruption of Blood, or Forfeiture except during the Life of the Person attainted.

Article. IV.

Section. 1.   Full Faith and Credit shall be given in each State to the public Acts, Records, and judicial Proceedings of every other State. And the Congress may by general Laws prescribe the Manner in which such Acts, Records and Proceedings shall be proved, and the Effect thereof.

Section. 2.   The Citizens of each State shall be entitled to all privileges and Immunities of Citizens in the several States.

A Person charged in any State with Treason, Felony, or other Crime, who shall flee from Justice, and be found in another State, shall on Demand of the executive Authority of the State from which he fled, be delivered up, to be removed to the State having Jurisdiction of the Crime.

No Person held to Service or Labour in one State, under the Laws thereof, escaping into another, shall, in Consequence of any Law or Regulation therein, be discharged from such Service or Labour, but shall be delivered up on Claim of the Party to whom such Service or Labour may be due.

Section. 3.   New States may be admitted by the Congress into this Union; but no new State shall be formed or erected within the Jurisdiction of any other State; nor any State be formed by the Junction of two or more States, or Parts of States, without the Consent of the Legislatures of the States concerned as well as of the Congress.

The Congress shall have Power to dispose of and make all needful Rules and Regulations respecting the Territory or other Property belonging to the United States; and nothing in this Constitution shall be so construed as to Prejudice any Claims of the United States, or of any particular State.

Section. 4.   The United States shall guarantee to every State in this Union a Republican Form of Government, and shall protect each of them against Invasion; and on Application of the Legislature, or of the Executive (when the Legislature cannot be convened) against domestic Violence.

Article. V.

The Congress, whenever two thirds of both Houses shall deem it necessary, shall propose Amendments to this Constitution, or, on the Application of the Legislatures of two thirds of the several States, shall call a Convention for proposing Amendments, which, in either Case, shall be valid to all Intents and Purposes, as Part of this Constitution, when ratified by the Legislatures of three fourths of the several States, or by Conventions in three fourths thereof, as the one or the other Mode of Ratification may be proposed by the Congress; Provided that no Amendment which may be made prior to the Year One thousand eight hundred and eight shall in any Manner affect the first and fourth Clauses in the Ninth Section of the first Article; and that no State, without its Consent, shall be deprived of it's equal Suffrage in the Senate.

Article. VI.

All Debts contracted and Engagements entered into, before the Adoption of this Constitution, shall be as valid against the United States under this Constitution, as under the Confederation.

This Constitution, and the Laws of the United States which shall be made in Pursuance thereof; and all Treaties made, or which shall be made, under the Authority of the United States, shall be the supreme Law of the Land; and the Judges in every State shall be bound thereby, any Thing in the Constitution or Laws of any State to the Contrary notwithstanding.

The Senators and Representatives before mentioned, and the Members of the several State Legislatures, and all executive and judicial Officers; both of the United States and of the several States, shall be bound by Oath or Affirmation, to support this Constitution; but no religious Test shall ever be required as a Qualification to any Office or public Trust under the United States.

Article. VII.

The Ratification of the Conventions of nine States, shall be sufficient for the Establishment of this Constitution between the States so ratifying the Same.

DONE in Convention by the Unanimous Consent of the States present the Seventeenth Day of September in the Year of our Lord one thousand seven hundred and Eighty seven and of the Independance of the United States of America the Twelfth In Witness whereof We have hereunto subscribed our Names,

Attest William Jackson Secretary

Go: Washington — Presidt.
and deputy from Virginia

Delaware
Geo: Read
Gunning Bedford junr
John Dickinson
Richard Bassett
Jaco: Broom

Maryland
James McHenry
Dan of St Thos. Jenifer
Danl Carroll

Virginia
John Blair—
James Madison Jr.

North Carolina
Wm. Blount
Richd. Dobbs Spaight.
Hu Williamson

South Carolina
J. Rutledge
Charles Cotesworth Pinckney
Charles Pinckney
Pierce Butler

Georgia
William Few
Abr Baldwin

New Hampshire
John Langdon
Nicholas Gilman

Massachusetts
Nathaniel Gorham
Rufus King

Connecticut
Wm: Saml. Johnson
Roger Sherman

New York . . . Alexander Hamilton

New Jersey
Wil: Livingston
David Brearley
Wm. Paterson.
Jona: Dayton

Pensylvania
B Franklin
Thomas Mifflin
Robt Morris
Geo. Clymer
Thos. FitzSimons
Jared Ingersoll
James Wilson
Gouv. Morris

ARTICLES in Addition to, and Amendment of, the Constitution of the United States of America, proposed by Congress, and ratified by the Legislatures of the several States, pursuant to the fifth Article of the original Constitution.

Article I.

Congress shall make no law respecting an establishment of religion, or prohibiting the free exercise thereof; or abridging the freedom of speech, or of the press; or the right of the people peaceably to assemble, and to petition the Government for a redress of grievances.

Article II.

A well regulated Militia, being necessary to the security of a free State, the right of the people to keep and bear Arms, shall not be infringed.

Article III.

No Soldier shall, in time of peace be quartered in any house, without the consent of the Owner, nor in time of war, but in a manner to be prescribed by law.

Article IV.

The right of the people to be secure in their persons, houses, papers, and effects, against unreasonable searches and seizures, shall not be violated, and no Warrants shall issue, but upon probable cause, supported by Oath or affirmation, and particularly describing the place to be searched, and the persons or things to be seized.

Article V.

No person shall be held to answer for a capital, or otherwise infamous crime, unless on a presentment or indictment of a Grand Jury, except in cases arising in the land or naval forces, or in the Militia, when in actual service in time of War or public danger; nor shall any person be subject for the same offence to be twice put in jeopardy of life or limb; nor shall be compelled in any criminal case to be a witness against himself, nor be deprived of life, liberty, or property, without due process of law; nor shall private property be taken for public use, without just compensation.

Article VI.

In all criminal prosecutions, the accused shall enjoy the right to a speedy and public trial, by an impartial jury of the State and district

wherein the crime shall have been committed, which district shall
have been previously ascertained by law, and to be informed of the
nature and cause of the accusation; to be confronted with the witnesses against him; to have compulsory process for obtaining witnesses in his favor, and to have the Assistance of Counsel for his
defence.

Article VII.

In Suits at common law, where the value in controversy shall exceed twenty dollars, the right of trial by jury shall be preserved, and
no fact tried by a jury, shall be otherwise reexamined in any Court
of the United States, than according to the rules of the common law.

Article VIII.

Excessive bail shall not be required, nor excessive fines imposed,
nor cruel and unusual punishments inflicted.

Article IX.

The enumeration in the Constitution, of certain rights, shall not
be construed to deny or disparage others retained by the people.

Article X.

The powers not delegated to the United States by the Constitution, nor prohibited by it to the States, are reserved to the States respectively, or to the people.

1792

Article XI.

The Judicial power of the United States shall not be construed to
extend to any suit in law or equity, commenced or prosecuted
against one of the United States by Citizens of another State, or by
Citizens or Subjects of any Foreign State.

1798

Article XII.

The Electors shall meet in their respective states, and vote by ballot for President and Vice-President, one of whom, at least, shall not
be an inhabitant of the same state with themselves; they shall name
in their ballots the person voted for as President, and in distinct ballots the person voted for as Vice-President, and they shall make distinct lists of all persons voted for as President, and of all persons
voted for as Vice-President, and of the number of votes for each,
which lists they shall sign and certify, and transmit sealed to the seat

of the government of the United States, directed to the President of
the Senate;—The President of the Senate shall, in the presence of the
Senate and House of Representatives, open all the certificates and
the votes shall then be counted;—The person having the greatest
number of votes for President, shall be the President, if such number be a majority of the whole number of Electors appointed; and if
no person have such majority, then from the persons having the
highest numbers not exceeding three on the list of those voted for as
President, the House of Representatives shall choose immediately, by
ballot, the President. But in choosing the President, the votes shall
be taken by states, the representation from each state having one
vote; a quorum for this purpose shall consist of a member or members from two-thirds of the states, and a majority of all the states
shall be necessary to a choice. And if the House of Representatives
shall not choose a President whenever the right of choice shall devolve upon them, before the fourth day of March next following,
then the Vice-President shall act as President, as in the case of the
death or other constitutional disability of the President.—The person having the greatest number of votes as Vice-President, shall be
the Vice-President, if such number be a majority of the whole number of Electors appointed, and if no person have a majority, then
from the two highest numbers on the list, the Senate shall choose
the Vice-President; a quorum for the purpose shall consist of two-
thirds of the whole number of Senators, and a majority of the whole
number shall be necessary to a choice. But no person constitutionally ineligible to the office of President shall be eligible to that of
Vice-President of the United States.

1804

Article XIII.

SECTION 1.   Neither slavery nor involuntary servitude, except as a
punishment for crime whereof the party shall have been duly convicted, shall exist within the United States, or any place subject to
their jurisdiction.

SECTION 2.   Congress shall have power to enforce this article by
appropriate legislation.

1865

Article XIV.

SECTION 1.   All persons born or naturalized in the United States,
and subject to the jurisdiction thereof, are citizens of the United
States and of the State wherein they reside. No State shall make or

enforce any law which shall abridge the privileges or immunities of citizens of the United States; nor shall any State deprive any person of life, liberty, or property, without due process of law; nor deny to any person within its jurisdiction the equal protection of the laws.

SECTION 2.   Representatives shall be apportioned among the several States according to their respective numbers, counting the whole number of persons in each State, excluding Indians not taxed. But when the right to vote at any election for the choice of electors for President and Vice President of the United States, Representatives in Congress, the Executive and Judicial officers of a State, or the members of the Legislature thereof, is denied to any of the male inhabitants of such State, being twenty-one years of age, and citizens of the United States, or in any way abridged, except for participation in rebellion, or other crime, the basis of representation therein shall be reduced in the proportion which the number of such male citizens shall bear to the whole number of male citizens twenty-one years of age in such State.

SECTION 3.   No person shall be a Senator or Representative in Congress, or elector of President and Vice President, or hold any office, civil or military, under the United States, or under any State, who, having previously taken an oath, as a member of Congress, or as an officer of the United States, or as a member of any State legislature, or as an executive or judicial officer of any State, to support the Constitution of the United States, shall have engaged in insurrection or rebellion against the same, or given aid or comfort to the enemies thereof. But Congress may by a vote of two-thirds of each House, remove such disability.

SECTION 4.   The validity of the public debt of the United States, authorized by law, including debts incurred for payment of pensions and bounties for services in suppressing insurrection or rebellion, shall not be questioned. But neither the United States nor any State shall assume or pay any debt or obligation incurred in aid of insurrection or rebellion against the United States, or any claim for the loss or emancipation of any slave; but all such debts, obligations and claims shall be held illegal and void.

SECTION 5.   The Congress shall have power to enforce, by appropriate legislation, the provisions of this article.

1868

Article XV.

SECTION 1.   The right of citizens of the United States to vote shall not be denied or abridged by the United States or by any State on account of race, color, or previous condition of servitude.

SECTION 2.   The Congress shall have power to enforce this article by appropriate legislation.

1870

Article XVI.

The Congress shall have power to lay and collect taxes on incomes, from whatever source derived, without apportionment among the several States, and without regard to any census or enumeration.

1913

Article XVII.

The Senate of the United States shall be composed of two Senators from each State, elected by the people thereof, for six years; and each Senator shall have one vote. The electors in each State shall have the qualifications requisite for electors of the most numerous branch of the State legislatures.

When vacancies happen in the representation of any State in the Senate, the executive authority of such State shall issue writs of election to fill such vacancies: *Provided,* That the legislature of any State may empower the executive thereof to make temporary appointments until the people fill the vacancies by election as the legislature may direct.

This amendment shall not be so construed as to affect the election or term of any Senator chosen before it becomes valid as part of the Constitution.

1913

Article XVIII.

SECTION 1.   After one year from the ratification of this article the manufacture, sale, or transportation of intoxicating liquors within, the importation thereof into, or the exportation thereof from the United States and all territory subject to the jurisdiction thereof for beverage purposes is hereby prohibited.

SEC. 2.   The Congress and the several States shall have concurrent power to enforce this article by appropriate legislation.

SEC. 3.   This article shall be inoperative unless it shall have been ratified as an amendment to the Constitution by the legislatures of the several States, as provided in the Constitution, within seven years from the date of the submission hereof to the States by the Congress.

1919

Article XIX.

The right of citizens of the United States to vote shall not be denied or abridged by the United States or by any State on account of sex.

Congress shall have power to enforce this article by appropriate legislation.

1920

Article XX.

SECTION 1. The terms of the President and Vice President shall end at noon on the 20th day of January, and the terms of Senators and Representatives at noon on the 3d day of January, of the years in which such terms would have ended if this article had not been ratified; and the terms of their successors shall then begin.

SEC. 2. The Congress shall assemble at least once in every year, and such meeting shall begin at noon on the 3d day of January, unless they shall by law appoint a different day.

SEC. 3. If, at the time fixed for the beginning of the term of the President, the President elect shall have died, the Vice President elect shall become President. If a President shall not have been chosen before the time fixed for the beginning of his term, or if the President elect shall have failed to qualify, then the Vice President elect shall act as President until a President shall have qualified; and the Congress may by law provide for the case wherein neither a President elect nor a Vice President elect shall have qualified, declaring who shall then act as President, or the manner in which one who is to act shall be selected, and such person shall act accordingly until a President or Vice President shall have qualified.

SEC. 4. The Congress may by law provide for the case of the death of any of the persons from whom the House of Representatives may choose a President whenever the right of choice shall have devolved upon them, and for the case of the death of any of the persons from whom the Senate may choose a Vice President whenever the right of choice shall have devolved upon them.

SEC. 5. Sections 1 and 2 shall take effect on the 15th day of October following the ratification of this article.

SEC. 6. This article shall be inoperative unless it shall have been ratified as an amendment to the Constitution by the legislatures of three-fourths of the several States within seven years from the date of its submission.

1933

Article XXI.

SECTION 1. The eighteenth article of amendment to the Constitution of the United States is hereby repealed.

SECTION 2. The transportation or importation into any State, Territory, or possession of the United States for delivery or use therein of intoxicating liquors, in violation of the laws thereof, is hereby prohibited.

SECTION 3. This article shall be inoperative unless it shall have been ratified as an amendment to the Constitution by conventions in the several States, as provided in the Constitution, within seven years from the date of the submission hereof to the States by the Congress.

1933

Article XXII.

SECTION 1. No person shall be elected to the office of the President more than twice, and no person who has held the office of President, or acted as President, for more than two years of a term to which some other person was elected President shall be elected to the office of the President more than once. But this Article shall not apply to any person holding the office of President when this Article was proposed by the Congress, and shall not prevent any person who may be holding the office of President, or acting as President, during the term within which this Article becomes operative from holding the office of President or acting as President during the remainder of such term.

SEC. 2. This article shall be inoperative unless it shall have been ratified as an amendment to the Constitution by the legislatures of three-fourths of the several States within seven years from the date of its submission to the States by the Congress.

1951

Article XXIII.

SECTION 1. The District constituting the seat of Government of the United States shall appoint in such manner as the Congress may direct:

A number of electors of President and Vice President equal to the whole number of Senators and Representatives in Congress to which the District would be entitled if it were a State, but in no event more than the least populous State; they shall be in addition to those appointed by the States, but they shall be considered, for the purposes of the election of President and Vice President, to be electors appointed by a State; and they shall meet in the District and perform such duties as provided by the twelfth article of amendment.

SEC. 2. The Congress shall have power to enforce this article by appropriate legislation.

1961

Article XXIV.

SECTION 1.   The right of citizens of the United States to vote in any primary or other election for President or Vice President, for electors for President or Vice President, or for Senator or Representative in Congress, shall not be denied or abridged by the United States or any State by reason of failure to pay any poll tax or other tax.

SEC. 2.   The Congress shall have power to enforce this article by appropriate legislation.

1964

Article XXV.

SECTION 1.   In case of the removal of the President from office or of his death or resignation, the Vice President shall become President.

SEC. 2.   Whenever there is a vacancy in the office of the Vice President, the President shall nominate a Vice President who shall take office upon confirmation by a majority vote of both Houses of Congress.

SEC. 3.   Whenever the President transmits to the President pro tempore of the Senate and the Speaker of the House of Representatives his written declaration that he is unable to discharge the powers and duties of his office, and until he transmits to them a written declaration to the contrary, such powers and duties shall be discharged by the Vice President as Acting President.

SEC. 4.   Whenever the Vice President and a majority of either the principal officers of the executive departments or of such other body as Congress may by law provide, transmit to the President pro tempore of the Senate and the Speaker of the House of Representatives their written declaration that the President is unable to discharge the powers and duties of his office, the Vice President shall immediately assume the powers and duties of the office as Acting President.

Thereafter, when the President transmits to the President pro tempore of the Senate and the Speaker of the House of Representatives his written declaration that no inability exists, he shall resume the powers and duties of his office unless the Vice President and a majority of either the principal officers of the executive department or of such other body as Congress may by law provide, transmit within four days to the President pro tempore of the Senate and the Speaker of the House of Representatives their written declaration that the President is unable to discharge the powers and duties of his office. Thereupon Congress shall decide the issue, assembling within forty-eight hours for that purpose if not in session. If the Congress, within twenty-one days after receipt of the latter written declaration, or, if Congress is not in session, within twenty-one days after Congress is required to assemble, determines by two-thirds vote of both Houses that the President is unable to discharge the powers and duties of his office, the Vice President shall continue to discharge the same as Acting President; otherwise, the President shall resume the powers and duties of his office.

1967

Article XXVI.

SECTION 1.   The right of citizens of the United States, who are eighteen years of age or older, to vote shall not be denied or abridged by the United States or by any State on account of age.

SEC. 2.   The Congress shall have power to enforce this article by appropriate legislation.

1971

Article XXVII.

No law, varying the compensation for the services of the Senators and Representatives, shall take effect, until an election of Representatives shall have intervened.

1992

Chronology

1751   Born March 16 (New Style) at the plantation of his maternal grandmother on the Rappahannock River opposite Port Royal in King George County, Virginia, the first child of James Madison and Nelly Conway Madison. (Father, born 1723, and mother, born 1732, married in September 1749.) Father owns Montpelier, plantation in Orange County, Virginia, that includes 2,850 acres and dozens of slaves, where he grows tobacco, wheat, and corn.

1753   Brother Francis born.

1755   Brother Ambrose born.

1758   Brother Catlett born and dies in infancy.

1760   Sister Nelly born.

1762   Brother William born. Madison begins attending boarding school kept by Donald Robertson, a graduate of the University of Edinburgh, in neighboring King and Queen County, where he studies English, Latin, Greek, arithmetic, algebra, geometry, geography, and French.

1764   Sister Sarah born.

1767   Madison begins to be tutored at home by the Reverend Thomas Martin, rector of the nearby Brick Church, the Anglican congregation attended by his family.

1768   Sister Elizabeth born.

1769   Madison enters College of New Jersey at Princeton, where he studies Greek and Latin literature, science, moral philosophy, rhetoric, logic, and mathematics. Lives in Nassau Hall, and forms friendships with fellow students William Bradford, Philip Freneau, and Hugh Henry Brackenridge.

1771   Brother Reuben born. Madison is awarded baccalaureate
            degree on September 25. Remains in Princeton for addi-
            tional study with John Witherspoon, president of the
            college.

1772–73   Returns to Montpelier in April, 1772. Worries about his
            health while continuing to read government and law.

1774   Visits Pennsylvania and New York in May and June, just
            as Americans are learning of the passage of the Parlia-
            mentary Coercive Acts punishing Massachusetts for the
            Boston Tea Party. Sister Frances born. Madison is elected
            on December 22 as a member of the Orange County
            Committee of Safety, formed to enforce the embargo on
            British imports adopted in October by the First Conti-
            nental Congress.

1775   Sister Elizabeth and brother Reuben die in late spring
            from dysentery. Madison participates in raising and
            drilling Orange County militia and is commissioned as a
            militia colonel on October 2, but never serves in the field
            because of his weak health.

1776   Elected on April 25 as a delegate from Orange County to
            the Virginia convention, which assembles in Williamsburg
            on May 6. Votes on May 15 for resolution instructing the
            Virginia delegates to the Continental Congress to pro-
            pose a declaration of independence. Serves on committee
            appointed to draft a declaration of rights, and secures im-
            portant amendment to its article concerning religious
            freedom during debate in the convention in June. Con-
            vention adjourns July 5 after adopting a constitution for
            the state; under its terms, the members of the convention
            become the first House of Delegates of the new General
            Assembly. Madison returns to Williamsburg for the first
            session of the General Assembly, October–December,
            where he meets Thomas Jefferson.

1777   Defeated for reelection to the House of Delegates on
            April 24. Elected by the General Assembly on November
            15 to the eight-man Council of State, which shares execu-
            tive power with the governor.

1778   Begins service on the council in January, acting as an ad-
        viser to Governor Patrick Henry. Elected to the House of
        Delegates in April, but election is annulled because of his
        membership on the council.

1779   Continues service on council when Jefferson succeeds
        Henry as governor in June. Elected by the General As-
        sembly on December 14 as a delegate to the Continental
        Congress.

1780   Writes essay on paper money and public finance. Travels
        to Philadelphia and takes seat in Continental Congress on
        March 20. Appointed March 22 to the Board of Admi-
        ralty, which oversees the navy, and serves until June 6. Be-
        comes involved in negotiations over the cession to
        Congress of Virginia land claims northwest of the Ohio
        River. Drafts instructions from Congress to John Jay, the
        American envoy to Spain, calling for the assertion of
        American navigation rights on the Mississippi.

1781   Ratification of the Articles of Confederation is completed
        on March 1. Madison proposes on March 16 that the Ar-
        ticles be amended to give Congress the power to coerce
        states that defy Congress or fail to meet their financial
        requisitions (proposal is referred to committee and never
        approved). Supports efforts by Robert Morris, the new
        superintendent of finance, to restore public credit. Partic-
        ipates in debates over instructions to American peace ne-
        gotiators in Europe. Reelected to Congress by the
        Virginia assembly on June 14.

1782   Continues active involvement in deliberations over west-
        ern land claims, peace terms, and public finance. Collab-
        orates with the Marquis de Barbé-Marbois, a member of
        the French legation, in writing an anonymous public
        letter defending the American alliance with France. Re-
        elected to Congress on June 15. Begins keeping detailed
        notes of debates in Congress in November.

1783   Plays major role in fashioning compromise measures de-
        signed to provide Congress with adequate revenue and to
        amend the revenue clauses of the Articles. Drafts address
        that accompanies financial measures proposed to the

states on April 18. Courts Catherine Floyd, 16-year-old daughter of New York delegate William Floyd. Takes up residence in Princeton with other delegates in late June after protests by unpaid Pennsylvania soldiers cause Congress to abandon Philadelphia. Catherine Floyd breaks off engagement during summer. Madison leaves Congress when his term expires on November 2 (under the Articles, delegates can serve for no more than three years out of six). Returns to Montpelier on December 5 for the first time since March 1780.

1784   Continues reading in law and government. Elected to the House of Delegates on April 22 and attends spring session of the assembly in Richmond, May–June. Travels with the Marquis de Lafayette to Fort Schuyler (now Rome, New York) in the Mohawk Valley to observe negotiations between American commissioners and the Iroquois, September–October. Returns to Richmond for the fall session of the assembly.

1785   Elected member of the American Philosophical Society on January 21. Returns to Montpelier in February and remains there until August. Reelected to the House of Delegates in April. Writes "Memorial and Remonstrance Against Religious Assessments" in June in opposition to proposed bill establishing a tax to support Christian ministers of all denominations. Travels to Philadelphia and New York, September–October, visiting George Washington at Mount Vernon during both his departure and his return. Takes seat in House of Delegates on October 25. Succeeds in preventing passage of the general assessment bill and in passing some of the laws drafted by Thomas Jefferson in 1778–79 as a revised statutory code for Virginia.

1786   Secures passage of revised version of the statute on religious freedom drafted by Jefferson in 1777 (writes to Jefferson that passage of the bill has "extinguished for ever the ambitious hope of making laws for the human mind" in Virginia). Assembly adopts resolution on January 21 calling for a general meeting of the states to consider adopting uniform commercial regulations and appoints Madison as one of the state's eight commissioners. Madison returns to Montpelier in March. Reelected to the

House of Delegates in April. Reads histories of ancient and modern confederacies and takes extensive notes on their strengths and weaknesses. Visits Philadelphia and New York, June–August. Becomes increasingly alarmed by sectional rift in Congress caused by the willingness of Secretary for Foreign Affairs John Jay and the northern states to yield American claims to navigation on the Mississippi in return for the negotiation of a treaty of commerce with Spain. Attends conference on commercial regulations, held in Annapolis, September 11–14. With only five states represented, the meeting adjourns after all 12 commissioners present adopt a resolution, drafted by Alexander Hamilton, proposing that a general convention meet in Philadelphia in May 1787 to consider constitutional changes. Madison returns to Virginia with James Monroe and visits Washington at Mount Vernon before taking his seat in the assembly in late October. Virginia assembly endorses call for a general convention, elects Madison as a delegate to Congress on November 7, and on December 4 appoints him as one of the state's seven delegates to the Philadelphia convention.

1787   Travels to New York and takes his seat in Congress on February 10. Reviews his studies of other confederations before drafting memorandum on the "Vices of the Political System of the United States." In letters to Jefferson, Washington, and Virginia governor Edmund Randolph, prepares a tentative agenda for the Federal Convention. Arrives in Philadelphia on May 5, the first delegate from any state other than Pennsylvania to appear. Joins with other members of the Virginia delegation in preparing the Virginia Plan, which Randolph proposes to the Convention on May 29. Plays leading role in debates while keeping detailed notes of the Convention proceedings from its first meeting on May 25 until adjournment on September 17. Returns to New York on September 24. Successfully resists efforts by Virginia delegate Richard Henry Lee to have the proposed Constitution amended by Congress before it is submitted to the states for ratification. Accepts invitation from Hamilton to assist him and John Jay in writing a series of essays supporting ratification, under the title *The Federalist* and the pseudonym "Publius." Publishes his first contribution to the series in the *New York Journal* on November 22.

1788   Remains in New York, attending Congress and complet-
              ing his contributions to *The Federalist*, eventually writing
              29 of its 85 essays. Returns to Virginia in early March and
              is elected as a delegate to the Virginia ratifying conven-
              tion on March 24. Maintains active correspondence with
              Federalist leaders in other states, including Hamilton in
              New York and Rufus King in Massachusetts. Takes seat in
              the Virginia convention at Richmond on June 3. Despite
              ill health, leads the Federalist defense of the Constitution
              against the wide-ranging criticisms of Antifederalist lead-
              ers Patrick Henry and George Mason. Reluctantly agrees
              to support form of ratification that calls for the new Con-
              gress to consider amendments to the Constitution. Con-
              vention approves the Constitution, 89–79, on June 25,
              making Virginia the tenth state to ratify. Leaves Rich-
              mond for New York on July 1, stopping en route at
              Mount Vernon. Despite his wishes, nominated by Vir-
              ginia Federalists for a seat in the new Senate, but is de-
              feated in the election held in the Virginia assembly on
              November 8. Returns to Virginia in December to cam-
              paign for election to the House of Representatives.

1789   Writes public letters announcing his support for the adop-
              tion of constitutional amendments protecting essential
              rights. Defeats his friend James Monroe, who had op-
              posed ratification in the Virginia convention, in the Feb-
              ruary 2 election, 1,308–972. Leaves Montpelier for New
              York in mid-February, stopping for ten days at Mount
              Vernon to discuss affairs with Washington. Congress
              achieves a quorum on April 6 and counts votes of presi-
              dential electors, who have unanimously chosen Wash-
              ington to be the first president. Madison introduces
              legislation in the House on April 8 to levy federal impost
              and tonnage duties. Advises Washington on his inaugural
              address and then drafts the House reply. Takes leading
              part in first constitutional debate in Congress, successfully
              arguing that the president has the power to remove exec-
              utive officials without obtaining the consent of the Sen-
              ate. Introduces series of constitutional amendments on
              June 8 and persuades the House to consider them during
              its first session. Congress submits 12 amendments to the
              states for ratification on September 25 (ratification of the
              third through the twelfth proposed amendments is com-
              pleted in 1791; the second proposed amendment is ratified

in 1992). Returns to Montpelier after Congress adjourns on September 29. Visits Monticello to see Jefferson, who has recently returned to the United States after five years of diplomatic service in Europe and is about to take office as secretary of state.

1790 Returns to New York, where he attends second session of the First Federal Congress from January until August. Secretary of the Treasury Alexander Hamilton submits plan to the House on January 14 for funding the national debt and for the federal assumption of state debts from the Revolutionary War. Madison gives speech on February 11 opposing Hamilton's plan for failing to discriminate between original holders of Continental securities and speculators who later purchased them at depreciated prices. House votes against discrimination, 36–13, on February 22 and begins debating assumption of state debts. Madison again opposes Hamilton's plan, arguing that it unfairly discriminates against Virginia and other states that have already paid much of their war debt. Assumption measure is defeated in the House, 31–29, on April 12. Congress continues to debate the site of the permanent national capital, with Madison strongly advocating its location along the Potomac River. In late June, Jefferson, Hamilton, and Madison agree that in exchange for southern support of a modified assumption measure, northern members of Congress will support moving the capital to Philadelphia for ten years and then permanently establishing it along the Potomac in 1800. Bills for moving the capital and for assuming state debts are passed in the House by narrow margins in July. Madison leaves for Virginia with Jefferson in early September. Reelected to the House of Representatives on September 6 with only minor opposition. Travels to Philadelphia in November for the third and final session of the First Congress, which convenes on December 6. Hamilton proposes on December 14 that Congress charter a national bank.

1791 Madison opposes chartering the bank, arguing in the House that the Constitution does not specifically give Congress power to issue charters of incorporation and that the incorporation of a bank is not necessary to the execution of any constitutionally specified powers. Advises Washington to veto the bank bill, which Congress passes, but the President instead follows Hamilton's advice and signs it on February 25. Congress adjourns March 3. In May and June Madison and Jefferson travel to Lake George and Lake Champlain in upstate New York, then return to New York City by way of Vermont and western Massachusetts. Encourages Philip Freneau to start a newspaper in Philadelphia opposed to Hamiltonian policies. Takes seat in Second Congress in Philadelphia on October 24. Publishes first of 18 unsigned essays in Freneau's *National Gazette* on November 21 (series continues until December 22, 1792).

1792   In conversation with Washington on May 5, Madison urges him to serve a second term as president. Returns to Virginia after Congress recesses on May 8. Drafts retirement address at Washington's request (Washington will use a portion of it in his 1796 farewell address). During the summer Hamilton publishes series of pseudonymous pieces in the press attacking Jefferson for hiring Freneau as a State Department translator while he was editing the partisan *National Gazette*. Madison and Monroe collaboratively write six unsigned articles defending Jefferson's conduct that appear in the Philadelphia *American Daily Advertiser*, September 22–December 31. Takes seat in new session of Congress on November 5.

1793   Returns to Virginia with Monroe after Congress adjourns on March 2. Reelected to the House on March 18 without opposition. Accepts honorary French citizenship conferred on him by the revolutionary National Assembly. After learning that France has declared war on Britain and consulting his cabinet, Washington issues proclamation on April 22 declaring American neutrality in the conflict. When Hamilton, writing as "Pacificus," defends presidential power to interpret treaties and issue proclamations of neutrality without consulting Congress, Jefferson urges Madison to respond. Madison writes five "Helvidius" essays, published August 24–September 18, defending the power of Congress to interpret treaties and proclaim neutrality. Brother Ambrose Madison dies October 3. Madison returns to Philadelphia for the Third Congress, which convenes on December 2. Jefferson retires as secretary of state on December 31, leaving Madison as the principal leader of the emerging Republican party opposed to Hamilton and his Federalist supporters.

1794   In support of report on foreign commerce submitted by Jefferson in December 1793, Madison introduces resolutions on January 3 imposing higher duties on British imports in retaliation for British policies discriminating against American commerce. Votes on March 4 for constitutional amendment removing from federal jurisdiction lawsuits brought against states by foreigners or by citizens of another state (ratification of the Eleventh Amendment is completed in 1795). Debate on commercial resolutions is interrupted in late March when Congress learns that the British have captured more than 250 American merchant ships engaging in commerce with the French West Indies. Washington appoints Chief Justice John Jay as special envoy to Britain on April 16 in effort to avoid Anglo-American war. Madison declines to be considered for appointment as American minister to France. Begins courtship of Dolley Payne Todd (b. 1768), widow of John Todd, a Quaker lawyer who died during the 1793 yellow fever epidemic in Philadelphia, and mother of John Payne Todd (b. 1792). Returns to Virginia after Congress adjourns on June 9. Marries Dolley Payne Todd on September 15 at Harewood in Jefferson County, Virginia (now West Virginia). Family returns to Philadelphia in October for the new session of Congress (Anna Payne, Dolley's younger sister, becomes member of Madison household until her marriage in 1804). During House debates in November Madison defends Democratic-Republican Societies after Washington accuses them of having fomented the Whiskey Rebellion in western Pennsylvania.

1795   Remains in Philadelphia after Congress adjourns on March 3. Reelected to the House on March 16 without opposition. Writes *Political Observations*, anonymous pamphlet strongly critical of administration policies, which is published in late April after Madison returns to Virginia. After secret debate, Senate votes 20–10 on June 24 to ratify treaty with Britain signed by Jay in November 1794. Terms of treaty, which provide for evacuation of British garrisons from frontier posts in the Northwest but contain few British concessions regarding neutral maritime rights or terms of Anglo-American trade, are widely attacked after its text is published on July 1. Washington signs the treaty on August 18. Madison drafts petition to the Virginia assembly protesting its terms that is printed in several newspapers in November. Returns with his family to Philadelphia, where the first session of the Fourth Congress convenes on December 7.

1796   Washington proclaims Jay Treaty to be in effect on February 29 and sends it to the House the following day. House begins debate on its constitutional role in ratifying treaties, with Madison and other Republicans arguing that since the House must appropriate money to implement the treaty, it has the right to review its merits, even though the Constitution explicitly vests the treaty power in the President and Senate. Madison joins majority when House votes 62–37 on March 24 to ask Washington for documents relating to the negotiation of the treaty. The President replies on March 30, withholding the papers while asserting that the House has no constitutional role in ratifying treaties; in his response, Washington refers to the understanding of the treaty power held by the Constitutional Convention in 1787. Madison continues to oppose the treaty and argues in speech on April 6 that the Constitution should be interpreted according to the prevailing understandings of the ratifying conventions in 1787–88. After intense debate, House votes 51–48 on April 30 to appropriate money for implementation of the treaty. Madison travels to Montpelier after Congress adjourns on June 1, then returns to Philadelphia in November for the second session of the Fourth Congress, which begins on December 5. His decision to retire from the House is announced in Fredericksburg, Virginia, newspaper on December 9. In the presidential election, Federalist candidate John Adams receives 71 electoral votes and is elected president, while Jefferson, the Republican candidate, receives 68 electoral votes and becomes vice-president.

1797   Fourth Congress adjourns on March 3. Madison returns to Montpelier in late April with Dolley and stepson John Payne Todd. Becomes actively involved in managing the plantation, which now includes 5,000 acres and over 100 slaves and produces wheat as its main crop. Studies scientific farming and undertakes renovation of the main house.

1798   Worsening relations between the United States and France and French seizures of American ships trading with Britain lead Adams and the Federalist-dominated Congress to begin undeclared naval war with France during the summer. Congress passes Alien Act, June 25, giving the president power to expel "dangerous" foreigners without judicial proceedings, and Sedition Act, July 14, making the publication of "false, scandalous, and malicious writing" attacking the Congress or the president a crime. Jefferson and Madison secretly draft resolutions condemning the Alien and Sedition Acts as unconstitutional and calling upon the states to oppose them. Kentucky legislature adopts Jefferson resolutions in modified form on November 10, and Virginia assembly adopts Madison resolutions on December 24.

1799   Madison writes essays on danger of British influence and the character of Franco-American relations which appear in the Philadelphia *Aurora General Advertiser* on January 23 and February 23. Elected as delegate from Orange County to the Virginia assembly on April 24. Meets with Jefferson and Monroe at Monticello in September to discuss plans for continued opposition to the Alien and Sedition Acts. Takes his seat in the assembly in December and begins writing extensive report on the response by other states to the Virginia Resolutions.

1800   Virginia assembly approves Madison's report in January. Madison is named to Republican ticket of presidential electors on January 30. Remains in Virginia throughout the year, maintaining active correspondence with Republican leaders in other states regarding the presidential election, in which Jefferson and Aaron Burr are opposing Adams and Charles Cotesworth Pinckney. Brother Francis Madison dies in April. Treaty signed in Paris on September 30 ends French-American hostilities. Madison casts electoral votes in Richmond on December 3 after Republicans win presidential election in Virginia. Voting by presidential electors nationwide results in tie between Jefferson and Burr as all 73 Republican electors divide their votes evenly between the two candidates, forcing the

presidential election into the Federalist-controlled House
of Representatives.

1801   House elects Jefferson president on February 17 after 36
        ballots; Burr becomes vice-president. During electoral
        crisis Madison remains at Montpelier, where his father
        dies on February 27 after weeks of failing health. Jefferson
        appoints Madison as secretary of state on March 5, but he
        remains at Montpelier for several weeks, suffering from
        rheumatism and attending to his father's estate. Arrives in
        the new capital of Washington, D.C., on May 1, where
        family stays for three weeks with Jefferson in the still-
        unfinished executive mansion. Takes oath of office on
        May 2 and begins attending to the extensive foreign and
        domestic administrative duties of the State Department.
        Advises Jefferson on patronage appointments (through-
        out Jefferson administration, Madison and Secretary of
        the Treasury Albert Gallatin serve as the President's clos-
        est advisers). Returns to Montpelier in July and remains
        there until early October (will continue to avoid extreme
        heat and humidity of Washington by spending summer
        months at Montpelier). Family moves into house at 1333 F
        Street N.W., two blocks from the executive mansion.
        Britain and France sign preliminary peace treaty on Octo-
        ber 1, ending war that began in 1793. Major foreign pol-
        icy issues confronting Madison include reports that Spain
        has secretly agreed to retrocede Louisiana to France and
        relations with Santo Domingo; administration decides to
        maintain trade with the island while withholding formal
        diplomatic recognition from the revolutionary regime of
        Toussaint L'Ouverture.

1802   French expeditionary force lands in Santo Domingo, and
        administration becomes concerned that French may send
        troops to occupy Louisiana. Madison instructs Robert R.
        Livingston, the American minister to France, to explore
        the possibility of the United States acquiring New Or-
        leans and the Floridas, which he believes may have also
        been ceded to France by Spain. French army on Santo
        Domingo suffers heavy losses from yellow fever and rebel
        attacks. Spanish intendant at New Orleans closes port to
        American commerce on October 16. Sister Nelly Madison
        Hite dies.

1803   Monroe is appointed as special envoy to France with in-
        structions to buy New Orleans and the Floridas. Madison
        and Gallatin advise Jefferson that although the Constitu-
        tion does not provide for the acquisition of foreign terri-
        tory, it can be acquired under the existing treaty-making
        power without the adoption of a constitutional amend-
        ment. Unable to send troops to Louisiana and anticipat-
        ing the renewal of war in Europe, Napoleon decides to
        sell the territory to the United States, and on May 2
        Monroe and Livingston sign a $15 million purchase agree-
        ment. War between Britain and France resumes on May
        18. When news of Louisiana Purchase reaches Washing-
        ton, Madison and Jefferson endorse decision by the
        American envoys to exceed their instructions, and Jeffer-
        son eventually agrees to have the purchase ratified with-
        out seeking a constitutional amendment.

1804   Administration asserts that eastern boundary of the
        Louisiana territory extends to the Perdido River (now the
        western boundary of the state of Florida), leading to de-
        teriorating personal relations between Madison and the
        Spanish envoy, Marquis de Casa Yrujo. Ratification of the
        Twelfth Amendment, which provides for separate ballot-
        ing in the electoral college for the president and vice-
        president, is completed on June 15. Madison protests
        impressment by the Royal Navy of seamen serving on
        American ships, but British refuse to stop practice of
        searching ships and seizing persons they claim are British
        subjects, regardless of whether they carry American citi-
        zenship papers. Jefferson defeats Federalist candidate
        Charles Cotesworth Pinckney of South Carolina in the
        presidential election with electoral vote of 162–14, while
        Republican vice-presidential candidate George Clinton is
        elected to succeed Aaron Burr.

1805   Spanish reject American claims to West Florida (the strip of
        Gulf Coast territory between Louisiana and the Perdido)
        and an offer to purchase East Florida. British admiralty
        court issues decision in *Essex* case strictly interpreting the
        "Rule of 1756," under which trade prohibited in time of
        peace cannot be opened to neutral shipping in time of war,
        and Royal Navy increases its seizures of American ships.
        Madison spends summer and early fall in Philadelphia,

where Dolley is being treated for an ulcerated tumor on her knee. Undertakes extensive research in international law in order to demonstrate that the Rule of 1756 is unjustifiable.

1806   Publishes 204-page pamphlet, *An Examination of the British Doctrine, Which Subjects to Capture a Neutral Trade, Not Open in Time of Peace.* Congress passes law in April restricting the importation of British goods (intended to go into effect in November 1806, its operation is suspended until December 1807 to allow negotiations to proceed). Administration appoints William Pinkney to join Monroe in London and attempt to secure limits on impressment and recognition of American neutral rights. Monroe and Pinkney sign treaty in December that does not address impressment issue.

1807   Madison and Jefferson receive text of the Monroe-Pinkney treaty in early March and immediately decide against submitting it to the Senate for ratification. British frigate *Leopard* fires on the American frigate *Chesapeake* off the Virginia coast on June 22, killing three men, and four seamen are then removed from the American ship. Administration bans British warships from entering American harbors while Madison instructs Monroe to obtain reparations and an end to impressment. British reassert their right to recover deserters from foreign ships as British and French seizures of American ships and cargoes increase. With strong support from Madison, Jefferson decides to exert economic pressure on European powers by embargoing all American overseas trade. Congress approves embargo measure on December 22.

1808   Madison engages in extensive but unproductive negotiations with George Rose, the special British envoy sent to discuss the *Chesapeake* affair. On January 23 the Republican congressional caucus selects Madison as their presidential candidate over George Clinton, who is supported by New York Republicans, and Monroe, who is backed by the conservative Virginia congressman John Randolph of Roanoke. Despite the increasing unpopularity of the embargo, Madison is elected president on December 7 with 122 electoral votes, while Federalist candidate Charles

Cotesworth Pinckney receives 47, mostly from New England, and Clinton six; in the balloting for vice-president, Clinton defeats Federalist candidate Rufus King.

1809   Congress repeals embargo and passes Nonintercourse Act, signed by Jefferson on March 1, which reopens American foreign commerce with all nations except Britain and France while authorizing the president to renew trade with either country if they remove their restrictions on American shipping. Madison is inaugurated on March 4. Prevented by opposition from Republican senators from appointing Gallatin secretary of state, Madison retains him as secretary of the treasury and names Robert Smith as secretary of state, William Eustis as secretary of war, and Paul Hamilton as secretary of the navy, while retaining Attorney General Caesar Rodney and Postmaster General Gideon Granger from the Jefferson administration. After successful negotiations with British envoy David Erskine, proclaims on April 19 that commerce with Britain will resume in June, but reimposes nonintercourse on August 9 after the British government repudiates agreement and recalls Erskine for exceeding his instructions. Continues to spend summer months at Montpelier when possible.

1810   With the Nonintercourse Act due to expire, Congress debates new measures and on May 1 passes legislation known as Macon's Bill Number 2, after Republican congressman Nathaniel Macon of North Carolina. The new act reopens commerce with Britain and France while authorizing the president to prohibit trade with one nation if the other removes its restrictions on American shipping. Following a rebellion by American settlers in West Florida, Madison issues proclamation annexing the territory to the United States (American occupation of the region is completed in 1813). After receiving dispatches from John Armstrong, the American minister in Paris, mistakenly reporting that Napoleon has rescinded decrees against American shipping, Madison declares on November 2 that commerce with Britain will cease in February 1811.

1811   Congress debates renewing charter of the national bank, which expires on March 4. Madison and Gallatin support renewal, but the House votes against it on January 24, and measure is also defeated in the Senate, February 20, with Vice-President Clinton casting the tie-breaking vote against renewal. Congress also defeats attempts by the administration to increase expenditures for the army and navy. Madison vetoes on constitutional grounds bills incorporating an Episcopal church in the District of Columbia and reserving land for a Baptist church in the Mississippi Territory. In March Madison obtains the resignation of Secretary of State Smith, who is widely considered to be incompetent and disloyal to the president, and replaces him with Monroe. On May 16 frigate *President* fires on British corvette *Little Belt* off the Virginia coast while on patrol to protect Americans against impressment, killing nine of her crew. British government threatens retaliation for new nonintercourse act passed in March and refuses to rescind Orders-in-Council directed against American shipping unless France revokes all decrees against neutral commerce and the importation of British goods into Europe. Renewed Indian warfare along the northwestern frontier in 1811 is widely blamed on the British presence in Canada. Madison increasingly believes war with Britain is inevitable, and summons Twelfth Congress into session one month early. Congress, which convenes November 4, includes as new members many younger Republicans who are willing to declare war on Britain. In message to Congress on November 5, Madison calls for an expansion of the army and navy. Appoints Joseph Story and Gabriel Duvall to the Supreme Court and names William Pinkney as attorney general after Rodney resigns.

1812   Congress approves measures for expanding the army but rejects increased appropriations for the navy. Vice-President Clinton dies April 20. Republican congressional caucus renominates Madison as its candidate for president. When dispatches received from Europe on May 22 indicate no change in British policy, Madison decides to seek declaration of war and sends message to Congress on June 1. Declaration is approved by the House, 79–49, on June 4 and by the Senate, 19–13, on June 17, then signed by the President on June 18. War is strongly opposed in much of New England, but Madison declines to ask for passage of a new sedition law despite the urging of some

Republican leaders. Learns that British cabinet suspended Orders-in-Council on June 23, but determines not to seek an armistice until British renounce impressment. American invasion of Canada ends in series of defeats in summer and fall, including surrender of garrison at Detroit on August 16. U.S. navy frigates win series of individual engagements with British ships. In electoral voting on December 2, Madison defeats De Witt Clinton of New York, an antiwar Republican supported by the Federalists, 128–89, while Elbridge Gerry, the Republican candidate, is elected vice-president. Secretary of War Eustis and Secretary of the Navy Hamilton resign amid widespread accusations of incompetence.

1813   Madison appoints John Armstrong as secretary of war and William Jones as secretary of the navy. Royal Navy imposes effective blockade along Atlantic coast from Delaware Bay south, reducing government revenues from import duties. Madison accepts offer of Russian mediation to end the war and sends Gallatin to Europe as chief peace negotiator (navy secretary Jones temporarily assumes his duties at the treasury). Fighting continues around the eastern Great Lakes. Madison falls seriously ill with "bilious fever" for several weeks in June and July. American naval victory in battle of Lake Erie on September 10 forces British withdrawal from Detroit, and battle of the Thames, fought in Ontario on October 5, ends in American victory and death of Tecumseh, Shawnee leader of Indian confederacy in the Northwest. Royal Navy extends blockade north to New York. American offensive against Montreal fails and British gain control of the Niagara Valley. In December Madison proposes and Congress adopts new embargo designed to stop American supplies from reaching British forces. British reject Russian mediation, but offer to open direct negotiations with the United States.

1814   Madison appoints John Quincy Adams, James Bayard, Henry Clay, Jonathan Russell, and Gallatin as peace commissioners and names George Campbell to replace Gallatin as secretary of the treasury. Nominates Richard Rush as attorney general when Pinkney resigns and Return Meigs as postmaster general after Granger is dismissed for political disloyalty. Asks for repeal of embargo on March 31 as defeat of Napoleon opens opportunities for American commerce in Europe. British extend naval blockade to cover New England ports and begin sending veteran troops from Europe to North America. Madison instructs peace commissioners on June 27 that they may sign a peace treaty that does not address impressment. American and British troops fight series of inconclusive battles along Niagara River, July–September. British occupy eastern Maine. Peace negotiations begin at Ghent, Belgium, on August 8. British land large raiding force at Benedict, Maryland, 30 miles southeast of Washington, on August 19. Madison, Monroe, Armstrong, and General William Winder attempt to arrange for defense of capital. Madison witnesses defeat of American forces at Bladensburg on August 24. British enter Washington and burn the White House, the Capitol, and several other government buildings before withdrawing on August 25. Madison returns to Washington on August 27. Names Monroe acting secretary of war to replace Armstrong (Monroe continues to serve as secretary of state). Insists that new session of Congress convene in Washington on September 19. American morale is raised by naval victory on Lake Champlain, September 11, and successful defense of Baltimore, September 12–14. Campbell resigns as secretary of the treasury as national finances approach bankruptcy. Madison replaces him with Alexander Dallas, who wins congressional approval for new internal taxes and proposes chartering a new national bank. Instructs negotiators on October 4 to seek peace on terms of a return to the status quo before the war began. Vice-President Gerry dies November 23. Nominates Benjamin Crowninshield as secretary of the navy after Jones resigns. British troops land on the Gulf Coast on December 13 and begin advance on New Orleans. Delegates appointed by Federalist-controlled legislatures in Massachusetts, Rhode Island, and Connecticut meet in Hartford on December 15 to consider constitutional changes designed to protect New England against southern and western domination of the federal government. After British drop demands for American territorial concessions, negotiators sign peace treaty at Ghent on December 24 that restores all territory captured during the war (with the exception of West Florida, which the United States retains) but does not address impressment or maritime rights.

1815   Hartford Convention recommends adoption of seven
          constitutional amendments on January 5. British attack on
          New Orleans is repulsed with heavy losses on January 8
          by forces under the command of Major General Andrew
          Jackson. News of victory reaches Washington on Febru-
          ary 4, and on February 14 Madison receives copies of the
          treaty of Ghent, which the Senate unanimously ratifies
          two days later. Madison declares an end to hostilities on
          February 17. Hartford resolutions fail to find support as
          treaty and Jackson's victory are widely acclaimed. Madi-
          son orders naval squadron commanded by Stephen De-
          catur to the Mediterranean, where it conducts successful
          campaign against the Barbary pirates. Appoints Gallatin as
          minister to France and John Quincy Adams as minister to
          Britain. Spends most of spring and summer at Mont-
          pelier. Appoints William Crawford as secretary of war in
          August. Submits annual message to Congress on Decem-
          ber 5, recommending consideration of a new national
          bank and adoption of a constitutional amendment to ex-
          plicitly authorize spending federal funds on roads, canals,
          and other internal improvements.

1816   Signs bills chartering a new national bank and establish-
          ing moderate protective tariffs. Republican congressional
          caucus endorses Secretary of State Monroe for presi-
          dent. Madison stays at Montpelier from early June to
          early October. Appoints Crawford as secretary of the
          treasury after Dallas resigns. Monroe defeats Federalist
          candidate Rufus King, 183–34, in the electoral voting on
          December 4.

1817   Congress passes Bonus Bill funding internal improve-
          ments in February, but Madison vetoes it on constitu-
          tional grounds on March 3. Monroe is inaugurated on
          March 4. Madison leaves Washington with Dolley on
          April 6, traveling part of the way to Montpelier by steam-
          boat (another passenger, James K. Paulding, is reminded
          by Madison "of a school Boy on a long vacation"). En-
          joys visits from extended family at Montpelier, but is in-
          creasingly distressed by the drinking and gambling habits
          of his stepson (will pay out approximately $40,000
          between 1813 and 1836 to cover his debts). Serves with
          Jefferson as active member of the Board of Visitors
          (trustees) of newly-chartered Central College, which

Jefferson hopes to transform into the University of Virginia. Becomes supporter of the American Colonization Society, founded in 1816, which advocates sending freed slaves to a colony in Africa.

1818   Sends New York publisher Jacob Gideon a list identifying the authors of the various *Federalist* essays. Delivers lengthy address on scientific agriculture to the Agricultural Society of Albemarle County, Virginia, which is later printed.

1819   Attends first meeting of the Board of Visitors of the University of Virginia and continues to work closely with Jefferson in choosing the faculty and curriculum for the new institution. Writes private letters opposing attempts to prohibit slavery in the new state of Missouri. Arranges his papers with the assistance of Dolley and brother-in-law John C. Payne (will continue to work on his papers into the 1830s). Continues active correspondence on political issues with Jefferson, Monroe, and others.

1823   Sister Frances Madison Rose dies.

1824   Visits with Lafayette at Monticello and Montpelier.

1825   Suffers increasing financial difficulties due to crop failures, bad weather, and falling prices for Virginia farm produce. University of Virginia begins holding classes in March. Jefferson, Madison, and Monroe visit the campus in the fall to chastise the students for incidents of drunken rioting (discipline improves after several students are expelled).

1826   Jefferson and John Adams die on July 4. Madison succeeds Jefferson as rector of the University of Virginia.

1827   Gives rare printed copies to Jonathan Elliot, who is preparing the state ratification debates of 1787–88 for publication, but declines to make corrections in accounts of his own speeches. Shares papers and reminiscences with historian Jared Sparks when he visits Montpelier (Sparks returns for second visit in 1830).

1828   South Carolina opponents of protective tariffs assert that Virginia and Kentucky Resolutions of 1798 support their doctrine of nullification. Madison writes public letters, published in December, that uphold the constitutionality of the tariff and deny that states have the power to nullify federal laws.

1829 Mother dies at Montpelier on February 11. Madison is elected as delegate from Orange County to Virginia state constitutional convention. Arrives in Richmond in October for three-month stay. Gives his only speech on December 2, advocating adoption of the federal three-fifths rule for counting slaves in legislative apportionment (measure, which would have reduced the power of counties with large slave populations, is not adopted).

1830 Writes letter to Edward Everett, published in the *North American Review* in October, opposing nullification and upholding the supremacy of federal law.

1831 Suffers increasingly from rheumatism, which at times prevents him from writing or walking. Monroe dies on July 4.

1832 Visited at Montpelier by President Andrew Jackson and Senator Henry Clay.

1833 Accepts honorary presidency of the American Colonization Society. Writes letters opposing doctrine of secession to Nicholas P. Trist, an aide to Jackson, and Virginia Senator William Rives, who draw upon them in preparing newspaper articles and speeches.

1834 Retires as rector of the University of Virginia. Writes political testament "Advice to My Country." Reluctantly sells 16 of his slaves to William Taylor, a relative in Louisiana.

1835 Draws up will in April, which does not provide for the manumission of any of his slaves.

1836 Dies at Montpelier on the morning of June 28. Buried on June 29 in the family plot on the estate.

Note on the Texts

This volume prints the texts of 197 letters, speeches, essays, messages, resolutions, and memoranda written or delivered by James Madison between 1772 and 1836. Although the majority of these documents existed only as autograph manuscript at the time of Madison's death, many of them were printed during his lifetime. Madison wrote numerous essays for newspaper publication, and his contributions to *The Federalist* were also published contemporaneously in book form; many of his speeches in the Virginia ratifying convention and in the Federal Congress were recorded by shorthand reporters and published by them in book form or in newspapers; and some of his writings, such as his report to the Virginia assembly in 1800, were printed as official government documents.

After his retirement from the presidency in 1817, Madison was able to obtain many of the letters he had written in earlier years to Thomas Jefferson, George Washington, James Monroe, Edmund Randolph, and other prominent Virginians. He also began to retain copies and drafts of letters he sent and, with the assistance of his wife, Dolley, and his brother-in-law John Coles Payne, to arrange and edit the notes he had made on the debates in the Continental Congress and in the Federal Convention of 1787. During his retirement Madison had some documents copied, wrote or dictated explanatory notes concerning his manuscripts, and destroyed some of his papers dealing with family matters.

In 1837, the year after her husband's death, Dolley Madison sold some of his papers from the 1780s to the United States for $30,000. Congress appointed Henry Dilworth Gilpin, the solicitor of the U.S. Treasury, to oversee their publication, and they were published in three volumes in 1840 as *The Papers of James Madison, purchased by order of Congress; being his correspondence and reports of debates during the Congress of the Confederation and His Reports of Debates in the Federal Convention*. In 1848 Dolley Madison sold all of the unpublished Madison papers in her possession to the United States for an additional $25,000, and in 1856 Congress asked William Cabell Rives, a former senator from Virginia who was writing a biography of Madison, to edit them. (A single volume, *Selections from the Private Correspondence of James Madison from 1813 to 1836*, was published in 1853 by James C. McGuire, the administrator of the Madison estate and a major creditor of his stepson John Payne Todd.) During the Civil War, while Rives remained in Virginia, Philip R. Fendall worked in Washington, D.C., on preparing the documents for publication with the assistance of McGuire, who had access to manuscripts that were not among the papers purchased by Congress in 1848. *Letters and Other Writings of James Madison Fourth President of the United States* was published in four volumes in August 1865. In preparing what subsequently became known as the "Congressional edition," Rives and Fendall altered Madison's spelling, punctuation, and capitalization, and sometimes omitted material from the documents they printed. Another edition, *The Writings of James Madison*, was published in nine volumes between 1900 and 1910. Edited by Gaillard Hunt, the head of the publications division of the Department of State, it included approximately 300 documents that had not appeared in the Gilpin, McGuire, or Congressional editions. Hunt also made changes in Madison's punctuation and capitalization, though he exercised greater editorial restraint than Rives and Fendall.

Work began in 1956 on *The Papers of James Madison*, a new edition sponsored by the University of Chicago and the University of Virginia (since 1971 the University of Virginia has been the sole sponsor of the project). The editors of *The Papers of James Madison* have collected more than 25,000 copies of documents relating to Madison's life from 250 archives. Publication of the initial series of 17 volumes, covering the period from Madison's birth in 1751 to his appointment as Secretary of State in 1801, began in 1962 and was completed in 1991. Two other series, *The Papers of James Madison: Secretary of State Series* (4 vols. to date, 1986–98) and *The Papers of James Madison: Presidential Series* (3 vols. to date, 1984–96), are still ongoing, and a series containing papers from the period of Madison's retirement (1817–36) is being planned. Documents are transcribed and printed without alteration in their spelling, capitalization, paragraphing, and punctuation, except for the substitution of periods for dashes used to end sentences and the omission of dashes in instances where a dash appears following a period. For the texts of Madison's contributions to *The Federalist*, the editors of *The Papers of James Madison* have used the first book edition, published in New York by John and Archibald McLean in two volumes on March 22 and May 28, 1788, shortly after Madison left the city to return to Virginia.

The present volume includes 151 documents from *The Papers of James Madison*. Another 42 documents, not so far included in that edition, are taken from *The Writings of James Madison*, edited by Gaillard Hunt. Four documents come from various other sources, either because they were not included in the Hunt edition, or, in the case of "Advice to My Country," because the alternative source offers a text based on the original autograph manuscript, which was unavailable to Hunt.

This volume prints texts as they appeared in these sources, but with a few alterations in editorial procedure. The bracketed conjectural readings of editors, in cases where original manuscripts or printed texts were damaged or difficult to read, are accepted without brackets in this volume when those readings seem to be the only possible ones; but when they do not, or when the editor made no conjecture, the missing word or words are indicated by a bracketed two-em space, i.e., [   ]. In cases where an obvious misspelling was marked by earlier editors with "[*sic*]," the present volume omits the "[*sic*]" and corrects the slip of the pen. (Two of Madison's errors in manuscript are corrected in this volume even though they were not marked by "[*sic*]" in the source: at 830.28, "to to" is changed to "to"; and at 833.7, "liberty a staked" is changed to "liberty staked.") Bracketed editorial insertions used in the Hunt edition to identify persons, clarify meaning, and supply passages from the Constitution referred to by Madison have been deleted in this volume. The text of the "Memorandum on the Battle of Bladensburg" presented in the Hunt edition prints in brackets words that were inserted into the text when the memorandum was copied in 1824, but this volume prints the text of the memorandum as written by Madison in 1814 and presents some of the material added in 1824 in the notes. In presenting the text of Madison's "Detached Memoranda" in *William and Mary Quarterly* (1946), Elizabeth Fleet printed canceled, but still legible, passages within brackets; in this volume, the canceled passages are omitted.

The following is a list of the documents included in this volume, in order of their appearance, giving the source of each text. The most common sources are indicated by these abbreviations:

Writings   *The Writings of James Madison*, edited by Gaillard Hunt (9 vols., New York: G. P. Putnam's Sons, 1900–10). Volumes 7, 8 (1908), Volume 9 (1910).

PJM   *The Papers of James Madison* (vols. 1–10, Chicago: University of Chicago Press, 1962–77; vols.11–17, Charlottesville: University Press of Virginia, 1977–91). Volumes 1, 2 (1962), Volume 3 (1963), Volume 4 (1965), Volume 6 (1969), Volume 7 (1971), edited by William T. Hutchinson and William M. E. Rachal; Volume 8 (1973), edited by Robert A. Rutland, William M. E. Rachal, Barbara D. Ripel, and Frederika J. Teute; Volume 9

(1975), edited by Robert A. Rutland and William M. E. Rachal; Volume 10 (1977), edited by Robert A. Rutland, Charles F. Hobson, William M. E. Rachal, and Frederika J. Teute; Volume 11 (1977), edited by Robert A. Rutland and Charles F. Hobson; Volumes 12, 13 (1979, 1981), edited by Charles F. Hobson and Robert A. Rutland; Volume 14 (1983), edited by Robert A. Rutland, Thomas A. Mason, Robert J. Brugger, Jeanne K. Sisson, and Frederika J. Teute; Volume 15 (1985), edited by Thomas A. Mason, Robert A. Rutland, and Jeanne K. Sisson; Volume 16 (1989), edited by J.C.A. Stagg, Thomas A. Mason, and Jeanne K. Sisson; Volume 17 (1991), edited by David B. Mattern, J.C.A. Stagg, Jeanne K. Cross, and Susan Holbrook Perdue. Copyright © 1962, 1963, 1965, 1969, 1971, 1973, 1975, 1977 by The University of Chicago. Copyright © 1977, 1979, 1981, 1983, 1985, 1989, 1991 by the Rector and Visitors of the University of Virginia. Reprinted with permission of the University Press of Virginia.

PJM: *The Papers of James Madison: Presidential Series* (3 vols.
Presi-   to date, Charlottesville: University Press of Virginia,
dential   1984–96). Volume 1, edited by Robert A. Rutland, Thomas A. Mason, Robert J. Brugger, Susannah H. Jones, Jeanne K. Sisson, and Frederika J. Teute (1984); Volume 3, edited by J.C.A. Stagg, Jeanne Kerr Cross, and Susan Holbrook Perdue (1996). Copyright © 1984, 1996 by the Rector and Visitors of the University of Virginia. Reprinted with permission of the University Press of Virginia.

THE REVOLUTION AND THE CONFEDERATION, 1772–1787

William Bradford, November 9, 1772. *PJM*, vol. 1, 74–76.

William Bradford, January 24, 1774. *PJM*, vol. 1, 104–6.

William Bradford, April 1, 1774. *PJM*, vol. 1, 111–13.

Amendments to the Virginia Declaration of Rights, May 29–June 11, 1776. *PJM*, vol. 1, 174–75.

Thomas Jefferson, March 27, 1780. *PJM*, vol. 2, 5–7.

Thomas Jefferson, April 16, 1781. *PJM*, vol. 3, 71–72.

Observations on State Territorial Claims, May 1, 1782. *PJM*, vol. 4, 200–2.

Memorandum on Conversation Regarding the Continental Army, February 20, 1783. *PJM*, vol. 6, 265–66.

Speech in the Continental Congress on Revenue, February 21, 1783. *PJM*, vol. 6, 270–72.

Edmund Randolph, May 1783. *PJM*, vol. 7, 59–62.

FRAMING AND RATIFYING THE CONSTITUTION, 1787–1789

Speech in the Federal Convention on Electing the Executive, July 17, 1787. *PJM*, vol. 10, 103–5.

Speech in the Federal Convention on Electing the Executive, July 19, 1787. *PJM*, vol. 10, 107–8.

Speech in the Federal Convention on Impeachment, July 20, 1787. *PJM*, vol. 10, 108.

Speech in the Federal Convention on Ratification, July 23, 1787. *PJM*, vol. 10, 112–13.

Speech in the Federal Convention on Electing the Executive, July 25, 1787. *PJM*, vol. 10, 115–17.

Speech in the Federal Convention on Suffrage, August 7, 1787. *PJM*, vol. 10, 138–40.

Speech in the Federal Convention on Control of Congressional Elections, August 9, 1787. *PJM*, vol. 10, 142.

Thomas Jefferson, September 6, 1787. *PJM*, vol. 10, 163–64.

George Washington, September 30, 1787. *PJM*, vol. 10, 179–81.

George Washington, October 18, 1787. *PJM*, vol. 10, 196–97.

Thomas Jefferson, October 24, 1787. *PJM*, vol. 10, 206–19.

George Washington, November 18, 1787. *PJM*, vol. 10, 253–54.

The Federalist No. 10, November 22, 1787. *PJM*, vol. 10, 263–70.

The Federalist No. 14, November 30, 1787. *PJM*, vol. 10, 284–88.

The Federalist No. 18, December 7, 1787. *PJM*, vol. 10, 299–304.

The Federalist No. 19, December 8, 1787. *PJM*, vol. 10, 305–9.

The Federalist No. 20, December 11, 1787. *PJM*, vol. 10, 320–24.

Edmund Randolph, January 10, 1788. *PJM*, vol. 10, 354–56.

The Federalist No. 37, January 11, 1788. *PJM*, vol. 10, 359–64.

The Federalist No. 38, January 12, 1788. *PJM*, vol. 10, 365–71.

The Federalist No. 39, January 16, 1788. *PJM*, vol. 10, 377–82.

The Federalist No. 40, January 18, 1788. *PJM*, vol. 10, 384–90.

The Federalist No. 41, January 19, 1788. *PJM*, vol. 10, 390–97.

The Federalist No. 42, January 22, 1788. *PJM*, vol. 10, 403–9.

The Federalist No. 43, January 23, 1788. *PJM*, vol. 10, 411–18.

The Federalist No. 44, January 25, 1788. *PJM*, vol. 10, 420–26.

The Federalist No. 45, January 26, 1788. *PJM*, vol. 10, 428–32.

The Federalist No. 46, January 29, 1788. *PJM*, vol. 10, 438–44.

The Federalist No. 47, January 30, 1788. *PJM*, vol. 10, 448–54.

The Federalist No. 48, February 1, 1788. *PJM*, vol. 10, 456–60.

The Federalist No. 49, February 2, 1788. *PJM*, vol. 10, 460–63.

The Federalist No. 50, February 5, 1788. *PJM*, vol. 10, 470–72.

The Federalist No. 51, February 6, 1788. *PJM*, vol. 10, 476–80.

The Federalist No. 52, February 8, 1788. *PJM*, vol. 10, 482–86.

The Federalist No. 53, February 9, 1788. *PJM*, vol. 10, 488–93.

The Federalist No. 54, February 12, 1788. *PJM*, vol. 10, 499–503.

The Federalist No. 55, February 13, 1788. *PJM*, vol. 10, 504–8.

The Federalist No. 56, February 16, 1788. *PJM*, vol. 10, 512–15.

The Federalist No. 57, February 19, 1788. *PJM*, vol. 10, 521–25.

CONGRESS AND THE REPUBLICAN OPPOSITION, 1789–1801

Thomas Jefferson, February 4, 1790. *PJM*, vol. 13, 18–21.

Benjamin Rush, March 20, 1790. *PJM*, vol. 13, 109.

Remarks in Congress During Debate on Militia Bill, December 16, 1790. *PJM*, vol. 13, 323.

Speech in Congress on Religious Exemptions from Militia Duty, December 22, 1790. *PJM*, vol. 13, 328–29.

Speech in Congress Opposing the National Bank, February 2, 1791. *PJM*, vol. 13, 373–81.

Thomas Jefferson, May 12, 1791. *PJM*, vol. 14, 22–23.

Population and Emigration, November 21, 1791. *PJM*, vol. 14, 117–22.

Consolidation, December 5, 1791. *PJM*, vol. 14, 137–39.

Dependent Territories, December 12, 1791. *PJM*, vol. 17, 559–60.

Public Opinion, December 19, 1791. *PJM*, vol. 14, 170.

Government, January 2, 1792. *PJM*, vol. 14, 178–79.

Charters, January 19, 1792. *PJM*, vol. 14, 191–92.

Parties, January 23, 1792. *PJM*, vol. 14, 197–98.

Universal Peace, February 2, 1792. *PJM*, vol. 14, 206–8.

Government of the United States, February 6, 1792. *PJM*, vol. 14, 217–18.

Spirit of Governments, February 20, 1792. *PJM*, vol. 14, 233–34.

Republican Distribution of Citizens, March 5, 1792. *PJM*, vol. 14, 244–46.

Fashion, March 22, 1792. *PJM*, vol. 14, 257–59.

Property, March 29, 1792. *PJM*, vol. 14, 266–68.

The Union: Who Are Its Real Friends?, April 2, 1792. *PJM*, vol. 14, 274–75.

Memorandum on Washington's Retirement, May 1792. *PJM*, vol. 14, 299–304.

George Washington, June 20, 1792. *PJM*, vol. 14, 319–24.

A Candid State of Parties, September 26, 1792. *PJM*, vol. 14, 370–72.

Who Are the Best Keepers of the People's Liberties?, December 22, 1792. *PJM*, vol. 14, 426–27.

Thomas Jefferson, June 13, 1793. *PJM*, vol. 15, 28–30.

"Helvidius" No. 1, August 24, 1793. *PJM*, vol. 15, 66–73.

Thomas Jefferson, September 2, 1793. *PJM*, vol. 15, 92–95.

Dolley Payne Todd, August 18, 1794. *PJM*, vol. 15, 351.

Speech in Congress on "Self-Created Societies," November 27, 1794. *PJM*, vol. 15, 390–92.

James Monroe, December 20, 1795. *PJM*, vol. 16, 168–71.

Speech in Congress on the Jay Treaty, March 10, 1796. *PJM*, vol. 16, 255–63.

Speech in Congress on the Jay Treaty, April 6, 1796. *PJM*, vol. 16, 291–301.

Thomas Jefferson, December 19, 1796. *PJM*, vol. 16, 432–33.

Thomas Jefferson, January 15, 1797. *PJM*, vol. 16, 455–56.

Thomas Jefferson, c. February 18, 1798. *PJM*, vol. 17, 82–83.

Thomas Jefferson, April 2, 1798. *PJM*, vol. 17, 104–5.

Thomas Jefferson, May 13, 1798. *PJM*, vol. 17, 130–31.

Virginia Resolutions Against the Alien and Sedition Acts, December 21, 1798. *PJM*, vol. 17, 188–90.

Thomas Jefferson, December 29, 1798. *PJM*, vol. 17, 191–92.

Foreign Influence, January 23, 1799. *PJM*, vol. 17, 214–20.

Political Reflections, February 23, 1799. *PJM*, vol. 17, 237–43.

Report on the Alien and Sedition Acts, January 7, 1800. *PJM*, vol. 17, 307–50.

Thomas Jefferson, January 10, 1801. *PJM*, vol. 17, 453–56.

SECRETARY OF STATE AND PRESIDENT, 1801–1817

Robert R. Livingston and James Monroe, July 29, 1803. *Writings*, vol. 7, 60–64.

James Monroe, July 6, 1807. *Writings*, vol. 7, 454–60.

First Inaugural Address, March 4, 1809. *PJM: Presidential*, vol. 1, 15–18.

Veto Message to Congress, February 21, 1811. *PJM: Presidential*, vol. 3, 176.

Thomas Jefferson, May 25, 1812. *Writings*, vol. 8, 190–92.

War Message to Congress, June 1, 1812. *Writings*, vol. 8, 192–200.

Second Inaugural Address, March 4, 1813. *Writings*, vol. 8, 235–39.

John Nicholas, April 2, 1813. *Writings*, vol. 8, 242–44.

John Armstrong, August 13, 1814. *Writings*, vol. 8, 286–91.

Memorandum on the Battle of Bladensburg, c. August 24, 1814. *Writings*, vol. 8, 294–97.

Memorandum on Armstrong's Resignation, August 29, 1814. *Writings*, vol. 8, 300–4.

Wilson Cary Nicholas, November 26, 1814. *Writings*, vol. 8, 318–20.

Message to Congress on Peace Treaty , February 18, 1815. *Writings*, vol. 8, 324–26.

Seventh Annual Message to Congress, December 5, 1815. *Writings*, vol. 8, 335–44.

Veto Message to Congress, March 3, 1817. *Writings*, vol. 8, 386–88.

RETIREMENT, 1817–1836

Robert Walsh, March 2, 1819. *Writings*, vol. 8, 425–33.

Robert J. Evans, June 15, 1819. *Writings*, vol. 8, 439–47.

Spencer Roane, September 2, 1819. *Writings*, vol. 8, 447–53.

Robert Walsh, November 27, 1819. *Writings*, vol. 9, 1–13.

Detached Memoranda, 1819? Elizabeth Fleet, "Madison's 'Detached Memoranda,'" in *William and Mary Quarterly,* 3rd. Ser., Vol. 3, No. 4. (October, 1946), 534–68. Reprinted with permission of the Omohundro Institute of Early American History and Culture.

James Monroe, February 10, 1820. *Writings*, vol. 9, 21–23.

Spencer Roane, May 6, 1821. *Writings*, vol. 9, 55–63.

Spencer Roane, June 29, 1821. *Writings*, vol. 9, 65–68.

Jonathan Bull and Mary Bull, c.1821. *Writings*, vol. 9, 77–85.

Edward Livingston, July 10, 1822. *Writings*, vol. 9, 98–103.

William T. Barry, August, 4, 1822. *Writings*, vol. 9, 103–9.

Edward Everett, March 19, 1823. *Writings*, vol. 9, 124–30.

Thomas Jefferson, June 27, 1823. *Writings*, vol. 9, 137–44.

Henry Lee, June 25, 1824. *Writings*, vol. 9, 190–92.

Peter S. DuPonceau, August 1824. *Writings*, vol. 9, 198–202.

Thomas Jefferson, February 8, 1825. *Writings*, vol. 9, 218–21.

Thomas Jefferson, February 24, 1826. *Writings*, vol. 9, 243–46.

Nicholas P. Trist, July 6, 1826. *Writings*, vol. 9, 247–48.

Henry Colman, August 25, 1826. *Writings*, vol. 9, 250–51.

Joseph Cabell, September 18, 1828. *Writings*, vol. 9, 316–40.

Speech in the Virginia Constitutional Convention, December 2, 1829. *Writings*, vol. 9, 358–64.

A Sketch Never Finished Nor Applied, 1830? *The Debates in the Federal Convention of 1787 Which Framed the Constitution of the United States of America*, edited by Gaillard Hunt and James Brown Scott (New York, Oxford University Press, 1920), 1–16.

Edward Everett, August 28, 1830. *Writings*, vol. 9, 383–403.

James Robertson, March 27, 1831. *Writings*, vol. 9, 444–47.

Jared Sparks, April 8, 1831. *Writings*, vol. 9, 447–51.

Jared Sparks, June 1, 1831. *Writings*, vol. 9, 469–70.

Mathew Carey, July 27, 1831. *Writings*, vol. 9, 462–64.

Nicholas P. Trist, May 1832. *Writings*, vol. 9, 478–80.

Andrew Stevenson, November 20, 1832. *Writings*, vol. 9, 488–89.

Nicholas P. Trist, December 23, 1832. *Writings*, vol. 9, 489–92.

William Cabell Rives, March 12, 1833. *Writings*, vol. 9, 511–14.

Advice to My Country, 1834. Irving Brant, *James Madison: Commander in Chief 1812–1836* (Indianapolis: The Bobbs-Merrill Company, Inc., 1961), 530–31. Copyright © 1961 by The Bobbs-Merrill Company, Inc. Reprinted with the permission of Simon & Schuster.

George Tucker, June 27, 1836. *Letters and Other Writings of James Madison*, edited by William C. Rives and Philip R. Fendall (Philadelphia: J. B. Lippincott & Co., 1865), volume 4, 435–36.

   This volume presents the texts of the editions chosen as sources here but does not attempt to reproduce features of their typographic design. Letters printed as superscript at the end of abbreviations in *The Writings of James Madison* have been printed on the line in this volume. Some headings have been changed, and James Madison's name at the end of letters has been omitted. The texts are printed without alteration except for the changes previously discussed and for the correction of typographical errors. Spelling, punctuation, and capitalization are often expressive features, and they are not altered, even when inconsistent or irregular. The following is a list of typographical errors corrected, cited by page and line number: 45.25, Constitution?; 183.16, abbè; 427.15, amendmends; 671.32, neogtiations; 754.8, subsequesnt; 754.9, effeebling; 758.23, scare; 763.40, pinciple; 769.34, *behaviour.*; 785.5, [inverted letter b]eing; 792.2, of, 56,; 828.35, Brittish; 832.20, embarrasments; 832.31, founnd.

Notes

In the notes below, the reference numbers denote page and line of this volume (the line count includes headings). No note is made for material included in standard desk-reference books such as Webster's *Collegiate*, *Biographical*, and *Geographical* dictionaries. Footnotes in the text are Madison's own. For further biographical background, references to other studies, and more detailed notes, see Irving Brant, *James Madison* (6 vols., Indianapolis: Bobbs-Merrill, 1941–61); Ralph Ketchum, *James Madison* (New York: Macmillan, 1971); *The Writings of James Madison*, edited by Gaillard Hunt (9 vols., New York: G. P. Putnam, 1900–10); *The Papers of James Madison*, edited by William T. Hutchinson et al. (17 vols., Chicago and Charlottesville: The University of Chicago Press and University Press of Virginia, 1962–91); *The Papers of James Madison: Secretary of State Series*, edited by Robert A. Rutland, et al. (4 vols. to date, Charlottesville: University Press of Virginia, 1986–98); *The Papers of James Madison: Presidential Series*, edited by Robert A. Rutland, et al. (3 vols. to date, Charlottesville: University Press of Virginia, 1984–96).

THE REVOLUTION AND THE CONFEDERATION, 1772–1787

3.1   William Bradford] Bradford (1755–95) received an A.B. from the College of New Jersey (Princeton) in 1772. He later served as attorney general of Pennsylvania, 1780–91, and as attorney general of the United States, 1794–95.

7.11–12   5 or 6 . . . religious Sentiments] Six Baptists were imprisoned in Culpeper County, Virginia, in 1773–74 for preaching without a license.

7.20   the Synod] The Synod of New York and Philadelphia of the Presbyterian Church.

8.10–11   bastards . . . Dod] In his letter of March 4, Bradford had written that Dod "was married to a Girl in Brunswick: but he put the Cart before the horse: he was a father before he was an husband."

8.35   your province] Pennsylvania.

9.33   Calpipnis Letters] A series of 20 letters by Jacob Duché, an Anglican minister in Philadelphia, that appeared over the signature "Tamoc Caspipina" in the *Pennsylvania Packet* beginning in March 1772. They were published in collected form as *Observations on a Variety of Subjects, Literary, Moral, and Religious* in 1774.

10.7–8   *Amendments . . . Rights*] Madison introduced these amendments during the debate in the Virginia convention on adopting the
Declaration of Rights that had been drafted primarily by George Mason. The
version of the article on religion submitted to the convention by the drafting
committee on May 27, 1776, read: "18. That religion, or the duty which we
owe to our CREATOR, and the manner of discharging it, can be directed only
by reason and conviction, not by force or violence; and therefore, that all
men should enjoy the fullest toleration in the exercise of religion, according
to the dictates of conscience, unpunished and unrestrained by the magistrate
unless, under colour of religion, any man disturb the peace, the happiness, or
the safety of society. And that it is the mutual duty of all to practice Christian
forebearance, love, and charity, toward each other." The first amendment
drafted by Madison was introduced by Patrick Henry, but was rejected by the
convention on the grounds that it would result in the disestablishment of the
Anglican Church in Virginia. Madison then framed the second amendment
printed here. In its final form, the article on religious freedom adopted by the
convention on June 12 read: "That religion, or the duty which we owe to our
CREATOR, and the manner of discharging it, can be directed only by reason
and conviction, not by force or violence; and therefore, all men are equally
entitled to the free exercise of religion, according to the dictates of conscience; and that it is the mutual duty of all to practice Christian forebearance, love, and charity, toward each other."

11.5   Charlestown]   Charleston, South Carolina.

11.29–31   old system . . . substituted]   The Continental Congress approved a plan on March 18, 1780, for retiring from circulation the heavily depreciated Continental currency first issued in 1775 and replacing it with $10
million in new paper money.

13.17–18   embargo . . . Delaware]   In 1780 Delaware had continued to
export foodstuffs despite an embargo designed to make provisions available
to the Continental Army.

16.16–17   *Memorandum . . . Army*]   This document is taken from the
notes Madison kept on the debates in the Continental Congress.

16.18–19   Mr. Fitzimmons . . . Mr. Carroll]   Thomas FitzSimons of
Pennsylvania, Nathaniel Gorham of Massachusetts, Alexander Hamilton of
New York, Richard Peters of Pennsylvania, and Daniel Carroll of Maryland
were delegates to the Continental Congress.

17.8   Genl.]   Madison canceled several words at this point in the manuscript. The canceled passage may have been "Gates' expert hand," referring
to General Horatio Gates.

17.25–26   *Speech . . . Revenue*]   The text of this speech is taken from the
notes Madison kept on the debates in the Continental Congress.

18.28–29   proposition . . . British Minister] The conciliatory proposal
was made by Lord North, the British prime minister, on February 20, 1775,
and was rejected by the Continental Congress on July 31.

20.16   propositions of Congress] On April 18, 1783, Congress proposed
to the states a new plan for restoring the public credit that called for levying
specific import duties and a general 5 percent impost for 25 years in order to
pay the interest and principal on the national war debt. At the same time
Congress proposed an amendment to the Articles of Confederation changing
the basis for apportioning requisitions from the states from property to population, with "other persons" (slaves) counted as three-fifths of "white and
other free citizens and inhabitants." The measures failed to receive unanimous approval from the state legislatures and never went into effect.

24.18–20   negroes . . . Treaty] The preliminary peace treaty signed in
Paris on November 30, 1782, required the British to return slaves they had
seized during the war.

29.22–23   Memorial . . . Assessments] Madison wrote the memorial in
opposition to the general assessment bill introduced in the fall 1784 session of
the Virginia assembly. Printed copies of the memorial were circulated in the
summer of 1785 and collected 1,552 signatures.

30.2–4   "that Religion . . . violence."] From Article 16 of the 1776
Virginia Declaration of Rights; see note 10.7–8.

31.24–25   "all men . . . independent,"] From Article 1 of the Virginia
Declaration of Rights.

36.22–23   proposed change . . . Confederation] The amendment, which
was introduced on March 28, 1785, would have given Congress the power to
levy duties on imports and exports. It was never submitted to the states for
their ratification.

39.30   Caleb Wallace] A friend of Madison's from the College of New
Jersey, Wallace was a lawyer in the Kentucky district of Virginia.

42.35–36   Lord Kaims] Henry Home, Lord Kames (1696–1782), Scottish
jurist and writer.

47.10–11   Revisall . . . Pendleton] The committee report on revising the
laws of Virginia prepared by Thomas Jefferson, George Wythe, and Edmund
Pendleton was submitted to the Virginia assembly in 1779 and printed in
1784.

47.19   the commercial propositions] The House of Delegates adopted a
resolution on November 30, 1785, instructing the Virginia delegates to
Congress to support proposals giving Congress the power to regulate commerce for 13 years. On December 1 the House rescinded its vote and tabled
the resolution.

55.34   *I almost despair*]   The italicized words in the text printed here were written in cipher in the original letter.

56.9   *Guardoqui*]   Diego de Gardoqui, the Spanish envoy to the United States.

56.29   *assent of nine states*]   The number required to ratify a treaty under the Articles of Confederation.

58.38–39   *we submit . . . project*]   Jefferson replied on December 16, 1786, that he would be unable to borrow the necessary money in France.

59.9   the business stated]   Monroe had written concerning the conclusion of the debate in Congress over revising instructions to Secretary for Foreign Affairs John Jay regarding negotiations with Spain. With all of the southern states opposed and Delaware absent, Congress voted 7–5 on August 29, 1786, to repeal its 1785 instructions requiring Jay to obtain free navigation of the Mississippi.

61.23   expedition . . . insurgents]   Massachusetts militia commanded by General Benjamin Lincoln routed the insurgents led by Daniel Shays at Petersham on February 4, 1787, ending the rebellion in western Massachusetts that began in September 1786 as a series of protests against farm foreclosures.

63.36   Governor of Virginia]   Edmund Randolph.

65.30   *favors the British*]   From here to the end of this letter, words in italics were in cipher in the original.

66.40   *Otto and de la forest*]   Louis-Guillame Otto, Comte de Mosley, the French chargé d'affaires, and Antoine de la Forest, the French vice-consul.

67.10   *Grayson*]   William Grayson, a Virginia delegate to Congress.

67.18   *Van Berkel*]   Pieter Johan van Berckel, the Dutch minister to the United States.

68.28   *Mr. H*]   Patrick Henry.

80.4–6   12. Impotence . . . States]   The manuscript breaks off at this point.

FRAMING AND RATIFYING THE CONSTITUTION, 1787–1789

89.1   *The Virginia Plan*]   These resolutions were drafted by Madison and the other Virginia delegates to the Convention. The text printed here, as well as the texts of Madison's speeches in the Convention included in this volume, are taken from the extensive notes Madison kept during the proceedings.

92.1–2   *Speech . . . Factions*]   Madison made this speech during the debate over a motion by Charles Pinckney of South Carolina to have the first branch of the national legislature elected by the state legislatures.

92.9–10   Sharman . . . objects mentioned] In a preceding speech Roger
Sherman had said that the "objects of the Union" were defense against foreign danger and internal disputes, treaties with foreign nations, and regulating and taxing foreign commerce.

94.3   the motion] James Wilson of Pennsylvania had moved to reconsider an earlier vote excluding the national judiciary from sharing revisionary
power over legislation with the national executive.

96.35   Mr. Adams' Book] *A Defence of the Constitutions of Government
of the United States of America* by John Adams. The first volume of the work,
which examined American state constitutions, was published in 1787, and two
more volumes appeared in 1788.

97.16–18   *too that . . . confederacy*] The italicized words were written in
cipher in the original letter.

98.3   motion (of Mr. Dickenson)] John Dickinson of Delaware had
moved that members of the second branch of the national legislature be chosen by the state legislatures.

99.21   the motion] Charles Pinckney had moved that the national legislature have the authority to negative all state laws it judged to be improper.

100.29   Mr. B.] Gunning Bedford of Delaware.

101.1–2   *Speech . . . New Jersey Plan*] On June 15 William Paterson of
New Jersey presented nine resolutions drafted by the New Jersey delegation,
with the assistance of delegates from Connecticut, New York, Delaware, and
Maryland. The resolutions called for giving the existing Congress power to
levy imposts and stamp taxes, regulate foreign and interstate trade, collect
requisitions from noncomplying states, and appoint an executive with the
power to compel a state to obey federal law. A federal judiciary would rule on
cases involving foreigners, treaties, and federal trade regulation and revenue
collection, and all acts of Congress and treaties would be "the supreme law
of the respective States."

112.6–7   the rule contended for] John Lansing of New York and
Jonathan Dayton of New Jersey had moved that the states be equally represented in the first branch of the national legislature.

117.16   Mr. E.] Oliver Ellsworth of Connecticut.

120.1–3   *Speech . . . Representation*] On July 2, 1787, the Convention appointed an 11-man committee to devise a compromise concerning state representation in the national legislature (Madison was not a member). The
committee reported a proposal on July 5 calling for each state to have one
representative for every 40,000 people, with slaves counted as three-fifths of
free citizens, in the first branch of the legislature, while in the second branch,
each state would have an equal vote.

121.34   a member] Gouverneur Morris of Pennsylvania.

135.29   *people of*] The italicized words in the text printed here were written in cipher in the original letter, with the exception noted below.

135.31   *Legislatures*] This word was underscored by Madison, but not
enciphered by him.

137.21   Mr. R. H. L.] Richard Henry Lee of Virginia.

138.18   Col. M] George Mason of Virginia, who, along with Edmund
Randolph and Elbridge Gerry, had refused to sign the Constitution at the
close of the Convention on September 17, 1787.

138.19   Me—— Smith] Melancton Smith of New York.

139.35   Genl. Pinkney] Charles Cotesworth Pinckney of South Carolina,
a second cousin of Charles Pinckney.

140.5   Mason's objections] George Mason first drafted his objections to
the proposed Constitution in mid-September, but chose not to formally present them to the Convention before it adjourned. He sent a revised and enlarged version to Washington on October 7, and they were printed in full in
the *Virginia Journal* on November 22, 1787, after circulating in manuscript
form for several weeks.

142.36   W.H. B.F.] William Hay, of Virginia, and Benjamin Franklin.

146.14–15   As I . . . opinion] In his letter to Jefferson dated March 19,
1787; see pp. 63–68 in this volume.

146.21   imperia in imperio] Governments within a government.

154.26   The Governour's party] Supporters of Governor George
Clinton, who opposed unconditional ratification of the Constitution.

154.32–34   Republican . . . Constitutional] Opponents of the 1776
Pennsylvania state constitution were known as "Republicans," while supporters of the state constitution were called "Constitutionalists."

155.11   Docr. Lee] Arthur Lee, brother of Richard Henry Lee.

155.40   Mr. Adams] John Adams had been serving as the American minister to Great Britain since 1785, and had been in Europe on various diplomatic missions since 1780.

156.4–8   *made . . . scruples*] The italicized words were written in cipher
in the original letter.

157.2   Mr. C. P.] Charles Pinckney of South Carolina.

158.26   Mr. Morris's] Robert Morris and Gouverneur Morris.

159.1   Mr. Gerry's . . . objections] Elbridge Gerry, a Massachusetts delegate to the Constitutional Convention, wrote a letter to the General Court

(Massachusetts legislature) on October 18 explaining why he had refused to sign the Constitution. It was published in the *Massachusetts Centinel* on November 3, 1787, and widely reprinted.

159.27–29   recognize one . . . fourth] Of the 85 *Federalist* essays published between October 27, 1787, and May 28, 1788, Alexander Hamilton wrote 51, Madison 29, and John Jay five. William Duer wrote a few essays that were not used in the series.

174.1   *Federalist No. 18*] In writing numbers 18, 19, and 20 of *The Federalist*, Madison drew upon the extensive notes on ancient and modern confederacies he had prepared in 1786, as well as material drafted by Hamilton.

175.29   Abbé Milot] Claude-François-Xavier Millot, author of *Élémens d'histoire générale . . .* (9 vols., 1772–73).

177.28   abbé Mably] Gabriel Bonnot de Mably, in *Observations sur l'histoire de la Grèce . . .* (1766).

183.15   Thuanus] Jacques-Auguste de Thou, author of *Historiarum sui temporis* (5 vols., 1604–8).

183.38   Pfeffel . . . d'Allemagne] A two-volume work published in 1776 by Christian Friedrich Pfeffel von Kriegelstein.

190.23   your letter . . . Assembly] The letter, in which Randolph gave his reasons for not signing the Constitution, was printed as a pamphlet on December 27, 1787.

193.7–8   Col. H. Lee . . . Wilkinson] In his letter to Madison of December 27, 1787, Randolph had written that Henry Lee had told James Wilkinson, a leader in the Kentucky district, that the new Congress under the Constitution would probably surrender American rights to navigation on the Mississippi.

204.11–13   One state . . . concurrence] Maryland did not complete ratification of the Articles of Confederation until March 1, 1781.

206.31   admissible] The texts of the *Federalist* essays printed in this volume are taken from the first book edition, published in 1788. This word appeared as "inadmissible" in the version printed in the New York *Independent Journal* on January 12, 1788.

215.39   But the operation] In the New York *Independent Journal*, January 16, 1788: "So far the national countenance of the Government on this side seems to be disfigured by a few federal figures. But this blemish is perhaps unavoidable in any plan; and the operation . . ."

246.16   Montesquieu] In *The Spirit of the Laws*, Bk. IX, ch. 2.

249.8   Montesquieu] In *The Spirit of the Laws*, Bk. IX, ch. 1.

274.35–39   "there can . . . powers,"] The quotations from Montesquieu in *Federalist No. 47* are from *The Spirit of the Laws*, Bk. XI, ch. 6: "Of the Constitution of England."

275.6–7   This would not have]   In the New York *Independent Journal,* January 30, 1788: "This would have."

279.10–11   officers]   In the *Independent Journal,* "offices."

283.14   without end.]   In the *New-York Packet,* February 1, 1788, this was followed by: "I might find a witness in every citizen who has shared in, or been attentive to, the course of public administrations."

283.27   "Notes . . . Virginia."]   Published in London in 1787. The passage quoted by Madison is from Query XIII.

285.24–25   number of members.]   The Pennsylvania constitution of 1776 established a 12-member supreme executive council, elected by the freemen of the state; the creation of seven new counties had increased its membership to 19 by 1788.

310.19–20   recently . . . sanction]   On April 18, 1783, the Continental Congress adopted an amendment to the Articles of Confederation changing the basis for apportioning treasury requisitions among the states from property values to population. By the time the Constitutional Convention met in 1787, all of the states except New Hampshire and Rhode Island had ratified the amendment.

322.35–323.2   With regard . . . universally.]   In the New York *Independent Journal,* February 16, 1788, this paragraph read: "The observations made on the subject of taxation apply with greater force to the case of the militia. For however different the rules of discipline may be in different states; They are the same throughout each particular state; and depend on circumstances which can differ but little in different parts of the same state."

324.39   *Burgh's Political Disquisitions]   James Burgh (1714–75), *Political Disquisitions* (3 vols., 1774–75).

339.18–20   "of a . . . indispensable."]   From the letter, dated September 17, 1787, and signed by George Washington as president of the Constitutional Convention, transmitting the Constitution to the Continental Congress.

353.1   *Eliza House Trist*]   Trist (1751–1828) helped her widowed mother, Mary House, keep a boarding house in Philadelphia where Madison stayed from 1780 to 1793. She became a lifelong friend of both Madison and Thomas Jefferson.

353.18–19   two federalists . . . elected]   In the election held on March 24, 1788, Madison received 202 votes, James Gordon Jr., 187, Thomas Barbour, 56, and Charles Porter, 42.

354.1   *Speech . . . Convention*]   The debates of the Virginia convention were recorded in shorthand by David Robertson, a Petersburg attorney, and published by him in *Debates and Other Proceedings of the Convention of Virginia* (1788–89; second edition, 1805).

354.33   my honorable friend]   Governor Edmund Randolph, who had spoken in support of ratification.

357.24   disgraceful insult]   Pennsylvania soldiers from the Continental Army surrounded the State House in Philadelphia, where Congress and the Pennsylvania executive council were meeting, on June 21, 1783, and demanded back pay. When the council decided not to use the militia to restore order, Congress left the city and reconvened in Princeton on June 26.

358.13–14   an eighth state]   South Carolina became the eighth state to approve the Constitution when its convention, meeting in Charleston, voted 149–73 in favor of ratification on May 23, 1788.

359.22   cessions to Spain]   In response to British victories in the South, Congress approved on February 15, 1781, new instructions allowing John Jay, the American envoy to Spain, to concede navigation rights on the Mississippi in return for a treaty of alliance. Jay made a conditional offer which the Spanish rejected, and after the British surrender at Yorktown in October 1781 the American claim to navigation on the Mississippi was reasserted by both southern delegates in Congress and the American peace negotiators in Europe.

359.38–39   state . . . nineteen]   The Massachusetts convention ratified the Constitution by a 187–168 vote on February 6, 1788.

366.14–15   clause . . . consideration.]   The convention had voted on June 3 to consider the Constitution clause by clause in a committee of the whole before voting on ratification.

367.26–27   treaty . . . majesty]   The Franco-American treaty of amity and commerce signed in Paris on February 6, 1778.

371.15–16   honorable gentleman]   James Monroe.

372.27   Mr. *Marshall*]   John Marshall.

380.5   honorable gentleman]   Patrick Henry.

381.2   opinion of a citizen]   Henry had said that Jefferson favored having nine states ratify the Constitution and four states reject it as a means of securing amendments, including a bill of rights.

385.3–4   honorable gentleman]   Patrick Henry.

393.5   the gentleman]   George Mason.

395.6   *feme covert*]   Married woman.

403.38–39   two . . . state]   Robert Yates and John Lansing, who withdrew from the federal convention after the July 10, 1787, session.

404.25–26   proposition . . . *Wythe*]   George Wythe proposed on June

24, 1788, that the convention ratify the Constitution and recommend the subsequent adoption of amendments. His resolution was adopted by an 89–79 vote on June 25.

407.21   number . . . alterations]   The convention had recommended the adoption of 40 amendments, 20 of which constituted a bill of rights.

408.7   Yours of yesterday]   Hamilton had written from Poughkeepsie, where he was attending the New York ratifying convention, to describe a proposal by Antifederalists for conditional ratification of the Constitution. When John Lansing moved on July 24 that the Constitution be conditionally ratified, Hamilton read Madison's letter of July 20 to the convention. The Lansing resolution was defeated, 31–28, and the convention voted 30–27 on July 26 to ratify the Constitution while recommending the subsequent adoption of amendments.

409.1–2   *Observations . . . Virginia*"]   Madison wrote these comments at the request of John Brown, an attorney living in the Kentucky district of Virginia, who hoped to use them in drafting a state constitution for Kentucky. They were written in response to the draft constitution published by Jefferson in *Notes on the State of Virginia* (1787).

416.27   *Stamen*]   Essential element.

418.15–419.30   *outfit . . . president*]   The italicized words were written in cipher in the original letter.

419.31   little pamphlet]   *The Ratifications of the New Fœderal Constitution Together with the Amendments Proposed by the Several States*, printed in Richmond, Virginia, in the late summer of 1788. The pamphlet collected the forms of ratification and recommended amendments adopted by the New York, Massachusetts, New Hampshire, Maryland, South Carolina, and Virginia conventions, as well as the amendments proposed by the North Carolina convention, which voted on August 2, 1788, to withhold ratification.

423.21–22   proceedings in Kentucky]   A convention that met in Danville in July 1788 had called for another convention to meet in November and propose a form of government for Kentucky.

425.24   appointments . . . Senate]   The Virginia General Assembly elected two Antifederalists, Richard Henry Lee and William Grayson, to the Senate on November 8, 1788. Lee received 98 votes, Grayson, 86, and Madison, 77.

427.12   *George Eve*]   A Baptist minister who was serving as pastor of Blue Run Church in Orange County, Virginia.

CONGRESS AND THE REPUBLICAN OPPOSITION, 1789–1801

433.1   *Speech in Congress*]   The texts of Madison's speeches in the House of Representatives are taken from newspaper accounts based on reporters' shorthand notes, with the exception of the speech on the Jay Treaty of March 30, 1796 (pp. 558–67), which is taken from Madison's handwritten manuscript.

433.2   *Presidential Titles*]   On May 9, a committee of the Senate proposed that the president should be formally addressed as "His Highness the President of the United States of America and Protector of the Rights of the Same."

434.16   (Mr. Parker)]   Josiah Parker, a representative from Virginia.

434.31–32   *Speech . . . Removal Power*]   On May 19 Madison proposed the establishment of departments of foreign affairs, the treasury, and war, and included in his motion a clause giving the president sole power to remove the officers heading these executive departments.

435.9   (Mr. Smith)]   William Loughton Smith, a representative from South Carolina.

435.21   (Mr. Bland)]   Theodorick Bland, a representative from Virginia, who had argued that removal required the consent of the Senate.

437.3–4   (Mr. Jackson)]   James Jackson, a representative from Georgia.

437.10–13   When I first . . . urgent business]   Madison had informed the House on May 4 of his intention to propose a set of amendments to the Constitution on May 25, but then delayed doing so as the House continued to debate revenue measures and the creation of executive departments.

438.17–18   loss of . . . time]   Representatives Roger Sherman of Connecticut, William Loughton Smith of South Carolina, and John Vining of Delaware had all expressed continued opposition to considering amendments while more pressing business was before the House.

440.4   those two states]   Rhode Island and North Carolina had both initially rejected the Constitution and were therefore not represented in Congress.

441.28   prefixed to the constitution]   The House discussed amending the Constitution by changing the text of the existing preamble and articles until August 19, when Roger Sherman proposed that the amendments be added as separate articles at the end, leaving the original text unaltered.

445.3–4   Great-Britain . . . declaration of rights]   After the overthrow of James II, the Convention Parliament offered the throne to William and Mary in February 1689 on the condition that they agree to a declaration of rights. William and Mary accepted, and the provisions of the declaration, which mostly concerned the rights of parliament, were incorporated into an act of December 16, 1689, commonly known as the Bill of Rights.

453.5–6   insertion . . . sentiment in law]   The House was debating a clause in the bill establishing a department of foreign affairs that made the secretary removable from office by the president.

457.38   (Mr. Sherman)]   Roger Sherman, a representative from Connecticut.

463.12–13   (Mr. Livermore)]   Samuel Livermore, a representative from New Hampshire.

467.11   Mr. Page]   John Page, a representative from Virginia.

467.19–20   *Remarks . . . Amendments*]   The House voted on July 21 to refer the amendments proposed by Madison on June 8 to a select committee whose 11 members included Madison and Roger Sherman. The committee delivered its report on July 28 and the House began to debate its provisions on August 13.

467.21–22   meaning of the words]   The clause on religious freedom in the committee report read: "No religion shall be established by Law, nor shall the equal rights of conscience be infringed."

468.2   omitting . . . these words]   Representative Thomas Tucker of South Carolina had moved to insert "to instruct their representatives" into the clause protecting freedom of speech and the press and the right of assembly.

469.8   honorable gentleman from Massachusetts]   Elbridge Gerry.

469.25   the committee]   The committee of the whole.

469.29   (Mr. Sumpter and Mr. Burke)]   Thomas Sumter and Aedanus Burke were Antifederalist representatives from South Carolina.

470.24–25   *Remarks . . . Amendment*"]   Madison was defending his proposed amendment to prohibit the states from infringing freedom of conscience, speech, press, or the right to trial by jury in criminal cases. The House adopted this amendment on August 24, but it was eliminated by the Senate in early September and not restored by the conference committee that established the final text of the 12 amendments submitted to the states on September 25, 1789.

471.1   *Richard Peters*]   Richard Peters had served with Madison in the Continental Congress in 1782–83 as a delegate from Pennsylvania; in 1789, he was a member of the Pennsylvania assembly.

471.7–8   "The wise . . . Guests"]   Verses satirizing Antifederalist opposition to the Constitution that Peters had enclosed in a letter of July 20, 1789.

472.23   *Memorandum . . . Slaves*]   A copy of this memorandum was sent by the Quaker architect and inventor William Thornton to Étienne Clavière, the president of the French Society for the Abolition of Slavery.

473.32   *To Thomas Jefferson*]   Some time after 1799 Madison made a revised transcript of this letter. The text printed here is of the letter sent to Jefferson in 1790.

477.23   the force . . . remarks]   In his letter of March 10, Rush had criticized Secretary of the Treasury Hamilton's plan for funding the national
debt and asserted that concern for public credit was an attribute of monarchical governments intent on waging wars.

477.27   Petitions . . . Slavery]   In February 1790 the House received petitions from several Quaker meetings asking Congress to take action against
the slave trade. The House voted 43–11 to refer the petitions to a select committee, whose report was adopted in amended form by the committee of the
whole in a 29–25 vote on March 23, with Madison voting in the majority. The
report reaffirmed the Constitutional prohibition against Congress banning
the importation of slaves into the United States before 1808 while asserting
the authority of Congress to "restrain" American citizens from supplying
foreigners with slaves and to provide for the "humane treatment" of slaves
being imported into the U.S.

478.10–11   *Remarks . . . Militia Bill*]   The pending bill to organize the
militia contained a clause exempting members of Congress from militia
service.

484.8   the Bank . . . former Congress]   In May 1781 the Continental
Congress had issued a charter to the Bank of North America; Madison voted
against the measure, on the grounds that the Articles of Confederation gave
Congress no authority to issue corporate charters.

489.28   the 11th. and 12th.]   The eventual Ninth and Tenth Amendments; see Chronology, 1789.

490.33   Payne's pamphlet . . . preface]   Jefferson had sent a copy of
Thomas Paine's pamphlet *Rights of Man* to Samuel Harrison Smith, a Philadelphia printer, along with a note endorsing Paine's sentiments; without
Jefferson's permission, Smith reprinted Jefferson's endorsement on the
frontispiece.

491.1–3   Mr. Adams . . . in a book]   See note 96.35.

491.7–8   antirepublican discourses]   *Discourses on Davila*, a series of essays by Adams attacking the French Revolution, was published in 1790–91.
Jefferson's criticism of "the political heresies which have sprung up among
us" in his note endorsing Paine was widely understood to be an attack on
Adams.

491.13   H. & B.]   Alexander Hamilton and George Beckwith, a British
army officer who served as an unofficial diplomatic emissary to the United
States.

491.16   Burke's pamphlet]   *Reflections on the Revolution in France* (1790).

491.22   Beckley]   John Beckley, the Clerk of the House of Representatives, a political ally of Madison and Jefferson.

491.28   Carrington] Edward Carrington, a former member of the Virginia assembly and the Continental Congress.

492.38   Stillingfleet and Bradley's] Benjamin Stillingfleet, *Miscellaneous Tracts Relating to Natural History, Husbandry, and Physick* (1759), and Richard Bradley, *A Philosophical Account of the Works of Nature* (1721).

494.23   Josiah Child] A governor of the East India Company and author of *A New Discourse of Trade* (1694).

495.13   John Sinclair] Madison draws on the calculations published by Sir John Sinclair in *Queries Drawn up for the Purpose of Elucidating the Natural History and Political State of Scotland* (1790).

495.27   Lord Sheffield] John Baker Holroyd, first Earl of Sheffield, in *Observations on the Commerce of American States* (1784).

501.8   requires] This word is possibly a printer's error for "acquires." In notes he made while preparing his essays for the *National Gazette*, Madison wrote: "This decides the question concerning a bill of rights, which acquires efficacy as time sanctifies and incorporates it with the public sentiment."

505.15–16   Rousseau . . . recommended] In 1761 Jean-Jacques Rousseau published a revised version of *Projet de paix perpétuelle* by Charles-Irénée Castel, which first appeared in 1712.

523.1   conduct . . . representation-bill] Adams had broken a tie in the Senate on December 15, 1791, in favor of an amendment to the apportionment bill which changed the ratio of representation in the House from 1:30,000 to 1:33,000.

523.13   claims of British creditors] While serving as secretary for foreign affairs, 1784–89, Jay had sought to have the states comply with article IV of the 1783 Treaty of Paris, which held Americans fully liable for pre-Revolutionary debts owed to British creditors. The article, which Jay had helped negotiate as one of the American peace commissioners, was especially resented by southern tobacco planters.

523.16   negociations . . . Spain] In a report to Congress in 1786 Jay recommended surrendering American claims to free navigation of the Mississippi for 25 or 30 years in return for the signing of a commercial treaty with Spain.

534.24   Decree of the Nat: Assemb.] On August 26, 1792, the French National Assembly had conferred citizenship on Madison and 16 other foreigners. Upon receiving this decree in April 1793, Madison wrote a letter accepting the honor.

534.36   apostacy of Dumourier] In April 1793 Charles François Dumouriez, the French commander in the Austrian Netherlands, defected to the

Austrians and called on the French people to restore the limited monarchy established by the constitution of 1791.

535.15   President's proclamation]   After learning that France had declared war on Britain, Washington consulted with his cabinet and then issued a proclamation of neutrality on April 22, 1793.

535.20–21   *engagements* . . . possessions of F.]   Under the terms of the 1778 treaty of alliance, the United States was pledged to help defend the French West Indies against attack.

536.19–20   Friend of our Friend]   In a letter of June 2, 1793, Jefferson had suggested that Madison urge Wilson Cary Nicholas, a Virginia politician, to inform his brother-in-law, Edmund Randolph, of the strength of pro-French sentiment in their native state.

537.13   Bartram]   William Bartram, the naturalist who kept a botanical garden outside of Philadelphia.

537.14   *"Helvidius" No. 1*]   Madison wrote five "Helvidius" essays; they appeared in newspapers from August 24 to September 18, 1793.

537.15   PACIFICUS]   The pen name used by Hamilton to publish seven essays between June 29 and July 27 supporting the proclamation of neutrality issued on April 22 and offering a broad defense of the prerogatives of the executive branch in conducting foreign policy.

538.32   casus federis]   Case of the treaty.

540.4   Wolfius, Burlamaqui and Vattel]   Christian Wolff, *Institutions du droit de la nature et des gens*, trans. Elie Luzac (Leiden, 1772); Jean Jacques Burlamaqui, *Principes du droit politique* (Amsterdam, 1751); Emmerich de Vattel, *The Law of Nations* (1760; originally published in French in 1758).

546.24–25   Federalist vol. 2, p. 273]   Madison quotes from *Federalist 75*, written by Hamilton.

547.1   Mr. D. R.]   David Meade Randolph.

547.3   conduct of Genèt]   In his letter of August 11, Jefferson informed Madison that the administration had decided to ask for the recall of Edmond Charles Genet, the first diplomatic minister sent to the United States by the French Republic. Genet had received an enthusiastic public welcome when he first arrived in April 1793, but soon angered the administration by arming and commissioning privateers in American ports in defiance of the neutrality proclamation issued by Washington on April 22, and then by threatening to make an appeal to the American public against the president's neutrality policy.

547.29–31   train of ideas . . . Richmond Resolutions]   On August 17, a Federalist-dominated meeting at Richmond, Virginia, had adopted resolutions denouncing Genet's conduct. While visiting James Monroe's home near

Charlottesville in late August, Madison and his host drafted a corresponding set of resolutions which praised Washington and the French Republic and denounced monarchical supporters of Great Britain while making no mention of Genet.

547.36   Mr. P.]   Edmund Pendleton.

547.39   A. Stuart]   Archibald Stuart, a former member of the Virginia House of Delegates.

548.9   the P.]   The President.

548.32–33   King . . . Walcot]   Senator Rufus King of New York; Supreme Court justice Thomas Johnson of Maryland; Edward Rutledge, a leading South Carolina Federalist; and Oliver Wolcott Jr. of Connecticut, the comptroller of the treasury.

548.34   my determination]   Not to replace Jefferson as secretary of state.

549.9   unfortunate appt. of G. M.]   Washington had appointed Gouverneur Morris as minister to France early in 1792.

549.14   Mr. W. N.]   Wilson Cary Nicholas.

549.16   E. R.]   Edmund Randolph.

549.25   Marshal]   John Marshall, the future secretary of state and chief justice, was the principal Federalist leader in Richmond.

549.27   great purchase from Fairfax]   Marshall and several of his relatives had formed a partnership to purchase more than 200,000 acres in northern Virginia from the Fairfax family.

550.19   his illness]   The illness of a French visitor to Montpelier.

551.3–4   Speech . . . "Self-Created Societies"]   The House was debating its reply to the president's annual message to Congress, which Washington had delivered on November 19. In his address, the President denounced "certain self-created societies" for having helped foment the Whiskey Rebellion in Pennsylvania earlier in the year, referring to the Democratic Societies, political clubs formed in 1793–94 by supporters of France. Thomas FitzSimons, a Federalist from Pennsylvania, moved to have a similar denuciation of "self-created societies" included in the House message reply.

551.15–17   President dissented . . . representatives)]   Washington used the presidential veto power for the first time on April 5, 1792, when he disapproved on constitutional grounds an apportionment bill that would have given some states more than one representative for every 30,000 persons.

551.22–23   gentleman from Georgia]   Abraham Baldwin.

553.8   expedition under St. Clair]   A military expedition commanded by General Arthur St. Clair was decisively defeated by Miami, Shawnee,

Potawatomi, and Chippewa Indians in the Northwest Territory on November 4, 1791.

553.16   *To James Monroe*]   Monroe served as minister to France, 1794–96. Italicized words in this letter were in cipher in the original.

553.26   Mr. Short]   William Short, the American minister to Spain.

553.31–32   Jay . . . Treaty]   See Chronology, 1794–95.

554.5   sub modo]   In a qualified sense.

554.6   Mr. Mason]   Stevens Thomson Mason, senator from Virginia.

554.29   predatory orders]   In July 1795 Washington learned that the Royal Navy was seizing American ships carrying grain to France. The order authorizing the seizures was withdrawn in September.

554.30   Mr. R's pamphlet]   Randolph had been forced to resign as secretary of state on August 19, 1795, after Washington came to suspect him of having solicited a bribe from the French. Randolph defended himself in a pamphlet, *A Vindication of Mr. Randolph's Resignation*, published on December 18, 1795.

554.34   Fauchet's intercepted letter]   The accusations against Randolph were based on a letter written by Joseph Fauchet, Genet's successor as French minister to the United States, that was intercepted by the Royal Navy and disclosed to the Washington administration.

555.27   *Sedgwick & Seagrove*]   Representatives Theodore Sedgwick of Massachusetts and Samuel Sitgreaves of Pennsylvania, both Federalists.

556.35   Senate . . . Rutledge]   On December 15, 1795, the Senate rejected Washington's appointment of John Rutledge to replace Jay as Chief Justice of the Supreme Court, in part because Rutledge had publicly criticized the Jay treaty.

558.20   the Committee]   The committee of the whole.

568.3   message . . . committed]   Thomas Blount of North Carolina moved on March 31 that the president's message of March 30, in which Washington refused the request by the House for documents relating to the negotiation of the Jay Treaty, be debated in a committee of the whole. Madison supported the motion, which was approved 55–37.

572.6   a member from Georgia]   Abraham Baldwin.

572.15–16   gentlemen from Connecticut and Maryland]   Federalist representatives Joshua Coit and William Vans Murray.

572.32–33   Judge Wilson]   Supreme Court justice James Wilson.

572.35–36   three gentlemen . . . convention]   John Rutledge, Charles

Pinckney, and Charles Cotesworth Pinckney; the last had in fact not attended the Charleston meeting in question.

572.38–39   very respectable citizen]   John Dickinson.

575.16   taken down . . . skilful hand]   David Robertson.

581.23   *Adams*]   From here to the end of this letter, words in italics were in cipher in the original.

581.27   intrigues . . . *setting P. above him*]   Alexander Hamilton had urged northern Federalist electors to divide their two votes evenly between Adams and Thomas Pinckney, while encouraging Federalists in South Carolina to vote for Pinckney and a candidate other than Adams.

581.37   answer . . . P.s. speech]   The reply by the House to Washington's annual message to Congress.

583.30   The special communication]   In his address of December 7, Washington had promised to submit a special message on French-American relations. The message was sent to Congress on January 19, 1797.

583.37   arrival of Pinkney]   Charles Cotesworth Pinckney, the new American minister, arrived in France on November 15, 1796.

584.21   the subject of arming]   A proposal authorizing the arming of American merchant ships trading with the West Indies was pending in Congress.

584.22–23   our hot-heated Executive]   Madison may have meant to write "hot-headed."

584.24–25   Managers for the Impeachment]   In the first impeachment proceedings under the Constitution, the House of Representatives had approved five charges against former senator William Blount of Tennessee, a Republican, on January 29, 1798, and then appointed a Federalist team of managers to prosecute the case in the Senate. The case was dismissed by the Senate in January 1799 for lack of jurisdiction (Blount had been expelled from the Senate on July 8, 1797, five days after being accused of conspiring with the British to seize Florida and Louisiana from Spain).

585.14   affair of Lyon & Griswold]   On January 30, 1798, Matthew Lyon, a Republican congressman from Vermont, spat on Roger Griswold, a Federalist representative from Connecticut, after Griswold made a remark impugning his courage. A Federalist attempt to expel Lyon from Congress failed to achieve the needed two-thirds majority on February 14; the next day, Griswold beat Lyon with a hickory cane in the House chamber.

586.6   Payne's letter]   Thomas Paine, *Letter to the People of France, and the French Armies, on the Events of the 18th Fructidor–Sep. 4–and Its Consequences* (1798).

586.7   The President's message] On March 19 Adams reported to Congress on the failure of the special diplomatic mission sent to France in 1797 and urged the adoption of measures to increase revenues and provide for the national defense.

586.12–13   the principle . . . the Treaty] See Chronology, March 24, 1796.

588.4–5   use of the Despatches] The dispatches sent by the diplomatic mission to France were published in April 1798 and revealed that three French diplomatic agents, identified in the dispatches as X, Y, and Z, had unsuccessfully solicited the American envoys for a $240,000 bribe as the precondition for negotiations.

591.23   The P.'s speech] Adams had delivered his annual message to Congress on December 8, 1798.

592.2–3   subtle partizan of England] Hamilton.

592.10–11   distinction between . . . *the Legislature*] Jefferson had sent Madison a draft of the Kentucky Resolutions on November 17, 1798, in which he asserted that a state legislature had the right to nullify unconstitutional federal laws. The resolutions adopted by the Kentucky legislature on November 10 did not mention nullification, but did declare the Alien and Sedition Acts to be "void, and of no force" and asserted that each state "has an equal right to judge for itself" whether the federal government had exceeded its delegated powers.

594.25   first minister . . . United States] John Adams.

598.18–19   foreign newspaper . . . British subject] *Porcupine's Gazette,* published in Philadelphia by William Cobbett.

610.8–9   the 12th amendment] The Twelfth Amendment proposed by Congress in 1789, which eventually became the Tenth Amendment.

615.22   the carriage tax] The constitutionality of the tax on carriages passed by Congress in 1794 was challenged on the grounds that, as a direct tax, it should be apportioned among the states according to population. In 1796 the Supreme Court upheld its constitutionality, ruling that it was an indirect excise tax.

663.11–12   the tie . . . Repub: characters] See Chronology, 1800–1.

663.34–35   letter to Coxe. . . T. Pinkney] In August 1800 a Republican newspaper printed a letter Adams had written to Tench Coxe in 1792 asserting that there had been "much British influence" in the appointment of Thomas Pinckney as minister to Great Britain during the first Washington administration. Adams subsequently wrote a letter of apology to Pinckney.

663.36   pamphlet of H] *Letter from Alexander Hamilton, concerning the Public Conduct and Character of John Adams, Esq., President of the United*

States, published in October 1800, described Adams as unfit to be president. Hamilton supported Charles Cotesworth Pinckney for the presidency.

664.7–8   meeting . . . Der. next]   The first session of the newly elected Seventh Congress would meet in December 1801.

664.23   French Convention]   The treaty signed on September 30, 1800, ending the undeclared naval war with France and suspending the 1778 treaty of alliance.

664.35   E. D. & Murray]   Oliver Ellsworth, William Davie, and William Vans Murray, the envoys who negotiated the Convention.

SECRETARY OF STATE AND PRESIDENT, 1801–1817

671.3   Treaty and two conventions]   See Chronology, 1803. The conventions covered matters ancillary to the purchase.

672.18–20   breach . . . St. Domingo]   See Chronology, 1802.

673.14   the Chief Consul]   Napoleon Bonaparte.

673.25–28   hostile attack . . . the Chesapeake]   See Chronology, 1807.

673.32   *This enormity*]   Italicized words in this letter were in cipher in the original.

675.4–5   *restoration . . . four seamen*]   One of the seamen, a British deserter from the Royal Navy, was court-martialed and hanged in August 1807. Of the three Americans taken from the ship, one died in a Halifax prison, while the other two were released in 1811 when the British government formally disavowed the attack on the *Chesapeake*.

675.10–11   Mr. Pinkney]   See Chronology, 1806.

677.38   Mr. Erskine]   David Erskine, British minister to the United States.

677.40   Mr. Canning]   George Canning, British foreign minister

678.1   new administration]   The ministry of the Duke of Portland, which came into office in the early spring of 1807.

684.5   B. & M. Decrees]   The Berlin and Milan decrees of Napoleon, issued respectively in 1806 and 1807, making American merchant ships trading with Britain subject to seizure.

684.9   O. In C.]   Orders in Council of Great Britain, imposing restrictions on American ships trading with areas of Europe under French control.

684.12   Mr. Barlow's wishes]   Joel Barlow, the American minister to France.

684.20   the Quids]   Led by John Randolph of Roanoke, the so-called

Tertium Quids were a conservative faction of the Republican party who opposed the administration's foreign policy.

690.1–3   a period . . . minister]   See Chronology, April–August 1809.

690.17   secret agent]   John Henry, a British businessman who was sent to New England in 1809 by Sir James Craig, the governor-general of Lower Canada, to report on whether New England Federalists would ally themselves with Britain in the event of an Anglo-American war. In February 1812 Henry sold his papers to the State Department for $50,000, and Madison submitted them to Congress on March 9. Federalists protested that nothing in the Henry papers implicated any American citizens in disloyalty.

696.10   *John Nicholas*]   A former Republican congressman from Virginia and brother of Wilson Cary Nicholas.

697.4   expedition under Hull]   General William Hull led an American army into Upper Canada in early 1812, but then retreated to Detroit, where he surrendered on August 16, 1812.

697.18   Mediation of Russia]   See Chronology, 1813.

699.20–22   Genl. Harrison . . . Jackson]   William Henry Harrison and Andrew Jackson.

700.24   General Winder]   General William H. Winder was commander of American forces in the military district surrounding Washington, D.C.

700.27–28   Genl. Armstrong]   Armstrong had been commissioned as a brigadier general in 1812, then appointed secretary of war in 1813.

700.30   Eastern Branch]   Of the Potomac River, also known as the Anacostia River.

700.33–35   Secretary of State . . . the Treasury]   James Monroe, William Jones, Richard Rush, and George Campbell.

701.4   Barney's corps]   A force of approximately 500 sailors and marines, led by Captain Joshua Barney, commander of the Chesapeake flotilla.

701.15–16   Secretary of War,]   When Madison had this memorandum copied in 1824, the following text was inserted at this point: "he lodged in the same house, with him."

701.35   duly attended to]   Inserted at this point in 1824 was: "in this case it had been requested in writing."

702.1   paper of instructions]   See pp. 697–700 in this volume.

702.10   to remove it]   Inserted at this point in 1824 was: "it was my purpose in case there should be time, to have the members of the Cabinet together in Bladensburg, where it was expected Genl. Winder would be, and in consultation with him to decide on the arrangements suited to the posture of things."

702.21   William Simmons]   The former accountant of the War Department.

RETIREMENT, 1817–1836

723.1   *Robert Walsh*]   A Philadelphia journalist and editor, Walsh was beginning work on *An Appeal From the Judgements of Great Britain Respecting the United States of America* (1819).

727.25–26   observations addressed . . . Albemarle]   The address Madison delivered to the Agricultural Society of Albemarle, Virginia, in May 1818.

727.31–33   the variance . . . the Federalist]   Madison had sent a list attributing authorship of the various *Federalist* essays to Jacob Gideon, a Washington printer, for his use in publishing a new edition of *The Federalist* in 1818. A different set of attributions appeared in the *New-York Evening Post* in 1817, based on a memorandum written by Hamilton shortly before his death. Modern scholarship accepts the accuracy of the attributions made by Madison in 1818.

728.28–29   recognised by the Constitution]   In the just compensation clause of the Fifth Amendment.

729.24   The Society]   The American Colonization Society, founded in 1816.

733.16   *Spencer Roane*]   Roane served as a judge on the Virginia court of appeals from 1794 to 1822.

733.20–21   case of M'Culloch . . . Maryland]   On March 6, 1819, the Court upheld 7–0 the constitutionality of the law chartering the Second Bank of the United States. Chief Justice Marshall's opinion for the Court endorsed the interpretation of the "necessary and proper" clause of the Constitution advanced by Hamilton and opposed by Madison in 1791.

741.34–36   N. W. Territory . . . Slaveholding]   Article VI of the Northwest Ordinance of 1787 prohibited slavery in the new Northwest Territory.

742.13   "the result . . . Concession"]   See note 339.18–20.

742.20–21   this mixed ratio . . . in Apl., 1783]   See note 20.16.

744.9   the Missouri question]   In February 1819 the House passed an amendment to the Missouri statehood bill that would have gradually abolished slavery in the new state. The measure was rejected by the Senate, and after extensive debate a compromise was adopted in March 1820 that allowed the admission of Missouri as a slave state while prohibiting slavery in the remainder of the Louisiana Purchase north of latitude 36° 30′ N.

744.40   your late volume]   See note 723.1.

745.14–15   return from France . . . Pennsylvania] In 1785.

746.23–24   anicdote . . . Presidts chair] During the signing of the
Constitution, Franklin observed that during sessions he had often been unable to tell whether the sun painted on the back of the chair Washington
presided from had been rising or setting, but that "now at length I have the
happiness to know that it is a rising and not a setting Sun."

747.22–23   Celebrated Dr. Fothergill] John Fothergill, an English
Quaker physician and botanist.

748.6–7   story . . . Abraham and the angels] Franklin's "A Parable
against Persecution."

749.16   Mr Dalton] Tristram Dalton, a Massachusetts Federalist.

751.34   179] 1791.

752.5   Mr. Giles] William Branch Giles, a leading Republican congressman from Virginia.

753.10   ut valeret quantum valere potuit]   So that it may be worth as
much as it could be worth.

754.21–22   printed ones in Freneau] The essays Madison published in the
National Gazette, edited by Philip Freneau, in 1791–92.

757.19   the year 178] 1784.

759.25   Religious Bill . . . 1786] See Chronology, 1786.

760.15   negatives . . . two bills] See page 683 in this volume. Madison
also vetoed a bill reserving land in the Mississippi Territory for a Baptist
church.

760.21   year by P. H.] 1784, by Patrick Henry.

761.8–9   a vote of . . . Jefferson dated] The amendment was defeated by
votes of 66–38 and 56–35. Madison may refer to his letter of January 22, 1786.

762.25   Obsta principiis] Resist the beginnings.

763.34–35   cum "maculis . . . natura."] With "faults which come from
negligence, or which human nature lets slip by."

767.21–22   I was outvoted] See Chronology, 1777.

769.14   memorandum . . . Mr Benson] Shortly before his fatal duel
with Aaron Burr, Hamilton reportedly left a memorandum identifying the
authors of the individual *Federalist* essays in the office of Egbert Benson, a
longtime political ally and prominent New York lawyer. The memorandum
was published in 1817; see note 727.31–33.

769.20   life of Mr. Jay by Delaplaine] Joseph Delaplaine, *Repository of
the Lives and Portraits of Distinguished American Characters* (1815).

771.5   Journals of the Convention] The journals of the Constitutional Convention, kept by its secretary William Jackson, were first published in 1819.

772.35   their late decision] In *Cohens* v. *Virginia* (1821) the Supreme Court unanimously reaffirmed its jurisdiction under the Constitution and Section 25 of the Judiciary Act of 1789 to decide appeals from state courts in matters relating to the Constitution or federal law.

776.29–30   Eleventh Amendment] Virginia had argued in *Cohens* that the Eleventh Amendment, removing from federal jurisdiction suits brought against a state by citizens of another state, precluded the Supreme Court from hearing the case (the Cohens were citizens of Maryland). Marshall rejected the argument, ruling that the amendment did not apply to suits begun by a state and then appealed by citizens with legitimate federal claims under Section 25.

777.26–27   "Algernon Sidney"] The pseudonym used by Roane in publishing five articles in the Richmond *Enquirer*, May 25–June 8, denouncing Chief Justice Marshall's decision in *Cohens* and asserting that the Supreme Court had no right to review the decisions of state courts.

786.20–21   Report . . . penal Code] *Report made to the General Assembly of the State of Louisiana of the Plan of the Penal Code for the said State* (1822).

790.1   *William T. Barry*] The lieutenant governor of Kentucky.

794.17   little pamphlet . . . "Europe"] *Remarks on the Censures of the Government of the United States Contained in the Ninth Chapter of "Europe"* by Christopher Gore, written in response to *Europe; or, A General Survey of the Political Situation of the Principal Powers, with Conjectures on their Future Prospects* by Alexander Hill Everett; both were published in 1822.

794.20   the Treaty of 1794] The Jay Treaty.

794.26   Rule of 1756] A principle of British maritime law forbidding neutrals from engaging in wartime in a trade they were excluded from in time of peace.

794.33   Sir Wm Scott] The leading judge on the high court of admiralty during the Napoleonic Wars.

795.15–16   your University] Harvard.

795.37   Govr. Livingston . . . Judge] William Livingston was governor of New Jersey, 1776–90, and a signer of the Constitution; his son Brockhurst Livingston was an associate justice of the U.S. Supreme Court, 1806–23.

798.15   your favor of the —— instant.] Jefferson had written Madison on June 13, enclosing a copy of his letter to Supreme Court Justice William Johnson of June 12.

799.38   Newburg letters written by Armstrong] John Armstrong, then a major in the Continental Army and later secretary of war under Madison, anonymously circulated two papers among the officers at the encampment at Newburgh, New York, on March 10 and 12, 1783. The addresses condemned Congress and called on the officers to rebel if their demands for pay were not met. Washington strongly condemned the addresses in a meeting held on March 15, and the officers adopted a resolution expressing loyalty to Congress.

800.1   Judge Cooper] Thomas Cooper, professor of chemistry at South Carolina College and a former Pennsylvania state judge.

800.20–23   more exceptions . . . same State] In his letter to Johnson, Jefferson had written that in these controversies, federal jurisdiction was limited to cases involving the use of paper money as legal tender, or the impairment of obligation of contracts.

802.1   Col: Taylor] John Taylor of Caroline, a leading Virginia theorist of states' rights who criticized Marshall's rulings on federal jurisdiction in *Construction Construed and Constitutions Vindicated* (1820).

802.22   seriatim opinions] Marshall had ended the previous practice of having each justice issue an individual opinion, replacing them with a single opinion for the entire Court.

802.27   connexion with Judge Todd] Lucy Payne Washington, Dolley Madison's widowed sister, had married Supreme Court Justice Thomas Todd in 1812.

804.19–20   "Life of Greene . . . Campaign of 1781."] In 1824 Lee published *The Campaign of 1781 in the Carolinas,* a defense of his father Henry "Light-Horse Harry" Lee against what he considered to be defamatory statements in Justice William Johnson's *Sketches of the Life and Correspondence of General Greene* (1822).

804.23   your discourse] Peter S. DuPonceau, *A Dissertation on the Nature and Extent of the Jurisdiction of the Courts of the United States* (Philadelphia, 1824).

806.23   per saltus] By a leap.

807.17   Mr Cabell] Joseph Cabell, a Virginia state senator and an influential member of the Board of Visitors of the University of Virginia.

807.20   Mr Barbour] Philip Pendleton Barbour, a prominent Virginia lawyer whom Madison had recommended as a candidate for professor of law at the University.

807.32   Sidney] Algernon Sidney, the author of *Discourses Concerning Government* (1698).

808.24   the Board]   The governing Board of Visitors of the University of Virginia.

809.33   Mr. Gilmour]   Francis Walker Gilmer, who Jefferson and Madison had hoped would accept appointment as professor of law at the University, died from tuberculosis on February 25, 1826.

810.4   Mr. Terril]   Dabney Terrill, a Kentucky attorney.

810.12   disclosures at Richmond]   Jefferson had asked the Virginia assembly for permission to sell his property by lottery in order to relieve his substantial private debts.

811.31   *Nicholas P. Trist*]   Trist was the grandson of Eliza House Trist (see note 353.1) and the husband of Jefferson's granddaughter Virginia Randolph. He later served as a secretary to President Andrew Jackson.

813.32   *Joseph Cabell*]   This letter was published, with Madison's permission, in the Washington *National Intelligencer* in December 1828.

814.10–11   "the power to regulate trade."]   In Article I, Section 8, the word "Commerce" is used, not "trade."

814.40   *"ex majori cautela"*]   With greater caution.

818.36   *Lloyd's Debates*]   Thomas Lloyd, *The Congressional Register; or, History of the Proceedings and Debates of the First House of Representatives Taken in Shorthand by Thomas Lloyd* (1789–90).

820.3   which says:]   The clause reads: "No State shall, without the Consent of the Congress, lay any Imposts or Duties on Imports or Exports, except what may be absolutely necessary for executing it's inspection Laws: and the net Produce of all Duties and Imposts, laid by any State on Imports or Exports, shall be for the Use of the Treasury of the United States; and all such Laws shall be subject to the Revision and Controul of the Congress."

822.23   Mr. Necker's work]   Jacques Necker, *Administration des finances* (1784).

824.3–4   the Committee]   The committee of the whole.

826.4–5   The Federal number]   The three-fifths ratio by which the enslaved population was counted for purposes of apportioning seats in the House of Representatives.

828.1   *A Sketch . . . Applied*]   Madison continued to work on this unfinished preface to his notes of debates in the Constitutional Convention during the 1830s.

833.39   Mr. Tyler]   John Tyler, a former speaker of the Virginia House of Delegates and father of President John Tyler.

835.12   Col: H.]   Hamilton.

835.29–30   pamphlet . . . Pelatiah Webster] Peletiah Webster, *A Dissertation on the Political Union and Constitution of the Thirteen United States of North America* (1783).

836.1   Longacre] James Longacre and James Herring, *The National Portrait Gallery of Distinguished Americans*, volume II (1835).

841.18   speech of Mr. Hamilton] Hamilton's long speech of June 18.

841.22   second day of May] Morris spoke at length on July 2.

842.10   *To Edward Everett*] Madison wrote this letter for publication; it appeared in the October 1830 *North American Review*.

847.1   the number of the "Federalist"] *Federalist 39*.

852.23–24   the 3d. Resolution . . . "alone,"] Cf. "the compact to which the states are parties," page 589.20 in this volume.

852.35–36   terms . . . "unconstitutional"] Cf. "that the acts aforesaid are unconstitutional, and that . . .," page 591.5 in this volume.

853.2–3   they were . . . original draft] The words were added at the suggestion of Jefferson by Wilson Cary Nicholas, to whom Madison had given his draft of the resolutions.

853.30   Pitkin's work] Timothy Pitkin, *A Political and Civil History of the United States of America, from the year 1763 to the close of the administration of President Washington, in March, 1797* (1828).

853.38–39   Judge Yates . . . Luther Martin] *Secret Proceedings and Debates of the Federal Convention* (1821), the first publication of the notes kept by Robert Yates (d. 1801); *The Genuine Information, Delivered to the Legislature of the State of Maryland Relative to the Proceedings of the General Convention Lately Held at Philadelphia* by Luther Martin (1788).

854.1   He left the Convention] See note 403.38–39

855.15–16   Chairman of the Committee] William Samuel Johnson.

857.28   Deane] Silas Deane, the American commissioner to France, whose recall by the Continental Congress in 1778 created a major factional controversy. Gouverneur Morris was a Deane supporter.

857.32   Col. Few] William Few of Georgia, who died on July 16, 1828.

858.2   Mr. Lansing who disappeared] John Lansing disappeared after leaving his hotel in New York City on December 12, 1829.

862.1   nolentem, volentem] Unwillingly, willingly; willy-nilly.

863.12   the late Proclamation] President Jackson's proclamation against nullification, issued on December 10, 1832.

Index

Library of Congress Cataloging-in-Publication Data

Madison, James, 1751–1836.
    [Selections. 1999]
    Writings / James Madison.
       p.   cm. — (The Library of America ; 109)
    Includes index.
    ISBN 1–883011–66–3 (alk. paper)
    1. Madison, James, 1751–1836.   2. United States—Politics
and government—1775–1783.   3. United States—Politics
and government—1783–1865.   I. Title.   II. Series.
E302.M192   1999
973.5′1′092—dc21   98–50372
                                                     CIP

THE LIBRARY OF AMERICA SERIES

The Library of America fosters appreciation and pride in America's literary heritage by publishing, and keeping permanently in print, authoritative editions of its best and most significant writing. An independent nonprofit organization, it was founded in 1979 with seed money from the National Endowment for the Humanities and the Ford Foundation.

1. Herman Melville, *Typee, Omoo, Mardi* (1982)
2. Nathaniel Hawthorne, *Tales and Sketches* (1982)
3. Walt Whitman, *Poetry and Prose* (1982)
4. Harriet Beecher Stowe, *Three Novels* (1982)
5. Mark Twain, *Mississippi Writings* (1982)
6. Jack London, *Novels and Stories* (1982)
7. Jack London, *Novels and Social Writings* (1982)
8. William Dean Howells, *Novels 1875–1886* (1982)
9. Herman Melville, *Redburn, White-Jacket, Moby-Dick* (1983)
10. Nathaniel Hawthorne, *Collected Novels* (1983)
11. Francis Parkman, *France and England in North America*, vol. I (1983)
12. Francis Parkman, *France and England in North America*, vol. II (1983)
13. Henry James, *Novels 1871–1880* (1983)
14. Henry Adams, *Novels, Mont Saint Michel, The Education* (1983)
15. Ralph Waldo Emerson, *Essays and Lectures* (1983)
16. Washington Irving, *History, Tales and Sketches* (1983)
17. Thomas Jefferson, *Writings* (1984)
18. Stephen Crane, *Prose and Poetry* (1984)
19. Edgar Allan Poe, *Poetry and Tales* (1984)
20. Edgar Allan Poe, *Essays and Reviews* (1984)
21. Mark Twain, *The Innocents Abroad, Roughing It* (1984)
22. Henry James, *Essays, American & English Writers* (1984)
23. Henry James, *European Writers & The Prefaces* (1984)
24. Herman Melville, *Pierre, Israel Potter, The Confidence-Man, Tales & Billy Budd* (1985)
25. William Faulkner, *Novels 1930–1935* (1985)
26. James Fenimore Cooper, *The Leatherstocking Tales*, vol. I (1985)
27. James Fenimore Cooper, *The Leatherstocking Tales*, vol. II (1985)
28. Henry David Thoreau, *A Week, Walden, The Maine Woods, Cape Cod* (1985)
29. Henry James, *Novels 1881–1886* (1985)
30. Edith Wharton, *Novels* (1986)
31. Henry Adams, *History of the United States during the Administrations of Jefferson* (1986)
32. Henry Adams, *History of the United States during the Administrations of Madison* (1986)
33. Frank Norris, *Novels and Essays* (1986)
34. W. E. B. Du Bois, *Writings* (1986)
35. Willa Cather, *Early Novels and Stories* (1987)
36. Theodore Dreiser, *Sister Carrie, Jennie Gerhardt, Twelve Men* (1987)
37. Benjamin Franklin, *Writings* (1987)
38. William James, *Writings 1902–1910* (1987)
39. Flannery O'Connor, *Collected Works* (1988)
40. Eugene O'Neill, *Complete Plays 1913–1920* (1988)
41. Eugene O'Neill, *Complete Plays 1920–1931* (1988)
42. Eugene O'Neill, *Complete Plays 1932–1943* (1988)
43. Henry James, *Novels 1886–1890* (1989)
44. William Dean Howells, *Novels 1886–1888* (1989)
45. Abraham Lincoln, *Speeches and Writings 1832–1858* (1989)
46. Abraham Lincoln, *Speeches and Writings 1859–1865* (1989)
47. Edith Wharton, *Novellas and Other Writings* (1990)
48. William Faulkner, *Novels 1936–1940* (1990)
49. Willa Cather, *Later Novels* (1990)
50. Ulysses S. Grant, *Personal Memoirs and Selected Letters* (1990)

This book is set in 10 point Linotron Galliard,
a face designed for photocomposition by Matthew Carter
and based on the sixteenth-century face Granjon. The paper is
acid-free Ecusta Nyalite and meets the requirements for permanence
of the American National Standards Institute. The binding
material is Brillianta, a woven rayon cloth made by
Van Heek-Scholco Textielfabrieken, Holland.
The composition is by The Clarinda
Company. Printing and binding by
R.R.Donnelley & Sons Company.
Designed by Bruce Campbell.